WEBSTER'S SPORTS DICTIONARY

Merriam-Webster Inc., Publishers
Springfield, Massachusetts, U. S. A.

A Merriam-Webster®

WEBSTER'S SPORTS DICTIONARY

Contents

Preface   5a

A Dictionary of Sports Terms   1

Appendix

   Abbreviations   492

   Referee Signals   496

   Scorekeeping   498

A GENUINE MERRIAM-WEBSTER

The name *Webster* alone is no guarantee of excellence. It is used by a number of publishers and may serve mainly to mislead an unwary buyer.

A *Merriam-Webster®* is the registered trademark you should look for when you consider the purchase of dictionaries and other fine reference books. It carries the reputation of a company that has been publishing since 1831 and is your assurance of quality and authority.

Weekly Reader Books offers several exciting card and activity programs. For information, write to WEEKLY READER BOOKS, P.O. Box 16636, Columbus, Ohio 43216.

This book is a presentation of **Just For Boys**,® Weekly Reader Books. Weekly Reader Books offers book clubs for children from preschool through high school. For further information write to: **Weekly Reader Books,** 4343 Equity Drive, Columbus, Ohio 43228.

Published by arrangement with Merriam-Webster Inc. Just For Boys and Weekly Reader are federally registered trademarks of Field Publications.

copyright © 1976 by Merriam-Webster Inc.
Philippines copyright 1976 by Merriam-Webster Inc.

Library of Congress Cataloging in Publication Data
Main entry under title:

Webster's sports dictionary

   1. Sports — dictionaries. 1. Title: Sports dictionary
GV567.W37   796'.03   75-42076
ISBN 0-87779-067-1

Printed and bound in the United States of America
   89 RRD 11

PREFACE

Webster's Sports Dictionary, like all other Merriam-Webster® dictionaries, is based on actual usage as recorded in a mass of examples from numerous printed sources. This dictionary defines terms normally used by the participants in various sports and by broadcasters and sportswriters as well as terms used in the playing rules of sports. The work is not aimed specifically at players, coaches, and sportswriters, for they are the people who daily use the terms this dictionary explains. The book is intended instead to serve as a handbook for the casual fan who wants a ready source of definitions of commonly used sports words and phrases, concise summaries of how particular games are played, or explanations of unusual game situations, types of plays, or special techniques. For the knowledgeable fan, the book can also serve as a handy reference for explanations of peculiarities in the playing rules and for specifications of playing areas and game equipment.

As a dictionary, this book gives definitions of terms but does not attempt to provide historical information or statistics, which is more properly the job of an encyclopedia. The book limits itself to terms actually peculiar to sports. Common terms of a general nature that are found in general dictionaries, though often used in describing sports action, have been omitted. Hunting and fishing terms are included, but the names of species of game animals and fish have been omitted. Their application is more widespread than just in the context of sports. Compound words and phrases which mean no more than the sum of the meanings of their component words have been omitted. Normally when a compound or a phrase is not entered in this dictionary, the important word in the compound or phrase will be entered.

The words in this dictionary are, for the most part, in widespread current use. Only a few terms that are no longer commonly used have been kept for their historical interest. The vocabulary is not limited to American sports or American usage. The principal sports of other English-speaking countries are also included, as are words and idioms of Australian, British, and Canadian usage. Since this book is based on citational evidence, some unusual local usages or esoteric terms may not be included here. Their absence from the book testifies to the lack of current evidence of their use in the extensive vocabulary files of Merriam-Webster Inc.

The term *sport* is difficult to circumscribe. The entries in this book cover the range of competitive games and activities such as baseball, football, tennis, rodeo, boxing, and wrestling; races by animals and by humans on foot and in vehicles; games requiring physical skill in maneuvering a ball for a score such as golf, bowling, and billiards; and outdoor recreational activities like hunting and fishing, hiking, skiing, and sailing. In general, sport, for the purpose of determining the scope of this dictionary, has been taken to include all activities one might reasonably expect to find treated in a sports publication or on the sports pages of a newspaper. Not included are terms from hobby activities, card and board games, and traditional children's games.

Where usage restricts a term or one sense of a term to a single sport, an italic subject label is given immediately before the definition in order to help the reader locate quickly the specific sense he is seeking. Terms specific to two or more sports are oriented within the definition. When the subject label appears before the sense numbers or subsense indicators, all the following senses or subsenses pertain to the sport indicated by the label. The senses are normally arranged alphabetically by subject label except where a sense is a direct borrowing from earlier use in another sport. In this case, the earlier use is listed before the borrowing. Unlabeled senses applicable to several sports are routinely listed before labeled senses, and simple cross-references usually follow labeled senses.

> ¹**pass 1** A transfer of the ball or puck in a goal game . . . .
> **2** A passing shot (as in tennis).
> **3** *baseball* . . . .
> **4** *court tennis* . . . .
> **5** or **passé** *fencing* . . . .
> **6** *track and field* . . . .
> **7** *waterskiing* . . . .
> **8** see PASE

Alternate definitions at specific senses are separated by a semicolon. The alternate definition may be another word or phrase that is used interchangeably with the preceding definition or may be a more specific application implicit in the preceding definition.

> **leg 1** A portion of a course or a series; the portion of a course or the total distance of a relay race that each member of a relay team must cover.

Where variants fall alphabetically in proximity to an entry, they are included in boldface along with the entry. Boldfaced variants applying only to a single sense are placed at the appropriate sense (as at ¹**pass 5** above). Where variants come at another alphabetical place in the dictionary, they are given in italics at the end of the definition.

hip circle or **hip pullover** or **hip swing**
gymnastics A movement....
(also called *belly grind, merry-go-round*)

Separate homographs marked by preceding raised numerals are given for noun, verb, and adjective/adverb definitions. The specific part of speech is distinguished by the wording of the definition. Homographs are generally arranged so that the one having the fuller treatment comes first. No distinction has been made in the definitions between transitive and intransitive uses of verbs, and none has been made for terms that may be used at one time as an adjective and at another time as an adverb.

Cross-references appear in small capitals and serve three principal functions. The "see" references direct the reader to a more common variant where the definition is given or to another entry where he will find additional information or a fuller treatment; "see also" references are used for parallel or related terms. The "compare" references direct the reader to contrasting terms.

Verbal illustrations have been used throughout the book to show the entry word in typical context. In many cases, these illustrations are actual quotations from general-interest and sports publications, sportswriters, and prominent sports figures.

An important part of *Webster's Sports Dictionary* is the inclusion of specifications for playing areas and game equipment. These are placed throughout the book either in the definitions themselves or in special charts. English measurements are used where they appear in the rules of a particular sport. Where the rules have metric measurements, these are given along with the approximate English equivalents.

Because of their frequent occurrence in sportswriting, a few trademarks are entered in this dictionary. Their treatment is based on a formula approved by the United States Trademark Association for use in *Webster's Third New International Dictionary*. Their inclusion in this dictionary is solely for the purpose of pointing out their status to the reader and should not be regarded as in any way affecting the validity of the trademark.

In addition to the basic A-Z vocabulary, this work includes a list of abbreviations commonly used in sportswriting, a section of referee's signals for football, basketball, and ice hockey, and a section of instructions on how to keep score in baseball and bowling.

Webster's Sports Dictionary has been written and edited with the assistance of James E. Shea, Assistant Editor, and E. W. Gilman, Senior Editor. Original artwork has been produced by J. A. Collier, Assistant Editor, and by Al Fiorentino and Harvey Kidder of Kirchoff/Wohlberg, Inc. Typing and clerical work has been handled principally by Frances W. Muldrew and Mildred C. Paquette of the Merriam-Webster staff under the direction of Evelyn G. Summers.

Robert Copeland
EDITOR

A Dictionary of Sports Terms

A

abaft   Toward or at the stern of a boat; aft.

abeam   At right angles to the fore-and-aft line of a boat; straight out from the sides of a boat.

aboard 1 *baseball* On base. ⟨struck out with 2 men *aboard*⟩
2 *boating* On, onto, or within a boat.

abseil   see RAPPEL

absence of blade   *fencing* The absence of contact between blades during a fencing phrase. Fencing with absence of blade may be a tactic to protect oneself from various attacks on the blade. — compare ENGAGEMENT

absolute pressure   *scuba diving* The combined pressure of a given depth of water plus that of the air at the surface. — compare GAUGE PRESSURE

abstain   *of a fencing judge* To refrain from voting on whether or not a hit has been made because of uncertainty as to whether a touch was made.

abstemmen   *skiing* The preliminary positioning of the body preparatory to making a stem turn which consists of pulling back the uphill shoulder and slightly stemming and weighting the downhill ski.

academic assault   *fencing* A demonstration bout in which hits are usually not counted.

academic seat   see CLASSICAL SEAT

acceptor   *British horse racing* A horse that remains entered in a race after the handicaps have been published and whose owner has in effect accepted the assigned weight.

accipiter   A short-winged hawk (as the goshawk or European sparrow hawk) used in falconry.

acclimatization   *mountain climbing* The process of becoming accustomed to high altitudes where the air is less dense than at sea level. This usually becomes necessary around 10,000 feet and usually involves climbing several lesser peaks and gradually working up to higher altitudes and longer excursions. Attempting to climb a high mountain without a period of acclimatization often results in mountain sickness.

accumulator   see PARLAY

¹ace 1 A point scored in a racket game (as badminton or racquets).
2 A serve in tennis or handball which is not touched by the receiver and which scores for the server.
3a An outstanding player; star. **b** The best pitcher on a baseball team.
4 *golf* see HOLE IN ONE

²ace 1 To score an ace against an opponent in a racket game; to score on a serve that is not returned.
2 *golf* To make a hole in one on a specific hole.

acey deucy   *horse racing* Having the right stirrup shorter than the left so that the jockey can more easily equalize his weight on the turns.

Acorn   A 1-mile stakes race for 3-year-old thoroughbred fillies that is one of the races in the filly Triple Crown. — compare COACHING CLUB AMERICAN OAKS, MOTHER GOOSE

across the board   *pari-mutuel betting* For win, place, and show.

action 1 The amount of resiliency and flexibility in a fishing rod in relation to its length and diameter.
2 The process of betting including offering and accepting bets and the determining of a winner.

action on the blade

3 Spin on a hit or stroked ball. ⟨almost chip the ball, putting as little *action* on it as possible so it lands softly — Jack Nicklaus⟩

4 The mechanism by which a firearm is loaded, fired, and unloaded. The action typically consists of the trigger, the firing pin, and the bolt which carries the firing pin, locks the cartridge in the chamber, and ejects the empty case after the weapon has been fired. Rifles are generally made with one of 4 types of action. The bolt action consists of a manually operated bolt which when slid to the rear ejects the empty case and exposes the chamber while at the same time cocking the firing pin, and when slid forward strips a new cartridge from the magazine and carries it into the chamber. The lever action works on a similar principle. When the lever is pulled down and forward it forces the bolt back, clearing the chamber and cocking the hammer. When the lever is returned to its original position, the bolt moves forward and carries a new cartridge into the chamber. Pump action or slide action guns are operated by a slide located directly under the barrel which when moved to the rear ejects the spent cartridge and cocks the firing pin and when moved forward loads a new cartridge. The automatic weapon utilizes a portion of the gases which propel the bullet or shot to drive the bolt to the rear, clearing the chamber and positioning a new round for the next shot. Shotguns employ the pump and automatic actions (the autoloading shotgun is in reality a semiautomatic) as well as a breakdown action which opens up at the rear of the chamber for loading and unloading by hand. The act of breaking the shotgun down cocks the firing pin. Most hand guns and some rifles use a spring-action hammer instead of a bolt.

action on the blade *fencing* Any movement by which a fencer makes contact with his opponent's blade and moves it so as to cause an opening for attack or to prevent a hit by the opponent.

activate To place or return a player who has been inactive (as because of injury, suspension, or absence from the active roster) to status as an active player eligible to participate in a contest.

active rope *mountain climbing* The rope used for belay between 2 climbers. — see ROPE

ad Short for *advantage* (*tennis*).

ad court Short for *advantage court.*

added money *horse racing* **1** Money that is added by a track or state racing association to the fees (as entrance, nomination, and starting fees)

that usually make up the purse for a race.
2 or **added** An added money race.

¹address 1 *archery* To stand ready to shoot with the body turned at right angles to the target.

2 *golf* To take one's stance over the ball and grip the club preparatory to hitting the ball.

²address The act of addressing; the position assumed in addressing.

Adolph *gymnastics* A trampoline stunt consisting of a forward somersault with 3½ twists.

adrift Not secured to a mooring; drifting.

¹advance 1 To move a ball or puck toward a goal.

2 To progress to the next round in a tournament.

3 *baseball* To move to the next base.

4 *fencing* To move forward toward the opponent by stepping first with the front foot and then bringing the other foot up the same distance.

²advance The act of advancing; a method of advancing.

advancing *field hockey* A foul that results when a player advances the ball with any part of the body instead of with the stick and that is penalized by awarding a free hit to the opposing team.

advantage 1 *tennis* The point scored immediately after deuce. Should the same player score the next point he wins the game. If his opponent scores the next point, the score reverts to deuce. (also called *vantage*) — see also DEUCE; IN, OUT

2 *wrestling* Control over one's opponent in which a wrestler is usually on top of and behind his opponent. A wrestler is awarded one point for accumulating a margin of one minute or more of advantage time over his opponent during a match.

advantage court or **ad court** *tennis* The left-hand service court. The ball is served into the left service court whenever one side or the other has the advantage.

advantage rule A provision in the rules of some games (as rugby or soccer) whereby play is not stopped for some infractions if the offending team has not gained an advantage on the play or if stopping play would impose a disadvantage on the offended team.

aerial 1 *football* A forward pass.

2 or **aerial cartwheel** *gymnastics* A flip that resembles a cartwheel but is done without the hands touching the floor or the balance beam.

3 *freestyle skiing* A category of competition in which competitors ski down a slope one at a time and perform various flips, twists, and turns as they jump over bumps on the course. — see also DAFFY, HELICOPTER, MOEBIUS FLIP; compare BALLET, MOGUL

aerial ball 1 *speedaway* A thrown or kicked ball that has not touched the ground or has bounced only once and may be played with the hands. **2** *speedball* A thrown or kicked ball that has not touched the ground since being kicked and may be played with the hands so long as it does not hit the ground. (also called *fly ball*) — compare GROUND BALL

aerial cartwheel see AERIAL (*gymnastics*)

aerofoil British term for *airfoil*.

aerostat A sports balloon.

afield 1 To or into the field; to a place for hunting. **2** Away from the concentrated center of action; toward the outer limits of a playing area.

afloat 1 Floating on the water. ⟨devices to keep you *afloat*⟩ **2** Aboard a boat. ⟨safety measures to be employed while *afloat*⟩

aft Toward or at the stern of a boat.

after Located in the stern of a boat. ⟨the *after* cabin⟩

age 1 The classification of a racehorse that approximates the chronological age of the animal. The universal birthday for racehorses is January 1st. A horse foaled in April will be classified as a yearling on the following January. Likewise, a horse foaled in December will be one year old a month later. **2** The classification of a racing greyhound that is identical to his chronological age.

age-group competition Competition (as in swimming or track and field) in which youths compete in categories according to their ages. Age-group competition usually serves as a training ground for athletes who eventually move into open competition.

agent Someone appointed to transact business for another. A racehorse owner may appoint his trainer to be his agent in buying, selling, and claiming horses. Professional athletes have agents to bargain with club owners on the terms of a contract, and jockeys have agents to secure mounts for them.

aground On or onto the shore or the bottom of a body of water.

ahead 1 In the lead. ⟨*ahead* by a score of 10–3⟩ ⟨coming to the wire he is *ahead* by 3 lengths⟩ **2** *baseball* Having the count in one's favor. When the pitcher has thrown more strikes than balls, he is ahead of the batter.

aid *equitation* A pull on the rein, shift of balance, or pressure with a leg which communicates an intended movement to a horse.

aikido A Japanese art of self-defense developed in the 20th century which emphasizes dodging and leading an attacker in the direction his momentum takes him to subdue him without causing injury. As a competitive sport, aikido involves mock fighting between 2 people on a mat approximately 9 meters (29½ feet) square for one or two 1-minute rounds. In one form of competition, one person is given a rubber knife and becomes the attacker for the first round; in the second round, the attacker and defender exchange roles. The object for the attacker is to attempt to score a point for a successful attack on the defender by striking him in the chest with the point of the knife. The defender seeks to parry the attack or to disarm or throw the attacker and thereby score a point for himself. There are other forms of competition in which the combatants fight for a single round without the knife. The competitor with the most points at the end of the bout is the winner. During the competition, the competitors wear a costume like the judo gi. The bout is supervised by a referee and scored by 2 judges. At the beginning of the match and at the end, the competitors bow to each other.

aikidoist Someone who engages in aikido.

¹aim To point a weapon at an object or target.

²aim 1 The pointing of a weapon at an object or a target. **2** The ability to hit the target. ⟨his *aim* was deadly⟩

air 1 *football* An offense or the part of an offense utilizing the forward pass. ⟨were stopped on the ground and were forced to take to the *air*⟩ **2** *scuba diving* Compressed air. ⟨find a place to buy *air*⟩ **— in the air 1** *baseball* For a fly ball. — usually used in the phrase *hit the ball in the air* **2** *football* As a forward pass. — usually used in the phrase *put the ball in the air*

air ball *basketball* A shot that completely misses the rim and the backboard. — compare GLASS BALL

air dribble *basketball* The act or an instance of tossing the ball in the air and touching it again before it touches the floor or before it is touched by another player. The rules formerly permitted a player to use one air dribble in conjunction with a regular bouncing dribble, with any number of steps permitted before the ball was touched again.

air embolism *scuba diving* A condition in which air bubbles forced into the bloodstream through ruptured capillaries in the lungs obstruct the cir-

3

culation. Air embolism is a common danger of failing to exhale compressed air while ascending.

airfoil A body (as an airplane wing) designed to provide a desired reaction force when in motion relative to the surrounding air. On airplanes, the wings are designed to provide lift. Airfoils for racing cars, either winglike devices mounted on the rear or deflectors usually mounted at the front, are designed to exert downthrust to increase traction and improve the cars' stability.

airplane racing see AIR RACING

airplane towing see TOWING

airplane turn *skiing* A change of direction made while in the midst of a jump (as over a mogul).

air racing or **airplane racing** The sport of racing airplanes usually over a closed course marked by pylons. A race consists of a specific number of laps with the winning plane being first to cross the finish line after covering the required number of laps. Planes compete within classes. — see also FORMULA ONE

air start *air racing* A starting procedure in which all competitors for a particular race are in the air and take up assigned positions behind a pace airplane to move to the starting line. This start is analogous to the flying start in auto racing.

air tank *scuba diving* A steel cylinder that holds compressed air for a diver. A typical tank holds approximately 71 pounds of compressed air. — see illustration at SCUBA DIVING

Alaskan canoe see KAYAK

Albion round *archery* A target round in women's competition in which each competitor shoots 36 arrows at a distance of 80 yards, 36 at 60 yards, and 36 at 50 yards. — compare ST. GEORGE ROUND

alee To leeward. ⟨put the helm *alee*⟩

Algonquin A modified bearpaw-type snowshoe with a wide front tapering to a rounded back.

all For each side; each. ⟨score is tied 15 *all*⟩

all-American A school or college athlete who is selected as one of the outstanding competitors in his sport in the United States.

alley 1 An area between the service court and the sideline on a doubles court (as for tennis or badminton) which is out of bounds in singles play. **2** A undefined relatively narrow unobstructed area on a playing field or court: **a** *football* An opening between linemen through which a defensive player may rush. **b** *baseball* The area between two outfielders when they are in their normal positions. ⟨youngsters who go to the *alleys* so well they've almost made triples extinct — Peter Gammons, *Boston Globe*⟩

3 *boccie* A strip of ground 75 feet long and 8 feet wide that is bounded by boards at the sides and ends and that serves as the playing area for the game; court.

4 *bowling* **a** A lane. **b** A building containing many lanes.

5 *field hockey* The area between the sideline and a line 5 yards (7 yards in men's play) inside and parallel to the sideline. All players are excluded from the alley during a push-in or roll-in from the sideline.

6 *squash racquets* An undefined area along the side walls close to the floor from which it is difficult to return a shot.

alley-oop shot *basketball* A shot made by a player who leaps high in the air near the basket to catch a lob pass and immediately drops or throws the ball in the basket before landing.

alley shot *squash racquets* A hard low drive that hits the front wall just above the telltale and rebounds very close to the side wall, bouncing twice before reaching the back wall.

¹all out With full vigor, determination, or resources. ⟨going *all out* to win⟩ ⟨an *all-out* effort⟩

²all out *of a cricket team* Retired because each batsman has been dismissed.

allowance *horse racing* A reduction in the amount of weight a horse must carry in an allowance or claiming race usually based on the horse's past performance, age, or sex. A horse that has not won a specified number or specified types of races or a specific amount of money during a designated period of time will be allowed to run with less weight. Weight allowances are usually given to 3-year-olds running against older horses and to fillies when they are entered against colts. An allowance called an apprentice allowance is also given to a horse being ridden by an apprentice jockey. — see also APPRENTICE ALLOWANCE

allowance race *horse racing* A race in which weight assignments are set by a formula tied to each horse's past performance or earnings. Horses running in allowance races are usually of better quality than those that normally run in claiming races but of lesser quality than handicap or stakes horses. — compare CLAIMING RACE, HANDICAP, STAKES RACE

all-play-all British term for *round robin*.

all-pro *football* A professional player selected to an all-star squad.

all-square British term for *tied*.

all-star A player named to a team composed

wholly of outstanding players. Selection to an all-star team is an honor accorded to outstanding performers usually by sportswriters, coaches, and fellow players, or sometimes by balloting among the fans.

all the way *football* For a touchdown. ⟨went *all the way* on a perfectly executed sweep⟩

all-time The best or hypothetically the best in a particular area in recorded sports history. ⟨the only active players . . . on the *all-time* list — Ted Williams⟩

alpenstock *mountain climbing* A long staff usually with a pointed metal tip that was formerly used as an aid to climbing but has today been generally replaced by the ice axe.

Alpine 1 Of or relating to downhill skiing or downhill competition.
2 Relating to a region of high mountains or mountain systems. ⟨*Alpine* wilderness⟩

Alpine Combined *skiing* A competition in which Alpine skiers are rated on the basis of scores made in the slalom and downhill events. The skier with the highest total wins the Combined regardless of the placing in the individual events. — compare NORDIC COMBINED

Alpinism Mountain climbing in high mountain ranges such as the Alps.

Alpinist A skier who competes in Alpine events; a skier who engages in skiing downhill rather than cross-country.

also eligible *horse racing* A horse entered in a race but not drawn as one of the limited number of starters. Such a horse may have a chance to start if another horse withdraws.

also-ran 1 A competitor (as a racehorse) that finishes out of the money.
2 A competitor who does not finish a contest or who is not expected to finish among the top prize or point winners; a competitor who is only moderately successful.

altered *drag racing* **1** A vehicle that is based on a standard automobile body but is modified practically without restriction.
2 A drag racing classification for these vehicles.

alternate Someone selected to take the place of a member of a team, squad, or group who is unable to participate.

alternate captain *ice hockey* A designated player who performs the duties of team captain when the captain is not on the ice.

alternate toe touch A calisthenic exercise that is started from an erect position with the feet apart and the arms extended to the sides and that consists of bending over to touch the toes with each hand alternately touching the toes of the opposite foot.

altimeter An instrument for measuring altitudes. The altimeter is basically a barometer that measures the air pressure at a given altitude and indicates this on a dial or gauge calibrated in feet or thousands of feet.

amateur 1 Someone who is not classified as a professional and who is eligible to participate in amateur competition as defined by the various governing and sanctioning organizations. The interpretation of amateur status is controversial and varies widely in different sports. The distinction between amateurism and professionalism in many situations is not clear. Some organizations bar all athletes who have ever received payment for participation in sports, even to the point of barring sports stars who capitalize on their fame for the promotion or advertising of sports equipment, yet permit or condone various forms of subsidies. These include training and traveling expenses and college scholarships which are based on a student's playing for a school and which end once the student's participation or eligibility ends. In some European nations where sports are under the control of the state, amateur subsidies resemble salaries and may include such bonuses as free use of apartments and automobiles. Though professionals are rarely allowed to compete in amateur competition, sports such as tennis and golf have open tournaments in which amateurs may compete with professionals and still retain their amateur status so long as they do not accept prize money.
2 Someone whose performance or ability is considerably below that exhibited by or expected of a professional.
3 *ice hockey* A player in an amateur league who receives payment and is usually supplied with room and board.

amateurism The status of an amateur; the fact of being an amateur.

ambient water *skin diving* The water that surrounds a diver at a given depth.

¹amble *equitation* An easy 4-beat gait that resembles a pace.

²amble *of a horse* To move at an amble.

American Legion Baseball A summer baseball league sponsored by the American Legion for youths aged 15–17. — compare BABE RUTH LEAGUE, LITTLE LEAGUE

American Road Race of Champions A program of races sponsored by the Sports Car Club of America for the winners of local club races from

American round

around the United States that is held at the end of the racing season to determine a champion in each automobile class.

American round *archery* A target round in which each competitor shoots 30 arrows at a distance of 60 yards, 30 at 50 yards, and 30 at 40 yards.

American ski technique see SKIING

American style see HOP-STEP

American twist *tennis* A serve in which the ball is struck with topspin at a point almost straight over the head so that it bounces unusually high and to the receiver's left when it hits the ground.

America's Cup A trophy awarded to the winner of a series of international races for 12-meter yachts. The trophy, originally called the Hundred Guineas Cup, was offered by the Royal Yacht Squadron of Great Britain in 1851 to the winner of a race around the Isle of Wight. This race was won by a seagoing schooner from America named "America," which beat 14 British yachts. The cup was eventually donated to the New York Yacht Club, its present owner, as a permanent trophy for perpetual international challenge races. Originally, challenging yachts had to sail on their own hulls to the site of the races, but

in 1956 that requirement was dropped and international 12-meter yachts were made standard.

amidships 1 To or in the part of a boat midway between the bow and the stern.

2 In the middle of a vehicle (as an automobile). ⟨a 12-cylinder engine mounted *amidships*⟩

anabolic steroid Any of a group of usually synthetic hormones that increase constructive metabolism and that are sometimes taken by athletes in training in order to increase the size of their muscles temporarily.

¹anchor 1 or **anchorman** A member of a team who is last to compete in a relay race (as in track or swimming).

2 or **anchor point** *archery* A point on an archer's face (as the cheek or chin) to which he brings the string hand each time the bow is drawn in order to ensure consistency in aiming and shooting.

3 *billiards* Any of the eight 7-inch-square areas on a balkline table at the intersections of the balklines and the cushions. The anchor is bisected by the balkline and serves to extend the restrictions of balk.

4 *boating* A heavy usually metal device in any of various shapes that is attached to the boat by

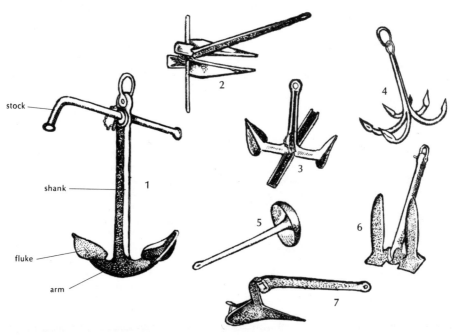

stock

shank

1

fluke

arm

2

3

4

5

6

7

anchor: 1 yachtsman's; 2 Danforth; 3 Northill; 4 grapnel; 5 mushroom; 6 Navy stockless; 7 CQR a cable or chain and that is cast overboard to keep the boat from drifting.

5 *mountain climbing* A point on a slope or rock face at which a belay is secured.

²anchor 1 To serve as an anchorman on a relay team.

2 *archery* To bring the string hand to the anchor point.

3 *boating* To secure a boat in place in the water by means of an anchor.

4 *mountain climbing* To establish a belay at an anchor.

anchor bend see FISHERMAN'S BEND

anchor leg The last leg of a relay. The anchor leg is the responsibility of the anchorman who is usually the fastest or strongest member of the team.

anchorman see ANCHOR

anchor point see ANCHOR (*archery*)

anchor rode *boating* A light rope attached to a boat's anchor.

¹angle 1 *football* A position to the side of an opponent from which a player may block the opponent more effectively.

2 *mountain climbing* A light piton with a U-shaped blade. — see illustration at PITON

²angle 1 To propel a ball in a diagonal direction.

2 To move at an angle.

3 To engage in fishing; fish.

angle block *football* A block made from the side and intended to drive the defender sideways; a block made at an angle on an opponent who is not lined up directly opposite the blocker.

angled *of the cueball in snooker* Blocked from the on ball by the corner of a cushion at the opening to a pocket.

angler A fisherman.

angling The sport of fishing.

angulation *skiing* A position used in traversing in which the skis are edged into the hill, the knees bent toward the slope, and the upper body held over the downhill ski.

animal round *archery* A round in field archery competition in which each competitor shoots at 28 life-size animal targets placed at distances from 10 yards to 60 yards around a field roving course. Three shots are allowed at each target, but the archer shoots only until one hit is made. Often the round requires shooting from varying positions (as kneeling, sitting, or standing), and scores are based on whether the scoring arrow was the archer's first, second, or third and on whether it hit a high or low scoring area.

ankle boot see BOOT (*harness racing*)

anorak A lightweight hooded, usually pullover-style parka.

anoxia *skin diving* Oxygen starvation which often results when a diver consciously represses the urge to breathe so as to extend the length of the dive and which often leads to shallow-water blackout.

antenna Short for *net antenna*.

ante-post *British horse racing* Relating to odds or betting prior to the day of the race. ⟨the *ante-post* favorite⟩

antiparachute ropes *ballooning* Lines that hold down the lower portion of a hot-air balloon envelope and prevent the lower half of a partially deflated balloon from rising into the upper half creating a parachute.

antisway bar see SWAY BAR

aperture sight A peep sight. — see SIGHT

apex *motor racing* The point in a turn at which the vehicle is nearest the inside edge of the roadway.

apparatus *gymnastics* The equipment (as parallel and horizontal bars, horses, rings, and beat boards) used in the performance of gymnastic and tumbling feats.

apparent wind *sailing* The wind as felt aboard a moving sailboat. It is a combination of the direction and magnitude of the true wind and the movement of the boat. Air resistance on a moving body creates a feeling of wind in the direction opposite the movement. A boat moving through the water at a speed of 4 knots experiences air resistance which seems like a wind of 4 knots. If the true wind is blowing from a similar direction, these 2 forces combine creating an apparent wind greater than the true wind and from a direction somewhat between that of the true wind and that of the air resistance. A flag or streamer fixed to the mast will blow in the direction opposite the apparent wind instead of opposite the true wind. When the direction of the true wind changes, the direction and magnitude of the apparent wind likewise changes. It is the apparent wind that is the total resultant force driving the boat and the wind to which the sails must constantly be trimmed.

appeal play *baseball* A situation in which a base runner commits a base-running infraction (as failing to touch a base in passing) but can be called out only if a member of the defensive team tags the player or touches the appropriate base while holding the ball and then appeals to the umpire before the next pitch. If no appeal is made, the infraction is ignored.

appearance money or **appearance fee** Money paid to a star performer (as a race car driver) or to a team for competing in a specific meet or competition. Appearance money may be a guarantee against winnings or may be paid in addition to winnings.

appel *fencing* A call to stop the bout made by a fencer by stamping his foot twice. The bout will be stopped immediately provided an attack is not underway.

apple A baseball. ⟨tried everything on the old *apple* but salt and pepper and chocolate sauce topping — Gaylord Perry⟩

apprentice allowance *horse racing* A reduction in the amount of weight a horse ridden by an apprentice jockey must carry in a race. Though the allowances are set by the individual state racing commissions, the following are those of the New York Jockey Club and are representative. Until the apprentice has ridden 5 winners, he is permitted to claim 10 pounds; he may claim an allowance of 7 pounds until he has ridden an additional 30 winners. If his first 35 winners come within his first year of riding, he is allowed to claim an allowance of 5 pounds for the remainder of the year. A 3-pound allowance is granted for an additional year provided he remains in the employ of his original employer. The apprentice allowance is indicated in the racing program by one or more stars or asterisks (popularly called *bugs*). The number of asterisks indicates the amount of the weight allowance.

apprentice jockey *horse racing* A novice jockey who is under contract to a trainer or owner for a period of from 3 to 5 years, who has been working for the trainer or owner for at least one year, and who is eligible to claim an apprentice allowance. — see also APPRENTICE ALLOWANCE

approach 1 *bowling* **a** A 16-foot-long section of the lane leading to the foul line, on which the bowler makes his approach in delivering the ball. **b** The steps taken and the motion made by a bowler in delivering the ball. Though 5-step and 3-step approaches are sometimes used, the 4-step approach is the most common.
2 *diving* The manner of moving to the starting position for a dive. For forward dives, the approach is normally a short run with a hurdle step to gain momentum and is usually judged on form.
3 *golf* An approach shot.
4 *gymnastics* The manner in which a performer moves to the apparatus to start a routine.

5 *track and field* The run by a competitor to the takeoff point (in vaulting or jumping) or up to the foul line (in throwing events) in order to gain momentum.

approach shot *golf* A shot made from the fairway to the putting green.

après-ski Social activity (as at a ski lodge) after a day's skiing.

apron 1 *auto racing* The inner edge of an oval racing track usually used by cars coming up to racing speeds on returning to the track from the pit area.
2 *boxing* The section of the ring floor extending beyond the ropes.
3 *golf* The area of closely-cut grass that surrounds the putting green. The apron is usually cut shorter than the fairway but not quite so short as the putting green.

¹aquaplane A flat board 5 to 6 feet long on which a rider stands to plane over the water when towed by a speedboat.

²aquaplane *of a car* To hydroplane.

aquaplaning The act or sport of riding an aquaplane.

aquatics Water sports including swimming, diving, surfing, skin diving, boating, and sailing.

arabesque A body position (as in gymnastics or skating) in which the performer balances on one leg, leans forward at the waist keeping the back arched, and holds the free leg horizontal. — see also SPIRAL, SCALE

Arabian or **Arabian jump** or **Arabian handspring** *gymnastics* A handspring started by jumping instead of falling into a handstand position.

arbiter A baseball umpire.

arch *gymnastics* A body position in which the body is bent backward so that the back is arched.

archer Someone skilled in the use of a bow and arrow or who engages in archery.

archer's paralysis *archery* A psychological state in which an archer is unable to aim directly at the center of a target or unable to loose the arrow when it is aimed at the center of the target. (also called *gold-shyness*)

archery The art, skill, or sport of shooting with a bow and arrow. Competitive archery encompasses target archery, in which all competitors take turns shooting groups of arrows at round targets at known distances, field archery, in which the competitors move in groups around a course laid out over the countryside or in a woods shooting a specified number of arrows at targets at unknown distances, and flight shooting, in which competitors seek to shoot their arrows as far as possible. In target archery, shooters are generally divided into groups of 4 archers for each target with one of the group serving as the target captain who orders the beginning and end of the shooting, designates the scoring value of each arrow in the target, and decides minor questions of interpretations of rules. Each archer usually shoots 3 arrows in turn and then yields his place to another member of the group. The end is scored after each shooter has shot 2 groups of 3 arrows each. This procedure is continued until the required number of arrows has been shot and scored from each distance according to the particular round being used. The principal rounds used in tournament competition are these: York, Hereford, St. George, Albion, Men's Western, Men's National, Western, National, Windsor, Columbia, and American rounds, and the FITA rounds for men and women. Archers are classified according to skill and age, and there are variations of many of these rounds for competitors in different age groups. — see also FIELD ARCHERY; CLOUT SHOOTING, FLIGHT SHOOTING, WAND SHOOTING

archery golf An adaptation of golf using a bow and arrow in which archers compete against each other on a specially prepared course or against golfers on a golf course following the basic rules of golf. The archer is limited to using one bow but he may use any number of arrows. The archer typically uses flight arrows for distance (driving) and field or target arrows for close range accuracy (the approach and putting). The archer counts one stroke for each arrow shot and he holes out by hitting a special target. The arrows used in the approach and in putting are specially prepared to prevent skidding; a lost arrow incurs the same penalty as a lost ball.

area blocking *football* Blocking any opponent in a particular area or zone instead of a designated player. (also called *zone blocking*)

area drive *hunting* A method of hunting in which some hunters wait along game trails while other hunters beat the woods to drive the game towards them.

arena 1 A building in which indoor sports (as basketball, ice hockey, and boxing) are held and which provides spectator accommodations and facilities (as dressing and shower rooms) for the participants.
2 *table tennis* see COURT

arête *mountain climbing* A sharp crested ridge of a mountain.

Arlberg strap or **Arlberg safety strap** *skiing* A strap attached to the ski binding and wrapped around the skier's ankle to prevent loss of the ski in the event the binding is suddenly released (as in a fall). (also called *safety strap*)

Arlberg system see SKIING

arm 1 Ability to throw or pitch. ⟨has one of the finest *arms* in the league⟩
2 The part of some anchors that extends out to either side from the shank.
3 Short for *firearm*.

arm bar see BAR ARM

arm guard *archery* A plastic or leather covering for the inner forearm of the bow arm to protect it from the bow string—see illustration at BOW.

armlock 1 *judo* A hold in which the opponent's arm is stretched out and held in that position with pressure applied to the back of the elbow.
2 *wrestling* Any hold in which the arm is held so that it cannot be moved.

arm pull *swimming* The pull of the arm through the water for propulsion.

armstand dive *diving* Any of a group of dives in which the diver begins in a handstand position at the end of the platform facing toward the platform and falls away toward the water. — compare BACKWARD DIVE, FORWARD DIVE, INWARD DIVE, REVERSE DIVE, TWIST DIVE

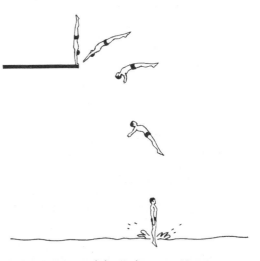

armstand dive in layout position

arm twist *wrestling* A counter in which a wrestler whose arm is grasped by an opponent straightens his arm then bends his elbow against his opponent's forearm and jerks free.

arm wrestling

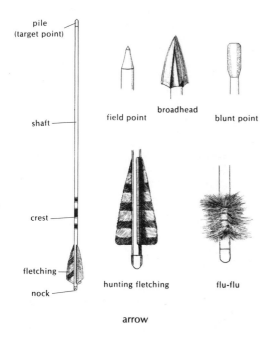

pile
(target point)

shaft

crest

fletching

nock

field point

broadhead

blunt point

hunting fletching

flu-flu

arrow

arm wrestling An activity in which 2 opponents sit face to face and grip each other's hand (usually the right hand) with the corresponding elbow set on a flat surface such as a table and attempt to force each other's arm down. (also called *Indian wrestling*) — compare WRIST WRESTLING

arrest *mountain climbing* The act or method of stopping a fall or slide by a climber. In belaying a fellow climber, a person usually allows the rope to pass around the body with each hand on it. The safest means of arresting a fall is to gradually tighten the grip on the rope, allowing it to run through the hands a little before pulling tight. This is known as the *sliding friction arrest;* with it much of the shock of the fall is absorbed by the movement of the rope through the belayer's hands instead of solely by the rope and the body of the fallen climber. The usual method of stopping a slide is the *self arrest* in which the sliding climber turns over on his stomach, digs his toes into the slope, and presses his ice axe or a staff into the dirt or snow. — see also BELAY

arrimada *jai alai* A shot returned to the front wall in such a way as to rebound close along the side wall where it is hard for the opponent to return.

arrow **1** *archery* A slender shaft of wood, metal, or fiberglass that is shot from a bow. The arrow is approximately $5/16$ inch in diameter and from 22 to 28 or sometimes 30 inches long. The length of the arrow used is determined usually by the length of the archer's arm or by the size of the bow. The arrow is composed essentially of four parts: pile, shaft, fletching, and nock. The pile may vary from the simple bullet-shaped point used in target shooting to the sharp broadhead used in hunting. The shaft is generally of equal diameter throughout its length and may be self (made of only one type of material) or footed (made with stronger material added at stress points). The fletching is the arrangement of feathers or the feathers themselves near the end of the arrow which give it stability in flight. The nock is a narrow groove in the end opposite the pile into which the bowstring fits.
2 An iceboat of a one-design class used chiefly for day sailing. It is 16 feet long, carries 80 square feet of sail, and weighs about 200 pounds.
3 *bowling* Any of the usually narrow triangular spots on the lane near the foul line.

arrowhead The pile of an arrow. — see ARROW

arrow plate *archery* A small inlaid or padded section on one side of the bow just above the arrow rest across which the arrow passes when shot. On target bows the plate is ornamental while a padded plate on hunting bows serves to deaden the sound of the shot.

arrow rest or **arrow shelf** *archery* A narrow ledge on the side of the bow which supports the arrow.

artificial climbing *mountain climbing* Climbing over rock or ice by means of artificial aids (such as pitons, chockstones, and étriers).

artificial fly see FLY

artificial respiration The restoration of breathing by manual or mechanical means. This consists essentially of forcing air into and out of the lungs rhythmically.

artificial route *mountain climbing* A route that can be abandoned conveniently by a traverse onto an easier route; a route that lies close to or parallel to an easier route which may be reached by relatively easy climbing.

ascender *mountain climbing* A mechanical device that can be slid along a rope in only one direction and that is used to connect loads to ropes so that they can be advanced up the rope without their sliding back down.

Ashes *cricket* A mythical trophy won by the winner of the England-Australia Test Matches.

Asian Games A program of amateur sports competition identical to the Olympic Games that is held every 4 years in the interval between Olympics among nations of Asia.

assault A fencing bout.

assist 1 An action by a player who assists a teammate in making a putout or in scoring a goal: **a** *baseball* A throw made to a teammate to enable him to make a putout. An assist can be awarded even though an error by the teammate prevents the putout. Example: the shortstop fields a batted ball and throws to the second baseman who steps on second base for a forceout and then throws to first base to complete the double play. Whether or not the double play is ultimately successful, the shortstop will get credit for an assist; the second baseman will be credited with a putout and, if the throw to first base was good and in time to retire the runner, an assist, even though the first baseman may have dropped the ball. **b** *basketball* A pass to a teammate who immediately scores a basket. An assist may be credited to a player even though the teammate may have to dribble the ball or dodge an opponent before shooting so long as the player continues his movement toward the basket after receiving the pass. No assist is given if the player receiving the pass holds the ball, dribbles it to get into position to shoot, or interrupts his movement. **c** *ice hockey* An instance of handling the puck immediately prior to a teammate's scoring. An assist is usually given to the 2 players who handled the puck just before the player who took the shot. In unusual circumstances, such as on a breakaway, it is possible for a goalkeeper to receive an assist. If the puck is deflected into the goal by an offensive player after a shot by a teammate, that player gets credit for the goal and the shooter receives an assist. **d** *lacrosse* A pass to a teammate who scores immediately without having to dodge a defensive player.
2 Credit given a player in statistical records for making an assist.

association croquet A version of croquet played in Great Britain between 2 sides of one or 2 players on a 28-by-35-yard court that has 6 wickets and a stake (peg), with the object for each side to drive its 2 balls in turn through each of the 6 wickets, first in one direction and then in the other, and finally hit the peg in the middle of the court. One point is scored for each wicket made and for hitting the peg; the first team to get 26 points (13 for each player) is the winner.

association football British term for *soccer.*

astern 1 Toward or at the stern of a boat; behind a boat.
2 In reverse; backward. 〈reversed the engines to move the boat *astern*〉

Astroturf A trademark used for a synthetic surface that is used in place of grass especially on football and baseball fields.

asymmetrical bars British term for *uneven parallel bars.*

at bat *baseball* An official turn as a batter charged to a player except when he gets a base on balls or a sacrifice hit, is hit by a pitched ball, or is interfered with by the catcher. The number of times at bat is used in computing a player's batting average. 〈3 hits in 5 *at bats*〉

athlete Someone who is trained to compete in exercises, sports, or games requiring physical strength, agility, or stamina. — used in Great Britain to refer to someone who competes in track and field sports

athlete's foot Ringworm of the feet that is characterized by softening and cracking of the skin between the toes accompanied by painful itching and that is spread especially through unsanitary conditions in a gymnasium.

athletics British term for *track and field* sports.

athletic supporter A usually elastic supporter for the genitals worn by men participating in sports.

athwart or **athwartships** Across or at right angles to the centerline of a boat.

atmosphere A unit of pressure equal to the pressure of the atmosphere at sea level; 14.7 pounds per square inch. 〈in seawater, the pressure increases one *atmosphere* for every 33 feet of depth〉

¹attack 1 An offensive or scoring action. 〈these players carried the *attack* deep into the opponent's territory〉
2 The offensive players on a team (as in lacrosse or Australian Rules football). — compare DEFENSE
3 *cricket* The action of a team in attempting to put out opposing batsmen and especially a team's bowling action. 〈turned his arm for 30.3 overs, capturing five wickets. . . . Last Saturday, he spearheaded Stafford's *attack* for 28 overs — *Wolverhampton (England) Express & Star*〉
4 *fencing* A movement or series of movements aimed at scoring a hit against an opponent. In foil and saber competition, a fencer must first parry an opponent's attack before he is permitted to initiate a counterattack.

²attack To mount an attack; to seek to score against an opponent.

attack block

attack block *volleyball* A block which forces the ball down into the opponents' court at such an angle as to give the opponents little chance of retrieving it.

attacker A player who is a member of a team's attack or a member of a team's offense.

attacking 1 Of or relating to a team's efforts to score.
2 Being the part of the playing area in which one team is attacking the opponent's goal. ⟨*attacking* half of the field⟩

attacking line *volleyball* A line parallel to and 10 feet from the net on each side of the court that divides the front court from the back court. A back line player who is in front of the attacking line is not permitted to jump up and spike the ball. To be able to spike, the back line player must start his jump from behind the attacking line. (also called *spiking line*)

attacking zone 1 *box lacrosse* The area in which the opponent's goal is located and which extends from the end of the box to the center zone. One team's attacking zone is the other team's defensive zone.
2 *ice hockey* The area in which the opponent's goal is located and which extends from the end of the rink to the nearest blue line. One team's attacking zone is the other team's defensive zone. — see also NEUTRAL ZONE

attackman *lacrosse* A player assigned to an offensive position or an offensive part of the field. — compare DEFENSEMAN

attack on preparation *fencing* An attack launched while the opponent is making a preparation of attack but before his attack has actually commenced. A successful attack on preparation can take the initiative and score before the opponent can adjust from offense to defense.

attack on second intent SEE FALSE ATTACK

attack on the blade *fencing* A preparation for attack in which the fencer attempts to move the opponent's blade to clear a line of attack or to obtain a reaction from the opponent which will create or suggest a line of attack.

attention *fencing* A position in which the fencer stands with his front foot pointed toward his opponent and the rear foot held at right angles while the sword arm is held straight and pointed at the floor at a 45 degree angle. This position is assumed by both fencers prior to the command to fence.

attrition The act of retiring from a race or the state of having retired. In auto racing, the car is usually retired because of an accident or me-chanical failure. Horses are retired from a steeplechase race usually because of a fall which delays them too much for them to have a chance of again being competitive.

audibilize or **audible** *football* To call an audible.

audible *football* A substitute offensive play or defensive formation called at the line of scrimmage especially because of the need to adjust to the formation of the opposing team. (also called *automatic*)

Australian crawl *swimming* A 2-beat crawl.

Australian doubles or **Australian formation** *tennis* An arrangement of doubles players in which the server's partner plays on the same side of the court as the server. It is normally used when the receiving player is especially strong on cross-court returns. (also called *I formation*)

Australian pursuit *cycling* A pursuit race between teams of up to 8 riders evenly spaced around the track. The race lasts for a stated number of laps or for a time period, and any rider who is passed by a member of the opposing team during the race is eliminated.

Australian Rules football A game played in Australia on an oval field approximately 180 yards long and 120 yards wide between 2 teams of 18 players each, with the object to move a rugby ball close enough to the opponent's goal to kick it between the uprights for a score and to prevent the opposing team from scoring. Fifteen of the players for each team maintain relatively fixed positions on the field while 3 players are permitted to move about the field following the play. One of these is the rover and the other 2 are the followers. Of the other members of the team, there are 3 full forwards who play nearest the opponent's goal, 3 half forwards who play midway between the goal and the middle of the field, 3 midfielders (a center and 2 wings) who occupy the middle of the field, 3 halfbacks, and 3 fullbacks playing nearest their own goal. Players may advance the ball by running, provided they bounce or touch the ball to the ground every 10 yards, or by kicking the ball or passing it to a teammate. The ball may be passed only by a kick or by punching the ball with the fist, not by throwing. Members of the opposing team attempt to prevent the advance of the ball by grabbing the ballcarrier and holding him so that he is forced to kick or pass the ball or by throwing him off balance so that he loses control of the ball. Players are not tackled, however, as they are in American football or rugby. At each end of the field are 4 upright posts side by side and each 7 yards apart. The 2 center posts are the goalposts and the outer posts are the behind posts. A goal, worth 6 points, is scored if the ball is kicked (by a punt, dropkick, or placekick) between the goalposts; if the ball passes inside the behind posts, it is a behind worth one point. Whenever a player is successful in catching a kicked ball in the air and calling out mark, the referee halts play and permits the player to make a free kick at the goal from the place of the catch. The game is played in four 25-minute quarters and play is continuous with no time-outs.

Austrian ski system   see SKIING

Autobol or **Autoball**   A game between 2 teams of 4 players each which is played according to the basic idea of soccer but in which the players all drive small automobiles and try to bump a 4-foot rubber ball into the goal.

autocross   An automobile gymkhana. In Great Britain the term is used of an automobile competition in which 2 or more competitors at a time compete in timed heats of 2 to 5 laps around a

Australian Rules football: FB fullback; HB halfback; C center; W wing; HF half forward; FF full forward; R rover; F follower

closed course up to ⅓ to ½ mile long laid out on grass. All competitors race against the clock with the one having the lowest lap time being the winner.

autodrome   An automobile racetrack.

autoloader   A automatic or semiautomatic firearm.

¹automatic   *of a firearm*   Employing the force of recoil or gas pressure and mechanical spring action to eject the empty cartridge case after a shot is fired, load a new cartridge from the magazine, fire, eject the spent case, and repeat the cycle as long as pressure on the trigger is maintained and there is ammunition in the magazine. — compare SEMIAUTOMATIC

²automatic   **1** An automatic or semiautomatic firearm.

2 *football*   see AUDIBLE

automatic reel   *fishing*   A fly reel that retrieves line by means of a spring device. — see illustration at REEL

automatic take   *baseball*   A situation with the count 3 balls and no strikes in which the batter almost always takes the next pitch in hopes of receiving a base on balls.

auto-pully tow   see TOWING

auto racing   The sport of racing automobiles. In the early days of the automobile, races were held over public roads, and the mechanic often rode in the car with the driver. Today practically all racing is done on closed courses specifically designed for racing, and the few races that are still run on public roads generally take place in Europe. Most auto racing can be divided into 3 major categories: drag racing, racing on oval tracks, and road racing. The automobiles used in each of these categories range from production-line passenger cars that are essentially unchanged from the way they are in the dealer's showroom through highly modified stock cars often retaining only the original body shape and the manufacturer's name to highly sophisticated racing machines which are powered by an engine built solely for racing. In all categories of racing, cars compete against one another within classes according to actual or potential speed, engine size, and modifications permitted. In endurance road racing, it is not uncommon for several different classes of cars to compete together, with the slowest cars seeking to beat out the other cars in their class without particular concern for their overall position. — see also DRAG RACING, ROAD RACING; FORMULA CAR, INDY CAR, STOCK CAR

auto tow see TOWING

avalanche A large mass of snow, ice, or earth sliding or falling down a mountainside.

avalanche cord *mountain climbing* A brightly colored cord 30 to 50 feet long that trails behind a climber walking or climbing near a potential avalanche site. If he should be caught in a snow slide, the cord could help others locate the buried climber.

avalement *skiing* The technique of allowing the knees to flex to absorb bumps and of pushing the feet slightly forward to keep the skis in constant contact with the snow when skiing and turning at high speed.

Avco Cup The championship trophy of the World Hockey Association.

average A ratio expressing the average performance of an individual or team computed according to the number of opportunities for successful performance and usually expressed as a number carried to three decimal places. — see BATTING AVERAGE, BOWLING AVERAGE, FIELDING AVERAGE, PASS COMPLETION AVERAGE; compare PERCENTAGE

away **1** Played at the opponent's home field, court, or ice. ⟨an *away* game⟩
2 *baseball* **a** *of a pitch* To the side of the plate away from the batter. ⟨pitch him low and *away*⟩ **b** Out. ⟨2 *away* in the ninth inning⟩
3 *of a golf ball* Lying farthest from the hole and therefore first to be played.

awayswinger see OUTSWINGER

axe *surfing* A wave that breaks directly over a surfer causing a wipeout.

axel or **Axel Paulsen** *skating* A jump from the forward outside edge of one skate with 1½ turns in the air and a return to the backward outside edge of the other skate.

azimuth see BEARING

B

Babe Ruth League A commercially sponsored baseball league for youths aged 13–15. — compare AMERICAN LEGION BASEBALL, LITTLE LEAGUE

baby A 2-year-old racehorse; juvenile.

baby split *bowling* A split that leaves either the 2 and 7 or the 3 and 10 pins standing. — see illustration of pin arrangement at BOWLING

babyweight *boxing* A boxer in one of the divisions below lightweight.

¹back **1** A primarily defensive player in many team games who is positioned behind his forward line and who generally must guard an opposing forward. The backs play near the goal they are defending. In polo these players are simply called backs. The backs in soccer and field hockey are traditionally the left and right fullbacks and the left, right, and center halfbacks. — compare FORWARD

2 *archery* The side of the bow away from the string. — compare BELLY

3 *football* **a** An offensive player who lines up at least one yard behind the line of scrimmage and who is responsible for advancing the ball toward the opponent's goal line by running with the ball, by throwing or catching forward passes, or by blocking for the ballcarrier. The 4 backs are generally the quarterback, fullback, and 2 halfbacks though other designations such as *tailback, running back, set back,* or *flankerback* are sometimes used in various formations. — see also FRONT LINE **b** see DEFENSIVE BACK

4 *rugby* Any of the 7 players who line up behind the scrum including the fullback, the halfbacks, and the threequarter backs. — compare FORWARD

5 *volleyball* Any of the 3 players stationed on the second row when the ball is served. Though the players have specific duties, they do not play set positions. The team rotates, with the players changing positions at a change of serve, so that each player will be a back during the course of the game.

²back **1** To bet on a competitor (as a racehorse).

2 *basketball* To defend against a player by playing directly behind him. — compare FRONT

3 *of a hunting dog* To stop and assume a pointing position behind another pointing dog automatically or on command.

4 *sailing* To brace a sail so that the wind presses upon the forward side checking headway or driving the bow over to a new course.

back alley *badminton* The area on a doubles court between the long service line and the back boundary line. A serve that falls within this area is a fault.

back-and-knee technique *mountain climbing* A method of climbing a chimney by placing the back against one side and bracing with the knees pushing against the opposite side.

backboard **1** *basketball* Either of 2 flat rectangular or fan-shaped surfaces which are supported above and perpendicular to the floor 4 feet inside the end line at each end of the court and to which the baskets are attached. The backboard serves to keep missed shots from going out of bounds and as a surface from which the ball can be made to rebound into the basket. Backboards may be of white rigid material or of transparent glass. Rectangular boards measure 6 by 4 feet and the fan-shaped board must be 54 inches wide. Transparent boards have a 24-by-18-inch rectangular outline centered just above the basket.

2 *ice hockey* The endboards of a rink.

3 *tennis* A wall against which players hit the ball for practice.

back boundary line *badminton* Either of the 2 lines parallel to the net that mark the end boundary of the court. In singles play, these lines also mark the rear boundary of the service courts.

backcast *fishing* A short backswing of the fishing rod immediately prior to the cast. In bait casting and spinning, the weight of the lure bends the rod tip back so that on the forward cast the forward spring of the rod helps propel the lure farther. In fly fishing, the backcast results in the entire line moving to the rear and is often used to lift the line from the water and to straighten it behind the caster in preparation for a forward cast.

back-check *ice hockey* To skate back toward one's own goal while defending against the offensive rush of an opposing player. Back-checking is usually done by forwards in their defensive zone. — compare FORE-CHECK
— **on the backcheck** In the act of back-checking.

back-checker A hockey player who back-checks.

backcourt **1** In net games, the part of the court farthest from the net. In badminton it is usually the area behind the short service line. In tennis, the area behind the service line is usually considered backcourt. In volleyball it is the area behind the attacking line.
2 In wall games, the half of the court farthest from the front wall; the area near the back wall. In handball it is usually the area behind the short line.
3 *basketball* **a** The half of the court which contains the basket at which the opponents shoot and in which a team plays defense. One team's backcourt is the other team's frontcourt. When a team gains possession of the ball in its backcourt (as after a goal or by means of a turnover), it has 10 seconds to move the ball across the division line. **b** The guard positions. ⟨he can play in the *backcourt*⟩ **c** The players who play guard positions. ⟨one of the best *backcourts* in the country — *Sports Illustrated*⟩

backcourt foul *basketball* A personal foul in professional play committed against an offensive player who is in his own backcourt for which the fouled player is awarded 2 free throws.

backcourtman A guard on a basketball team.

backcourt violation *basketball* A violation resulting from a team's failure to move the ball into their frontcourt within 10 seconds of having gained possession of it in the backcourt or from dribbling, throwing, or knocking the ball over the division line into the backcourt for which the opposing team is awarded possession of the ball.

back crawl see BACKSTROKE (*swimming*)

back dive see BACKWARD DIVE

backdoor or **backdoor play** *basketball* A play in which an offensive player cuts away from the defender and moves behind the defense to receive a quick pass under the basket.

backdrop *trampolining* A stunt in which the performer jumps in the air, lands on his back with his legs and arms in the air, and returns to his feet.

backed bow *archery* A bow that has a strip of material laminated to the entire length of the back for added strength.

backer-up **1** *baseball* A defensive player who backs up a teammate fielding a ball.
2 *football* see LINEBACKER

backfield **1** *football* **a** The player positions behind the linemen. **b** The offensive backs (as halfbacks, fullbacks, and quarterbacks) who line up behind the offensive linemen and who are primarily responsible for running with the ball, throwing and receiving forward passes, blocking, and sometimes kicking. **c** The defensive players (as cornerbacks and safeties) who line up behind the defensive linemen and who are primarily responsible for defending against runs and passes and who sometimes return kicks.
2 *field hockey* A team's defensive players including the goalkeeper.
3 *soccer* The primarily defensive players including halfbacks, fullbacks, and the goalkeeper.

backfield line *football* The vertical plane one yard behind and parallel to the offensive team's line of scrimmage. The offensive backs with the exception of the quarterback must line up behind the backfield line.

backfist *karate* A punch thrown by swinging the forearm away from the body with the hand turned so that the target is hit with the back of the fist.

back flip A backward somersault; a backward dive in which the diver performs a single somersault in a layout position and enters the water feetfirst.

back float *swimming* A floating position in which the swimmer lies on his back with his arms extended to each side.

back four *soccer* The 4 defenders who play in the defensive half of the field in a modern lineup. — see illustration at SOCCER.

back glide *swimming* A gliding maneuver performed in the back-float position with arms at the sides and started by pushing off with the feet from the side or bottom of the pool.

¹**backhand** **1** A stroke (as in tennis) made with the arm across the body and the back of the hand turned toward the direction of movement. — compare FOREHAND
2 *baseball* A catch made by reaching across the body and turning the hand so that the palm is toward the ball.
3 *box lacrosse* A shot made by a player facing away from the goal by throwing the ball back over the shoulder.

4 *ice hockey* A shot or pass made with the back of the blade and with the back of the controlling or lower hand facing the direction of movement.

backhand stroke

²backhand **1** To hit a ball or puck with a backhand stroke.

2 *baseball* To make a backhand catch of a ball.

backhand cast *fishing* A cast made (as in fly fishing) with the casting arm across the body with the rod moving forward from the opposite side of the body.

backhander *ice hockey* A shot made with a backhand stroke.

back header **1** *diving* A backward dive in which the diver enters the water headfirst.

2 *soccer* A header made by hitting the ball with the back of the head.

backheel *wrestling* A takedown in which a wrestler standing behind his opponent locks his hands around the opponent's waist, places his feet against the opponent's heels, and pulls the opponent backward to the mat.

backing **1** *archery* A thin strip of material bonded to the back of a bow to improve the cast or to help strengthen the bow.

2 *fishing* Line wound on a reel under the casting line to help fill the reel and to serve as a reserve supply in the event a hooked fish makes a long run.

3 *horse racing* The total amount bet on a horse before a race.

back iron *basketball* The metal plate at the back of the basket rim by means of which it is attached to the backboard.

back jackknife *diving* An inward dive in a jackknife position.

back judge A football official who takes a position in the defensive backfield on the same side of the field as the line judge and who is primarily responsible for watching for clips and pass interference on deep plays, noting when and where the ball goes out of bounds on his side of the field, and ruling on field goals along with the field judge.

backlash *fishing* A snarl in the line on the spool of a bait casting reel caused by the spool's revolving faster than the line is traveling out. A spool will start revolving too fast if a heavy lure imparts too much momentum to the spool at the start of the cast. Proper pressure must be exerted on the spool by the thumb to prevent backlash.

backlift *cricket* The backswing of the bat prior to the swing at the ball.

back line **1** The line of backs (as in volleyball or water polo).

2 *curling* see BACK SCORE

3 *ice hockey* A team's defensemen.

4 *polo* The boundary at each end of the field. The goals are centered on the back lines.

backliner A defenseman on an ice hockey team.

back man British or Australian term for *back* (as in soccer or Australian Rules football).

back marker *auto racing* A competitor who is far behind the leaders in a race.

back nine *golf* The second half of an 18-hole course.

back off *auto racing* To decelerate (as when going into a turn) by letting up on the throttle.

back out *surfing* To pull back from a wave that could have been caught.

¹backpack A hiking or camping pack often made of nylon or canvas that is carried on the back and used to hold equipment and provisions. Modern hiking packs are usually supported by a lightweight frame typically made of aluminum. Packs used by mountain climbers are generally small packs with smooth profiles so that there are no projections to get caught on rocks or ledges.

²backpack To carry food or equipment by means of a backpack; to hike with a backpack.

backpacker Someone who hikes with or carries equipment in a backpack.

back pass A pass (as in soccer or field hockey) from a player to a teammate behind him.

backpedal To retreat or move backward (as in boxing or football) while facing an opponent or a play.

back pocket A fullback in Australian Rules football.

back room *tennis* The area between the base-

packframe
pack

climbing
pack

backpacks   rucksack

line and the fence or wall that bounds a court. The area recommended for tournament play is 21 feet deep.

back rope *mountain climbing* A technique sometimes used in traversing in which the last man on a rope is protected from a possible fall by employing a second rope from the leader through a running belay at the beginning of the traverse. As the last man moves across the traverse, the leader takes up the main rope while playing out the second rope. When the climber reaches the end of the traverse, the second rope is released at one end and pulled through the belay and retrieved. This technique protects the last climber by keeping him from swinging like a pendulum in the event of a fall.

back sacrifice throw *judo* A throw in which the defender grabs the lapels of the attacker, falls to his back pulling the attacker toward him and, placing a foot in the attacker's stomach, pushes the attacker upward and over his head.

back score or **back line** *curling* The line across the rink at the rear edge of the house. A stone which comes to rest behind this line is out of play and is removed from the rink.

backspin A backward rotary motion imparted to a ball (as a golf ball, tennis ball, billiard ball, or table tennis ball) that causes the ball to stop abruptly or bounce backward upon making contact with a surface or another ball. (also called *underspin*)

backstay *sailing* A rope or wire cable extending from the top of the mast to the rear of the boat

to help hold the mast upright. — compare HEAD-STAY, SHROUD

backstop **1** A screen or fence (as behind home plate in baseball or behind the baseline of a tennis or platform tennis court) for keeping a ball from leaving the field of play.
2 A player (as the catcher in baseball or the wicketkeeper in cricket) whose position is behind the batter.
3 A goalkeeper in ice hockey.

backstraight *motor racing* A long straight on the far end of a racecourse typically away from the grandstands and often parallel to the front straight.

backstretch The straight on the side of a racetrack opposite the homestretch and the finish line.

backstroke **1** *cricket* A batting stroke in which the batsman steps back with his rear foot just before swinging. — compare FORWARD STROKE
2 *polo* A stroke that sends the ball in the direction opposite to that in which the horse is heading.
3 *swimming* **a** Either of 2 strokes executed in a supine position: (1) A stroke that combines a frog kick and a double arm pull in which the arms are extended beyond the shoulders and moved together to the hips. (also called *elementary backstroke*) (2) A stroke that combines the flutter kick and alternate arm pulls in which each arm is extended beyond the shoulders and pulled to the hips alternately. This is the form of backstroke used in competition. (also called *back crawl, racing backstroke*) **b** A competitive event or a leg of a medley in which the backstroke is used. The most common distances for the backstroke as a separate event are 100 and 200 meters and 100 and 200 yards.

backstroker *swimming* Someone who swims the backstroke especially in competition.

backswing The movement of an implement (as a club or racket) or an arm backward to a position from which the forward or downward swing is made. Body rotation is combined with the backswing whose purpose is to give momentum and extra power to the stroke.

back-to-back Consecutive. ⟨won *back-to-back* championships⟩

back umpire *Canadian football* An official whose duties are similar to those of the umpire in American football.

[1]backup or **backup ball** *bowling* A ball that has spin opposite that of a hook and that curves toward the same side as the hand delivering it

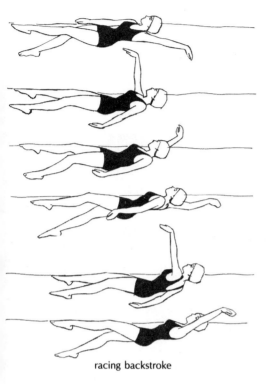

racing backstroke

elementary backstroke viewed from above

to hit the pins from the opposite side. (also called *reverse hook*)

²backup Substitute. ⟨*backup* quarterback⟩

back up **1** To move to a position near or behind a teammate to be in position to assist on a play if necessary (as by stopping a missed ball).
2 *of the nonstriker in cricket* To move forward of the crease as the bowler is delivering the ball so as to be in a better position to run if the striker hits the ball. Backing up is analogous to a base runner's taking a lead in baseball.

backup ball see BACKUP (*bowling*)

back uprise see UPRISE

backward dive or **back dive** *diving* One of a group of competitive dives which is started from a position facing toward the board or platform and in which the diver jumps up and turns backward to enter the water feetfirst facing toward the board or headfirst facing away from the board. — compare ARMSTAND DIVE, FORWARD DIVE, INWARD DIVE, REVERSE DIVE, TWIST DIVE

backward hit *rounders* A batted ball that is not hit into the forward area and that is not in play. A backward hit is analogous to a foul ball in baseball.

backward pass see LATERAL (*football*)

backward somersault A somersault performed by turning backward; a dive in which the diver leaves the board facing toward the board and turns a backward somersault before entering the water. On a full somersault the diver enters the water feetfirst. If the dive involves an additional half revolution so that the diver enters the water headfirst, it is a back 1½ (somersault).

backwash **1** The motion of water thrown back by the oars or propeller of a boat.
2 Water rushing back to the sea after a wave washes up on shore.

backward dive in layout position

backwater

¹backwater *canoeing* A stroke in which paddles are pushed forward in order to drive a boat backward.

²backwater *canoeing* To drive a boat backward by pushing the paddles forward.

backwind *sailing* To sail in such a position that the wind deflected from one's sails adversely affects a following boat. This deflected wind approaches the other boat from more nearly head on with the result that the second boat cannot point as high into the wind as the first boat and consequently cannot move as fast.

badminton A court game played as a singles or doubles game with light, long-handled rackets with which a shuttlecock is volleyed over a high net. The court marked for both singles and doubles play measures 44 by 20 feet and has designated service areas. Play is started by one player or side serving to the other side with the shuttlecock volleyed over the net until one side fails to make a good return. Points are scored only by the serving side; if the serving side fails to make a good return, the service goes to the other side. Men's singles and doubles games are played until one side scores 15 points; women's singles games are to 11 points. In all forms of the game, there is a method of extending the game, called *setting the score,* if the game is tied at a particular score. — see also COURT

baffy *golf* An old name for a number 5 wood.

¹bag 1 *baseball* A square white stuffed canvas bag secured to the ground for use as a base.
2 *boxing* The heavy bag.
3 *hunting* The amount of game taken during a particular period or during a hunt. — see also BAG LIMIT

²bag To take animals as game; shoot.

bag limit The maximum number of fish or game animals permitted by law to be taken by one person in a given period.

¹bail 1 *cricket* Either of a pair of short wooden bars that are laid atop the 3 stumps of a wicket. The batsman is out if the bails are dislodged by a bowled ball, by a defensive player holding the ball before the batsman reaches the crease, or by the batsman himself in swinging or running.
2 *fishing* A U-shaped metal arm attached to the revolving cup of a spinning reel which catches the line and winds it on the spool when the reel handle is turned. The bail is locked out of the way for casting and springs into position when the handle is turned.

²bail To remove water from a boat.

bailer *boating* An opening at the stern of a boat

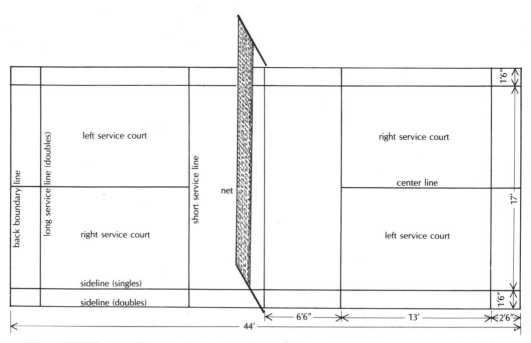

badminton court

through which shipped water is drained while the boat is moving forward at speed.

bail lock A device on a spinning reel which can be engaged to prevent the handle and bail from being turned backward. When the bail lock is engaged, it produces a clicking sound as the handle is turned forward.

bail out 1 *baseball* **a** To fall away from the normal batting stance or from the batter's box to avoid being hit by a pitched ball. **b** To make a pronounced step away from the plate as part of one's batting stride; to step in the bucket.
2 *surfing* To jump or dive away from a surfboard when a wipeout appears imminent so as to be as far as possible from the board when surfacing to avoid injury.

¹bait *fishing* Food attached to a hook to attract fish as opposed to an artificial lure used for the same purpose. Bait ranges from live or dead bait fish and worms to insects, corn kernels, and doughballs.

²bait *fishing* To place bait on a fishhook.

bait casting 1 *fishing* The casting of bait or an artificial lure using a casting rod and a bait casting reel. A relatively heavy lure is required to overcome the inertia of the revolving-spool reel, and control of the rate of revolution of the spool with the thumb is therefore an important art in bait casting. — compare FLY CASTING, SPINNING
2 Tournament competition in which a lightweight practice plug is cast at target rings placed at various distances using bait casting, spinning, or spin casting equipment. A ⅜- or ⅝-ounce practice plug may be used with bait casting equipment but only the ⅜-ounce plug is permitted with spinning or spin casting equipment. The caster makes 10 casts — 2 at each of 5 targets or one at each of 10 targets placed at distances from 40 to 80 feet from the caster. A perfect cast is worth 10 points and one point is deducted for each foot from the target the cast lands. There is no time limit for the caster to make his 10 casts. — see also FLY CASTING, SKISH

bait casting reel *fishing* A reel that has a wide revolving spool mounted at right angles to the direction of the cast, that has a gear arrangement to increase the turning ratio to about 4 to 1, and that often has a level wind mechanism. During the cast, the weight of the lure must overcome the inertia of the reel before it will revolve, and the speed with which it revolves has to be controlled with the thumb. Some bait casting reels have a device to disengage the gears for casting.

bait casting rod *fishing* A casting rod that is designed to be used with a bait casting reel.

bait fish *fishing* A small fish (as a minnow, chub, or herring) used as bait.

bait fishing Fishing with bait rather than an artificial lure at the end of the line.

baiting The practice of spreading food at or near a hunting or fishing site in order to induce game or fish to the area so that they may be easily caught or killed. The practice is illegal in many places though it is an accepted method of deepsea fishing.

baiting duck *hunting* A live duck whose movements are restricted so it can serve as a decoy. Live decoys are now illegal.

bait the hole *football* To disguise a trap play by making it appear to be another kind of play (as a pitchout) so that a sophisticated defensive lineman will not hesitate to rush through the hole between offensive linemen and can be trapped.

balaclava A knitted covering for the head and neck with an opening for a portion of the face or with small openings for the eyes and mouth and sometimes for the nose that is worn by hikers, climbers, and skiers for protection from the wind and cold. A similar garment of fire-resistant material is worn by auto racing drivers.

balance beam *gymnastics* **1** A wooden beam 5000 millimeters (approximately 16 feet) long and 100 millimeters (4 inches) wide that is supported in a horizontal position 1000 to 1200 millimeters (approximately 4 feet) above the floor and is used for balancing feats in competition.

balance beam

balance climbing

2 An event in women's competition in which a 1½- to 2-minute routine that includes walking, running, jumping, turning, standing, sitting, and lying is performed on the balance beam.

balance climbing *mountain climbing* A rock-climbing technique by which a climber is able to move up an extremely steep rock face on small footholds by using the hands only to maintain balance instead of to pull up and support the body's weight.

balanced line *football* An alignment of the offensive line in which there are an equal number of players on either side of the center.

balanced seat see FORWARD SEAT

balanced tackle *fishing* The proper combination of rod, reel, line, and lure to provide maximum efficiency.

balestra *fencing* A short jump forward usually followed by a lunge. In moving close enough for a lunge, the balestra offers more speed and surprise than a step.

¹balk **1** *baseball* An illegal motion by the pitcher committed with one or more runners on base for which each base runner is advanced one base. A balk may be called for the following actions (among others): pitching from a stretch without first coming to a set position; failure to make a pitch after making a body movement habitually associated with the delivery; feinting a throw to home plate or to first base; throwing to a base in an attempt to pick off a base runner without first stepping toward that base; assuming the pitching position on or near the pitcher's rubber when not holding the ball; pitching the ball when the catcher is not in the catcher's box; making more than 2 pumps during a windup; making a quick pitch or any other illegal pitch. If a balk is committed when there are no runners on base, a ball is called by the umpire.

2 *billiards* A specific restricted area on a billiard table which governs play in certain situations in different games. On a pocket billiards table, balk is the area between the head string and the head rail. On English billiards and snooker tables, it is the quarter of the table between the balkline and the bottom rail. In pocket billiards and English billiards, when an object ball is within balk and the cue ball is in hand and to be played from balk, the object ball is either spotted or not shot at on the play. In snooker, balk gives no such protection to an object ball. On a table marked for balkline games, balk is the area between a balkline and the nearest parallel cushion. When both object balls are within the same balk area,

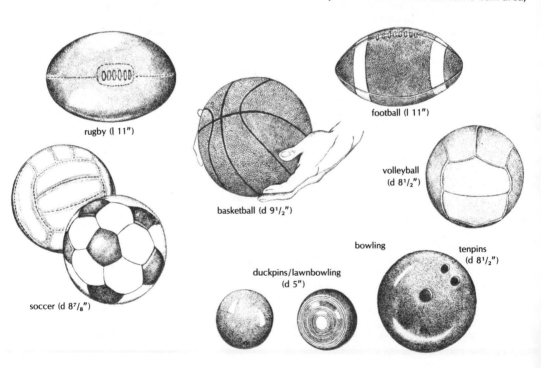

rugby (l 11")

football (l 11")

basketball (d 9¹/₂")

volleyball (d 8¹/₂")

bowling

tenpins (d 8¹/₂")

duckpins/lawnbowling (d 5")

soccer (d 8⁷/₈")

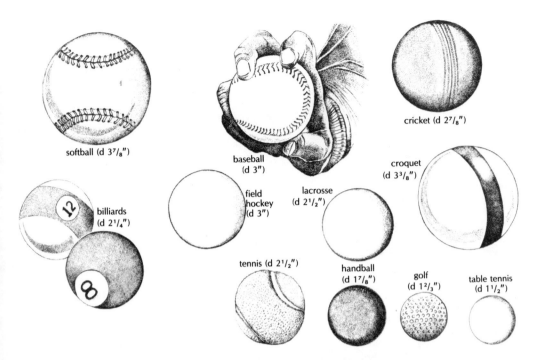

softball (d 3⁷/₈″)

baseball (d 3″)

cricket (d 2⁷/₈″)

croquet (d 3³/₈″)

billiards (d 2¹/₄″)

field hockey (d 3″)

lacrosse (d 2¹/₂″)

tennis (d 2¹/₂″)

handball (d 1⁷/₈″)

golf (d 1²/₃″)

table tennis (d 1¹/₂″)

a player is restricted in the number of points he may make before being required to drive one or both balls out of balk.

3 a Illegal interference with an opponent in a racket game. **b** *badminton* A fault which results when a player makes a feint during or before the serve.

²balk *of a baseball pitcher* To make a balk.

balkline 1 *billiards* **a** A line on a snooker or English billiards table parallel to the bottom rail and midway between the bottom rail and the center of the table which serves as the boundary of balk. — see illustration at BILLIARD TABLES **b** Any of the 4 lines parallel to and 14 or 18 inches from the cushions on a balkline table which mark the boundaries of the balk areas. **2** *croquet* Either of the two 13-yard-long lines on an association croquet court parallel to and one yard out from either end of the court on which the balls are placed to begin play.

balkline spot A spot in the exact center of the balkline on a snooker table on which the brown ball is placed at the beginning of the game. — see also BILLIARD SPOT, CENTER SPOT, PYRAMID SPOT

ball 1 A typically round object that is carried, thrown, kicked, dribbled, hit, or rolled as the principal action in a number of games. Balls are generally spherical. Football and rugby balls are exceptions. They have an oval outline, with the football having somewhat more pointed ends. The bowl used in lawn bowling is not perfectly spherical but has a bias on one side causing it to curve slightly when rolled. Balls may be classified into one of 4 groups according to the type of construction: some, like the football, rugby ball, basketball, and soccer ball, are inflated usually with a bladder inside a leather or rubber cover; others are made of solid or hollow rubber, like the lacrosse ball, handball, squash racquets ball, and tennis ball; still others are made of solid wood or hard plastic or composition material such as the billiard, bowling, croquet, and polo balls; and there are those built up of many layers of thread or yarn wound around a solid center and covered with a rubber or leather cover, like the baseball, cricket ball, pelota (jai alai), and softball. — see also JACK, PUCK, STONE, SHUTTLECOCK

2 A game in which a ball is used and especially the game of baseball. ⟨play *ball*⟩

3 The manner, style, or quality of play in a ball game. ⟨played almost errorless *ball* and scored three touchdowns and three field goals on fourth-down plays — Joe Jares, *Sports Illustrated*⟩

ball

BALL

Abbreviations: c circumference, d diameter. Figures in parentheses are approximate diameter sizes for ease of comparison.

game	size	weight	construction
Australian Rules football	11" length 29½" long c 22¾" short c (7" d)	16–17 oz	similar to rugby ball
baseball	9–9¼" c (3" d)	5–5¼ oz	rubber or cork center wound with yarn and covered with a white leather cover with raised seams
basketball	29½–30" c (9½" d)	20–22 oz	inflated bladder with cemented leather or rubber cover, usually in natural brown color
billiards			
American pocket	2¼" d	5½–6 oz	solid ivory or hard composition rubber
carom, balkline	2²⁷⁄₆₄" d	7–7½ oz	
snooker	2⅛" d	5–5½ oz	
English billiards	2¹⁄₁₆–2³⁄₃₂" d	5 oz	
boccie	4½–4¾" d	up to 2 lb, 12 oz	hard wood or hard composition rubber
bowling (tenpins)	up to 27" c (8½" d)	up to 16 lbs	plastic or hard composition rubber
box lacrosse	8" c (2½" d)	6 oz	solid rubber (white, orange, or red)
Canadian fivepins	same as for duckpins		
Canadian football	same as for football		
candlepins	up to 4½" d	up to 2 lb, 7 oz	hard composition rubber
court tennis	2⁷⁄₁₆–2⁹⁄₁₆" d	2½–2¾ oz	numerous layers of yarn wrapped tight and covered with soft cloth
cricket	8¹³⁄₁₆–9" c (2⅞" d)	5½–5¾ oz	cork center wrapped with yarn covered with red leather stitched with raised seams
croquet			
American lawn	3⅜" d	12 oz	solid hard wood or hard composition rubber
regulation	3¼" d	12 oz	
association	3⅝" d	15¾–16¼ oz	
duckpins	5" d	up to 3 lb, 12 oz	hard composition rubber

ball

game	size	weight	construction
field ball	same as for basketball, soccer, or volleyball		
field hockey	8¹³⁄₁₆–9¼" c (3" d)	5½–5¾ oz	cork center wrapped with twine and covered with a stitched or cemented white leather or rubber cover
fives	5¾" c (1⅞" d)	1½ oz	cork center wrapped with twine and covered with white leather
football	11–11¼" length 21¼–21½" short c 28–28½" long c (6⅞" d)	14–15 oz	oval with somewhat pointed ends, inflated bladder covered with pebbled grain leather, reversed seams
Gaelic football	27–29" c (9¼" d)	13–15 oz	inflated bladder with stitched leather cover, reversed seams
golf *American*	not less than 1.68" d	1.62 oz	compressed solid rubber or a solid or liquid-filled rubber center wrapped
English	not less than 1.62" d		with rubber strips and having a dimpled hard composition rubber cover
handball	1⅞" d	2.3 oz	solid black rubber
hurling	9–10" c (3⅛" d)	3½–4½ oz	cork center wrapped with twine and covered with stitched leather with a raised seam
jai alai (pelota)	2" d	4½ oz	hard rubber center wrapped with strips of rubber and then linen twine covered with 2 layers of stitched goatskin
lacrosse	7¾–8" c (2½" d)	5–5¼ oz	solid rubber (white or orange)
lawn bowling (bowl)	4¾–5⅛" d	up to 3 lb, 8 oz	hard wood or hard composition rubber (black or brown)
paddleball	same as for handball or racquetball		
paddle tennis	may be a punctured tennis ball or a platform tennis ball		
platform tennis	2½" d		orange sponge rubber
polo	up to 3¼" d	4¼–4¾ oz	solid willow or bamboo root
racquetball	2¼" d	1.4 oz	hollow black rubber
racquets	1" d	1 oz	cork center wrapped with twine and covered with cemented leather
roller hockey	9" c (2⅞" d)	5½ oz	composition rubber or compressed cork

25

ballast

game	size	weight	construction
roque	3¼" d		hard composition rubber
rounders	7½" c (2⅜" d)	2½–3 oz	similar to a baseball
rugby	11–11¼" long 24–25½" short c 30–31" long c (8⅛" d)	13½–15 oz	oval, inflated bladder, covered with stitched leather, with reversed seams, natural tan or brown color
soccer	27–28" c (8⅞" d)	14–16 oz	inflated bladder, covered with stitched leather, reversed seams, natural color or white, or white and black
softball			
regular	11⅞–12⅛" c (3⅞" d)	6¼–7 oz	kapok or cork and rubber center wrapped with yarn and covered with a stitched white leather cover, flat seams
16 inch	15¾–16¼" c (5⅛" d)	9–10 oz	
speedaway	same as for soccer		
speedball	same as for soccer		
squash racquets			
singles	1.70–1.75" d	1.10–1.15 oz	hollow black rubber
doubles	1.70–1.75" d	1.05–1.10 oz	
table tennis	1.46–1.50" d	37–39 grains (approx ⅒ oz)	hollow white celluloid or similar plastic
team handball	23–24" c (7⅝" d)	15–17 oz	inflated bladder with cemented leather cover
tennis	2½–2⅝" d	2–2¹⁄₁₆ oz	hollow rubber with cemented fuzzy white or yellow cloth cover
volleyball	25–27" c (8⅝" d)	8⅞–9⅞ oz	inflated bladder with cemented white leather or rubber cover
water polo	27–28" c (8⅞" d)	15–17 oz	inflated bladder with cemented gold or yellow rubber fabric cover

4 A hit or thrown ball; a delivery of a ball. ⟨swung at a low *ball*⟩ ⟨foul *ball*⟩ ⟨a bowler is allowed 2 *balls,* if needed, in each frame⟩
5 *baseball* A pitch that does not pass through the strike zone and that is not swung at by the batter and that is added to the count in the batter's favor during a time at bat. — compare STRIKE
— **on the ball** *Australian Rules football* Play-

ing in a ruck position so as to follow the ball anywhere in the field of play.
ballast 1 *ballooning* Heavy material such as sand bags that can be dumped to lighten the gondola of a gas-filled balloon and enable it to rise.
2 *boating* Heavy material fitted in the bottom of a boat for stability in the water.
ball back *rugby* A situation in which a player,

in an attempt to find touch, kicks the ball out of bounds without its first touching the ground in-bounds and which results in the formation of a scrum at the point from which the ball was kicked.

ball boy **1** *baseball* A boy who retrieves foul balls and brings new balls in to the umpire during a game.

2 *basketball* A boy who looks after the balls and other equipment for a team.

3 *tennis* A boy who retrieves balls for the players.

ballcarrier The player who runs with the ball (as in football or rugby). In football the term usually refers to running backs who receive the ball on the snap or on a handoff from the quarterback. Though a pass receiver may run quite a distance after catching a pass, the designation *receiver* rather than *ballcarrier* is generally applied to him.

ball control **1** The ability to manuever a ball (as by dribbling or cradling) while maintaining control of it.

2 An offensive or defensive strategy (as in basketball) in which a team attempts to maintain control of the ball for extended periods in order to prevent the opposing team from having an opportunity to score. A team may engage in ball control throughout a game in an attempt to force an obviously stronger team to change its usual style of play and commit errors or openings on defense, or it may use such a tactic only at the end of the game when it wishes to run out the clock to protect a lead.

3 *football* The ability of a team to maintain continuous possession of the ball for long stretches especially by accumulating consecutive first downs.

ball cushion *bowling* The padded back wall of the pit at the end of the lane which absorbs the force from a pin or ball to prevent its rebounding back onto the lane.

ballet *freestyle skiing* A category of competition in which each skier performs graceful ballet- or skating-like movements to music on a gentle slope. — compare AERIAL, MOGUL

ball game A game played with a ball.

ball girl A girl who performs the duties of a ball boy.

ball handler A player who is handling the ball at a given point during a game; a player who is skilled in controlling and especially in dribbling or cradling and passing the ball.

ball handling Control and maneuvering of the ball during the course of a game (as basketball or soccer). Ball handling is usually considered an offensive technique by which the ball is maneuvered into position to score or to a player who will attempt a shot. Good ball handling involves not only the ability to maintain control of the ball when dribbling but the ability to make accurate passes to teammates.

ball hawk **1** A good defensive player (as in football and basketball) who makes steals and interceptions, blocks passes or kicks, and recovers fumbles and loose balls.

2 *baseball* An outfielder who is exceptionally good at chasing and catching fly balls.

ball hawking The action of a ball hawk; good defensive play.

¹balloon A large nearly spherical air- or gas-filled balloon that has a gondola suspended from the bottom and that is flown in the sport of ballooning. The inflated balloon is not steerable and drifts along with wind currents. However, the pilot often can ascend or descend until he finds a wind blowing in the direction in which he wishes to travel. Practically all balloons used for sport today are hot-air balloons.

²balloon To fly a balloon; to ride in a balloon.

ballooner see BALLOON JIB

ballooning The sport of riding in or flying a balloon.

balloonist A person who ascends in a balloon; a balloon pilot.

balloon jib or **ballooner** *sailing* A large full-cut triangular sail used in place of the regular jib when sailing before the wind.

ball park An area in which ball games are played; a baseball stadium.

ball player Someone who plays a ball game; a baseball player.

ball return or **ball return track** *bowling* The usually enclosed track that runs beside or under a lane and along which the ball rolls in returning to the bowler.

¹ball up *Australian Rules football* A method of putting the ball in play (as at the beginning of a quarter or after a goal or scrimmage) in which the field umpire bounces the ball and the opposing centers jump up to try to gain possession. (also called *hit-out*)

²ball up *of a crampon or the sole of a climbing boot* To become packed with soft or wet snow with the result that secure contact with the slope is difficult or impossible.

Baltimore chop *baseball* A batted ball that hits home plate or the ground in front of the plate and bounds high into the air. By the time the ball comes down to a fielder he will usually not have time enough to make a putout at first base.

banana ball *golf* An exaggerated slice.

banana blade *ice hockey* A stick blade with an exaggerated curve.

bandage *horse racing* A narrow length of material wrapped around a horse's leg for treatment of injury or infection or for support.

bandages *boxing* Protective wrappings for a boxer's hands formed usually from lengths of 1½- or 2-inch-wide gauze wrapped around the hand and taped at the wrist.

banderilla *bullfighting* A decorated barbed dart about 24 inches long which is thrust into the bull's neck or shoulder during a bullfight. Usually 2 or 4 pairs of banderillas are stuck into the charging bull by the banderilleros or by the matador in order to weaken the neck and shoulder muscles of the bull so that at the end of the fight the bull's head will be low enough for the matador to kill him with one thrust of the sword.

banderillero *bullfighting* A member of the matador's cuadrilla who thrusts the banderillas into the bull.

bandy A game played on a large ice surface between 2 teams of 11 players wearing ice skates with the object to hit a small ball with a curved stick and drive it past an opposing goalkeeper into the goal for a score and to prevent the opposing team from scoring. Though bandy is considered a possible forerunner of ice hockey, the play more closely resembles that of field hockey.

banjo hitter *baseball* A weak hitter and especially one who cannot hit for distance.

¹bank **1** A banked turn on a racecourse.
2 *lawn bowling* A mound of earth rising from the ditch at each end of the green to serve as the end boundary of the rink. The bank extends at least 9 inches above the surface of the green.

²bank To cause a ball to rebound from a cushion or backboard.

banked track A racetrack (as for bicycles or automobiles) that has banked turns.

banked turn A turn on a racecourse or track that is constructed to slope inward. Banked turns are common on cycling tracks, indoor running tracks, and on some automobile racecourses and they allow the competitors to move through the turn at greater speed because centrifugal force has been largely counteracted.

banking A banked turn; the degree of inclination of a banked turn.

bank line *fishing* A line attached to the shore and not constantly attended by the fisherman. The bank line is illegal in many states.

bank shot A shot in which a ball is caromed off a wall, cushion, or backboard.

bantamweight A boxer or weight lifter who competes in the bantamweight division. — see DIVISION

banzai *drag racing* An all-out effort.

bar Short for *bar arm, crossbar, horizontal bar.*

barani or **baroni** *gymnastics* A front somersault with a half twist.

bar arm *wrestling* A hold in which an opponent's upper arm is partially encircled and held in the crook of the elbow. (also called *arm bar*)

barb A sharp projection extending backwards from a point (as of a fishhook) to prevent easy extraction from a wound. — see illustration at FISHHOOK

barbell *weight lifting* An adjustable weight device consisting of a steel bar 5 or 6 feet long fitted with disc weights held in place by adjustable collars. The weights are usually placed near the ends of the bar and the bar gripped anywhere between the weights.

bareback riding *rodeo* An event in which contestants are required to ride a bucking wild horse for 8 seconds holding on with one hand to a handle attached to a strap around the animal's chest. The rider may not touch the horse, the strap, or the handle with his free hand, and he must swing his legs forward beyond the horse's front legs on each jump. (also called *bronc riding*) — see also SADDLE BRONC RIDING

barebow *archery* Using no aiming or sighting device on the bow. ⟨*barebow* shooting⟩

barge *surfing* A large awkward surfboard.

barging *yacht racing* The action of a boat attempting to sail between a leeward boat and the marker on the starting line in violation of the rules of racing. Boats to windward are burdened and must give way to leeward boats on the same tack. The rules of racing require the windward boat to give way unless there exists sufficient room between the other boat and the marker. Once the starting signal has sounded, however, the "anti-barging rule" no longer applies and the leeward boat is not permitted to point higher in order to cut off the windward boat. Differences of opinion as to just what constitutes barging often lead to protests after a race.

barmaid see SLEEPER

barnburner An unusually close or exciting contest.

baroni see BARANI

barrage *fencing* A fence-off between 2 fencers who are tied at the end of a qualifying round.

barrel **1** The tube of a firearm from which the projectile is discharged.
2 The thicker part of a baseball bat with which the ball is hit.

barreled shaft *archery* An arrow shaft that is thicker in the middle than at the ends. Used chiefly in the construction of flight arrows, the barreled shaft is tapered toward the ends in order to reduce weight and yet maintain the proper spline for the bow being used.

barrel knot see BLOOD KNOT

barrel roll **1** *track and field* see STRADDLE
2 *wrestling* see FIREMAN'S CARRY

barrier **1** *horse racing* The starting gate.
2 *track and field* A hurdle.

¹bascule *equitation* The ideal arc made by a horse as it jumps a fence.

²bascule *of a horse* To jump a fence in a bascule.

base **1** Any of the 4 objects that mark the corners of a baseball or softball diamond and that must be touched or occupied by a base runner before he can score. Though home plate is a base within the broad compass of the rules, the term is usually limited to the 3 bases located around the infield. First and third bases are placed on the infield side of their respective baselines with one side on and parallel to the baseline. Second base is centered at the intersection of 2 lines perpendicular to the baselines along the rear edges of first and third bases. The bases themselves are white canvas bags 15 inches square that are filled with soft material. In baseball, the bases are set 90 feet apart (60 or 75 feet apart for younger players) and in softball they are set 60 feet apart.
2 *skiing* **a** A foundation of packed snow. **b** A tar-base wax that is applied directly to the running surface of a touring ski for protection from moisture and wear. — see also BINDER, RUNNING WAX
— on base *of a baseball player* Occupying a base. A player who has reached a base but has not scored remains on or near that base to avoid being tagged out. He may advance to the next base, if it is unoccupied, anytime the ball is in play but he generally does so only when the batter hits the ball or when he is attempting a steal.

baseball **1 a** A game played between 2 teams of 9 players using a bat and a ball on a field having an infield or diamond — a 90-foot square with a base located at each corner — at one end.

These bases mark the route an offensive player must take in order to score. At the corner of the field is home plate and the other 3 bases, in the order in which they must be run, are first base, second base, and third base. Each team takes turns playing on offense and defense. The team on defense has 4 players stationed around the infield: a first baseman near first base, a second baseman between first base and second base, a third baseman near third base and a shortstop between third base and second base. There are 3 players stationed in the outfield: a left fielder, a center fielder, and a right fielder. A pitcher approximately in the middle of the diamond pitches to a catcher who is behind home plate. The batter, an offensive player, stands beside home plate and attempts to hit a pitch into fair territory away from the fielders so that he can run to one or more bases without being put out. The ways a player may be put out include striking out, hitting a ball in the air that is caught before it hits the ground, being tagged with the ball while off base, and having a base that one is forced to advance to touched by a player holding the ball. The pitcher is encouraged to pitch the ball over home plate where it is easier for the batter to have a chance to hit it; if he throws 4 pitches that are not over the plate and that are not swung at by the batter (*balls*), the batter is permitted to advance to first base (a *base on balls*). The batter is encouraged to try to hit any pitch that passes over home plate; if he fails to hit one of 3 good pitches over the plate (*strikes*), he strikes out.

Once a player reaches base safely, he may stay on that base without danger of being put out unless he is forced to advance when the batter hits the ball. If an offensive player is able to progress around all bases without being put out and to touch home plate, he scores a run for his team.

The game is under the control of an umpire stationed behind the catcher who rules on whether a pitch is a ball or a strike, calls fair and foul balls, rules on plays at home plate, and has the authority to decide whether a game is to be forfeited or called because of rain or darkness. This umpire is assisted by umpires at each of the bases who call plays at their respective bases. Play begins when the umpire-in-chief calls "play ball," and the ball is in play at all times unless it is knocked out of the playing area or unless an umpire calls time-out.

Play proceeds by innings, each of which con-

baseball

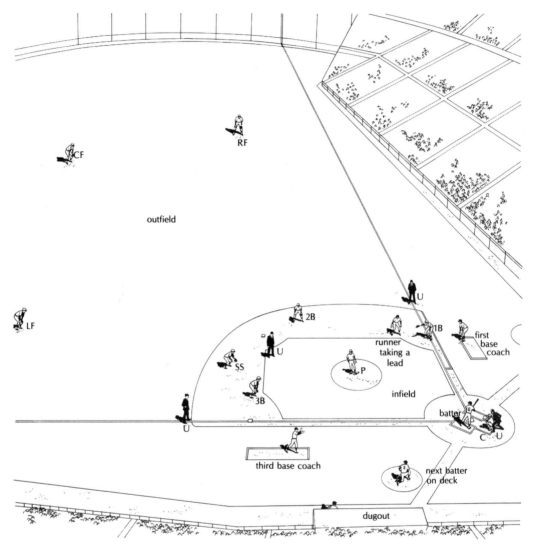

baseball: P pitcher; C catcher; 1B first baseman; 2B second baseman; 3B third baseman; SS shortstop; LF left fielder; CF center fielder; RF right fielder; U umpire

sists of a turn on offense and on defense for each team. A team's turn on offense continues with the players batting in rotation until 3 men have been put out. That team then takes the field while the other team comes to bat. A game normally consists of 9 innings with the team having the most runs at the end of the game being the winner. If the home team (which always bats in the second half of each inning) is leading after 8½ innings, the game ends without the home team batting again. If the home team scores the winning run during the ninth inning, the game ends immediately regardless of the number of outs; the team's margin of victory is only the winning run unless it is scored as a result of a home run. In that event, all runs knocked in by the home run are counted. If the score is tied after 9 full innings, the game continues in extra innings until one team is leading after a full inning. Occasionally a game cannot be played for the full number

basketball

of innings because of rain or darkness. A game is considered complete if at least 5 full innings have been played or if the home team is leading after 4½ innings. If the game is stopped at any time after 5 full innings, the final score stands as it was at the end of the last full inning played.

When the game is played by younger players, a smaller playing field is used. The bases are usually set 60 or 75 feet apart instead of 90 feet, and there is a corresponding reduction in the distance the pitcher stands from home plate. The game is also shortened to 6 or 7 innings instead of 9 innings. — see also BALL, FORCE PLAY, INFIELD FLY, STRIKE; AMERICAN LEGION BASEBALL, BABE RUTH LEAGUE, LITTLE LEAGUE **b** The ball used in the game of baseball. — see BALL

2 A variation of pocket billiards played with 21 object balls numbered from one to 21. The object of the game is for each player to pocket as many balls as possible in 9 successive innings. Each ball is worth points corresponding to the number on the ball. On all shots after the break shot, the player must call both the ball he intends to pocket and the pocket. A player's inning ends when he scratches, fouls, or fails to pocket the called ball.

3 *pari-mutuel betting* A method of betting (as on the daily double) in which a horse in one race is individually paired with each horse in the next race.

Baseball Annie A girl or young woman who follows or seeks the companionship of professional baseball players.

baseballer A baseball player.

baseball grip see GRIP (*golf*)

baseball pass A pass in which a ball (as a basketball) is thrown overhand with one arm while the body weight shifts to the opposite foot.

baseball throw A competitive event in which a baseball is thrown for distance.

base hit *baseball* A hit into fair territory which allows the batter to reach base safely without benefit of an error or a fielder's choice. The term is sometimes used of any safe hit from a single to a home run, though a single is most often referred to.

baseline 1 The boundary line at either end of a court for a net game (as tennis or volleyball) behind which a player must stand when serving. **2** *baseball* **a** Either of the lines leading from home plate to first base and third base that are extended into the outfield as foul lines. **b** A basepath. **3** *basketball* Either of the end lines on the court;

the area just inbounds along the baseline.

baseline game *tennis* A style of play in which a player stays on or near the baseline playing ground strokes and seldom moves to the net. — compare NET GAME

baseliner *tennis* A player who plays a baseline game.

baselinesman *tennis* A linesman who calls the play (as balls out of play and foot-faults) at a baseline.

base on balls *baseball* An advance to first base awarded to a batter who during his turn at bat receives 4 pitches outside the strike zone that he does not swing at. (also called *walk, pass*)

base path *baseball* The area between bases used by base runners. Runners generally run in a direct line between bases, and though they may run far out of the way to avoid interfering with a player attempting to field a batted ball, they may not go more than 3 feet away from a direct line to avoid being tagged.

base runner *baseball* A player of the team at bat who is on base or who is attempting to reach base.

baserunning *baseball* The action of running the bases; skill at running bases and at taking a lead and sliding.

bases-empty *of a hit in baseball* Made with no men on base. ⟨a *bases-empty* homer⟩

bases-loaded *of a hit in baseball* Made with men on first, second, and third bases. ⟨a *bases-loaded* single⟩

basket 1 *basketball* **a** A goal which consists of a cord net suspended from an 18-inch diameter metal ring. When the game was invented, peach baskets were used as goals. Although the goals have been considerably refined since then, the term basket persists. **b** A field goal. ⟨shot the winning *basket* at the buzzer⟩ **2** *skiing* A ring around the ski pole about 4 to 6 inches above the base that is held to the pole by straps and that serves to keep the pole from sinking too deep into the snow. (also called *snow ring*)

basketball 1 A game played on a court between 2 teams of 5 players with the object to score by tossing an inflated ball through a goal, which consists of a basket mounted 10 feet above the floor on a backboard, and to attempt to prevent the opponents from scoring. Players may dribble the ball or pass it to a teammate, but they may not walk or run with the ball. Players are not allowed to hit, shove, hold, or tackle opponents to prevent their scoring, but they may intercept

basketball

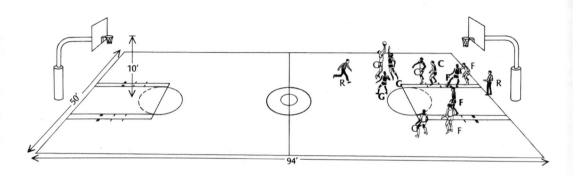

basketball: G guard; F forward; C center; R referee

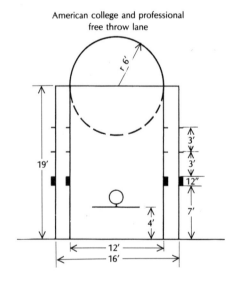

American college and professional free throw lane

international free throw lane

passes, block shots, bat away the ball when it is being dribbled, or wrest it from an opponent. Illegal contact between opposing players is a foul which usually results in the other team's gaining possession of the ball or in the fouled player's shooting a free throw — an unhindered shot at the basket from a line 15 feet away. Players charged with more than the permitted number of fouls are put out of the game. A team is normally made up of 2 guards who are responsible for bringing the ball up the court and working it to teammates near the basket and who customarily play near the backcourt, 2 forwards who usually play on the sides near the basket, and a center who is usually the tallest player and who usually plays in the middle of the frontcourt around the free throw lane where he can relay passes to teammates, shoot, and be in a position to get rebounds. The game is conducted by 2 referees (one is officially the umpire) who have equal responsibility for calling violations and fouls. Each period of the game is started by a jump ball in the center of the court (only the first period in professional basketball), and play is continuous except for time-outs, violations, and fouls. When one team scores, the other team must put the ball in play from outside the end line underneath the basket. If a player commits a violation such as walking with the ball or losing the ball out of bounds, the other team puts the ball in play by a throw-in from the sideline. Two points are usually scored for each field goal and one point for a free throw. The game is divided into 4 quarters or 2 halves and the team with the most points at the end of the playing time is the winner. If the score is tied at the end of regulation play, a short overtime period is played. As many overtime periods as necessary are added until at the expiration of the overtime period one team has a lead. In professional play the game consists of four 12-minute quarters; a college game consists of two 20-minute halves. High school games last four 8-minute quarters. Overtime periods for college and professional play are 5 minutes long; for high school play, 3 minutes. — see also FREE THROW, JUMP BALL, PERSONAL FOUL, TECHNICAL FOUL, VIOLATION

2 The ball used in the game of basketball. — see BALL

basketballer A basketball player.

basketball throw A competitive event in which a basketball is thrown overhand for distance.

basket catch *baseball* A catch of a fly ball made with the glove held palm up at waist level.

basket-hanger *basketball* A player who remains near his own basket when the opponents have the ball at the other end of the court so that when his teammates get the ball he can receive a quick pass and attempt to score before the opponents can get back to defend against him.

basket sled A small dogsled used especially in dogsled racing. The sled has an open hardwood framework that extends up to form a handbar at the rear and encloses a slat platform on which a passenger may ride or equipment may be hauled. The runners of the sled extend 2 or more feet behind the body of the sled to enable the driver to stand on them and ride during portions of a run. Runners on competition sleds are often finished with plastic or fiberglass or with steel strips.

bass bug *fishing* A bug used in fishing for bass. — see BUG

¹bat **1** *baseball* A rounded stick usually made of one-piece solid hardwood that is used by the batter to hit the ball. The diameter may not exceed 2¾ inches nor the length 42 inches though 36 or 37 inches is rarely exceeded. (Little League bats are limited to a maximum of 33 inches long with a 2¼-inch diameter.) The bat tapers toward

one end to a diameter of approximately one inch so that it may be comfortably gripped. The handle may be wrapped up to 18 inches from the end with tape or a composition material to improve the grip. Tubular metal bats are approved for use in amateur competition.

2 *softball* A solid hardwood or tubular metal stick not more than 34 inches long with a diameter not greater than 2¼ inches. The handle is covered with a 10- to 15-inch grip of tape, cork, or composition material. Tubular metal bats have wood or metal inserts at the handle end and a usually rounded rubber insert at the large end.

3 *cricket* A narrow paddlelike wooden implement used by the batsman to hit the ball. The blade of the bat is approximately 2 feet long, no wider than 4¼ inches, and varies in thickness from approximately 3½ inches near the end to approximately 2 inches near the handle. Though the maximum overall length is 38 inches, a common length is around 35 inches.

4 *horse racing* The short whip used by a jockey.

5 A table tennis or paddle tennis paddle.

6 Batting ability (as in baseball). ⟨like to have his *bat* in the lineup⟩

— **at bat** *baseball* As a batter.

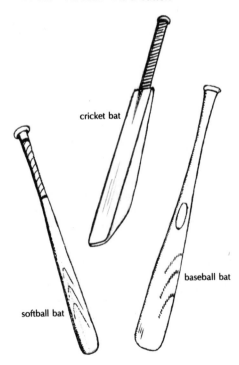

cricket bat

baseball bat

softball bat

bat

²**bat** **1** To assume the position of batter or batsman; to attempt to hit pitched or bowled balls.
2 To have a player bat in a specified order in the lineup. ⟨*bat* him fourth⟩
3 To advance a base runner by batting.
4 To have a specific batting average. ⟨*batting* .500⟩

bat around *of a baseball team* To have all the players in the lineup get a turn at bat in a single inning.

bat boy *baseball* A boy who looks after the bats and equipment of a team.

bat girl A girl who performs the duties of a bat boy.

baton *track and field* A hollow cylinder of wood, metal, plastic, or cardboard approximately 12 inches long that is carried by each runner in a relay race. The baton must be handed to the man running the next leg of the race and the last runner must carry it across the finish line. The transfer of the baton takes place within a defined exchange zone and if the baton is dropped the runner must pick it up before continuing the race.

batsman **1** *baseball* A batter.
2 *cricket* The player whose turn it is to bat; the player who stands by one of the wickets and who attempts to hit bowled balls and score runs by running to the other wicket without being put out. There are 2 batsmen on the pitch at one time, each stationed by a wicket. The bowler bowls a series of balls at one wicket at a time attempting to cause the batsman to be out especially by knocking down the bails or stumps of the wicket defended by that batsman. When the batsman hits the ball, he is not required to run but the 2 batsmen must exchange places in order to score a run on a hit ball. The more times they can exchange places the more runs they can score. When a batsman has been put out, his turn is over for the innings and another batsman takes his place. — see also STRIKER, NONSTRIKER

batten *sailing* A flat strip of wood or plastic inserted into pockets in the leech of a sail to help it keep its shape.

batten down *boating* To secure (as equipment or clothing) especially by covering and tying down.

batter *baseball* The player whose turn it is to bat; the player who stands in the batter's box by home plate and attempts to get on base and score a run by hitting a pitched ball into fair territory away from a fielder or beyond the boundaries of the outfield. The batter is out if a batted ball is caught on the fly or if he has 3 strikes charged against him. Once a batted ball touches the ground in fair territory, the batter is considered a base runner.

batter's box **1** *baseball* Either of two 6-by-4-foot rectangles marked on the field on either side of and 6 inches from home plate within which a batter must stand. (Little League specifications are 5½ by 3 feet and 4 inches from home plate.) The middle of the long side is in line with the center of home plate. — see illustration at HOME PLATE
2 *softball* Either of two 7-by-3-foot rectangles marked on the field on either side of and 6 inches from home plate within which a batter must stand. The front edge extends 4 feet beyond the center of home plate.

battery **1** *baseball* The pitcher and catcher.
2 *horse racing* see JOINT

battery wall *court tennis* The inner wall along one long side of the court below the penthouse.

batting The action of hitting a ball; the use of or the ability to use a bat.

batting average **1** *baseball* A number between 0 and 1 carried to 3 decimal places that is obtained by dividing the number of base hits by the number of official times at bat and that is used as a measure of the batting effectiveness of a player or team. Example: a player who has 98 base hits in 310 times at bat has a batting average of .316.
2 *cricket* A number obtained by dividing the total number of runs scored by a batsman by the number of innings in which the batsman made out that is used as a measure of the batting effectiveness of a player.

batting cage *baseball* A large movable steel wire cage which is open at one side and under which a batter stands during batting practice. The cage serves to contain fouled balls.

batting order The order in which batters or batsmen take their turns at bat. A baseball team's batting order is fixed at the start of the game and is not changed. A substitute takes the place in the batting order held by the player he replaces. The order in which cricket batsmen appear is not so rigidly fixed. Cricket batsmen come to bat only once during an innings (which often constitutes the entire match), and the order of those batsmen who have not yet batted may be changed during the course of the innings.

batting practice *baseball* Practice in batting held usually before a game.

battle clouts *archery* A field archery variation

of clout shooting in which 36 broadhead arrows are shot from a distance of 200 yards at a target with a 12-foot center.

battle royal *cockfighting* A battle to the finish among a number of cocks at one time. The bout ends with one cock victorious and all others disabled or killed.

bat weight *baseball* A doughnut-shaped weight slipped onto a bat to make the bat heavier for warm-up swings. Players often like to swing a heavy bat, or several bats, so that the bat they use in batting will seem lighter and easier to handle. The bat weight enables the player to swing one heavy bat instead of two or 3 regular bats in warming up. (also called *doughnut*)

baulk British spelling of *balk*.

bay A horse that is light to dark reddish brown with a black mane and tail and usually with the lower legs also black. — compare CHESTNUT

bay reel *fishing* A smaller version of a big-game reel holding from 100 to 400 yards of line.

beam *boating* 1 The widest part of a boat.
2 The side of a boat; the direction outward from the side of a boat.
— **on the beam** At right angles to the fore-and-aft line of a boat.

beam reach see REACH

bean *baseball* To hit a batter in the head with a pitch.

beanball *baseball* A pitch that hits a batter in the head or one that is deliberately thrown at a batter's head and is intended to intimidate the batter. — compare BRUSHBACK

bear in *of a racehorse* To tend to move toward the rail while racing.

bearing The relative position of one point with respect to another; the horizontal direction of an object from an observer measured usually clockwise from a reference direction (usually north) in degrees from 0 to 360. Compasses are also generally calibrated in 360 degrees, but since the needle points to the north magnetic pole instead of to the geographic north pole, there will be an error, called *declination* or *variation,* between the reading of the compass and the north direction on a map. A bearing is said to be a *true bearing* when it is calculated with reference to a map. A bearing determined solely with reference to a compass is a *compass bearing.* The true bearing can be determined by adding or subtracting the declination for that particular geographic area from the compass bearing. Example: An object in the distance is determined by means of a compass to have a bearing of 72° (due east would to 90°). If the declination for the area is 10° west, the 10° is subtracted from the compass bearing giving a true bearing of 62°. If the distance is known, the object now may be located on a map since its bearing is known to be 62° with reference to true north, the reference used in map making. (also called *azimuth*)

bear off *sailing* To turn to leeward.

bear out *of a racehorse* To tend to move toward the outside especially on a turn thereby not running along the shortest route and often losing ground to the field. — compare LUG IN

bearpaw A short oval snowshoe with a slightly turned up front and a rounded tailless back. The bearpaw is popular in mountains or on rocky terrain. — see illustration at SNOWSHOE

beartrap see BINDING (*skiing*)

bear up *sailing* To turn to windward.

Bear Valley *fishing* A spinner that consists of a Colorado blade on a shaft containing red beads and that is designed to be fished without any additional lure or bait.

¹beat 1 To defeat an opponent in a contest.
2 **a** To outmaneuver a defender and get free. **b** To score a goal against a goalkeeper. **c** To reach base ahead of a throw.
3 *hunting* see DRIVE
4 *sailing* To sail to windward by means of a series of tacks. A skipper seeks to sail as close to the wind as possible, but the minimum angle is about 45 degrees.

²beat 1 *fencing* A sharp tap of one's blade against the opponent's blade to deflect it in parrying an attack or to make an attack on the blade.
2 *rowing* The number of strokes per minute. The stroke or coxswain sets the beat for the crew, which may vary from 30 to 40 during a race and sometimes goes as high as 44 at the drive for the finish. (also called *cadence*)
3 *sailing* A course to windward; tack. — compare REACH, RUN
4 *swimming* The number of leg kicks to a cycle of arm strokes. In the 6-beat crawl, since the arm strokes are alternate, there are 3 kicks with each arm stroke.
5 The rhythm at which the feet of a horse strike the ground in a particular gait.

beat board *gymnastics* An inclined springboard approximately 25 by 30 inches that is 4 inches high in the front and that serves as a takeoff board in vaulting, tumbling, and in mounting an apparatus.

beat out 1 To gain a position, rank, or honor by

performing better than one's rivals. ⟨the rookie *beat out* three veterans for a starting assignment⟩

2 *baseball* To turn what appears to be a routine groundout into a base hit by beating the throw to first base. ⟨*beat out* a grounder to shortstop⟩

beat the gun see JUMP THE GUN

becket bend see SHEET BEND

bed **1** The flat level top of a billiard table. On top quality tables the bed is made of slate at least one inch thick and is covered with wool cloth.

2 The part of a trampoline on which a performer jumps and which is usually made of canvas webbing.

bedpost *bowling* A split that leaves the 7 and 10 pins standing. (also called *goalpost, fencepost*)

¹behind *Australian Rules football* A score of one point made when the ball is kicked between a behind post and a goalpost, passes between the goalposts after hitting a post or being deflected by a player, or is knocked or kicked through the goalposts by a defending player.

²behind **1** *baseball* Having the count to one's disadvantage. The pitcher is behind the hitter if he has thrown more balls than strikes.

2 *wrestling* To the rear of the opponent in the referee's position.

behind post *Australian Rules football* Either of 2 vertical posts at each end of the field 7 yards on either side of the goalposts. A ball kicked between a behind post and a goalpost scores a behind worth one point.

¹belay *mountain climbing* **1** An object (as a rock, chockstone, tree, or piton) to which a climber ties himself for security or around which a running belay is passed.

2 A method of holding or securing a rope for a moving climber. There are 2 principal methods, the body belay and the running belay. In the body belay, the active rope, which leads directly from one climber to another, is passed around the waist or shoulder of the belayer and is held in each hand. He takes up the slack or plays out the rope to the climber by moving one hand at a time along the rope. With both hands holding the rope, the belayer can then make an arrest if the other climber falls. The running belay may or may not be used during a climb, but it does not substitute for the body belay. In the running belay, the leader attaches the active rope to a piton or passes it around a rock or chockstone along the route. Since the rope is secured to a belay which is much nearer the climber than his

running belay

belay: top, second belaying the leader; bottom, leader belaying the second

partner is, the climber will have a shorter distance to fall if he slips, and some of the shock of the fall will be borne by the running belay instead of solely by the belayer.
— **belay on** or **on belay** *mountain climbing* A call to inform another climber that one has belayed himself and is ready to tend the rope for that climber.

²**belay 1** *boating* To secure a line to a cleat.
2 *mountain climbing* **a** To tie oneself to a belay point as a stationary member of a roped party in order to manage the active rope and safeguard a moving climber. **b** To safeguard a moving climber at the end of a rope by putting tension on the rope, by playing it out to a climber moving ahead or taking it in from a climber moving from below, and by holding the rope in order to stop a fall.

belayer *mountain climbing* A climber who has secured himself on a ledge and who is handling the rope for a moving climber.

bell 1 *boxing* A bell that is sounded to mark the beginning and the end of each round. ⟨failed to answer the *bell* for round 5⟩ ⟨saved by the *bell*⟩
2 *fencing* see GUARD

bell buoy see BUOY

bell guard see GUARD (*fencing*)

bell lap The last lap of a race (as in track or cycling) indicated by the ringing of a bell as the leader begins the last lap.

belly 1 *archery* The side of a bow nearest the bowstring. — compare BACK
2 *fishing* The thickest part of a tapered fly line.
3 *football* An offensive play in which the quarterback hands off to a running back by shoving the ball into his belly.
4 *surfing* The underside of a surfboard.

belly back *of a ballcarrier in football* To move away from the line of scrimmage momentarily while running a sweep in order to run around blockers or to get away from onrushing linemen.

belly board *surfing* A small surfboard about 3 feet long that one propels with swim fins.

belly flop see BELLY WHOPPER

belly grind see HIP CIRCLE

belly roll see STRADDLE

belly series *football* A series of offensive plays in which the quarterback hands off to a running back by thrusting the ball into his stomach or fakes such a handoff often with the intention of passing.

belly whopper or **belly flop** A fall or dive in which the front of the body lands flat against a surface (as the surface of water or the ground or the top of a coasting sled). ⟨the shortstop made a *belly whopper* to glove the hot liner⟩

Belmont Stakes A 1½-mile stakes race for 3-year-old thoroughbred racehorses that has been held annually at Belmont Park in New York since 1867 and that is the third race in horse racing's Triple Crown. — see also KENTUCKY DERBY, PREAKNESS STAKES

below *boating* Beneath the deck.

belt To hit forcefully. ⟨*belted* his opponent against the ropes⟩ ⟨he *belted* his 30th homer — *New York Times*⟩

¹**bench 1** A bench or row of chairs on which team members sit when they are not playing in the game.
2 The substitute or reserve players on a team. ⟨the *bench* contributed a lot toward their win⟩
3 *weight training* A low often padded bench on which a lifter can sit or lie while performing various lifts.

²**bench 1** To remove a player from and keep him out of a game.
2 To cause a player to be unable to play. ⟨*benched* by a back injury⟩
3 To replace a player as a regular starter.

bench jockey 1 *baseball* A player who rides his opponents from the bench or dugout.
2 see BENCH WARMER

bench minor penalty or **bench penalty** A minor penalty in ice hockey or box lacrosse imposed on a team that is guilty of unnecessary delay of the game, that has too many men on the ice or the floor, or whose members, including players, managers, trainers, or club executives, use profane language or gestures. The 2-minute penalty is served by any player designated by the manager or coach in the same manner as for a regular minor penalty.

bench-press *weight training* To lift a usually specified weight in the bench press.

bench press *weight lifting* A competitive lift or an exercise in which a lifter lies on his back on a horizontal bench and pushes a barbell up from his chest to arm's length and then lowers it to his chest.

bench racing The practice of analyzing, second-guessing, and arguing about drag racing among drivers or fans.

benchrest *shooting* A small pedestal placed on a sturdy table or platform and held in place by sandbags that supports a heavy target rifle in order to provide maximum steadiness in firing.

bench warmer or **bench jockey** A substitute

player who seldom gets into a game and therefore spends most of his time on the bench.

¹bend **1** A knot that unites 2 rope ends. — compare HITCH

2 A turn in a racecourse.

3 The usually curved part of a fishhook between the shank and the barb.

²bend *boating* To fasten one rope to the end of another; to fasten a sail to a spar.

bends *scuba diving* A condition in which gas bubbles (as of nitrogen) come out of solution in the body tissues and blood too rapidly to be passed off in normal respiration and lodge in the tissues and joints causing pain and crippling and sometimes impairing circulation. The gases that make up the air are forced into solution in the body as the diver descends and the water pressure on the diver increases. These gases begin coming out of solution as the diver ascends and the pressure decreases. The bends is a common danger present when a diver breathes compressed air at depths greater than 33 feet and fails to decompress properly on ascending. (also called *caisson disease, decompression sickness*)

benighted Caught by darkness on a climb, hike, or ski trek and forced to return to camp in the dark or to bivouac.

bergschrund *mountain climbing* A crevasse or series of crevasses formed where a glacier breaks away from a mountain.

Bermuda rig *sailing* A fore-and-aft rig with tall triangular sails. (also called *Marconi rig*)

berth **1 a** A mooring for a boat. **b** A place to sleep on a boat.

2 A playing position on a team; a position on the starting team.

3 A place in an elimination tournament; an opportunity to play in a tournament.

besom *curling* The broom used for sweeping the ice.

best-ball *golf* **1** A match in which one player plays his ball against the best score of 2 or 3 players making up the other side. Each of the players making up the partnership which opposes the individual player plays his own ball but only the best score counts.

2 see FOUR-BALL

bettor Someone who makes a bet.

bias *lawn bowling* **1** A peculiarity in the shape of a bowl that causes it to swerve when rolled on the green.

2 The swerve of a bowl.

biathlon An athletic contest in which competitors ski over a 20-kilometer cross-country course

stopping at designated points to fire a rifle at stationary targets. The contest is a race against the clock with time added to an individual's run as a penalty for missed targets.

bib *fencing* The throat protector attached to the bottom of a fencing mask.

bicycle kick An exercise performed while lying on one's back with the hips and legs in the air and the hips supported on the hands that consists of moving the legs up and down as if pedaling a bicycle.

bicycle motocross Bicycle racing for youngsters using rugged bicycles with short frames, high handlebars, and small wheels on a closed, dirt course with hills, jumps, banked turns, and mud.

bicycle racing see CYCLING

Biddy Basketball Basketball designed for play by youngsters using a smaller than regulation court, a smaller ball, and baskets that are 8½ feet high.

big bag see HEAVY BAG

big ball *bowling* A delivery with sufficient action to produce a strike nearly anywhere it hits the pin setup.

big-bore *of a firearm* **1** Having a large or relatively large caliber; larger than .22 caliber.

2 Involving the use of large-caliber firearms.

big fill *bowling* A good pinfall on the first ball bowled following a spare.

big four *bowling* A split that leaves the 4, 6, 7, and 10 pins standing.

big game **1** *fishing* Large marine game fish such as marlin and tuna.

2 *hunting* Large game animals such as deer, elk, and bear.

big-game reel *fishing* A heavy-duty bait casting reel often having variable gear ratios and holding up to 1000 yards of heavy line.

big gun **1** A player who is a threat to score or to produce scores. ⟨looking for some way to stop the other team's *big guns*⟩

2 A large heavy surfboard.

bight The loop formed when a rope is doubled.

big league **1** A baseball major league.

2 The top level of a sports enterprise or athletic competition. ⟨a *big league* racetrack⟩

big leaguer **1** *baseball* Someone who plays in the major leagues.

2 A top-notch performer; someone whose performance is equal to the best in his field.

big man The center on a basketball team.

bike **1** A bicycle or motorcycle.

2 *harness racing* A sulky with pneumatic bicycle-type tires.

biker A bicycle or motorcycle rider.

billiards

bilge The bottom of a boat as distinguished from the sides; the part of a boat lying between the sides and the keel.

bilge board *sailing* A usually retractable plane fitted to the bilge on either side of a shallow-draft racing boat so as to extend nearly vertically into the water when the boat is heeling at a desired angle. Bilge boards usually have a smaller area and are more effective than a single centerboard.

bilge board scow *sailing* A sloop-rigged shallow-draft racing boat with bilge boards instead of a centerboard.

billiard see CAROM

billiards Any of several games played on a rectangular table with or without pockets by driving small balls against one another or into the pockets at the sides of the table with a cue. In American use, the term often refers to carom billiards as distinguished from pocket billiards. There are 4 major forms of billiards, each discussed separately and each having individual variations. In each game the player strikes only the cue ball with the cue driving the cue ball into one or more of the object balls.

1 *English billiards* A form of billiards popular in Great Britain that is played between 2 players or 2 pairs of players on a 12-by-6-foot table with 6 pockets using a white, a spot white, and a red ball. The object is to score points for making a cannon (driving the cue ball against both object balls), a winning hazard (driving the white or the red object ball into a pocket), or a losing hazard (caroming the cue ball off either the red or white object ball and into a pocket). A winning hazard in which the red ball is pocketed counts 3 points; if the white ball is pocketed it counts 2 points. A losing hazard is worth 3 points if the cue ball first caroms off the red ball and 2 points if off the white ball. A cannon counts 2 points, and any combination of cannon and hazards made on a single stroke is counted. Players alternate turns, but each continues a turn (called a *break*) as long as he continues to score points. The rules limit the number of successive cannons or hazards that a player may make. — see also RUSSIAN POOL

2 a *pocket billiards* An American form of billiards, popularly called *pool,* played usually by 2 players on an 8-by-4-foot or a 9-by-4½-foot table with 6 pockets using a white cue ball and 15 colored balls numbered from one to 15. The object is to drive the cue ball against one or more of the object balls, knocking them into the pockets. The player scores points for each of the ob-

ject balls pocketed, but if his cue ball is pocketed or leaves the table, he has scratched and he loses his turn, forfeits any points made on that stroke, and is penalized one point. Players alternate turns (called *innings*), but a player continues to shoot as long as he continues to score points. On the break shot, when all 15 object balls are in a triangular arrangement and the cue ball is to be played from hand, the player is required to pocket a ball or to drive 2 or more object balls plus the cue ball to a cushion. A player is credited with any balls pocketed on the break shot. On all shots after the opening break, a player is required to state which ball or balls he intends to pocket, but he is not required to designate the pocket. If the player pockets the called ball, he is entitled to all other balls pocketed on the same stroke. If the called ball is not pocketed, however, he loses his inning and forfeits any balls that are pocketed on that stroke. One point is scored for each ball legally pocketed. The first player to pocket 8 balls is the winner.

b *14.1 continuous* or *14 point 1 continuous* A variation of basic pocket billiards played in championship competition. This game differs from basic pocket billiards chiefly in 2 respects. First, the player is required to designate both the ball he intends to pocket and the pocket. Failure to make the called shot is a miss and ends his inning. Second, once 14 balls have been pocketed, they are racked again. The player continues play by pocketing the 15th ball and caroming the cue ball into the racked balls or by driving a called ball from the racked balls into a pocket. Each time 14 balls have been pocketed, they are reracked and play continues to the end of the game. The number of points set for a game is usually 125 or 150. Any time a player fails to make a called shot, his inning ends. He is penalized for a foul if he fails to make the cue ball contact some other object ball, with that object ball and the cue ball both subsequently hitting a cushion. If a player scratches, he loses his inning and is penalized one point. After scratches in 3 successive turns, the player is penalized an additional 15 points and play begins again from the opening break. (also called *straight pool*)

c *fifteen ball* A variation of basic pocket billiards in which players are not required to call their shots. A player gets a number of points for a pocketed ball corresponding to the number on the ball (one point for the one ball, 7 points for the 7 ball, etc.) and the first player to score 61 points wins the game.

billiards

d *rotation* A variation similar to fifteen ball with the number of points for each ball equal to the number of the ball and with 61 points needed to win. In rotation, the balls must be played in rotation — in numerical order starting with the lowest numbered ball on the table. Any balls pocketed as a result of or subsequent to contact with the proper object balls are credited to the player, even if the first object ball is not pocketed. Failure to first contact the proper object ball, however, constitutes a miss and ends the player's inning. Any balls pocketed on a miss are returned to the table and spotted.

e *eight ball* A popular variation of pocket billiards in which one side is required to pocket the balls numbered from 1–7 and the other side the balls numbered from 9–15. Which group a player takes is determined by the first ball pocketed in a game. A player may pocket the balls in his group in any order and he is not required to call the ball or the pocket. If a player pockets a ball from the other player's group, the other player gets credit for the ball. Failure of a player to pocket any ball in his group on a turn constitutes a miss and ends his inning. The first player to legally pocket all the balls in his group and then pocket the 8 ball in a called pocket is the winner. If a player pockets the 8 ball before he has pocketed all his balls or, when trying for the 8 ball, fails to shoot directly at it, fails to drive it at least to a cushion or carom the cue ball into a cushion, scratches the cue ball, or pockets the 8 ball in the wrong pocket, he loses the game.
— see also BASEBALL, BOTTLE POCKET BILLIARDS, COWBOY, CRIBBAGE, FORTY-ONE, GOLF, LINE-UP, MR. AND MRS., NINE BALL, ONE AND NINE BALLS, ONE POCKET, PILL POOL, POKER POCKET BILLIARDS

3 a *carom billiards* An American form of billiards, sometimes called *French billiards,* played usually by 2 players on a 9-foot by 4½-foot or a 10-foot by 5-foot table, without pockets using a white, a spot white, and a red ball. The object of the game is to score points by driving the cue ball into each of the 2 object balls in succession. Failure to contact both object balls is an error which ends the player's turn. If a player makes an illegal shot or drives the cue ball off the table, he has fouled and he loses one point. (also called *straight rail*)

b *3-cushion billiards* A carom billiards game in which a player is required to drive the cue ball to 3 cushions before or while making caroms off the 2 object balls. For each 3-cushion carom, the player scores one point.

c *balkline* A variety of carom billiards played on a table marked with 4 balklines 14 or 18 inches from and parallel to each cushion. The lines mark off 8 balk areas near the cushions. Whenever both object balls lie within the same balk area, a player is limited to only one or 2 shots, depending on the particular game, before being required to drive at least one of the balls out of balk. This is to prevent a player from corralling all the balls in one corner and making caroms indefinitely. Failure to make a carom on a shot or to drive one of the object balls out of balk when it is required is an error and ends the player's turn. At the point where each balkline meets the cushion is a 7-inch square, known as the *anchor.* This has restrictions similar to those of balk to prevent a player from continually playing one ball just over the balkline but close to the rail in order to avoid the balk restrictions. The games are designated both by the distances of the balklines from the cushions and by the number of points that may be made before driving a ball out of balk. 14.2 balkline, for example, indicates the balklines are 14 inches from the cushions and when both balls are in the same balk area, one ball must be driven out of balk when trying for the second point. 14.1 has a one-shot rule. The games of 18.1 and 18.2 have the same 1- and 2-shot restrictions, but are played on a table with the balklines 18 inches from the cushions.

4 *snooker* A game played by 2 players or sides on a 12-by-6-foot or 10-by-5-foot table marked as for English billiards with a white cue ball, 15 red object balls, and 6 object balls of different colors. The object of the game is to pocket a red ball and a colored ball alternately (each time returning the colored balls to the table until all the red balls have been pocketed) and finally pocket each of the colored balls in the order of their numerical values. Red balls legally pocketed are never returned to the table, even if a player fouls on the stroke. A player receives points for each ball he pockets on a legal stroke and for fouls committed by his opponent; his turn continues as long as he continues to score points. Each red ball is worth one point and the colored balls are valued as follows: yellow 2 points, green 3, brown 4, blue 5, pink 6, and black 7. The ball that is next to be struck at any given time during the game is referred to as *on.* At the beginning of a player's turn and after he has pocketed a numbered ball, a red ball is on. The player is not required to indicate which red ball he intends to pocket or the pocket. After pocketing a red ball, a player designates a colored ball which he intends to pocket — this ball is now on — but he does not have to call the pocket. If at any time during the game a player is unable to shoot directly at the ball he is on because other balls are in the way, he is snookered. When a player is snookered he must make the cue ball strike the on ball before striking any other ball. If the player fails to hit the on ball first or fails to hit any other ball on the table he fouls and when he does so, he forfeits any balls made on the stroke and his opponent gets 7 points (or, in certain instances in English snooker, the value of the on ball or the incorrectly hit ball). After an opponent has fouled, the player, in addition to gaining points, has the option of playing the balls as they have come to rest on the table or of requiring his opponent to play again. The game ends when all the red balls are off the table and all numbered balls have been pocketed in proper order. The player with the highest total of points for pocketed balls and fouls by his opponent is the winner.

billiard spot A spot on an English billiards table 12¾ inches from the center of the top cushion on which the red ball is placed at the beginning of the game and after being pocketed. In

snooker, the black ball is placed on the billiard spot at the beginning of the game and after being pocketed. — see also BALKLINE SPOT, CENTER SPOT, PYRAMID SPOT

billiard table Any of several tables designed for billiards and pocket billiards games. A pocket billiards table is 4 by 8 feet or 4½ by 9 feet and has 6 pocket openings approximately 5 to 5½ inches wide, one at each corner and one in the middle of each long side. The table for carom billiards is 4½ by 9 feet or 5 by 10 feet with no pockets. A balkline table has balklines marked 14 or 18 inches from each cushion and anchors marked at the intersections of the balklines and the cushions. An American snooker table is 4½ by 9 feet or 5 by 10 feet and is marked like an English billiards table. The 6 pockets in a snooker table are approximately 3½ to 4½ inches wide. The height of all American tables is 31 inches. An English billiards table is 12 feet long and 6 feet wide, stands 33½ to 34½ inches high, and has 6 pockets, one at each corner and one in the middle of each long side. A balkline is marked across the table parallel to and 29 inches from the bottom cushion. From the middle of the balkline, a semicircle with a radius of 11½ inches, called the D, is marked within the balk. In the exact center of the table is a center spot. A pyra-

4½' x 9' pocket billiards table at opening break

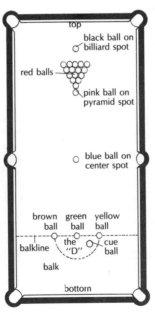

6' x 12' English billiards table arranged for snooker

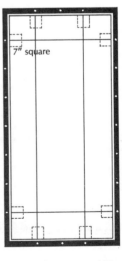

5' x 10' carom billiards table with 14" balklines

mid spot lies midway between the center spot and the middle of the top cushion, and a billiard spot is 12¾ inches from the middle of the top cushion.

¹bind *fencing* An attack on the blade or a riposte in which an opponent's blade is forced diagonally across the body in a semicircular movement to another line by pressure on his blade. The bind is usually followed immediately by a lunge. (also called *liément*) — compare CROISÉ, ENVELOPMENT

²bind or **bind to** *of a falcon* To seize prey in flight by grasping with the talons.

binder *skiing* A wax that is sometimes applied between the base and running waxes.

binding **1** *skiing* A fastening device by which the boot is attached to the ski. The binding commonly employed in ski touring and cross-country racing is a pin type consisting of a metal plate with usually 3 vertical pins that fit into holes in the sole of the boot and a wire clamp that holds the toe of the boot in place. For Alpine or downhill skiing the binding is usually a step-in type consisting of metal clamps for the toe and heel. Each clamp is adjustable so that it releases the boot with a given amount of twisting force to prevent injury in case of a fall. Less popular for Alpine skiing is the cable binding, which consists of a toe clamp like that of the step-in binding and a spring cable which fits a groove in the heel of the boot and holds the boot snugly against the toe clamp. The cable is usually equipped with a device to release the boot in a fall. Another binding employing the cable is called a *beartrap* and has a flat plate in front with upturned edges that hold the sides of the boot in place. The beartrap is an old binding still popular for touring but seldom used in Alpine skiing since it does not release the foot in a fall.

2 An arrangement of usually rubber or leather straps that secure the boot to a snowshoe.

3 *track and field* An area on a javelin or a vaulting pole wrapped with cord or tape to serve as a grip.

4 *water skiing* A usually adjustable device that holds the foot of the skier to the ski. The binding usually consists of a wide rubber strap that fits over the instep and a cupped rubber section that fits against the heel. The rubber holds the foot snugly against the ski but is flexible enough to allow the foot to be pulled free in a fall.

biner Short for *carabiner*.

bingle *baseball* A base hit.

bird **1** A shuttlecock.

2 A clay pigeon.

3 A birdie.

birdcage *football* A facemask that has several bars around the front and a vertical bar running up to the middle to the front of the helmet and that is generally worn by linemen.

bird dismount SEE HECHT DISMOUNT

bird dog SEE GUN DOG

¹birdie *golf* A score of one stroke less than par for a hole.

²birdie *golf* To score a birdie on a hole.

bird's nest **1** *gymnastics* A stunt performed on the rings by raising the legs, hooking the feet in the rings, and then turning the body over so as to hang by the hands and feet with the front of the body toward the floor.

bird's nest

2 A backlash on a fishing reel.

birling A sport in which 2 people try to maintain balance on a floating log with each seeking to rotate the log in such a way as to unbalance the other person. Competition is usually an elimination series with 2 or 3 trials and often involves the use of logs with progressively smaller diameters. (also called *log rolling*)

bisque A handicap that is to be taken at a time of the player's choosing; one or more strokes in golf which may be subtracted from a player's score at any time during a round in match play. The handicap may be used on the hole or holes designated by the handicap player, but he must announce his choice to use bisque on a hole before play begins on that hole.

bit *equitation* The mouthpiece of a bridle. The

2 most common bits are the snaffle and the curb bit. The snaffle bit consists of a bar of metal, wire, or rubber which has large rings at each end to which the bridle and reins may be attached. The pull from the reins is direct and pressure on the horse's mouth is light. The curb bit consists of a bar usually with a bend in the middle that is attached to 2 long braces which form an elongated H. The reins are attached to the lower ends of the braces so that leverage is applied to the mouth. If a strap or curb chain is attached to the upper end of the braces, considerable pressure can be exerted on the horse's jaw.

— on the bit *of a horse* Easily accepting the bit in his mouth; responsive to the reins.

bite 1 *auto racing* The traction of tires against the pavement.
2 *fishing* The act of a fish's taking bait or a lure.
3 *golf* Backspin on a ball.

bitter *curling* A stone that just touches the outer ring of the house.

bitt *boating* One or more vertical posts on board a boat to which lines are secured.

bitter end *boating* The last part of a line or the last link of a chain.

¹bivouac A temporary encampment often with little or no shelter.

²bivouac To make a temporary camp (as for the night) usually without prior planning by taking advantage of whatever shelter (as a boulder, log, or snow cave) is available. Though mountain climbers may at times plan to bivouac on a difficult part of a climb, most bivouacking is forced when a hiker, camper, or hunter is benighted away from camp or transportation.

bivouac sheet A light canvas or plastic sheet that can be carried easily and can serve as a ground sheet or an emergency tent if one is forced to bivouac.

black belt 1 A black belt awarded to one who has earned a rating of expert in any of the Oriental arts of self-defense (as judo and karate).
2 An expert in an Oriental art of self-defense.

black-flag *motor racing* To signal a driver to come into the pit by the waving of a black flag.

black flag *motor racing* A solid black flag that is shown with a vehicle number to indicate that the officials are requiring the designated vehicle or driver to return to the pits.

blackguard *fives* A service that strikes the front wall without first hitting a side wall. The receiver has the option of playing a blackguard or not, but he may not return a blackguard if he needs only one point to win. The receiver wins a point au-

tomatically if 3 successive blackguards are served and none is played.

black ice 1 Thin transparent ice formed over freshwater or saltwater. The water seen through the ice gives it a dark appearance.
2 Dark-colored glacial ice formed from silt-laden water. The mixture of silt makes this ice extremely hard.

blackout An instance of having a televised sports event blacked out in an area.

black out To prohibit the telecasting of a sports event (as a football game or an auto race) to the area in which the event or a similar event is taking place. A football game may be blacked out in the local area in order to ensure maximum attendance at the game; in the case of a local high school or college game played at the same time as a nationally televised game, the televised game may be blacked out to avoid affecting attendance at the local game.

blade 1 a The wide flat part of a paddle or oar which exerts force against the water to propel a boat. **b** The thin flat part of a fishing spinner that spins on the shaft as it is drawn through the water.
2 The striking surface of an iron golf club or of a field hockey or ice hockey stick.
3 a The part of a fencing sword that extends from the guard to the tip. **b** The flat or V- or U-shaped part of a piton that is driven into a crack.
4 The thin strip of metal on the bottom of an ice skate that glides on the ice.

bladework *rowing* The action of the blade of the oar against the water on a stroke; the manner in which the blade is moved through the water.

blank *baseball* To hold an opposing team scoreless; shut out. ⟨*blanked* the Birds on 3 hits⟩

blank end *curling* A scoreless end.

blanket *sailing* To sail in such a position as to block the wind from a leeward boat's sails.

blanket finish An extremely close finish to a race.

¹blast *golf* To hit a ball out of a sand trap by striking the sand slightly behind the ball. The ball is forced out by the explosive pressure of the sand and is not actually touched by the club.

²blast *baseball* A hard-hit ball; a home run.

blast valve *ballooning* A valve on the burners that releases a large flame and provides maximum heat to the air in the balloon for quick climbs. — compare CRUISE VALVE

¹blaze A mark on a tree usually made by chipping off a piece of bark.

²blaze To make a mark on a tree usually by chipping off a piece of bark; to mark a path or trail by blazing various trees along the route.

bleach box see BURNOUT PIT

bleacherite Someone who sits in the bleachers.

bleachers A section of stands consisting typically of tiered planks unprotected from the sun and rain that afford relatively inexpensive and usually unreserved seating for spectators (as at a ball park or racetrack). Bleachers are often nonpermanent uncovered stands as distinguished from grandstands. When used in conjunction with grandstands, the bleachers are usually located in an area affording a less comprehensive or less advantageous view (as beyond the outfield walls at a baseball park).

bleeder 1 *baseball* A batted ball that just gets through the infield for a base hit.

2 *boxing* A boxer noted for being easily cut by punches.

blind *hunting* A concealing enclosure from which a hunter may wait undetected for approaching game and especially for waterfowl. Blinds are often constructed on the ground and in holes dug in the ground, though floating blinds and blinds built over the water are sometimes used for duck hunting. The principal method of camouflaging the hunter is with natural vegetation such as grasses and branches.

blind bridle *horse racing* A bridle provided with blinkers.

blinders see BLINKERS

blind gate A closed gate on a slalom course. — see GATE

blind hole *golf* A hole or green that cannot be seen when making a normal approach shot.

blind pass 1 A pass made by a player to a teammate without looking at the teammate.

2 *track and field* A baton pass in a relay race in which the receiving runner does not look back at the passer.

blind score *bowling* A score that is added to a team's score for a game when a member of the team is absent or has been disqualified and no substitute is available. A typical blind score would be the absent bowler's average less 10 pins.

blind-side To hit a player on his blind side. ⟨bound to be *blind-sided* . . . sooner or later — Ken Willard⟩

blind side 1 The side away from which a player is looking.

2 *rugby* The side of the scrum nearest the touchline.

blinkers *horse racing* Shields often in the form of half cups attached to a bridle to block a

horse's view to the sides and rear. Blinkers are sometimes used on a horse that might be skittish on seeing movement of another horse approaching him from the rear. (also called *blinders, rogue's badge*)

blip *motor racing* To rev an engine momentarily.

¹blitz *football* A rush into the offensive backfield at the snap by one or more linebackers or defensive backs. The blitz is normally used only when a pass play is anticipated. When it is successful, the passer will be tackled before he can throw the pass, or he will be forced to rush the pass with the result that it is incomplete or even intercepted. A blitz is sometimes successful in stopping a running play when an extra defensive player suddenly appears in the offensive backfield. The blitz is a gambling maneuver which creates weaknesses in the team's defensive structure and is therefore employed only on strategic plays. If the blitzing player is blocked or unable to stop the ballcarrier, he has left a hole in the secondary through which the ballcarrier may be able to run for a long gain. The blitz is sometimes defeated with the calling, by an alert quarterback, of a short pass over the middle of the line to a receiver in the area left vacant by the blitzing player. If the blitz is made by a safety instead of by a linebacker, it is called a *safety blitz*. (also called *red dog*)

²blitz 1 *box lacrosse* To double-team an opponent who is already tied up by a defender in an attempt to dislodge the ball from his stick before he can pass off or get free.

2 *football* **a** *of a linebacker or defensive back* To rush across the line on a blitz. **b** To have one or more linebackers or defensive backs blitz.

blitzer *football* A linebacker or defensive back who blitzes.

¹block 1 To stop or deflect a shot, pass, kick, or return.

2 To impede the movement or progress of an opposing player: **a** *basketball* To move illegally into the path of an opposing player. — see BLOCKING **b** *football* To legally impede or interfere with the movement of an opposing player or to knock him down or off balance by hitting him with the shoulders or the body. Offensive players block defensive players to prevent their reaching the ballcarrier or the passer or in order to drive the defensive player out of position to create a hole for the ballcarrier. The offensive player is prohibited from using his hands and, in college play, the blocker must keep his hands

shoulder block   body block

against his chest in making a straight shoulder block. — compare TACKLE, CHARGE, CHECK

c *squash racquets* To interfere illegally with the movements of an opponent; to hinder an opponent.

3 To catch or deflect an opponent's hand, arm, or leg (as in boxing or karate) to prevent a punch or kick from reaching the target.

4 *racquetball* see SCREEN

5 *soccer* see TRAP

6 *wrestling* To prevent the successful application of a hold especially by quick maneuvers.

²block 1 The act or an instance of stopping or deflecting a shot, kick, pass, or return.

2 The act or an instance of legally or illegally impeding an opponent.

3 The act or an instance of stopping a kick or a punch or of preventing the application of a wrestling hold.

4 A frame enclosing one or more pulleys.

5 *billiards* A unit of a match in championship play which continues until one player reaches a specific number of points (as 150).

— **in the blocks** *of a sprinter* At the starting line with feet in the starting blocks waiting for the starting signal. — **on the block** *of a professional athlete* Subject to being traded to another team.

blocker 1 *football* An offensive player who obstructs an opponent by means of legal body contact; a player who precedes the ballcarrier in order to block potential tacklers.

2 *volleyball* A player who attempts to block a spiked ball.

block heel *horse racing* A horseshoe made with

a raised heel to prevent the horse from running down.

blocking 1 *basketball* Body contact which results when a player illegally moves into the path of an opposing player in such a manner that the other player is unable to stop or change direction to avoid him. The usual instance in which blocking occurs is when a defensive player moves into the path of the ball handler though blocking is sometimes called when an offensive player sets a screen too close to a defensive player or fails to come to a complete stop before the defensive player runs into him. A player must have an opportunity to see and react to the presence of a player in his path. If a player fails to establish position, subsequent body contact is blocking and the player is charged with a personal foul. — compare CHARGING

2 *football* **a** The action of preventing opponents from reaching the passer or ballcarrier. **b** The protection or interference provided by blockers.

blocking parry see PARRY

block out see BOX OUT

block the plate *of a baseball catcher* To take up a position on the baseline between the base runner and home plate while attempting to tag the runner. This forces the runner to try to run wide of the catcher to avoid the tag or to run or slide into the catcher; the catcher usually runs the risk of having the ball knocked out of his hands in the collision or of being injured.

blood To expose a hunting dog to the scent or taste of the blood of its prey.

blood knot A knot used typically to join two ends of monofilament fishing line that is made by twisting each end around the other standing part usually 3 or more times and then pushing the ends through the center twist so that they lie opposite each other and at right angles to the standing part. (also called *barrel knot*) — see illustration at KNOT

blood sport British term for a sport in which game is killed (as hunting, gunning, or coursing).

¹bloop *baseball* To hit a fly ball just beyond the infield. ⟨*blooped* a double down the left field line⟩

²bloop Made on a blooper. ⟨a *bloop* single⟩

blooper *baseball* **1** A pitch that is lobbed to the batter.
2 A fly ball hit barely beyond the infield; Texas leaguer.

¹blow *bowling* A failure to make a spare when there is no split; error.

²blow **1** To fail to make an easy play; to waste an advantage. ⟨*blew* the lay-up⟩ ⟨*blow* a 16-point lead⟩
2 To move quickly around an opponent. ⟨*blew* past him for a lay-up⟩
3 *of a baseball pitcher* To throw the ball hard. ⟨*blew* a fastball past him for a strike⟩
4 *motor racing* **a** *of a racing engine* To fail under the stress of racing. **b** *of a driver* To have one's engine fail. ⟨*blew* an engine⟩

blow in *football* To charge through the line (as on a blitz). ⟨linebacker was going to *blow in* and nail the quarterback⟩

blown *of a racing engine* Supercharged. ⟨their engines are either *blown* or fuel-injected⟩

blown out *of surf* Whipped by high winds so as to be too choppy for surfing.

blow off the floor (court, track, ice) To defeat an opponent by a wide margin; outclass.

blowout *horse racing* A brief workout held a day or two before a race.

blue flag *motor racing* A solid blue flag shown to a particular competitor to indicate that another vehicle is following him closely. When waved, the blue flag calls for the slower vehicle to give way to the faster one trying to pass.

blue line *ice hockey* Either of the two 1-foot-wide blue lines that extend the width of the rink and that are located 60 feet from and parallel to the goal lines. The blue lines divide the rink into the defensive, attacking, and neutral zones. — see also OFFSIDE (*ice hockey*)

blueliner A defenseman on an ice hockey team.

blueprint *motor racing* To rebuild a stock engine to the manufacturer's exact design specifications. An assembly-line engine will usually

have minor irregularities and variances from the specifications which mean its performance will not be as high as possible. Racing shops and engine specialty shops take a production engine or the engine block and major parts and machine and align the parts so that the entire engine will conform exactly to the manufacturer's specifications. In this way the power of the engine can be significantly increased without modifying or changing the engine.

blunt *archery* An arrow with a blunt or flat tip for use in hunting birds and small game. The flat pile increases the shocking power of the arrow yet reduces the chance of mangling the animal, a danger present when sharp penetrating points are used.

bo *karate* A long wooden staff that is used in training as a weapon by advanced students.

¹board **1** *racquets* A wooden board across the front wall of a court 27 inches up from the floor which marks the lower edge of the playing area of the front wall.
2 *skiing* A ski.
3 *squash racquets* see TELLTALE
4 Short for *diving board, scoreboard, springboard, surfboard, tote board.*
— **off the board** *of pari-mutuel odds* Greater than 99–1. Tote boards have facilities for listing odds only as high as 99 so higher odds can only be shown as 99–1.

²board *ice hockey* To board-check an opponent.

board-check To body-check an opponent into the boards in ice hockey and box lacrosse. A major or minor penalty may be imposed when unnecessary violence is involved in board-checking the puck carrier or ball handler. If the player board-checked is other than the puck carrier or ball handler, a penalty is automatically called.

board check The act or an instance of body-checking a player into the boards.

board checking or **boarding** The act of illegally board-checking an opponent which results in a major or minor penalty.

boarding ladder A small portable ladder designed to hang over the side of a boat to facilitate boarding from the water by a water-skier or swimmer.

boards **1** A wooden wall between 3 and 4 feet high that encloses an ice hockey rink or a box lacrosse box. The boards along the side are often called *sideboards* and those at the ends, *endboards.* Along the top of the boards is a protective screen or unbreakable glass designed to pro-

tect the spectators from an errant puck or ball.
2 *basketball* Backboards. The term is normally used in reference to rebounding. ⟨dominated the *boards* with 14 rebounds⟩ ⟨crashing the *boards*⟩
3 *track and field* An indoor competition area and especially the track itself.

board-surfer *surfing* Someone who rides the surf on a surfboard as distinguished from a body-surfer.

boast *squash racquets* A shot from the back corner of the court that hits first a side wall then the front wall at the diagonally opposite corner and then the floor near or at the crease.

boat **1** *fishing* To bring a hooked fish into a boat.
2 *rowing* To enter a crew in competition. ⟨the heaviest crew the school had ever *boated*⟩

boat hook *boating* A staff with a metal hook and point at one end that is used to push off or to pull the boat into place or to pick up a mooring.

boating **1** The act or sport of riding in or navigating a boat for pleasure.
2 *rowing* The seating arrangement of a crew.

boat net *fishing* A landing net with a long handle for use when fishing from a boat.

boat rod *fishing* A usually short stout rod typically used with a bay reel in saltwater fishing from a boat.

bob Short for *bobsled, ski bob.*

bob and weave *boxing* To move up and down and side to side quickly and repeatedly in order to present a moving target to one's opponent.

bobber *fishing* A float (as of plastic or cork) tied to the line between the bait and the pole to keep the bait at the desired depth and to indicate, when it is pulled under, that a fish is biting. (also called *dobber*)

bobbing *swimming* The action of alternately rising above the surface for breaths of air and submerging while maintaining a usually vertical position in the water. The submerging is usually aided by raising the arms out of the water which forces the head under and the rising is aided by a kick and a downward sweep with the arms. Bobbing is often used as a training aid to help beginning swimmers become accustomed to the water and as a technique by which advanced swimmers rest in the water for long periods when too exhausted to swim or tread water.

¹bobble **1** *baseball* To fumble or mishandle a batted ball when attempting to field it.
2 *waterskiing* To momentarily lose balance and make a quick recovery.

²bobble The action or an instance of bobbling in waterskiing or of mishandling a batted ball in baseball.

boblet A 2-man bobsled.

bobrun *bobsledding* A narrow ice-covered chute usually 1500 meters (1635 yards) long that has high walls and numerous banked turns and that is used as a course down which bobsleds are raced one at a time.

bobsled A large racing sled that has two pairs of runners in tandem, a long seat for 2 or 4 riders, and a hand brake and that is steered by means of a steering wheel or ropes connected to the front runners. Bobsleds for 4 men are up to 12½ feet long and approximately 2 feet wide and weigh up to 460 pounds. Two-man bobsleds are approximately 8½ feet long and 2 feet wide and weigh up to 360 pounds.

4-man bobsled

bobsledding The sport of racing bobsleds. The bobsleds are given a push start at the beginning of the run by the crew members who then must jump aboard. The front rider does the steering and the rear rider does the braking; the entire crew must cooperate on balance and precisely timed weight shifts. Competition is in the form of heats and the team with the fastest time after usually 4 heats is the winner.

bobsleigh British term for *bobsled.*

bocce The ball used in boccie. — see BALL

boccie or **bocci** An Italian bowling game somewhat resembling lawn bowling that is played on a dirt court 75 feet long and 8 feet wide bounded on all sides by boards. A team consists of 2 players stationed at opposite ends of the court. To start play, one player tosses or rolls a small ball, a *pallino,* to the opposite end of the court and then, alternating turns with an opponent, rolls or tosses 4 larger balls at the pallino to score points for each ball his team has closer to the pallino than the opponents. After the balls have been played from one end and scoring tallied, the teammates play from the other end. It is permissible to knock the opponent's ball out of position or to knock the pallino away. The boards around the court keep all balls in play and playing rebounds from these walls is a part of the game. The game is usually played to 12 points.

boccie out or **bocci out** *boccie* To knock the pallino or an opponent's ball out of position.

boccino see PALLINO

body block *football* A block made by hitting the opponent usually with the side of the torso instead of with the front of the shoulders. In making a body block, a player is not required to keep his hands or arms in contact with his body. (also called *crab block, cross-body block*) — compare SHOULDER BLOCK

body-check **1** *ice hockey* To block the puck carrier or an opponent going for the puck by hitting him from the front or side and above the knees with the upper part of the body. To make a legal body check a player must not take more than 2 strides before hitting an opponent and he must not leave his feet while hitting him.
2 *lacrosse* To check or block the ball handler, a potential pass receiver, or an opponent who is within 5 yards of the ball by hitting him from the front or side and above the knees with the upper part of the body while keeping at least one foot on the ground.

body check The act or an instance of body-checking an opponent in hockey or lacrosse.

body checker *ice hockey* A player noted for his body-checking.

body drop *judo* A throw made by grasping an opponent, turning so as to have one's back to him, and pulling him down over an outstretched leg.

body English The instinctive attempt to influence the movement of a propelled object (as a ball or puck) by contorting one's body in the direction of desired movement.

body press *wrestling* A hold in which a wrestler is lying on top of a supine opponent on the mat with all his weight on the opponent in an attempt to secure a fall.

body slam *wrestling* An illegal throw in which an opponent's body is lifted and brought down hard to the mat.

bodysurf To engage in body surfing.

bodysurfer Someone who engages in body surfing.

body surfing The act or sport of riding a wave without a surfboard by planing on the chest and stomach.

boeckl *skating* A jump from the forward inside edge of one skate with one and a half turns in the air and a return to the backward outside edge of the same skate.

¹bogey *golf* **1** A score of one over par for a hole.
2 A standard score that an average or occasional player playing under ordinary weather conditions might hope to achieve and that is somewhat higher than par. In Britain, a course may have a bogey rating; in the United States, bogey is usually an average of one over par for each hole for the round.

²bogey *golf* To score a bogey on a hole.

boiler plate A frozen crusty surface of snow.

bollard **1** *boating* An upright post (of wood or metal) on a pier to which mooring lines can be attached.
2 *mountain climbing* A narrow upright projection of rock or a similar feature cut in ice that serves as a belay point.

¹bolt **1** A part of the action of a firearm that slides back and forth in the breech to position the cartridge in the chamber and to extract the used case and that carries the firing pin. — see also ACTION
2 A short arrow shot from a crossbow.
3 *mountain climbing* A short solid metal bar with threads and a nut at one end that is sometimes used for a belay on rock faces which have no cracks for inserting a piton. The climber must drill a hole into the rock and then hammer in the bolt. The soft metal at the end of the bolt expands to fit the hole and provides a permanent anchor. A bracket which accepts a carabiner fits over the threaded end and is secured by the nut. (also called *expansion bolt*)

²bolt **1** *of a hunting dog* To force an animal (as a fox or otter) from a lair.
2 *of a racehorse* To veer from a direct course while running in a race.

bolt action see ACTION (*firearms*)

¹bomb **1** *basketball* A shot at the basket from approximately 20 or more feet away.
2 *football* A long forward pass and especially one that results in a touchdown.
3 *surfing* A wipeout.

²bomb **1** To defeat overwhelmingly.
2 *basketball* To shoot successfully from long range.
3 *box lacrosse* To shoot the ball hard.
4 *football* To throw bombs.

boom

bomb out **1** *skydiving* To dive headlong from a plane at the start of a jump.
2 *surfing* To be wiped out by a wave.

bomb squad see SPECIAL TEAM

bong *mountain climbing* A wide U-shaped piton that often has holes in the sides to reduce weight. — see illustration at PITON

bonspiel A curling tournament.

bonus **1** or **bonus free throw** *basketball* An additional free throw awarded to a fouled player when the opposing team has exceeded the number of team fouls permitted during a period of play. In high school and college play the bonus applies only to those personal fouls that normally involve one shot. If the free throw is made, the player is given another free throw. If the original free throw is missed there is no second chance. This situation is known as *one-and-one*. There is no bonus for 2-shot fouls. Professional rules differ in that the bonus applies to both 1-shot and 2-shot fouls. In the bonus situation what is normally a 1-shot foul becomes a 2-shot foul — 2 chances to score 2 points. On a normal 2-shot foul the player is given 3 chances to score 2 points; if he misses the first shot, he still has 2 more chances. The bonus free throw was instituted to cut down on the number of deliberate fouls committed usually late in a game by a team that would sacrifice the one point of a free throw in return for possession of the ball and an opportunity to make 2 points. With the bonus situation, nothing is gained by the deliberate foul since the team still has the opportunity to make the 2 points. — see also PERSONAL FOUL, TEAM FOUL
2 *bowling* An addition to a bowler's score awarded for a strike or spare. The bonus for a spare is the number of pins knocked down with the first ball in the next frame; for a strike it is the number knocked down with the next 2 balls. The bonus is added to the score for the spare or strike in the previous frame as well as counted in the frame in which it was rolled.

bonus baby A player who receives a large bonus when he signs his first professional contract.

bonus free throw see BONUS (*basketball*)

bonus situation *basketball* A situation in which one team has exceeded the permitted number of team fouls for the period with the result that for each subsequent personal foul the other team will receive a bonus free throw. (also called *penalty situation*)

¹book **1** A store of knowledge about the strengths and especially the weaknesses of an opponent. ⟨what they all were saying was that there was no accurate *book* on me — Ted Williams⟩ **2** A prerace estimate of probable odds. ⟨*book* favorite⟩ **3** The basic or conventional principles and techniques of a sport. ⟨contest between a slugger and a *book* fighter⟩ ⟨*book* strategy⟩

²book *of a British rugby or soccer referee* To record in a book the name of a player or players guilty of flagrant fouls or unsportsmanlike conduct. The player is reported to the league officials and if that player is booked a number of times during the season, he is subject to disciplinary action by the league. When a player is booked during a game, it often serves as a caution to the player that repeated violations or similar conduct will result in his being disqualified. A player who is sent off during the game usually will also be booked.

bookmaking The action or process of taking and paying off wagers as a private business as distinguished from similar action by a racetrack or a government agency. In England, bookmaking is the only legally recognized method of handling betting on horse racing and the bookmakers are licensed by the government. The bookmaker sets individual odds for each of the competitors and keeps a record of the wagers as they are made. He keeps his book balanced so that no matter which of the competitors wins, he will make a profit because the amount to be paid out to winning bettors is covered by that taken in on losing wagers. The bookmaker will pay off a wager at the odds as they were at the time the wager was made regardless of how they are ultimately changed. There may be times when the bookmaker will have to place a bet of his own with another bookmaker as insurance against being wiped out by a heavily backed favorite. This is known as *laying-off* and there are usually special lay-off centers established among bookmakers just for this purpose. Wagering on boxing matches is commonly handled in the same manner as for horse racing with one competitor usually getting higher odds than the other. But for games like football or basketball, the bookmaker usually establishes a point spread instead of setting separate odds for each team. His odds remained fixed (requiring a wager of 6 dollars to win 5 or 11 dollars to win 10) but he will vary the point spread as necessary to balance the betting on either side and to ensure himself a profit. — see also POINT SPREAD, VIGORISH; compare PARI-MUTUEL BETTING

boom *sailing* The horizontal pole to which the

foot of a sail is attached. The boom is attached to the mast at one end and is used to hold the sail at the proper angle in the wind.

boom vang *sailing* A short line that runs from the bottom of the boom to the deck near the base of the mast to help keep the boom and mainsail down against the action of heavy winds when sailing before the wind.

¹boot 1 A usually ankle-high foot covering that is worn when one needs more protection or support than a shoe can give. Boots worn for skiing fall chiefly into 2 categories: boots for downhill skiing and boots for cross-country or tour skiing. The downhiller's boots are typically insulated and form fitting, often custom-fitted by injecting quick-setting foam while the foot is in the boot. They have a flat rigid 1-piece sole and provide total rigid support to the foot and ankle. The ski touring boot is usually a low-cut light-weight leather boot with a heel and a flexible sole that extends beyond the upper at the toe and on the underside has 3 holes that accept the pins of the binding. The touring boot offers no support to the ankle but is flexible to allow the heel to rise from the ski when making long strides. Boots worn by mountain climbers and hikers are constructed typically of 1-piece leather uppers, are often lined and padded on the inside, and have a scree collar and a rigid molded-lug sole. The more rugged the planned climbing, the more rigid the sole must be. — compare SHOE
2 A kick (as in football or soccer).
3 *baseball* An error made in attempting to field a grounder.
4 *harness racing* Any of a variety of usually leather or rubber coverings for a horse's hoof or leg that are used to aid him in maintaining balance or gait or to protect the hoof or leg if the horse habitually kicks himself. *Elbow boots* are usually lamb's-wool-lined leather coverings for the elbow that are held in place by straps which go over the horse's back and that protect against kicks from the front hooves when a high-gaited horse picks up his front legs. *Knee boots* protect the knees from kicks from the opposite front hoof (as when the horse is running around a turn) and *shin boots* protect the rear legs from being kicked by the front hooves. A *tendon boot* is essentially a shin boot with padding at the rear that is worn on the front legs. An *ankle boot* may be worn by pacers to protect the inside and rear of the front legs. It gives greater freedom of movement than the tendon boot. The *quarter*

boot is a small covering for the rear of the front hooves of a trotter and for the rear hooves and the inside of the front hooves of a pacer. Pacers often wear *scalpers,* doughnut-shaped pieces of rubber, that slip over the rear hooves, to protect against kicks from the front legs. If the horse kicks just above the hoof or above the area protected by the scalper but below the shin, it may require *speedy cut boots.* A popular boot for use on a trotter's front legs for balance is the *bell boot.* It is a wide band of rubber that is more secure than the quarter boot or the scalper, which it often replaces.

²boot 1 To kick a ball (as in football, rugby, or soccer) especially in a scoring attempt.
2 *baseball* To mishandle the ball in attempting to field a grounder.
3 *horse racing* To ride a horse in a race. ⟨*booted* home 4 winners today⟩

booter 1 A kicker in football.
2 A soccer player.

bootie *skin diving* A neoprene rubber foot covering that is sometimes worn as part of a wet suit.

¹bootleg *football* An offensive play in which the quarterback fakes a handoff, hides the ball on his hip, and rolls out to the opposite side to run or pass.

²bootleg *football* To run a bootleg play; to make a gain on a bootleg play. ⟨*bootlegged* 18 yards round his right end — *New York Times*⟩

boot top or **boot topping** The part of a boat above the waterline.

bore 1 The inside diameter of the barrel of a firearm. — see also CALIBER, GAUGE
2 The diameter of a cylinder of an internal-combustion engine.

boresight To align the sight and barrel of a firearm on a single point usually by sighting a target through the barrel of a rigidly mounted firearm and then adjusting the sight on the target.

¹borrow *golf* The distance a putt will veer from a direct line on a sloping putting green.

²borrow *golf* To putt to the left or right of a direct line to the hole to allow for the slope of a green.

bosey Australian term for *googly,* named after its originator, B. J. T. Bosanquet.

boss *archery* A compact circular mat of straw used as a backing for a target. (also called *matt*)

bote corrido *jai alai* A ball played against the front wall so that it rebounds to the floor and bounces very high.

bote pronto *jai alai* A ball that is scooped up immediately from a bounce. The bote pronto is somewhat analogous to a half-volley in tennis.

bottle pocket billiards A variation of pocket billiards played with a cue ball, 2 object balls numbered one and 2, and a shake bottle. The object of the game is to be first to score exactly 31 points by making caroms off both balls (one point) and by pocketing the object balls (one or 2 points). A carom off both balls which knocks over the shake bottle, balanced upside down in the middle of the table, is worth 5 points. If a player goes over 31 points, he must begin again with the number of points by which he exceeded 31. Any carom which causes the shake bottle to flip over and come to rest upright automatically wins the game.

bottom *baseball* The last part. ⟨the *bottom* of the eighth inning⟩

bottom bouncing *fishing* A method of fishing from a boat in which the lure or sinker is allowed to bounce repeatedly on the bottom and raise small puffs of sand or mud.

bottom rig *fishing* A terminal rig designed to hold the bait on or near the bottom. Bottom rigs commonly employ a sinker attached at the end of the line so as to rest on the bottom and a leader and hook that can be moved up or down the line depending on the depth to be fished. An important advantage to this rig is that the fish will not feel the weight of the sinker when taking the bait.

bottom time *scuba diving* The amount of time a scuba diver has been underwater. The depth of the dive and the bottom time are used in computing decompression stops and the amount of time a diver must spend on the surface between dives. (also called *down time*)

bounce *baseball* To hit the ball so that it bounces before reaching an infielder. ⟨*bounced* out to the shortstop⟩

bounce pass A pass made in basketball or box lacrosse by directing the ball at the floor at a point between the passer and the receiver.

bouncer **1** *baseball* A bouncing ground ball.
2 *cricket* see BUMPER

bounce-shot *lacrosse* A shot in which the ball is directed at the ground in front of the goal so that it will be harder for the goalkeeper to stop and will bounce into the goal.

boundary *cricket* An award of usually 4 runs to a batsman who hits a ball beyond the boundary of the playing field. If the ball crosses the boundary on the fly, the batsman is automatically awarded 6 runs. This is analogous to a home run in baseball.

boundary umpire *Australian Rules football* An umpire on the sidelines who signals the field umpire when the ball goes out of bounds.

bounder *baseball* A bounding ground ball.

bounds see INBOUNDS, OUT OF BOUNDS

bout **1** *boxing* A contest between 2 boxers which consists of a specified number of rounds and which usually ends in a decision by the judges or by a knockout or a technical knockout. Amateur bouts usually last for three 3-minute rounds and professional bouts for up to fifteen 3-minute rounds.
2 *fencing* A contest between 2 fencers which ends when one contestant scores a designated number of hits or at the end of a time limit. A bout for women usually consists of 4 hits or a 5-minute limit; for men a bout usually lasts for 6 minutes or until 5 hits are made. If the time limit expires before the designated number of hits has been made, the score is advanced for each fencer so that the winner's score will show the required number of hits. Example: if time runs out with the score 4–2, the scores will be advanced to read 5–3. If the score is tied, as at 2–2, it will be advanced to 4–4, and the fencers will continue without time limit until the final point is won.

¹bow **1** *archery* **a** A strip of flexible material that has a hand grip in the middle and tapers at both ends, that is drawn in an arc by means of a bowstring attached between the ends, and that is used to propel an arrow. The ends of the bow are called *limbs* and are usually flat on each side. The side toward the target is called the *back* and the side near the string is the *belly*. Though some bows (called *self bows*) may be constructed of a single piece of material, most modern bows are a composite of wood and fiberglass and are usually recurved or constructed so that the tips curve toward the back when the bow is not strung. A straight bow is one whose tips are straight when it is not strung. Bows generally range from 52 to 72 inches in length though target bows are commonly 64 to 70 inches long. The element most important in the selection of a bow is draw weight — the force required to pull the bow to full draw. A hunting bow may have a draw weight of 50 or more pounds while the target bow rarely exceeds 45 pounds for men or 30 pounds for women. **b** The third circle out from the center of a clout target.
2 *squash racquets* A shot from the corner of the court hitting first the rear of one side wall then the other side wall in the diagonally opposite

bow

recurved bow at full draw with stabilizer bars on the back

corner of the court and finally hitting the front wall just above the telltale.

²bow The front or forward end of a boat.

bow arm *archery* The arm that supports the bow in shooting.

bow fishing Fishing with a bow and arrow instead of a rod and reel. The arrows used in bow fishing are usually equipped with a special pile having a hinged or spring barb. The feathers of the fletching are either absent or replaced with rubber vanes that are not affected by the water. The line is attached to the pile and is wound on a nonrevolving spool that resembles the spool of a spinning reel. The spool is attached to the back of the bow and allows the line to come off freely when the arrow is shot.

bow hand *archery* The hand that holds the bow in shooting.

bow hunter Someone who hunts game with a bow and arrow.

bow hunting The sport of hunting game with a bow and arrow.

bowknot A knot that is used chiefly to join 2 pieces of line and that is tied in basically the same way as a square knot but with the second overhand knot formed with loops. — see illustration at KNOT

¹bowl **1** A cast or delivery of a bowl down the green, a bowling ball down the alley, or a cricket ball to a batsman; a turn to bowl.

2 A bowl-shaped athletic stadium often constructed by excavation.

3 A shallow area where the surf breaks unusually hard and fast.

4 or **bowl game** *football* A postseason game between specially invited teams or between teams of specially invited players.

5 *lawn bowling* The hardwood or hard rubber composition ball that is rolled at the jack. The bowl is between 4¾ and 5⅛ inches in diameter and weighs 3½ pounds. It is biased, that is, constructed slightly less than perfectly spherical, so as to curve several feet in the length of the green.

²bowl **1** To roll a bowl or a bowling ball at the target with an underhand motion.

2 To propel a cricket ball at the far wicket with an overhand motion while keeping the arm straight. The bowler is permitted to bend his wrist but he must not throw the ball by allowing his elbow to bend. In the very early days of cricket, it was customary to bowl the ball with an underhand motion. Gradually players began to move the arm higher and higher in bowling the ball until today the delivery is straight overhand. The term *bowling* has remained and the distinction between throwing the ball and bowling it is a matter of keeping the elbow straight during the delivery.

3 *rounders* To throw a ball underhand to the batter.

4 a To participate in a game of bowling; to complete a game in bowling. ⟨*bowl* a string⟩ **b** To achieve a specified score in bowling. ⟨*bowled* a 175⟩

bowled *of a cricket batsman* Out when a bowled ball is not hit but knocks the bails from the defended wicket.

— bowled for a duck *of a cricket batsman* Bowled out without having scored.

bowler **1** Someone who participates in the sport of bowling or lawn bowling.

2 *cricket* A player who bowls the ball at the defended wicket in an attempt to put out the batsman. The bowler's job is somewhat analogous to that of the pitcher in baseball. The bowler, however, delivers only 6 or 8 balls at a time (an *over*) and must then relinquish the bowling to another player who bowls the next over in the opposite direction. Any player may bowl as many overs from either end as the team captain decides so long as one bowler does not bowl 2 consecutive overs.

bowler's thumb *bowling* A painful muscle strain in the thumb of the bowling hand that results from wrenching the thumb as it leaves the thumb hole.

bowl game see BOWL (*football*)

bowline A knot that is tied like a sheet bend to form a fixed loop in the end of a rope that will not slip or jam. The bowline is used for mooring or hoisting and by mountain climbers in attaching a belay or in tying on to the climbing rope. — see illustration at KNOT

bowline on the bight A bowline knot that is formed in the middle of a rope when the ends are inaccessible and that is tied by passing the bight through the loop formed on the standing part and then over the second loop and up to the standing part. — see illustration at KNOT

bowling 1 A sport in which individuals compete against one another or as members of a team against another team in rolling a ball down a 60-foot-long alley in an attempt to knock down 10 pins arranged in the form of a triangle. The object is to have the highest individual or team score, that is the greatest number of pins knocked down, at the end of the game. A game

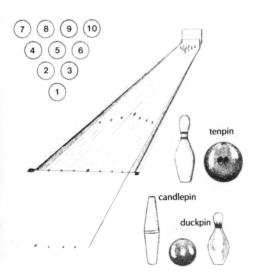

bowling: upper left, pin arrangement; center, bowling lane; right, pins and balls

is divided into 10 frames each of which consists of 2 attempts to knock down the pins. If all 10 pins are knocked down with one ball (a *strike*) or with 2 balls (a *spare*), a bonus of the number of pins knocked down with the bowler's next one or 2 balls is added to his score for that frame. If a strike or a spare is rolled in the 10th frame, a total of 3 balls can be rolled for that frame to provide the bonus. The highest possible score for a game, 12 consecutive strikes, is 300. Bowlers must roll the ball from behind a foul line and they are allowed to take several steps in bowling so long as they do not cross the foul line. A bowler usually rolls one frame at a turn except in match play where 2 frames are normally bowled; one bowler is not permitted to interfere with another bowler. — see also CANDLEPINS, DUCKPINS; compare LAWN BOWLING

2 *cricket* The action of bowling the ball at the wicket defended by the batsman. The bowler may run before bowling the ball but he may not cross the popping crease until the ball is released. Though the ball may be thrown directly at the wicket, it is commonly made to bounce a short distance in front of the batsman. The bowler typically imparts spin to the ball to make it harder for the batsman to anticipate how the ball will bounce.

bowling average 1 *bowling* The average score of a bowler determined by dividing the total number of pins credited to him (including bonuses) by the number of games bowled during a period (as a week or a season). Example: a bowler who is credited with 8006 pins in 36 games has a bowling average of 222.

2 *cricket* A number that is obtained by dividing the number of runs scored against a particular bowler by the number of wickets taken by the bowler and that is used as a measure of the effectiveness of a bowler. The smaller his bowling average, the more effective he is.

bowling bag A small bag in which a bowling ball and sometimes bowling shoes are carried.

bowling crease *cricket* Either of 2 parallel lines 8½ feet long and 66 feet apart on which the wickets are centered and behind which the bowler must keep his rear foot in bowling the ball. — compare POPPING CREASE, RETURN CREASE

bowling on the green or **bowls** The game of lawn bowling.

¹bowman An archer; a bowhunter.

²bowman The paddler who is in the bow of a canoe. — compare STERNMAN

bow rudder *canoeing* A maneuver in which the

paddler in the bow inserts his paddle alongside the bow on the side on which he has been paddling so that the paddle can act as a rudder to steer the canoe around obstacles. — compare CROSS BOW RUDDER

bowsight *archery* An adjustable aiming device attached usually to the upper limb of the bow. It has either a single thin point or a peep hole extending to the side which the archer lines up with the target. As the distance from the target increases the pointer is moved farther down so that the arrow is pointed higher.

bow sock *archery* A dark cloth covering that prevents a hunting bow from reflecting light.

bowstring *archery* The synthetic or waxed linen string attached to the two ends of a bow usually by loops. When pulled, the string causes the two limbs of the bow to bend evenly so that when the string is released it snaps forward to its original position and thereby propels the arrow.

bow weight *archery* The draw weight of a bow.

bow window see STRING PICTURE

¹box 1 Any of the 6 designated areas on a baseball diamond where the batter, pitcher, catcher, and coaches stand. — see BATTER'S BOX, CATCHER'S BOX, COACH'S BOX, MOUND

2 The enclosed playing area for box lacrosse which is generally an ice hockey rink with a floor instead of an ice surface. At each end of the box is a goal 4 feet high and 4½ feet wide that is backed with a net that comes to a point on the floor 3 to 4 feet behind the goalposts. Surrounding each goal is a circular goal crease with a radius of 10 feet. At the rear of the goal the arc meets a straight line parallel to and 6 feet behind the front of the goal which forms the rear of the crease. Outside each crease is a broken semicircular free throw line with a radius of 24 feet. The box is divided into 3 zones by 2 lines that cross the middle of the playing area 22 feet apart forming the center zone. In the exact middle of the center zone is a face-off circle. There is a face-off circle surrounded by a 12-foot restraining circle in each corner of the box centered 16 feet from the sideboards and 30 feet from the goal line. On one side of the center zone in front of the penalty bench is a semicircle with a 10-foot radius known as the *referees' crease.*

3 *bowling* A square on a score sheet; frame.

4 *pari-mutuel betting* A grouping of several competitors in all the possible combinations (as in quiniela or perfecta betting).

5 *track and field* The rectangular hole with a sloping bottom which is in front of the pole vault pit and in which the pole is planted at the start of the takeoff. (also called *planting pit*)

6 Short for *penalty box, service box, starting box.*

7 British term for the *penalty area* in soccer.

— in the box *of a racing sailboat* Behind an opposing boat and in its wind shadow so as to receive very little wind.

²box 1 To engage in boxing.

2 or **box in** To surround and hem in a competitor in a race (as in track or horse racing) so that he must drop back and go wide to pass.

3 *baseball* To field a batted ball clumsily.

4 *pari-mutuel betting* To bet on all the possible combinations involving a certain number of competitors (as in a quiniela or perfecta).

box-and-one *basketball* A defense in which 4 players form a square zone defense on either side of the free throw lane while the fifth player guards the other team's best scorer man-to-man.

box defense *box lacrosse* A defensive formation used by a team when shorthanded in which 4 players form a square in front of the goalkeeper.

boxer Someone who engages in boxing. The term is often used to contrast one especially skilled in defensive tactics — moving in to deliver a blow and quickly moving back out of range to avoid being hit — with a slugger or puncher.

box in see BOX

boxing The art of fighting with the fists; a sport in which 2 opponents fight each other with gloved fists inside a usually elevated ring — a square canvas-covered mat surrounded by ropes — for a specified maximum number of rounds with each attempting to win by knocking out or scoring more points than his opponent. The sport has developed from bare-knuckle fighting, in which a round lasted until one fighter was knocked down, to a contest conducted in 3-minute rounds with 1-minute rest periods between rounds and having the emphasis on tactics of attack and defense. A boxer is not permitted to use any part of his body other than his fist in attacking or his arms and hands in blocking and parrying blows. To be legal, all blows must land above the waist on the front and sides of the body and head. A referee in the ring supervises the fight, separating the fighters when they clinch and ensuring that the blows are fair. If one fighter is knocked down, he is given 10 seconds in which to rise or he will be counted out by the referee. If the round ends before the count is finished, however, the count may be stopped and the fighter is then "saved by the bell." During a knockdown, the other fighter must retire to a neutral corner. The rules forbid kicking or wrestling with an opponent or hitting an opponent when he is down. The referee has the power to stop the fight at any time if he feels one fighter is unable to continue or is in danger of suffering a possibly severe or permanent injury. The other fighter then wins on a technical knockout. If no knockout or technical knockout is scored, the winner is determined by the decision of usually 3 or more judges. There is no universal scoring system. Some fights are scored on the basis of the number of rounds won, some on points — the boxer who wins the round gets a given number of points and the other fighter is given fewer points and the one with the most points at the end is the winner — and some on both round-by-round and a points system. When both systems are used, it is technically possible for one boxer to win more rounds but lose the fight on points. Because of the obvious advantage enjoyed by a large man in a bout with a smaller opponent, boxing is conducted in weight divisions. — see also DIVISION (*boxing*), FIVE POINT MUST SYSTEM, MARQUIS OF QUEENSBURY RULES, TEN POINT MUST SYSTEM

box lacrosse or **boxla** A version of lacrosse played between 2 teams of 6 players usually indoors on an ice hockey rink with a wooden floor in place of the ice. A team consists of a goalkeeper, 2 defensemen, and 3 forwards. The goals are 4 feet high and 4½ feet wide. The game is played in 3 periods of 20 minutes and a team must take a shot in 30 seconds or lose possession of the ball.

boxman *football* A member of the chain crew who handles the down box.

box out *basketball* To position oneself between an opponent and the basket so as to make it more difficult for an opposing player to get a rebound. (also *block out, screen out*)

box score A printed summary of a game usually in tabular form giving the essential details of play (as names and position of players and individual performances).

boy *horse racing* A jockey.

Boy's Baseball A commercially sponsored summer baseball league for boys aged 13 and 14 that was formerly known as Pony League.

brace *archery* To string a bow.

bracer *archery* An armguard.

bracket **1** *skating* A figure that resembles a bracket and that is formed by turning the body away from the curve being skated and changing

from one edge to the other on the same skate so as to have the cusp outside the curve; a jump made in this way.
2 A pair of parallel lines connected at one end used to show the pairings in an elimination tournament; a pairing in an elimination tournament.

brain bucket A crash helmet used especially in motor racing.

brake bar *mountain climbing* A short metal bar with a hole in one end and a notch in the other end that is braced crosswise in a carabiner to provide friction and serve as a brake for a rope especially in rappeling.

brakeman *bobsledding* The member of a bobsled team who rides at the rear and who operates the brake.

brassie *golf* An old name for a number 2 wood.

¹break **1** To make a sudden movement or dash; to change direction suddenly. 〈*broke* for the plate〉
2 To do better than an existing record or standard. 〈couldn't *break* par〉 〈*broke* 3 world records〉
3 To open the breech of a shotgun for loading or unloading by raising the rear of the barrel away from the stock.
4 *of a propelled ball* To swerve, drop, or change direction.
5 *of a baseball pitcher* To cause a pitch to break. 〈*broke* a curve over the plate〉
6 *billiards* To separate the racked balls by hitting them with the cue ball to start a game.

BOX SCORE

HAWKS	ab	r	h	rbi	LIONS	ab	r	h	rbi
Garcia 2b	4	2	2	1	White lf	3	0	1	1
Collins ss	4	0	2	0	Howe ss	4	0	0	0
C Martin cf	3	0	2	0	Maddox cf	4	0	1	0
O'Brien rf	5	1	2	1	Rice 1b	5	0	2	0
Robinson lf	2	0	0	0	Scott 3b	4	0	2	0
J Martin 1b	3	1	1	1	McMillan 2b	3	0	1	0
Wilson c	3	1	1	2	Perez c	3	1	0	0
Thompson 3b	3	0	1	0	Jones rf	2	2	2	1
Miller p	2	0	0	0	Ash p	2	0	0	0
Jones p	0	1	0	0	Curtis p	1	0	0	0
Smith ph	1	0	0	0	Simmons p	0	0	0	0
					Bell ph	1	0	0	0
					Ford ph	1	0	1	1
Totals	30	6	11	5	Totals	33	3	10	3

Hawks	001 032 000	6
Lions	000 200 010	3

E—Howe. DP—Lions 1. LOB—Hawks 6, Lions 2. 2b—Garcia, O'Brien, J. Martin. 3b—Scott. HR—Wilson. SB—Garcia, Rice. WP—Jones. LP—Curtis.

typical box score of a baseball game

7 *of boxers* To separate from a clinch on command from the referee.

8 *cricket* **a** To bowl a ball with spin so that it breaks. **b** To knock the bails from a wicket with the bat or with the ball.

9 *cycling* To speed up and begin the sprint after a period of slow circling of the track trying to get position in a sprint race.

10 *football* **a** To get through the defense for a long gain. **b** To get out of a tackle.

11 *of a harness horse* To go off gait and begin to gallop with the result that the driver must pull to the outside and slow up until the gait is regained.

12 *of a racehorse* To leave the starting gate. ⟨his horse *broke* on top⟩

13 *of a hunting dog* To leave a point and begin to retrieve game.

14 *tennis* To win a game against the opponent's service.

15 *track and field* **a** To make a false start by moving off the starting line before the starting signal is given. **b** To move to the inside lane after running a specified distance in a race begun with a staggered start.

16 *of a wave* To crest and fall over in surf.

²break **1** A sudden movement or dash. ⟨made a *break* for second⟩

2 British term for a sequence of successful shots (as in croquet or billiards).

3 The deviation of a propelled ball from a straight line; a sudden swerving or dipping movement of a pitched baseball.

4 *basketball* Short for *fast break*.

5 *billiards* A shot that separates the racked balls at the beginning of the game.

6 *bowling* An open frame following a series of marks.

7 *boxing* The act of separating after a clinch.

8 *cricket* The change in the direction of flight of a bowled ball after it bounces on the pitch that is caused by spin imparted by the bowler.

9 *harness racing* An instance of a horse's going off his gait.

10 *horse racing* The act of the horses leaving the starting gate.

11 *ice hockey* A quick offensive drive toward the goal in an attempt to score before the defense can set up.

12 *surfing* The collapse of a wave into surf; the point at which a wave collapses.

13 *tennis* Short for *service break*.

14 *track and field* **a** An instance of moving off the starting line before the gun is fired. **b** The

mark made when a jumper lands in the pit that is used for measuring the distance of a long jump or triple jump.

breakable crust *skiing* A snow surface that is hard but not strong enough to support the weight of a skier.

breakage *pari-mutuel betting* The odd cents over an established payoff figure (usually the next lower 10 cents) that are not paid to a winning pari-mutuel bettor and that are retained by the track or divided between the track and the state. — see PARI-MUTUEL BETTING

breakaway **1** An offensive drive in hockey or lacrosse in which one or more offensive players get a jump on the defense so that they are moving in on the goal with fewer defenders than attackers.

2 *basketball* A fast break.

3 *football* A run that goes through the defense for a long gain. A breakaway runner is one who is elusive and adept at broken field running.

break back *tennis* To break an opponent's service on the very next game after he has broken your service.

break ball *billiards* The last object ball on the table after the first 14 balls have been pocketed in the game of 14.1 continuous pocket billiards which is to be pocketed on the break shot for continuation of the game after the other 14 balls have been racked.

break cover *of a fox or hare* To leave the protection of brush or an earth and run when hunted by hounds.

breakdown *wrestling* The act or an instance of breaking an opponent down.

break down **1** *of a racehorse* To suffer an injury or lameness during a race.

2 *wrestling* To force an opponent who is on the mat to his stomach or side by knocking or pulling his arm or leg support from under him. If a wrestler is able to break his opponent down he has a good chance of pinning him.

breakfall A technique of falling (as in tumbling or judo) in which the arms or legs absorb part of the impact especially by slamming against the mat or floor.

break ground *fencing* To retreat.

breaking pass A pass to a breaking teammate (as in ice hockey).

break one's duck *of a cricket batsman* To score the first run during one's innings and thereby avoid being out for a duck.

break one's fall To absorb part of a fall (as in tumbling or judo) by flexing the arms or legs or by slamming an arm down on the mat just as the shoulders land.

break one's wrist *baseball* To roll the wrist as a part of the swing of the bat. The swing is not considered completed if the wrist is not broken so it is possible for a batter to begin to swing at a pitch but change his mind and if he stops before turning his wrist, and if the pitch is not over the plate, he will not be charged with a strike.

breakout *ice hockey* An offensive play designed to get the puck out of a team's defensive zone.

break point *tennis* A situation when the score is love–40, 15–40, or 30–40 or when the receiving side has the advantage in which the receiving player or side will break the opponent's service by winning the next point; the point won in this situation.

break service *tennis* To win a game that an opponent is serving. Because the server is generally conceded to have an advantage, the winning of a game on the opponent's serve is an important step toward winning the set.

break shot *billiards* An opening shot in a game in which the cue ball is driven into a group of racked balls to separate some or all of them.

break the wind *of a cyclist* To push aside the air and create a slipstream which makes it easier for another cyclist pedaling immediately behind.

breast *track and field* To hit the tape at the finish line with one's chest in winning a race.

breaststroke *swimming* **1** A stroke executed in a prone position which combines the frog kick, a glide with the arms outstretched overhead, and a double arm pull downward and to the side.
2 A competitive event or a leg of a medley in which the breaststroke is used. The most common distances are 100 and 200 meters and 100 and 200 yards.

breaststroker *swimming* Someone who swims the breaststroke; a swimmer who competes in breaststroke events.

breech The part of a firearm at the rear of the barrel where the cartridge chamber is located.

breechblock The steel block which closes the rear of the barrel of a firearm against the force of the charge.

breeder One who breeds animals (as horses or dogs). The breeder of a racehorse is the one who owns the dam at the time the horse is foaled.

breeze *horse racing* To exercise a horse at its own brisk pace without encouraging it to run faster.

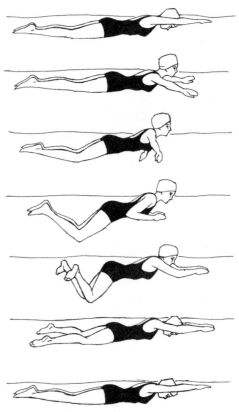

breaststroke with frog kick

¹bridge **1** A position (as in gymnastics, tumbling, or wrestling) in which the body is supported in a supine position with the back arched away from the mat and only the feet and hands or the feet and head on the mat.
2 *billiards* **a** The position of the hand in supporting the tip end of the cue in shooting. The most common bridge is formed by placing the heel of the hand on the table, spreading the fingers in front, and placing the thumb beside the index finger to form a notch for the cue or making a loop between the index finger and the thumb into which the cue fits. **b** A long stick that resembles a cue with a notched semicircular plate attached to the tip. This bridge is used for shooting over another ball or for long shots where the hand bridge cannot be used. (also called *mechanical bridge, stick bridge*)
3 *bowling* The distance between the inside edges of the finger holes in a ball. — compare SPAN

bridge

bridges: top, billiard player's hand bridge; center, mountain climber bridging a chimney; bottom, wrestler's bridge

4 *lacrosse* A strip of material (as cord, gut, or rawhide) at the throat of a stick between the guard and the flat wooden section to prevent the ball's becoming lodged too securely in the pocket.

5 *mountain climbing* The action or an instance of climbing a chimney by spanning the opening with the legs.

²bridge 1 *billiards* To support the end of a cue especially with a mechanical bridge.

2 *mountain climbing* To climb a chimney by supporting the body with the feet on opposite walls. The pressure of the feet and hands is often directed outward against the face of the wall instead of downward on holds.

3 *wrestling* To arch one's back into a bridge to avoid being pinned.

bridle 1 A set of leather straps that fit over a horse's head and that hold the bit in place. The bridle also includes the reins and a curb chain if one is used.

2 The ropes and rings in a dogsled to which the gangline is attached.

3 *sailing* A slack line between 2 fittings on the stern of a sailboat to which is attached a block through which the main sheet runs. The bridle serves the same function as a traveler.

bring down 1 To tackle a player in football or rugby.

2 *Australian Rules football* To catch a kicked ball overhead and take a mark.

3 *hunting* To shoot down game.

bring in *baseball* To score a base runner on a base hit.

bring up *mountain climbing* To provide a belay from above for a climber who is moving up toward the belayer. The climber moves up by himself with only the security of the belay, not a hoist up.

bring up a flag *Australian Rules football* To score a behind which the goal umpire signals by raising one flag.

bring up two flags *Australian Rules football* To score a goal which the goal umpire signals by raising 2 flags.

broach or **broach to** *of a boat* To swing or be thrown sideways to the direction of the waves in a heavy sea.

broadhead *archery* An arrowhead used on hunting arrows that consists of 2 or more blades; an arrow with a broadhead. — see illustration at ARROW

broad-jump To make a long jump to compete in the long jump.

broad jump see LONG JUMP

broad jumper see LONG JUMPER

broadside *motorcycle racing* To slide sideways through a turn.

broken field *football* The area beyond the line of scrimmage where defenders are normally spread out. In contrast to plunges through the line which are largely attempts to run through the holes made by offensive linemen, broken-field running usually requires the ballcarrier to maneuver to dodge defenders often without the aid of blockers.

bronc riding see SADDLE BRONC RIDING, BAREBACK RIDING

Bronx cheer A sound of derision made by protruding the tongue between the lips and expelling air forcibly to produce a vibration.

bronze medal A bronze-colored medal awarded for third place in a competition.

broodmare A mare that is used for breeding.

Brooklyn *bowling* A hit on the side of the headpin opposite to the hand delivering the ball — on the left side for a right-handed bowler or on the right side for a left-handed bowler. (also called *crossover, Jersey*)

broom *curling* A broom used to sweep the ice ahead of the moving stone. The skip will usually place his broom on the ice as a target for members of his team to aim at. (also called *besom*)
— **on the broom** *of a shot in curling* Directly on a line with the skip's broom.

broomball A variation of ice hockey that is played on ice without skates using brooms and a soccer ball instead of sticks and a puck.

broomballer Someone who plays broomball.

¹brush *fox hunting* The tail of a killed fox taken as a trophy.

²brush **1** *of a harness horse* To go at top speed one or more times during a race.
2 *of a racehorse* To strike and injure the fetlock of one foot with another hoof.

brush and rails *equitation* An obstacle for show jumping which consists of a section of brush topped by one or 2 rails.

brushback *baseball* A pitch thrown high and inside ostensibly to force a batter who is crowding the plate to move back. The brushback is not usually thrown to hit the batter, only to make him move if he seems to be digging in to hit a long ball or if the pitcher thinks the batter is looking for a pitch on the outside. The distinction between a brushback and a beanball is often a matter of point of view; the pitcher's brushback may look like a beanball to the batter. ⟨don't

expect to scare anybody or make him hit the dirt when I throw a *brushback* — Bob Gibson⟩

brush back *baseball* To attempt to move a batter away from the plate by throwing high and inside.

brush block *football* A light block intended to delay the opponent briefly rather than take him out of the play. The brush block is used when the blocker has to perform a second assignment (as catch a pass).

brushoff A screen in lacrosse.

bubble *soaring* A thermal that consists of a small area of heated air that breaks loose from the ground and rises like a balloon.
— **on the bubble** *of a race car driver* Having qualified a car in the last starting position in a race having a limited number of entries and subject to being knocked out of the race if someone subsequently qualifies with a faster speed.

bucket **1** *bowling* A leave of the 2, 4, 5, and 8 pins for a right-handed bowler or the 3, 5, 6, and 9 pins for a left-hander. — see illustration of pin arrangement at BOWLING
2 *basketball* **a** The goal; basket. ⟨made his move toward the *bucket*⟩ **b** A field goal; basket. ⟨scored the winning *bucket* with 2 seconds left⟩
— **in the bucket** *of a baseball batter's front foot* Drawn away from the plate in making the stride. This is generally considered bad form because it opens the stance and makes outside pitches harder to hit. It has, however, been a characteristic of some outstanding pull hitters.

bucket step *mountain climbing* A large step cut in snow or ice and used mainly as a stance or for resting.

buck fever Excitement of a novice hunter at the sight of large game that unnerves him and often results in his failing to shoot or in his missing the shot.

buckshot *hunting* Coarse lead shot usually ranging from $1/4$ to $1/3$ inch in diameter.

bucktail *fishing* A wet fly that is tied on a long shanked hook and dressed with hair to resemble a minnow. — compare STREAMER

buddy breathing *scuba diving* The systematic sharing of one tank of air by 2 divers (as when forced to ascend because one diver's air is exhausted). The divers normally pass the mouthpiece back and forth taking only one or 2 breaths at a time.

buddy line *scuba diving* A line that is usually not over 10 feet long that is tied to 2 divers so they will not become too widely separated when diving at night or in water with poor visibility.

buddy system   An arrangement whereby individuals are paired for safety (as in swimming or scuba diving). An individual is expected to always know where his buddy is and whether or not he is in need of aid.

¹bug   **1** *fishing* A small surface plug intended to resemble a large insect.

2 *horse racing* A star or asterisk in a racing program that indicates an apprentice allowance.
— see also APPRENTICE ALLOWANCE

²bug   To fish using a bug as a lure.

bug boy   *horse racing* An apprentice jockey.

bug taper   *fishing* A weight-forward fly line suitable for casting bugs.

build a house   *curling* To deliver the stones so that they will be placed in position to protect each other and block off the opponents' stones.

¹bulge   *mountain climbing* A usually small rounded overhang on a face or ridge.

²bulge   *of a rising fish* To make a noticeable bulge in the surface of the water when feeding on nymphs just below the surface.

bulkhead   A vertical partition on a boat.

bull   Short for *bull's-eye.*

bulldog   *rodeo* To throw a steer by seizing it by the horns and twisting the head to one side and down.

bulldogging   see STEER WRESTLING

bullet   **1** A lead projectile fired from a firearm (as a rifle or pistol). — see also RIFLED SLUG

2 a A fast and accurately thrown ball and especially one with a relatively flat trajectory. **b** *baseball* A fastball.

bullfight   A single event in bullfighting.

bullfighting   The ceremonial fighting and usually killing of a bull in a ring by a matador and his cuadrilla. The bullfight is a Spanish, Portuguese, and Latin-American spectacle full of tradition and pageantry. The bulls used in the ring are a specially bred stock of spirited animals known for continuous attacking often without provocation. An afternoon's program (*corrida*) usually consists of 6 fights with 3 matadors each working with 2 bulls. The corrida begins with a colorful procession of all the participants. When the first bull is led out, the 3 matadors often take turns leading the bull in basic passes after which the picadors, mounted on horseback, fend off charges by the bull with pointed poles. The picadors attempt to thrust the points into the neck and shoulder muscles to weaken them so that at the end of the fight the bull's head is lowered. After the picadors come the banderilleros who thrust barbed banderillas into the bull's neck to further weaken the muscles. (Some matadors plant their own banderillas.) The final part of the fight is the confrontation between the weakened bull and the matador who leads the bull in a series of dangerous and graceful passes working as close to the bull as possible, and finishes with a thrust of his sword into the bull's neck. If well executed, one sword thrust causes almost instant death.

bull pen   *baseball* **1** A place on the field usually in the outfield and usually fenced off from the playing area where relief pitchers warm up during a game.

2 The relief pitchers of a team. ⟨a terrific *bull pen* with the best short relievers in baseball — Pete Rose⟩

bullrider   *rodeo* Someone who competes in the bullriding event.

bullriding   *rodeo* An event in which competitors are required to ride a jumping and twisting bull for 8 seconds while holding on with one hand to a rope attached to a band around the bull's chest.

bull ring   **1** The arena in which bullfighting takes place.

2 An extremely small oval racing track that is usually no more than half a mile long.

bull's-eye   The center of a target.

bully   **1** *field hockey* A method of putting the ball in play (as at the beginning of a period or after a goal) in which 2 opponents stand over the ball facing each other and opposite sidelines and strike their sticks to the ground beside the ball and then together over the ball, repeating the sequence 2 more times, and then attempt to gain possession of the ball or to pass it to a teammate.

2 *soccer* Confused play with several players close together attempting to gain possession of the ball, especially in front of the goalmouth.

¹bump   *volleyball* A forearm pass.

²bump   *volleyball* To pass the ball by means of a forearm pass.

bump and run or **bump and go**   *football* A defensive maneuver in which a cornerback playing opposite a wide receiver hits the receiver as he comes off the line and then runs with him to defend against a pass. The bumping is designed to upset the receiver's timing and concentration but in professional play, the defender is permitted only one bump after the receiver gets 3 yards downfield.

bump ball   *cricket* A batted ball that bounces high in the air.

bumper *cricket* A ball that is bowled short so that it bounces often to chest or head height usually to intimidate the batsman. The bumper is analogous to baseball's brushback and sometimes to the beanball. (also called *bouncer*)

bumper pool or **bumpers** *billiards* A game played usually on a relatively small table with a hole at each end and cushioned pegs on the playing surface. The pegs or bumpers necessitate extensive use of bank shots.

bump pass *volleyball* A forearm pass.

bump start *motorcycle racing* A start in which the riders push their bikes at the starting signal and then jump on them, shift into gear, and let out the clutch to start the engine. — compare CLUTCH START

bunch start see CROUCH START

¹bunker *golf* An area of bare ground on a course that constitutes a hazard for the golfer. At one time the term was used to designate natural hazards such as large mounds, but today practically all bunkers are sand traps. — compare WATER HAZARD

²bunker *golf* To hit one's ball into a bunker. ⟨faced with a seemingly impossible putt after *bunkering* his drive — *London Evening News*⟩

bunkered *of a golfer* To have one's ball in a bunker.

bunkering The design and layout of the bunkers on a golf course.

bunny hop *skating* A short leap from one skate to the toe of the other skate with a quick step again to the first skate.

¹bunt *baseball* A batted ball that is hit usually with the bat held relatively motionless and is intended to roll slowly along the ground. The bunt is usually used as a sacrifice play to advance a runner from first base to second but if it catches the infield by surprise and is well placed it may be beaten out for a base hit. — compare SWINGING BUNT

²bunt *baseball* **1** To make a bunt; to hit a ball for a bunt.
2 To advance a base runner by bunting. ⟨*bunted* him to second⟩

bunter *baseball* A player who bunts; one adept at bunting.

bunting *baseball* The technique of tapping a pitched ball so that it rolls slowly within the infield.

buoy An anchored float used to mark a channel or to indicate the location of a submerged danger (as a rock or shoal). Buoys are usually distinguished by their shape or by their action. The 2 most common types of buoys are the cylindrical can buoy and the conical nun buoy. The *can buoy* is typically used to mark the port limits of a channel (when approaching from the sea) and is painted black or has a black top band and carries odd numbers. The *nun buoy* is used to mark the starboard limits of the channel and is painted red or has a red top band and carries even numbers. When other buoys are used in place of the can or the nun only the color, not the shape, is important. Where it is necessary for the buoy to be seen at night, a *light buoy* which gives off a red light for starboard or a green light for port is used. *Bell, gong,* and *whistle buoys,* sounded by the action of the waves and wind, are also used. Sometimes a *spar buoy,* a large spar anchored at one end, is used in place of some other buoy when there is a danger that another buoy might be destroyed by a severe storm.

buoyage A series or system of buoys; a system of fixed or floating markers other than lightships or lighthouses that mark a channel or hidden dangers.

burdened *of a boat* Required by the Rules of the Road to maneuver so as to be clear of another boat when meeting or overtaking the other boat. Powerboats are generally burdened when meeting a sailing boat; when 2 sailing boats meet the one that is to windward, that is overtaking, or (if both are running free), that is on the port tack is burdened. — compare PRIVILEGED

burgee *boating* A small triangular or swallow-tailed flag which usually bears the insignia of a yacht club.

bunt

burladero *bullfighting* A wooden shield set parallel to the wall in a bull ring behind which bullfighters can take shelter if pursued.

¹burn **1** To gain a distinct advantage on an opponent (as in football or ice hockey); to beat or score on a defender.
2 To illegally interfere with a stone or jack in curling or lawn bowling.

²burn The act or an instance of heating the air in a hot-air balloon in order to gain lift.

burner *ballooning* A propane heater located at the top of the gondola and just under the opening of the envelope of a hot-air balloon which heats the air inside the balloon so that the balloon can rise.

burn in *skiing* To heat a base wax that has been applied to the running surface of a ski until it is liquid enough to penetrate the wood.

burn off *cycling* To tire a competitor by setting an unusually fast pace in the early part of a race.

buttending

burnout *drag racing* A brief spinning of the rear tires of a drag racer in a small puddle of water or laundry bleach just before the start of a race. The friction created by the burnout heats up the tires and softens the rubber so that they will have increased traction during the race.

burnout pit *drag racing* A designated section of the staging area where burnouts are performed. (also called *bleach box*)

bush Not up to the standards associated with the top level of sports competition or promotion; characteristic of or suggestive of the bush leagues; unprofessional. ⟨the travesty was not that the speedway went the show-business

route, but that the execution was so *bush* — John S. Radosta, *New York Times*⟩

bushes The bush leagues.

bush league **1** A small baseball minor league; a minor league of a low classification.
2 A minor, small-time, or mediocre level of a sports enterprise or competition. ⟨*bush league* racetracks⟩

bushwhacking The making of one's way through the woods without following a trail.

bute The medication phenylbutazone which is often administered to racehorses to kill pain. In some states use of the drug on racehorses is prohibited, but in other states the drug may be used provided that it is out of the horse's system before the race.

¹butt **1** The end part of the handle of a stick, racket, or cue.
2 The end part of the stock of a rifle or shotgun that fits against the shoulder; the bottom part of a pistol grip.
3 The handle of a fishing rod.
4 A mound or embankment that serves as a backstop behind an archery target.

²butt To hit an opponent with the top of one's head.

butt-end To jab an opponent with the butt end of the stick in ice hockey or box lacrosse.

butt-ending The act of jabbing an opponent with the butt end of an ice hockey or box lacrosse stick which results in a major or minor penalty.

butterfly or **butterfly stroke** *swimming* **1** A stroke executed in a prone position that combines a dolphin kick and a double overarm pull with the arms and face coming out of the water on the recovery.
2 A competitive event or a leg of a medley in which the butterfly is used. The most common distances are 100 and 200 meters and 100 and 200 yards.

butterflyer A swimmer who swims the butterfly or who competes in butterfly events.

butterfly knot *mountain climbing* A knot that may be used by a climber to tie on in the middle of a rope and that is formed by twisting the rope once to form a loop and then twisting the loop to form a figure eight and then passing the bight over the rope and back through the first loop. — see illustration at KNOT

butterfly stroke see BUTTERFLY

butting *boxing* The act or an instance of hitting an opponent with one's head (as while in a clinch). Butting is illegal and the boxer may be penalized.

butterfly stroke with dolphin kick

button **1** *curling* The first circle out from the center of the house.
2 *fencing* A covering for the blunted tip of a blade.

3 *rowing* A usually leather ring or collar on the handle of an oar to prevent its slipping through the oarlock.

buttonhook *football* A pass pattern in which the receiver runs straight downfield and then abruptly turns back toward the line of scrimmage. (also called *comeback, comebacker*)

butt plate A metal plate fitted to the butt section of a rifle or shotgun stock.

buttress *mountain climbing* A projecting part of a mountain or hill usually defined by gullies on either side.

butt ring The ring guide closest to the handle of a fishing rod.

butt shaft *archery* A target arrow.

buy the rack *pari-mutuel racing* To bet every possible combination in a race or series of races for a pool which requires the correct selection of 2 or more finishers (as in the daily double or a perfecta).

buzzer **1** A loud buzzer sounded at the end of a game or a period (as of basketball).
2 see JOINT

bye **1** The position of a participant in an elimination tournament who has no opponent after participants are paired and who advances to the next round without playing. — see ELIMINATION TOURNAMENT
2 *cricket* A run that is scored when a bowled ball passes the wicket without being hit allowing the batsmen to exchange places. The run counts toward the team's score but not to the batsman's credit. — compare LEG BYE, WIDE
3 *soccer* A shot that crosses the goal line wide of the goal.

bye hole *golf* Any of the holes remaining after the match has been decided in match play. If one contestant has a lead greater than the number of holes left, these bye holes are not played.

caber

caber A wooden pole about 17 feet long and weighing about 90 pounds that is tossed in competition in the Highland Games. The caber, which is slightly tapered, is balanced vertically on the smaller end by the contestant who runs with it and attempts to toss it so that it lands on the larger end and falls away from him.

cabin *boating* A small compartment below decks usually used for sleeping and eating.

cable *boating* A heavy rope or chain usually used for towing or as an anchor rode.

cable binding see BINDING (*skiing*)

cable-laid *of a rope* Made up usually of 3 strands twisted together in a left-handed direction. — see ROPE

cab squad see TAXI SQUAD

cactus league *baseball* The major league teams that have their spring training in the southwestern United States and that play exhibition games against each other. — compare GRAPEFRUIT LEAGUE

¹caddie or **caddy** *golf* Someone who assists a player especially by carrying his clubs and helping to locate his ball and sometimes by giving advice.

²caddie *golf* To serve as a caddie.

cadence 1 *fencing* The rhythm in which a sequence of movements is made during a phrase.
2 *football* The rhythm used by a quarterback in calling signals.
3 *rowing* see BEAT

cadge *falconry* A wooden frame on which falcons and hawks are transported to and from the field.

¹cage 1 A goal structure enclosed with netting (as for hockey, soccer, or lacrosse).
2 A large building (as on a college campus) designed for winter practice of baseball and often track and field and typically having a dirt floor, glass roof, and running track. At one time, long completely enclosed batting cages were used in gymnasiums for practice in throwing and hitting baseballs. When schools began to build special buildings just for baseball practice, the term *cage*

was carried over. Some of the buildings have portable seats and removable floors for basketball competition. — compare FIELD HOUSE
3 The game of basketball. In the early days of professional basketball, some games were played on small courts enclosed in chicken wire and later netting to keep the ball from going out of bounds. It was during this period that basketball began to be known as the cage game and the players as cagers.
4 Short for *batting cage, birdcage.*

²cage To drive a ball or puck into a goal.

cager A basketball player.

cagoule A usually calf-length hooded pullover parka worn especially for hiking in rain. It may be designed to allow the bottom to be buttoned up out of the way in fair weather.

cairn A small usually triangular pile of stones used to mark a trail or to indicate the summit of a mountain or a peak.

caisson disease see BENDS

calendar A schedule of events for a season (as of racing).

calf machine *weight training* A device used to develop the calf muscles that typically consists of bars attached to a wall at one end from which are hung adjustable weights. The lifter rests the bars on his shoulders and pushes up against the force of the weights as he does toe raises.

calf roping *rodeo* An event in which a mounted rider pursues a calf into the arena and attempts to rope the calf from horseback, tie the rope to the horn of his saddle, dismount and throw the calf, and tie any 3 of the calf's legs together in the shortest possible time. The cowboy is required to throw the calf; if the calf is already down, he must permit it to rise and then throw it. The calf is given a head start, but the cowboy seeks to reach his starting line at a gallop by the time the calf crosses the scoreline. If he is too early, the cowboy is penalized 10 seconds on his final time. — see also TEAM ROPING

caliber The diameter of the bore of a rifle or pistol typically given in hundredths or thousandths of an inch. ⟨.22⟩ ⟨.45⟩ ⟨.375⟩ — compare GAUGE

calisthenics Systematic rhythmic body exercises generally performed without apparatus or weights that consist of bending, twisting, swinging, kicking, and jumping movements and such specific exercises as push-ups, sit-ups, and chin-ups.

calk or **calkins** or **caulk** A short wedge- or cone-shaped projection on the bottom of a horseshoe.

¹call **1 a** An announced description of a race (as of horses or dogs) giving the positions of the participants at various stages of the race. **b** A point at which the order of participants is announced. ⟨moved in front by the stretch *call*⟩ **2** A decision or ruling made by an official in a contest; an instance of calling a foul or infraction. ⟨had to admit that the referee had made a good *call*⟩ **3** A device used by a hunter to produce a sound that imitates the natural call of a game animal or bird. **4** A yell by the shooter in skeet or trapshooting to announce that he is ready for the targets to be released. **5** *fencing* A call to stop the bout; appel. **6** *football* An assignment to carry the ball on a running play. ⟨the fullback got the *call*⟩ **7** *tennis* The score at any given time during a game.

²call **1** To make a ruling or decision on a play as an official in a contest. ⟨the linesman *called* the ball out⟩ ⟨the umpire *called* him safe⟩ **2** *baseball* **a** *of an umpire* (1) To indicate and keep track of balls and strikes. (2) To call off or postpone a game or to stop play before the end of a game (as because of rain or darkness). **b** *of a catcher* To indicate to the pitcher which pitches to throw to the batter. **3** *football* **a** To call out the offensive or defensive signals at the beginning of a down. **b** To direct a team's offense during a game especially by choosing plays. ⟨the coach *called* the game from the sidelines⟩ **4** *hunting* To produce a sound that imitates the natural call of a game animal or a bird.

called ball *billiards* The object ball a player designates as the one he intends to pocket.

called pocket *billiards* The pocket in which a player intends to make a called ball.

called shot *billiards* A shot in which a specific object ball has been designated to be pocketed or both the ball and the pocket have been designated.

called strike *baseball* A pitch that is not hit or swung at by the batter but that passes through the strike zone and is called a strike by the umpire.

caller A track announcer who calls a race (as of horses or dogs) over the track's loudspeaker system.

call one's shots *billiards* To specify the object ball that one intends to pocket and the pocket as required in certain games (as straight pool).

call time To suspend play as an official by signaling a time-out; to request a time-out from an official.

camber **1** The upward curvature from front to back of the bottom of a ski that gives springiness to the ski and that helps distribute the skier's weight over the entire length of the ski. **2** *surfing* see ROCKER

camel or **camel spin** *skating* A spin performed with the body in an arabesque position.

¹camp **1** An area of temporary shelter especially for a hiker, mountain climber, or hunter. **2** The tents and other shelters that constitute the living quarters of a camp.

²camp To pitch a camp; to occupy a camp.

¹campaign A season of sports competition. ⟨closed out the football *campaign* with an upset victory⟩

²campaign **1** To engage in a season of competition. **2** To enter a horse or dog in a series of races. ⟨was *campaigned* very little as a 2-year-old⟩

campo A boccie court.

campsite A place suitable for the site of a camp.

Canadian canoe see CANOE

Canadian fivepins A version of bowling similar to duckpins in which a 5-inch ball is rolled down an alley at 5 small pins (which resemble duckpins) arranged in a triangle. The game is played in the manner of other bowling games with spares and strikes and with a maximum of 3 deliveries allowed in a frame; a game consists of 10 frames. The bowler gets points equal to the scoring value of the different pins. The headpin is worth 5 points, the next 2 pins are worth 3 points, and the rear pins are worth 2 points each.

Canadian football A game played essentially like American football and having the same terminology with the following rule differences: Canadian football is played on a field 110 yards long between goal lines and 65 yards wide with the goalposts placed on the goal lines and with the end zones 25 yards deep. There are 12 players on a team instead of 11, with the twelfth man playing in the backfield or as a flanker on offense and as a linebacker or defensive back on defense. The neutral zone is one yard wide so that the defensive linemen must line up one yard away from the ball. There is no restriction on the number of backs that may be in motion at the snap nor on the directions in which they may run. A team is allowed only 3 downs in which to advance the ball 10 yards. On a punt, the receiver may not make a fair catch and teammates may not block for him, but opponents must remain 5 yards from him until he catches or fields the ball. The punter or another player on his team who was behind the ball when it was kicked is eligible to recover the punt before it is touched by the opponents. If a player fails to run a punt out of the end zone, the punting team is awarded a point, called a *rouge*. All other scoring is the same as in American football. After a touchdown, the extra point, called a *convert,* may be scored by kicking the ball between the goalposts or by running or passing it over the goal line. Most of the penalties in Canadian football are for 5 or 10 yards with only clipping, unnecessary roughness, and unsportsmanlike conduct penalized with 15 yards. Kickoffs are made from the 45 yard line, and either team may recover the ball after it travels 10 yards. The game is played in four 15-minute quarters, and there are no time-outs during the game.

can buoy see BUOY

cancha A jai alai court which measures 176 feet long and 40 feet wide and has a 40-foot-high wall at the front, back, and on one side. — see JAI ALAI

candlepin A slender wooden bowling pin. In contrast to the duckpin and the tenpin, the candlepin is nearly cylindrical having a diameter at the waist of 2¾ inches and tapering to a diameter of 2 inches at each end. It is about 15 inches high.

candlespins A bowling game in which small balls without finger holes are rolled at candlepins. The game is played with a maximum of 3 balls instead of 2 allowed in a frame, and deadwood is normally not swept away but is left to be played.

candlestick *gymnastics* A balancing stunt in which the body is supported upside down with one shoulder on the balance beam.

Cane Pace A 1-mile stakes race for 3-year-old pacers that is named in honor of William H. Cane, a former standardbred owner and racetrack president, and that is one of the races in the pacing Triple Crown. — see also LITTLE BROWN JUG, MESSENGER STAKES

¹cannon *billiards* **1** British term for *carom.*
2 A stroke in English billiards in which the cue ball is caromed off the 2 object balls without any of the balls being pocketed and which counts 2 points. If the cue ball hits the second object ball directly after striking the first ball without first hitting a cushion, it is a *direct cannon.* If the cue ball hits a cushion before striking the second object ball, it is an *indirect cannon.*

²cannon To make a cannon in English billiards.

cannonball **1** *swimming* A feetfirst jump into the water (as from a board) in a tuck position.
2 *tennis* A hard flat serve.

¹canoe A narrow lightweight boat with the sides coming to a point or edge at both ends that is propelled by a paddle. As it applies to competition, the term *canoe* refers to 2 kinds of boats. One is the open boat in which the paddler or paddlers normally kneel, which is paddled by a single-bladed paddle, and which is associated with the American Indians. It is officially known as the *Canadian canoe.* The other is covered except for a small opening in which the paddler or paddlers sit, is propelled by a double-bladed paddle, and is commonly known as the *Alaskan canoe* or the *kayak.* In normal use, the term *canoe* refers to the Canadian type as distinguished from the kayak. Canoes are normally constructed of aluminum or fiberglass or of a wooden framework covered with waterproofed canvas. For recreational use, canoes are usually 15 to 17 feet long and hold 2 or 3 people.

²canoe To travel in or propel a canoe.

canoeing The art or sport of paddling a canoe for recreation, as an adjunct to some other activity such as fishing or hiking, or in competition. Canoeing competition is normally conducted in the Canadian canoe and kayak events. Canoe races are normally held on flat water for 1-, 2-, and 4-man or woman teams over distances of 500, 1000, and 10,000 meters for men and 500 meters for women. Kayak events are held on both flat water courses and on white-water slalom courses for 1-, 2-, and 4-man and woman crews. The flat water distances are the same as for the canoe. The winner is determined solely by time. In the slalom events, the individual or team is judged both on the time required to navigate through the gates and the manner in which one covers the course, with penalty points for hitting or failing to pass a gate added as seconds to the competitor's time.

canoeist A person who paddles a canoe; someone who engages in canoeing.

canoe polo A version of water polo played on water in an area 33 yards long and 22 yards wide between 2 teams of 5 players in kayaks. At each end of the playing area is a goal 13 feet wide and 5 feet high that is defended by a goalkeeper. Players are permitted to use their paddles to stop the ball in the air or to move it over the water. For passing and shooting, the ball is played with the hands.

canoe slalom A slalom event in canoeing.

can of corn *baseball* A high fly ball.

cant 1 *archery* To tilt a bow while aiming so that the limbs are no longer vertical.

2 *shooting* To tilt a rifle while aiming by rotating slightly on the axis of the barrel so that the sights are to the right or left of vertical.

¹canter A 3-beat gait of a horse that is identical to the gallop except that it is slower and is usually performed with the horse collected.

²canter 1 *of a horse* To move at a canter.

2 To ride a horse at a canter.

cantle The upward projecting rear part of a saddle.

canvas *boxing* The canvas-covered mat which forms the floor of the ring.

canvasback *boxing* A boxer who is easily or often knocked out.

¹cap 1 A head covering that has no brim but usually has a visor to shade the eyes from the sun and that forms a part of the uniform for various sports (as baseball) or the costume of a jockey. Caps worn by water polo players have no visor and are strapped under the chin. They have numbers prominently displayed and serve to identify the players.

2 A cap awarded to a player in a team sport (as soccer or rugby) who is selected to play on a national team in international competition (as the World Cup or test matches). ⟨he is 30 with over 40 *caps* and was Sweden's striker in the Mexico World Cup — Doug Gardner, *Sportsworld*⟩

²cap To select a player to play on a national team in international competition. ⟨took the scrum half position, in which he was so often *capped* for Great Britain — Vivian Jenkins, *London Times*⟩

capework The art of the bullfighter in working the bull with the cape.

capriole *equitation* A vertical leap of a horse with a backward kick of the hind legs at the peak of the leap.

capsize To overturn a boat.

¹captain A member of a team who is elected or appointed to represent the team as its spokes-man and to make certain decisions for the team. The captain is the only player permitted to confer with officials on matters of rule interpretation. In such sports as hockey, lacrosse, and football a captain must be within the playing area at all times, and therefore these teams may have several captains or alternate captains. The captain of a football team must inform the officials of the decision to accept or decline a penalty. In games such as bowling and cricket the captain is essentially a playing coach or team manager, while in baseball or basketball the designation may be little more than an honor accorded a respected player.

²captain To serve as captain of a team.

carabiner *mountain climbing* An oblong or D-shaped ring with an inward opening spring catch on one side. The carabiner has such uses as joining ropes to pitons, connecting a rope to a belay point or to a sling to provide a smooth running surface, or joining a belay or climbing rope to a climber's waistline or harness. (also spelled *karabiner;* also called *snaplink, snap ring*)

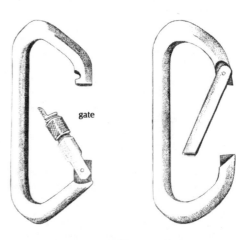

gate

carabiner

caracole *equitation* A half turn to one side or the other by a horse.

carbine A lightweight short-barreled rifle.

carburetor restrictor plate *auto racing* A plate fitted over the air intake of the carburetor of some racing engines to reduce the amount of air taken into the engine and consequently reduce the power produced by the engine. The size of the holes in the plate varies according to a formula based on engine displacement and design.

The plates are used to handicap the larger engines in stock car racing and provide a more competitive field.

¹card **1** Short for *scorecard.*

2 A sports program (as of boxing or horse racing).

²card To make a specific score (as on a hole or round of golf).

career **1** The entire time during which one has participated formally in a sport. ⟨never fouled out of a basketball game in his entire *career*⟩

2 The time during which one has participated formally in a sport at a particular level. ⟨playing the last game of his college *career*⟩ ⟨undefeated in his *career* as a professional⟩ ⟨had a *career* batting average of .367⟩

¹carom The act or an instance of a ball's rebounding from a wall, cushion, or another ball:

1 *billiards* A shot in carom billiards in which the cue ball rebounds from one object ball into another with or without having struck a cushion. (also called *billiard*)

2 *jai alai* A ball played against the side wall so that it then strikes the front wall, then the court floor, and finally the screen on the side in front of the spectators.

²carom To cause an object (as a ball, disk, or puck) to rebound from another object or a surface.

carom shot **1** *croquet* A shot in regulation croquet in which a ball is banked off a wall before striking another ball or before going through a wicket. (also called *wall shot*)

2 *shuffleboard* A shot in which one disk strikes another disk and usually replaces it.

¹carry **1** To allow an obviously weaker opponent to make a good showing by lessening one's opposition.

2 To perform well enough to make up for the poor performance of one's partner or teammates.

3 To allow a ball or shuttlecock to rest momentarily in the hands (as in volleyball) or on a racket (as in badminton) during a rally in violation of the rules.

4 To hold and run with the ball (as in football or rugby) in order to advance it toward the opponent's goal line in an attempt to score; to rush with the ball.

5 *basketball* To allow the ball to rest in the hand momentarily during the dribble in violation of the rules; palm the ball.

6 *bowling* To knock down one or more pins.

7 *of a hit or thrown ball* To travel a long often specified distance on the fly. ⟨a pass . . . that *carried* 45 yards. —*Sports Illustrated*⟩⟨balls don't *carry* here. It's a very tough place for hitters — Mike Epstein⟩

8 *of a golf shot* To pass a specified object or place. ⟨his approach shot *carried* the pond easily⟩

9 *hockey* To propel and control the ball or puck along the playing surface; dribble.

10 *of a soccer goalkeeper* To take too many steps while holding the ball.

²carry **1** The distance a ball travels on the fly.

2 *football* The act or an instance of rushing with the ball. ⟨averaged 4 yards per *carry*⟩

carry one's bat *of a cricket batsman* To end the innings or the period of play without being out.

car-top To transport a small boat on top of a car.

cartopper A small boat that may be transported on top of a car.

cartridge A unit of ammunition consisting of the case containing the primer, the powder charge, and the bullet or shot.

cartwheel A revolution of the body sideways from feet to hands to feet performed with the arms and legs spread. The cartwheel is made by leaning to the side, touching first one hand and

cartwheel

then the other on the floor, passing momentarily through a handstand, and landing on the feet.

case The paper, metal, or plastic container for the primer, powder, and shot or bullet of a shell or cartridge.

¹cast 1 *archery* **a** The elasticity of a bow represented by the distance an arrow travels or by the speed of the arrow as it leaves the bow. **b** The right to shoot first in competition as a result of having won the last shot or end.
2 *falconry* A number (as 2) of hawks or falcons released together by the falconer.
3 *fishing* **a** The act or method or an instance of throwing a lure or baited hook into the water. **b** British term for *leader*. **c** A place in which to fish.
4 *gymnastics* A preliminary movement of the legs forward so that greater momentum is gained in the backswing thus aiding the gymnast in pulling himself up from a hang to a support position or, when in a support position, to move the body above the point of support. The term *cast* is sometimes also used to refer to a kip performed from a front swing. — see also KIP
5 *hunting* **a** A number of dogs working together in pursuit of game. **b** The ranging over an area by dogs in search of game.

²cast 1 *fishing* To throw the lure or baited hook out into the water.
2 *gymnastics* To perform a cast; to move the body from a hang to a support position or to a position above the point of support by a swing initiated with a cast or by a kip.
3 *of a hunting dog* To search an area for scent of game.

caster Someone who fishes by casting or who participates in casting competition.

casting The act or technique of propelling a lure or a fly line in fishing or in competition. In bait casting and spinning, the weight of the lure pulls out the lightweight line from the reel while in fly casting the relatively heavy line is propelled carrying with it a nearly weightless fly. In casting tournaments there are distance and accuracy events for ⅜- and ⅝-ounce plugs and for wet and dry flies. — see BAIT CASTING, FLY CASTING, SKISH

casting rod A fishing rod that is usually 4 to 6 feet long, is used to cast bait or lures, and is designed for the reel to be mounted on the top in front of the handle so that the thumb can control the line during the cast. The rod used for bait casting is typically stouter than a spin-casting rod and if designed as a 2-piece rod will usually separate

at the butt section whereas the spin-casting rod may separate in the middle of the rod. The ring guides on a spin-casting rod are usually larger and set higher than those on a bait-casting rod.

castle *cricket* The wicket defended by the striker.

cast off *boating* To untie a line or knot; to untie a boat from a mooring.

casual water *golf* Any temporary accumulation of water on the course (as after a heavy rain) that does not constitute a hazard. If the player elects to take relief, he may drop the ball away from the water without penalty.

catamaran A boat that has 2 hulls or planing surfaces side by side.

catamaran with crew hiking with a trapeze

catapult British term for *slingshot* (the weapon).

catboat A sailboat that has a centerboard, a single fore-and-aft sail with no jib, and the mast set well forward.

¹catch 1 To seize or intercept and hold an object moving through the air. In common sports usage one catches a hit or thrown ball in one's bare or gloved hands, in one's arms, or in a device (as a basket or lacrosse stick) attached to or held in one's hands. Important in the concept of catching is the idea of holding onto the ball, for merely

catch

to stop a ball without gaining control is not to catch it. In both baseball and football, the concept of catching the ball is commonly restricted to a ball that is on a downward path and especially one that has not touched the ground since it was given initial impetus. One catches a fly ball but generally picks up or fields a grounder; a pass is caught, but a fumble is picked up or recovered.

2 Overtake. ⟨*caught* the leader at the wire⟩

3 *baseball* **a** To play the position of catcher; to serve as catcher for a specified pitcher. ⟨couldn't find anyone willing to *catch* him⟩ **b** To put out a base runner who is off the base or who is attempting to steal. ⟨he was *caught* trying to steal second⟩

4 *fishing* To hook and land a fish.

5 *surfing* To maneuver into position to be pushed toward shore by a wave. ⟨*catch* the crest⟩

²catch **1** The act or an instance of catching a ball. ⟨made a running *catch*⟩

2 A game or pasttime between 2 or more people in which a ball is thrown and caught. Ball players often play catch as a means of warming up before practice or a game.

3 The initial force of an oar or a swimmer's hand against the water at the beginning of a stroke; the entry of the hand or oar into the water.

4 *fishing* A fish that is caught; the number of fish caught.

5 *gymnastics* The act of grabbing the bar of an apparatus after a swinging, twisting, or somersault maneuver during which the bar is released.

catch a crab *rowing* To accidently dip an oar in the water or have it hit by a wave on the recovery stroke. The force of the oar hitting the water can stun an oarsman or knock him out of his seat or even completely check the forward movement of the shell.

catch a rail *surfing* To have a rail of the surfboard catch in the water while the board is sliding sideways on a wave with the result that the surfer is thrown from the board.

catch-as-catch-can see FREESTYLE (*wrestling*)

catch driver *harness racing* A driver who drives for another owner or trainer for a fee. Most trainers do their own driving, but some hire a catch driver on a race-by-race basis. The catch driver is somewhat analogous to flat racing's jockey.

catcher **1** *baseball* A player who is stationed behind home plate and who catches pitches not hit by the batter. The catcher wears a special mitt that differs from the gloves worn by the other players and he wears a face mask, chest protec-

tor, and shin guards as protection against fouled balls. He is required to remain within the catcher's box until the pitch is delivered but when the ball is hit he may cover the area from behind home plate to the pitcher's mound or to first or third bases in attempting to catch or field a ball and regularly backs up the first baseman on routine putouts. The catcher normally directs the team's defense especially by signaling for specific pitches and designating a particular fielder to catch a pop fly, makes plays on runners attempting to score, and throws to bases to try to prevent a runner from stealing. (also called *receiver*)

2 *boxing* A boxer relatively unskilled at defense who takes a lot of punches. ⟨I'm not a *catcher*. I don't just stand in the middle of the ring and get hit with everything a guy throws — George Chuvalo⟩

catcher's box *baseball* A rectangular area behind home plate within which the catcher must stand until the pitcher releases the pitch. The catcher's box is 4 feet wide and extends 6 feet behind the rear edge of the batter's box.

catch fence *auto racing* A fence, such as a chain link fence, erected at a dangerous area on a racecourse that is designed to stop a car that hits it by giving to absorb much of the impact of a collision and to prevent the car's being thrown back onto the course or the car's bouncing over it and off the course.

catching glove *ice hockey* A glove that resembles a baseball first baseman's mitt and is used by a goalkeeper to catch the puck shot at the goal. — see illustration at GLOVE

catch-up A style of play necessitated when a team that is considerably behind is attempting to catch up. When a team has to play catch-up ball, it often abandons its normal style of play and is sometimes forced to gamble or take chances it would not normally take.

Catenaccio system *soccer* A formation characterized by the use of 2 strikers, 3 midfielders, a line of 4 defenders in the defensive half of the field, and a sweeper who plays in front of the goalkeeper to plug any holes that develop in the line of defenders.

cauliflower ear *boxing* An ear deformed by injury (as from repeated blows) and excessive growth of reparative tissue.

caulk see CALK

caution flag *auto racing* A yellow flag used to warn the drivers of danger ahead on the course.

cavalletto One of a series of adjustable timber

jumps used for schooling horses. — when used in the plural, the Italian form *cavalletti* is commonly used

caving   The sport of exploring caves; spelunking. The sport is similar to mountain climbing, and it employs the same techniques and much of the same terminology as mountain climbing.

ceding parry   *fencing*   A parry of an attack on the blade made by offering no resistance as the blade is forced to a new line and then blocking the lunge with the blade in this new line.

ceiling shot or **ceiling ball**   A stroke in handball or racquetball in which the ball is made to hit the ceiling usually 2 to 3 feet in front of the front wall. The ball picks up backspin and on hitting the front wall, drops sharply to rebound high into a back corner or hit low off the back wall.

cellar   Last place in league, conference, or division standings.

¹center   **1** A player who occupies a middle position on a team: **a** *Australian Rules football* A player who plays in the middle of the center line and who participates in the ball up. **b** *basketball* The usually tallest member of a team who normally plays the pivot and takes part in the center jump. **c** *box lacrosse* A player who normally takes the middle position on the attack and who takes part in the center-zone face-off. **d** *football* An offensive lineman who plays in the middle of the line and who snaps the ball between his legs to a back to start a down. **e** *ice hockey* A primarily offensive player who plays in the middle of the forward line and who normally takes part in the face-off to start a period. **f** *lacrosse* A player who plays near the middle of the field on both offense and defense and who normally takes part in the face-off.
2 The position played by a center.
3 *skating* The starting point for a school figure; the part of the figure where 2 circles meet.
4 A pass made from the side of the field to the area in front of the goal.
5 Short for *center field, center threequarter back.*

²center   **1** To play a ball or puck (as in lacrosse, soccer, or hockey) from an area near the sidelines back toward the center of the playing area and especially in front of the opponent's goal.
2 To play the center position on a line or squad (as in ice hockey).
3 *football* To snap the ball to begin a down.
4 *skating* To maintain a spin in one place without moving over the skating surface.
5 *soaring* To locate the outer limits of a thermal

in order to keep a sailplane within it and most effectively utilize its lift.

center back   A player who plays in the center of a back line (as in volleyball).

centerboard   *sailing*   A retractable keel which serves to stabilize a small boat and keep it from heeling. The centerboard pivots on one corner and is raised and lowered in a fore-and-aft slot. — compare DAGGERBOARD

centerboarder   *sailing*   A boat that has a centerboard.

center circle   **1** *Australian Rules football* A 10-foot circle in the middle of the field in which the umpire bounces the ball for a ball up. Only the 2 opposing centers are permitted inside the circle during the ball up.
2 *basketball* **a** A 4-foot circle in the center of the court that is divided by the division line. The opposing jumpers are required to have at least one foot on or within the circle when the ball is tossed up for a jump ball. **b** The center restraining circle on a court marked off for international rules.
3 *soccer* A 20-yard circle in the middle of the playing field from which the kickoff is made. The opposing players are excluded from the center circle until the ball is kicked.

center face-off spot   see CENTER ICE SPOT

center field   *baseball*   **1** The part of the outfield beyond second base and between right field and left field.
2 A player position for covering center field.

center fielder   *baseball*   The player who plays center field.

center-fire   **1** *of a cartridge* Fired by the striking of the hammer or firing pin against the center of the base.
2 *of a firearm* Designed for center-fire cartridges. — compare RIMFIRE

center forward   **1** **a** A player in the center of the forward line (as in volleyball or water polo). **b** *field hockey* A primarily offensive player who plays in a lane midway between the sidelines and who normally takes part in the bully at the start of play. **c** *soccer* A primarily offensive player who plays in a lane midway between the sidelines and who normally takes part in the kickoff.
2 The position played by a center forward.

center halfback or **center half**   **1** A primarily defensive player in soccer or field hockey who plays in a lane midway between the sidelines and who normally guards the opposing center forward.
2 see HALFBACK (*Australian Rules football*)

center half forward see HALF FORWARD

center ice The neutral zone of an ice hockey rink.

center ice circle *ice hockey* The face-off circle in the center of the rink.

center ice spot or **center face-off spot** *ice hockey* The face-off spot in the center of the ice and within the center ice circle.

center jump *basketball* A jump ball usually between opposing centers that takes place at the center of the court at the beginning of a period and after a double foul.

center line **1** The line that runs across the middle of a field, court, rink, or pool from side to side and that divides the playing area in half. — see also DIVISION LINE

2 *Australian Rules football* The 3 players, including the center and 2 wingmen, who play near the middle of the field on both offense and defense.

3 *badminton* The line that runs from the midpoint of the short service line to the midpoint of the back boundary line and that divides the court into right and left service courts.

4 *curling* The line that runs from the midpoint of the hog line through the tee to a point 12 feet in back of the tee. The hack is centered on this line at the point where it terminates.

5 *table tennis* The line that runs the length of the table parallel to and equidistant from the sidelines to divide each side of the table into 2 service courts for doubles play.

centerman A center (as on an ice hockey team).

center mark *tennis* A short line that extends inward from the midpoint of the baseline and that marks the edge of the area in which a player stands when serving.

center opening *court tennis* The opening in the corridor under the penthouse that is in the middle of the court opposite the net post. A ball knocked into this opening makes a chase.

center service line SEE HALF COURT LINE

center spot **1** A spot in the exact center of an English billiards, carom billiards, or pocket billiards table. The blue ball is spotted on the center spot at the beginning of play and after it has been pocketed in snooker. — see also FOOT SPOT, HEAD SPOT; BALKLINE SPOT, BILLIARD SPOT, PYRAMID SPOT

2 *box lacrosse* The center face-off circle.

center strap or **center strop** *tennis* A strip of canvas that runs down the middle of the net and that is anchored to the court to hold the bottom of the net in place and to keep the top of the net at the proper height.

center stripe The center line on a lacrosse field.

center threequarter back *rugby* Either of the 2 threequarter backs who play in the middle lane of the field.

center zone **1** *box lacrosse* The 22-foot-wide area in the middle of the box between the 2 attacking zones which is analogous to the neutral zone in ice hockey. When a face-off is held in the center zone, all players except the 2 taking part in the face-off must be outside the center zone.

2 *ice hockey* The neutral zone.

centurion *cricket* A player who gets 100 or more runs during an innings; one who gets a century.

century *cricket* A score of 100 or more runs by a batsman in one innings.

cesta *jai alai* A narrow curved wicker basket that may be 2 to 2½ feet long, that is fitted to the hand by means of a glove-like feature on the back, and that is used to catch and hurl the ball.

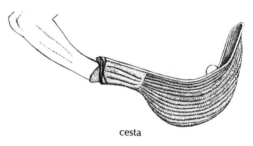

cesta

chain *football* A 10-yard length of chain that is used to measure the distance the ball must be advanced during a series of downs. Each end of the chain is attached to a rod for ease in handling and moving. (also called *yardage chain*)

chain crew *football* A group of assistants to the officials who handle the measuring chain and the down box and who mark the progress of the ball for a series of downs.

chain plate A metal plate which is attached to the side of a boat and to which the shrouds are fastened by means of a turnbuckle.

chair British term meaning to carry someone (as the coach or a player) from the field of play on the shoulders of other players after a victory.

chair lift A motor-driven conveyor consisting of a series of seats suspended from an overhead moving cable and used for transporting skiers or sightseers up or down a long slope or mountainside.

¹chalk **1** *billiards* A small cube of chalk rubbed

on the tip of a cue to prevent the tip from becoming too smooth and slippery during play.

2 *horse racing* The late odds on a race; the favorite. The term comes from the use of chalk and chalkboards by bookmakers at the tracks before the institution of pari-mutuel betting systems which show the odds electronically. ⟨the *chalk* horse⟩ ⟨*chalk* player⟩

3 *skittles* A turn of 3 throws for a player.

4 *tennis* Powdered chalk used to mark the lines on a court; a line on a court. ⟨a hard drive that hit the *chalk*⟩

²chalk *billiards* To rub the tip of a cue with chalk.

chalk talk or **chalk session** see SKULL SESSION

chalk up To attain; register; score. ⟨*chalked up* his 22nd win of the season⟩ ⟨*chalk up* a 4 to 1 lead⟩

challenge round A contest between a defending champion or titleholder and a challenger who has survived an elimination tournament aimed at providing a single challenger. The distinctive aspect of challenge-round competition is that the defending champion is not required to play before the challenge round and therefore is not subject to losing in the early stages of competition.

chamber The part of a firearm tooled to receive the cartridge.

chambered *of a firearm* Designed to use a specified cartridge.

champion The winner of first place or first prize in competition by defeating the other contestants in his area or division or in a contest or tournament, by defeating a defending champion (as in a challenge round or championship fight), or by being first in the standings (as of a league or division) or in accumulated points (as in auto racing) at the end of a season; one who is recognized as champion by a sanctioning organization (as a boxing commission).

championship **1** The designation as champion; the title held by a champion.

2 A contest held to determine a champion. ⟨Eastern-conference *championship* will begin today⟩ ⟨a *championship* fight⟩

championship car see INDY CAR

chance **1** *baseball* An opportunity to catch or field a batted ball and make a putout or make a play on a base runner that results in either a putout, assist, or error and that is used in determining fielding average.

2 *cricket* An opportunity for a fieldsman to put out a given batsman. ⟨a marathon innings of 261 not out by Geoffrey Boycott . . . [who] batted

more than a day and a half, 9½ hours in all. He never offered a *chance* and by my reckoning he played and missed only twice — Michael Carey, *Sportsworld*⟩

chancery see HEADLOCK

change beat *fencing* A beat made after a change of engagement.

change of edge *skating* A movement in which the skater shifts from one edge to the other of the same skate without turning the body.

change of engagement *fencing* An action by which on opponent's blade is moved to a new line and which usually consists of passing the point under or over the opponent's blade and engaging it on the opposite side.

change of leg *equitation* A movement in which the horse is required to change the lead from one foot to the other in a canter.

change-over *tennis* A pause in the match when the players change sides of the court after the odd numbered games during which the players have a few moments to rest, have something to drink, and towel off. (also called *crossover*)

change spin *skating* A spin during which the skater changes from one foot to the other.

change-up **1** or **change of pace** *baseball* A slow pitch thrown for deception with the same motion as a fastball. (also called *letup*)

2 *skiing* A technique by which cross-country skiers rest their arms by skipping every other thrust of the poles.

channel **1** *boating* A deeper part of a body of water (as a river or harbor) where the main current flows and which affords the best passage.

2 *bowling* see GUTTER

3 *mountain climbing* A piton with a U-shaped cross section. — see illustration at PITON

channel ball see GUTTER BALL

chap and lie The bowling or sliding of a bowl or curling stone so that it knocks away another bowl or stone and stops in or near its place.

¹charge To run into an opponent to upset his balance in any of several contact sports. In certain sports (as soccer, lacrosse, and rugby) charging is permitted, with certain restrictions. In soccer, for example, it is legal to bump an opponent who is in control of the ball or who is attempting to gain control of the ball if it is done shoulder to shoulder. If a player charges an opponent who is not within playing distance of the ball or when he is not upright or does not have at least one foot on the ground or if he charges an opponent from behind, he is guilty of a foul which is penalized by a free kick. In certain other sports (as basketball or ice hockey) charging means illegally running into or bumping an opponent. — compare BLOCK

²charge The act or an instance of charging; a foul called as a result of charging. ⟨trying to draw the *charge*⟩

charging The act of running into an opponent:
1 A foul in ice hockey or box lacrosse that results when a player skates, runs, or jumps into an opponent from the rear or after taking 2 or more strides and that is a minor or major penalty, depending on the severity of the act.
2 *Australian Rules football* A foul that results when a player runs into or bumps an opponent who is more than 5 yards away from the ball and that is penalized by a free kick.
3 *basketball* A personal foul that results when a player who has control of the ball or who has just taken a shot or made a pass runs into a defensive player who has already established position on the court or who has established a path of movement. If the offensive player has established a path, he is entitled to continue along that path even after making a shot. However, if the defender has reached a certain spot on the floor before the offensive player, subsequent contact is charging. The defensive player may not move into the path of the offensive player if that player is in the air as a result of making a shot. Charging will not usually be called for contact made after a dribbler has his head and shoulders beyond the defender. — compare BLOCKING

charity line or **charity stripe** The free throw line in basketball.

charity shot A free throw in basketball; a foul shot.

charity stripe see CHARITY LINE

charley horse A muscular strain or bruise especially in the thigh that is characterized by pain and stiffness.

charreada A Mexican form of rodeo.

¹chart 1 *boating* A map of an area of water usually including adjacent land that gives such information as the various depths of the water and the location of channels, buoys, and obstacles and that is intended to be used as an aid to navigation. (also called *nautical chart*)
2 *horse racing* A published report of a race usually giving a summary of the race, listing the conditions under which the horses were entered, and showing the order of finish of the horses and their positions at various points during the race. It also provides information about the jockeys and the condition of the track, gives fractional times, comments on how each horse ran, and usually gives pari-mutuel payoff prices. (also called *race chart*)

²chart *baseball* To make a pitching chart for a particular pitcher.

¹chase 1 *court tennis* A rally which ends with the ball bouncing twice on the floor and which must be replayed. Whenever a player allows the ball to bounce twice, instead of losing the point, he makes a chase which he must defend before the game is decided. A chase is named for the chase lines within which it falls. These lines are marked on the floor of the court at half-yard intervals from the end wall on the serving side of the court and from the service line on the hazard side. A chase is made whether a player intentionally or unintentionally allows the ball to fall. It is usually a strategic tactic employed when the player believes the ball will bounce a second time far from the end wall. Since the chase is a point which has not yet been decided, it must be played off before the game is ended. Players change sides with the original server becoming the receiver and the original receiver now becoming the server. A single chase is played off when one player's score has reached 40 and the next point could win the game. If 2 chases are made in a single game, the players change sides to play it off immediately. To win a chase, a player must hit a winning stroke (as by driving the ball into the grille or the dedans) or hit the ball so that it will fall nearer the end wall, if not returned, than where the chase was made. If the ball falls farther from the wall than his chase, the player has failed to defend the chase and he loses the point. Once the players change courts to play off a chase, they stay in that position for the remainder of the game.
2 Short for *steeplechase*.

²chase *baseball* To cause an opposing pitcher to be removed from the game because of a batting rally.

chase line *court tennis* Any of the lines on the floor of the court parallel to the end walls that are used in marking chases.

chaser A horse that competes in steeplechases.

chassé *skating* A movement in which the free foot is placed on the surface beside the skating foot, the weight is momentarily shifted to the free foot, and then a new thrust is made on the original skating foot.

chatter Noise produced by the vibration of a ski during a turn on hard snow or by a surfboard in choppy water.

RACE CHART

NINTH RACE
Belmont
SEPTEMBER 3, 1975

6 FURLONGS. (1.08⅗) CLAIMING. Purse $7,500. Fillies, 3-year-olds. Weight, 122 lbs. Non-winners since August 16 allowed 2 lbs. July 20, 4 lbs. July 5, 6 lbs. Claiming price $15,000; for each $1,000 to $13,000, 2 lbs. (Races where entered for $11,000 or less not considered.)

Value of race $7,500, value to winner $4,500, second $1,650, third $900, fourth $450. Mutuel pool $133,382, OTB pool $106,784. Track Triple Pool $162,186. OTB Triple Pool $254,148.

Last Raced	Horse	Eqt.A.Wt	PP	St	¼	½	Str	Fin	Jockey	Cl'g Pr	Odds $1
27Aug75 ^{9}Bel^{1}	Dawny Baby	3 113	7	8	6^{4}	$3^{\frac{1}{2}}$	$1^{\frac{1}{2}}$	$1^{1\frac{1}{4}}$	Baeza B†	13000	1.70
21Jly75 ^{9}Atl^{6}	Bit O' The Sea	3 112	8	7	$4^{\frac{1}{2}}$	$4^{\frac{1}{2}}$	$3^{\frac{1}{2}}$	$2^{2\frac{1}{2}}$	Castaneda M	13000	12.10
28Aug75 ^{5}Bel^{3}	Aunt Bud	3 111	9	9	$2^{\frac{1}{2}}$	1^{hd}	2^{1}	$3^{3\frac{1}{2}}$	Long J S^{7}	14000	2.10
22Aug75 ^{1}Sar^{6}	Funny Belle	3 112	2	5	8^{1}	8^{3}	6^{hd}	4^{nk}	Velasquez J	13000	6.50
8Aug75 ^{7}Sar^{7}	Squad Girl	3 112	6	2	1^{hd}	2^{1}	4^{3}	$5^{1\frac{1}{4}}$	Amy J	13000	25.40
8Aug75 ^{1}Sar^{6}	Cool Maid	3 112	4	4	9	9	9	$6^{1\frac{1}{4}}$	Turcotte R	13000	22.10
25Jly75 ^{3}Bel^{1}	Barney's Baby	3 112	5	3	$5^{1\frac{1}{2}}$	6^{2}	7^{2}	7^{2}	Imparato J	13000	12.50
22Aug75 ^{2}Sar^{1}	Dry Sherry	3 109	1	1	3^{1}	5^{2}	5^{1}	$8^{1\frac{3}{4}}$	Martens G^{7}	15000	20.40
15Aug75 ^{5}Mth^{6}	Pat G.	3 116	3	6	$7^{\frac{1}{2}}$	$7^{1\frac{1}{2}}$	$8^{1\frac{1}{2}}$	9	Vasquez J	15000	8.10

OFF AT 5:38 EDT Start good, Won driving. Time, :23⅖, :47⅕, 1:12⅕ Track fast.

$2 Mutuel Prices:			
8-(H)-DAWNY BABY	5.40	3.60	2.80
9-(I)-BIT O' THE SEA		9.20	5.00
10-(J)-AUNT BUD			3.00

$2 TRIPLE 8-9-10 PAID $151.00.

B. f, by Proudest Roman—Summer Rerun, by Summer Tan. Trainer Imperio L. Bred by Ferrara V R (Fla).

DAWNY BABY loomed boldly from the outside leaving the turn and outfinished BIT O' THE SEA under good handling. The latter, sent up between horses leaving the turn, continued on with good energy to be second best. AUNT BUD, rushed into contention after breaking slowly, dueled for the lead to midstretch and gave way. FUNNY BELLE failed to seriously menace. SQUAD GIRL was used up vying for the lead. BARNEY'S BABY tired. DRY SHERRY tired badly from her early efforts. PAT G. had no apparent excuse.

Owners— 1, Brodsky Elaine M; 2, Walder M; 3, Pace Eleanor; 4, Shirley Stable; 5, Arkay Stable; 6, Karutz W S; 7, Preski B J; 8, Rapid Rise Stable; 9, Giordano A J.

Trainers— 1, Imperio L; 2, Campo J P; 3, Jerkens H A; 4, Trovato J A; 5, Imperio D A; 6, Jacobs E; 7, Sazer D; 8, Johnson P G; 9, Horn P J Jr.

† **Apprentice allowance waived:** Dawny Baby 7 pounds.
Overweight: Dawny Baby 1 pound.
Dawny Baby was claimed by Sommer S; trainer, Martin F.
Scratched—Real Decoy (16May75 ^{6}Aqu^{5}).

A sample results chart of a horse race. The horses are listed in the order of finish followed by an indication of any unusual equipment (Eqt), the age (A) of each horse, the weight (Wt) assigned to each, and the post position (PP) and position of each horse at the start (St) and at various points in the race, including the quarter-mile and half-mile points, the beginning of the stretch, and the finish. The small raised numbers and fractions indicate the number of lengths by which each horse was leading the one just behind it. The abbreviations hd, nk, and no stand for head, neck, and nose. Since this race was a claiming race, the last part of the chart gives the claiming price and dollar odds for each horse.

cheap shot An act of deliberate roughness against an opponent usually committed when the opponent is not expecting it or cannot defend himself and often intended to cause injury.

cheap-shot artist or **cheap shotter** A player who is prone to take cheap shots at opponents.

cheat **1** To move too far to one side in attempting to defend an area (as in football or tennis) to be able effectively to cover the other side of the area; to edge toward one side in anticipation of a play's being to that side.
2 *skating* To complete part of the turn of a jump after landing instead of while in the air.
3 *surfing* To attempt to hang five without actually moving the body weight forward (as by squatting and stretching one leg toward the front of the board).
4 *weight training* To employ additional mus-

cles or another part of the body as an aid in lifting a weight. Cheating is a common technique for squeezing out a couple of extra repetitions of an exercise when the primary muscles are too fatigued to lift the weight without aid. A common example of cheating is pulling the torso back when making a biceps curl so that the movement of the body starts the weight moving upward and the arm muscles can continue the lift without having to overcome inertia at the beginning of the lift.

cheater five *surfing* A hang five made by cheating.

cheat sheet *golf* A course diagram and yardage chart.

¹check **1** *Australian Rules football* **a** To guard or mark an opponent closely. (also *watch*) **b** see SHEPHERD

2 *basketball* To keep one hand on an opponent who is controlling the ball or to continually bump or shove him with one hand while guarding him. (also *hand check*)

3 *of a hunting dog* To stop the chase when the scent is lost.

4 *of a falcon or hawk* To turn from the proper game and fly after something else.

5 *football* To block an opponent with a brush block.

6 *ice hockey* To defend against an opponent who has the puck or who is going for the puck by a stick check or a body check.

7 *lacrosse* To defend against an opponent who has the ball or who is going for the ball by a crosse check or a body check.

8 *skating* To move the body or an arm or leg in such a way as to have more control or to counter the natural rotation of the body in making a turn.

9 *skiing* To slow oneself while skiing downhill by edging or stemming the skis, by sideslipping, or by raising the body to create more air resistance.

²check The act or an instance of checking; a stick check, body check, or crosse check.

checker A player who checks an opponent.

checkered flag *motor racing* A black and white checkered flag shown at the finish line first to the winner of the race and subsequently to all other competitors to signal the end of the race.

check mark or **checkpoint** *track and field* Any temporary mark or object placed next to the track or runway that may be used to assist an individual in gauging his approach to a scratch line (as in the long jump or javelin throw) or to

assist a pair of relay runners in the timing of their exchange of the baton.

check off *football* To change the play at the line of scrimmage by calling an audible.

checkpoint **1** *motor sports* A point at the end of a leg of a rally or off-road race at which contestants stop to have their time for that leg recorded by the officials before continuing with the next leg. In some rallies and races and especially in long-distance events, the contestants may have an allotted amount of time at certain checkpoints for eating, sleeping, or making repairs before beginning the next leg.

2 *orienteering* One of several points which a competitor must pass during the course of the race. The checkpoints are usually not manned but have a device for marking or punching a card carried by the competitor to show that he actually passed the checkpoint. (also called *control point*)

3 *track and field* see CHECK MARK

checkrein A rein that goes over a horse's head and serves to hold his head up or back.

check side British term for *draw* (billiards).

cheekpiece A part of the stock of some firearms against which a shooter may rest his cheek while aiming and firing.

¹cheer **1** A shout of applause, enthusiasm, or encouragement.

2 A group of words to be used as a cheer.

²cheer **1** To urge on or encourage a performer or team especially with shouts.

2 To applaud a performer or team with shouts.

cheerleader Someone who calls for and directs organized cheering for a team.

cheese A flat round disk 8¾ inches in diameter that weighs 10 to 12 pounds and may be used in the game of skittles.

cheesecake *bowling* A lane on which high scores are common or on which strikes are easy to make.

cherry *bowling* An error caused by hitting the front pin in such a way that it misses one or more pins of a relatively simple leave.

cherry flip see TOE LOOP JUMP

chest **1** *soccer* To trap the ball with one's chest. **2** *track and field* To hit the tape at the finish line with one's chest.

chestnut A horse that is brown or reddish brown with mane, tail, and lower legs of the same or a lighter color. — compare BAY

chest pass A pass (as of a basketball) that is made by holding the ball in front of the chest with 2 hands and extending the arms quickly and snapping the wrists to push the ball out and away from the body.

chest protector *baseball* A usually stuffed pad worn over the chest by a catcher or plate umpire for protection from fouled balls. The catcher's chest protector extends from the top of the shoulders to the waist or sometimes to the crotch. The umpire's protector may be identical to that used by a catcher or may be a foam rubber or inflated shield held in front of the body.

chest roll *gymnastics* A roll down onto the chest from a handstand position.

chest trap *soccer* A trap made with the chest.

chicane *motor sports* **1** An obstacle around which one must maneuver in the slalom competition of an automobile gymkhana.

2 A pair of tight turns in opposite directions usually less than a car length apart in an otherwise straight stretch of a road-racing course usually designed to reduce slightly the speed of the cars along the straight.

chic chac *jai alai* A shot that rebounds from the front wall to the floor very close to the back wall, hits the back wall, and then falls again to the floor.

chicken coop *equitation* An obstacle for show jumping which resembles an A-shaped roof.

chicken-fight *football* To repeatedly block a defensive lineman from an upright position on a pass play.

chicken wing *wrestling* A hold in which the aggressor, in a position above and behind his opponent, bends his opponent's arm at the elbow so that the wrist is near the side either in front or in back and thrusts his own arm under

chicken wing

the opponent's forearm and over his shoulder or across the back exerting upward leverage. This hold is legal so long as pressure is not applied parallel to the long axis of the opponent's body.

¹chimney 1 *mountain climbing* A steep and narrow cleft in the face of a cliff or mountain that is wide enough for a climber to get inside. Chimneys are often climbed by bridging or by placing the back against one wall and the feet against the other wall and alternately moving the back and feet. — compare CRACK, GULLY

2 *soaring* A thermal composed essentially of a vertical column of rising air.

²chimney *mountain climbing* To climb up a chimney.

chin To pull oneself up while hanging by the hands until the chin is level with or just above the support; to perform a chin-up.

chinaman *cricket* An off-break bowled by a left-handed bowler to a right-handed batsman. — compare GOOGLY

chine The intersection of the sides and the bottom of a flat- or V-bottomed boat.

chinning bar A horizontal bar.

chin-up The act or an instance of pulling oneself up while hanging by the hands until the chin is level with or just above the support. A bar is normally placed at a height sufficient to permit one to hang without being able to touch the floor. Chin-ups are often performed in groups as a conditioning exercise and may be performed while hanging by one hand. (also called *pull-up*)

¹chip 1 *curling* A very thin hit on the edge of another stone. (also called *rub*)

2 *golf* A chip shot.

3 *soccer* A high lobbed pass.

4 *tennis* A return made by slicing the ball usually with backspin and aiming it at the opponent's feet.

²chip To make a chip or a chip shot.

chippie 1 *basketball* An easy uncontested shot under the basket.

2 *golf* A chip shot from off the green that goes into the hole thereby winning a bet for the player in informal play.

chip shot *golf* A short usually low approach shot that lofts the ball to the green and allows it to roll. (also called *pitch and run*)

chock A usually metal fitting (as on the bow or stern of a boat) with 2 short horn-shaped arms curving inward between which ropes or hawsers may pass for mooring or towing. — compare CLEAT

chockstone *mountain climbing* A stone

wedged in a crack and used as a hold, stance, or belay point. The chockstone may be naturally wedged into the crack or be placed there by the climber.

choctaw *skating* A half turn from forward to backward or from backward to forward and from one foot to the other that involves a change of edge (as from inside to outside or outside to inside).

¹choke 1 a A slight narrowing of the bore of a shotgun barrel just before the muzzle that serves to concentrate the shot pellets as they leave the muzzle. The degree of choke is usually determined by the percentage of shot pellets hitting within a 30-inch circle at 40 yards. There are 3 standard degrees of choke: *full choke,* which provides the narrowest pattern but the longest effective range; *modified choke,* giving intermediate pattern and range; and *improved cylinder,* which gives a wide shot distribution and a relatively short effective range. **b** An adjustable choke that fits over the muzzle of a shotgun. **2** or **choke hold** *judo* A hold by which pressure is applied to an opponent's throat to cut off the blood supply to his head. The choke is essentially a submission hold designed to win by forcing the opponent to surrender. When properly applied, the choke affects only the blood supply, not the breathing, and can produce momentary unconsciousness in less than 10 seconds.

²choke or **chock up 1** *baseball* To shorten one's grip on the handle of the bat; to grip the bat nearer the barrel than normal in order to reduce the effective weight for better control. **2** To lose one's composure and fail to perform effectively in a crucial situation. ⟨just want to get far enough ahead so I can still *choke* and win — Lee Trevino⟩

choke hold see CHOKE (*judo*)

choose up To form sides for an informal game by having designated captains alternately choose from available players.

choose-up game An informal game (as of basketball, softball, or touch football) played by teams formed by choosing up.

¹chop 1 To hit a ball with a short downward stroke with the palm of the hand or the face of a racket or paddle facing up so as to impart backspin to the ball. **2** *baseball* To swing down on a pitch to hit the ball to the ground. **3** *track and field* To shorten one's stride (as to avoid hitting the heels of a runner immediately ahead).

²chop 1 A hit or stroke made by chopping a ball. **2** *karate* A blow made with the hand held open and stiff and swung level or downward so that the side of the hand strikes the target.

chopper *baseball* A high-bouncing batted ball.

christie or **christy** or **christiania** *skiing* A turn that is used for altering the direction of descent or for stopping and that is executed usually at high speed by leaning forward, unweighting the skis, and skidding into a turn with the skis parallel.

Christmas tree 1 *bowling* A split that leaves the 3, 7, and 10 pins for a right-hander and the 2, 7, and 10 pins for a left-hander. Sometimes a leave of the 1, 7, and 10 pins is also called a Christmas tree. — see illustration of pin arrangement at BOWLING **2** *drag racing* A set of paired colored lights arranged in 2 columns on a vertical pole in front of the starting line and used for starting each race. There is a set of lights for each competitor. The top light is white and indicates that the competitor's car has not yet reached the starting position. The second light, also white, lights up when the car is staged, that is, in the exact position for the start. The next 5 lights are amber and are designed to flash from top to bottom in sequence at half-second intervals to allow the driver to anticipate the green starting signal. If a driver incorrectly times his start and leaves the line before the green comes on, a red light signals that he has fouled and is disqualified for that race. The lights can be programmed to flash independently so that one driver gets the green ahead of the other in handicap races.

christy see CHRISTIE

¹chuck 1 To throw a ball; to throw rather than bowl a cricket ball to the batsman. **2** *football* To block or bump a pass receiver by shoving him with the forearms held in front of the chest. In professional play, a defensive player may chuck a receiver any number of times while he is within 3 yards of the line of scrimmage. Beyond that 3-yard area, the receiver may be chucked only once.

²chuck 1 A throw; a delivery in cricket in which the ball is thrown rather than bowled. **2** *football* The act or an instance of chucking a pass receiver.

chucker *cricket* A bowler suspected of throwing rather than bowling the ball.

chukker or **chukkar** or **chukka** *polo* A period of play usually lasting 7½ minutes. A game normally consists of 6 chukkers with a 3-minute rest period between chukkers and a 5-minute rest at halftime. Important matches often consist of 8 chukkers. Players usually change ponies between chukkers and in the course of a 6-chukker game will generally use 3 ponies.

chula *jai alai* A shot aimed to rebound from the front wall, strike the base of the back wall where it meets the floor, and come out along the floor without bouncing.

¹**chum** *fishing* Food such as chopped or ground fish, grains, or live bait fish thrown into the water to attract fish. Chum amounts to a free handout to the fish to get them in a feeding mood so they will take the fisherman's hooked offering.

²**chum** To throw chum overboard to attract fish; to attract fish with chum.

chumming Attracting fish by throwing out chum from shore or from a boat. Chumming is illegal for inland fishing in many states but is often used in saltwater fishing (as for tuna).

chute **1 a** A straight extension of the track at the beginning of the straightaway portion of the homestretch and backstretch of a racetrack or at the beginning and end of the front straightaway of a running track to permit the starts of certain races to be made on a straight portion of track rather than on a turn. **b** The straightaway portion of a racetrack.

2 The starting line or starting area for a drag race or a dogsled race.

3 *cross-country* The narrow passage at the small end of a funnel-shaped area set up at the finish line of a large meet through which finishers must pass so that their exact order of finish can be recorded.

4 *rodeo* A narrow stall with a gate which opens at one side into the arena in which an animal that is to be ridden (as a bull or a bronco) is held so that the rider can mount it.

5 *sailing* A spinnaker.

6 Short for *parachute.*

Cigarette or **Cigarette hull** A large inboard racing powerboat that is used for offshore racing and that has an open cockpit for a 3-man crew.

Cincinnati *bowling* A split that leaves the 8 and 10 pins standing. — see illustration of pin arrangement at BOWLING

¹**circle** **1** *curling* One of the rings which comprise the house.

2 *football* A pass pattern in which the receiver runs across the line of scrimmage and circles toward the middle of the field.

3 *gymnastics* A rotary movement of the body or a part of the body around a support (as a

horizontal bar, the uneven parallel bars, or the pommel horse). A true circle involves a 360-degree revolution and may be done forward or backward.

4 Short for *center circle, face-off circle, free throw circle, restraining circle, striking circle, throwing circle.*

²**circle** **1** To run or move in a curving path.

2 *football* **a** To run a circle pattern. **b** To have a receiver run a circle pattern.

circle dodge *lacrosse* A dodge made by pivoting away from an opponent rather than past him.

circle eight *skating* A school figure which requires the skater to skate a full circle on one skate in one direction and then a full circle in another direction on the other skate so that the 2 circles form a figure eight.

circle pass *football* A pass thrown to a receiver running a circle pattern.

circuit **1** A league or conference.

2 A series of professional contests (as tournaments or races) held in different places and usually competed in by the same participants.

3 A racecourse for auto racing.

4 *horse racing* The tracks under the authority of a single racing commission that usually share the allotted racing days and that generally have the same horses or same quality horses racing all year long.

circuit clout A home run in baseball.

circuit training A method of performing conditioning exercises (as calisthenics) or weight training in which one moves from one exercise to another, usually to a different station for each exercise, with the object of performing the entire group of exercises as rapidly as possible with no rest between. As the the circuit of exercises is completed, the exercises increase in difficulty, or the allotted time is reduced so that the athlete constantly performs at or near his peak potential. The speed factor provides cardiorespiratory stress so often absent when the athlete is allowed to rest between exercises.

circular parry *fencing* A parry made by moving the blade in a circle so that it will catch the opponent's blade in whatever line it is attacking and force it away from the line of attack. (also called *counter* or *counter parry*)

circus catch A catch (as of a hit baseball or a football pass) that involves extraordinary or spectacular effort such as diving and rolling on the ground.

claim *horse racing* To make a formal written commitment to purchase a specific horse entered in a claiming race for the published claiming price before the start of the race. Only registered owners of horses running at the meeting in which the claiming race is held or their agents may claim a horse.

claimer *horse racing* **1** A claiming race.
2 A horse that runs in claiming races.

claiming race *horse racing* A race in which each horse is entered to run against horses of the same estimated monetary value with each horse subject to being claimed for a stipulated claiming price by another owner or trainer before the race. If a claim is made, the owner is obligated to sell the horse after the race and the purchaser is obligated to buy; the original owner gets the purchase price as well as any money won by the horse. Claiming races are run by horses of the poorest quality, yet, they make up the majority of races run by thoroughbreds and trotters in America. The claim keeps top quality animals out of races with horses of lesser quality and helps to ensure consistency in the quality of the racing. Because the trainer seeks to run his horse at the level at which he can win a purse now and then, he will not continually overvalue his horse when he cannot win against better quality animals, nor will he run the risk of losing the horse to a claim by habitually running him against obviously inferior opposition. — compare ALLOWANCE RACE, HANDICAP, STAKES RACE

clamp and rake *lacrosse* A maneuver to gain control of the ball on a face-off in which a player rotates his stick to force the opponent's stick to the ground and clamps the ball between the sticks and then pulls his stick back to rake the ball from the opponent's net.

class **1** A category into which race machinery or vessels are grouped on the basis of power or potential speed. In air racing, the classes are for various types of propeller-driven airplanes, from the tiny formula one to the class for single engine planes with unlimited engines. The classes in karting and motorcycle racing are based on engine size while those in powerboat racing group boats of similar size and type. In yacht racing, there are one-design classes in which all boats of a particular class must be identical, classes which group boats according to a complex formula or meter rule which includes calculations of the boat's measurements, shape, weight, and sail area, and classes for offshore cruising yachts based chiefly on overall size.
2 A top performer with proven superior ability, competitive spirit, and fortitude. ⟨still looks the

class of the Yankee Conference — Dave Warner, *Coach & Athlete*⟩ ⟨it is rare for a *class* trotter — over the age of 3 — to pass up a shot at the $22,500 top prize — Pat Putnam, *Sports Illustrated*⟩
3 *trapshooting* A category into which shooters are grouped for competition based on their abilities as determined by the average percentage of targets they have broken in competition.

classic **1** Any of the 5 famous traditional English races for 3-year-old thoroughbreds including the Derby, the Oaks, the 2000 Guineas, the St. Leger, and the 1000 Guineas. The term is often used in reference to some of the older American horse races such as those making up the Triple Crown.
2 A large or important annual sports event. The term has been used as part of the name of various golf and basketball tournaments.

classical seat A posture of the rider in the saddle in dressage events characterized by an erect body and head, legs slightly bent at the knees and in slight contact with the horse, and arms close to the body with the forearm held nearly level.

clay A tennis court with a clay surface or a synthetic surface that resembles clay.

clay pigeon A thin saucer-shaped target 3 to 4 inches in diameter that is made of asphalt and that is thrown from a trap in skeet and trapshooting.

¹clean **1a** Affording no chance of being fielded or misplayed. ⟨a *clean* single to center with none out in the fifth inning—*Sporting News*⟩ **b** Without a fumble or a misplay.⟨have to come up *clean* with the ball and throw on the run — Rod Carew⟩
2 *of a racing car* Having a smooth body contour for aerodynamic efficiency.
3 a *of a skating turn* Made with no flats. **b** *of a skating jump* Made without a turn of the skate on the surface at the takeoff or landing.

²clean *weight lifting* To lift a weight from the floor to shoulder height in a single continuous motion. The lifter normally uses an extension of his knees and a pull of his back to start the weight moving up and then makes a short lunge or squat to bring the arms under the bar.

³clean *weight lifting* The act of cleaning a weight; an exercise in which a weight is cleaned.

clean-and-jerk *weight lifting* To lift a usually specified amount of weight in the clean and jerk.

clean and jerk *weight lifting* A lift in which the lifter cleans the weight to shoulder level, pauses

clean and jerk

momentarily and usually on signal from the referee thrusts the weight overhead so that his arms are straight. The lifter is not restricted in the movement of his feet during either phase of the lift, and he normally employs a slight lunge to get his body under the weight. The lift is completed when the weight is held straight overhead for a specified length of time (as 3 seconds) with the feet together. — compare PRESS, SNATCH

clean the bases or **clear the bases** *baseball* To hit a home run with men on base thus driving them all home and leaving the bases empty.

cleanup *of a baseball batter* Batting in the fourth position in the team's batting order. The cleanup hitter is traditionally a strong hitter placed in this position to clean the bases should the first 3 men get on base.

¹clear To throw or kick a ball or to pass or drive a puck away from the defended goal.

²clear 1 The act or an instance of clearing the ball; a cleared ball.

2 *badminton* A shot hit high and deep into the opponent's court. — compare DRIVE

clear one's ears *skin diving* To equalize the pressure on both sides of the eardrum when diving especially by blowing gently while pinching the nose closed.

clear the bases see CLEAN THE BASES

clear the bench 1 *of a coach* To put all the reserves in a game once the outcome is no longer in doubt.

2 *of an official* To require all reserve players to leave the players bench and the immediate playing area or return to the dressing room because they are disrupting the game (as by too much heckling).

¹cleat 1 A fitting on a boat usually consisting of 2 short horn-shaped arms projecting outward around which a line may be secured. — see also JAM CLEAT; compare CHOCK

2 A usually rubber or plastic projection extending downward from the sole and heel of a shoe used in field sports (as football, soccer, or lacrosse) to provide traction. Cleats are typically flattened or rounded cones usually no thicker or longer than ½ inch. (also called *stud*)

²cleat 1 To secure a line to a cleat.

2 To equip a shoe with cleats.

cleats Shoes equipped with cleats. — compare SPIKES

cleek *golf* **1** An old name for the number 4 wood.

2 An old name for the number one iron.

clerk of the course An official who acts as executive secretary to the board of judges for horse races and track and field sports.

clerk of the scales An official who weighs jockeys and their gear before and after a horse race.

clew *sailing* The after lower corner of a sail. — see illustration at SAILBOAT

click A catch on a fishing reel that prevents the reel from revolving too fast and that usually produces a clicking sound as the spool revolves.

cliff hanger *mountain climbing* A narrow hook about 4 inches long which may be hooked on a small bump or crack too small to serve as a foothold or handhold and to which a foot stirrup or sling may be attached for temporary support.

¹climb **1** To move up an incline or slope on one's feet without the use of the hands for support or balance. A hiker may climb a small mountain by walking up a trail, or a skier may climb a slope by means of special stepping techniques or with the aid of climbing waxes or climbers.

2 To progress up a mountain or rock face by using the hands extensively for grasping, pulling, or more commonly for balancing. Special techniques in climbing and working with equipment (such as a safety rope, pitons, or ice axes) distinguish climbing from simple hill walking or hiking.

²climb The act or an instance of climbing a mountain; an ascent made by climbing.

climber **1** Someone who climbs mountains using special techniques and usually carrying special equipment (as ropes, pitons, and carabiners).

2 *skiing* A strip of material (as sealskin or mohair) that can be attached to the running surface of a ski to prevent backward movement while going uphill. The bristles on the bottom of the climber point toward the rear so as to catch in the snow and retard backward slipping while allowing the ski to be moved forward easily. (also called *creeper*)

climbing boot A boot used in mountain climbing. — see BOOT

climbing iron see CRAMPON

climbing pack or **climbing sack** *mountain climbing* A usually small lightweight backpack that can be worn comfortably while climbing and that is used to carry essential equipment for the climb. The climbing pack is usually designed without outside pockets and with a strap to hold an ice axe.

climbing wax *skiing* A gummy wax especially designed to allow a skier to walk up a slope without sliding back down.

¹clinch **1** To win a title or championship before the end of normal play by virtue of an insurmountable lead. A team has clinched first spot in league standing when it is mathematically impossible for any rival team to finish with a better season record even if the first place team should lose all remaining games. — see also MAGIC NUMBER

2 *boxing* To hold or tie up an opponent with one or both arms so that no blows or only short-range blows can be exchanged. A boxer may resort to a clinch when hurt or tired, and it is up to the referee to separate the fighters to keep the fight from stalling.

3 *fencing* To move close to an opponent so that there is body contact or so that normal fencing actions are impossible. While forcing a clinch is allowed as a tactic in épée, it is not allowed in other competition and may lead to a warning or penalty.

²clinch The act or an instance of clinching in boxing or fencing.

clinch knot A knot that is used to tie a hook to the end of fishing line and that is formed by passing the end of the line through the eye of a hook, turning the end around the standing part 3 or 4 times, and then pushing the end through the loop formed by the first turn from the eye of the hook. An improved clinch knot is formed in the same way except that after the end is pushed through the first loop it is tucked back between the standing part and the large loop formed when the end is pushed through the first loop. — see illustration at KNOT

clinker A broad-headed nail used on the edge of the sole of a climbing boot.

¹clip *football* To block an opponent (other than the ballcarrier) from behind especially by hitting or throwing the body across the back of the opponent's legs. It is legal for a player to clip an opponent in the vicinity of the line of scrimmage within a specified clipping zone so long as the player doing the clipping was within the zone at the start of play. If a player clips outside the legal zone or if he was outside the zone at the beginning of the play and comes inside to clip, he is charged with a clipping foul.

²clip **1** A magazine for a firearm.

2 *football* An instance of clipping an opponent.

clipping *football* The act of clipping an opponent during a free kick down or outside of the legal clipping zone during a scrimmage down which results in a 15-yard penalty.

clipping zone *football* The zone around the line of scrimmage which extends approximately 4

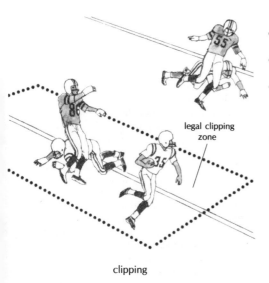

legal clipping zone

clipping

yards on either side and 3 yards in front and in back of the offensive center and within which a player may legally clip an opponent. (also called *free-blocking zone*)

¹clock **1** A clock that is usually visible to the players and spectators and that indicates the amount of official playing time left in a period.
2 A clock that indicates the amount of time the attacking team has left to take a shot; shooting clock. ⟨the NBA uses a 24-second *clock*⟩
— **against the clock** *of competition* With each competitor individually timed while competing alone and the competitor with the best time winning.

²clock To time a competitor over a predetermined distance with a stopwatch or electronic timer during competition or in a practice, time trial, or workout.

clocker **1** A timer for a race (as in swimming or track and field).
2 Someone who times racehorses during workouts and who records the times and other information that may be of use in handicapping the horses.

¹close **1** Very near. ⟨played *close* to his man⟩
2 Difficult to call or uncertain in outcome. ⟨a *close* play at second⟩ ⟨a *close* game⟩
— **in close** Near the goal; inside.

²close **1** To move up or gain on the leaders especially near the finish of a race.
2 To alter one's stance or position from more open to more closed.
3 To have specified odds as the betting stops for

the start of the race. ⟨his horse *closed* at 2–1⟩

close aboard *boating* Near an object or another boat.

close a port *curling* To block an opening between 2 stones.

close attack *lacrosse* The 3 attackmen, including the in home, out home, and first attack, who play near the opponent's goal. — compare CLOSE DEFENSE, MIDFIELD

closed **1** *of a stance* Having the front foot closer to the line of play of the ball (as in baseball or golf) than the rear foot.
2 *of an archery string picture* Having the string appear near the center of the limb of a bow.
3 *of a slalom gate* Set up with the 2 poles in line with or parallel to the line of descent. — see illustration at GATE
4 *of a contest, league, or tour* Open only to competitors of a particular sex, age group, amateur or professional status, or club affiliation or from a designated geographical region.
5 *of a racket* Swung with the face slightly downward and the top nearer the net or front wall than the bottom.
6 *of a line in fencing* Blocked because of the position of the opponent's arm or sword.
7 **a** *of a skating position* With an individual's hips or shoulders turned toward the skating foot or with the free leg slightly ahead of the skating foot; with ice dancing partners facing each other.
b *of a skating figure* Performed with an individual's body in a closed position.
8 *of a racecourse* Forming a continuous path and having the starting and finishing point at the same place.

closed-circuit see SCUBA

close defense *lacrosse* The 3 defensemen, including the point, cover point, and first defense, who play near their own goal. — compare CLOSE ATTACK, MIDFIELD

closed season A period during which game or fish are protected by law and may not be legally caught or killed.

close-hauled *of a sailing boat* Sailing as nearly against the wind as the boat will go.

close in *fencing* To move into a clinch.

close-out *surfing* A wave or series of waves that are too big to ride or that collapse right at the shore and cannot be ridden.

closing odds *pari-mutuel betting* The odds at the time the betting stops.

¹clothesline **1** A line drive in baseball.
2 *football* A tackle that is made by extending an arm out straight to catch the ballcarrier by the

head and neck unawares. It is now illegal.

²clothesline To hit and knock down a player with an outstretched arm.

clout 1 *archery* A target that is 12 times the size of a standard target and is laid out on the ground for use in clout shooting. The overall size is 48 feet and the center, which is 1½ feet, is marked by a small flag. The rings are marked in the same proportion and have the same scoring value as those of the standard target.

2 *baseball* A hard-hit ball.

clout shooting *archery* Competition in which arrows are shot at a target clout from distances of 120 to 180 yards. Each competitor shoots a round of 36 arrows.

clove hitch A knot that is used to secure a rope to an object (as a post) temporarily and that is formed by making a full turn around the object, crossing the standing part, making a second turn in the same direction and tucking the end under the second turn. — see illustration at KNOT

clown *rodeo* A clown who is in the arena to entertain the crowd and to distract the bull from thrown riders.

club 1 a An amateur or professional organization devoted to a particular sport. A club may consist of both management and contract athletes, as a baseball club, or merely be a sponsoring organization for which athletes perform as in track and field or swimming. A club for golf or tennis may be little more than an organization which provides playing facilities for members and guests. A sports car club may hold regular meetings and conduct races and rallies for its members or in conjunction with other clubs. **b** A team or group of athletes that represent a club or school in competition.

2 *golf* An implement used to hit the ball that consists of a long slender shaft with a small usually wooden or metal head at one end. A golfer carries a variety of clubs, each with a different degree of loft, for use in a variety of shots. The greater the degree of loft, the higher and shorter the flight of the ball. The woods, traditionally made with thick hardwood heads, are generally used for shots off the tee and occasionally for long fairway shots. The irons, which normally have shorter shafts and thin metal heads, are usually used for fairway and approach shots. The putter, a club without loft, is used to roll the ball across the putting green. The clubs are numbered in order of increasing loft, with the woods numbered from one to 5 and the irons numbered usually from 2 through 9. Two important clubs

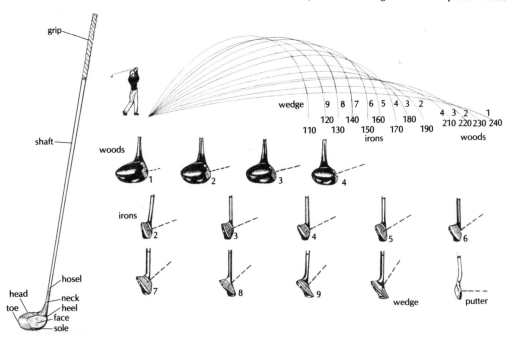

golf clubs: left, parts of a club; top, average ranges of various clubs; bottom, lofts of clubfaces

that are classed as irons but that are not usually numbered are the pitching wedge and the sand wedge, both of which have loft somewhat greater than that of the number 9 iron. A golfer is limited to carrying 14 clubs and those normally carried include 3 or 4 woods, 7 or 8 irons, plus a pitching wedge, a sand wedge, and a putter.

clubface The face of a golf club.

club fighter *boxing* A boxer developed at a neighborhood boxing club and especially one noted for his persistent slugging style and ability to absorb punishment.

clubhead The head of a golf club.

clubhouse 1 A building adjacent to a golf course providing such facilities as a locker room, pro shop, and restaurant.

2 A section of the grandstand at a racetrack generally located between the finish line and the first turn that usually provides the choicest seats and often includes such facilities as a restaurant and a bar.

3 A baseball team's dressing room.

— **in the clubhouse** *of a professional golfer* Having finished a tournament while others are still on the course. ⟨was the leader *in the clubhouse* at 5 under par⟩

clubhouse turn *horse racing* The turn on a racetrack just past the finish line and nearest the clubhouse. — compare FAR TURN

clubmate Someone who competes for the same athletic club as another.

club player A tennis player who regularly plays at a club rather than on a professional tour.

club sport An intercollegiate sport that is not a part of the regular school athletic program and that is not funded by the school but is run wholly by the student participants and supported chiefly by fund-raising activities.

¹clutch A tight or crucial situation when the outcome of a game is at stake. — often used to describe a player who can make the big play in the clutch fairly consistently ⟨*clutch* shooter⟩ ⟨*clutch* hitter⟩

²clutch or **clutch up** To psych oneself to the point of failing in a clutch situation; choke. ⟨can tell by her face that she's *clutched* — she imagines herself double-faulting — and sure enough, she double-faults — Billie Jean King⟩

clutch start *motorcycle racing* A start in which the motorcycles are at the starting line with the engines running and in gear and the riders only have to engage the clutch at the starting signal. — compare BUMP START

¹coach 1 A person who instructs or trains performers or players in the fundamentals and various techniques of a sport. In such sports activities as gymnastics and figure skating, a coach usually works closely with an individual performer in perfecting various maneuvers and in creating practically flawless performance of a routine. In team sports, a coach usually teaches fundamentals and techniques, conducts practices, develops plays, and runs the game (as by directing offensive or defensive strategy and making substitutions). A coach in a team sport may be a player who directs team play, a non-player who has to perform all the various duties of a coach alone, or a member of a large coaching staff who generally concentrates on a particular limited aspect of play (as pitching in baseball or defensive play in football). Where there is a large coaching staff, the conduct of the game is ultimately under the control of the head coach. — compare MANAGER, TRAINER

2 or **coacher** *baseball* Either of 2 members of the team at bat who are allowed to stand in the coach's boxes adjacent to first and third bases and relay signals from the manager to the batter and base runners and direct the runners in running the bases. Members of the coaching staff usually perform these duties in professional ball, while in amateur competition the coaches are typically players who are not in the game.

²coach To be a coach; to have the duties of a coach. ⟨*coached* football for 10 years⟩

coacher see COACH (*baseball*)

Coaching Club American Oaks A 1¼-mile stakes race for 3-year-old thoroughbred fillies that is one of the races in the filly Triple Crown. — compare ACORN, MOTHER GOOSE

coach's box *baseball* Either of 2 rectangular areas adjacent to first and third bases within which the coaches must stand when the ball is in play. The areas are marked 8 feet outside the baselines and extend from the bases toward home plate for 20 feet. On a softball field, the coach's boxes are 15 feet long and marked 6 feet outside the baselines.

coaming *boating* A slightly raised frame around a cockpit above the level of the deck to keep out water.

coast see FLOAT (*track and field*)

cock Short for *gamecock.*

cock feather *archery* The feather set perpendicular to the nock of the arrow so that it sticks away from the bow when the arrow is drawn. The cock feather is in reality no different from the other feathers, known as *hen feathers,* but it is often of a contrasting color to facilitate locating the position of the nock.

cockfighting or **cocking**   The matching of specially bred gamecocks to fight each other for a designated time or until one cock has killed or disabled its opponents. The fight, called a *bout*, usually takes place in a circular area known as a *pit* that is bounded by a low wall. The cocks are usually fitted with sharp metal spurs or gaffs on their legs with which they slash at the other cocks. A program of bouts is a *main*. Though there is prize money to be won by the owner of the victorious bird in each of the bouts, betting on the outcome is a major aspect of cockfighting. Cockfighting is illegal in most states of the United States, Canada, Great Britain, and most Latin American countries.

cockpit   **1** *auto racing*   The compartment in which the driver sits in a racing car.
2 *boating*   **a** An open area behind the decked part of a small boat in which the skipper and crew or passengers sit and from which the boat is steered.   **b** The small hole in the middle of a kayak in which the kayaker sits.   **c** The open area in a racing shell in which the crew sits.

codeball   **1** Either of 2 games formerly played by kicking a 6-inch inflated ball: **a** A game that resembles handball played on a 4-wall court.   **b** A game resembling golf played on a field having 14 holes.
2 The ball used in codeball.

cody   *trampolining*   A backward somersault in a tuck position performed on the trampoline from a front drop position with a landing on the feet.

coffee grinder   **1** *gymnastics*   A single leg circle performed in a squatting position with both hands on the floor.
2 *sailing*   A 2-hand winch with handles on both sides that is used for hoisting a sail (as a spinnaker).

coffin corner   *football*   Any of the 4 corners of a field formed by the intersection of the sideline and goal line. The punting team may attempt to kick the ball out of bounds near the coffin corner to prevent a return and to force the receiving team to put the ball in play from very close to its own goal line.

coincident penalty   A penalty in ice hockey and box lacrosse assessed to players of both teams simultaneously which does not result in either team's playing at a disadvantage. On coincident minor penalties, substitution is not allowed and the scoring of a goal does not affect the duration of the penalty. For coincident major penalties, the teams may substitute for the penalized players and do not have to play below normal strength as a result of the penalty. The most common coincident penalty is for fighting, which results in both players being penalized equally.

collapse   *of a defensive team in basketball*   To close in on the opposing pivotman when he gets the ball in the free throw lane in order to tie him up or to prevent him from passing or shooting effectively.

¹collar   The throat of a lacrosse stick.

²collar   *of a cricket batsman*   To score easily off a particular bowler or a particular kind of bowling.

collect   To cause a horse to assume a posture in which it is erect and responsive to the bit and has its hocks well under its body so that the center of gravity is toward the rear.

collection   The act of collecting a horse. — compare EXTENSION

colledge   *skating*   A jump from an outer forward edge of the skate with one and a half turns in the air and a return to an inner backward edge of the same foot.

color   Analysis of game action or strategy, statistics and background information on participants, and often anecdotes provided by a sportscaster to give variety and interest to the broadcast of a game or contest. — compare PLAY-BY-PLAY

Colorado   *fishing*   **1** A broad teardrop-shaped spinner blade.
2 A spinner with a Colorado blade. (also called *Idaho*)

colorman or **colorcaster**   A sportscaster who provides the color for the broadcast of a game or contest.

colors   see SILKS

colt   A young male horse:
1 A thoroughbred of age 4 or less.
2 A standardbred of age 3 or less.
— compare HORSE, GELDING; FILLY

Columbia round   *archery*   A target round in women's competition in which each competitor shoots 24 arrows at a distance of 50 yards, 24 at 40 yards, and 24 at 30 yards.

combination   **1** *boxing*   A series of blows delivered in rapid succession usually in a practiced pattern. ⟨a left-right *combination*⟩
2 *pari-mutuel betting*   A ticket that combines win, place, and show betting in a single purchase for the same price as 3 individual tickets and that is sold as a convenience to bettors.

combination shot   *billiards*   **1** A shot in pocket billiards in which the cue ball drives one object ball into another in a chain reaction until the called ball is pocketed.

2 A shot in English billiards in which the player scores in 2 ways (as by cannoning and pocketing a ball).

combined grasp *gymnastics* A grasp on the horizontal bar with one hand turned palm away from the performer and one turned toward him.

come about see TACK

comeback see BUTTONHOOK

come back 1 To perform or attempt to perform at or near a previous high level after a period of poor play or inactivity (as because of retirement or an injury).

2 To overcome a disadvantage and often go on to win. ⟨*came back* to win 3 straight sets and the match⟩

comebacker 1 *baseball* A grounder hit directly to the pitcher.

2 *football* see BUTTONHOOK

come in *of a baseball pitcher* To throw a particular pitch over the plate. ⟨got to *come in* with that pitch. And it's always the same speed — Reggie Jackson⟩

come off To have just had or played a specific kind of game or season. ⟨*coming off* a poor season to lead the league in home runs⟩

come off the ball see MOVE OFF THE BALL

comma position *skiing* A body position used in traversing in which the knees are bent slightly and angled toward the slope while the upper body is turned away from the slope.

commissioner The administrative head of a professional sport or of a sports league or conference.

committee boat *yacht racing* A boat which usually serves as one end of the starting line and the finish line and from which the race committee conducts a race.

common foul *basketball* Any personal foul that is not a part of a double or multiple foul and that is not committed against a player shooting a field goal. A common foul is normally penalized by the awarding of the ball to the offended team out of bounds. In a bonus situation, the fouled player is awarded a bonus free throw except when the foul is an offensive or player control foul.

Commonwealth Games A program of amateur sports competition that is similar to the Olympic Games and that is held every 4 years among British Commonwealth nations. The Games normally include competition in badminton, boxing, cycling, fencing, lawn bowling, rowing, swimming, track and field, weight lifting, and wrestling

and are usually held in the middle of the 4-year interval between Olympics. — see also OLYMPIC GAMES

compass bearing see BEARING

compensator A device fitted to the muzzle of a firearm to reduce recoil by directing a part of the powder gases through a series of lateral vents.

Competition Eliminator see ELIMINATOR

complete *football* To throw a forward pass that is caught by the intended receiver. ⟨has *completed* 53 per cent of his passes — *New York Times*⟩

complete game *baseball* A game that the starting pitcher finishes and that is credited to the pitcher in permanent records.

completion *football* A forward pass that is caught by the receiver and that is credited to the passer in statistical records. — compare RECEPTION, INTERCEPTION

composite average *bowling* The bowling average for one who bowls in more than one league determined by dividing the total number of pins credited in all leagues by the total number of games bowled in all leagues.

compound attack or **composite attack** *fencing* An attack that combines 2 or more successive movements (as a feint followed by a thrust) and that is intended to deceive an opponent and cause him to change his guard and leave open a line of attack.

compound parry *fencing* Two or more parries used in combination.

compound riposte *fencing* A riposte made with one or more feints.

compulsories see SCHOOL FIGURES

compulsory *of a dive, movement, or school figure* Required to be performed by all competitors as part of formal competition. Diving, skating, and gymnastics competition all involve compulsory as well as optional sections with each section performed separately from the other. The compulsory aspect of the competition may be predetermined by the rules or by the judges (as in gymnastics or skating) with the performer having no choice. In diving the performer may choose from a list of compulsory dives, and the performance is judged on the degree of difficulty of the dive as well as its execution.

compulsory freestyle *skating* An event in which all contestants are required to perform certain required movements in conjunction with a freestyle program and which counts toward the overall scores.

concede To acknowledge that an opponent has

won before the end of a contest; to credit a golf opponent with a holed ball before the opponent's ball is actually holed. ⟨*concede* a putt⟩

conditional race   *harness racing*   A race in which specific conditions (as a specified gait, age, sex, or amount of money or number of races won) limit the horses eligible and thereby provide relatively even competition. — compare CLAIMING RACE, STAKES RACE

condition book   *horse racing*   A publication put out by a racetrack giving the conditions for every race of every program and sometimes including information on track rules, the jockeys that regularly ride at that track, and track records.

conditions   *horse racing*   The provisions and restrictions under which a race is run that determine the eligible horses. The conditions state the distance and type of race (as maiden, allowance, handicap, or claiming race), the age and sometimes sex of eligible horses, and in some cases the standard weights to be carried and weight allowances that may be claimed. A claiming race may be open, for example, to all horses 3 years old and older for a specified claiming price, or it may be open only to 3-year-old fillies. An allowance race might be open to horses which have won no more than 2 allowance races in the past year with horses that have won fewer than the maximum number of races eligible to claim specific weight allowances.

conference   An association of athletic teams or clubs usually in a particular geographic region. A conference may be an independent association such as a conference of colleges or universities that normally play each other during a season for a championship, or it may be a major subdivision of a league, as is the case in many professional sports where the clubs compete against each other more often than against clubs outside the conference and where the conference champion usually advances to the league play-off series. — see also DIVISION

connect   **1** To make a successful hit, shot, punch, or throw. ⟨*connected* for a triple⟩ ⟨*connected* on 60 percent of his shots and on 10 of 11 free throws — *New York Times*⟩ ⟨*connected* with a right to the jaw⟩ ⟨*connected* on an 85-yard pass play⟩
2 *baseball*   To hit a home run.

consecutive climbing   *mountain climbing*   A method of climbing difficult pitches on rock or snow in which only one climber moves at a time because a fall could not be held by a moving

climber. The usual technique is for the leader to climb and then bring up the second before continuing up. If another climber is on the rope, he will be brought up by the second before the second moves again to join the leader. — compare CONTINUOUS CLIMBING

consolation   A contest held for competitors who have lost in early competition or who failed to qualify for a contest. ⟨*consolation* game⟩ ⟨*consolation* race⟩

consolation double   *pari-mutuel betting*   A provision in some daily doubles whereby holders of combinations that include the winner of the first race and a horse that is scratched from the second race are paid a proportion of the money bet on the pool.

consy   *auto racing*   A consolation race.

contact sport   A sport (as football, boxing, ice hockey, basketball, or judo) in which individuals or teams compete against each other directly with each side permitted to hinder the other side and in which some physical contact between opponents is a part of play.

contain   To hold an opponent in check; to prevent an opponent from scoring, advancing, or mounting a successful attack.

contender   **1** An individual or team that has a good chance of winning a championship.
2 A boxer good enough to provide suitable opposition to or possibly defeat a champion.

Continental grip   see GRIP (*tennis*)

continuation   *basketball*   The continuous movement to the basket for a shot and the shot itself made by a player who is obviously committed to making the shot (as a driving lay-up) but who is fouled by an opponent before he actually shoots the ball. Continuation is recognized in professional play, and if the player makes the shot, he is awarded a free throw with a chance for a 3-point-play; if he misses the shot he is awarded 2 free throws as if fouled in the act of shooting. In college ball, play is terminated by the call and the foul is treated only as a common foul.

continuous   *of a climbing route*   Having rock unbroken by patches of grass or bushes.

continuous climbing   *mountain climbing*   A method of climbing relatively easy routes on rock or snow in which all climbers move at the same time and maintain the interval between them. This technique is sometimes used to advance quickly over a route where there are sufficient points for running belays and where a fall might easily be arrested even though the other climbers are not belayed. — compare CONSECU-TIVE CLIMBING

continuous pool or **continuous pocket billiards** see BILLIARDS

contraction parry *fencing* A combination of a simple parry and a circular parry.

control *baseball* The ability of a pitcher to throw a pitch with accuracy.

control flag *skiing* Any of the flags which mark the edges of a downhill or slalom course or which indicate a slalom gate.

control point see CHECK POINT

conventional grip see GRIP (*bowling*)

conversion 1 *basketball* The making of a free throw.

2 *football* The scoring of one or 2 extra points after a touchdown.

3 *rugby* The making of 2 points on a goal after a try.

¹convert 1 To take a pass or a rebound and immediately shoot and score a goal.

2 *basketball* To make a successful free throw.

3 *bowling* To knock down all the remaining pins with the second ball to score a spare.

4 *football* **a** To make good on a try for point after a touchdown. If the ball is kicked over the crossbar, one point is scored; if the ball is run or passed over the goal line, 2 points are scored in school or college play or one point in professional play. **b** To train a player to play a position other than one he formerly played.

5 *rugby* To make good on a kick for 2 points after a try.

6 *soccer* To make a successful penalty kick.

²convert *Canadian football* The point after touchdown scored by kicking the ball over the crossbar or by running or passing it over the goal line.

cookhole A section in the floor of some tents designed especially for winter camping that can be opened when cooking so that spilled liquids will run directly onto the ground or snow.

cooler *horse racing* A light blanket placed over a horse after a race or workout while he is being walked to cool off.

cool out *horse racing* To walk a horse after a race or workout to allow him to cool off before he is returned to his stall.

cop A policeman in ice hockey.

coquille *fencing* The bowl-shaped guard of a foil or épée.

¹corner 1 The area of a court or playing field near the intersection of the sideline and the goal line or baseline. ⟨hit a jumper from the *corner*⟩

2 *baseball* Either side of home plate. ⟨a fastball over the outside *corner*⟩

3 *boxing* Any of the 4 corners of a ring. The boxers are assigned opposite corners where they rest and are attended by seconds between rounds. In the event of a knockdown, the standing boxer must retire to a neutral corner while the count proceeds.

4 *field hockey* A free hit awarded a member of the attacking team from a spot on the sideline or goal line 5 yards from the corner of the field when a defender drives the ball beyond his own goal line. (also called *long corner*) — compare PENALTY CORNER

5 *football* The outside of a formation; the edge of a line of blockers or potential tacklers. ⟨turned the *corner* and started upfield⟩

6 *ice hockey* Any of the 4 rounded corners of the rink including the adjacent section of the sideboards.

7 *motor racing* A turn on a road course.

8 *mountain climbing* A place where 2 walls join at nearly right angles.

9 *soccer* see CORNER KICK

²corner *motor racing* To negotiate a corner.

corner area *soccer* A quarter circle with a 3-foot radius drawn inside the playing field at each corner where the touchlines and goal lines meet. The ball is placed in the corner area for a corner kick.

cornerback *football* A defensive back who plays outside the linebacker 3 to 10 yards off the line of scrimmage and whose duties include defending against sweeps and covering a wide receiver.

corner crew *auto racing* A group of people who are stationed at each turn on a road course to signal to the drivers to warn of dangerous conditions ahead which they cannot see (as an accident or an oil spill) and to assist drivers who have gone off the track. Members of the corner crew signal a driver who has spun off the course when it is safe for him to return to the course, and if a car is wrecked, they help get the driver out, push the car away from the track, and if necessary put out a fire.

corner flag *soccer* A flag placed at each corner of a field.

corner kick or **corner** *soccer* A free kick awarded the attacking team from the corner area when a defender drives the ball beyond his own goal line.

cornerman 1 A forward on a basketball team.

2 A cornerback on a football team.

3 A wing on an ice hockey team who is adept at getting the puck out of the corner.

4 Either of 2 attacking players in box lacrosse who position themselves in the corners of the attacking zone near the center zone.

corner shot A shot in racquetball or squash racquets that is aimed at a front corner of the court so as to hit the side wall and then low on the front wall and drop to the floor.

corner throw **1** *team handball* An unhindered throw of the ball from the corner of the field awarded to the attacking team when any member of the defending team other than the goalkeeper drives the ball over his own goal line.

2 *water polo* A free throw from the corner of the pool awarded to the attacking team when a defender drives the ball beyond the goal line.

cornice *mountain climbing* An overhanging mass of snow or ice resembling a breaking wave that is formed on the leeward side of a ridge by the wind.

corn snow *skiing* Granular snow formed by alternate thawing and freezing. (also called *spring snow*)

corps à corps *fencing* Body contact between opponents which prevents effective use of the weapons and which causes the bout to be stopped; clinch.

corrected time *yacht racing* A boat's elapsed time less the handicap allowance.

corrida or **corrida de toros** A program of usually 6 bullfights.

corridor see GATE

cortada *jai alai* A shot from off the court that hits low on the front wall and then on the floor.

Cotton Bowl A postseason college football bowl game played in the Cotton Bowl stadium in Dallas between specially invited teams of which one is often from the Southwest Conference.

cough up To lose possession of a ball or puck especially because of the action of defenders.

coulé see GLIDE

couloir *mountain climbing* A deep gorge in a mountainside often bounded by steep rock walls. A couloir offers a relatively easy route for climbers, but since it is a natural channel for falling rocks and avalanches it can become quite dangerous when the higher portions become warmed by the sun.

count **1** *baseball* The number of balls and strikes charged to a batter in one turn at bat. The count is normally given with the number of balls stated first. Example: after 2 strikes and 3 balls, the count on the batter is 3 and 2.

2 *billiards* The score for a successful shot. In carom billiards games a count is one point for a carom. In some pocket billiards games a count is one point for each ball pocketed, and in other games it is equal to the number on the pocketed ball.

3 *bowling* **a** The number of pins knocked down with the first ball of a frame following a spare or strike that is used in determining the bonus for the earlier mark. **b** A failure to knock down the maximum number of pins in a frame; a frame in which all of the pins have not been knocked down.

4 *boxing* The calling off of the seconds from one to 10 when a boxer has been knocked down; the number of seconds counted against a boxer. ⟨was up at the *count* of 3⟩

¹counter **1** or **counterpunch** *boxing* A punch thrown while blocking an opponent's lead.

2 *curling* A stone that is resting within the rings closer to the tee than any opposing stone.

3 or **counter parry** *fencing* see CIRCULAR PARRY

4 *football* An offensive play in which the ball-carrier runs in a direction opposite the flow of the play.

5 *skating* **a** A turn from forward to backward or backward to forward on the same edge with the rotation against the curvature of the edge being skated. **b** A school figure consisting of 3 connected circles that is performed on a single edge by executing a counter turn at the junction of each of the 3 circles.

6 *wrestling* A maneuver that counteracts the opponent's attack and provides a hold on the opponent.

²counter **1** *boxing* To block an opponent's lead and immediately throw a punch.

2 *wrestling* To block an opponent's attacking move and immediately apply a hold.

counterattack **1** An offensive action begun immediately after gaining control of the ball or puck from the opposing team.

2 *fencing* An attack made in direct response to an opponent's attack. Since the rules of foil and saber fencing give the attacker the right of way until his attack is either completely avoided or parried, the hit on a counterattack must land before the completion of a compound attack or the counterattack must be made after or while parrying the opponent's attack if it is to be valid. — see also STOP HIT, TIME THRUST

counter-disengagement *fencing* A movement made in direct response to a change of engagement whereby the blade is moved around the opponent's blade so as to engage it in the original line.

counter jump *skating* A jump with a half turn in the air made with the landing on the same edge of the same skate as on the takeoff but facing in the opposite direction so that the movement on landing begins a curve in a different direction.

counter parry see CIRCULAR PARRY

counterpunch see COUNTER (*boxing*)

counterpuncher A boxer who uses a counter as his normal style; one who normally allows his opponent to throw the first punch so he can strike in the area left vulnerable by the attack. ⟨I don't punch until the other guy do ... I'm really a *counterpuncher* when I go to the body — Joe Frazier⟩

counter-riposte *fencing* An attacking movement made immediately after parrying an opponent's riposte or counter-riposte.

counterrotate *skiing* To twist the shoulders in the direction opposite that in which one intends to turn the skis in making a turn.

counterrotation *skiing* The action of rotating the shoulders in a direction opposite to that of the feet and legs in making a turn. Counterrotation, performed while the skis are unweighted, provides a equal and opposite reaction to the turn of the skis and theoretically gives a smoother and more effective turn. (also called *reverse shoulder*)

counter-time see FALSE ATTACK

count out *of a boxing referee* To indicate a knockout of a boxer who is down by completing an audible count of 10 seconds before the boxer rises.

country club A usually suburban or outlying club or clubhouse providing recreation facilities (as for swimming, golf, and tennis) and social activities for members.

coup British term for *scratch*.

coupé see CUTOVER

¹course **1** The route taken or to be taken by participants in a race. The course may consist of a cross-country route used in running or skiing, a track used for running, horse racing, or motor racing, a path to be followed through gates in a slalom race, or a route around markers or buoys used in boat racing. **2** Short for *golf course*.

²course *of a hunting dog* To pursue game by sight rather than scent.

coursing **1** The sport of pursuing game (as hare or deer) with dogs that course (as greyhounds). — compare FOX HUNTING **2** The modern sport of racing greyhounds.

court **1** The playing area for a number of games and especially those in which a ball is driven back and forth over a net or is rebounded from a wall. A court may be a rectangular floor or surface marked with lines within which the players or the ball or both must remain during play, or it may encompass an entire room with the floor and the walls and sometimes the ceiling being part of the playing area.
a *badminton* A rectangular area divided by a 5-foot-high net into 2 equal areas. A doubles court is 20 feet wide and 44 feet long and is usually marked with a line 18 inches inside and parallel to each sideline to mark the side limits of the service court and the court for singles play. Parallel to the net and 6½ feet from it is a *short service line* on each side of the net. A *center line* extends from the middle of the short service line to the *back boundary line* and marks 2 service courts on each side. Two and a half feet inside the back boundary lines is a *long service line* that marks the back of the service courts for doubles play.
b *basketball* A rectangular area usually divided by a line across the middle, marked with a 12-foot *restraining circle* in the center and each end, and having a restricted *free throw area* in the shape of a rectangle or trapezoid extending 19 feet in from each end line. At each end of the court a metal ring is fixed to a backboard and supported 10 feet above the floor. The optimum size of a court is 94 feet long and 50 feet wide (84-by-50-feet for high school play). For major competition it is laid out on a hardwood floor in a gymnasium or indoor arena. Dirt and asphalt courts are common in playgrounds.
c *boccie* A rectangular area 75 feet long and 8 feet wide of packed clay or sand that is bounded on all sides by a wooden wall 12 inches high on the sides and 18 inches high at the ends.
d *court tennis* A rectangular area approximately 110 feet long and 39 feet wide enclosed by 4 walls 17 feet high and divided by a net across the middle that is 3 feet high at the center and 4½ feet high at the ends. Around the base of the 2 end walls and one long wall is a roofed corridor approximately 7 feet wide and 7 feet high. The roof of the corridor slopes up to the outer wall at an angle of about 30 degrees. The ball is served and played off this sloping roof,

which is called the *penthouse*. The corridor at the server's end of the court contains a spectator's area, called the *dedans*. At the opposite end of the court, the corridor is totally enclosed except for a small opening on one side near the penthouse roof. This opening is known as the *grille*. On the long side of the court, the corridor has 9 openings to the court from 3 to 9 feet wide. The 4 openings on either side of the *center opening* are known as the *first gallery, door, second gallery,* and *last* or *winning gallery*. On the receiver's side, the main wall projects into the court about 1½ feet creating a vertical surface, called a *tambour,* off which the ball may be played for unusual rebounds. On most of the server's side and part of the receiver's side, the floor of the court is marked with lines parallel to the end walls and spaced ½ yard apart. These are called *chase lines* and are used to designate the value of chases made during play. The floor and walls are usually made of concrete.

e *croquet* (1) *lawn croquet* A marked or unmarked rectangular area on a lawn that is usually 60 feet long and 30 feet wide and that contains a wooden stake at each end and 9 wire arches (*wickets*) arranged so that there are 2 wickets directly in front of each stake, one wicket in the center of the court, and a wicket on each side of the court about 15 feet from each end. (2) *association croquet* A rectangular area 115 feet long and 84 feet wide laid out on a lawn with a wooden stake (*peg*) in the exact center and 6 wire arches (*wickets*) arranged with one on either side of the peg and one near each corner of the court. (3) *regulation croquet* A rectangular area 75 feet long and 40 feet wide that is laid out on a hard clay surface bounded by a low wall and that contains a wooden stake at each end and 10 wickets arranged as on a roque court.

f *deck tennis* A rectangular area 40 feet long and 18 feet wide (12 feet wide for singles) that is divided by a net 4½ feet high across the middle. On each side of the net and 3 feet from the net is a line marking the *neutral zone* which is out of play. Both sides of the court are identically marked with serving areas formed by a line running from the neutral zone back to the baseline midway between the sidelines. A doubles court usually has a line on each side 3 feet inside each sideline marking the side boundaries of the court for singles play. Courts are often marked on ship decks and on playgrounds.

g *fives* A rectangular area 28 feet long and 18 feet wide enclosed by 4 walls. The front wall is 15 feet high and the back wall 6 feet high. Each side wall descends from the front to the back wall in a series of steps. Across the front wall 2½ feet above the floor is a wooden board which marks the lower boundary of the playing area of the front wall. The court is typically made of concrete.

h *handball* (1) A rectangular area 40 feet long and 20 feet wide enclosed on 3 sides by a 20-foot-high wall and by a 12-foot-high wall in the back. A ceiling extends along the top of the 20-foot walls and to the plane of the back wall and is part of the playing area. A *service area* is marked on the floor 15 feet from the front wall by 2 parallel lines 5 feet apart. One is the *service line* and the other the *short line*. A line between these lines 1½ feet from and parallel to each side wall marks the *service boxes* on each side of the court. Five feet behind the service area, a line 3 inches long is marked up from the floor on each side wall to indicate the *receiving zone*. Some courts may be constructed with glass walls above a height of 12 feet on all walls but the front wall in order to provide more spectator viewing areas. (2) A rectangular area of the same dimensions as the 4-wall court but with only a front wall and 2 side walls. There is no back wall and there may or may not be a ceiling as part of the court. A variation of the 3-wall court is one similar to a jai alai court of the same size as a 4-wall court with a front wall and a back wall and only one side wall. Along the open side, an *outside line* running the length of the court marks the out of bounds area on the open side. There is a *serving line* marked on the floor 5 feet on either side of the *short line* so that the players may turn around and play in the opposite direction, with the front wall becoming the back wall, after each game. This prevents one player with a particularly strong side from maintaining an advantage for more than one game. (3) A rectangular area 34 feet long and 20 feet wide with a single wall at one end 16 feet high. The back of the court is marked by a *long line*. Sixteen feet from the wall is a *short line*. *Service markers* 6 inches long are marked on the floor midway between the short line and the long line and these, along with the short line and the sidelines, indicate the *service zone*. The *receiving zone* extends from the short line to the long line.

i *horseshoes* A rectangular area 50 feet long and 10 feet wide with a 6-foot-square pitching box at each end. In each pitching box is a metal stake 14 inches high angled slightly toward the other stake. The stakes are 40 feet apart, and the area of the pitching box around the stake is composed of soft clay, dirt, or sand.

j *jai alai* A rectangular area 176 feet long and 40 feet wide that has a 40-foot-high wall enclosing 3 sides with the fourth side open to spectators. A screen separates the spectator area from the court itself. The side wall is the long side of the court. At regular intervals along the side wall are numbered lines dividing the court into 15 distinct zones. The *serving area* is between the fourth and seventh lines. Around the front and back walls and along the top of the side wall is a foul area, painted red, which marks the out of bounds area. Between the court and the screen is a 10-foot-wide strip for the officials. The court floor and walls are made of concrete with the front wall constructed of granite blocks.

k *paddleball* Same as for *handball* (4-wall).

l *paddle tennis* A rectangular area 44 feet long and 20 feet wide with a net 2½ feet high dividing the court into 2 areas, each having identical service areas. A line on each side of the court 2 feet inside and parallel to the sidelines marks the sides of the service courts and the sidelines for singles play. Twelve feet on each side of the net is a *service line;* a line connecting the middle of the 2 service lines marks the service courts. Courts are typically laid out on playgrounds and on gymnasium floors.

m *platform tennis* Same as for paddle tennis but enclosed by a 12-foot-high fence of taut chicken wire 8 feet back of the *end lines* and 5 feet outside the sidelines off which the balls may be played. The net is 2 feet 10 inches high. Platform tennis courts are constructed on a wooden platform.

n *racquetball* Same as for *handball* (4-wall).

o *racquets* A rectangular area 60 feet long and 30 feet wide enclosed by 4 walls. The front wall and the side walls are 30 feet high; the back wall is 15 feet high. On the front wall 27 inches above the floor is a wooden board above which the ball must hit to be in play. Across the front wall at a height of 9 feet 7½ inches is a *service line* or *cut line.* Thirty-five feet 10 inches back of the front wall and parallel to it is a *short line* extending across the court. A *fault line* extends from the middle of the short line to the middle of the back wall dividing the rear portion of the court into 2 service courts. At the points where the short line meets the 2 side walls are *service boxes* 5 feet 3 inches square extending into the service courts.

p *roque* A rectangular area with cutoff corners that is 60 feet long and 30 feet wide and that has a stake at each end and 10 wire arches arranged with 2 in front of each stake, one near each corner of the court, and 2 set crosswise in the center of the court. The court surface is hard-packed clay and it is bounded all around with a low wall off which the balls may be banked during play.

q *shuffleboard* A rectangular area 52 feet long and 6 feet wide that has a triangular scoring area at each end. The scoring areas are 10½ feet long and are 6½ feet from the baselines. There are 2 *dead lines* 12 feet apart across the middle of the court 20 feet from each end. Courts are marked out on the decks of ships, floors, and asphalt or concrete areas.

r *squash racquets* (1) *American singles* A rectangular area 32 feet long and 18½ feet wide enclosed on 3 sides by a 16-foot-high wall and by a 6½-foot wall at the back. Across the front wall 6½ feet above the floor is a *service line;* across the bottom of the front wall at a height of 17 inches is a metal strip known as the *telltale.* On the floor parallel to the back wall and 10 feet from it is the *service court line;* a line extending from the middle of the service court line to the middle of the back wall divides the rear portion of the court into 2 service courts. At the points where the service court line meets the side walls are 2 service boxes — arcs with a 4½-foot radius drawn in the service courts. (2) *British singles* A rectangular area 32 feet long and 21 feet wide enclosed by 4 walls. The front wall is 15 feet high and the back wall 7 feet high. The top edges of the 2 side walls extend in a diagonal line from the top of the front wall to the top of the back wall. The *telltale* runs along the base of the front wall extending up to a height of 19 inches. Six feet above and parallel to the floor on the front wall is a *service line.* Across the floor 14 feet from the back wall is the *short line;* from the middle of this line to the middle of the back wall runs a *half court line* dividing the rear portion of the court into 2 *service courts.* At the points where the short line meets the side walls are 2 *service boxes* 5 feet 3 inches square extending into the service courts. (3) *doubles* A rectangular area 45 feet long and 25 feet wide enclosed on 3 sides by a 20-foot-high wall and in the back by a 7-foot wall. The court is marked like an American singles court but with the *service line* on the front wall 8 feet 2 inches high and the *service court line* 15 feet from the back wall.

s *squash tennis* Same as for American squash racquets except that the back wall is only 5 feet high.

t *team handball* A rectangular area 38–44 meters (126–147 feet) long and 18–22 meters (60–73 feet) wide that has a goal 3 meters (9 feet 10¼ inches) wide and 2 meters (6 feet 6¾ inches) high on each goal line and that is divided by a center line. In front of each goal is a semicircle that extends 6 meters from the goalposts to mark the goal area within which only the goalkeeper is allowed. Beyond this area is another semicircle outside of which a free throw must be taken. Directly in front of each goal and 7 meters out is a penalty mark.

u *tennis* A rectangular area 78 feet long and 36 feet wide with a net 3 feet high dividing the court into 2 equal areas. Parallel to and 4½ feet inside the sidelines is a *service sideline* on each side which marks the boundary of the service courts and serves as the sideline for singles play. Twenty-one feet on each side of and parallel to the net is a *service line;* a line connecting the middle of the 2 service lines marks 2 service courts on each side of the net. Courts are usually marked off on grass, clay, asphalt, or synthetic surfaces outdoors and usually on synthetic surfaces indoors.

v *volleyball* A rectangular area 60 feet long and 30 feet wide that is divided across the middle by a net 8 feet high (7 feet 4½ inches for women's play). Directly under the net runs a center line. Ten feet from and parallel to the net on each side is an *attacking line.* Courts are usually laid out on beaches, lawns, or gymnasium floors.
2 The part of a court on either side of the net.
3 A service court.
4 *table tennis* The area surrounding a table and extending for approximately 12 feet at each end and 6 feet at each side of the table. In major competition, the court is usually marked by 2½-foot barriers. (also called *arena*)

courtesy runner *baseball* A player who is permitted sometimes in informal competition and in special circumstances in college play to run whenever a teammate (as the pitcher) gets on base without requiring that the substituted player be removed from the game.

court game A game that is played on a court and especially one in which a ball or shuttlecock is alternately hit over a net (as in badminton, tennis, and volleyball) or toward a front wall (as in handball, jai alai, and squash racquets).

court hinder see HINDER

court player *team handball* A player other than the goalkeeper who is on the court at a given moment.

courtside The area at the edge of a court (as for tennis or basketball). ⟨had his pro at *courtside* to give tactical suggestions — *World Tennis*⟩ ⟨*courtside* television cameras⟩

court tennis A game which resembles tennis and from which tennis developed that is played on a rectangular court approximately 110 feet long and 40 feet wide divided by a net and enclosed by 4 walls off which the ball may be played. For the most part, court tennis is played and scored like tennis except that all serving is done from one side of the net and all serves must be made off the penthouse. There are 2 other distinctive features of court tennis: (1) a rally may be won immediately by hitting the ball into one of several openings in the walls known as the *dedans,* the *grille,* and the *winning gallery,* and (2) a point is not lost immediately if the ball bounces twice on the floor. It is called a *chase* and must be replayed, after the players change courts, before the point is decided. A game consists of 4 points, as in tennis; a set is won when one side wins 6 games and a match is won by the first side to win 2 of 3 or 3 of 5 sets. (also called *real tennis, royal tennis*) — see also CHASE, GALLERY, PENTHOUSE

cousin *baseball* An opponent who is regularly or easily defeated. This may be a team that a pitcher regularly beats or a pitcher who is easy for a batter to hit. One team's cousin, however, is not necessarily easily or regularly defeated by other opponents.

¹cover 1 a To play defense in an assigned position or where the play dictates. ⟨supposed to talk to each other and decide who will *cover* deep on the option — Ray Nitschke⟩ **b** *baseball* To move into or be in position to receive a throw and make a play at a base. ⟨fielded the ball and tossed to the pitcher who was *covering* first base⟩ **c** To move about a court to be in position to return an opponent's shots (as in squash or handball).
2 To guard an opponent. ⟨forced to throw to his backs because his wide receivers and tight end were *covered* — St. Louis Post-Dispatch⟩
3 *fencing* To protect a part of the body or a line of engagement by the position of the sword.
4 *yacht racing* To duplicate the tacking movements of a following boat in order to blanket that boat and prevent it from passing.

²cover 1 *hunting* Vegetation that affords concealment for game or birds.

2 *skiing* A surface of snow.

coverage Defensive responsibility; the manner in which a defense or defender covers a player, an area, or a play. ⟨going over what the other people's defensive backs have been doing on their *coverage* — Vince Lombardi⟩

cover drive *cricket* A drive to the off side in the general direction of the cover point position.

covered *fencing* Having the blade so positioned that a direct thrust by the opponent would be deflected without the fencer's having to move.

cover point **1** *cricket* A player position on the off side somewhat between point and mid-off but usually quite distant from the batsman. — see illustration at CRICKET

2 *lacrosse* A member of the close defense who normally lines up in front and to the side of the crease and within the goal area on a face-off.

covert A thicket affording cover for game.

cover up *of a boxer* To assume a defensive stance by protecting the head and body as much as possible with the arms.

cowboy **1** A variation of pocket billiards played with a cue ball and 3 object balls numbered one, 3, and 5 in which players score points by making caroms off 2 or all 3 of the object balls and by pocketing the object balls. A 2-ball carom is worth one point; a 3-ball carom, 2 points. The pocketed object balls score their number. A winning score is 101 points. The first 90 points may be scored by caroms and pocketed balls, the next 10 points by caroms only, and the final point only by caroming the cue ball off the one ball and into a called pocket.

2 Someone who competes in rodeo events.

cradle

crab ride

cox *rowing* To serve as coxswain for a crew.

coxswain or **cox** *rowing* A usually smaller and lighter member of a crew who does not row but who sits in the stern facing forward, steers the shell, and directs the strategy of the race especially by setting the beat.

C.Q.R. A trademark for a style of anchor. — see illustration at ANCHOR

crab block see BODY BLOCK

crab ride *wrestling* A hold in which a wrestler who is behind and facing in the same direction as his opponent has his arms around his opponent's waist or has an arm lock on his opponent and has his toes hooked under his opponent's knees.

crack *mountain climbing* A narrow fissure in a rock face that is usually only wide enough for one or 2 fingers or occasionally an arm or leg to be inserted for a jam or hold. — compare CHIMNEY

crackback *football* An illegal blind-side block on a linebacker or defensive back by a pass receiver who starts downfield and then cuts back toward the middle of the line.

crack back *football* To make a crackback block.

¹cradle **1** *trampolining* A stunt performed on the trampoline which consists of a half forward somersault from a back drop position with a half twist so that the performer winds up again on his back.

2 *lacrosse* The act or technique of cradling the ball.

3 *wrestling* A hold in which a wrestler holds the opponent in a doubled-up position by circling the opponent's head and one leg with his arms and locking his hands in front of the opponent's body.

crawl stroke with flutter kick

²cradle *lacrosse* To keep the ball in the pocket of the crosse by rocking the crosse back and forth.

cradler A lacrosse player who is skilled at cradling the ball.

crampit or **crampet** *curling* A sheet of iron formerly placed behind the house for a curler to stand on when sliding his stone. Today a hack, or foothold cut in the ice, is used instead.

¹crampon *mountain climbing* A steel framework that fits to the bottom of a boot and that has usually 10 pointed spikes projecting downward to allow a climber to move up slopes of hard snow or ice without having to cut steps. (also called *climbing iron*)

²crampon *mountain climbing* To climb with the aid of crampons.

crampon on a climbing boot

crash box *auto racing* An unsynchronized transmission.

crawl or **crawl stroke** *swimming* A stroke executed in a prone position that combines a usually 6-beat flutter kick with alternate arm pulls in which each arm recovers out of the water and reenters the water ahead of the body. This is the fastest stroke and the most popular one for recreational swimming and freestyle competition. In competition the swimmer's head remains in the water, and breaths are taken with the head rolled to one side so that the mouth is just out of the water.

crawling *football* An attempt by the ballcarrier to advance the ball by crawling or wriggling along the ground after he has been tackled that results in a 5-yard penalty. College rules prohibit moving forward with the ball after any part of the body other than the feet or hands has touched the ground.

crawl stroke see CRAWL

cream To hit a ball hard.

creance *falconry* A light line used as a leash on a hawk especially during training.

crease 1 *cricket* see GROUND
2 *squash racquets* The intersection of the wall and the floor of the court.
3 Short for *bowling crease, goal crease, popping crease, return crease.*

crease attackman or **creaseman** *lacrosse* An attackman who normally plays in front of the goal crease.

crease defenseman *lacrosse* A defenseman who plays in front of the goal and who guards the opposing crease attackman.

creaseman 1 *box lacrosse* A winger who plays to one side of the opponent's goal near the goal crease.
2 see CREASE ATTACKMAN

creel *fishing* A bag or basket that usually hangs on a shoulder strap and that may be worn by a wading fisherman to hold fish which have been caught.

¹creep *of an arrow* To move forward just before being released and as a result fall short of the mark.

²creep *archery* The slight forward movement of an arrow just prior to its being released.

creeper 1 *bowling* A slow rolling ball.
   2 *cricket* A bowled ball that stays low after pitching.
   3 *skiing* see CLIMBER

creeping *archery* The moving of a drawn arrow forward of the anchor point just before release. This is a fault in the archer's form, for it adversely affects the accuracy of the shot.

crest or **cresting** *archery* A series of colored bands painted around the shaft of an arrow just below the fletching that serves to identify an archer's set of arrows and sometimes aids in locating lost arrows.

crevasse *mountain climbing* A crack in the surface of glacier ice caused usually by a change in the course of movement of the glacier or by a change in the angle of the slope over which the glacier moves. A crevasse may vary in size from a small crack narrow enough to step over to a huge chasm too wide to cross. The crevasse may be open and visible or masked by a light crust of snow, and some crevasses may be spanned by a bridge of snow.

¹crew 1 *rowing* **a** A team of oarsmen and coxswain who man a racing shell. **b** or **crew racing** The sport of rowing. 〈a collegiate standout at both wrestling and *crew*〉
   2 *sailing* Someone who assists the skipper (as by trimming or setting sails and hiking out) while sailing and especially during a race. The term crew is used even when a single individual is referred to.

²crew *sailing* To serve as crew on a boat.

crewman A member of a rowing crew and especially of a men's crew.

crew racing see CREW

crewwoman A member of a women's rowing crew; an oarswoman.

cribbage A pocket billiards game in which players seek to accumulate points or cribbages by pocketing 2 balls in a single inning whose combined total scoring value is 15 points. The 15 ball may be shot at and pocketed only after all other possible cribbages have been scored. The player with the most cribbages is the winner.

cricket A game played between 2 teams of 11 players with a bat and ball on a large field in the center of which are 2 wickets placed 66 feet apart. The area around each wicket, behind a white line (*popping crease*) 4 feet in front of each wicket, serves as a base for the batsman; there is one batsman stationed at each wicket. So long as the batsmen are behind their respective popping creases, they cannot be put out; if either is beyond the crease, he may be put out by a fieldsman who knocks down the wicket while holding the ball. One team is stationed in the field while members of the other team take turns as batsmen. The bowler, a member of the fielding team who is analogous to the pitcher in baseball, runs up behind one wicket and bowls the ball overhand at the opposite wicket usually causing it to bounce (*pitch*) in front of the wicket. If the bowled ball knocks the bails off the wicket or hits the batsman in front of the wicket, the batsman is out. The batsman stationed at that wicket (the *striker*) tries to hit the ball in any direction away from the fielders so that he and the other batsman (the *nonstriker*) can exchange places and score a run. One run is scored each time the batsmen are able to change places. The batsman does not have to run if he thinks he cannot safely do so. The batsman can be put out in a number of ways such as by having a hit ball caught in the air (as in baseball), by allowing a bowled ball to hit the wicket behind him, or by a fielder's breaking the wicket with the ball while he is beyond the popping crease or running between wickets. As one batsman is put out a new batsman takes his place until all 11 players have batted and 10 have been dismissed. That ends a team's innings and then it takes the field while the other team comes to bat. After a bowler has bowled 6 balls at one wicket (an *over*) another player bowls an over in the opposite direction. A bowler may bowl as long as his team captain wants but he may not bowl 2 successive overs. If an even number of runs are scored by the batsmen, the striker will be back at the same wicket to receive the next delivery of the over; if an odd number of runs are scored, the nonstriker is at the wicket to which the bowler is delivering the ball and he becomes the striker for the next delivery. Only runs scored as a direct result of a hit ball are counted for the batsman, though anytime the batsmen can run and change wickets (as because a bowled ball passes the wicketkeeper) runs are added to the team's score.

cricketer

A cricket match often starts in the late morning with a break for lunch and another break later for tea. Major matches usually consist of two innings for each team and are played over 2 or 3 days. Many matches are played for a designated number of overs or with a time limit. The teams normally alternate in taking their innings. In a match of 2 or more innings, the team batting second may be required to begin its second innings right after the end of its first innings (to *follow on*) if the team that batted first has a substantial lead and feels that the second team cannot in 2 innings equal or surpass the first team's score of one innings. If the second team does not surpass the first team's score, the first team wins without having to bat again. If the second team does surpass in 2 innings the first team's score of one innings, the first team can then have its second innings. A team can, at any time it feels it has sufficient runs to beat the other team, declare its innings closed. If the other team is successful in scoring more runs, however, the team which declared will not later be able to finish its innings. — see also BOUNDARY, BOWLING, BYE

cricketer Someone who plays cricket.

cripple *baseball* A pitch thrown when the count is 3–0 or 3–1. Because he does not want the batter to get a base on balls, the pitcher must concentrate on throwing a strike, and quite often he has to throw the kind of pitch the batter likes to hit.

criterium *cycling* A race of a specific number of laps on a closed course laid out over public roads closed to normal traffic.

critical point *ski jumping* The point on the landing hill where the gradient decreases to the point of being unsafe for landing; the point of maximum distance for a safe jump. — compare NORM POINT

croisé *fencing* An attack on the blade or a riposte in which the opponent's blade is moved to a new line on the same side of the body by means of pressure on the blade. The blade is moved with a semicircular movement which is

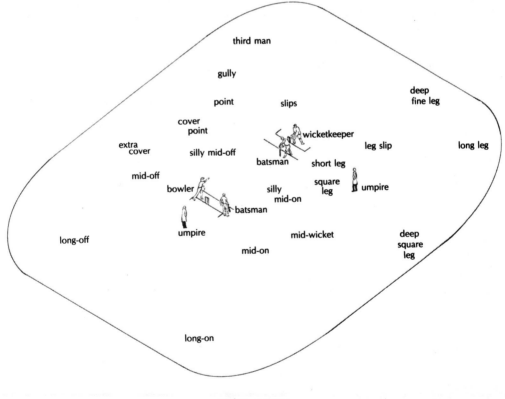

cricket positions

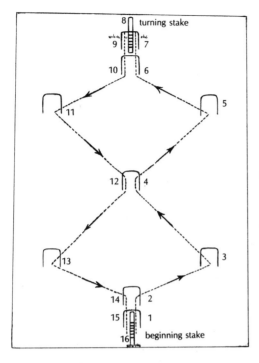

8 turning stake
9 7
10 6
11
5
12 4
13 3
14 2
15 1
16 beginning stake

lawn croquet court

usually followed immediately with a lunge. — compare BIND, ENVELOPMENT

¹croquet 1 A game which is usually played informally on a lawn and in which each player in turn hits his ball with a long-handled mallet and tries to drive it from one stake to another and back through a series of 9 wire wickets in a specified sequence. A player receives bonus strokes when his ball hits a stake, passes through a wicket, or strikes an opponent's ball. The striking of another ball (a *roquet*) gives the player the option of playing 2 strokes after placing his ball a mallet head's length away from the other ball or of driving the other ball away and playing one additional stroke. No more than 2 additional strokes may be accumulated by a player at one time, but a series of successful wickets and roquets could enable a player to complete the entire course in a single turn. The first player or side to complete the course wins. (also called *lawn croquet*)
2 A version of lawn croquet played outdoors especially in organized croquet associations as a singles or doubles game using a short-handled mallet on a hard-surface rectangular court that has 10 wickets laid out as for roque and that is

bounded by a concrete wall which can be used for making bank shots. Points are scored for each wicket made, and games may be decided on the basis of finish as in lawn croquet or on the basis of number of points after a predetermined number of innings. (also called *professional croquet, regulation croquet*)
3 see ASSOCIATION CROQUET
4 The driving away of another's ball in croquet by hitting one's own ball placed in contact with it. The player places his foot on his own ball to keep it in place while driving the other ball away.
²croquet To drive away an opponent's ball by placing one's own ball in contact with the opponent's ball and holding it in place with the foot while striking it with the mallet.
¹cross 1 *boxing* A hook thrown over an opponent's lead.
2 *football* A pass pattern in which receivers run downfield on opposite sides of the formation and then cut to the inside so that their paths cross.
3 *gymnastics* **a** A position in which the breadth axis of the performer is at right angles to the long axis of the apparatus. — compare SIDE **b** A position in which the gymnast supports himself upright between the rings with his arms holding the rings straight out to each side. (also called *crucifix, iron cross, Roman cross*) — compare INVERTED CROSS, LEVER
4 *soccer* A pass made by kicking the ball from one side of the field to the other.
²cross 1 *boxing* To hit an opponent with a cross.
2 *of 2 football pass receivers* To run downfield

cross

from opposite sides of the formation and cut toward the inside so that the paths cross.

3 *soccer* To pass a ball to the opposite side of the field.

crossbar **1** A horizontal bar that connects the goalposts of various goals and marks the upper limit of some and the lower limit of others. — see also GOAL

2 A light bar (as of metal or wood) approximately 12 to 14 feet long and one inch thick that rests on small supports or pins extending from the back of 2 upright standards and that has to be cleared by high jumpers and pole vaulters in order to advance in their respective events. Crossbars typically have a triangular or circular cross section; circular bars have squared ends so that they will rest more securely on the supports of the uprights.

3 The traverse member of a hurdle.

cross block *football* To block a defensive lineman from the side rather than head-on (as when blocking assignments have been switched).

cross-body block see BODY BLOCK

cross-body ride *wrestling* A hold in which a wrestler is usually to the rear of his opponent and has a scissors or grapevine on one leg and a lock on the opposite arm.

crossbody ride

crossbow *archery* A weapon that consists of a short bow mounted crosswise near the front of a stock which resembles a rifle stock. The bow is drawn by hand, and the string is held back by a device attached to a trigger. When the trigger is released, the string carries a short arrow called a *bolt* down a channel or barrel on the stock of the weapon.

crossbowman An archer who uses a crossbow.

cross bow rudder *canoeing* A maneuver in

which the paddler in the bow inserts his paddle alongside the bow on the side opposite the paddling side without changing his grip so that the paddle can act as a rudder to steer the canoe around obstacles. — compare BOW RUDDER

cross buck *football* An offensive play in which 2 running backs charge diagonally into the line of scrimmage at opposite angles so that their paths cross. The quarterback fakes a handoff to one and gives the ball to the other.

cross buttocks see HIPLOCK

¹cross-check **1** *ice hockey* To hit an opponent illegally with the stick held in both hands in front of the body and with no part of the stick on the ice.

2 *lacrosse* To check an opponent with the part of the stick between the butt and the throat.

²cross-check An instance of cross-checking.

cross checking The act of cross-checking an opponent which results in a penalty.

crosscorner shot *squash racquets* A shot played into the diagonally opposite front corner so as to return to the same side of the court.

cross-country **1** Distance running over variable terrain (as hills, wooded areas, and roads) rather than around an oval track. The courses generally range from 2 to 6 miles in length depending on the level of competition. Cross-country is essentially a team sport. A team member's order of finish determines his contribution to the team score (one point for first place, 2 points for second, etc.), and the team with the lowest total score is the winner. The cross-country event in the Modern Pentathlon covers a course 4 kilometers (2.48 miles) long with a total climb of 60 to 100 meters (65 to 109 yards). Competitiors run the course individually at intervals, and they are scored on the basis of how many seconds slower or faster than the arbitrary standard time of 14 minutes 15 seconds they finish.

2 a Ski racing across the countryside over courses up to 50 kilometers (31 miles) in length usually requiring equal amounts of uphill, downhill, and level skiing. The skis are narrow and lightweight. The boots are lightweight and low cut and are attached to the ski only at the toe. **b** see SKI TOURING

3 An endurance event in equestrian competition in which each competitor at a designated interval rides his horse over a 5-to-8-kilometer (3-to-5-mile) course laid out over the countryside with obstacles to be jumped at approximately every 250 meters. Each competitor is judged on the time taken to traverse the course and may receive bonus points for being under the time limit and penalty points for exceeding the time limit or for missing or failing to jump an obstacle.

¹crosscourt To or toward the opposite side of the court (as in basketball) or to the diagonally opposite court (as in tennis). ⟨*crosscourt* pass⟩ ⟨a *crosscourt* backhand⟩

²crosscourt To hit a shot crosscourt; to make a crosscourt shot.

crosscourt shot *squash racquets* A shot hit to the front wall so as to land in the other side of the court.

crosse see STICK (*lacrosse*)

crosse-check *lacrosse* To hit the stick of an opposing player who has possession of the ball or one who is attempting to gain possession of the ball with one's own stick in order to knock the ball loose or to prevent the opponent from gaining possession of the ball. It is legal to crosse-check the opponent only if he is within 5 yards of the ball.

crosse check *lacrosse* The act or an instance of crosse-checking. (also called *stick check*)

cross face *wrestling* A hold in which a wrestler positioned to the side of or behind his opponent places his forearm across his opponent's face and with the same hand grasps the opponent's far arm just above the elbow.

¹crossfire *baseball* A sidearm pitch that comes across the plate at an angle.

²crossfire *of a pacer* To strike a forefoot with the diagonally opposite hind foot while racing.

cross-handed With the hands crossed or held in the reverse of the normal manner. ⟨bats *cross-handed* but can still hit the ball hard⟩

cross handle *curling* The position of the stone at rest with the handle parallel to the tee line.

cross-kick *rugby* A kick which sends the ball to the other side of the field where a teammate will have fewer defenders to dodge.

crossover **1** or **crossover step** A step in which one leg is crossed over the other especially when one is moving sideways or quickly changing direction. — compare SHUFFLE

2 *bowling* see BROOKLYN

3 *skating* A technique for gaining thrust when skating an edge that consists of crossing the free foot in front of the skating foot, placing it down to the inside of the curve and shifting the weight to it, and as the other foot is moved back around into skating position again, giving a thrust so as to glide on the original skating foot.

4 *tennis* see CHANGE-OVER

5 *track and field* A style of approach in throwing the javelin in which at a predetermined point near the end of the runway the thrower brings the javelin back to a throwing position and turns his body toward the javelin as he steps with his right foot (if a right-handed thrower), brings his left foot slightly in front of his right, crosses over the left foot with the right foot, and then strides forward with the left as he throws the javelin. (also called *Finnish Style, Finnish crossover, front crossover, front cross-step*) — compare HOP-STEP

6 *wrestling* A takedown maneuver in which a wrestler standing behind his opponent with his arms locked around his opponent's waist crosses one leg over the other, drops to the opposite knee, and pulls his opponent backward to the mat over his outstretched leg.

cross pilot *shuffleboard* A pilot shot placed near the tip of the scoring area on the opponent's side. — compare TAMPA PILOT

crossover step

cross roll *skating* A roll made by crossing the free foot over the skating foot and placing it to the inside of the roll being made.

cross set see SET (*volleyball*)

cross-step see CROSSOVER (*track and field*)

cross stroke *skating* The thrust used in a crossover or cross roll.

cross support *gymnastics* Support of the body in a cross position by the hands on the parallel bars.

crotch **1** The intersection of 2 playing surfaces (as 2 walls or one wall and the floor) on a court (as for handball or racquetball).
2 *billiards* **a** A 4½-inch square at each corner of a carom billiards table which restricts the number of caroms which may be made when both balls are within the area. **b** A situation in straight rail billiards in which both object balls lie within the same crotch and only 3 consecutive points may be scored before one of the balls must be driven out.
3 *sailing* A brace with a fork at the top to support the boom when the boat is not being sailed.

crotch ball or **crotch shot** A shot (as in handball or paddleball) that hits a crotch.

crotched *of a billiard ball* Lying within a crotch.

crotch hold *wrestling* A hold in which the wrestler encircles his opponent's upper thigh with his hand and forearm or hooks his arm through his opponent's crotch.

crotch shot see CROTCH BALL

crouch start *track and field* A position normally assumed at the start of a dash, hurdles race, or short relay race in which the runner crouches with one foot placed under his body and the

crouch start from starting blocks

other extended to the rear and places both hands on the track immediately behind the starting line. The distance between the front and rear feet determines the type of crouch start. In the *bunch start* the toes of the rear foot are about 12 inches behind the toes of the front foot; in the *medium start* the knee of the rear leg is next to the toes of the front foot; in the *elongated start* the knee of the rear leg is next to the heel of the front foot. Starting blocks are usually used with a crouch start.

croup *gymnastics* The end of a vaulting horse nearest the vaulter as he approaches; the end of a pommel horse to the right of the gymnast as he approaches the apparatus. — compare NECK, SADDLE

crowd the plate *of a baseball batter* To stand as close to home plate as possible while within the limits of the batter's box.

crown The title representing a championship in a sport. ⟨won the batting *crown*⟩

crown green bowls A game essentially identical to lawn bowling except that it is played between 2 players on a large green approximately 40 yards square that is higher in the center than at the sides. Normally several different games will be in progress at one time on a single green.

crucifix **1** *gymnastics* see CROSS
2 *wrestling* see GUILLOTINE

cruise valve *ballooning* A valve on the burners that supplies heat to the balloon at a steady rate for cruising. — compare BLAST VALVE

cuadrilla *bullfighting* A team assisting a matador in a ring and usually consisting of 3 banderillas and 2 or 3 picadors.

Cuban fork ball *baseball* A pitch suspected of being a spitball. ⟨I use a *Cuban fork ball*. I learned to use it while I was swimming in the Mediterranean Sea — John Wyatt⟩

cubes *motor sports* Cubic inches of engine displacement.

cub hunting *fox hunting* Hunting for fox cubs usually conducted in the late summer or early autumn to train young hounds to hunt and to teach fox cubs to run from the hounds.

cuddy *boating* A small decked shelter usually smaller than a cabin.

cue **1** or **cue stick** *billiards* A long tapering stick usually made of wood with a leather tip that is used to strike the cue ball. Cues measure up to 57 inches in length and usually weigh between 14 and 22 ounces. The leather tip enables the player to impart spin to the ball.
2 *shuffleboard* A long stick with a concave or

forked head that is used to shove the disks. Cues come in varying lengths up to 6 feet 3 inches.

cue ball *billiards* The usually white or ivory-colored ball that is stroked with the cue and driven into the object ball.

cue stick see CUE (*billiards*)

Cunningham *sailing* A grommet in the mainsail about 12 inches above the tack in certain classes of small boats that is fitted with a line which acts like a downhaul to flatten the sail.

cup 1 A plastic or metal insert for some athletic supporters to provide extra protection for the wearer.

2 *curling* The concave area on each side of the stone.

3 *fishing* The cup-shaped part of a spinning reel which holds the bail and which revolves around the spoon as the handle is turned.

4 *golf* The hole in the putting green. ⟨tapped the ball into the *cup*⟩

cup of coffee *baseball* A brief stay in the major leagues by a minor-league player usually near the end of the regular season.

cuppy Marked by small depressions. ⟨a *cuppy* racetrack⟩ ⟨his ball was in a *cuppy* lie⟩

curb *track and field* The usually raised inside border of a track.

curb bit see BIT

curb chain A chain attached to the upper end of a curb bit and running under a horse's jaw that is used to exert pressure on the horse's lower jaw when the reins are pulled. — see also BIT

¹curl 1 or **curl-in** *football* A pass pattern in which a receiver runs downfield and then cuts back toward the line of scrimmage to catch the ball. The curl is often used when a team is willing to forego a long gain in order to prevent an interception.

2 *surfing* A hollow arch of water formed where the crest of a breaking wave spills forward. (also called *tube, tunnel*)

3 *weight lifting* An exercise in which a weight held at thigh level is raised to chest or shoulder level and then lowered without moving the shoulders or upper arms.

²curl 1 To engage in curling; to slide a curling stone with slight rotation.

2 *football* To run a curl pattern.

curler Someone who plays curling.

curl-in see CURL (*football*)

curling A game that resembles shuffleboard or lawn bowling played on a 138-foot-long and 14-foot-wide strip of ice (a *rink*) between 2 teams of 4 players with each in turn sliding 2 curling stones down the ice toward a series of concentric circles at the other end of the rink. A team scores one point for each stone it places nearer the center of the rings than its opponent. After all players on both teams have delivered their stones to one end of the rink (an *end*) the stones are scored and then delivered to the opposite end. Curling involves considerable strategy in the placing of a team's stones in or around the tee and in the displacing of an opponent's stones. A unique aspect of curling is sweeping. Team members customarily sweep the ice ahead of a moving stone to remove foreign objects that might slow up or deflect the stone or because they believe the sweeping has an effect on increasing the length of the delivery. Though a match may be played to a stipulated number of points, most are played for a designated number of ends (as 14, 17, or 21). — see also HACK, HOUSE

curling stone A large polished circular stone usu-

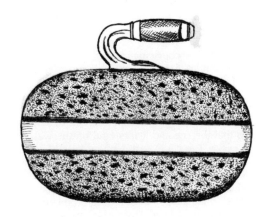

curling stone

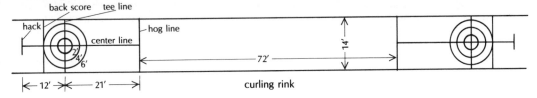

curling rink

ally of hone or granite about 12 inches in diameter that weighs 42–44 pounds, has a handle at the top, and is delivered along the ice in curling. The stone is rough on one side and smooth on the other side and the handle is removable so that either side may be used. Each side of the stone has a concave area near the center so that only a small portion of the stone's surface area actually touches the ice.

Curtis Cup International golf competition held every 2 years between 6-woman amateur teams from the United States and Great Britain. The competition has been held since 1932 and is named for Harriot and Margaret Curtis, former American champion amateur golfers.

¹curve 1 or **curveball** *baseball* A pitch thrown with sufficient downward or sideward rotation to make it veer from the trajectory it might have been expected to follow. When thrown with the right hand, the ball will tend to break toward the left and when thrown with the left hand, to the right. When thrown with a straight overhand motion, the ball will tend to break down rather than to either side since the rotation imparted will be mostly downward. — compare FASTBALL, SCREWBALL, SLIDER

2 *bowling* A bowled ball that rolls to the opposite side of the alley in a continuous sweeping movement; one that curves to the left when bowled by the right hand. — compare HOOK

3 *skating* see EDGE

²curve 1 *of a propelled object* To deviate from a straight-line course by moving gradually to one side without a sharp change of direction.

2 To cause a propelled object to curve.

3 *baseball* To throw a curve to a batter.

curveball see CURVE (*baseball*)

curve cast *fishing* A usually side cast of a fly line so that the line and leader land on the water in a curve. The curve cast is often desirable when a fast current would cause excessive drag if the line were cast straight out.

cushion 1 *billiards* A felt-covered rubber pad fitted to the inside rim of a billiard table to keep the balls on the table. The cushion extends in 1½ to 2 inches but is angled back from the top so that balls strike it only at the top. Balls may be caromed off the cushion in all billiards games.

2 Canadian term for the surface of an ice hockey rink.

cusp *skating* The point in a turn (as a three turn or bracket) at which a skater changes from one edge to the other on the same foot.

¹cut 1 A quick change of direction to get free of

a defender or to move at an angle toward a goal or an opening in a defensive formation.

2 a The dropping of a player from a roster; the eliminating of a prospective player after a tryout. **b** The elimination of competitors who fail to qualify after one or 2 rounds in a tournament in which there are more entrants than can be accommodated in the competition; elimination from a tournament of those golfers whose scores after usually 2 rounds of play are over a prescribed limit.

3 A shot (as in tennis) with a great deal of sidespin or backspin.

4 *baseball* A swing at a pitch.

5 *cricket* see LATE CUT, SQUARE CUT

6 *fencing* A hit made with the edge of a saber.

7 *gymnastics* The swinging of one leg under a hand which is supporting the body (as on a pommel horse) by momentarily shifting the weight to the other hand and lifting the hand so that the leg may pass under it.

²cut 1 To make a sudden change of direction (as to avoid a defender) especially by planting one foot and pushing off to one side in a new direction; to move at an angle toward a usually specified area especially to receive a pass from a teammate. ⟨ran downfield, gave a quick fake, and *cut* to the sideline⟩ ⟨*cut* toward the baseline, took a pass, and made a lay-up⟩

2 To eliminate a player from a roster or from a tournament for failure to meet certain standards.

3 a To hit a ball (as in tennis) with a glancing stroke so as to impart spin. **b** *billiards* To drive an object ball at a sharp angle by a very thin hit. **c** *cricket* To hit a bowled ball with a glancing stroke to drive it to the off side beside or behind the wicket.

4 *of a pitch in baseball* To pass over a usually specified corner of home plate. ⟨*cut* the outside corner for a called strike⟩

5 *gymnastics* To swing one leg under a supporting hand by momentarily shifting the weight and lifting the hand.

cutaway *diving* A dive from a position facing the diving board in which the diver springs up and back but rotates forward toward the board; inward dive.

cutback 1 *football* A sharp cut upfield or back toward the middle of the line by a ballcarrier after running laterally behind the line usually made to avoid a defender.

2 *surfing* To turn back toward the breaking part of a wave.

cut back *of a ballcarrier in football* To make a

sharp cut especially in the opposite direction or toward the middle of the line.

cut block *football* A block by which a pass receiver is tripped as he starts downfield. In professional play it is illegal to block a receiver below the waist once he crosses the line of scrimmage.

cut down 1 *baseball* To throw out a base runner especially when he is trying to steal or reach an extra base on a hit. ⟨was *cut down* at the plate⟩ **2** *football* To knock an opponent to the ground.

cut line see SERVICE LINE (*squash racquets*)

cut man *boxing* A second who specializes in stopping the bleeding of cuts.

cut off *baseball* The interception by an infielder of a ball thrown from the outfield toward home plate. On hits out of the infield when there is a possibility of a base runner's scoring, the outfielder will usually throw the ball directly to home plate in an attempt to put out the potential scorer. If the throw is wide or if there appears to be no chance of preventing the run from scoring, the infielder, often at the direction of the catcher, will catch the ball and relay it to the catcher or sometimes try to prevent another base runner from advancing.

cutoff block *football* A block made on a defensive lineman (as a defensive tackle) by the offensive center on a running play, especially when a guard has pulled to lead the play, that usually consists of falling in front of the opponent to trip him.

cutover *fencing* A change in the line of engagement made by passing one's blade over the point of the opponent's blade. (also called *coupé*) — compare DISENGAGE

cutter A single-masted sailboat that resembles a

cutover

sloop but has the mast stepped farther aft and that typically carries 2 foresails.

cutthroat An informal game (as of handball or billiards) in which each of 3 people plays for himself against the other 2.

cut-under *fencing* A change in the line of engagement made by passing one's blade under the point of the opponent's blade.

cycle *baseball* A series of a single, double, triple, and home run hit by one player during one game. — usually used in the phrase *hit for the cycle*

cycling The sport of racing bicycles. The most common forms of cycle racing are road racing over public roads, often without restricting normal traffic, and track racing on specially built usually high banked tracks used only for bicycle races. Track racing falls into 2 major categories: sprint racing and pursuit racing between individuals or teams. The lightweight bicycles used in road racing are essentially the same as the common touring bicycles and are equipped with variable speed gears and brakes. Track bikes commonly have shorter frames than road bicycles, are equipped with a single gear ratio and no brakes, and have straps that hold the cyclist's feet to the pedals. Track bikes are not made with a free-wheeling provision so that the cyclist can pedal forward or backward and at times actually remain practically stationary by slightly moving the pedals forward and backward. — see also CRITERIUM, PURSUIT, ROAD RACE, SPRINT

cyclist Someone who rides a bicycle for recreation or in competition.

cyclo-cross A bicycle race that somewhat resembles a motocross and that usually requires the cyclist to ride over natural terrain and occasionally to carry his bicycle over certain hazards (as through stretches of mud, over fences, or up a set of stairs).

cylinder 1 The turning chambered breech of a revolver.

2 *scuba diving* The aluminum or steel container that holds compressed air for the diver. — see also VALVE, REGULATOR

Cy Young Award An annual award made to the outstanding pitcher in major-league baseball named in honor of Cy Young who had a total of 509 victories in his 22-year career which ended in 1911. Up until 1967 the award was given to only one major-league pitcher but is now given to the outstanding pitcher in both the American and National Leagues.

Czech see MOORE

D

D **1** Defense. ⟨defense has generally been the key to championship teams. The Big *D* usually wins out — John Havlicek⟩
2 *billiards* A semicircle drawn in the balk from the middle of the balkline on an English billiards table. The cue ball is played from the D after a losing hazard.

Daffy *freestyle skiing* A stunt in aerial competition performed at the peak of a jump which consists of separating the legs with one in front and one in back and keeping the legs straight and the skis nearly vertical. If the performer switches the position of the legs in the air having first one forward and then the other, he performs a double Daffy.

daggerboard *sailing* A retractable keel that serves to stabilize a small boat and that is raised and lowered by hand in a fore-and-aft slot. — compare CENTERBOARD

daily double *pari-mutuel betting* A betting pool in which bettors must pick the winners of 2 stipulated races or contests (usually the first and second races) in order to win.

dan **1** The expert level in Oriental arts of self-defense (as judo and karate) that is divided usually into 10 ranks from first degree dan (lowest) to tenth degree dan and that is distinguished by the black belt worn on the costume.
2 Someone who is an expert in an Oriental art of self-defense.

dance skating A form of competitive skating in which a man and woman skate together performing dance movements to music. Competition involves a program of compulsory movements and a freestyle program usually 4 minutes long in which the couple perform the dance movements to music of their choice. In addition to the performance of dance movements rather than jumps and figures, dance skating differs from pairs freestyle competition in that the dance couple do not at any time separate during the course of the program.

Danforth A trademark used for a style of anchor. — see illustration at ANCHOR

dangerous play *soccer* A foul that is charged against a player for making certain plays (as heading the ball when it is below the waist or kicking the ball with a hitch kick) when an opponent is near and that results in an indirect free kick for the opposing team.

dapping *fishing* A method of fly fishing in which the fly is suspended from the end of the rod on a relatively short leader and is repeatedly allowed to touch the water lightly without any part of the line or leader touching the water. — compare SKITTERING

dart A short missile that has a weighted pointed shaft at one end and feathers for stability in flight at the other and that is thrown at a dart board in the game of darts.

dart board A circular board usually of cork or bristle that is divided into 20 scoring sectors that radiate out from a pair of concentric center circles. The center circles are 1¾ inches and ½ inches in diameter with the larger one having a scoring value of 25 points and the smaller inner one worth double that. Each of the scoring sectors is numbered from one to 20 to indicate the point value of each. At a distance of 2⅞ inches out from the center circles is a ⅜-inch-wide treble ring, and around the outside edge of the scoring sectors is a ⅜-inch-wide double ring. A dart in the double ring scores twice the value of that sector and one in the treble ring, 3 times the scoring value of the sector.

darts A singles or doubles game especially popular in the public houses of Great Britain in which each player or side takes turns throwing 3 darts at a dart board from a distance of 8 feet (in the United States) or 9 feet (in Great Britain). After each turn, the scores for the darts thrown, determined by scoring areas on the dart board, are subtracted from the side's beginning score (as 301 or 501 points); the object of the game is to be first to reduce one's score to exactly zero. The scoring is started only by getting a dart in the double ring and it is necessary to finish the game on a double. If the player gets more points than

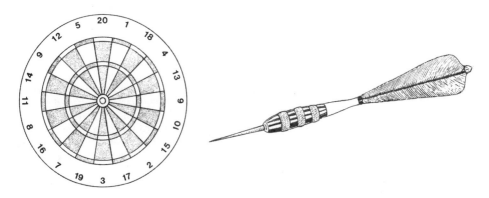

dartboard and representative dart

he needs to reach exactly zero or if he reduces his score to one point, he forfeits that turn and his score reverts to what it was before that turn. On his next turn he again attempts to reach zero on a double. Because of the importance of reducing one's score systematically especially in the later stages of the game, strategy and precise aiming play a major part in the game.

dash **1** *harness racing* A race that is decided in a single trial rather than in heats.

2 *track and field* A race other than a hurdles or relay race during which contestants run at or near full speed throughout. Dashes run indoors are commonly contested at distances of 50, 60, 300, and 440 yards. Outdoor dashes are commonly run at 100, 220, and 440 yards and 100, 200, and 400 meters.

dasher *ice hockey* The ledge at the top of the boards.

dashman *track and field* A runner who competes in dashes.

Davis Cup An international tennis tournament that is played annually between national teams and that includes singles and doubles competition for men. The original format included a challenge round, but a recent change has resulted in competition in which all teams compete from the beginning. Semifinalists are winners in 3 geographic regions: the Eastern Zone (Asia, Australia, New Zealand), the American Zone (North and South America), and the European Zone (2 separate semifinalists from the nations of Europe).

day cruiser A small powerboat that may have a small cabin but is not equipped for sleeping aboard.

daylight *football* An opening in the opposing team's defensive line. ⟨run to *daylight*⟩

day sailer A small pleasure sailboat that is not specifically designed for racing and is not equipped for sleeping aboard.

dead **1** *of a ball* **a** Temporarily out of play and not subject to being hit, kicked, bowled, shot, advanced, or returned in accordance with the rules. A ball may be dead as a result of a foul or infraction of the playing rules by one or more players, as a result of a let, or as a result of having been driven out of bounds. Time is not necessarily suspended during the interval when the ball is dead. In basketball, for example, the clock is stopped on all fouls and violations when the ball is dead; in football, however, the ball is dead after every down but the clock may continue to run. The ball is dead whenever the playing time for a game or a period has expired. Any progress or score made when the ball is dead does not count. **b** Having little or no spin; stopping immediately on landing or on striking another ball. **2** *of a baseball* Having little resilience and not traveling very far when hit; not lively. **3** *of a bowling delivery* Being relatively ineffective in knocking down pins. **4** *of a clay pigeon* Broken or at least having a visible piece broken away by a shot. **5** *of play* Stopped by an official because the ball or puck is unplayable or because of a foul or infraction. ⟨they bang together in front of the net as play is whistled *dead* — Neil Offen, *Sport*⟩

dead-ball line *rugby* Either of the 2 lines parallel to and 25 yards (6–12 yards in Rugby League play) behind the goal lines that mark the extreme limits of the playing field.

dead-heat

dead-heat To finish a race in a dead heat.

dead heat A situation in which 2 or more competitors finish a race exactly even.

dead lift *weight lifting* A lift in which the weight is lifted from the floor to hip level and then lowered by the power of the back or the back and legs. In one version the arms and legs are held straight throughout the lift, while in another version the weight is grasped while the knees are bent and then lifted by straightening first the legs and then the back.

dead line **1** *Canadian football* Either of 2 lines parallel to and 25 yards behind the goal lines that mark the extreme limits of the playing field and the end of the end zones.
2 *shuffleboard* Either of 2 lines that extend across the court 3 feet in front of the scoring areas. A disk which fails to reach the far dead line is removed from play.

deadman *mountain climbing* A thin metal plate approximately 9 inches square that is usually constructed with 2 holes in the center through which a wire sling is fastened and that is used for making a belay in snow. The deadman is driven into the snow at such an angle that any force exerted on a rope attached to the sling tends to pull the deadman deeper into the snow.

dead man's float *swimming* A prone floating position in which the arms are extended forward. (also called *prone float*)

dead mark *bowling* A strike or spare rolled with the last ball of the tenth frame.

dead wood *bowling* Pins that have been knocked down but that remain on the alley. In candlepins, the dead wood remains on the alley and is in play.

death spiral *skating* A maneuver performed by a couple in pairs skating in which the man spins in place while holding the outstretched arm of the woman who spirals around him supported

death spiral

on one skate, gradually increasing the radius of the spiral and lowering herself to the surface so that her body is level and her head is just above the surface.

decathlete *track and field* An athlete who competes in the decathlon.

decathlon *track and field* A 10-event contest in which individuals are awarded points according to their performance in relation to a predetermined standard for each event. The events are held over a 2-day period in the following order: first day — 100 meter dash, long jump, shot put, high jump, and 400 meter dash; second day — 110 meter hurdles, discus throw, pole vault, javelin throw, and 1500 meter run. For the running events, points are deducted from the maximum possible (as 1200) for each fraction of a second the competitor is slower than the arbitrary standard time. In the throwing and jumping events, points are deducted for each centimeter or fraction that the competitor falls short of the standard distance. The competitor with the highest total of points at the end of the competition is the winner. — compare PENTATHLON; MODERN PENTATHLON

deceive *fencing* To move one's blade in such a way as to avoid a parry or to avoid having the blade controlled by the opponent. ⟨*deceive* the parry⟩

deception *fencing* The act of deceiving an opponent.

deciding *of a score* Being the one to determine the outcome of a game; winning. ⟨one-out bloop single with the bases loaded drove in the *deciding* run — Sam Goldaper, *New York Times*⟩

¹decision **1** *boxing* The awarding of a bout to the boxer with the most points or with the most rounds won when there is no knockout or technical knockout.
2 *wrestling* The awarding of a match to the wrestler with the most points when there is no fall.

²decision To defeat a boxing or wrestling opponent by a decision.

deck The horizontal platform within or over the hull of a boat that serves as a floor and a covering for the area below (as a cabin or stowage area). — **on deck** **1** On or onto the deck of a boat. **2** Waiting one's turn to compete (as in track and field or swimming). **3** *of a baseball player* Due to bat next after the present batter.

deck tennis A singles or doubles game played on a 40-by-18-foot court in which players toss a 6-inch ring of rope or rubber over a net approximately 4½ feet high. The game is started by one side serving to the other by tossing the ring over the net. The ring is caught and tossed back and forth until one side fails to make a successful return. Only the serving side scores points, and a game usually consists of 15 points. Deck tennis became popular as a recreation on board ocean liners.

declare **1** *cricket* To forego completion of one's team's innings in order to have a chance to retire the 10 opposing batsmen before the expiration of a time limit. If the team that bats last has not concluded its innings by the end of the allotted playing time, the contest ends in a draw regardless of the difference in the scores. A team with a large number of runs may declare and gamble on being able to put out the opposing 10 batsmen before they surpass the team's total in runs in order to prevent a draw.
2 *horse racing* **a** To confirm that a horse previously entered in a race will actually start. **b** To withdraw a horse previously entered in a race within the allotted time. — compare SCRATCH

declination The difference between magnetic north indicated by a compass and true north on which maps are based. The declination for an area is commonly indicated on topographical maps and is expressed in degrees east or west of true north. By adding the declination to or subtracting it from the compass reading, the reading can be corrected to correspond to a map. (also called *variation*) — see also BEARING

decline board An inclined board that has a strap attached at the higher end and that is used for sit-up exercises. The feet are hooked under the strap for greater efficiency in the exercise.

decompress *scuba diving* To ascend slowly or to pause at certain depths for a specified period of time when ascending to allow gases which have been forced into the blood and body tissues while under pressure to come gradually out of solution and be passed off in respiration.

decompression *scuba diving* **1** The decrease of water pressure experienced by a diver when he ascends.
2 The process of decompressing.

decompression diving *scuba diving* Diving at such depths and for such lengths of time as to require planned decompression.

decompression sickness see BENDS

decompression stop *scuba diving* A brief stop at a specified depth made when ascending from a deep or lengthy dive in order to allow the body to become desaturated by allowing air forced into the system under pressure gradually to come out of solution. On dives requiring extended decompression stops, extra compressed air tanks are often placed beforehand at appropriate depths to provide air required at these stops.

decompression tables A group of tables (as those prepared by the U.S. Navy) that indicate what dives require decompression and specify how much time must be spent at each decompression stop. In addition there are charts that provide information on surface desaturation intervals and on how to compute decompression requirements for repetitive dives.

decoy *hunting* A wood, plastic, or rubber imitation of a bird used to attract live birds (as waterfowl) to the area where they may be shot by hunters hiding in a blind.

decoy shooting *hunting* A method of hunting in which one sets out decoys and then waits in a blind for birds to be attracted to the area by the presence of the decoys.

dedans *court tennis* An opening in the end wall on the service side of the court under the penthouse which is protected by a screen and which is a spectators' gallery. A ball hit into the dedans wins a point for the player hitting it.

deep **1** Away from a center of action or an implied front (as the direction a side normally faces during play): **a** Near the rear limits of a playing area or of a player's normal area of play. ⟨lobbed the ball *deep* to the baseline⟩ ⟨returned the kick from *deep* in his own territory⟩ ⟨the entire infield was playing *deep*⟩ **b** Far to the rear and distant from an offensive or defensive formation. ⟨played the safetymen *deep* in an obvious passing situation⟩
2 Relatively close to an opponent's goal. ⟨a defenseman who likes to carry the puck in *deep*⟩ ⟨had to worry about defending against both short and *deep* passes⟩
3 Near the midpoint of a turn on a racecourse. ⟨drove his car *deeper* into the corner before braking⟩
4 *fencing* Close to the target. ⟨feints should be made *deep*⟩
5 **a** *of a team* Having good players or performers all the way down the roster and not having to rely on only a few stars; having one or more good substitutes for any position. **b** *of a pitching staff* Having a number of good pitchers and especially relief pitchers.

deer rifle *hunting* A large-bore rifle (as a .30–30, .30–06, or .308) commonly used for hunting big game.

¹default The failure of an individual or side to compete in a contest which results in an automatic win credited to the opponent.

²default To lose a contest because one is not able or not permitted to begin or to continue (as because of illness, tardiness, or improper conduct).

¹defeat The loss of a contest.

²defeat To win against an opponent; beat.

defend **1** To attempt to prevent an opponent from scoring at a particular goal. ⟨will *defend* the south goal⟩

2 To play defense or be on defense. ⟨*defend* against the long pass⟩

3 To compete as current titleholder in a competition to retain a title. ⟨decided not to *defend* his title this year⟩

defender A player who plays defense or is assigned a defensive position.

defending zone see DEFENSIVE ZONE

¹defense **1** The act, action, or state of attempting to protect oneself or one's side from an opponent's attack or of attempting to disrupt the opponent's offense, to prevent the opponent from scoring, and usually to gain possession of the ball or puck in order to mount one's own offense. ⟨since [they] admittedly won't have as much power as in the past, they'll have to do it with pitching, speed, and *defense* — Jack Herman, *Sporting News*⟩ ⟨on *defense* [he] is just as deceptive. He receives service far behind the baseline and is actually retreating (rather than advancing) as he hits the ball — Curry Kirkpatrick, *Sports Illustrated*⟩

2 The means or method of defending against offensive play; a defensive alignment; a style or pattern of play incorporating basic principles of defense. ⟨moved a safetyman up to the line of scrimmage, in effect adding a fourth linebacker to create a *defense* that sometimes showed as a 6–2–3 alignment, sometimes as a 4–3–4 — William N. Wallace, *New York Times*⟩ ⟨learning to read *defenses*⟩

3 A defensive team or members of a team who customarily play defense. ⟨an alert *defense* took over, turning four of the Steelers' miscues into scores — Associated Press⟩

4 Defensive play or ability. ⟨ability to disrupt an entire rival team's offense with his shot-blocking and tough *defense* — Phil Elderkin, *Sporting News*⟩

5 The act or an instance of competing as a champion against a challenger. ⟨roadwork, the early training for his third title *defense* — Robert Lipsyte, *New York Times*⟩

6 *cricket* The act or state of being the batsman and attempting to defend the wicket to prevent the opposing bowler from knocking it down with a bowled ball. — compare OFFENSE

²defense To take specific defensive action against an opposing team or player. ⟨forces the defense to *defense* us in depth — Ara Parseghian⟩

defense kick see GOAL KICK

defenseman A player (as in ice hockey or lacrosse) other than the goalkeeper assigned to a defensive zone or position.

defensive **1** Engaged in or employed in attempting to prevent an opponent from scoring. ⟨*defensive* team⟩ ⟨*defensive* plays⟩ ⟨a fine *defensive* tackle⟩ ⟨*defensive* strategy⟩

2 Relating to the playing of defense. ⟨a *defensive* slump⟩ ⟨had *defensive* problems behind the plate last season — *Sporting News*⟩

3 Being the part of the playing area in which a team must play defense. ⟨the *defensive* half of the field⟩

defensive back *football* **1** One of the usually 4 members of the defensive team including the cornerbacks and the safeties who normally line up behind the linebackers and whose primary duties are to defend against passes and breakaway runs. (also called *back*)

2 The position played by a defensive back.

defensive board *basketball* The backboard of the goal a team is defending.

defensively **1** In respect to defense or defensive play. ⟨has improved *defensively* and is steady under pressure — *Sports Illustrated*⟩

2 In a defensive capacity. ⟨used *defensively* in two games — *Sporting News*⟩

defensive rebound *basketball* A rebound taken by a defensive player off the backboard of the goal his team is defending.

defensive zone **1** *box lacrosse* The area in which the goal a team is defending is located and which extends from the end of the box to the center zone. One team's defensive zone is the other team's attacking zone.

2 or **defending zone** *ice hockey* The area in which the goal a team is defending is located and which extends from the end of the rink to the nearest blue line. One team's defensive zone is the other team's attacking zone. — see also NEUTRAL ZONE

deflation port *ballooning* A large valve at the top of a hot-air balloon that can be opened to allow the air to excape so that the balloon can be quickly deflated (as after landing).

deflection *ice hockey* A shot or pass that strikes

something (as a skate or stick) and rebounds in the direction of the net.

degree of difficulty *diving* A factor based on the relative difficulty of each competitive dive by which a diver's preliminary scores are multiplied to determine his final score. The factor may range from 1.2 to 3.0 depending on the position in which the dive is performed and the height from which the dive begins.

dejada *jai alai* A shot that is lobbed to the front wall so that it hits just above the foul line and drops to the floor.

¹deke To fake an opponent out of position in ice hockey or box lacrosse.

²deke A fake in ice hockey or box lacrosse

¹delay *football* An offensive play in which the ballcarrier or receiver delays momentarily as if to block before receiving a handoff or running a prescribed pattern.

²delay *of a football player* To hesitate or pause momentarily before carrying out an assignment (as making a block or running a pass pattern).

delayed offside *ice hockey* A situation in which the calling of an offside in the attacking zone is deferred because a defending player intercepts the puck when it is passed into the zone and immediately after it crosses the blue line. If the defending player carries or passes the puck out of the zone the offside is ignored, but if he loses possession of the puck before it crosses the blue line the offside is called.

delayed penalty *ice hockey* 1 A penalty that is deferred when its immediate assessment would result in there being fewer than 4 men on the ice for the penalized team because 2 or more players are already in the penalty box. Since a team must play with at least 4 men on the ice, the penalized player is sent to the penalty box immediately but his place is taken on the ice by a substitute. The timing of the offending player's penalty does not begin until the end of the first of the prior penalties which affected the numerical strength of the team, at which time the substitute leaves the ice.
2 A penalty which is called on the defending team and which is not imposed until the attacking team loses possession of the puck or a goal is scored. A minor penalty is not enforced if a goal is scored on the play.

delayed steal *baseball* A steal that is not made at the moment the pitcher delivers the ball but is delayed until the catcher returns the ball to the pitcher or until a play is made for another base runner (as on a double steal).

delayed whistle *ice hockey* 1 A delay by the official in blowing the whistle to signal offside on a delayed offside. (also called *slow whistle*)
2 A delay by an official in blowing the whistle to stop play when a foul has been committed by a defending player until the attacking team has shot the puck or has lost possession of the puck so as to avoid penalizing the fouled team when a goal appears likely. A minor penalty will not be enforced if a goal is scored on the play.

delay of game or **delay of the game** *football* An infraction in which a team delays the progress of a game (as by failing to put the ball in play within a specified time or by crawling or deliberately attempting to advance the ball after it is dead) and which results in a 5-yard penalty.

deliberate Characterized by the use of set plays and usually by slow and careful play. ⟨*deliberate* offense⟩

deliver To send something aimed or guided to an intended target or destination. ⟨*delivered* a right to the jaw⟩ ⟨*delivered* a fastball⟩ ⟨the bowler should keep his shoulders straight as the ball is *delivered*⟩

delivery 1 The act, action, or manner of throwing, pitching, serving, or bowling. ⟨developing a smooth *delivery*⟩
2 A thrown, pitched, or bowled ball.

delta wing kite see ROGALLO WING

demand regulator see REGULATOR

demolition derby A contest in which skilled drivers ram old cars into each other until only one car remains operable.

de-peg *mountain climbing* To remove a piton from a crack.

depth Good players or performers throughout the roster who contribute to the team effort. ⟨relied on team *depth* to notch their fourth championship — *NCAA News*⟩

depth gauge *scuba diving* A gauge, usually designed to be worn on the wrist, that measures water pressure and indicates it on a dial calibrated in feet.

derby 1 A contest open to all comers or to those in some special category (as a certain age group) with prizes usually awarded to winners. ⟨fishing *derby*⟩
2 A field trial for hunting dogs classified as 2-year-olds.

Derby A 1½-mile stakes race for 3-year-old thoroughbred racehorses held annually at Epsom Downs, Surrey, England, that is one of the English Classics and one of the races of the English Triple Crown. The race was named for the twelfth earl of Derby, who originated the race in 1780 and who was also the originator of the Oaks. The name *Derby* has since been taken as part of the name of other horse races, notably the Kentucky Derby.

dérobement *fencing* A maneuver in which a fencer who has extended his arm in preparation for an attack avoids the opponent's attempt to take the blade or make an attack on the blade by moving his blade out of the way by using only finger manipulation without having to withdraw his arm and give up the right of attack. (also called *evasion*)

derrick lift *weight lifting* A straight-legged dead lift.

descendeur *mountain climbing* A small metal device that attaches to a waist line or harness and around which a rope is wound to provide friction to control the rate of descent in rappelling especially in Alpine climbing.

descending ring *mountain climbing* A small metal ring which is secured at the top of a rock face (as by a sling) and through which the rope runs when the party must descend by rappelling.

Desi Short for *designated hitter.*

designated hitter *baseball* A player designated at the start of the game to bat in place of the pitcher without causing the pitcher to be removed from the game. When a designated hitter is used, the pitcher does not come to bat, and the designated hitter does not play defensively in the field.

designated tournament *golf* A tournament designated by a players' association as one in which all the top players are required to compete.

de-stroke To reduce the length of the stroke of the pistons in an internal-combustion engine as a method of reducing the engine displacement (as in preparing an overlarge engine for racing).

detachment parry *fencing* A parry made by deflecting the attacker's blade and then immediately pulling the sword away from it.

detune To adjust an internal-combustion engine to run at less than peak performance (as by altering ignition and valve timing and reducing the compression ratio) in order to reduce speed and engine wear or to allow the engine to run on less fuel or a lower grade of fuel.

¹deuce 1 A tie (as in tennis) after each side has a score of 40 when one side must score 2 consecutive points to win the game. The point scored after deuce is called *advantage.* If the next point is scored by the same side, that side

wins the game; if by the other side, the score reverts to deuce.
2 *golf* A score of 2 strokes on a hole.

²deuce To tie the score (as in tennis or badminton) at a point where one side must score 2 consecutive points to win the game or where one side has the option of setting the game.

deuce court *tennis* The right-hand service court. It is so called because the ball is served into this court whenever the score is deuce.

deuce set *tennis* A tie after each side has won 5 games in the same set which requires one side to win 2 consecutive games to win the set when a tiebreaker is not in use.

development *fencing* A principal attacking movement consisting of a thrust, made by straightening the sword arm, followed by a lunge.

deviation *boating* The deflection of the needle of a compass caused by magnetic influences within the boat on which it is mounted.

diagonal *ski touring* A technique of striding in which a kick with one leg is accompanied by a push off with the pole held by the opposite hand. — compare PASGANG

diagonal pass A pass that is made at an angle to a direct line between teammates and that is often a lead pass.

diagonal serve *handball* A serve made to hit the front wall close to the corner and rebound on the side wall and back to the diagonally opposite corner where it comes off the side wall almost parallel to the back wall.

diamond *baseball* **1** The infield portion of the playing field consisting of a large square that has a base at each corner and that resembles a diamond when viewed from home plate.
2 The entire playing field.

¹dice *auto racing* A close contest between 2 or more drivers for position during a race. In a dice the drivers may frequently change position as the one in back attempts to pass and the other tries to keep from being passed.

²dice *of racing drivers* To engage in a dice.

die 1 *of a base runner in baseball* To be left on base when a side is retired.
2 of a hit ball To fail to bounce or to bounce very low; to stop rather suddenly.

¹dig 1 To hit a ball (as in volleyball or handball) just before it hits the floor.
2 To run hard.
3 *ice hockey* To battle for control of the puck (as in the corners) until possession is gained.
4 *surfing* To paddle hard.

²dig The act or an instance of digging:
1 The successful return of a low difficult shot in handball.
2 A pass made in volleyball by digging.

digger **1** A player who digs: **a** A volleyball player adept at digging the ball **b** A hockey player who is adept at gaining control of the puck away from another player in the corners.
2 *drag racing* A dragster.

dig in *of a baseball batter* To dig a small depression in the dirt in the batter's box with the spikes so that the rear foot can be more firmly planted and give more power to the swing. ⟨[his] wildness works to his advantage. The hitters don't really know where he's gonna be throwing the ball. You don't *dig in* against him unless you are an imbecile — John Roseboro⟩

dimple One of the usually 336 small depressions on the surface of a golf ball that reduce drag on the ball in flight.

ding A damaged area on a surfboard.

dinger A home run in baseball.

dinghy A small open boat that is often carried aboard a larger boat and that is usually propelled by oars.

¹dink A soft hit that falls just beyond the net (as in volleyball or tennis).

²dink To hit a dink against a particular opponent. ⟨I try to *dink* him around, pull him to the net, then mix garbage with passing shots — Rod Laver⟩

dip dodge *lacrosse* A variation of the face dodge in which the stick is shifted from one hand to the other and which is often started with a quick dip on one leg.

dipsey sinker or **dipsie sinker** or **dipsy sinker** *fishing* A tear-shaped lead sinker that usually has a swivel at the top.

direct *of a fencing attack or parry* Made in the line of engagement.

direct cannon see CANNON

direct English see FOLLOW

direct free kick *soccer* A free kick awarded a team at the point of the foul when an opposing player commits a foul such as holding, tripping, or kicking an opponent or a major infraction such as playing the ball with the hands. A goal may be scored directly from a direct free kick. — compare INDIRECT FREE KICK, PENALTY KICK

director **1** *fencing* The official who is in charge of conducting the bout and who makes the final decision on awarding hits. (also called *president*)
2 *lawn bowling* A player who is at a given time in charge of the head for his team.

dirt-track car A large heavy front-engined open-wheel racing car that is used on dirt tracks. The drive shaft runs underneath the driver's seat and the driver sits upright near the rear axle. — see also SPRINT CAR, MIDGET; compare ROADSTER

dirt track racing *motor racing* Racing on a closed dirt track as distinct from racing on a paved track or from off-road racing. Dirt tracks for automobiles are typically ¼ to ½ mile long and the races are characterized by a sideways sliding of the vehicles when making turns.

disabled list *baseball* A list containing the names of players injured severely enough to require their missing a number of games. When a team places a player on the disabled list, that player remains a part of the team's roster but he is not permitted to play for a specified number of days (as 15 or 21 days), during which time the team may add another player to the roster to temporarily replace the injured player.

discus *track and field* **1** A disk that is usually made of wood or plastic with a metal rim and metal plates attached to the sides, that is thicker in the middle than at the perimeter, and that is used in the discus throw.
2 Short for *discus throw*.

DISCUS
---

college and international competition	men	women
diameter	219–221 mm (8⅝–8¹¹/₁₆ in)	180–182 mm (7³/₃₂–7⁵/₃₂ in)
weight	2 kgs (4 lbs, 6⅔ oz)	1 kg (2 lbs, 3¼ oz)
thickness		
center	44–46 mm (1¾–1¹³/₁₆ in)	37–39 mm (1¹⁵/₃₂–1¹⁷/₃₂ in)
rim	12 mm (½ in)	12 mm

high school boys	
diameter	8¼–8⁵/₁₆ in
weight	3 lbs, 9 oz
thickness	
center	1⅝ in
rim	½ in

---

discus throw *track and field* A field event in which a discus is hurled for distance with one hand from within a throwing circle which is 8

discus thrower

feet 2½ inches in diameter. In order to qualify as a legal throw, the discus must land in the throwing sector formed by 2 lines extending out at a 60 degree angle (90 degrees for high school) from the center of the throwing circle. Each competitor is allowed 3 trials in the finals; in large meets, a prior set of 3 trials is used to determine the finalists. The best effort of the competitor in either the trial or the finals is credited to him in determining the final standings.

discus thrower An athlete who competes in the discus throw.

discus throw

¹disengage *fencing* To pass one's blade under the opponent's blade to another line in making an attack.

²disengage or **disengagement** *fencing* An attack made by passing one's blade under the opponent's blade to a new line. — compare CUT-OVER

disgorger *fishing* A device that is used to remove a hook from the mouth or gullet of a fish.

dish rag *gymnastics* A position in which the body is draped across a balance beam.

disk 1 Any of the 8 wooden or rubber composition disks 6 inches in diameter and one inch thick that are used in shuffleboard.
2 An ice hockey puck.

dislocate *gymnastics* A movement performed on the rings from an inverted pike position in which the gymnast thrusts his legs up and out, straightens his body and arches his back, and turns over to swing down while at the same time pushing his arms out and rotating them so that the palms are turned out as the body turns over.

dismiss *cricket* To cause a batsman to be out. There are a number of ways in which a batsman may be dismissed: by hitting the wicket with a bowled ball, by catching a hit ball in the air, or by breaking a wicket that a batsman is running to before he reaches the crease, a procedure which is somewhat analogous to putting out a runner in baseball on a force play.

¹dismount *gymnastics* A movement by which a gymnast gets off an apparatus. The dismount is an integral part of the routine and usually involves a graceful jump or flip in which the gymnast lands on his feet a short distance away.

²dismount To get down from a horse or a gymnastics apparatus.

displacement The size of an internal-combustion engine measured as the total volume displaced by each piston on a single stroke and usually measured in cubic centimeters or cubic inches.

displacement hull *boating* A hull designed to remain in the water and to displace a constant amount of water regardless of the speed of the boat. — compare PLANING HULL

disqualify 1 To bar a competitor from competition for infractions of certain rules or for an excessive number of infractions and especially for flagrant misconduct. Disqualification may be only for the duration of the competition or meet, or depending on the sport, the ruling authority, and the nature of the violation, it may prevent the competitor from entering competition for a stated period (as a month).

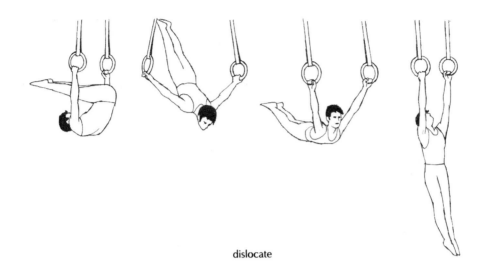

dislocate

2 To make ineligible to win a contest or a particular prize because of a rule infraction; to drop a competitor to a lower finishing position than the one where he actually finished because of an infraction (as in horse racing).

disqualifying foul A foul (as a deliberate attempt to harm an opponent) for which a player may be disqualified.

dissent *soccer* Disagreeing with the referee's decision or arguing with a referee for which a player may be booked or sent off.

distance **1** A distance race; the length of a distance race. ⟨there were horsemen who wondered if the colt could go a *distance* — Whitney Tower, *Sports Illustrated*⟩ ⟨ran the finest *distance* double in history, touring the mile in 3:56.8 and the three mile in 13:06.4 — Ron Reid, *Sports Illustrated*⟩
2 The duration of a contest. — usually used in the phrase *go the distance*
3 *fox hunting* The number of miles covered by a hunt. — compare POINT
4 *horse racing* A length of the track indicated by a post or flag at a set distance from the finish line which a horse in a heat race must reach by the time the winner crosses the finish line in order to qualify for later heats.
— in distance *fencing* Near enough to one's opponent to score a hit merely by lunging. —
out of distance *fencing* Far enough from one's opponent to require an advance and a lunge in order to score a hit.

distance man *track and field* A runner who competes in a distance race.

distance medley *track and field* A medley relay which consists of legs of ¼, ½, ¾, and one mile respectively.

distance race Any race of more than a mile. (also called *long distance race*)

distance runner *track and field* An athlete who competes in distance races. ⟨entered her in everything from the 100-yard dash to the mile and finally decided to make her a *distance runner* — *Newsweek*⟩

ditch *lawn bowling* A small excavation 6–8 inches deep and 8–11 inches wide at each end of the rink that is bordered on one side by the bank. Bowls in the ditch are no longer in play; if the jack is in the ditch, it remains in play.

¹dive **1** A headfirst leap or plunge: **a** A plunge into water (as from a diving board or platform) executed in a prescribed manner. Most dives begin from a standing position with the diver turning headfirst after takeoff. The diver may enter the water headfirst directly from the board or may continue in one or more revolutions entering the water headfirst or feetfirst. **b** *gymnastics* A leap in which the gymnast lands usually on the hands or arms and continues immediately with a roll.
2 *boxing* A faked knockout. — used in the phrase *take a dive*
3 *football* An offensive play in which the ballcarrier plunges headfirst into the line for short yardage.
4 A period of skin diving or scuba diving.
²dive **1** To make a headlong leap or plunge; to engage in competitive diving.
2 To engage in skin diving or scuba diving; to

engage in skin diving or scuba diving in a specified area or around a specified submerged object. ⟨this wreck had never been . . . *dived* before — *Skin Diver*⟩

diver Someone who dives or who engages in diving.

diver's flag or **diver-down flag** *scuba diving* A red flag with a white stripe running diagonally from the upper shaft corner that is mounted on a boat or float to warn boatmen to stay clear of the area because there are divers below.

dive schedule A chart in decompression tables that lists combinations of bottom times and various depths for use by divers in calculating no-decompression dives, repetitive dive categories, and decompression stops.

diving **1** The act or practice of plunging into water especially from a diving board or platform. Competitive diving is an adjunct to major swimming meets and consists of divers performing a number of required and optional dives for which their form is judged and scored by a group of judges. Dives are commonly performed from the 1- and 3-meter springboards and the 10-meter platform. All aspects of the dive including the preparatory stance, run-up and hurdle, takeoff, position in the air, and entry are judged. Each dive is evaluated for excellence on a scale of 0 to 10 points. The score for each dive is multiplied by a degree-of-difficulty factor, and the diver with the highest score at the end of the competition is the winner.
2 The act or sport of swimming underwater usually with face mask, swim fins, and snorkel and often with scuba equipment. — see also SKIN DIVING, SCUBA DIVING

diving board A flat somewhat flexible board that is secured at one end and mounted on a fulcrum so as to extend over the edge of a diving or swimming pool and that is used by divers to gain height for dives; springboard.

diving well The deep section of a swimming pool under the springboards or diving platforms that is deep enough that a diver will not hit bottom while diving.

division **1** A class or category into which competitors are grouped on the basis of weight (as in boxing or weight lifting).
2 A unit of a professional sports league or conference in which teams in one major geographic area are grouped to provide regional rivalries. The teams within a single division usually compete against each other more regularly than against teams in other divisions with the best

team or teams in the division eligible for play-off berths.
3 The upper or lower group of teams in a league standing. ⟨first time in 3 years they finished in the first *division*⟩
4 *horse racing* Any of the 2 or more separate races into which the entrants for a particular stakes or handicap race must be divided when there are too many horses entered to run at one time.

division boards *bowling* The area on an alley where the dark and light boards meet.

division line *basketball* A line parallel to and equidistant from each end line that divides the court into 2 equal areas and that distinguishes a team's backcourt from its frontcourt. (also called *midcourt line, time line*) — see also BACKCOURT VIOLATION

divot *golf* A piece of sod cut out of the fairway by the club head just after it hits the ball.

dobber see BOBBER

¹dodge A maneuver (as in lacrosse or field hockey) by which an offensive player with the ball gets away from a defender while maintaining possession of the ball. In lacrosse, a dodge is commonly made by feinting in one direction and moving in another. In field hockey, where the ball is not actually carried, a common dodge is made by shoving the ball past a defender on one side and then running around the defender on the other side to retrieve the ball.

²dodge To maneuver around a defender by employing a dodge.

dodger *lacrosse* A player who is at a given moment making a dodge.

dodo split *bowling* A leave that has the headpin and either the 7 or the 10 pin standing. — see illustration of pin arrangement at BOWLING

¹dog To defend against an opponent closely and persistently.

²dog **1** *football* Short for *red dog*.
2 *horse racing* Any of the rubber cones (formerly wooden sawhorses) placed around the track near the rail to keep horses in the middle of the track and prevent their churning up the inside portion of the track during morning workouts.
3 or **dogger** A hot dog skier.

dogleg *golf* A fairway that has a sharp bend.

dog paddle *swimming* An elementary stroke performed in a prone position with the head out of the water, the legs kicking, and the arms alternately reaching forward without going out of the water and pulling down and back.

WEIGHT DIVISIONS

(maximum weights)

boxing

	amateur	professional
light flyweight	48 kgs (106 lbs)	—
flyweight	51 kgs (112 lbs)	112 lbs
bantamweight	54 kgs (119 lbs)	118 lbs
featherweight	57 kgs (125 lbs)	126 lbs
junior lightweight	—	130 lbs
lightweight	60 kgs (132 lbs)	135 lbs
light welterweight	63.5 kgs (139 lbs)	—
junior welterweight	—	140 lbs
welterweight	67 kgs (147 lbs)	147 lbs
light middleweight	71 kgs (156 lbs)	—
junior middleweight	—	154 lbs
middleweight	75 kgs (165 lbs)	160 lbs
light heavyweight	81 kgs (178 lbs)	175 lbs
heavyweight	unlimited	unlimited

weight lifting

	Olympic lifting	powerlifting international	US
flyweight	52 kgs (114½ lbs)	52 kgs	—
bantamweight	56 kgs (123½ lbs)	56 kgs	123½ lbs
featherweight	60 kgs (132¼ lbs)	60 kgs	132¼ lbs
lightweight	67.5 kgs (148¾ lbs)	67.5 kgs	148¾ lbs
middleweight	75 kgs (165¼ lbs)	75 kgs	165¼ lbs
light heavyweight	82.5 kgs (181¾ lbs)	82.5 kgs	181¾ lbs
middle heavyweight	90 kgs (198¼ lbs)	90 kgs	198¼ lbs
100 kgs class	—	100 kgs	—
heavyweight	110 kgs (242½ lbs)	110 kgs	220¼ lbs
light super heavyweight	—	—	242½ lbs
super heavyweight	unlimited	unlimited	unlimited

dog racing The sport of setting specially bred greyhounds to race each other in pursuit of a mechanical rabbit. The races of usually ¼ or ⅜ mile are run on a small oval dirt track. The mechanical rabbit makes an effective lure because the greyhound depends on sight rather than on smell in chasing its prey. The speed with which the rabbit moves is controlled by a worker at the track who keeps it several yards ahead of the running dogs. Greyhounds race in classes (grades) that reflect their past record of victories. As with horse racing, pari-mutuel betting is a major attraction of dog racing.

dogsled A sled used in dogsled racing. — see SLED

dogsled racing The sport of racing teams of sled dogs pulling lightweight sleds over special trails in the snow. The driver usually runs behind the sled, sometimes pushing the sled over rough areas, sometimes riding on the runners. Races are run in varying distances, some from one town to another, others over courses 5–10 miles long. Championship dog teams may average 15 miles per hour.

dohyo A 15-foot ring in which sumo wrestling takes place. The ring is on a 2-foot-high mound of clay and is bounded by a large rope partially buried in the floor which is covered with sand.

dojo A school for training in various arts of self-defense (as judo and karate).

dollar odds *pari-mutuel betting* The amount of money a bettor would profit for each dollar wagered. The dollar odds do not include the amount of the wager. Example: a bettor wagers $2 on a horse that pays $6.60 to win. The payoff ($6.60) includes the original $2 wager, so the profit is $4.60 for dollar odds of $2.30. (also called *equivalent odds*)

dolphin kick *swimming* A kick used in the butterfly stroke in which the legs are moved up and down together with the knees slightly bent on the upward movement.

donkey baseball or **donkey softball** Baseball or softball played by players who must ride donkeys while playing in the field and while running bases. It is typically played as a fund-raising program by a charitable organization.

donkey raise *weight training* An exercise for the calf muscles that is usually performed in a device that requires the lifter to stand and bend forward, supporting with his back a platform with adjustable weights, and do toe raises against the resistance of the weight.

donkey softball SEE DONKEY BASEBALL

door *court tennis* An opening in the corridor under the penthouse on each side of the net beside the first gallery and farther from the net than the first gallery. A ball hit into the door makes a chase.

¹dope *horse racing* **1** Information or speculation regarding the likely outcome of a race especially when it is not common knowledge and is purported to come from an informed and usually reliable source.
2 A stimulant or depressant drug that is illegally administered to a racehorse before a race to alter his performance.

²dope To illegally drug a racehorse before a race.

dormie *golf* Ahead in match play by the same number of holes as remain to be played. As soon as the dormie team wins one more hole, it wins the match, and the remaining holes are not played since the other side then could not possibly win or tie. ⟨he and his partner were *dormie* three when he aced the 16th—Jimmy Martin, *Leicester (England) Mercury*⟩

¹double **1** Victories in 2 events or races on the same program by the same individual.
2 *baseball* A base hit on which the batter reaches second base safely. (also called *two-base hit, two-bagger*)
3 *bowling* Two strikes in succession. — compare TURKEY
4 *cricket* The scoring of 1000 runs as batsman

and the taking of 100 wickets as bowler by one individual in a single season.
5 *curling* The removal of 2 opposing stones with a single shot.
6 *fencing* An attacking movement that consists of 2 successive disengagements in the same line followed by a lunge.
7 *fishing* The catching of 2 fish at the same time on one line.
8 a A daily double. **b** *jai alai* A pool in which a bettor must pick the winners of 2 consecutive games in order to win.
9 A double-barreled shotgun.
10 Two targets released at the same time in skeet or trapshooting.

²double **1** To enter 2 different competitive events (as 2 races or 2 field events) in a single meet. ⟨I also wanted to *double,* but it's going to be hard enough just to run the three mile now — Steve Prefontaine⟩
2 *baseball* **a** To hit a double. ⟨*doubled* to left center field⟩ **b** To cause a base runner to score or a run to be scored by a double. ⟨*doubled* in one run during the sixth inning rally — *Springfield (Mass) Union*⟩ **c** or **double up** To put out a base runner in completing a double play. ⟨was *doubled* off second — *Boston Herald Traveler*⟩
3 *of a double-barreled shotgun* To fire both rounds simultaneously.

³double **1** Involving 2 complete turns or rotations of the body. ⟨*double* axel⟩ ⟨*double* backward somersault⟩
2 *of a wrestling hold* Made by using both arms, legs, or hands. ⟨*double* bar arm⟩ ⟨*double* grapevine⟩
3 *of a knot* Formed with 2 turns instead of one; formed with an additional turn or loop. ⟨*double* sheet bend⟩
4 *of an archery round* Consisting of twice as many ends as a single round. ⟨*double* Hereford⟩
5 *of a gymnastics movement* Involving both legs or both arms. ⟨*double* leg circles⟩
6 Involving 2 people. ⟨*double* sculls⟩

double action SEE ACTION

double-barreled shotgun A shotgun with 2 separate barrels mounted side-by-side and fired independently by 2 triggers or by a single trigger when a small selector device is employed. — compare OVER AND UNDER

double blade or **double paddle** A canoe or kayak paddle with blades at each end which are usually set at different angles. The paddle is normally gripped in the middle, and each end is alternately dipped in the water on opposite sides of the boat, producing a steady propelling action.

double-bogey *golf* To score a double bogey on a hole.

double bogey *golf* A score of 2 strokes over par for a hole.

double-cover see DOUBLE-TEAM

double coverage Coverage of one offensive player by 2 defensive players.

[1]**double dribble** *basketball* An infraction that results when a player dribbles the ball with both hands simultaneously or continues a dribble after allowing the ball to come to rest in one or both hands and that results in loss of possession of the ball.

[2]**double dribble** To commit a double dribble.

double eagle *golf* A score of 3 under par for a hole.

double elimination tournament A version of an elimination tournament in which an individual or team must lose twice before being eliminated.

double-ender *surfing* A surfboard that has both ends of the same shape.

double-fault *tennis* To lose the point by committing 2 consecutive faults while serving.

double fault *tennis* Two successive faults committed while serving which result in the loss of the point.

double figures A number (as of points) that is 10 or more. ⟨6 players scored in *double figures*⟩

double foul *basketball* Two fouls committed simultaneously by opponents against each other with the result that the penalties offset each other. If the double foul involves personal fouls, both players are charged with the foul, but it is not charged as a team foul. Play is restarted by a jump ball if the double foul occured during loose ball play or if one of the players involved had control of the ball. If the foul was committed away from the ball, the team in control puts the ball in play by a throw-in. — compare MULTIPLE FOUL

doubleheader Two games, contests, or events held consecutively on the same program for the same admission price. Baseball teams may play 2 successive games on one day often to make up previously postponed games. A doubleheader may also consist of 2 games played by different pairs of teams (as in basketball). Doubleheaders are especially common in tournament competition. Some doubleheaders, notably in auto racing, may include 2 different events on consecutive days for a single admission price.

double hit **1** A stroke (as in squash racquets or badminton) in which the ball or shuttlecock is struck twice. This is illegal and the player loses the point or the serve.

2 *fencing* A double touch.

double hook *fishing* A hook that has 2 bends, points, and barbs and that is usually formed from a single piece of wire so that it has a double shank and a single eye.

double in *gymnastics* A move by the gymnast from the end of the pommel horse to the middle while performing flank circles.

double nelson *wrestling* A full nelson. — see NELSON

double out *gymnastics* A move by the gymnast from the middle of the pommel horse to the end while performing flank circles.

double oxer *equitation* An obstacle for show jumping which consists of an oxer with an additional rail behind the brush.

double paddle see DOUBLE BLADE

double pinochle *bowling* A split that leaves the 4, 6, 7, and 10 pins standing. — see illustration of pin arrangement at BOWLING

double play *baseball* A play in which 2 players are put out. Two players may be forced out on one ground ball that is quickly relayed to 2 bases, or the batter may fly out and the runner be thrown out before he can return to the base or while he is attempting to advance, or the batter may strike out and the runner be thrown out attempting to steal.

double-pole *ski touring* To move oneself forward by pushing off with both poles simultaneously.

double-pump *of a baseball pitcher* To make 2 pumps during a windup.

double reverse *football* An offensive play which consists of a reverse with another handoff so that the ultimate ballcarrier is running in the direction in which the play originally started.

doubles **1** A form of play in court games (as tennis, badminton, table tennis, squash racquets, or handball) between 2 pairs of players with 2 players on a side. The court is sometimes larger for doubles play than for singles. The rules specify the order in which partners serve and receive service but, with the exception of table tennis, after the service is returned, either partner may hit a ball or shuttlecock. Doubles play requires a player to cover only half the court, but it also requires a high degree of teamwork between partners.

2 Competition (as in luge or waterskiing) involving 2 people competing together.

double steal *baseball* A play in which each of

2 base runners steals a base. The most common situation for a double steal is with men on first and third bases. The player on first attempts to steal second. When the catcher throws to second base, the runner on third breaks for home.

double taper SEE FLY LINE

double-team **1** To block or guard an opponent with 2 players at the same time.

2 To assist a teammate to block or guard an opponent; to block or guard an opponent who is also being blocked or guarded by a teammate. (also *double-cover*)

double three *skating* A school figure that consists of a three turn performed twice on each circle. — see illustration at SCHOOL FIGURE

double touch or **double hit** *fencing* A situation in which a touch is made by both fencers at or near the same time. In foil and saber, a hit is scored only for the one having the right of way if this can be determined. In épée, a hit is scored for each fencer.

double up **1** To double-team a player.

2 see DOUBLE (*baseball*)

double wing *football* **1** A variation of the single wing formation utilizing 2 wingbacks with one on each side of the formation.

2 An offensive formation characterized by a split end and the 2 halfbacks placed wide as receivers. In a common version of the double wing, one halfback plays as a slotback.

double wood *bowling* A leave in which one pin is left standing directly behind another.

doughnut SEE BAT WEIGHT

¹down **1** Trailing an opponent (as in points scored). 〈were *down* by 2〉

2 *of a doubles player in badminton* Having lost the serve by failing to score. When one player is down, his partner serves until the side again fails to score at which time the side is out and the serve passes to the opponents.

3 *baseball* Out. 〈2 *down* in the bottom of the seventh〉

4 *of a boxer* Not standing and ready or able to fight; subject to being counted out. The boxer is considered down if any part of his body except his feet touches the canvas or if he is outside the ropes. Once he is down and the count begins, it continues until the boxer is standing or is counted out or sometimes until the round ends. The boxer is considered down even when he is rising.

5 *of a cricket wicket* Broken so that the batsman is out.

6 *of the ball in football* Not in play because of

wholly stopped progress or because the officials have stopped the play. 〈marked the ball *down* on the 15-yard line〉

7 *of a game fish* Hiding or staying on or near the bottom and not actively feeding (as when frightened).

8 *of a golfer* Having putted the ball into the hole. 〈hit that into a trap, took three to get *down* and wound up with a bogey — *Sports Illustrated*〉

9 *of a shot in squash racquets* Not legally playable because of having bounced twice or having hit the telltale; not up.

²down **1** *badminton* Failure to score and loss of the serve by one partner in doubles competition.

2 *football* **a** A complete play to advance the ball which begins with a free kick (a *free kick down*) or a center snap (*scrimmage down*) and ends when the ball is dead. **b** One of a series of 4 attempts (3 in Canadian football) to advance the ball 10 yards. 〈second *down* and 8 yards to go〉 **c** A situation usually calling for a particular strategy. 〈an obvious passing *down*〉

—on downs *of a team's acquiring possession of the ball in football* As a result of the opposing team's having failed to advance the ball 10 yards in 4 downs. 〈failed to get the first down and their opponents took over *on downs*〉

³down **1** To bring a ballcarrier to the ground by tackling (as in football or rugby).

2 *football* To cause the play to end and the ball to be dead at a particular spot without attempting to advance the ball especially by touching the ball to the ground or touching one knee to the ground while holding the ball. An offensive player may down the ball in the end zone for a touchback after receiving a kick rather than attempt to advance the ball. Members of the kicking team often try to down a punt which is not caught by a member of the receiving team to prevent it from bouncing back upfield or to keep it from going into the end zone for a touchback.

down-and-in *football* A pass pattern in which the receiver runs straight downfield and then cuts sharply to the inside usually after a fake.

down-and-out *football* A pass pattern in which the receiver runs straight downfield and then cuts sharply to the outside usually after a fake.

down box or **down indicator** *football* A device consisting of a 5- to 6-foot rod on top of which is mounted a series of numbered cards. The rod is handled by an assistant to the head linesman and is placed along the sideline to mark the spot of the ball at the beginning of each down. The cards are used to indicate the number of the down (from 1 to 4) that is to be played.

downcourt *basketball* In or into the opposite end of the court; into a team's frontcourt. ⟨took down the rebound, turned, and fired the ball *downcourt*⟩

downfield In or into the part of the field toward which the offensive team is headed. ⟨scooped up the loose ball and raced *downfield*⟩

downhaul *sailing* A line that is used to hold down a mast or the bottom of a sail (as to provide a good shape to the sail in a strong wind or to keep the sail from riding too high).

¹downhill *skiing* A race against time down a 1½-to-3-mile-long course that has a vertical drop of at least 2000 feet in 1½ miles with each competitor seeking the fastest most direct route down the slope while staying within the boundaries of the course. The competitors normally start one at a time at 1-to-2-minute intervals. — compare SLALOM

²downhill 1 Of, relating to, or used in downhill skiing. ⟨*downhill* equipment⟩
2 Lower; nearer the bottom of an incline. ⟨the *downhill* ski⟩ ⟨your *downhill* shoulder⟩
3 Downwind. ⟨a *downhill* spinnaker run — *New York Times*⟩

downhiller 1 *golf* A putt that must roll down a sloping green to the cup. ⟨while I am not hesitant at a relatively straight-in putt, I do prefer caution on . . . *downhillers* — Arnold Palmer⟩
2 *skiing* A skier who competes in downhill events and especially in the downhill. ⟨at best a second-rate *downhiller* — *Skiing International Yearbook*⟩

downhill skiing Skiing that consists essentially of gliding down a slope after being towed to the top. Since in downhill skiing the skier is not concerned with climbing the slope or with moving on relatively flat areas, the run down the slope and the maneuvers and turns he makes during the run provide the enjoyment for the skier. Modern developments in ski equipment have led to a greater repertoire of sophisticated turns and maneuvers, which add to the challenge of the slope. Competitive events in downhill skiing, often called *Alpine* events, involve racing downhill against the clock in the downhill, slalom, and giant slalom. — see also SKIING; compare SKI TOURING

down indicator see DOWN BOX

downsman *Canadian football* An official on the sideline who marks the position of the ball after each down. The downsman's job is identical to that of the official in American football who is responsible for handling the down box.

downswing The forward and downward swing of an implement (as a golf club) to hit a ball after a backswing.

down the line *of a shot in net games* Made from the side of the court and directed across the net near the edge of the court on the same side. — compare CROSSCOURT

down-the-line shooting British term for *trapshooting*.

down time see BOTTOM TIME

downwind In the direction that the wind is blowing; with the wind aft. ⟨sailing the *downwind* leg⟩ ⟨sailing *downwind*⟩ — compare WINDWARD

¹draft 1 The depth of a boat beneath the water; the depth of water required for a boat to float.
2 An arrangement among professional sports teams in a league or association whereby exclusive rights to new players are apportioned among the teams so that all the teams will not be in competition for the same players. The draft system provides that teams with poorer season records have a chance to select players before the teams with better records. It is designed to ensure that weak teams will have a chance to improve with the addition of top players and that the strong teams cannot continue to acquire the best players simply because they have more money to offer. Draft rights are negotiable and are often traded for established players.
3 The act or an instance of following close behind another racer in drafting.

²draft 1 To select a prospective new player in a professional sports draft. In drafting a player, a team gets exclusive rights to negotiate with that player. If a player is unable to come to terms with the team that drafted him, he may be able to negotiate a contract with another team providing that team satisfactorily compensates the original team (as by trading a player).
2 To engage in drafting.

drafting The art or practice of driving or riding close behind another racing car at high speed to take advantage of the reduced air resistance just back of it and move at the same speed while using much less energy. As a body moves forward, it cuts through a wall of air, forcing the air to move around the body and leaving an area of temporarily reduced air pressure to the rear. A certain amount of energy is required merely to overcome air resistance, so if a racing driver can ride close enough to another to stay in the low pressure area, he will receive a tow enabling

drag

him to move at the same speed as the leading car while conserving power to pass the car at some strategic point. The leading car also benefits somewhat from the drafting as the second car breaks up the backward suction which ordinarily would slow the lead car. The strategy of staying close behind another competitor to conserve energy is also employed in competition other than auto racing, notably bicycle racing. (also called *slipstreaming*)

¹drag **1** *billiards* Backspin imparted to the cue ball to cause it to stop after striking the object ball. — compare DRAW, FOLLOW

2 *fishing* **a** A device to vary the tension on the winding mechanism of a reel to control the rate at which the spool will revolve backward when line is being pulled out by a hooked fish. The drag commonly consists of a series of metal and usually composition washers which, when the control is tightened, are pressed closer together, increasing friction and making it harder for the spool to turn. **b** The condition of an artificial fly traveling through or over the water faster than the speed of the current that results when a portion of the line is caught in a swift flow causing the fly to be pulled downstream.

3 *fox hunting* **a** The scent left on the ground by a fox. **b** An artificial trail for hounds to follow produced by dragging a sack filled with a strong smelling substance (as aniseed) over the ground.

4 *wrestling* A takedown maneuver in which an opponent's upper arm is grasped and he is pulled to the mat.

5 Short for *drag race.*

²drag **1** *of an artificial fly* To be pulled over or through the water by drag.

2 To participate in a drag race.

3 *baseball* To make a drag bunt.

drag bike A motorcycle specifically designed for drag racing.

drag boat A powerboat used in or specifically designed for drag boat racing.

drag boat racing A sport in which specially designed or modified powerboats compete in acceleration contests over a ¼-mile course. — see also DRAG RACING

drag bunt *baseball* A bunt made with the object of getting on base rather than sacrificing. In attempting a drag bunt, the batter tries to catch the pitcher and infielders by surprise, so he usually drops the bat in front of the ball without squaring around as is normally done in making a sacrifice bunt. The drag bunt is most commonly attempted by left-handed batters who turn the

body and start for first base allowing the bat to trail behind them to tap the ball.

dragger Someone who competes in drag races.

drag hunt A hunt with hounds following an artificial drag instead of the trail of a live fox. This may be resorted to for exercise when no fox is available or when the area is too congested to permit a safe hunt of a fox.

drag line *ballooning* A rope that is trailed from a hot-air balloon as it approaches a landing spot to help slow the drift of the balloon and to be used by the ground crew in pulling the descending balloon to earth.

Dragon A sloop-rigged keelboat of a one-design class that is 29 feet long, has a sail area of 267 square feet plus 325 square-foot spinnaker, and carries a crew of 3.

drag race An acceleration contest between vehicles (as automobiles) usually over a ¼-mile course.

drag racing The sport of holding acceleration contests for vehicles over a straight usually ¼-mile-long course. While there are acceleration contests held for a wide range of motor-powered vehicles from motorcycles to powerboats, drag racing's most common and most popular format is the racing of modified, specially designed automobiles. Competition is conducted in elimination heats with 2 contestants at a time racing against each other. The first one across the finish line is the winner. As the competition progresses during a program, winners from earlier heats are matched within their categories in later heats until only one competitor in each class is left. — see also ELIMINATOR

dragster **1** **a** A specially built vehicle for use in drag racing that has a narrow lightweight tubular frame with small front wheels for steering of the type used on bicycles and huge wide rear tires for traction, that has one or sometimes 2 supercharged engines located just ahead of the rear wheels and a single-seat open cockpit usually between or just behind the rear wheels, and that is run on fuel or commercial gasoline. Some of the newer dragsters are designed with the cockpit ahead of the engine. **b** Any vehicle designed or modified for drag racing.

2 Someone who participates in a drag race; one who drives a dragster.

drag strip or **dragway** A site for a drag race; a paved strip that is wide enough for 2 vehicles to race side by side and long enough to have a racing area ¼ mile long with sufficient room beyond the finish line for the competitors to be

dragster

able to bring their vehicles to a stop safely. There are a few drag strips that provide a racing area only ⅛ mile long.

¹draw 1 A match (as in cricket, boxing, or wrestling) that ends in a tie.

2 A face-off in lacrosse or hockey.

3 a The process by which competitors' names are drawn at random and paired on a tournament draw sheet after the seeded competitors have been placed. **b** The arrangement of the names of competitors on a tournament draw sheet usually in the order drawn; the match-ups for a tournament.

4 *archery* The act or an instance of pulling the string back and tensing the bow in preparation for shooting the arrow. **b** The condition in which the string is pulled and the bow is tensed. ⟨at full *draw*⟩

5 *billiards* Backspin imparted to a cue ball to cause it to come back after striking an object ball. (also called *reverse English*) — compare DRAG; FOLLOW

6 or **draw stroke** *canoeing* A stroke made by drawing the paddle into the side of the canoe to steer the canoe toward the paddle side.

7 or **draw play** *football* An offensive play in which the quarterback drops back as if to pass and then hands off to a back who runs straight ahead past the pass rushers.

8 *golf* A shot in which the ball is intentionally made to curve to the side opposite the dominant hand of the player. — compare HOOK; FADE

²draw 1 a To cause a propelled ball to veer in an intended direction usually by imparting a particular spin. **b** *golf* To cause a ball to veer to the side opposite to the dominant hand of the player. ⟨*drew* the ball to the left⟩ **c** *billiards* To impart backspin to the cue ball to cause it to return after striking the object ball.

2 To gain a draw or tie in a contest; to finish a contest with a draw.

3 To make some movement or action that provokes or causes a specific response or reaction from an opponent. ⟨*drew* his opponent offside⟩ ⟨took a long lead hoping to *draw* the throw to first⟩ ⟨*drew* the foul⟩

4 To have a particular placing or specific opponent for a round in a tournament as a result of the draw. ⟨*drew* the top-seeded player in the first round⟩ ⟨*drew* a bye⟩

5 *archery* To pull back the bowstring and tense the bow in preparation for shooting an arrow.

6 *canoeing* To make a draw stroke.

7 *curling* **a** *of a stone* To slide down the ice all the way to the tee line. **b** To deliver a stone with sufficient force to cause it to reach the tee line. **c** To slide a stone in such a way that it winds up behind a previously delivered stone.

8 *football* To use a particular player as the ball-carrier on a draw play.

9 *horse racing* To withdraw or scratch a horse from a race.

draw first blood To be the first side to score in a contest.

drawing hand *archery* The string hand.

drawman *box lacrosse* A player who usually takes part in a center face-off; center.

draw play see DRAW (*football*)

draw sheet An official listing of tournament competitors on the basis of the draw, usually indicating individual matches to be held during the various rounds. The draw sheet for an elimination tournament is a chart listing the contestants and individual contests in the first round with brackets for successive contests leading eventually to a single undefeated winner. As each winner advances, his name is entered on the next line usually along with the score of his victory.

draw shot

Draw sheets for other types of tournaments (as round robin) usually list the competitors and opponents of each for the different rounds and usually also provide for the scores of individual contests as well as the overall won-lost record for each competitor.

draw shot *billiards* A shot in which draw is applied to the cue ball causing it to come back after striking the object ball. — compare FOLLOW SHOT

draw stroke see DRAW (*canoeing*)

draw weight **1** *archery* The force (measured in foot-pounds) required to pull a bow to full draw for a given arrow length.

2 *curling* The precise momentum a stone needs to travel to the opposite tee. — compare HITTING WEIGHT

dressage An equestrian event in which a rider takes his horse through a series of formal and graceful maneuvers that demonstrate the horse's obedience, submission, and training and the ability of the horse and rider to work together so that the horse proceeds smoothly through several difficult movements in response to barely perceptible moves of the rider's hands and legs and shifts in the rider's weight. Among the maneuvers required of the horse are changes from leading on one foreleg in a canter to leading on the other foreleg, a backward walk, changes of direction, diagonal movements, trotting in place, pirouettes, and school figures. The horse and rider are permitted 12 minutes to perform all of the required maneuvers of the test, and they are awarded points from 0–10 on how well the maneuvers are executed; points are deducted for errors, omissions, and exceeding the time limit.

¹**dribble** **1** To impel a ball or puck with a series of light taps with the hand or foot or with a stick while maintaining possession: **a** *basketball* To bounce the ball with successive taps of one hand. A player is not permitted to walk or run with the ball in his possession unless the ball is dribbled; while the ball is being dribbled there is no limit to the number of steps that may be taken between bounces. Once the dribbled ball is allowed to come to rest in one or both hands the dribble ends, and the player may not dribble again until he loses and then regains possession of the ball (as after having passed to a teammate or after a shot at the basket). — see also AIR DRIBBLE **b** *field hockey* To advance the ball with successive light taps with the flat side of the stick

dribbling: basketball; ice hockey; soccer; water polo

blade. **c** *ice hockey* To move the puck along the ice with successive taps with either side of the stick blade. **d** *soccer* To move or advance the ball along the ground with successive light kicks. **e** *water polo* To advance the ball over the water keeping it in front of the head and between the arms by tapping it lightly with the head or the arms while swimming a modified crawl stroke.

2 To advance or move by dribbling a ball or puck. ⟨*dribbled* to the top of the key⟩

3 *of a ball* To travel relatively slowly and only a short distance by bouncing as a result of being poorly hit. ⟨heard the cannon go off on his downswing and nearly fell off the tee while his ball *dribbled* about 30 yards — *Sports Illustrated*⟩

4 To hit a ball poorly so that it dribbles. ⟨*dribbled* a single between shortstop and third base — *Sporting News*⟩

²dribble The act or an instance of dribbling a ball or puck.

dribbler **1** A player who is dribbling a ball or puck.

2 *baseball* A poorly hit ball that dribbles. (also called *squibbler*) ⟨hit a *dribbler* down the third base line⟩

¹drift **1** *archery* Lateral deviation in the flight of an arrow caused by the wind.

2 *auto racing* A cornering technique in which the car is allowed to slide sideways slightly in order to go through the turn at the highest possible speed. The drift is controlled by means of the throttle; an increase in power increases the drift with the car sliding more toward the outside of the turn while a decrease in power reduces the drift. The drift is a very delicate maneuver, for if the driver goes through the turn too slow, he may lose time; if he attempts to go through too fast, the car may lose adhesion to the road and spin out. Though some degree of drift is employed in nearly all forms of racing, it is most obvious and most effective on dirt tracks.

²drift *auto racing* To allow a racing car to slide sideways while going through a turn.

drift fishing Fishing from a boat that is allowed to drift with the current. (also called *float fishing*)

¹drill A practice maneuver or session concentrating on perfecting skills (as shooting, passing, blocking, or tackling) by repetition.

²drill **1** To take part in a drill; to train players in a particular action by means of drills.

2 To throw, kick, or hit a ball or shoot a puck with great speed and great accuracy especially so as to penetrate a defense. ⟨*drilled* a 65-footer past the goalie⟩ ⟨thinks that with his arm there is no pass that he can't complete, that he can just *drill* it through — Fran Tarkenton⟩

3 *wrestling* To bring an opponent to the mat with great force.

¹drive **1** **a** To propel a ball, puck, or shuttlecock with force. ⟨*drove* the ball through the infield⟩ ⟨*drive* the ball to the baseline⟩ **b** *cricket* To hit a drive against a particular bowler. **c** *golf* To hit the ball from the tee especially with a driver.

2 or **drive in** *baseball* To cause a run or a runner to score because of a hit ball. ⟨singled to *drive* the winning run home⟩

3 To make a quick move toward the goal with the ball in an attempt to score. ⟨*drove* in for a lay-up⟩

4 To frighten game and force it toward waiting hunters. (also *beat*)

5 **a** To ride in and control a racing car. **b** To ride in or on a horse-drawn vehicle as opposed to riding on horseback; to control a racing harness horse while riding in the sulky.

²drive **1** A hard stroke or hit that travels in a relatively flat trajectory: **a** A hard shot (as in squash or handball) that rebounds from the front wall nearly parallel to the floor. **b** *badminton* A hard hit that sends the shuttlecock in a straight line parallel to the floor barely clearing the net. — compare CLEAR, SMASH **c** *golf* A ball hit from the tee toward the green. **d** *tennis* A hard ground stroke that just clears the net. — compare LOB, SMASH

2 A quick offensive move toward the goal with the ball.

3 A form of hunting in which game is forced (as by people who move forward in a line beating the bushes) into or past an area in which hunters are waiting.

4 *cricket* A hit ball that travels generally straight out from the batsman. A drive directly beyond the far wicket is called a *straight drive;* a drive to the off side is called an *off drive;* one to the leg side is on *on drive.* — see *also* COVER DRIVE

5 *football* A sustained offensive effort (as a series of successful plays) resulting in a steady advance toward the opponent's goal. ⟨a 7-yard touchdown pass capped the 80-yard *drive*⟩

6 *harness racing* A job driving a harness horse in a race.

7 *horse racing* A ride in which the horse is urged to an all-out effort with heavy whipping, especially in the homestretch.

drive in see DRIVE (*baseball*)

driven partridge A form of clay pigeon shooting popular in Britain in which targets are propelled in pairs without warning from behind an opaque screen. — compare HIGH PHEASANT, RUNNING RABBIT, SPRINGING TEAL

driver **1 a** Someone who operates and especially steers a powerboat or an automobile in a race. **b** A person who rides a sulky and controls a harness horse in a race. **c** A person who rides in front of and steers a bobsled. **d** A person who controls a dogsled team.
2 *golf* A number one wood normally used in driving from the tee.

drive serve *badminton* A fast low serve often used for deception in doubles competition.

drive the green *golf* To drive a ball from the tee to the green in a single stroke.

drive-volley *tennis* A volley executed in the manner of a forehand drive.

driving *of a racehorse* Winning a race under the intense urging of the jockey rather than easily with a comfortable lead.

driving bit *harness racing* A snaffle bit commonly used on harness horses.

driving iron *golf* An old name for a number one iron.

driving range *golf* A field usually equipped with distance markers in which one can practice driving.

¹drop **1** A drop shot.
2 *baseball* A curve that is thrown overhand so that it suddenly drops as it approaches the plate; an overhand curve.
3 *football* **a** A defensive move away from the line of scrimmage to defend against a forward pass. ⟨can spin out of a block and has good *drops* on passes — Don McCafferty⟩ **b** The act or an instance of dropping back to pass. ⟨look for a quick *drop* and a quick release and . . . speed and agility in retreating to the throwing area — *Sports Illustrated*⟩
4 *golf* The act, an instance, or the opportunity of dropping one's ball away from an unplayable lie.
5 *gymnastics* A maneuver in which the performer makes a controlled fall to a lower level or position (as from a position supported by the arms to a hang or from a standing to a kneeling or lying position) on an apparatus, mat, or trampoline.

²drop **1** To knock down or tackle an opponent. ⟨he was *dropped* with a left hook⟩ ⟨*dropped* on the 2-yard line⟩
2 To make a drop pass, drop shot, or dropped goal.
3 To outdistance an opponent (as in cycling).
4 To cause a ball to roll or fall into a hole or through a basket. ⟨*dropped* in a 20-foot putt⟩ ⟨drove in for a lay-up and *dropped* it in⟩
5 Lose. ⟨*dropped* 3 games in a row⟩
6 *cricket* To drop a ball hit in the air by a particular batsman. ⟨*dropped* Dennis Amiss with the score at 30 in the Test trial at Worcester today — Bob Downing, *Wolverhampton (England) Express & Star*⟩
7 *golf* To pick up a ball from an unplayable lie and drop it over one's shoulder 2 club lengths from the original place or anywhere farther from the hole often with a penalty of one stroke.
8 or **drop in** *surfing* To slide down the face of a large wave to pick up speed before maneuvering along the face of the wave at an angle.

drop a goal *rugby* To kick a dropped goal.

drop-back *of a passer* Being one who normally drops back and passes from the pocket.

drop back *of a football quarterback* To move straight back from the line of scrimmage in preparation for throwing a forward pass. — compare ROLL OUT

drop ball *soccer* A method of restarting play after a temporary suspension (as because of an injury or when 2 opponents simultaneously knock the ball out of bounds) in which the referee drops the ball between 2 opponents, each of whom attempts to kick or gain control of the ball after it has hit the ground.

drop goal see DROPPED GOAL

drop in see DROP (*surfing*)

dropkick **1** A kick made by dropping a ball and kicking it as it bounces. The dropkick is commonly used in rugby and speedball but changes in the shape of the football have resulted in almost total abandonment of the dropkick in American football in favor of the placekick.
2 *speedball* A score of 4 points made by dropkicking the ball between the goalposts over the crossbar. — compare FIELD GOAL

drop-kick To make a dropkick; to propel a ball by means of a dropkick.

drop line see HANDLINE

drop mohawk *skating* A figure that consists of a mohawk followed by a change back to the original skating foot.

drop off *of a defensive player* To move away from a primary man or area of coverage in order to help cover another man or area. ⟨*dropped off* to double-team the receiver⟩

dropkick

drop-out *rugby* A dropkick made from within the 25-yard line by the defending team to put the ball in play after it has been kicked or carried over the touch-in-goal or dead ball lines or after a touchdown.

drop pass A pass (as in hockey or basketball) that is left for a trailing teammate rather than directed to a teammate. In hockey, the puck carrier stops the puck and skates past it usually attempting to draw away a defender. In basketball, the dribbler commonly moves away from the ball, allowing a teammate to move up and continue the dribble.

dropped goal or **drop goal** *rugby* A goal made by drop-kicking the ball between the goalposts and over the crossbar during play.

dropped three or **drop three** see WALTZ THREE

dropper *fishing* A short section of leader material tied to the middle of a leader so that 2 or more flies can be fished on a single line.

dropper fly *fishing* A fly that is tied to the end of a dropper. The dropper fly may be a wet fly fished with a streamer or a dry fly that serves as a locator or indicator when one is fishing a wet fly or nymph.

drop-shot To hit a drop shot. ⟨having lobbed brilliantly or *drop-shotted* cannily — *World Tennis*⟩

drop shot **1** A soft shot (as in tennis, badminton, or volleyball) that just clears the net and then drops suddenly.
2 *squash racquets* A soft shot that hits the front wall just above the telltale and drops suddenly.

drop volley *tennis* A drop shot made on a volley.

drop zone *skydiving* An area (as a large field often near an airfield) in which skydivers can land.

dry fly *fishing* An artificial fly that is designed to float on the surface of the water and that is usually tied with hackles that stick out at right angles from the hook.

dry-sail To remove a wooden sailboat from the water after each day's sailing so that its hull will not absorb water and become heavier.

dry skiing Practice (as indoors or during the off-season) of basic movements and positions used in skiing.

dry suit A waterproof rubber suit sometimes worn by scuba divers for protection from extremely cold water. The diver is kept warm by a layer of air trapped in warm underclothing. Any leak or rip in the rubber therefore reduces the effectiveness of the dry suit. — compare WET SUIT

dry sump A type of engine oil circulating system on some racing cars in which oil is stored in a special cooling radiator instead of in a reservoir at the base of the engine.

dual meet A meet (as for track and field, wrestling, or swimming) between 2 teams in which each team's score is the sum of the scores of the individual members. — see also MEET

¹dub A poor or inept player.

²dub *golf* To hit the ball poorly.

duck *cricket* A situation in which a batsman is retired without having scored a single run. The term comes from the British expression *duck egg* for zero recorded on the score sheet for the batsman. ⟨a true sportsman. He laughs when he makes a *duck* and looks dashed pleased with himself when he hits a boundary—*Sporting Life*⟩

duck-hook *golf* To hit a duck hook. ⟨*duck-hooked* his tee shot on the 18th hole — *Sports Illustrated*⟩

duck hook *golf* A low exaggerated hook.

ducking Hunting for ducks.

duckpin A short squat bowling pin used in the game of duckpins. The duckpin has the same general shape as the tenpin but it is only about 9½ inches tall and has a maximum diameter of approximately 4¼ inches tapering to 1⅜ inches at the base.

duckpins A game of bowling in which small balls without finger holes are rolled at duckpins. The bowler is allowed a maximum of 3 balls instead of 2 in a frame.

duckunder see UNDERARM SNEAK

dud A shotgun shell that fails to fire properly.

duffer One who has only mediocre skills at a recreational activity or game (as golf) especially because of limited experience or participation (as only on weekends).

dugout A low roofed shelter constructed on either side of a baseball diamond that is usually enclosed at the sides and back and that contains the players bench. The dugout is designed so that it does not block the view of the playing field from the stands. The floor of the dugout is typically below ground level, and there is usually a direct passage connecting the dugout and the team's dressing room.

dumbbell *weight training* A weight device consisting of a short bar with identical weighted spheres or adjustable disk weights on each end. The disks are held in place by adjustable collars; the middle part of the bar serves as a handle. Dumbbells are usually used in pairs and are popular for exercises in which the arms are moved alternately or in opposite directions.

¹dummy 1 *football* A heavy stuffed cylindrical bag (as of canvas) that is used in blocking or tackling practice.
2 A fake by the player with the ball.

²dummy British term meaning to make a fake. ⟨the player putting [the ball into the scrum] shall not hesitate or *dummy* and after putting it in he shall immediately retire behind his own pack of forwards — *Rugby Football League Laws*⟩

dump 1 To deliberately lose a game or contest.
2 *bowling* To release the ball with the fingers and thumb at the same time with the result that the ball fails to hook.
3 *drag racing* To defeat an opponent.
4 *football* **a** To tackle a quarterback before he can throw a pass; sack. **b** To throw a short pass to a back especially to counteract a blitz or when the primary receivers are covered. — often used with *off*
5 *ice hockey* To hit the puck into the attacking zone away from the goal and especially into a corner so that a teammate will have a chance to go after it.
6 *skydiving* To pull the ripcord.

dumped *of a surfer* Knocked off the board by a wave; wiped out.

¹dunk To throw a basketball into the basket with the hand above the level of and over or within the rim.

²dunk or **dunk shot** *basketball* A shot made by jumping high into the air and throwing the ball down through the basket with one or both hands.

dunk shot

dust 1 or **dust off** *baseball* To throw a pitch high and inside to a batter ostensibly to make him move back from the plate.
2 To hit a clay pigeon in skeet or trapshooting just enough to produce a puff of dust without breaking it. If there is no piece broken from the target, the target does not count in the shooter's score.

duster *baseball* A pitch that is intentionally thrown high and inside to a batter.

dust off see DUST (*baseball*)

Dutch 200 or **Dutchman** *bowling* A game with a score of 200 made by bowling alternate strikes and spares.

dynamic belay *mountain climbing* A method of arresting a fall in which the belayer allows the rope to run under friction around his waist while progressively increasing the tension with his hands. The dynamic belay absorbs much of the shock of the fall which might otherwise possibly break the rope, pull the belayer off his stance, or even kill the falling climber.

dynamometer *motor racing* A device that measures the power produced by an engine and that is used especially by engine builders to determine what tuning adjustment or design characteristics produce the maximum horsepower for a given engine.

dynasty A strong team or club that dominates its league or association for a number of successive years.

E

¹eagle *golf* A score of 2 strokes less than par for a hole.

²eagle *golf* To make an eagle on a hole. ⟨*eagled* the 16th hole⟩

early closing race *horse racing* A race for which the horses must be entered at least 6 weeks prior to the date of the race. All fees are forfeited if the horse is subsequently declared. A horse that is eligible at the time of the closing remains eligible regardless of its subsequent record. — compare OVERNIGHT

early foot *horse racing* Greater than usual speed at the beginning of a race.

earned run *baseball* A run scored before the defensive team has had a chance to make the third putout in an inning that is a result of an offensive or defensive action (as a base hit, stolen base, or fielder's choice) which did not result in an error and that is used in computing a pitcher's earned run average. A run that scores on a fielding error, a run scored by a base hit after a team has failed to get the third out because of an error, or a run scored by a runner who reached base on an error is not an earned run.

earned run average *baseball* The average number of earned runs per 9-inning game scored against a pitcher determined by dividing the total number of earned runs charged against him by the total number of innings pitched and multiplying by nine. Example: a pitcher who is charged with 76 earned runs for 314 innings has an earned run average of 2.18 ($76 \div 314 \, (= .242) \times 9 = 2.18$).

¹earth *fox hunting* An underground burrow of a fox.

²earth **1** *fox hunting* To drive a fox to hiding in an earth.

2 *of a fox* To hide in an earth.

earth stopper *fox hunting* Someone employed by a hunt to cover the area of the hunt the night before and stop up the drains and earths while the fox is out hunting so that it will not be able to seek refuge in these when chased by the hounds.

eased-up *of a racehorse* Slowed somewhat and not running all out (as in a race or workout).

easily *of a racehorse* Winning a race by a comfortable margin without having to be urged on by the jockey.

Eastern cut-off *track and field* A variation of the scissors in which the high jumper crosses the bar on his back in a horizontal position instead of in a sitting position so that his center of gravity is higher.

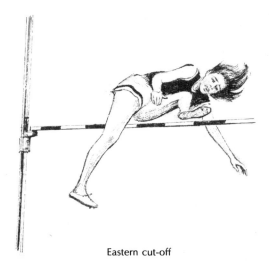

Eastern cut-off

Eastern grip see GRIP (*tennis*)

Eastern roll *track and field* A variation of the Eastern cut-off in which the jumper rolls over after crossing the bar and lands on his trailing leg.

eat the ball *of a football quarterback* To be tackled with the ball rather than throw a bad pass.

Eclipse Award An award presented to the outstanding jockey of the year.

¹edge **1** *skating* **a** Either of the 2 edges of an ice skate blade where the side and bottom surfaces meet that is made sharp by hollowing a groove along the bottom surface. **b** (1) A curve skated on one foot made by tilting the foot in the direction of desired movement and balancing the body over the skating foot. In skating an edge on ice skates, only the edge of the skate blade is in contact with the ice. In contrast, the wheels of a roller skate are designed to turn in the direction in which they are weighted so that during an edge all 4 wheels are in contact with the floor. Edges are called inside or outside edges depending on whether the foot is tilted to the inside or outside. Edges are normally designated by letters (as RFI or LBO) as to whether they are skated on the right or left foot, are skated forward or backward, and are inside or outside edges. (also called *curve*) (2) The figure made by an edge.

2 *skiing* Either of the 2 bottom edges of a ski that are dug into the slope especially to control sideslip in traversing or making turns and that are often reinforced with metal strips.

²edge 1 To defeat an opponent by a very narrow margin.

2 *skiing* To force one edge of the ski deeper into the snow by leaning the ankle to one side when traversing, turning, or stopping.

edge-set *skiing* The act of edging the skis at the beginning of a turn.

Edison see JOINT

Edward J. Neil Award An award given to the outstanding boxer of the year.

eeph *lacrosse* A single motion in which the ball is scooped up from the ground and passed to a teammate.

egg position *skiing* A tight crouch in which the skier's head is near his knees and his poles are tucked under his arms that is employed in downhill racing and in sliding down a jumping ramp as a means of increasing speed by reducing wind resistance.

eight *rowing* **1** An 8-oared racing shell.

2 The crew of an 8-oared shell.

eight ball see BILLIARDS

eighth pole see POLE (*horse racing*)

800 or **800-meter run** *track and field* A race run over a distance of 800 meters.

880 or **880-yard run** *track and field* A race run over a distance of 880 yards.

eights *rowing* Competition for 8-oared shells. ⟨Radcliffe, the favorite in the *eights* before the regatta began — *Sports Illustrated*⟩

ejector A mechanism in the action of a firearm that ejects the empty cartridge case.

elapsed time The actual time taken in traveling over a course (as in racing). In drag racing, each competitor is separately timed, and the one with

the shortest elapsed time is the winner. In yacht racing, where boats of widely differing sizes and speeds are competing together so that handicaps must be used, the winner is determined on the basis of corrected time, and the one with the fastest elapsed time may not necessarily be the winner.

elbow see GATE

elbow boot see BOOT (*harness racing*)

elbowing The act of hitting an opponent with the elbow in ice hockey or box lacrosse which results in a major or minor penalty.

electric épée *fencing* An épée that has a spring-loaded electrical contact at the button which is connected ultimately to an electrical scoring device at the scorer's table. A wire runs through the blade and connects outside the guard to a body wire which runs up the fencer's sword arm and around to his back to another wire which leads to the end of the piste. As the fencer moves forward and back, the slack in the wire is taken up by a spring-loaded spool at the end of the piste. The electrical device records all hits on target and only the first hit if the other fencer subsequently hits the target. If the hits are made within 1/25 of a second, the device registers a double hit. Electrical scoring is used in all major épée competition and because of its accuracy has eliminated the need for judges.

electric foil *fencing* A foil that has a spring-loaded electrical contact in the button and that is wired like the electric épée. In foil competition the target is limited to the trunk, so in order for the scoring device to distinguish between valid and invalid hits, the fencers wear metallic jackets which cover the target area. Hits made on the metallic jacket are recorded by a colored light and those made off target (as on the mask or an arm) by a white light. The device used with electric foils does not give priority to hits made at virtually the same time, so the judge is not completely eliminated.

elementary backstroke see BACKSTROKE (*swimming*)

elephant's foot see FOOTSACK

elevation 1 The height of the muzzle of a firearm in relation to the breech or the height of the pile of an arrow in relation to the nock when aiming at a target.

2 An adjustment on a sight which moves the sight up or down and thereby makes a corresponding change in elevation when the weapon is aimed.

elevator *wrestling* A move in which a wrestler

131

forces his leg under his opponent's leg and raises it to lift the opponent off balance.

eleven A football, soccer, cricket, or field hockey team.

eligible receiver *football* An offensive player who is permitted by the rules to catch a forward pass. At the time the pass is thrown only the backs and the 2 ends may legally catch a pass. If the pass is subsequently touched or tipped by a defensive player, all offensive players are then eligible. — see also FORWARD PASS

elimination heat *harness racing* One of 2 or more heats to qualify horses for a final heat.

elimination tournament A tournament set up with pairs of participants competing against each other and with losers being eliminated and winners advancing to compete against other winners until a single champion emerges. The most common form of elimination tournament is a single elimination in which competitors are eliminated by a single loss. The participants are paired on a draw sheet in the order of the draw with the winner of one pairing advancing to face the winner of the adjacent pairing. The elimination tournament is the most popular tournament format for sports in which individuals or teams compete against one another, and great interest is often placed on the semifinal and final rounds. In order for the tournament to come out even, that is to have 4 competitors in the semifinals and 2 in the finals, the number of entrants should be a power of 2 (as 4, 8, 16, 32, 64). Where the number is greater or less than a power of 2, some entrants will draw byes and will advance to the next round without competing. The number of byes is determined by subtracting the number of entrants from the next higher power of 2. Example: with 29 entrants in a single elimination tournament, 3 entrants (32 minus 29) will draw first-round byes and advance to the second round. The remaining 26 will compete producing 13 winners that will advance. The second round will then have 16 participants. — see also BYE, DRAW, SEEDING; compare ROUND-ROBIN

Eliminator *drag racing* 1 A car that wins its heat. 2 Any of eight categories in which winners in the various classes are grouped for the final heats. Four of the groups are designated as professional and 4 as sports-racing. The Top Fuel and Top Gas Eliminators are 2 categories that include the most powerful fuel- or gasoline-powered dragsters that are essentially unrestricted as to modifications in engine or drive train or to the design of the car. Some dragsters even use 2 engines.

The Funny Car Eliminator category represents fuel-powered funny cars, and the Pro Stock Eliminator category includes standard late-model production cars with modifications in the engine and body. These 4 categories make up the professional group. In the sports-racing group, the Eliminator categories are made up of class winners from many different classes grouped on the basis of elapsed times. Because of the range of classes competing together, handicap starts are normally used in this group. The Competition Eliminator category represents an assortment of specially designed and built drag racing cars, including smaller and less powerful dragsters, that are run on either gasoline or fuel. The gasoline engines may be supercharged. The Modified Eliminator category represents various nonsupercharged gasoline-powered hot rods that are essentially extensive modifications of automobiles originally built for street use. The Super Stock Eliminator and Stock Eliminator categories are for production cars that are not extensively modified beyond stronger clutches and flywheels, custom exhaust systems, and special drag racing tires.

elite *rowing* 1 Being an oarsman who has rowed in a winning boat in a major championship meet; being one who has won a major championship. 2 Being an event for crews made up of or having elite oarsmen. A crew which has at least one elite oarsman is not permitted to compete in any but elite events.

elongated start see CROUCH START

emery ball *baseball* A ball illegally roughened on one side with powdered emery or with emery cloth so that the rough side will be more air-resistant and cause the ball to curve abnormally when pitched.

encroaching *of a football player* Having any part of the body illegally over the scrimmage line when lining up for the snap; making illegal contact with an opposing player after lining up for the snap but before the ball is put in play. Encroaching is penalized by a loss of 5 yards.

encroachment *football* The act or infraction of encroaching.

end 1 *archery* A number of arrows shot and scored as a group. Six arrows shot in 2 groups of 3 constitute an end in tournament shooting in the United States; in international competition an end is 3 arrows. 2 *cricket* The wicket defended by a particular batsman. ⟨to score a run the batsmen must exchange *ends*⟩

3 *curling* The play of all stones to the house at the opposite end of the rink. After the last stone has been played, the end is scored, and a new end is begun in the opposite direction.
4 *football* **a** Either of 2 players who line up at the extremities of the offensive or defensive line. On offense the ends may be played close to or away from the other players on the line; usually a team plays one end tight and the other split. Offensive ends are primarily used as blockers and pass receivers, though they may on occasion carry the ball on such plays as the end around. On defense the ends normally rush the passer and try to contain running plays coming to the outside. **b** The position played by an end.
5 *lawn bowling* The play of the jack and all bowls from one end of the rink to the other. After the last bowl has been played, the end is scored, and a new end is begun in the opposite direction.
6 *speedball* **a** Either of the 2 offensive players who play on the outside of the forward line and who are analogous to the outside forwards in soccer or the wings in field hockey. **b** The position played by an end.
7 *tennis* The side of the court occupied by one player or side. ⟨the players change *ends* after odd-numbered games⟩
end around *football* A reverse in which an end cutting back through his own backfield receives a handoff and runs around the opposite end of the line.
endboards *ice hockey* The boards at the ends of the rink.
end kick or **end goal** *speedball* A score of one point that results when a ground ball is kicked over the end line but not between the goalposts. The end kick is an optional means of scoring in men's speedball, but it is not used at all in the women's game.
end line **1** Either of 2 lines at the extreme ends of a court or playing field perpendicular to the sidelines that mark the end boundaries of the playing area.
2 *fencing* Either of 2 lines 40 feet apart that mark the rear limits of the fencing area on the piste.
endo *auto racing* A crash in which a car turns end over end.
end run *football* An offensive play in which the ballcarrier attempts to run wide around the flank of the formation.
end strings A set of strings that can be adjusted to vary the depth of the pocket of a lacrosse stick. — see STICK (*lacrosse*)

endurance race A race of long duration (as 6, 12, or 24 hours) or over a long distance (as 500 miles or 1000 kilometers) that is designed to test the ability of a competitor or machine to withstand extended periods of stress. Endurance racing is an important aspect of motor sports and especially of auto racing. The races are generally run over a closed course, with the winner being the one that covers the greatest distance in the allotted time or that finishes first (in a fixed distance race). The cars are run continuously, usually stopping only for fuel or to change drivers. In very long races the drivers normally spend no more than 3 to 4 hours at a time driving.
enduro An endurance race.
end zone **1** *box lacrosse* The zone at either end of the box that extends from the center zone to the boards behind the goal; the attacking or defensive zone.
2 *Canadian football* A 25-yard-deep area at either end of the field between the goal line and the dead line.
3 *football* A 10-yard-deep area at either end of the field between the goal line and the end line.
4 *ice hockey* The zone at either end of the rink that extends from the blue line to the boards behind the goal; the attacking or defensive zone.
5 *lacrosse* The playing area at either end of the field behind the goal.
enforcement spot see SPOT OF ENFORCEMENT
enforcer *ice hockey* A strong tough player who is known for retaliating against unusually rough play by members of the opposing team. (also called *policeman*) — compare HATCHETMAN
engagement *fencing* Contact between the blades when the fencers are on guard.
en garde see ON GUARD
English Spin usually around the vertical axis imparted to a ball by striking it to the right or left of center (as in billiards) or by twisting the hand when releasing it (as in bowling). — see also DRAW, FOLLOW
English billiards see BILLIARDS
English hand balance *gymnastics* A handstand performed on the balance beam with the body in line with the lengthwise axis of the beam, the heels of the hands placed on top of the beam, and the fingers against the sides of the beam.
English saddle see SADDLE
en marchant *of a fencing action* Made while advancing.
enter To formally register oneself or another in a competition by filling out an entry form and paying the required entry fee.

entertain To play against an opposing team on one's home field, court, or ice. ⟨the way tonight's . . . playoff picture unfolds as Montreal *entertains* Chicago in game no. 1 — *Syracuse Herald-Journal*⟩

entry **1** A competitor entered in competition.

2 *diving* The act of entering the water at the completion of a dive. The entry, during which the body must be straight and essentially vertical, is judged on form as a part of the dive.

3 *horse racing* A single betting unit of 2 or more horses running in the same race that have the same owner, stable, or trainer. The horses will usually have the same number with the second horse carrying in addition a letter designation (as entry 1 and 1A). A bet made on the entry will pay off if either horse finishes in the position picked. The entry designation, however, is only for betting purposes and does not affect the running of the race or the distribution of the purse.

4 *skating* The point at which a skater begins a jump or spin.

entry fee A fee that may be required of all competitors entered in a competition. The entry fee is normally paid at the time a competitor is entered in the competition, and it is used to help defray the expenses involved in staging the competition or as a partial source of the purse.

entrymate *horse racing* A horse that is entered in a race as part of the same entry as another.

envelope *ballooning* The usually nylon bag that holds the air or gas of a sports balloon.

envelopment *fencing* An attack on the blade or a riposte in which the opponent's blade is moved in a complete circle ending with the blades in the original line of engagement. The envelopment is usually followed immediately by a lunge. — compare BIND, CROISÉ

épée **1** A fencing sword with a bowl-shaped guard and a relatively rigid blade with a triangular cross section that has no cutting edge and that tapers to a blunted point. The épée is a thrusting rather than a cutting weapon derived from the dueling sword. Its overall length is about 43 inches and it weighs up to 27 ounces. On the point is a tiny 3-pronged device (*pointe d' arrêt*) that catches on the clothing and keeps the point from glancing off before a hit can be registered. — see also ELECTRIC ÉPÉE; compare FOIL, SABER

2 The art or sport of fencing with an épée; competition in which the épée is used. In épée, unlike foil and saber, the entire body is a valid target, and there is no definite sequence of play or convention that must be followed. For this reason, épée fencing more closely resembles dueling, and the first point to reach the target scores a hit. If both fencers hit simultaneously, both are declared hit on the analogy that in a duel both would be wounded or dead.

épéeist Someone who fences with an épée.

equalise British term meaning to score an equalizer.

equalizer A goal, run, or point that ties the score. ⟨scored an *equalizer,* then assisted on a second goal — *Soccer News*⟩

equestrian events The competitive events in riding and handling a horse that include cross-country riding, dressage, and show jumping and are held as separate events or together make up the One and Three Day Events.

equipment bag A bag (as a duffle bag) in which a player or a team carries equipment (as bats, gloves, masks, helmets, and pads).

equitation The art or sport of riding and handling a horse in competition in dressage events.

equivalent odds see DOLLAR ODDS

¹error **1** *baseball* A defensive misplay other than a wild pitch or passed ball made when normal play would have resulted in an out or would have prevented the advance of a base runner. It is charged against the player and against the team in statistical records. An error is normally charged against a player who drops a fly ball, makes a wild throw to a base, or is unable to field a batted ball cleanly. A batted ball that, in the judgment of the scorer, could not have been fielded even though it was touched by the fielder's glove is not charged as an error.

2 *billiards* Failure by a player to make a called shot that ends the player's inning.

3 *bowling* Failure to make a spare on a leave other than a split; blow, miss.

4 Failure of a player to make a successful return of the ball during play (as in tennis, handball, or squash).

²error *baseball* To make an error.

errorless *baseball* Having no error charged against a player or a team during a designated period. ⟨have put together a string of 90 consecutive *errorless* innings — *Sport*⟩

¹escape *wrestling* The act or an instance of regaining a neutral position after a takedown by one's opponent or from a position of disadvantage; a maneuver that brings about an escape. An escape is worth one point to the wrestler. — compare REVERSAL

²escape *wrestling* To maneuver out of a position in which one's opponent has an advantage; to regain a neutral position especially after a take-down.

Eskimo roll *kayaking* A stunt roll in a skirted kayak in which the kayaker leans over to one side causing the kayak to capsize and then rights the kayak with a movement of the hips so that he surfaces on the other side and completes a full circle in one continuous motion.

ess or **esses** *motor racing* Two turns in opposite directions located close together on a road racing course; an S-shaped turn. ⟨stay in that gear through Turn 2, a medium speed left-right *ess* — Jackie Stewart⟩

ethyl chloride A local anesthetic that rapidly chills an injured area (as a bruise or sprain) when sprayed on the area.

étrier *mountain climbing* A short rope ladder with up to 4 steps that is usually used in pairs especially to serve as a foothold in artificial climbing. An étrier may also be made of webbing with 3 or 4 loops through which the foot or leg may fit.

Euler *skating* A jump from the backward outside edge of one skate with a full turn in the air and a return to the backward inside edge of the opposite skate. (also called *half loop*)

European Cup Soccer championship competition among representative teams of the member nations of the European Football Association.

European Cup Winner's Cup Soccer championship competition among the various national champions of the European Football Association.

evasion see DÉROBEMENT

even court *badminton* The right service court. It is so named because the serve is made from the right court when the server's score is love or an even number.

even money An equal amount on both sides of a bet; a bet without odds that would return a profit equal to the amount wagered.

even par *of a golfer* Having scored par for a hole or a round.

event Any of the individual contests that comprise a sports program.

even time A running time of exactly 10 seconds for the 100-yard dash.

eventing Equestrian events or competition.

evident superiority *wrestling* A situation in which one wrestler has scored at least 8 points more than his opponent and has therefore won the match.

exacta see PERFECTA

exchange **1** *track and field* The process of transferring the baton in a relay race from one runner

to a teammate within a designated exchange zone. The next runner starts to run before his teammate reaches the passing zone so that the exchange can be made when he is running at full stride. The exchange may be either visual or non-visual, depending usually on the length of the relay. The nonvisual exchange involves the transfer of the baton to an outgoing runner, who does not watch the transfer, from either hand of the incoming runner to the opposite hand of the outgoing runner, which is extended backward with the palm facing down. The nonvisual exchange is used primarily when speed of transfer is essential (as in 440-yard relay), and it is the incoming runner who is responsible for the success of the exchange. The visual exchange also is made on either side of the lane but involves watching of the incoming runner by the receiver who takes the baton with the palm of his hand facing either up or down. The visual exchange is most often used in longer relays when the incoming runner is fatigued or when the runners lack a sufficient degree of timing to effect the nonvisual exchange; it is the receiver who is responsible for the successful completion of a visual exchange. **2** A rally in racquetball.

exchange zone or **exchange lane** *track and field* An area 20 meters (65 feet, 7.4 inches) long marked in each lane of the track within which the exchange of the baton must take place in a relay race. (also called *passing zone, takeover zone*)

execute To perform properly or skillfully the basic techniques or fundamentals of a sport or a particular play. ⟨they ran away from us because we just weren't *executing* on defense⟩

executive course or **executive length course** A golf course that is considerably shorter and less demanding than a regulation course with par for each hole based on shorter distances and that is usually built for use by older players.

exempt player *golf* A player who is exempt from having to qualify for a tournament usually by virtue of his past performance. A touring professional will have to qualify for the weekly tournaments unless he has won a tournament during the past 12 months, currently ranks in the top 60 money winners on the tour, or has survived the cut in the previous week's tournament. It is also possible for a player to be exempt for a specific tournament as a result of having been among the top 25 finishers in the same tournament the previous year.

exercise boy *horse racing* A rider who is employed by a stable or a trainer to exercise racehorses.

exhibition 1 A public performance of a competitive or noncompetitive sport staged essentially as a demonstration of skills with the performers often not going all out to win and usually with no decision made as to a winner. ⟨a karate *exhibition*⟩ ⟨2 former heavyweight champions sparring in a 2-round *exhibition* bout⟩
2 A professional wrestling match.

exhibition game An unofficial game played between 2 professional teams usually as a benefit or as one of a series of preseason games that are part of the training program. Exhibition games are played under regular game conditions, often in a city that does not have a franchise, so that fans in that city will have a chance to see the teams in action. Winning in exhibition games is important, but since the results are of no importance to league or conference standings, the games usually offer the coaches a chance to try out new strategies or to observe the play of less experienced players under game conditions.

exotic bet *pari-mutuel betting* Any of several betting schemes which depend on the position of more than one competitor at the finish (as the perfecta) or the results of more than one race (as the daily double), which have extremely high odds against the success of any one combination, and which usually have very high payoffs.

expansion bolt see BOLT (*mountain climbing*)

expansion team or **expansion club** A professional sports team formed when a league or conference expands by granting additional franchises. An expansion club is typically created in a special draft of available players from all of the other teams in the league. Each of the established clubs is normally allowed to protect a given number of players (usually equal to the starting lineup plus several substitutes), and the remaining players are then available to be drafted by the expansion clubs.

expedite rule *table tennis* A rule designed to speed up play in championship games and to encourage strong offensive play in order to prevent long games in which players with good defensive skills are able to keep the ball in play for long rallies with neither side scoring. If a game is not concluded within 15 minutes, the format changes so that each side alternates in serving after each point, and if a rally goes for 13 exchanges without a score, the receiver is automatically awarded the point.

Experimental Free Handicap *horse racing* A rating of the top thoroughbreds expected to be racing the following season which consists of assigning weight handicaps to each of the horses as if they were all running in a handicap race. The rating is usually made during the winter for horses that will be racing the following season as 3-year-olds and is based on their performances as 2-year-olds. Fillies and colts are rated together with fillies normally receiving a 5-pound weight allowance.

explosion shot *golf* A shot in which the club strikes the sand just behind the ball and blasts it out of the sand trap.

explosive 1 *of a team or an offense* Known for the ability to produce a sudden strong offensive or scoring effort especially after a period of relatively ineffective or low scoring play.
2 *of a football running back* Known for the ability to exploit available openings in the line or elsewhere in the defensive formation to make a long gain.

exposure *mountain climbing* The condition of being or the climber's awareness of being in an open position on a steep cliff or mountain with only open space below.

expulsion foul *lacrosse* A foul (as for striking or attempting to strike an opponent, coach, or official) which results in a 3-minute penalty charged against the player and his immediate expulsion for the duration of the game. A substitute is permitted to take his place after the 3-minute penalty time has expired.

extend 1 To exert or push oneself to full physical capacity.
2 *equitation* To cause a horse to move with a full-length stride.
3 *gymnastics* To stretch out the body or to straighten the arms and legs.

extended hold see HAND-IN-HAND POSITION

extension The act of extending a horse. — compare COLLECTION

extra *cricket* A run made whenever the batsmen are able to exchange places without having hit the ball (as on byes, wides, or no-balls). The runs count in the team's score but not as part of the batsman's record.

extra-base hit *baseball* A base hit good for more than one base (as a double, triple, or home run).

extra cover *cricket* 1 A fielding position on the off side between cover point and mid-off but usually farther from the batsman than cover point.
2 The fieldsman covering this area.

extractor A mechanism in a firearm that extracts the empty case from the chamber so that it can be ejected.

extra inning *baseball* Any full inning played beyond the number (as 9) constituting a regulation game in order to break a tie.

extra man *lacrosse* One more player than an opposing team has on the field because one of its players is in the penalty box. ⟨will be playing with an *extra man* for the next 3 minutes⟩

extra period Any period played after the end of a regulation game in order to break a tie; overtime.

extra point *football* A point scored on a successful try for point after a touchdown; point after touchdown.

extra time Playing time added to the end of a game (as of soccer or rugby) because of unusual delays during the game for which there are no permitted time-outs.

eyas or **eyess** *falconry* A young hawk or falcon taken from the nest for training as distinguished from one caught wild. — compare HAGGARD

eye 1 A loop at the end of the shank of a fishhook.
2 A hole in a piton through which a carabiner is attached.
3 A loop in the end of a bowstring.
4 Skill or ability dependent upon eyesight or judgment of distance (as in aiming a firearm or in determining whether a pitched baseball is or is not in the strike zone).

F

¹face **1** The front or principal side or part of something: **a** The exposed nearly vertical surface of a rock cliff. **b** The sloping front portion of a wave down which surfers plane. **c** The part of the blade of a hockey stick that normally makes contact with the ball or puck. **d** The flat part of a racket or paddle that makes contact with the ball or shuttlecock. **e** The painted side of an archery target. **f** The belly of an archery bow. **g** The flat part of a golf club that makes contact with the ball and that is set at a different angle for each club. **h** The sloping part of a bunker on a golf course. **i** The end of a croquet or roque mallet head that makes contact with the ball. **2** Short for *face-off*.

²face **1** To put the puck or ball in play in a face-off. ⟨*face* the puck at center ice⟩
2 *baseball* To bat against a particular pitcher. ⟨struck out all of the twenty-one batters who *faced* him — *Current Biography*⟩

face dodge *lacrosse* A dodge that is made by bringing one's stick up and faking a pass and, as the defensive player brings up his stick to block the pass, swinging the stick in front of the face to the other side.

face guard see FACE MASK

face hold *wrestling* An illegal hold in which the mouth, nose, or eyes are covered.

face mask **1** A device that consists usually of steel or molded plastic and that is worn by players in

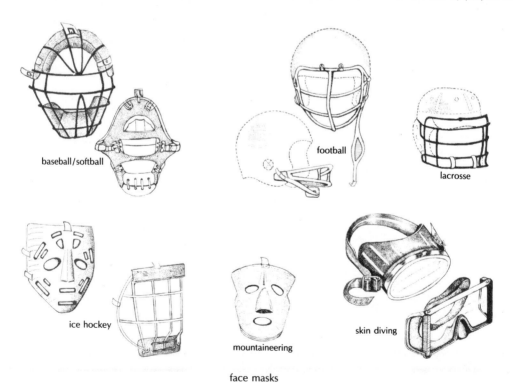

baseball/softball

football

lacrosse

ice hockey

mountaineering

skin diving

face masks

a number of sports to protect the face and especially the nose and mouth from injury: **a** A steel or plastic cage that is attached to a helmet (as in football, lacrosse, or ice hockey) to protect the player's face especially during physical contact. (also called *face guard*) **b** *ice hockey* A molded plastic covering for the face usually with holes for the eyes and mouth that is held in place by straps and that is worn by a goalkeeper for protection in the event he is hit in the face by the puck. **c** *baseball* A steel cage that is padded and held in place by straps and that is worn by the catcher and home-plate umpire to protect them from injury especially from foul tips.

2 A piece of skin diving or scuba diving equipment that consists of a piece of flat clear glass or sometimes plastic that is fitted to a flexible molded rubber skirt which forms a watertight fit around the diver's eyes and nose to keep out water and permit undistorted vision underwater. The nose is covered both to aid the diver in breathing through his mouth and to permit equalization of pressure inside the mask by exhaling through the nose.

3 A usually leather covering for the face, chin, and neck that has openings for the eyes, nose, and mouth, that is held in place by straps, and that is used by skiers and mountaineers for protection from the wind and cold. — compare BALACLAVA

¹face-off 1 *ice hockey* The method of putting the puck in play (as at the start of each period or after a goal) in which 2 opponents face each other (each with his back to his own goal) with stick blades usually held flat on the ice and, when the puck is dropped or thrown down by an official, attempt to gain possession of the puck or hit it to a teammate. Although a face-off may occur at any place on the ice exclusive of the area within 20 feet of the goal and 15 feet of the boards, it often will be held at one of the 9 face-off spots.

2 *lacrosse* A method of putting the ball in play (as at the start of each period or after a score) in which 2 opponents face each other (each with his back to his own goal) with sticks flat on the ground and with the ball balanced between the 2 sticks and attempt to gain possession of the ball or to pass it on to a teammate at a signal from the referee.

3 *water polo* A method of putting the ball in play (as after a double foul) in which the referee tosses the ball into the water midway between 2 opposing players. Play resumes as soon as the ball touches the water, but the face-off players are not permitted to touch the ball before it strikes the water.

ice hockey face-off

²face-off To take part in a face-off. ⟨the opposing centers *face-off* after a goal⟩

face-off circle 1 *box lacrosse* Any of 5 circles 2 feet in diameter that are used as the location for a face-off. There are 2 face-off circles in each end zone located 30 feet from the goal lines and 16 feet from the sideboards. There is one face-off circle located in the middle of the center zone. A pair of lines tangent to the circles and parallel to the sideboards are used as restraining lines for the players taking part in the face-off. Circles 12 feet in diameter surround the end-zone face-off circles and restrain the players not taking part in the face-off. During a center-zone face-off, only the 2 men taking part in the face-off are allowed in the center zone.

2 *ice hockey* Any of the 5 restraining circles centered on the face-off spots at center ice and in the end zones of the rink. The circles are drawn on a 15-foot radius for professional play and a 12-foot radius for amateur play. Only the referee and the 2 players taking part in the face-off are permitted inside the circles during the face-off. — see also FACE-OFF SPOT

face-off spot 1 *ice hockey* Any of 9 circular spots used as the location for a face-off when the puck has to be moved from the point at which play was stopped (as when the stoppage occurs within 20 feet of a goal or within 15 feet of the sideboards) or when play resumes in a different zone. There are 2 red face-off spots in each end zone that are 2 feet in diameter and that are located 20 feet from the goal lines (15 feet in amateur hockey) and 22 feet from an imaginary line connecting the centers of the two goals (15 feet from the sideboards in amateur hockey). There are 4 red face-off spots in the neutral zone, 2 at each end of the zone, that are 2 feet in diameter (one foot in amateur hockey) and that are located 5 feet from the blue lines and 40 feet apart; in the exact center of the rink is a 1-foot blue spot (a 2-foot red spot in amateur hockey). The end-zone face-off spots are used most often when icing is called, when a defensive player causes the puck to be lodged in the back of the net, when a stoppage of play occurs close to the sideboards or to the goal, or after an unsuccessful penalty shot attempt. The center face-off spot is used most often at the start of each period and after a goal is scored. The neutral-zone face-off spots are used most often when a player in his attacking zone commits an infringement of the rules or causes a stoppage of play and when an offside is called.

2 *lacrosse* The point on the field at which a face-off takes place marked by an X in the middle of the center line.

faceplate The glass or plastic front of a skin diver's face mask.

factory team *motor racing* A racing team that is supported by the manufacturer of the vehicles it races. A factory team may be one that is under the direct sponsorship and control of the manufacturer, or it may be an independent team under contract to prepare and race the manufacturer's equipment under the team's name with major technical and financial support coming from the manufacturer. (also called *works team*)

FA Cup The postseason championship tournament and the championship trophy of the British Football Association (soccer).

¹fade 1 *of a hit, thrown, or rolled ball* To swerve to the right or left of a straight course.

2 or **fade back** *of a football quarterback* To move back from the line of scrimmage with the ball in preparation for throwing a forward pass.

3 *golf* To deliberately cause the ball to swerve in flight to the same side as one's dominant hand (as to the right when hit by a right-hander) especially to avoid obstacles. ⟨I used to have to *fade* the ball to be accurate — Gay Brewer⟩ — compare SLICE, DRAW

²fade *golf* The act or an instance of causing a ball to fade.

¹fadeaway 1 *baseball* Early name for a screwball. The term was first used of a pitch developed by Christy Mathewson. ⟨every time I throw the *fadeaway* it takes so much out of my arm . . . so I save it for the pinches — Christy Mathewson⟩

2 *handball* A ball hit to the front wall in such a way as to rebound very close to the side wall.

²fadeaway see FALLAWAY

fadeaway slide *baseball* Early name for a hook slide. (also called *fallaway slide*)

fade ball *bowling* A backup ball.

faena *bullfighting* A series of final passes made by the matador that leads to the kill.

fair *baseball* In or into fair territory.

fair ball *baseball* A batted ball that lands within the foul lines or that is within the foul lines when bounding to the outfield past first or third base or when going beyond the outfield for a home run.

fair-catch *football* To make a fair catch of a kick. ⟨punts of 57, 43 and 52 yards into the end zone and another of 47 yards that was *fair-caught* on the 12 — Ron Reid, *Sports Illustrated*⟩

fair catch 1 *football* A catch of a ball kicked by the opposing team made by a player who signals his intention to the officials and does not attempt to advance the ball after the catch and who is free from being hit or tackled by members of the kicking team. The player must signal for a fair catch by raising or waving one arm overhead while the ball is in flight. A fair catch is most often employed in catching a punt when the player catching the ball feels he may be tackled immediately after catching the ball and risks dropping the ball. When a fair catch is made, the ball becomes dead and is next put in play from that point by a scrimmage play or, in professional play only, by a free kick. If a fair catch is signaled but the ball is not caught, the ball becomes dead where it comes to rest or where downed by a member of the kicking team. If a fair catch is muffed, it is a loose ball and may be recovered by either team.

2 *rugby* A catch of the ball made directly from a kick, knock-on, or throw-forward by the opposing team before it hits the ground. In making the fair catch the player must call out "mark" and at the same time make a mark in the ground with his heel. The referee then stops play and allows the player catching the ball to make a free kick from the point of the mark or from any point behind the mark but the same distance from the touchline as the mark. The kick, which can be a punt, dropkick, or a placekick, is toward the opponent's goal, and until the player begins his kick or places the ball on the ground (for a place-kick), opposing players must remain behind the point of the mark. Any form of kick is useful for gaining ground (moving the ball closer to the opponent's goal), for a team does not automatically give up possession of the ball by kicking it providing a member of the kicking team gets to the ball first; if the free kick is a placekick or a dropkick (but not a punt), a goal can be scored if the ball passes between the goalposts. (also called *mark*)

fair territory *baseball* The part of the playing field lying within the foul lines.

fairway **1** The navigable part of a river or bay; an open channel.

2 The well-mowed area of a golf course between the tee and the putting green exclusive of hazards.

faja A colorful sash worn as part of the uniform of a jai alai player.

¹fake A simulated action (as a pretended kick, pass, or jump) or a quick movement in one direction before going in another that is intended to deceive an opponent. ⟨gave . . . a hip *fake,* two leg *fakes,* a couple of shoulder *fakes,* a hatful of head *fakes,* and a few eye blinks — *Sports Illustrated*⟩

²fake **1** or **fake out** To give a fake to an opponent; to draw an opponent out of position with a fake. ⟨*faked* two defenders and the onrushing goalie before calmly placing the ball into the middle of the net — *North American Soccer News*⟩

2 To pretend to do something in order to deceive an opponent. ⟨*faked* a field goal⟩

falcon Any of several long-winged hawks and especially the peregrine that are trained for use in falconry. The term *falcon* is commonly limited to the female falcon. — compare TIERCEL

falconer Someone who engages in falconry; one who trains and hunts with hawks.

falconry The art or sport of keeping, training, and hunting with hawks or falcons or occasionally eagles. Though young hawks may be raised and trained as eyases, it is usually easier to train and hunt with adults caught in the wild. Training usually is a matter of conditioning the bird to respond to and come to the falconer on command since the attacking of the quarry is natural to the hawk. In hunting the hawk may be flown at the quarry directly from the fist, or it may be allowed to soar high overhead while a dog flushes the game. The short-winged hawk usually kills its prey with its talons while the long-winged falcon merely uses the talons to grip the prey, often killing it on the ground by severing its neck with its notched beak. Hawks do not retrieve game. Once a hawk has downed its quarry, it is necessary for the falconer to retrieve the game, either after allowing the bird to eat some of it or by substituting other raw meat. The game sought in falconry is usually pheasant, quail, partridge, duck, or rabbit. (also called *hawking*)

¹fall *of a shot in tennis* To bounce twice without having been returned.

²fall *wrestling* A situation in which a wrestler is able to pin his opponent's shoulders to the mat for a designated time (as one second in collegiate or 2 seconds in high school competition) and thereby win the match. A fall wins the match regardless of the individual point scores of the wrestlers.

fallaway *of a shot in basketball* Made while a player is moving or falling away from the basket. ⟨a *fallaway* jumper⟩ (also *fadeaway*)

fallaway slide see FADEAWAY SLIDE

fall line *skiing* The natural slope of a hill; the most direct line from a given point on a slope to the bottom of the hill.

false attack *fencing* An attacking action that is meant to be parried or to provoke a specific response from the opponent so that the attacker can score on a redoublement, counter-riposte, or stop hit. (also called *attack on second intent, countertime*)

false-cast *fishing* To make a false cast.

false cast *fishing* A forward cast of the line in fly fishing with the rod pulled back so that the line returns before it hits the water. Several false casts may be made to dry off the fly or to extend the length of line being cast.

false double foul *basketball* Fouls charged against opposing players where the second foul is not simultaneous with the first as in a double foul but occurs before play is restarted following the first foul. Each foul carries its own penalty, and play is resumed with a center jump.

false edge *fencing* The first third of the back edge of a saber blade.

false grip *gymnastics* A grip by which a gymnast hangs from an apparatus (as the rings) that is characterized by the wrist being bent so that the heel of the hand rests on the apparatus.

false keel A thin strip attached below the keel of a boat to increase the lateral resistance or to serve as protection for the main keel.

false multiple foul *basketball* Two or more

fouls committed against one player by more than one opponent where the second foul is not simultaneous with the first as in a multiple foul but occurs before play is restarted following the first foul. Each foul is penalized with a free throw.

false start 1 Movement across the starting line or off the blocks before the starting signal is given in a race. A competitor may be disqualified for excessive false starts (as 2 in track and 2 or 3 in swimming depending upon the length of the course). A competitor who fails to comply promptly with the starter's commands may also be charged with a false start.

2 *football* Movement made by an offensive player after he has assumed a set position but before the ball is snapped that feigns a charge or shift or that simulates the beginning of a play. The offending team is penalized 5 yards, and any charge of encroaching by the opponent as a result of the false start is nullified.

¹fan 1 An enthusiastic follower, supporter, or spectator of a sport.

2 *football* A pass pattern in which the receiver on the strong side runs downfield a short way and then cuts sharply to the outside.

²fan 1 a *of a baseball batter* To strike out. ⟨nobody likes a pinch-hitter who *fans* — *Sporting News*⟩ **b** *of a baseball pitcher* To strike out a batter. ⟨walked only one man and *fanned* five — *Sport*⟩

2 *of an ice hockey player* To miss the puck when attempting to make a shot or a pass. — usually used with *on* ⟨he *fanned* on the shot⟩

far *wrestling* Relating to or being an arm or leg on the side of the body farthest from the opponent.

farm A minor league club (as in professional baseball or hockey) that is associated with a major league club and that provides a place for young players to get training and playing experience until they are needed by the parent club. ⟨*farm* team⟩

farm out To send a baseball player to a farm club.

fartlek *track and field* A system of endurance training in which the runner alternates periods of sprinting or striding with periods of jogging.

far turn *horse racing* The turn on a racetrack to the left of the grandstand and opposite the clubhouse turn.

fast 1 *of a playing surface* So hard or slick that a ball will move along the surface very quickly or will bounce quickly without perceptible slowing.

2 *of a bowling lane* Having a finish that allows

the ball to slide farther than normal before beginning to hook.

3 *of a dirt racetrack* Dry and firm enough to allow horses to run, trot, or pace their fastest. — compare GOOD, HEAVY, MUDDY, SLOPPY, SLOW

fastball *baseball* A pitch that is thrown at full speed and that rises or sinks slightly as it nears the plate. — compare CURVE, KNUCKLEBALL, SLIDER, SINKER, SCREWBALL, CHANGE-UP

fastballer *baseball* A pitcher who relies chiefly on a fastball.

fastballing *of a baseball pitcher* Being a fastballer. ⟨a *fastballing* left-hander⟩

fast bowler *cricket* A bowler who specializes in bowling the ball at top speed. A fast bowler normally relies on speed rather than a particular spin or bounce of the ball to get the batsman out.

fast-break To execute a fast break.

fast break A quick offensive drive toward the goal after gaining possession of the ball (as in basketball or lacrosse) in an attempt to score before the opposing team has time to set up its defense. The fast break normally results in the offensive players outnumbering the defensive players momentarily.

fast pill *horse racing* An illegal stimulant intended to make a horse run faster.

fast pitch softball see SOFTBALL

¹fat 1 *of a pitch in baseball* Easy to hit. ⟨knew the pitch was *fat* and took his let's-put-the-ball-away cut — Whitey Ford⟩

2 *of a golf stroke* Made with the clubhead lower than intended so that the ball travels high but short of the intended target. ⟨I was a little anxious and I hit it a little quick and I hit it *fat* — Gene Littler⟩

²fat *golf* The broad part of a putting green away from the hole.

fault 1 A violation of the rules of a court or racket game and particularly the rules of service whereby the server fails to serve the ball, ring, or shuttlecock properly or into the proper service court, drives it into the net or out of the playing area, fails to make it rebound from the wall past a designated line (as the short line), or steps out of a designated area while making the serve (*foot fault*):

a *badminton* Any violation of the rules of the game committed by either the server or the receiver. A single fault results in loss of service if by the server or loss of a point if by the receiver.

b *court tennis* A violation of the service rules. Two consecutive faults by the server (a *double* *fault*) result in loss of a point but not loss of service.

c *deck tennis* A violation of the service rules. Two consecutive service faults result in loss of service but not loss of a point.

d *handball* A violation of service rules. A double fault results in loss of service but not loss of a point.

e *jai alai* A violation of service rules which results in loss of a point and loss of service.

f *paddle tennis* A violation of service rules which results in loss of a point but not loss of service.

g *platform tennis* Same as paddle tennis.

h *racquets* A violation of service rules. Two consecutive faults result in loss of sevice but not loss of a point.

i *squash racquets* A violation of the service rules. A double fault results in loss of service and loss of a point.

j *squash tennis* Same as racquets.

k *table tennis* A violation of service rules which results in loss of a point but not loss of service.

l *tennis* A violation of service rules. Two consecutive faults result in loss of a point but not loss of service.

m *volleyball* A violation of service rules which results in loss of service but not loss of a point. — see also FOOT FAULT

2 *equitation* A penalty point deducted from the score of a horse and rider in jumping competition. Typical deductions are 3 faults for the first instance of disobedience by the horse, 4 faults for knocking down an obstacle or failing at the water jump, 6 faults for the second instance of disobedience, and 8 faults for a fall by horse and rider.

fault line *racquets* A line on the court perpendicular to the short line that extends from the middle of the short line to the back wall and that divides the rear of the court into 2 service courts.

favorite A competitor (as a racehorse or a ball team) judged by a handicapper or by bettors most likely to win. ⟨morning-line *favorite*⟩ ⟨a 3-point *favorite*⟩ — compare UNDERDOG

¹feather *archery* Any of the 3 or more feathers attached to the shaft of an arrow near the nock to stabilize the arrow in flight. If 3 feathers are used, they are spaced 120 degrees apart, with one (the *cock feather*) placed perpendicular to the nock. The cock feather is not necessarily from a male bird, nor are the other 2 feathers (the *hen feathers*) necessarily from a female bird. For ease and speed in nocking the arrow, the cock

feather is normally a different color from the hen feathers. It is important for all the feathers to have the same natural curve and to be attached to the shaft at the same angle for maximum stability.

²feather **1** *archery* To furnish an arrow with feathers.

2 To turn an oar or paddle so that the blade is horizontal in order to move it forward or backward with a minimum of air or water resistance. An oar is normally feathered at the end of a stroke and during recovery.

3 To use a very light touch (as in propelling a ball or puck or in increasing or decreasing the pressure on the throttle of a racing car).

feathered *of a double paddle* Having the 2 blades placed at different angles so that when one is pulling against the water the other is recovering with minimum air resistance.

featherweight A boxer or weight lifter who competes in the featherweight division. — see DIVISION

feature The most important event on a day's program. The seventh or eighth race is normally the feature on a horse racing program; the final boxing match is normally the feature on a card.

¹feed To pass a ball or puck to a teammate who is in position or who has an opportunity to score.

²feed A pass made to a teammate who is in position to score.

feeder A player who feeds a teammate.

¹feint **1** A quick movement (as of the head, hand, or body) in one direction before going or passing the ball or puck in another direction made in an effort to deceive an opponent; fake.

2 *badminton* see BALK

3 *boxing* A quick movement of the hand as if to punch that is intended to cause the opponent to move away or try to block and thereby leave an opening for a real punch.

4 *fencing* A simulated attack made usually by extending the sword arm with the intention of drawing a reaction from the opponent that will leave him open to a genuine attack.

5 *gymnastics* **a** A movement on the uneven parallel bars in which a gymnast holding the higher bar swings into the lower bar and flexes her hips as they hit the bar but does not release the grip on the higher bar. **b** A movement on the pommel horse in which the gymnast supporting himself with his hands on the pommels swings one leg around the end of the horse until he is straddling the end of the horse and then swings it back. This movement is often performed quickly as a preliminary to a swinging movement (as a flank circle).

²feint To deceive an opponent by making a feint.

fell race A single event in fell running.

fell running A form of cross-country running similar to orienteering and popular in the highland areas of Great Britain in which competitors race over long distances (up to 20 miles) from one landmark to another with each competitor free to pick his own route, finding his way with a map and compass.

¹fence To engage in fencing.

²fence 1 A wall that encloses and marks the boundaries of a playing area; boards. ⟨any unnecessary contact with a player playing the puck . . . which results in that player being knocked into the *fence* is boarding — *National Hockey League Rules*⟩ 2 An obstacle to be jumped by a horse in a steeplechase or jumping competition.

fence buster *baseball* A batter who is capable of hitting the ball to the outfield fences consistently; a power hitter.

fence-off *fencing* A bout for breaking a tie for first place in a competition.

fence off *fencing* To conduct or engage in a fence-off. Competitors usually fence off only a tie for first place; the placing of competitors tied for other positions is normally done in favor of the one who has received the fewest touches.

fencepost see BEDPOST

fencer A person who engages in fencing.

fencing The art or sport in which 2 opponents engage each other in combat with blunted swords on a narrow strip approximately 40 feet long and 6 feet wide. A bout is conducted until one opponent has scored a prescribed number of hits (as 5 for men or 4 for women) or until the expiration of a time limit (usually 6 minutes for men and 5 for women). Though the tips of all fencing swords are blunted, the fencers wear special cloth garments and a special wire-mesh mask for protection. A fencer is not permitted to use any part of his body but must rely solely on his sword for attacking and for parrying his opponent's attacks while moving up and down the strip into and out of attacking range. To be valid a hit must be made on the target area, which varies with the weapon used. In foil, which is engaged in by both men and women, the target is the torso and touches on the head, arms, or legs are not valid hits. The target in épée, usually engaged in only by men, is the entire body including the head, arms, and legs while that for

saber, also usually limited to men, is the entire body above the top of the hips, including the head and arms. A director or president, positioned just off the strip, supervises the bout, awarding hits to the fencers when they make valid touches on target. Competition in foil and épée is conducted with electric weapons which register valid hits on an electric device. In competition in which electric weapons are not employed, notably in saber and in less formal competition in épée and foil, the director is usually assisted by 4 judges who stand on either side of the strip and watch for hits. Fencing with foil and saber involves complex rules of attack (or *right of way*), which is the right of the first fencer who has extended his arm in attack to continue his attack until it is parried by the opponent. Only after the opponent's attack has been parried may a fencer launch a counterattack. Any hit made by a fencer while his opponent has the right of attack will be disallowed. Épée fencing, which developed from early training in dueling, has no such rules. It has retained the character of the duel, with the result that it is a more freestyle form of fencing.

fencing measure The distance that fencers normally maintain between each other for most effective swordplay.

fencing position The position in which a fencer stands on guard covering a particular line of attack.

fencing time The amount of time required to perform a simple fencing action.

fender *boating* A usually cylindrical cushion fixed to a rope that is hung over the side of the boat to protect it when docking or when it is alongside another boat.

¹fetch *sailing* To reach an objective usually despite adverse wind or tide and without making an additional tack.

²fetch *sailing* The distance a boat will travel by its own momentum when headed into the wind.

fid A pointed wooden tool that is used to open the strands of a rope.

¹field 1 The playing area for an outdoor game or sport:
a *Australian Rules football* An oval field 150–200 yards long and 120–170 yards wide with goals at each end consisting of 4 upright posts 7 yards apart. A rectangle 7 yards wide and 10 yards deep extends from the 2 inner posts of each goal toward the middle of the field. In the exact center of the field is a 10-foot circle.
b *baseball* A large field with 2 foul lines that

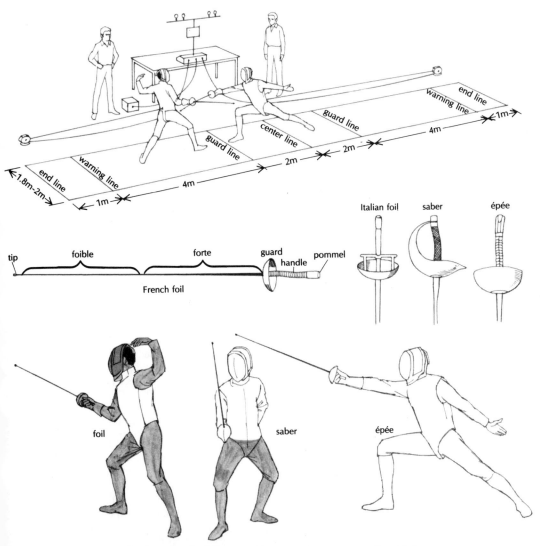

fencing: piste for foil competition; swords; target areas (in white)

meet at right angles at one edge and an outfield that extends out generally in an arc from foul line to foul line. The distance to the outfield boundaries differs from field to field but those of a representative major league park would be a minimum of 325 feet along the foul lines and 400 feet to dead center field. At the intersection of the foul lines is a 5-sided rubber slab 17 inches wide (*home plate*) which forms one corner of a 90-foot square which has a 15-inch-square base at each of the other 3 corners. Near the center of

this square is a small mound 10 inches high which has a 24-inch by 6-inch rubber slab near its center (the *pitcher's rubber*). This rubber is located 60 feet 6 inches from the rear corner of home plate. Batter's boxes 6 feet by 4 feet are marked on either side of home plate and beside the baselines near first and third bases are coach's boxes 20 feet long and 5 feet wide located parallel to and 8 feet outside the baselines. On grass fields, the areas around home plate, the pitcher's mound, and the base paths

field

and a wide arc from behind first base to behind third base are dirt. Behind home plate there must be an unobstructed space for a distance of 60 feet. For young players, the size of the field is reduced. The Little League has the following specifications:

distance between bases: 60 feet
distance from home plate to pitcher's mound: 46 feet
distance to outfield boundaries: approximately 200 feet
batter's boxes: 5 feet 6 inches by 3 feet
coach's boxes: 8 feet by 4 feet located 6 feet from the baseline

c *Canadian football* A rectangular field 160 yards long and 65 yards wide with a goal line at each end located 25 yards inside and parallel to each end line (*dead line*). There is an H-shaped or squared-Y-shaped goal consisting of 2 upright goalposts connected by a 10-foot-high crossbar located on the middle of each goal line. The field is marked with lines parallel to the goal lines every 5 yards just as in American football. Along each side of the field 24 yards from each sideline are inbounds lines.

d *cricket* A generally oval or rectangular field with no specific dimensions. A representative British cricket field may be 200 yards long and 120 yards wide. Near the center of the field is a firm closely-cut strip 22 yards long and 10 feet wide (the *pitch*) at each end of which is erected a wicket. On the ground through each wicket is an 8-foot-8-inch line (the *bowling crease*) and 4 feet in front of and parallel to each bowling crease is a popping crease of unlimited length but usually marked no longer than 10 feet. All 4 lines are parallel. Extending back at right angles from the ends of each bowling crease is a return crease. The return creases and the bowling crease mark the area in which the bowler must have his rear foot when delivering the ball; the popping crease marks the forward edge of the batsman's ground.

e *field hockey* A rectangular field 90–100 yards long and 50–60 yards wide that is divided by a center line across the middle of the field and 2 broken lines (the *25-yard lines*) across the field 25 yards from each end line. Along each side of the field is a broken line 5 yards inside and parallel to the sidelines (7 yards for men's play). Goals 12 feet wide and 7 feet high are located in the middle of each end line, and immediately in front of each goal is a 15-yard semicircle (16 yards for men's play) called the *striking circle*.

f *football* A rectangular field 120 yards long and 53$^1/_3$ yards wide that has a goal line 10 yards inside and parallel to each end line. The area between the end line and the goal line is the *end zone*. A goal in the shape of an H or squared Y consisting of 2 upright goalposts connected by a 10-foot-high crossbar is located in the middle of each end line. Lines are marked across the field parallel to the goal lines at 5-yard intervals. At right angles to the yard lines are a series of short inbounds lines 53 feet 4 inches from the sidelines for college play and 70 feet 9 inches from the sidelines in professional play.

g *Gaelic football* A rectangular field 160 yards long and 100 yards wide with an H-shaped goal located in the middle of each end line. Across the field is a center line, and there are restraining lines 14 yards, 21 yards, and 50 yards from each end line. Immediately in front of each goal is a rectangular area 15 yards wide and 5 yards deep (the *parallelogram*) which is analogous to the goal area and penalty area in soccer.

h *hurling* A field marked the same as for Gaelic football except that there are two 70-yard lines instead of 50-yard lines.

i *lacrosse* A rectangular field 110 yards long and 60 yards wide. Across the field is a center line; on each side of the center line is a line parallel to the center line that is 40 yards long and 20 yards from the front of each goal. From each end of this line, a line runs to the end line forming a rectangular goal area surrounding each goal. Across the center line parallel to the sidelines are 2 restraining lines that extend 10 yards on either side of the center line. These are marked 20 yards from the center of the field. Eighty yards apart at each end of the field are 2 goals 6 feet wide and 6 feet high, which are surrounded by 18-foot circles (the *creases*).

The field for women's play has no boundary lines, has goals located 100 yards apart, and is marked by 3 circles: a 17-foot crease around each goal and a 20-yard restraining circle in the middle of the field. Inside the center circle is a 4-yard-long line parallel to the goal lines.

j *polo* A rectangular field 300 yards long and 160 yards wide surrounded by a safety zone 10 yards wide on each side and 30 yards wide at each end. In the middle of each back line is a goal which consists of 2 upright goalposts at least 10 feet high and 8 yards apart. Across the field at each end are lines 30 and 60 yards from and parallel to the back line, and directly in front of each goal 40 yards out is a mark. These lines and the mark are used for certain penalty hits.

k *rugby* A rectangular field 160 yards long and 75 yards wide that has a goal line at each end 25 yards inside and parallel to the end lines (*dead-ball lines*). The area between the dead-ball line and the goal line is the *in-goal* area analogous to the end zone in football. An H-shaped goal consisting of 2 upright goalposts connected by a 10-foot-high crossbar is located in the middle of each goal line. Across the middle of the field is a *halfway line* and 10 yards in either side of and parallel to the halfway line are *10-yard lines*. Another line (the *25-yard line*) is marked across each end of the field 25 yards from the goal lines. Along the side of the field 5 yards from and parallel to each touchline is a broken restraining line.

The field used for Rugby League play is essentially the same except that the in-goal area is only 6 to 12 yards deep and the restraining lines along each side of the field are 10 yards from the touchlines.

l *soccer* A rectangular field from 100 to 130 yards long and 50 to 100 yards wide. A representative field may be 120 yards long and 75 yards wide. The field is divided by a halfway line across the middle. In the middle of the halfway line is a 20-yard restraining circle. A goal 24 feet wide and 8 feet high is located in the middle of each goal line. In front of each goal is a rectangular goal area 20 yards wide and 6 yards deep and surrounding the goal area is a rectangular penalty area 44 yards wide and 18 yards deep. Directly in front of each goal is a penalty kick mark 12 yards out from the goal. The penalty area is enlarged by an arc drawn 10 yards from the penalty kick mark.

The field used for women's play is typically 100 yards long and 60 yards wide with a restraining line 5 yards on either side of the halfway line instead of a center circle and with a semicircular penalty area marked on a radius of 15 yards from the goalposts.

m *softball* A field generally like that used for baseball with the following specifications:

distance between bases: 60 feet (16-inch slow pitch: 55 feet for men, 50 feet for women)

distance from home plate to pitcher's rubber: 46 feet for men, 40 feet for women (16-inch slow pitch: 38 feet)

distance to outfield boundaries at foul poles: 200 feet, minimum (slow pitch: 275 feet, minimum; 16-inch slow pitch: 250 feet, minimum)

batter's boxes: 7 feet by 3 feet

coach's boxes: 15 feet long located 6 feet outside the baselines

n *speedaway* A field hockey field.

o *speedball* A college football field.

p *team handball* see COURT

2 The area enclosed by a running track on which field events are held; infield.

3 Any of the 3 parts of a baseball outfield. ⟨hits to all *fields*⟩

4 a All of the competitors in a contest. ⟨a near record *field* of 20 Derby starters — *Boston Sunday Advertiser*⟩ **b** All of the competitors in a contest except the favorite or the winner. ⟨had a 36-point lead on the *field* — Don O'Reilly, *Auto Racing*⟩ **c** *pari-mutuel betting* Any competitors that do not make up the first 11 betting interests and that are grouped as a single betting unit. Pari-mutuel machines can handle only 12 betting interests, so in races which have more than 12 competitors or 12 separate betting interests — 2 horses with the same owner or trainer constitute a single betting interest — all those over 11 are grouped as the field, and a bet on the field, Number 12, pays off if any one of the field horses finishes in the money. Because of the increased possibilities of winning with a single field bet, only longshots are placed in the field. (also called *mutuel field*)

5 Any of the scoring rings on an archery target.

6 *cricket* **a** A fieldsman; all of the fieldsmen of a team. **b** The arrangement of the fieldsmen on the field.

7 *fox hunting* The people other than the master and his staff who make up the hunt.

²field **1** To play as a fielder or fieldsman.

2 a To play a ball that is in the air. ⟨every player is assigned an area of the court and is expected to allow his teammates to *field* balls that are out of his area of play — Allen E. Scates & Jane Wade, *Volleyball*⟩ **b** To pick up and control a ball on the ground. ⟨*field* a grounder⟩ ⟨*fielded* a punt⟩

3 To enter something in competition. ⟨more recently, the Giants have *fielded* some dreadful teams — Pete Axthelm, *New York*⟩ ⟨from his own viewpoint [his] highest level in racing was reached when he *fielded* his own Formula 1 Eagle and became the first American to capture a Grand Prix in a car of his own design — Jeff Scott, *Auto Racing*⟩

field archery Archery competition in which the archers move around a course laid out in a wooded area to simulate hunting conditions and shoot at targets of various sizes set up at different distances. Competition usually includes a field round, hunter's round, and animal round and is normally divided into freestyle shooting, in which there are no restrictions on aiming devices on the bows, and barebow or instinctive shooting, in which aiming devices are not permitted. The archer with the highest aggregate score is the winner. — see also FIELD ROVING COURSE

field arrow *archery* An arrow intended for field archery use and normally having a constant-diameter shaft, a field point, and large feathers. — compare FLIGHT ARROW

fieldball or **field handball** A game played on a soccer field by 2 teams of 11 players with the object to move the ball (as a soccer ball or basketball) upfield by passing, catching, and dribbling it with the hands as in basketball and attempting to score by throwing or punching the ball past the opposing goalkeeper into the goal. The game originated in Germany and has generally been replaced by a revised version called *team handball.*

field captain 1 see CAPTAIN
2 The chief official of an archery tournament.

fielder 1 *baseball* A player other than the pitcher or catcher who occupies a defensive position in the field while the opposing team is batting.
2 *cricket* A fieldsman.
3 *lacrosse* A field player.

fielder's choice *baseball* A situation in which the batter reaches base safely on a batted ball because the fielder attempts to put out another runner on the play. On a fielder's choice the batter is not credited with a base hit but is charged with a time at bat.

field event *track and field* An event other than a race including the high jump, pole vault, long jump, triple jump, shot put, discus throw, javelin throw, hammer throw, and weight throw.

field game A sports game (as baseball, football, lacrosse, soccer, or polo) that is played on a field.

field general A football quarterback.

field goal 1 *basketball* A score of usually 2 points made by throwing the ball through the basket during play. In some professional play, a field goal made from 25 or more feet away from the basket is worth 3 points.
2 *football* A score of 3 points made by dropkicking or placekicking the ball through the goalposts over the crossbar from scrimmage.
3 *rugby* A dropped goal.

4 *soccer* A score of 2 points in women's play made by driving the ball into the goal during play.
5 *speedball* A score of 3 points made by driving a ground ball with any part of the body other than the hands through the goal under the crossbar during play. — compare DROPKICK

field handball see FIELDBALL

field hockey A game played on a rectangular field 90–100 yards long and 50–60 yards wide between 2 teams of 11 players with the object to propel a ball along the ground using a curved stick and score by hitting the ball past the opposing goalkeeper into the goal and to prevent the opponents from scoring. Players are not permitted to obstruct opponents physically though they may seek to knock the ball out of the opponent's control. A team is made up of a goalkeeper and 2 fullbacks who are defensive players, 3 halfbacks who are primarily defensive players, and 5 forwards who are offensive players. Hitting, shoving, and tripping an opponent as well as striking, hooking, or holding down an opponent's stick are fouls which are usually penalized by a free hit or a penalty corner — an unhindered stroke at the ball — awarded to the opposing team. The game is normally played in two 30-minute halves with no time-outs except for injuries. Play is started at the beginning of each period and after each goal with a bully which is analogous to the face-off in ice hockey.

field horse *horse racing* A racehorse that is in the mutuel field for betting purposes and that often starts from an outside post position.

field house 1 A large building on a college campus used for cold- or bad-weather practice of field sports such as football, soccer, and baseball and often for indoor track and field competition, physical education classes, and intramural activities. A field house typically consists of a single room from 150 to 200 feet wide and 300 to 400 feet long with a synthetic surface or a dirt floor. Some field houses may have permanent or movable stands enabling them to be used for assemblies and, with the addition of a wooden floor, basketball games.
2 A building on or near an athletic field used for storing equipment.

fielding 1 The act or practice of catching or picking up a batted ball (as in baseball or cricket) and usually attempting to put out a runner or batsman.
2 *field hockey* The act of stopping and gaining control of a ball.

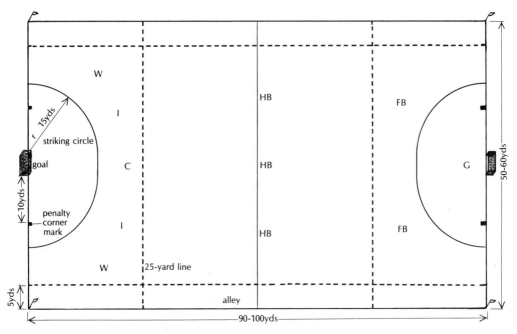

field hockey: G goalkeeper; FB fullback; HB halfback; W wing; I inner forward; C center forward

fielding average *baseball* The ratio of putouts and assists to the total number of chances expressed as a number between 0 and 1 carried to 3 decimal places and used as a measure of the success of a fielder or a team. Example: a player who is credited with 521 putouts and assists in 545 chances has a fielding average of .956.

field judge A football official who takes a position in the defensive backfield several yards away from the line of scrimmage and who is primarily responsible for covering the play on punts and deep pass plays, looking for pass interference, indicating when and where the ball is out of bounds, noting fair catches, and ruling on field goals with the back judge. The field judge also counts the 30 seconds that a team is allowed before snapping the ball and times the time-outs and halftime intermission.

field of play 1 A field on which a game is played. **2** A fencing piste.

field player A player other than a goalkeeper in a team sport.

field point *archery* A tapered point used in place of hunting or target points for general shooting in the field or woods. — see illustration at ARROW

field position *football* Position of the line of scrimmage with respect to the goal line at which a team is attempting to score.

field round *archery* A round in field archery that consists of 56 arrows, 28 in each group of 14 targets, shot from different positions and from distances of from 15 yards to 80 yards. Some of the targets call for a single shot while at other targets the archer will have to make 4 shots, each from a different position and from a different distance.

field roving course *archery* A course laid out usually in rolling wooded terrain to simulate the conditions encountered in bow hunting. A course has a total of 28 targets, usually in 2 groups of 14, ranging in size from 6 inches to 24 inches and set up so that the archers move from one shooting position to another much as golfers move around a golf course from hole to hole.

fieldsman *cricket* A player other than the bowler or wicketkeeper who occupies a position in the field when the opposing team is batting.

field trial A competition for hunting dogs held under actual or simulated hunting conditions in which the dogs are judged on such traits as scenting, pointing, flushing, and retrieving.

field umpire 1 *Australian Rules football* The umpire on the playing field who follows the

149

progress of the ball and who has sole control over the game. — compare BOUNDARY UMPIRE, GOAL UMPIRE

2 *baseball* see UMPIRE

fifi-hook *mountain climbing* A small hook that is attached to the top of an étrier (as by a carabiner) so that moving the étrier from a lower piton to a higher one is simplified.

15 or **fifteen** The first point made in a tennis game. (also called *five*)

fifteen ball see BILLIARDS

1500 or **1500-meter run** *track and field* A race run over a distance of 1500 meters.

50 or **50-yard dash** *track and field* A race run over a distance of 50 yards.

56-pound weight *track and field* An implement that consists of a heavy metal ball attached to a handle by a welded steel link, that is no more than 16 inches in overall length, and that is used in the 56-pound weight throw.

56-pound weight throw *track and field* A field event in which the 56-pound weight is hurled for distance with 2 hands from within a throwing circle 7 feet in diameter. In order to qualify as a legal throw, the weight must land in the throwing sector formed by 2 lines extending out at a 45-degree angle from the center of the throwing circle.

50-yard line *Gaelic football* Either of 2 lines across the field parallel to and 50 yards from the goal lines from which an offensive player puts the ball in play by a free kick when it is driven over the end line by a defending player.

fight A boxing match; bout.

fighter A boxer.

fighting chair *fishing* A heavy chair with an integrated footrest and a usually reclining back that is mounted on a swivel post to the deck of a sportfishing boat to provide the big-game fisherman with a secure place from which to play the fish.

figure see SCHOOL FIGURE

figure eight or **figure of eight** A movement, maneuver, or stunt (as in parachuting, stunt flying, or skating) in which the performer moves in a pattern resembling the numeral 8. — see also SCHOOL FIGURE

figure eight knot or **figure of eight knot** A stopper knot that is tied like the overhand knot with a twist in the loop. — see illustration at KNOT

figure 8 race *auto racing* A race run on a short figure 8-shaped track and characterized by the lead cars usually having to dodge slower cars at the crossing point.

figure 4 or **figure 4 scissors** *wrestling* A scissors hold in which the foot of the encircling leg is locked behind the knee of the opposite leg.

figure 4 scissors

figure skate see SKATE

figure skater Someone who engages in figure skating.

figure skating Competitive or recreational skating in which the skaters move in distinctive circular patterns based on the figure eight. Figure skating encompasses both ice skating and roller skating, and competition includes individual competition in school figures and freestyle skating, pairs competition in both compulsory figures and a freestyle program, and dance skating with compulsory and freestyle dance movements. Performers are required to perform a series of compulsory school figures as well as a freestyle program which consists of jumps and footwork in a smooth routine set to music of the skater's choice. In the compulsory section, a skater is required to trace each of the required school figures usually 3 times. In ice skating, the skater must create the pattern in the ice with his skate blade and attempt to duplicate it. In roller skating the pattern is painted on the floor to be followed by the skater. Skaters are judged on how well they duplicate the pattern, and in ice skating on how well they trace circles in the ice, and on smoothness of execution as well as on body position. Ice skating competition, in addition to the compulsory figures and the freestyle skating program, has a compulsory freestyle section in which each competitor is required to perform a number of required jumps in a coordinated sequence.

fill *bowling* The number of pins knocked down on the next ball following a spare.

filly A young female racehorse:

1 A thoroughbred of age 4 or less.

2 A standardbred of age 3 or less.

— compare COLT; MARE

¹fin **1** A swim fin.

2 A skeg on the bottom of a water ski or surfboard.

²fin *swimming* To move the hands back and forth through the water in propelling oneself; scull.

finalist A player or team that competes in the finals of a sports competition.

finals The deciding match, heat, game, or trial; the last round in a tournament to select a champion.

find *of a hunting dog* To pick up the scent of the quarry.

find the handle *of a baseball fielder* To hold onto a batted ball when fielding it. — used negatively when a fielder repeatedly drops the ball in attempting to field and throw it hurriedly

find touch *rugby* To punt the ball so that it will bounce out of bounds up the field nearer the goal line and will then be put in play by a scrum or line-out where it goes out of bounds. Finding touch is a strategic move intended to advance the ball quickly but not allow the opposing team an opportunity to catch the kick and run it back before one's teammates can move up the field. In the scrum and line-out each team has an equal opportunity to recover the ball.

fine **1** *of an athlete or animal* Physically trained or hardened close to the limit of efficiency. ⟨said he trained too long and too hard last winter . . . and as a result was down too *fine* when the season began — Ray Fitzgerald, *Boston Globe*⟩

2 *baseball* Precisely on the edge of the strike zone. ⟨gets himself in trouble, because then he tries to get too *fine* with his pitches — Bill Freehan⟩

3 *of a hit ball in cricket* Hit to the rear of the batsman nearly in a straight line with the line of the delivery. ⟨the greater scoring medium would be to sweep it *fine*. So when he sees that particular ball coming along, the striker instinctively knows the sweep to fine leg will offer the greatest reward — Sir Donald Bradman⟩

fine leg *cricket* A fielding position to the rear of the batsman and just on the leg side.

finesse **1** To hit a ball with delicate skill and careful placement rather than with raw power. ⟨*finessed* his fairway shots to the middle of the green⟩

2 To beat an opponent or take him out of position by deception and skillful maneuvering rather than by brute force.

finger hold *wrestling* An illegal hold that involves any bending of the opponent's thumb or fingers except when grasping the opponent's hand in an attempt to break a hold.

finger horse *harness racing* The favorite which is sometimes indicated on a scratch sheet by a hand with a pointing finger.

finger play or **fingering** *fencing* Manipulation of the sword by using only the thumb and fingers of the sword hand rather than the wrist and arm. Finger play is used to make most circular movements of the blade.

finger stall or **finger tip** *archery* A small thimble-like leather covering worn for protection on the tips of each of the string fingers.

finger tab *archery* A flat piece of leather with a notch at one side and one or more finger holes at the other that is worn to protect the string fingers from abrasion by the bowstring.

finger tip see FINGER STALL

finger-tip grip see GRIP (*bowling*)

¹finish **1** The end of a race.

2 *rowing* The end of a stroke when the oar is lifted from the water and the recovery is begun.

²finish **1** To reach the finish line. ⟨they *finished* in a dead heat⟩

2 To end a season or one's career with a specified standing or record. ⟨the team *finished* in last place for the second year in a row⟩

finisher A competitor that finishes in a specified place or position. ⟨the top four *finishers*⟩

finish line An actual or imaginary line that marks the end point of a race. The finish line is usually marked on the surface of a paved course or a running track, but on a racetrack for horse racing, the line is usually indicated by an overhead wire stretched across the track. The finish line for races on snow or ice (as in skiing, bobsledding, or dogsled racing) is typically indicated by an overhead banner. The finish line for races on open water (as in sailing or rowing) is often an unmarked direct line between 2 points on opposite sides of the course (as between 2 floating markers or between a floating marker and a committee boat). On a closed course where a race may involve many laps of the course, the finish line is always in place and is usually also the starting line. Each time the competitors pass the finish line, a lap has been completed. Though usually only a part of a competitor's body or a vehicle or craft must cross the line to qualify as having reached the finish line, (for the purpose of determining which of several reached it first), the body, craft, or vehicle must subsequently be

finish tape

wholly over the line in order to qualify as a finisher. In track it is the torso, not the arms, legs, or head, that determines when a competitor has reached the finish line.

finish tape or **finish yarn**   see TAPE (*track and field*)

Finn or **Finn Dinghy**   *sailing* A cat-rigged centerboard boat of a one-design class that is approximately 15 feet long, has a sail area of 114 square feet, and carries a crew of one.

Finnish Style or **Finnish crossover**   see CROSS-OVER (*track and field*)

fire   **1** To discharge a firearm.
2 To propel a ball or puck straight and hard. ⟨*fired* a slap shot wide⟩ ⟨*fired* a strike past the batter⟩

firearm   A weapon (as a rifle, shotgun, or pistol) from which a shot is discharged by gunpowder.

fireballer   *baseball* A pitcher who relies chiefly on or who is noted for his fastball; fastballer.

fireballing   *of a baseball pitcher* Being a fireballer. ⟨won ten games in a row and became a kind of *fireballing* folk hero — *Time*⟩

fireman   *baseball* A relief pitcher.

fireman's carry or **fireman's lift**   *wrestling* A takedown maneuver in which a wrestler holds his opponent's arm over one shoulder and with the opposite arm gains a crotch hold so as to lift his opponent onto his shoulders and then proceeds to kneel or sit and bring the opponent to the mat. (also called *barrel roll*)

fire out   *of an offensive lineman in football* To move off the ball quickly and forcefully at the snap.

firepower   The scoring action or potential of a team.

firing line   *shooting* A line which is a specified distance in front of targets and behind which competitors must remain in shooting.

firing pin   The part of a firearm action that strikes the cartridge primer.

first   **1** *baseball* First base. ⟨2 outs and a man on *first*⟩
2 *football* First down. ⟨*first* and 10 on the 35-yard line⟩

first attack   *lacrosse* **1** A chiefly offensive player and a member of the close attack.
2 The position played by a first attack.

first base   *baseball* **1** The base that is positioned on the baseline on the right side of the field and that is to be touched first by a base runner.
2 The player position for covering the area around first base. ⟨plays *first base*⟩

first baseman   *baseball* A player stationed usu-

ally to the left of first base who is responsible for covering the area around first base and taking throws from other infielders and making putouts.

first-class cricket   Cricket played by clubs at the highest level of national competition. In Great Britain, it involves clubs representing the counties and universities and usually includes both amateur and professional players.

first defense   *lacrosse* **1** A chiefly defensive player and a member of the close defense.
2 The position played by a first defense.

first down   *football* **1** The first of a series of 4 downs (3 in Canadian football) in which a team must net a 10-yard gain to retain possession of the ball.
2 A gain of a total of 10 or more yards within 4 downs (3 downs in Canadian football) giving the team the right to start a new series of downs.

first gallery   *court tennis* An opening in the corridor under the penthouse beside the center opening on either side of the net. A ball hit into the first gallery makes a chase.

first home   *lacrosse* **1** A chiefly offensive player and a member of the close attack in women's play.
2 The position played by a first home.

first sacker   A first baseman in baseball.

1st slip   see SLIP

first-string   Being a regular as opposed to a substitute. ⟨*first-string* catcher⟩

first team   The players on a team who regularly start a contest; the first-string players.

fish   **1** To attempt to catch fish; to engage in fishing.
2 To attempt to catch fish in a particular place. ⟨*fished* both sides of the stream⟩
3 To use a particular bait or lure in fishing. ⟨*fishing* a minnow skillfully has its arts — Maury Delman, *Fishing World*⟩

fishable   *of a body or section of water* Suitable, promising, or legally open for fishing.

fisherman   Someone who engages in fishing.

fisherman's anchor   A small mushroom anchor.

fisherman's bend   A knot that is used to secure a rope to a spar or a ring and that is formed by passing the end twice around the spar or through the ring and passing the end around the standing part and back under both turns. The knot is usually finished by making a half hitch or by lashing the end to the standing part. (also called *anchor bend* — see illustration at KNOT

fisherman's knot   A knot that is used to join 2 lines end to end and that is formed by overlapping the ends of 2 lines and tying overhand knots in each line so that each knot encloses the opposite line. — see illustration at KNOT

fishfinder *fishing* **1** A sonar-like device that is used to locate schools of fish.

2 or **fishfinder rig** A rig that is typically used in surf fishing and that normally consists of a pyramid-shaped sinker attached to the ring on the line so that the line will slide freely through the attaching ring. The weight is used for casting and for holding the bait near the bottom, but the ring permits the bait to be moved around by the current without being held down by the position of the sinker.

fishhook A relatively small hook usually made of stout steel wire that has a usually barbed point on one end and that is used to catch fish. Fishhooks are made in hundreds of different patterns and sizes but a typical hook consists of a point, barb, bend, shank, and eye. The point is the part

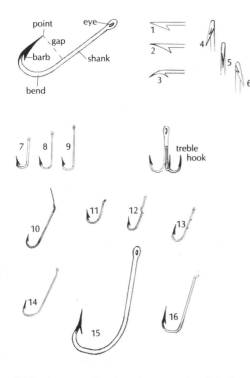

fishhooks: type of points: 1 spear point; 2 hollow point; 3 rolled point; 4 kirbed point; 5 straight point; 6 reversed point; wire sizes: 7 2x stout; 8 normal; 9 2x long; hook styles: 10 Aberdeen (snelled); 11 salmon egg; 12 humpshank; 13 baitholder shank; 14 Limerick (turned up eye); 15 O'Shaughnessy; 16 sneck (turned down eye)

that penetrates the mouth of the fish. Points are typically made in either the spear, hollow, or rolled-in point design, and if the point is offset to the side it is either a kirbed or a reversed point. The barb is the backward projection at the rear of the point which helps keep the point embedded. The bend is the curved portion of the hook, and it is one of the most noticeable single differences between the various hook styles. The shank is the straight part of the hook opposite the point, and the eye is a loop that may be formed on the end of the shank for attaching the line or leader. The eye may be either straight or turned up or down. For each hook size and pattern there is usually a standard wire thickness and shank length. A hook of a particular pattern that differs in some way from the standard is usually indicated by an x number. A hook made with a thicker or thinner wire may be indicated as a 2x or 3x stout or fine, meaning that the wire is the size normally used on a hook of the same pattern 2 or 3 sizes larger or smaller. Different shank lengths are indicated in the same manner. A 2x long hook has a shank of the length normally found on a hook 2 sizes larger.

fishing The sport or pastime of attempting to catch fish with a hook and line. — see also BAIT CASTING, FLY CASTING, SPINNING, TROLLING

fishing chair *fishing* A chair on the deck of a fishing boat in which one sits while fishing; fighting chair.

fishing rod A flexible tapering pole of split bamboo or fiberglass that has a handle with a place to mount a reel at the larger end and that normally has ring guides along its length through which the fishing line passes. On bait casting and spin casting rods the guides are mounted on the top while they are mounted on the bottom of spinning and fly rods.

fish out To exhaust the supply of fish in a particular spot by fishing.

fishplate see HANGER

fishtail *of a racing car* To lose traction (as in a turn) so that the rear end swings from side to side usually out of control. (also *squirrel*)

fist To punch a ball with the fist; to drive a ball by hitting it with the fist.

fistic Of or relating to boxing. ⟨the biggest *fistic* attraction that Rocky Mountain city has ever had — *Sports Record Weekly*⟩

fistmele *archery* The distance between the handle of a braced bow and the bowstring at the serving. This distance is commonly between 6 and 7 inches. Formerly this was measured as the

FITA round

distance between the bottom of the fist and the tip of the outstretched thumb, but today it is normally checked with a ruler to ensure consistency. If the bow is braced too much, a few twists are removed from the end of the bowstring to lengthen it and reduce the tension. If too little, a few additional twists will shorten the string and increase the tension.

FITA round *archery* **1** A target round in men's competition in which each competitor shoots 36 arrows at a distance of 90 meters, 36 at 70 meters, 36 at 50 meters, and 36 at 30 meters. **2** A target round in women's competition in which each competitor shoots 36 arrows at a distance of 70 meters, 36 at 60 meters, 36 at 50 meters, and 36 at 30 meters.

fitting Any of the hardware items on a boat (as a lamp, turnbuckle, or cleat).

five or **5** **1** A basketball team.
2 see FIFTEEN

500 or **500-yard run** *track and field* A race run over a distance of 500 yards.

five-man line *football* A defensive line that consists of 2 ends, 2 tackles, and a middle guard. The five-man line is less popular in professional play than the four-man line.

5–0–5 *sailing* A sloop-rigged centerboard boat of a one-design class that is 16½ feet long, has a sail area of 172 square feet plus a 220-square-foot spinnaker, and carries a crew of 2.

5.5 meter *sailing* A sloop-rigged keelboat of a one-design class that is approximately 32 feet long, has a sail area of 300 square feet plus a spinnaker, and carries a crew of 3.

5 point must system *boxing* A scoring system in which the winner of a round is given 5 points and the loser any number less than 5. In practice, the difference between the 2 scores is seldom more than one point. If the round is scored even, each boxer is given 5.

5 point system *boxing* A scoring system in which the winner of a round is given from one to 5 points while the loser of the round is given any number less than that awarded to the winner. In practice, the difference between the 2 scores is seldom more than one point. If a round is scored even, each boxer is given zero.

fives An English form of handball developed at Rugby school and played as a singles or doubles game on a 4-wall court. Play is begun by one side serving the ball—throwing it against one side wall so that it then hits the front wall above the board and rebounds. The server may serve the ball directly against the front wall (a *black-guard*) but the receiver is not required to play such a serve. In fives, unlike handball, only the receiving side can score points. If the receiver wins the rally, he wins a point. If the server wins the rally, he becomes the receiver. A game is played to 15 points or, if both sides are tied at 14, to 16 points. (also called *Rugby fives*) — see also BLACKGUARD

five-second rule *basketball* A rule in amateur play which requires a player who is closely guarded in his frontcourt to advance toward the basket or pass the ball within 5 seconds. A violation is a held ball.

5000 or **5000-meter run** *track and field* A race run over a distance of 5000 meters.

five-yard line *field hockey* A line inside and parallel to each sideline on a field marked for women's play which indicates the alley and serves as a restraining line for roll-ins.

¹fix **1** An instance of collusion in which one or more regular participants in a contest agree to lose the contest especially so that another individual or group can win a bet. **2** A contest whose outcome is illegally prearranged.

²fix To arrange for the outcome of a contest to be in one's favor especially by collusion with one or more participants.

fixed spool A spool of a fishing reel (as a spinning or spin casting reel) that is mounted with its axis parallel to the rod and that is open at the front so that it need not revolve when the line is wound on it or cast off it.

fixture An annual or traditional sports event. ⟨the *fixture,* which is run at a mile and a sixteenth . . . brought out seven horses — *New Yorker*⟩ ⟨Henley-on-Thames is famous for its regatta, which is the annual international *fixture* of the rowing world — *British Isles*⟩

¹flag **1** Any of a series of flags of different colors used to signal the competitors on the course in motor racing or yacht racing. **2** A small flag or foam rubber cylinder on a flexible wire pole that is placed at the corners of a playing field (as for football or soccer). **3** A marker used by the officials in a sport or contest. In rugby and Australian Rules football, the officials carry small flags on short poles which they raise to signal that an infraction has been committed, that the ball has gone out of bounds, or that a score has been made. In horse racing an official stationed at the starting line drops a flag when the horses pass the line — not when the starting gate opens — to signal the start

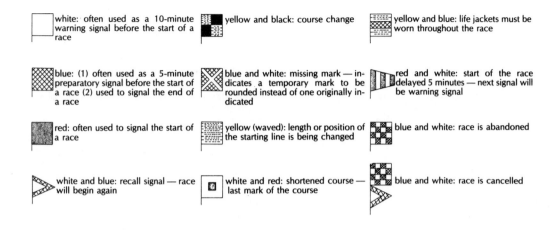

white: often used as a 10-minute warning signal before the start of a race

yellow and black: course change

yellow and blue: life jackets must be worn throughout the race

blue: (1) often used as a 5-minute preparatory signal before the start of a race (2) used to signal the end of a race

blue and white: missing mark — indicates a temporary mark to be rounded instead of one originally indicated

red and white: start of the race delayed 5 minutes — next signal will be warning signal

red: often used to signal the start of a race

yellow (waved): length or position of the starting line is being changed

blue and white: race is abandoned

white and blue: recall signal — race will begin again

white and red: shortened course — last mark of the course

blue and white: race is cancelled

flags used in yacht racing

of the race. The official in water polo has a short stick with a different color flag at each end to represent the different teams. This he uses to indicate which team is guilty of an infraction or which team is permitted to put the ball in play (as by a free throw). Football officials all carry a bright red or gold handkerchief weighted at one end which they throw in the air to signal an infraction or a foul.

4 *flag football* A strip of material usually 3 inches wide and 16 to 20 inches long that is attached to a special belt worn by all players and that is to be removed from the belt of the ballcarrier by an opponent in place of tackling.

5 *football* A pass pattern in which the receiver runs straight downfield and then cuts diagonally toward the goal line flag at the corner of the field.

²flag **1** To signal to a competitor (as in motor racing) by displaying or waving a signal flag.

2 *of a football official* To call a foul or infraction on a particular player. ⟨was *flagged* for holding⟩

3 *of a competitor* To tire in the later stages of a race.

flag football A variation of football played usually with 6 or 9 players to a side in which blocking is allowed but tackling is not and in which a defensive player must remove a flag from the ballcarrier's clothing to stop play. Each team is given 4 downs in which to score or lose possession of the ball, and each member of a team is eligible to catch a forward pass. All players wear flags usually attached to special belts, but sometimes the game is played with handkerchiefs

hanging from hip pockets instead of with the special flags. (also called *tail football*)

flagman **1** *horse racing* An official at the starting pole who drops a red flag as the horses pass to signal the start of the race.

2 *motor racing* The starter or a member of a corner crew who holds or waves racing flags to signal to the drivers.

3 *rodeo* An official who waves a flag to signal the beginning or the end of a timed period for certain events (as calf roping and steer wrestling) and judges on the legality of the catch, throw, or tying.

4 *rugby* A touch judge.

flagstick *golf* A thin pole usually having a numbered flag at the top that stands in the cup on a putting green to mark its location. The flagstick is removed from the hole while the players are putting. (also called *pin*)

flake *mountain climbing* A thin flat piece of rock that sticks out from a rock face and that can be used as a belay point or a handhold or foothold.

flameout *ballooning* A cessation of operation of the burner (as when the fuel is exhausted or when the pilot light becomes extinguished).

¹flank *football* Either end of a formation.

²flank *football* To line up wide of the formation.

flank circle *gymnastics* A double leg circle performed on the pommel horse while the performer faces continuously in one direction.

flanker **1** *Australian Rules football* A halfback or half forward who normally plays on either side

flankerback

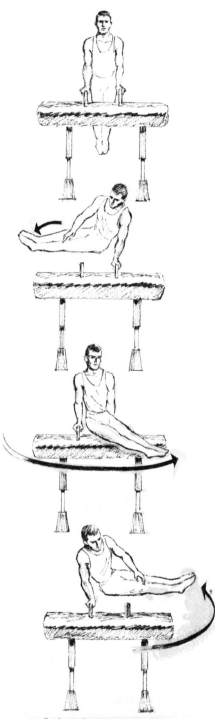

flank circle on a pommel horse

of the center halfback or center half forward. **2** *football* An offensive player who lines up wide of the formation; a halfback who lines up just back of the line of scrimmage several yards wide of the formation and who acts chiefly as a pass receiver. **3** *rugby* A wing forward.

flankerback *football* A halfback who plays as a flanker.

flank forward see WING FORWARD

flank speed *sailing* The maximum possible speed. ⟨had slammed at *flank speed* into North East Rock, one of a string of low, unmarked islets rising abruptly from deep water—Carleton Mitchell, *Sports Illustrated*⟩

flank vault *gymnastics* A vault sideways over a vaulting horse in which the gymnast goes over the horse with his legs out to one side and pushes off with one hand.

flare *football* A short pass thrown to a back who is running toward the sideline at or behind the line of scrimmage.

¹flat 1 *fishing* A level stretch of land alternately covered and uncovered by the tide that is a popular area during high tide to fish for marine game fish such as tarpon and bonefish. **2** *football* The area to either side of an offensive formation. ⟨the halfback circled out to the *flat* for a short pass⟩ **3** *ice skating* A movement made with the skate blade flat so that both edges contact the ice simultaneously; a tracing made by a flat. — **on the flat** British term meaning *in flat racing.*

²flat 1 a *of a hit ball or shuttlecock* Moving in a relatively straight line with little or no arc. **b** *of a stroke* Made so as to impart little spin to the ball. **c** *of a racket or paddle head* Held perpendicular to the intended line of flight of a ball or shuttlecock when making a stroke so as to hit it in a flat trajectory or with little spin. **2** *of a sail* Taut with little or no curve. **3** *of surf* Calm with low waves unsuitable for surfing.

flat ball 1 or **flat apple** *bowling* A dead ball. **2** *football* A ball placed on the ground in preparation for a placekick with its long axis parallel to the goal line instead of teed up.

flat bow *archery* A bow made with the same thickness throughout its length. — compare LONGBOW

flat kill *handball* A kill shot made to rebound very low off the front wall.

flatlander A person who is inept at body surfing.

flat-out As fast or as hard as possible; at maximum speed. ⟨the Ferrari plan is to run *flat-out* to win instead of the previous tactic of husbanding an engine for 24 hours — *New York Times*⟩

flat pass **1** *football* A pass made to a receiver in the flat.
2 *ice hockey* A pass made so that the puck does not leave the surface of the ice.

flat race *horse racing* A race for horses ridden on a relatively level course without obstacles as distinguished from a steeplechase or a harness race.

flat racing The sport of racing thoroughbred horses over dirt or grass courses having no obstacles or barriers to be jumped. — see also HORSE RACING

flat racing seat The posture of a jockey riding a horse in a flat race characterized by an extreme forward lean that places his head very near and the hands alongside the horse's neck and by a tight crouch necessitated by extremely short stirrups.

flats **1** Flat races. — compare TROTS
2 Light track shoes without spikes.

flatten **1** *boxing* To knock out an opponent.
2 *handball* To hit the ball so that it rebounds low from the front wall and quickly dies.

flea-flicker *football* A razzle-dazzle pass play:
1 A play that starts out like a double reverse with the ball coming back to the quarterback who then throws a long pass.
2 A long pass that is caught by the receiver who then laterals the ball to a trailing teammate.

flèche *fencing* A running attack sometimes employed in épée or saber fencing in which the attacker attempts to score a hit as he runs past his opponent. In this all-out effort, the attacker sacrifices any defense or follow-up attack since the action is stopped when one fencer passes another.

fleet *yacht racing* A group of boats competing in a race.

Flemish bend A knot that is used to join 2 ropes end to end and that is formed by tying a figure eight knot in the end of one rope and then threading the other rope through the knot in the reverse direction. — see illustration at KNOT

fletch *archery* To fix feathers to the shaft of an arrow.

fletching or **fletch** *archery* The feathers attached to an arrow to stabilize it in flight — see also ARROW

flic-flac or **flip-flop** *gymnastics* A back handspring.

¹flick **1** A stroke (as in badminton or table tennis) made with a quick snap or roll of the wrist at the moment of contact.
2 *field hockey* A shot made without backswing but with a slight twist of the stick to cause the ball to rise off the ground slightly and curve.

²flick **1** To hit or shoot a ball or shuttlecock with a flick.
2 *of an arrow in flight* To make a sudden deviation from the line of flight.
3 *lacrosse* To catch a pass and then pass or shoot the ball with a flip of the stick without first cradling the ball.

flick kick *soccer* A kick in which the ball is hit with the outside of the foot by snapping it outward quickly at the moment of contact. (also called *jab kick*)

flick pass *Australian Rules football* A pass made by snapping the wrist to hit the ball.

flick serve *badminton* A fast low serve made with a flick of the wrist at the moment of contact. It is commonly used for deception in order to pass an opponent who is playing close to the net.

flick shot *lacrosse* A shot made by flicking the ball.

fliffis *trampolining* A stunt performed on the trampoline which consists of a double somersault forward or backward with a full twist.

¹flight **1** *cricket* The movement in flight of a bowled ball that drops to the ground more quickly or carries farther than the batsman expects. — compare SWING
2 A hurdle to be jumped in a hurdles race (in horse racing or track and field).
3 *track and field* A round of trials in a field event.

²flight *cricket* To bowl a ball in such a way as to cause it to drop suddenly or to carry a little beyond the point at which the batsman expects it to bounce.

flight arrow *archery* An arrow designed for flight shooting and normally having a barreled shaft for weight reduction, a field point, and large feathers.

flights *archery* The feathers attached to the shaft of an arrow for stability; fletching.

flight shooting *archery* Competition in which arrows are shot for distance but not at targets. There is usually competition with regular bows as well as freestyle competition with no restrictions on bow size in which competitors often use foot bows.

¹flip **1** The act or an instance of turning over in the air; a somersault that is performed in the

flip

air (as in diving, gymnastics, or freestyle skiing).
2 *football* A short quick pass.
3 *skating* **a** A jump from the backward outside edge of one skate with a half turn in the air and a return to the forward inside edge of the same skate. **b** A jump from the backward inside edge assisted by a toe pick or toe point from the free foot with a full turn in the air and a return to the backward outside edge of the opposite skate.
4 *track and field* A long-jumping technique in which the jumper makes a forward somersault while in the air.

²flip 1 To propel a ball or puck (as in passing or shooting) by a quick snap of the wrist instead of drawing back to throw, hit, or kick it. ⟨*flipped* a pass to a teammate in front of the goal⟩
2 To make a short quick toss. ⟨scooped up the grounder and *flipped* to the pitcher covering the bag⟩

flip dodge *lacrosse* A dodge made especially after faking a pass by flipping the ball to the ground just beyond the defenseman and running around him and scooping up the ball.

flip-flop see FLIC-FLAC

flip pass 1 A pass made (as in ice hockey or lacrosse) by flipping the ball or puck with the stick. In ice hockey the puck is raised off the ice especially to get it over an opponent's stick or skate.
2 *basketball* A short pass made especially with an underhand motion or a flip of the wrists.

flipper 1 A long jumper who uses the flip.
2 see SWIM FIN

flip shot *ice hockey* A wrist shot in which the puck is flipped through the air.

flip turn *swimming* A turn made by the swimmer at the end of the pool which involves his turning forward in a half somersault and half twist underwater as he nears the wall and then pushing off the wall with his feet and gliding in the opposite direction ready to resume the stroke as he surfaces.

¹float 1 To be carried down a stream or river by the current.
2 *of a hit or thrown ball* To move through the air relatively slowly with little or no spin or rotation; to move in a relatively high arc.
3 To hit or throw a ball so that it floats. ⟨*floated* a backhand lob deep to the baseline — *New York Times*⟩
4 *swimming* To rest at the surface of the water through natural buoyancy. The most common methods of floating are lying on one's back with the body just at the surface and the face out of

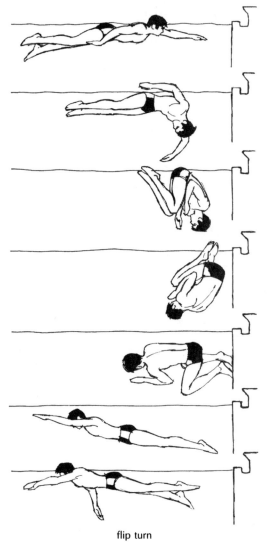

flip turn

the water, lying prone with the face down and the arms extended beyond the head, and tucked in a ball with the face down and just the shoulders out of the water.
5 *track and field* To settle into a relaxed pace during the middle of a race to conserve energy for a kick at the end. (also *coast*)

²float 1 A device (as a plastic ball or a cork) that buoys up a baited fishing line; bobber.
2 A floating platform anchored near a shore for use by swimmers or for tying up boats or one attached to a dock or pier to serve as an exten-

sion or as a platform that will be constantly at water level.

3 The act or an instance of floating; a period during which one floats.

4 A buoyant wooden or plastic object that supports a rope used to make a lane for swimming competition.

floater 1 A sailplane that has a lightweight structure that allows it to stay aloft under a variety of lift conditions but that is not suited to distance competition. — compare LEAD SLED

2 A pitched, thrown, or hit ball (as a baseball pitch, a football pass, or a volleyball serve) that floats.

3 A large buoyant surfboard.

4 see HANGER (*ice hockey*)

float fishing 1 A method of still fishing in which a bobber is used on the line.

2 A method of fishing popular especially in the Ozarks in which participants float down a large river in a boat, fishing as they go.

3 A method of fishing that involves securing a baited line to a floating object (as a jug, bottle, or large cork) and leaving it unattended. This is illegal in many states.

flood *football* To send more than one pass receiver into the same defensive area in order to have more receivers in the area than there are defenders to cover them.

¹floor The playing area of a basketball court. — **from the floor** *basketball* In field goals as opposed to foul shots. ⟨hit 63% *from the floor*⟩

²floor *boxing* To knock down an opponent.

floor exercise *gymnastics* A competitive event in which each performer executes a number of ballet and tumbling movements in a coordinated routine on a floor space 12 meters or 42 feet square without the use of apparatus. The routine is timed and in women's competition is accompanied by music.

floor hockey A version of ice hockey played by children on a floor without the use of skates.

¹flop *track and field* A method of high jumping in which the athlete goes over the bar backwards and headfirst and lands on his back. — compare STRADDLE, WESTERN ROLL

²flop *of an ice hockey goalkeeper* To fall to the ice in an attempt to stop a shot.

flopper 1 *ice hockey* A goalkeeper who frequently falls to the ice to make a save.

2 *track and field* A high jumper who uses the flop.

flu-flu or **floo-floo** *archery* An arrow originally designed for bird hunting that usually has a blunt

flop

point and special fletching which consists of feathers spiraled around the shaft so as to resemble a feather duster. The special fletching allows the arrow to fly straight for a short distance and then drop suddenly. — see illustration at ARROW

fluke The pointed part of an anchor that is usually attached to the stock and that digs into the bottom to hold the anchor in place. — see illustration at ANCHOR

¹flush 1 *of a game bird* To fly up suddenly from a place of concealment.

2 To cause a game bird to flush.

²flush see GATE

flutterball see KNUCKLEBALL

flutterboard see KICKBOARD

flutter kick *swimming* A kick used in the crawl and backstroke in which the legs are alternately moved past each other.

¹fly 1 A piece of material (as nylon or canvas) that covers the roof of a tent to protect the tent from rain or direct rays of the sun.

2 *fishing* An artificial lure that consists of a hook dressed with feathers, fur, tinsel, or yarn and that is intended to represent an insect or small bait fish. A dry fly is usually tied with hackle feathers sticking away from the hook at right angles to keep the body of the fly above the surface of the water. A wet fly is a small fly that is designed to be fished under the surface of the water; its feathers normally lie relatively flat against the hook. Streamer flies and bucktails are much larger versions of the wet fly that are intended to represent small fish. A nymph is a hook dressed with fur, tinsel, or yarn but without feathers; it represents the nymph or larval form of various aquatic insects. (also called *artificial fly*) — see also BUG

3 *football* A pass pattern in which the receiver runs straight downfield.

4 Short for *butterfly, fly ball.*

— **on the fly 1** *of a hit, thrown, or served ball* Being still in flight and without having bounced. ⟨once hit a ball between my legs so hard that my center fielder caught it *on the fly* backing up against the wall — Dizzy Dean **2** *of substitution in ice hockey* Made without interrupting the play of the game; made while play continues rather than when the puck is dead.

²fly To hit a ball high in the air; to hit a fly ball. ⟨*fly* the ball to the green⟩ ⟨*flied* to center field⟩

flyaway *gymnastics* A dismount from the horizontal bar or the rings in which the gymnast performs a full backward somersault in the air after releasing the apparatus at the end of a forward swing.

fly ball 1 *baseball* A ball that is hit into the air in a high arc and that usually travels to the outfield. (also called *fly*) — compare GROUND BALL, POP FLY

2 *handball* A ball that is played before it hits the floor.

3 *speedball* see AERIAL BALL

fly book *fishing* A flat wallet with felt or lamb's wool pages or with plastic envelopes for storing wet flies and streamers.

fly box *fishing* A plastic or metal box often with individual compartments for storing dry flies.

fly bridge see FLYING BRIDGE

fly casting 1 The casting of artificial flies in fishing using a fly rod and a relatively heavy line. Fly casting differs from other forms of casting such as bait casting or spinning notably in the fact that the weight of the lure does not pull out the line. Instead it is the line that is being cast, and the moving line carries the relatively weightless fly. The reel is not employed as it is in other forms of casting. It serves normally only for storage of the line. For casting, the line is usually first pulled off the reel by hand.

2 Tournament competition in which an artificial wet or dry fly, with the hook cut off, is cast for accuracy at 5 target rings at various distances. The caster makes 2 casts at each target ring. A perfect cast is worth 10 points, and one point is deducted for every foot from the target the fly

lands. The rings are scattered on the water at distances from 20 to 50 feet away for dry casting and placed all in a straight line at distances from 35 to 55 feet away for wet fly competition. The caster has 8 minutes for his 10 casts in dry fly casting and a 5-minute limit in wet fly casting. In addition to the scoring for accuracy on the casts, the caster is also subject to penalty points deducted from his score for such things as allowing the fly to touch the water between casts, exceeding the time limit, using an improper retrieve, and for permitting a dry fly to sink. — see also BAIT CASTING; SKISH

fly dope *fishing* A dressing used to make a dry fly water-resistant so that it will float.

fly-fish To engage in fly fishing.

fly fishing A method of fishing in which artificial flies are used and in which fly casting is normally employed.

fly half see STAND-OFF HALFBACK

flying 1 Traversed or to be traversed (as in speed-record trials) from a flying start. ⟨*flying* kilometer⟩

2 *of a skating spin* Begun by a jump. ⟨*flying* camel⟩

flying bridge or **fly bridge** An open deck on a cabin cruiser or sportfishing boat located above the bridge on the cabin roof and usually having a duplicate set of navigating equipment.

Flying Dutchman *sailing* A sloop-rigged centerboard boat of a one-design class that is approximately 20 feet long, has a sail area of 200 square feet plus a 190-square-foot spinnaker, and carries a crew of 2.

flying mare *wrestling* A throw in which the wrestler, while facing his opponent, grasps his opponent's wrist, turns, drops to one knee, and pulls the opponent over his back to the mat.

flying rings *gymnastics* Rings allowed to swing while a performer is executing movements on them. At one time flying rings were used in gymnastic competition, but today the rings must be kept still.

flying start *auto racing* A start of a race in which the competitors are already moving as they cross the starting line or receive the starting signal. (also called *running start*) — compare STANDING START, GRID START

flying wedge *football* An obsolete offensive formation in which blockers formed a wedge surrounding the ballcarrier and moved upfield usually holding special handles sewed to each other's pants. The flying wedge was directly responsible for numerous serious injuries to defensive players, and it was finally outlawed in 1906 when the forward pass was legalized. — compare WEDGE

flying wing *Canadian football* An offensive back who is the twelfth player on the team.

fly kick *rugby* The act or an instance of kicking the ball while it is in the air without first catching it.

fly kill *handball* A kill shot made by hitting the ball before it bounces.

fly line *fishing* A relatively thick coated line that is used with a fly rod in fly casting. Fly lines come in a variety of diameters with the lines of larger diameter having more weight and requiring larger and stiffer rods to cast properly. They are typically made of plastic-coated nylon or polyester and are designed either to float or to sink. Floating lines are normally used in dry fly fishing and where the fish are feeding close to the surface; sinking lines are used to carry a wet fly down to fish several feet below the surface. A level line is one that is manufactured with a constant diameter throughout its length. The double taper line tapers symmetrically from a fine tip at each end to a relatively heavy belly. The double taper is the most popular shape for dry fly fishing because the fine tip allows a delicate presentation of the fly. Since the 2 ends of the double taper line are identical, it can be reversed when one end wears out. The third common shape is the weight forward line (commonly known as a *torpedo taper, bug taper,* or *shooting head*), which tapers from a fine tip up to a heavy section about 20 feet from the tip and back to an intermediate diameter for the rest of its length. The heavy section concentrated in the forward part of the line makes this line popular where long casts are necessary or when heavy or large air-resistant lures (as bass bugs) are used. Because of the large size of fly lines, a relatively long leader is used between the line and the fly.

fly reel A simple fishing reel used on a fly rod to hold the line. The fly reel, normally a single-action or automatic reel, plays no part in the casting since the length of line to be cast is first stripped from the reel. The spool is large but narrow. The narrow spool eliminates the need for a level wind device, and the large diameter accommodates the bulky fly line and allows a faster retrieve. — see illustration at REEL

fly rod A relatively long usually hollow fiberglass or split bamboo fishing rod that is flexible enough to cast fly line. A fly rod is normally made in 2 or 3 sections, with popular sizes ranging from 7 to 9½ feet, and has the reel seat behind the grip.

fly rodder A fly fisherman.

fly shooting *handball* The hitting of the ball after it rebounds from the front wall but before it hits the floor.

fly tying The art or practice of tying various materials (as hair, fur, feathers, wool, yarn, or tinsel) to a fishhook to create artificial flies or bugs.

flyweight A boxer or weight lifter who competes in the flyweight division. — see DIVISION

foamie A ski boot that is custom-fitted with injected foam that sets following the shape of the foot.

foible *fencing* The half of a sword blade nearest the tip. — see illustration at FENCING; compare FORTE

foil **1** A fencing sword with a shallow bowl-shaped guard and a flexible blade of rectangular cross section that tapers to a blunted point. The foil has no cutting edge and is basically a thrusting weapon. Its overall length is about 43 inches, and it weighs up to 17 ounces. There are 2 basic handles commonly found in foils. The French foil has a plain handle about 8 inches long that is slightly curved to fit in the palm of the sword hand. The Italian foil has a shorter, straight handle with a bar crossing it about 2 inches below the guard. It is secured to the hand with a strap. — see also ELECTRIC FOIL; compare ÉPÉE, SABER **2** The art or sport of fencing with a foil; competition in which the foil is used. Foil fencing is governed by convention and complex rules of attack and defense. The first fencer to mount an attack has the right of way, and his opponent may not counterattack until the initial attack has been parried. The target in foil is the torso, and hits that land on the head, arms, or legs are not counted.

foilsman or **foilist** Someone who fences with a foil.

foldboat A collapsible kayak that consists essentially of an assembled frame usually of wood that is fitted inside a rubber-covered canvas hull. The foldboat may be broken down and stored or carried in one or more bundles like a tent.

follow *billiards* Top spin imparted to a cue ball to cause it to continue rolling forward after striking an object ball. (also called *direct English*) — compare DRAW, DRAG

follower see RUCKMAN

follow on *of a cricket team* To begin a second innings immediately after completing the first at the option of the opposing captain when behind by a specified number of runs (as 150 in a 3-day

follow shot

match). The captain of the team that batted first in the first innings may request the opposing team to follow on when he thinks his team has sufficient runs to win without batting again. If a team follows on and surpasses the first team's total, the first team may then have its second turn at bat.

follow shot *billiards* A shot in which the cue ball is made to continue forward after striking an object ball. — compare DRAW SHOT

follow the string *of an archery bow* To assume a pronounced set toward the string.

follow-through **1** The act of following through. **2** The continuation of a stroke following the striking of an object.

follow through **1** To continue a stroke or motion (as in swinging a club) after hitting, kicking, or throwing an object. Following through gives the motion full power and smoothness that would be sacrificed if the muscles were tensed to stop the action once the object was on its way. **2** *archery* To hold the position of the string hand for a moment after the release to ensure smoothness and accuracy.

foot **1** The part of something that is opposite the head; the lower part of a sail. **2** *archery* The first circle of a clout target. **3** A racing car driver.

football **1** A game played between 2 teams of 11 players using an inflated oval ball on a rectangular playing field 120 yards long and 53¹/₃ yards wide having a goal at each end in which the object is to move the ball across the opponent's goal line by running or passing the ball or to kick the ball over the goal crossbar for a score and to prevent the opposing team from scoring. Defensive players may tackle the ballcarrier and may shove players out of the way to get to him. Offensive players are permitted to block their opponents but may not use their hands to keep them away from the ballcarrier or the passer. Play is not continuous; it stops whenever the ballcarrier is tackled, when a pass is incomplete, or after a score is made. The ball remains in the possession of one side (unless the other side recovers a fumble or intercepts a pass), and that side has 4 downs — opportunities to advance the ball — in which to make a net gain of 10 yards — a first down — or lose possession of the ball to the other side. Play is started at the beginning of each half and after a score by one team's kicking the ball to the other team. Subsequent play is started from the line of scrimmage — the point at which the ballcarrier was tackled — by

one player's snapping the ball back between his legs to a teammate behind him.

Each squad normally uses separate offensive and defensive teams. There are restrictions on how the members of the offensive team may line up. There must be 7 offensive players on the line of scrimmage when the ball is snapped. They are the center, 2 guards, 2 tackles, and 2 ends. In the backfield, at least one yard behind the line, are 4 backs — a quarterback, a fullback, and 2 halfbacks. Any player may run with the ball, but only the 2 ends and the backs are eligible to catch a forward pass. Normally the linemen do the blocking, and the backs run with the ball and throw and catch passes. The defensive line is not restricted in lining up, but there are normally 4 or 5 linemen — 2 tackles and 2 ends and sometimes a middle guard — on the line of scrimmage and behind them 2 or 3 linebackers and 4 defensive backs — 2 cornerbacks and 2 safeties.

Even though the game is called football, kicking plays a relatively minor role other than in attempting a field goal or point after touchdown. Normally a team kicks the ball to give the other side possession as far as possible from the goal such as on a kickoff or by a punt when a first down seems unlikely. Though tackling, shoving, and blocking are normally permitted, unusually rough play and illegal use of the hands (as holding) are fouls usually penalized by a loss (or gain for the other side) of 5, 10, or 15 yards or by loss or replay of the down. If a team carries or passes the ball over the goal line, it scores a touchdown worth 6 points and has an opportunity to kick the ball over the crossbar or carry it over the goal line again for one or 2 extra points. A field goal — a kick over the crossbar other than when after a touchdown — is worth 3 points, and a safety — made when a team tackles an opposing player with the ball behind his own goal line — counts 2. The game is played in four 15-minute quarters (12-minute quarters in high school play) with the teams changing goals after each quarter. The team with the highest score at the end of the playing time wins. In professional play, ties may be played off in one or more 15-minute sudden-death overtime periods. **2** Any of several games in which kicking a ball is an integral part of the game. — see AUSTRALIAN RULES FOOTBALL, CANADIAN FOOTBALL, GAELIC FOOTBALL, RUGBY, SOCCER **3** The ball used in football.

footballer Someone who plays a form of football and especially soccer.

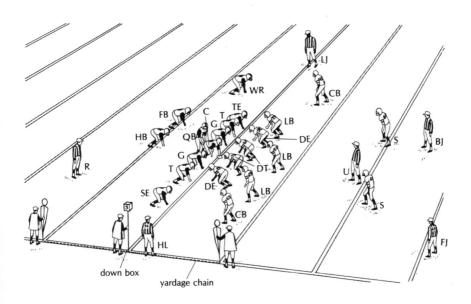

football: HB halfback; FB fullback; QB quarterback; WR wide receiver; SE split end; T tackle; G guard; C center; TE tight end; DE defensive end; DT defensive tackle; LB linebacker; CB cornerback; S safety; R referee; U umpire; HL head linesman; LJ line judge; FJ field judge; BJ back judge

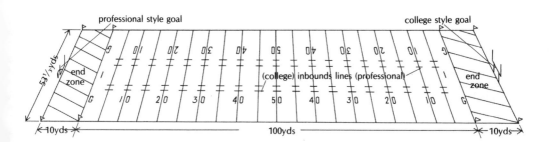

football roll see SHOULDER ROLL

foot bow *archery* A bow that is drawn by an archer who sits on the ground, places his feet on either side of the handle, and pulls the string back with both hands. This bow is popular in freestyle flight shooting competition.

foot court *shuffleboard* The end of the court from which the players shoot during the first half of a round.

footed *of an arrow* Having a stronger material inserted at a stress point (as just behind the pile).

foot fault **1** An infraction of the service rules in various games that results from illegal placement of the server's feet and that is penalized as any other fault:

a An infraction in handball or racquetball that results when the server steps out of the service zone before the serve passes the short line.

b *paddleball* An infraction that results when the server steps out of the service zone or when his doubles partner steps out of the service box before the serve passes the short line.

c *squash racquets* An infraction that results when the server steps out of the service box or fails to have his feet on the floor when the ball is hit.

d *tennis*. An infraction that results when the server steps on or over the baseline before the ball is hit.

e *volleyball* An infraction that results when the

server steps on or over the end line when serving.

2 *lawn bowling* An infraction that results when the bowler does not have one foot in contact with the mat when the bowl is delivered. For a second offense (after a warning by the umpire) the bowl is declared dead and removed from play.

foothold *mountain climbing* Something on which to place the foot for support in climbing.

footing *horse racing* The condition of a racetrack.

footpass *Australian Rules football* A pass made by kicking the ball to a teammate.

footprint *auto racing* The amount of surface area of an automobile tire tread that is in contact with the road at a given time.

footrace A race run by persons on foot.

footsack A short bag insulated like a sleeping bag that is used especially by a mountaineer on a bivouac to keep his feet and legs warm. The footsack is smaller and lighter than a full sleeping bag which is generally not required since in cold areas the climber will usually wear a long insulated parka. (also called *elephant's foot*)

foot score SEE HACK LINE

foot spot A spot midway between the center spot and the middle of the foot cushion on a carom or pocket billiards table. The first ball of the racked balls is placed on the foot spot at the beginning of a pocket billiards game; any balls illegally pocketed are returned to the foot spot.
— see also CENTER SPOT, HEAD SPOT

foot sweep *judo* A throw in which the defender grabs the attacker by the lapels as the attacker is stepping forward and sweeps his front foot out from under him just as he is shifting his weight to it.

footwork 1 The action or manner of moving the feet in coordination with other body movements for maximum efficiency and balance.

2 *skating* The sequence of steps and edges that move a skater over a surface and that are used as a link between jumps and spirals in a freestyle program.

foozle A bungling stroke (as in golf).

¹force 1 To try to complete a pass (as in football or basketball) by throwing the ball toward a teammate who is surrounded or blocked off by defenders.

2 To make a shot or series of shots (as in tennis) that puts an opponent on the defensive or out of position for a subsequent shot.

3 *baseball* **a** To cause a base runner to be put

out on a force play. ⟨was *forced* at second⟩
b *of a pitcher* To cause a runner to score or a run to be scored by the opposing team by giving up a base on balls with the bases full. ⟨*forced* in the tying run⟩

4 *basketball* To attempt a shot when there is little chance for success (as when off balance, out of position, or closely guarded).

²force 1 *baseball* A force-out.

2 *billiards* A shot in which the cue ball is struck off center so that it stops or rebounds at a desired angle after striking an object ball.

force dodge *lacrosse* A variation of the roll dodge in which the player leans against the defender to force him back.

force-out *baseball* A play in which a runner is put out on a force play.

force play *baseball* A situation in which a base runner loses the right to occupy a base and must attempt to reach the next base because the batter has hit a fair ball that is not caught in the air and has himself become a base runner. Once the batter hits a fair ball, he must attempt to reach first base. Any base runner occupying a base that a runner behind him is forced to try to reach is himself forced to run. On a force play, it is not necessary for a fielder to tag the runner; he only has to touch the base the runner is attempting to reach while holding the ball for the runner to be out. The force play ceases to exist once all base runners have advanced one base or when the batter (or a runner behind a given base run-

forehand stroke

ner) has been put out. Only a fair hit by the batter can create a force play. Example: with a runner on first base, the batter hits a grounder to the first baseman who throws to the shortstop covering second base. The shortstop catches the ball, steps on second making the force-out on the runner, and throws the ball back to first base completing a double play. Because the runner on first was forced to run, the shortstop did not have to tag him. If the first baseman had fielded the ball and stepped on first base (to put out the batter) before throwing to second, the shortstop would then have had to tag the runner, for the force play situation ends once the batter is put out.

forcing shot A shot (as in tennis) that forces an opponent to be on the defensive or out of position for a subsequent shot.

¹fore *golf* A traditional warning cry to alert anyone ahead that a shot is to be played.

²fore To or toward the bow of a boat; forward.

fore-and-aft Lying or running in the general line of the length of a boat.

fore-and-aft rig *sailing* A rig in which most or all sails are set on masts or on stays in a fore-and-aft line.

forearm balance A position (as in gymnastics or tumbling) in which the body is supported on the forearms with the legs usually together in the air. — compare HANDSTAND

forearm pass *volleyball* A pass made by holding the arms straight out with the forearms together and contacting the ball with both forearms simultaneously. (also called *bump* or *bump pass*)

forecaddie *golf* A caddie stationed down the fairway to point out where the ball lands.

fore-check *ice hockey* To check an opponent in his defensive zone while he has control of the puck. — compare BACK-CHECK

forechecker A hockey player who fore-checks.

forecourt 1 *badminton* The part of the court nearest the net.
2 *squash racquets* The frontcourt.
3 *tennis* The area in front of the service line.

fore-end The part of the stock of a firearm located under the barrel and ahead of the trigger guard.

forehand 1 A stroke (as in tennis) made with the palm of the hand turned in the direction of movement. — compare BACKHAND
2 *ice hockey* A shot or pass made with the front of the blade and with the palm of the lower or controlling hand facing the direction of movement.

forerunner *skiing* A skier who skis the course just before the start of competition to check for possible hazards, to see that control flags are set up and officials are ready, and to clear the course of spectators.

foresail *sailing* A usually triangular sail set forward of the mast.

forestroke A forward stroke; a stroke in polo that drives the ball in the direction in which the horse is heading.

¹forfeit 1 To lose a contest because of a serious breach of the rules (as refusal to obey an official) or for refusal or inability to begin or continue the contest (as because of injury, tardiness, or lack of a sufficient number of players). When an individual or team forfeits, the opponent is automatically awarded the victory. The rules of certain sports specify a score to be recorded for a forfeited game: baseball, 9–0; basketball, the actual score if the forfeiting team is behind, otherwise 2–0; football, 1–0; ice hockey, 1–0; softball, 7–0; volleyball, 15–0; water polo, 1–0; wrestling, the same as awarded for a fall. — see also DEFAULT, DISQUALIFICATION
2 *billiards* To have points subtracted from one's score or added to an opponent's score as a penalty for various fouls.

²forfeit A forfeited contest.

fork ball *baseball* A pitch that is thrown with the index and middle fingers spread wide and that breaks downward as it nears the plate.

form 1 Ability, readiness, or condition to perform at one's best.
2 *horse racing* **a** A horse's past performance.
b or **form sheet** A printed chart giving past performances of horses entered in a racing program along with conditions of the race, probable odds, jockey assignments, and often a handicap rating or a brief comment for each horse. (also called *racing form*)
3 see KATA

formation *football* An alignment of players on offense or defense at the beginning of each play. (also called *set*)

form sheet see FORM

formula A set of regulations governing the construction of a racing vehicle or craft (as a car, airplane, or yacht) that includes such things as size, length, weight, type and displacement of engine, and sail or wing area. In automobile and airplane racing, the formula specifies the overall length and weight, maximum permissible engine size and engine type, and size of fuel tanks and type of fuel. Sailing formulas are actually com-

formula A

plex mathematical formulas which include length, girth, and sail area measurements to arrive at a number that is usually expressed in meters. Boats built to conform to the meter rule therefore may differ considerably from one another in certain design characteristics, but because a change in one dimension will require an adjustment at some other point, the boats are essentially equal for competition.

formula A see FORMULA 5000

formula Atlantic *auto racing* A British formula car identical to the American formula B.

formula B *auto racing* A formula car powered by a nonsupercharged production engine of from 1100 to 1600 cc displacement and run on gasoline. The formula B is a smaller and lighter car than the formula 5000.

formula C *auto racing* A formula car powered by a nonsupercharged racing engine of up to 1100 cc displacement and run on gasoline.

formula car *auto racing* A racing car constructed according to a formula set up by a racing authority and typically having a tubular or wedge-shaped body without fenders, a single-seat open cockpit in which the driver sits in a reclining position, and the engine located behind the driver but ahead of the rear wheels.

turbocharged engine and must run on gasoline. There is much similarity between the formula 5000 and the formula one car, which is also eligible to race in this category.

formula Ford see FORMULA F

formula kart An enduro kart with a full body that encloses all of the driver but his head.

formula one or **formula I** **1** *air racing* A formula airplane that is approximately 18 feet long, has a wingspan of approximately 16 feet and a wing area of 66 square feet, and is powered by a 200-cubic-inch engine which develops 100 horsepower.

2 *auto racing* A formula car run on commercial gasoline and powered by a nonsupercharged V-8 or V-12 racing engine of from 1600 to 3000 cc (97.6–183 cubic inches) displacement or a supercharged racing engine of up to 1500 cc (91.5 cubic inches) displacement which usually develops up to 450 horsepower. The formula one is a low essentially wedge-shaped car in which the driver reclines in a single-seat open cockpit ahead of the engine. The fuel tanks and usually the radiators are located on the sides of the car, which weighs a minimum of 530 kilograms (1166 pounds) and is run on extremely wide treadless tires mounted on 13-inch wheels.

formula car

formula F or **formula Ford** *auto racing* A formula car powered by a nonsupercharged 1600 cc English Ford or Ford Pinto engine and run on gasoline.

formula 5000 *auto racing* A formula car powered by a racing engine of from 1600 to 3000 cc or a production V-8 engine of up to 5000 cc (305 cubic inches) displacement. The formula 5000 is not permitted to have a supercharged or

The formula one has a self-starter and a transmission with 4 or 5 forward gears plus reverse. At the rear behind the engine is an airfoil to increase traction. The formula one is designed for the World Championship of Drivers — Grand Prix — series and many of the characteristics of the formula one are found in the smaller formula car designs. (also called *international formula one*) — compare INDY CAR

formula Super Vee *auto racing* A formula car that uses a Volkswagen 1600 cc engine and gearbox and runs on gasoline.

formula three or **formula III** *auto racing* A formula car run on gasoline and powered by a non-supercharged production-car engine of up to 1600 cc (97.6 cubic inches) with certain air intake restrictions.

formula two or **formula II** *auto racing* A formula car run on commercial gasoline and powered by a nonsupercharged 4-cylinder production-car engine of from 1300 to 1600 cc (79.3–97.6 cubic inches) displacement. The formula two, somewhat smaller and lighter than the formula one, is popular in Europe, and many of the Grand Prix drivers compete in formula two races. The formula two is similar to the formula B, which is raced in the United States. (also called *international formula two*)

formula Vee *auto racing* A formula car that runs on gasoline and that uses a Volkswagen 1200 cc engine, gearbox, suspension, and wheels.

forte *fencing* The half of the sword blade nearest the handle. — see illustration at FENCING; compare FOIBLE

40 or **forty** **1** The third point made in tennis. When both players reach this score, it is called deuce.
2 A dash of 40 yards usually used as a method of evaluating the relative speed of football players. ⟨ran the *40* in 4.5 seconds⟩

forty-one A pocket billiards game in which each player at the beginning of the game shakes a numbered counter from a shake bottle that becomes his private number. The object of the game is for each player to score points corresponding to the numbered balls, which when added to his private number, unknown to the other players, will total 41 points. If a player goes over 41 total points on a stroke, he has burst and must replace all balls previously scored and begin again.

¹forward **1** A primarily offensive player in many team games who normally plays near the goal his team is attacking. Forwards are usually designated by position as the left, center, and right forwards in water polo; the full forwards and half forwards in Australian Rules football; the center, inside, and outside forwards in soccer; the center forward, inners, and wings in field hockey; and the center and left and right wings in ice hockey.
2 *basketball* Either of 2 players who normally play on either side of the pivot near the basket.
3 *rugby* Any of the 8 (6 in Rugby League) play-

ers who line up in the scrum and attempt to gain possession of the ball and pass it back to the backs.
4 *volleyball* Any of the 3 players stationed near the net when the ball is served.

²forward To or toward the bow of a boat.

forward area *rounders* The area of the field forward of the batting area into which the ball must be hit to be in play and which is analogous to fair territory in baseball.

forward cast *fishing* A cast which propels the bait, lure, or line forward.

forward dive *diving* Any of a group of competitive dives from a position facing out from the diving board in which the diver springs up and rotates forward and enters the water headfirst facing toward the board or feetfirst facing away from the board. (also called *front dive*) — compare ARMSTAND DIVE, BACKWARD DIVE, INWARD DIVE, REVERSE DIVE, TWIST DIVE

forward dive in pike position

forward line The forwards on a team (as in soccer, speedball, hockey, or Australian Rules football).

forward pass *football* A pass that is thrown in a direction forward of the passer. Only one forward pass may be thrown during a down, and for it to be legal the passer must be behind the line of scrimmage, though the ball does not have to cross the line of scrimmage to be a forward pass. While any defensive player may intercept a forward pass, only designated offensive players are eligible to catch one. If not caught, the pass is incomplete and the ball is dead, with the next down beginning at the original line of scrimmage. — compare LATERAL

forward seat The position of a rider in the saddle for hunting or for jumping events that is characterized by a forward lean of the body with the knees well bent and the legs in contact with the horse. (also called *balanced seat, hunting seat, jumping seat, modern hunting seat, military seat*)

forward stroke *cricket* A batting stroke in which the batsman steps forward with his front foot just before swinging. This is analogous to the batter's taking a stride before swinging in baseball. — compare BACKSTROKE

Fosbury Flop see FLOP (*track and field*)

¹foul 1 An infraction of the rules of various games or contests that normally involves illegal play or interference with an opponent for which a penalty is assessed against the guilty individual or his team:

a *basketball* An infraction of the rules including illegal physical contact (as charging, blocking, holding, or pushing another player), procedural infractions (as taking too many time-outs or delay of the game), and unsportsmanlike conduct. Each foul is charged against the guilty individual and is penalized by awarding the other team possession of the ball or by awarding one or more free throws. — see PERSONAL FOUL, TECHNICAL FOUL; compare VIOLATION

b *billiards* A stroke that is made in violation of the rules of the particular game being played (as stroking the cue ball more than once, knocking a ball off the table, failing to keep one foot on the floor when making a shot, hitting a moving ball, and in some games scratching the cue ball or shooting at the wrong ball). A foul ends the player's turn and results in forfeiture of any points made on the foul stroke and often the loss of one or more additional points.

c *bowling* The act or an instance of stepping over the foul line or of allowing any part of the body to touch anything beyond the foul line during a delivery that is penalized by counting the delivery as one of the 2 or 3 allowed during the frame but not counting the pinfall made on the delivery. If the foul is made with the first ball of the frame, any pins knocked down must be replaced.

d *boxing* An illegal punch (as one below the belt or at the back of the neck or one made with the back of the hand or while the opponent is down or out of the ring) or an illegal action (as butting the opponent with the head, wrestling, or hitting on the break). For the first offense the boxer is usually warned; for a subsequent offense he may lose points or be disqualified.

e *fencing* An instance of making body contact with one's opponent, of using the free hand either in attacking or in defense, or of deliberate roughness. On the first offense the guilty fencer may be warned and for subsequent offenses penalized one hit. If the director believes a foul to be deliberate, he may immediately disqualify the fencer.

f *field hockey* An infraction of the rules including obstructing, charging, shoving, or tripping an opponent, playing the ball with the stick above shoulder level, advancing the ball with the body instead of the stick, or picking up or throwing the ball with the hands which is penalized by a free hit, a corner, a penalty bully, or a penalty flick depending on the severity of the infraction.

g *football* An infraction of the playing rules including procedural violations (as having too many players on the field, illegal use of the hands, and offsides), personal fouls (as tripping, hitting, or clipping an opponent, hitting an opponent who is obviously out of the play or after the ball is dead, running into the kicker, or grabbing an opponent's face mask), and unsportsmanlike conduct (as disrespect to an official or attempting to conceal the ball under the clothing) which is penalized by loss of 5, 10, or 15 yards and often also by loss of the down. For flagrant fouls the offending player may be immediately disqualified.

h *Gaelic football* Illegal interference with an opponent including pushing, kicking, tripping, holding, or charging a player from behind or one who is not playing the ball which is normally penalized by awarding the opposing team a free kick, or if the foul is committed within the parallelogram, a penalty kick.

i *hurling* Illegal interference with an opponent including pushing, kicking, tripping, charging a player from behind or one who is not playing the ball, or deliberately touching a player with the hurley which is normally penalized by awarding the opposing team a free puck at the point of the foul.

j *ice hockey* An infraction of the playing rules including illegal interference with an opponent (as charging, tripping, or board checking), improper use of the stick (as slashing, butt-ending, spearing, cross checking, or high sticking), and unsportsmanlike conduct. Fouls are commonly referred to as penalties, and they are penalized by a temporary suspension of the guilty player usually for 2 minutes — a minor penalty — or 5 minutes — a major penalty. — see MAJOR PENALTY, MINOR PENALTY

k *lacrosse* An infraction of the playing rules including procedure violations (*technical fouls*) and rough or unsportsmanlike play (*personal fouls*) for which a team loses possession of the ball or for which a player may be temporarily suspended for from 30 seconds to 3 minutes of playing time. — see PERSONAL FOUL, TECHNICAL FOUL

l *polo* Dangerous play or improper use of the mallet such as riding off or bumping an opponent at a dangerous angle, reaching across or under an opponent's pony to hit the ball, striking the legs of an opponent's pony, and hooking the opponent's stick above shoulder level or when the ball is on the other side of the opponent which is generally penalized by awarding the other team a free hit often from the spot of the foul. If the foul is committed to prevent a goal, the penalty is usually the awarding of an automatic goal (*penalty goal*) to the other side.

m *rugby* An infraction of the rules including playing the ball or being involved in the play while offside, deliberate disobedience of the rules, obstructing an opponent, or foul play (as tripping, striking, or hacking an opponent) which is penalized by awarding the fouled player a penalty kick.

n *soccer* A violation of the rules including illegal interference with an opponent (as striking, kicking, tripping, or holding the opponent or charging the opponent from behind or one who is not playing the ball), dangerous play, playing the ball with the hands, and unsportsmanlike conduct which is penalized by awarding a free kick to the opponent. — see DIRECT FREE KICK, INDIRECT FREE KICK; PENALTY KICK

ō *speedball* An infraction of the rules including illegal obstruction of an opponent (as kicking, tripping, charging, or holding the opponent), unnecessary roughness, procedural infractions (as illegal substitution, taking too many time-outs, delay of the game), and unsportsmanlike conduct which is penalized by awarding the opposing team a free kick or penalty kick. — see PERSONAL FOUL, TECHNICAL FOUL; compare VIOLATION

p *swimming* An infraction of the rules including walking on the bottom of the pool, making an illegal start or turn, or impeding another swimmer for which the guilty swimmer may be disqualified at the discretion of the referee. If a foul affects the chances of another swimmer, the referee may allow that swimmer to advance automatically to the next heat; if the foul occurred in the final heat, the referee may order the race to be swum again.

q *track and field* (1) Interference with another runner or stepping out of the lane or off the track during a race for which a runner or his relay team may be disqualified. If another runner's chances are affected by the foul, he may be advanced automatically to the next heat; if the foul occurs in the final heat, it may be run again. (2) The act or an instance of stepping on or outside the boundaries of the throwing area or on the stop board in making a throw or of stepping over the takeoff board in making a jump. As a penalty, the trial counts as one of usually 3 trials permitted each competitor but the results are not counted.

r *volleyball* A violation of the rules such as hitting the ball with a part of the body other than the hand, fist, or arm, touching the net or hitting the ball while it is beyond the net, hitting the ball more than 3 times on one side or twice in succession by one player, blocking or spiking the ball by a back line player in front of the attacking line, screening the server from the opponents, or unsportsmanlike conduct. Each foul is penalized by loss of the point if committed by the receiving side or loss of the serve if committed by the serving side.

s *water polo* An infraction of the rules including illegal interference with an opponent (as holding, pulling, or dunking an opponent), impeding an opponent who does not have the ball, holding the ball underwater, standing or walking on the bottom of the pool, punching the ball, or being within 2 meters of the goal, unless the ball is closer to the goal, which is penalized by a free throw awarded to the other team. — see PERSONAL FOUL, TECHNICAL FOUL

t *yacht racing* An infraction of the rules such as failing to give another boat right-of-way or not attempting to avoid a collision for which the fouled boat or another boat may lodge a protest with the race committee and for which the guilty skipper and boat may be disqualified.

2 *baseball* see FOUL BALL

3 *fishing* A tangle of the line on or off the reel.

²foul **1** **a** To commit a foul; to commit a foul against a particular opponent. **b** *of a boat* To

foul

collide with another boat in yacht racing.

2 *baseball* **a** To hit a foul ball. **b** or **foul off** To hit a pitch for a foul ball.

3 *of a line in boating or fishing* To become tangled or jammed.

³**foul** **1** Constituting a foul. ⟨a *foul* punch⟩

2 *of a batted ball in baseball* Outside the foul lines. ⟨hit it *foul*⟩

foul ball or **foul** *baseball* A batted ball that lands in foul territory or that is outside the foul lines when passing first or third base. A batted ball that lands in fair territory but rolls foul before passing first or third base is a foul ball. If a foul ball is caught on the fly, the batter is out, and runners may try to advance at their own risk; one not caught on the fly counts as a strike against the batter unless he already has 2 strikes.

foul hooked *of a fish* Caught with the hook going through the mouth from the outside.

foul line **1** *baseball* Either of 2 straight lines that extend at right angles from the rear corner of home plate through the outer edges of first and third bases respectively to the boundary of the outfield. The foul lines enclose fair territory.

2 *basketball* A free throw line.

3 *bowling* A line on the alley 60 feet from the head pin separating the lane from the approach. The bowler commits a foul if any part of his body is on or over this line or if he touches anything beyond this line during or after the delivery.

4 *deck tennis* Either of 2 lines on either side of the net, each parallel to and 6 feet from the net, that mark the neutral zone. A ring falling in this zone does not count in scoring.

5 *track and field* A line over which a contestant in a field event must not step if he is to have his throw or jump qualify for measurement.

foul out **1** *of a baseball batter* To be out when a foul ball is caught on the fly.

2 *of a basketball player* To be put out of a game for exceeding the number of fouls permitted.

3 *of a jai alai player or team* To lose the point because of a foul.

foul play *rugby* Any action (as tripping, kicking, or obstructing an opponent or holding a player not in possession of the ball) which constitutes a foul for which a penalty kick is awarded and for which the guilty player may be sent off.

foul pole *baseball* Either of 2 vertical poles placed at or near the boundary of the field on the foul line that serve as a vertical extension of the foul line to aid the umpire in determining whether a ball hit to the outfield is fair or foul.

foul shot see FREE THROW

foul territory *baseball* All the area not enclosed by the foul lines.

foul throw *track and field* A throw that is counted as a trial but is not measured because the competitor fouled.

foul tip *baseball* **1** A fouled ball that goes straight back from the bat to the catcher's hands and is caught direct from the bat. It counts as a strike (as if the bat had not touched it) and the ball is in play. A foul tip made with 2 strikes on the batter becomes the third strike and the batter is out. If the ball is not caught directly, is trapped, or is dropped, it is not a foul tip and is counted merely as a foul ball.

2 Any fouled ball that goes straight back.

foundation *bowling* A strike in the ninth frame.

four **1** *cricket* A boundary hit that is worth 4 runs.

2 *rowing* **a** A 4-oared racing shell. **b** The crew of a 4-oared shell.

four-bagger A home run in baseball.

four-ball *golf* A match in which 2 players that make up one side match their better score for each hole against the better score of the 2 players that make up the other side.

440 or **440-yard dash** or **440-yard run** *track and field* A race run over a distance of 440 yards.

four-handed game A doubles game; a game in which 2 players compete as a partnership or side against 2 other players.

four horsemen *bowling* A leave of the 1, 2, 4, and 7 or the 1, 3, 6, and 10 pins. — see illustration of pin arrangement at BOWLING

400 or **400-meter dash** or **400-meter run** *track and field* A race run over a distance of 400 meters.

four quarter hold *judo* A pinning hold in which one player places his body over his supine opponent in such a way as to hold him down at both shoulders and at both sides of the hips.

fours **1** *lawn bowling* Competition for teams composed of 4 players.

2 *rowing* Competition for 4-oared shells.

3 *skating* Competition in which 2 couples skate at one time.

foursome *golf* **1** A match in which 2 players who make up one side compete against 2 players making up the other side with each side playing only one ball and the partners taking turns hitting the ball. (also called *Scotch foursome*)

2 A group of 4 golfers playing together with each

playing his own ball and each competing against the others.

14.1 continuous see BILLIARDS

14-yard line Either of 2 restraining lines on a Gaelic football or hurling field parallel to and 14 yards from the goal lines. In Gaelic football, a penalty kick is taken from the middle of the 14-yard line.

four-waller Someone who plays 4-wall handball.

four-yard line *water polo* Either of 2 unmarked lines across the pool between markers on the sides of the playing area parallel to and 4 yards in front of the goal lines. A player making a penalty throw must be positioned in front of the goal on the 4-yard line.

fowling piece *hunting* A light gun used in hunting birds and small animals.

fox hunting A sport or pastime in which mounted horsemen follow and observe a pack of hounds that search for and pursue a fox. When the fox is caught, it is customarily killed and eaten by the hounds though the fox's head (*mask*), tail (*brush*), and feet (*pads*) are taken as trophies. The hunt is under the direction of the master, who is customarily assisted by the huntsman who is in charge of the hounds, and usually by 2 whippers-in, who help keep the pack together. Fox hunting is primarily a social pastime for the well-to-do that is steeped in tradition and etiquette; the primary appeal is the required horsemanship. In following the hounds, the horsemen often cover much ground with hard riding and frequent jumps over hedges, walls, and fences. Traditionally, all members of the hunt participate at the invitation of the master, even though they may pay for the privilege. The normal hunt costume is a scarlet coat, white breeches, a top hat, and riding boots. The master and members of his staff normally wear black velvet caps, as do some women members of the hunt.

fox race A pastime in which people gather round a campfire at night to listen to the sounds made by their hounds chasing a fox. An important aspect of the fox race is the ability of an owner to pick out the distinctive voice of his own hound and determine the dog's position in the race by the sounds it makes.

fractional time or **fraction** *horse racing* The cumulative time of the leader for a given point in a race. Results charts normally give times at each quarter mile and at the finish.

frame **1** An inning in baseball.

2 *bowling* **a** One of the 10 squares on a score sheet in which a bowler's running score is recorded; box. **b** A player's turn in bowling.

3 *snooker* A period of play in which all the balls are pocketed.

¹free **1** *of an offensive player* Unguarded or not closely guarded by opponents. ⟨trying to get *free* for a shot⟩

2 *of a sailboat* Sailing with the wind aft; sailing before the wind.

3 *skating* Of or relating to the skater's foot that is not in contact with the surface at a given time. ⟨*free* foot⟩ ⟨*free* leg⟩ — compare SKATING

4 *of a weapon in shooting competition* Having few restrictions with respect to caliber, barrel length, trigger operation, or accessories. ⟨*free* pistol⟩ ⟨*free* rifle⟩

²free *swimming* Short for *freestyle*.

free agent A professional athlete or potential professional athlete who is not under contract to any club.

free ball **1** *basketball* A ball that is in the air (as during a pass or on a rebound) or on the floor not in possession of any player and recoverable by any player on either team.

2 *football* A live ball that is not in possession of a player or team. A lateral pass, a fumble, or a muffed kick is normally a free ball and may be caught or recovered by any player on either team. On a free kick, the ball must travel at least 10 yards forward before it can be recovered by the kicking team, but the kicking team may not interfere with the opposing team's attempt to catch the kick. A forward pass, though it may be caught by players of either team, is technically not a free ball, since the passing team retains possession of the ball if the pass is incomplete.

3 *volleyball* A ball that may be easily played or controlled. Normally a free ball is one that travels over the net in an upward direction in contrast to a spike.

free-blocking zone see CLIPPING ZONE

freeboard The part of a boat that is above the waterline; the distance from the waterline to the gunwale.

free climbing *mountain climbing* A form of mountain climbing in which artificial aids (as pitons or bolts) are not employed along a pitch but may be employed at various belay points.

free dance *skating* The part of a dance skating competition in which each couple performs a program of dance movements of its choice to music.

free diver Someone who engages in free diving.

free diving Skin diving in which a diver takes a breath at the surface before each descent.

free drop *golf* A drop permitted without penalty when a ball lands in a part of the course declared unplayable by course rules or tournament officials.

free exercise An exercise (as swinging the arms, rotating the trunk, or doing push-ups) performed without weights or apparatus.

free fall *skydiving* The period during a jump before the parachute is opened in which the jumper falls earthward usually while performing various stunts and maneuvers (as rolling, turning, or gliding down at an angle). For expert jumpers, free fall may last as long as 30 seconds depending on the height at which the jump was started.

free-for-all *harness racing* **1** A horse that has won a given amount of money and must race with the fastest horses.
2 a A race for free-for-all horses that is filled usually by invitation instead of by a speed or earnings limitation. **b** A race open to all horses regardless of earnings.

free handicap *horse racing* A handicap race in which horses may be nominated and entered without payment of any fees until the weight assignments have been accepted.

free hit **1** *field hockey* An unhindered hit at a stationary ball awarded to a team when an opponent commits a foul. All players other than the one taking the free hit must be at least 5 yards from the ball.
2 *polo* An unhindered shot at the goal awarded to a team for certain fouls by the opponent. The distance from the goal varies with the seriousness of the foul.
3 *roller hockey* An unhindered opportunity to play a stationary ball in any direction that is awarded to a player for infractions or fouls by the opponents. For minor fouls, the player is awarded an indirect free hit off which a goal may not be scored directly. All other players must be at least 9 feet from the player making the free hit. On a direct free hit, all players must be 15 feet away, and a goal may be scored directly.

free kick **1** An unhindered kick of a stationary ball in any direction used as a method of putting the ball in play (as in Gaelic football, soccer, or speedball) after the opponent has committed a foul or infraction. — see DIRECT FREE KICK, INDIRECT FREE KICK; compare PENALTY KICK
2 *Australian Rules football* An unhindered kick toward the goal awarded to a player when an opponent commits a foul or infraction.

3 *football* A kick (as a placekick or a punt) made with restrictions which prohibit either team from advancing beyond restraining lines until the ball is kicked. The ball is put in play at the beginning of each half and after a field goal or a try for point after touchdown by a free kick (normally a placekick) from the kicking team's 35-yard line in professional play and 40-yard line in high school and college play. After a safety, the team giving up the safety puts the ball in play by a free kick (usually a punt) from its own 20-yard line. In professional play a free kick may follow a fair catch, and a field goal can be scored directly from such a free kick.
4 *rugby* A dropkick, placekick, or punt toward the opponent's goal made by a player who has made a fair catch. The kick is made from any point behind the player's mark along a line the same distance from the touchline as the mark, and the opponents are not permitted to rush the kicker until the ball has been placed on the ground for a placekick or until the kicker moves forward to begin a dropkick or punt. If the ball is drop-kicked or placekicked, a goal worth 3 points (2 points in Rugby League play) may be scored directly from the free kick.

free-legged *of a pacer* Not wearing hobbles while racing.

free play *lacrosse* A method of starting play after a player has thrown or carried the ball out of bounds that consists of the referee's placing the ball in the stick of an opposing player at the point where the ball went out of bounds and signaling play to resume.

free position **1** *diving* A diver's choice of positions for a dive which includes one or more of the basic layout, tuck, and pike positions.
2 *lacrosse* A method of starting play in women's play after a player has fouled that consists of the referee's placing the ball in an opponent's stick and signaling play to resume.

free puck *hurling* An unhindered opportunity to hit the ball awarded to a player when an opponent fouls. Opposing players are required to remain 21 yards from the ball during a free puck.

free safety or **free safetyman** *football* A defensive back who normally lines up on the weak side 8–10 yards deep and who does not have a specific pass receiver to cover but is free to follow the play and help out other defensive players or defend against a pass as the situation dictates.

free skating *skating* The part of competition in which each competitor performs an individual program of his choice consisting of jumps, spins, spirals, and footwork to music. The performer is graded on the execution of the various movements and on the style, grace, and rhythm of the performance. (also called *freestyle*)

free-spool *of a spool in a fishing reel* To revolve freely without contact with other parts of the mechanism (as during a cast).

free spool A spool in a fishing reel that can be disengaged so as to revolve free of other parts of the mechanism (as in casting).

freestyle **1** *archery* **a** Target competition in which some form of aiming device or sight is used on the bow. **b** Flight shooting competition in which competitors are not limited to shooting with specified methods or equipment. Many competitors employ foot bows for record distances in freestyle shooting.
2 *skating* SEE FREE SKATING
3 *surfing* Competition in which maneuvers of the surfer's choice are performed while riding a wave.
4 *swimming* **a** Competition in which each competitor may use the stroke of his choice instead of a specified stroke. Since the crawl is the fastest competitive stroke, it is invariably used in freestyle competition. **b** The crawl stroke.
5 *wrestling* Competition in which the wrestlers are permitted to use any legal holds, including leg holds and tripping movements but may not hit or butt an opponent or use dangerous holds (as the stranglehold). If there is no fall, the wrestler with the most points at the end of the bout is the winner. (also called *catch-as-catch-can*)
— compare GRECO-ROMAN WRESTLING, SAMBO

freestyler A swimmer who competes in freestyle events.

freestyle skiing Skiing competition in which competitors are individually judged on style and execution in 3 separate events: downhill skiing over extremely bumpy terrain (*mogul*), performing artistic ballet-like movements on a very gradual slope (*ballet*), and performing acrobatic stunts off jumps (*aerial*). (also called *exhibition skiing, hot dog skiing*)

free throw **1** *basketball* An unhindered shot at the basket from behind the free throw line that is awarded to a player when an opponent has committed a personal or technical foul. A successful free throw scores one point. Other players normally line up, except after a technical foul, at designated spaces on either side of the free throw lane to be in position to play the ball in the event the attempt is unsuccessful. After a

successful throw, the ball is put in play by the opposing team outside the end line; after an unsuccessful throw, the ball is in play just as after a missed field goal attempt. For certain fouls, the player is awarded 2 free throws; the ball is not in play after the first throw whether it is successful or not. For a technical foul, the ball is not in play; it is put in play, usually by the team shooting the free throw, at the sideline after the free throw attempt. — see also PERSONAL FOUL, TECHNICAL FOUL; BONUS SITUATION
2 *box lacrosse* An unhindered pass or shot awarded a player when his team is given possession of the ball (as when the opposing team fails to make a shot in 30 seconds). No other player may be within 9 feet of the player making the free throw and no attacking player is permitted to make the throw from inside the opponent's free throw line.
3 *team handball* An unhindered throw of the ball in any direction awarded to a team when a member of the opposing team has committed a minor infraction of the rules (such as illegally playing the ball). The throw is taken by a player from outside the free throw area. Opposing players must be 3 meters (approximately 10 feet) from that player until the ball leaves his hand, and they usually line up between him and the goal. A goal can be scored directly from a free throw.—compare CORNER THROW, PENALTY THROW
4 *water polo* An unhindered opportunity to throw the ball to a teammate or to begin dribbling the ball that is awarded to a player as a method of restarting play after an opponent has committed a foul or has knocked the ball out of bounds. A goal may not be scored directly from a free throw; the ball must be intentionally touched or played by 2 players before a goal can be scored. — compare CORNER THROW, PENALTY THROW

free throw area *basketball* The free throw lane sometimes including also the free throw circle.

free throw circle *basketball* Either of the 2 restraining circles that are bisected by the free throw lines.

free throw lane *basketball* A lane marked on each end of the court that extends from the free throw line to the end line. The lane is a rectangular area 19 feet long by 12 feet (16 feet in professional play) wide; in international rules the lane is 5.80 meters (19 feet) long by 3.80 meters (12 feet) wide at the free throw line and 6 meters (19 feet 8¼ inches) wide at the end line. Players line up on either side of the lane during a free throw attempt, and they are not permitted to be in the lane until the ball touches the rim, the backboard, or the basket. An offensive player is not permitted to remain in the free throw lane for more than 3 consecutive seconds while the ball is in his frontcourt and his team is in control of the ball. (also called *three-second area, three-second lane*) — see illustration at BASKETBALL

free throw line **1** *basketball* A straight line 12 feet long which is marked at each end of the court 15 feet in front of the backboard and parallel to the end line behind which a player must stand while attempting a free throw.

2 *box lacrosse* A broken line marked on the floor in a semicircle 24 feet from the center of the goal beyond which an attacking player must stand in making a free throw.

3 *team handball* An arc outside each goal area which extends from each side of the field around to the front of the goal, which is no closer than 2.5 meters (8 feet 3 inches) to the goal area, and outside of which an offensive player stands when awarded a free throw.

free ticket or **free trip** A base on balls in baseball.

free wheel To coast on a bicycle by means of momentum or the force of gravity (as in going round a corner or downhill) without moving the pedals.

free-wheeling Characterized by fast loose play which takes advantage of opportunities without having set patterns. ⟨*free-wheeling* offense⟩

¹freeze **1** To attempt to retain continuous possession of the ball or puck without an attempt to score in order to prevent the opponents from gaining possession and scoring. The tactic is often employed near the end of the game in order to let the playing time expire while protecting a small lead, but it is sometimes used throughout a contest by an obviously inferior team that hopes to keep the score low and thereby gain a better chance for an upset victory. A team that is freezing the ball may simply make continual passes between teammates (as in basketball, hockey, or lacrosse) or may limit play (in football) to short runs taking the maximum allowable time between plays.

2 *ice hockey* To hold the puck against the boards with the stick or the skates thereby stopping play and forcing a face-off.

3 *of a curling stone* To come to rest immediately in front of and touching another stone.

²freeze The act or an instance of freezing a ball or puck; stall.

French billiards see BILLIARDS

French ski method see SKIING

friction climbing *mountain climbing* A technique of rock climbing in which a climber utilizes the friction between his boot soles or his hands and the rock face often employing the principle of opposing forces (as in bridging or laybacking). Friction climbing is commonly employed where there are no suitable handholds or footholds. The climber often has to make use of climbing momentum to help him progress where he would not be able to stand still.

friction knot A knot (as the prusik knot) that is used to attach the end of a rope to a spar or pole, to the standing part of another rope, or to its own standing part and that can be slid in one direction but will not slide in the direction of tension.

friendly British term for a friendly game (as of soccer or cricket) between 2 international teams usually before the beginning of regular international competition.

Frisbee A trademark used for a plastic disk several inches in diameter that is sailed between players by a flip of the wrist. The Frisbee, which has a rounded top and somewhat resembles an inverted saucer or pie pan, is used in games of catch.

Frisbee football see ULTIMATE FRISBEE

frog balance *gymnastics* A position of balance in which the gymnast is supported solely by his hands with his body in a relatively horizontal plane and his knees bent and drawn up just outside his elbows so that his upper arms and thighs are in contact. (also called *squat balance*)

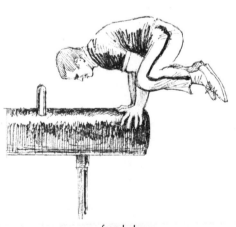

frog balance

frog head balance *gymnastics* A position identical to the frog balance but with the head touching the mat for additional support.

frog kick *swimming* A kick used primarily in the breaststroke and the elementary backstroke in which the knees are brought up almost level with the hips, the feet are kicked out, and the legs are quickly pulled together all in one continuous movement.

froissement *fencing* A quick deflection of the opponent's blade with a grazing action just preparatory to an attack. (also called *graze*)

¹front *football* Defensive line. ⟨5-man *front*⟩

²front *basketball* To play in front of an opposing pivotman instead of between him and the basket in order to prevent him from receiving passes from teammates.

frontcourt **1** The forward part of a court; the part of a court nearest the front wall or the net: **a** The area of the court (as for handball or paddleball) in front of the short line. **b** The area of the court (as for squash racquets) in front of the service line. **c** *volleyball* The area between the net and the attacking line.
2 *basketball* **a** The half of the court in which the goal at which a team shoots is located. One team's frontcourt is the other team's backcourt. **b** The center and forward positions on a team. ⟨decided to try him in the *frontcourt*⟩

frontcourtman A center or forward in basketball.

front crossover or **front crossstep** see CROSS-OVER (*track and field*)

front dive see FORWARD DIVE

front drop A trampoline stunt that consists of jumping up and turning forward, landing on the stomach with the head up and the arms and legs spread, and returning to the original upright position.

frontenis A game of Mexican origin that closely resembles handball or squash racquets and is played with rackets and a hard rubber ball on a 3-wall court that is much like a jai alai court.

front four *football* The players who make up a 4-man defensive line.

front grip *gymnastics* A method of grasping the horizontal bar that is characterized by having the palms turned away from the gymnast. — see GRIP

front header *diving* A forward dive in which the diver enters the water headfirst often after one or more somersaults.

frontis *jai alai* The front wall of the court. The frontis is made of solid granite blocks to withstand repeated hitting by the ball.

front-line First-string; regular. ⟨*front-line* catcher⟩

front line **1** *basketball* The center and forwards on a team.
2 *football* The linemen on a team.
3 *volleyball* The players who line up on the front row at the serve.

frontliner A player who plays on a front line.

front nine *golf* The first 9 holes on an 18-hole course.

fronton A jai alai auditorium usually consisting of the court and a tiered spectator area at one side with facilities for pari-mutuel betting on the game.

front race A race in which a particular competitor's strategy is to maintain the lead throughout.

front raise *weight training* An exercise performed with dumbbells in which they are raised from thigh level to a position in front of the body at arm's length and approximately shoulder height and then lowered.

front runner A contestant that runs best when in the lead and setting the pace instead of when trying to catch up to and pass the leaders near the end of the race.

front scale see SCALE

front service line see SHORT SERVICE LINE

front straight The straightaway on a racecourse on which the starting line and finish line are usually located and which is usually nearest the main grandstand.

front uprise see UPRISE

front wall The wall of the court (as in squash, handball, or jai alai) which is normally faced by the players and against which the ball is served and must ultimately be played for a good return.

frostbite **1** Of or relating to sailing in cold weather.
2 Engaged in frostbite sailing. ⟨*frostbite* sailors⟩

frostbiter A sailboat used in frostbite sailing.

frostbiting The sport of frostbite sailing.

frozen *of a billiard ball* Resting against another ball or against a cushion. In most billiard games the situation in which one ball is frozen to another does not affect play. In carom games, however, the rules require that when the cue ball is frozen to an object ball, the player must shoot away from the object ball or respot the balls in the same positions as for the break.

frozen rope A line drive in baseball.

fuel *motor racing* A combustible liquid typically consisting of a blend of methanol and nitromethane, with small amounts of various additives (as benzene, acetone, ether, or gasoline) which serve as igniters, that is used instead of gasoline for certain racing cars.

fueler *drag racing* A dragster that is run on fuel. — compare GASSER

fuel injection *motor sports* A system by which gasoline or racing fuel is sprayed directly into the individual combustion chambers of an internal-combustion engine at the instant the air in the chamber is under maximum compression as distinguished from being drawn in with the air through the carburetor by suction created by the movement of the piston. Fuel injection is typically used on racing engines and where permitted on modified production engines because it is more efficient than a carburetor and permits the engine to develop more power than a carburetor does.

full **1** *of a dive, jump, or gymnastic stunt* Involving a complete twist or somersault. ⟨*full* gainer⟩
2 *of the bases in baseball* Each occupied by a base runner; loaded. ⟨popped up with the bases *full* and two out in the fifth inning—Leonard Koppett, *New York Times*⟩
3 *of a stroke in golf* Made with the sweet spot of the clubhead in contact with the ball.

fullback **1** A primarily defensive player (as in soccer, field hockey, rugby, or Australian Rules football), who normally plays nearest the goal his team is defending. In games where there is no goalkeeper (as rugby or Australian Rules football), the fullbacks are the last line of defense.
2 *football* An offensive back who normally plays directly behind the quarterback. Fullbacks tend to be bigger and heavier than halfbacks and are used primarily for blocking and for carrying the ball especially on plunges into the line.
3 The position played by a fullback.

full bore At maximum speed or effort; flat-out.

full choke The narrowest degree of choke on a shotgun. — see CHOKE

full count *baseball* A count of 3 balls and 2 strikes on the batter.

full draw *archery* The position of an arrow when it is nocked and drawn back its full length ready to be shot.

full forward **1** Any of 3 offensive players who play nearest the goal they are attacking in Australian Rules football or Gaelic football.
2 The position played by a full forward.

full gainer *diving* A reverse dive that incorporates a somersault.

full nelson see NELSON

full pitch or **full toss** *of a delivery in cricket*

Made straight at the wicket in the air all the way rather than so as to bounce.

full roller *bowling* A delivery in which the ball is held with the fingers at the side and released with a sharp lift that causes the ball to slide down the alley with rotation perpendicular to the line of travel. The ball slows up on nearing the pins, and the rotation causes the ball to hook into them. — compare FULL SPINNER, SEMI-ROLLER, STRAIGHT BALL

full spinner *bowling* A delivery in which the ball is held with the fingers near the top and released with a snap of the wrist which causes the ball to slide down the alley spinning like a top. This is the least effective delivery for a hook. — compare FULL ROLLER, SEMI-ROLLER, STRAIGHT BALL

full toss see FULL PITCH

¹fumble **1** *baseball* A misplay of a grounder.
2 *box lacrosse* A dropped pass.
3 *football* **a** The accidental loss of control or possession of the ball when handling or running with it as opposed to when attempting to catch a pass or a kick. A fumble is not limited to a player's dropping the ball. Loss of possession because an opponent has snatched the ball from the ballcarrier's grasp is also a fumble, and the ball normally belongs to the team that is able to gain possession of it. In professional play, the ball remains in play following a fumble, and any player recovering the ball before or after it touches the ground may advance it. In college play, an offensive player may advance a fumble at any time, but a defensive player may only advance a fumble if it is caught before it strikes the ground. — compare MUFF **b** A fumbled ball. ⟨fell on the *fumble*⟩

²fumble To make a fumble; to lose control or possession of the ball; to misplay the ball.

fundamentals The basic skills necessary to the playing of a game or sport.

fungo *baseball* A fly ball hit to players for practice by tossing the ball in the air and hitting it as it falls.

fungo bat *baseball* A relatively thin bat with a short barrel and a long handle that is designed for hitting fungoes.

fungo circle *baseball* Either of 2 circles on the field beside the baselines near home plate that are used by players or coaches hitting fungoes before the start of the game.

funny car *auto racing* **1** A racing car that is unusual or unorthodox or that has been modified beyond the limit of its class.

2 A specialized drag-racing car that has a 1-piece molded body which resembles a mass-produced car, that is powered by a highly modified super-charged engine, and that is normally run on fuel. The body is hinged to the chassis at the rear and opens from the front. The engine is normally located in the middle, and the driver sits where the back seat of a conventional car would be located.

furl To roll or fold a sail and tie it to a boom.

furlong *horse racing* One eighth of a mile.

fuselage **1** The body of an airplane or sailplane. **2** The body of an iceboat.

futurity or **futurity race** *horse racing* A stakes race usually for 2-year-olds for which the competitors are nominated at or before birth.

G

gad *horse racing* A jockey's whip.

Gaelic football A game that is played between 2 teams of 15 players on a large rectangular field with an H-shaped goal at each end with the object to drive a round ball resembling a soccer ball by kicking or punching it past a goalkeeper into a goal for a score and to prevent the opposing team from scoring. One point is scored if the ball is driven over the crossbar of the goal and 3 points if the ball is driven under the crossbar (a *goal*). The ball may be advanced by kicking or punching it and by dribbling it with the hands (as in basketball) or with the feet (as in soccer). Players are not permitted to throw or run with the ball and only the goalkeeper is permitted to pick up the ball from the ground. A player may not hold, trip, or push an opponent and fouls are penalized by awarding a free kick to the fouled team. Practically every other form of physical collision is permitted, however, and Gaelic football is noted for its furious action and rough play. Games are usually played in two 30-minute halves though the championship in Ireland is usually played in 40-minute halves. — see also FIELD, FREE KICK, GOAL

¹gaff 1 *cockfighting* A metal spur about 2½ inches long that is attached to a gamecock's leg in place of its natural spur.
2 *fishing* A large barbless hook with a handle that is used to hold and lift a fish while it is being landed or boated.
3 *sailing* A spar on the after part of the mast that supports the head of a 4-sided sail.

²gaff 1 To fit a gamecock with a gaff.
2 *fishing* To use a gaff on a fish; to hook or hold a fish with a gaff.

gaff-headed *of a sail* Having 4 sides and requiring a gaff to support the head.

gaff-rigged *of a sailboat* Employing a gaff-headed mainsail.

gaggle *soaring* A group of gliders or sailplanes flying together.

¹gain *football* The number of yards the ball is advanced on a play.

²gain *football* To advance the ball. ⟨a sweep that *gained* 5 yards⟩ ⟨the team *gained* 200 yards through the air⟩ ⟨*gained* 27 yards on 6 carries⟩

gainer see REVERSE DIVE

gain ground 1 *fencing* To advance toward one's opponent; to force one's opponent back. — compare RETREAT
2 *rugby* To kick the ball forward where there is a chance of catching or recovering it nearer the opponent's goal line.

gait A discrete sequence in which the hooves hit the ground as a horse moves forward. A gait may be a steady 2 beats with 2 hooves hitting the ground at a time as in the trot or pace, 3 beats with first one hoof, then 2 more and finally the last followed by a definite pause as in the canter or gallop, or a steady 4 beats in which each hoof hits the ground separately as in the rack. — see also CANTER, GALLOP, PACE, RACK, TROT

gaited *of a horse* Having a particular kind of gait; trained to use particular gaits. ⟨high-*gaited*⟩ ⟨a five-*gaited* horse⟩

gaiter *hiking* A usually zippered covering worn over the top of hiking boots and the bottom of pants legs to keep dirt, snow, and water from getting inside the boots.

gaiting strap *harness racing* A leather strap that is stretched between one shaft tip and the front of a sulky to prevent the horse from moving his hind end too far sideways. A wooden pole which serves the same purpose is called a *gaiting pole*.

gallery 1 a An area for spectators at the side or back of a court (as for tennis, squash racquets, or handball). **b** The spectators (as at a tennis match or golf tournament).
2 *court tennis* Any of the 3 openings on each side of the net along one side wall under the penthouse including the first galleries, second galleries, and last or winning galleries. A ball hit into a winning gallery on either side automatically wins the point; one into any of the other galleries makes a chase. — see also DOOR

galley A kitchen on board a boat.

¹gallop 1 A fast 3-beat gait in which the horse

comes down first on one hind leg, then on the other hind leg and the diagonally opposite foreleg simultaneously, and finally on the other foreleg. The cycle is followed by a brief period of suspension during which all 4 feet are off the ground

2 A period of riding a horse at a gallop.

²**gallop 1** To ride a horse at a gallop; to cause a horse to run at a gallop.

2 *of a horse* To run at a gallop.

game 1 A sport which is conducted according to set rules and in which participants playing usually in direct opposition to each other or as a team in direct opposition to another team throw, hit, roll, carry, or kick an object such as a ball, puck, shuttlecock, ring, or horseshoe so as to score and often try actively to prevent the opponent from scoring.

2 A single competition in a sport which terminates when each side has completed a specified number of turns (as in baseball or bowling), when a time limit expires (as in basketball or football), or when one side reaches a predetermined score (as in badminton or horseshoe pitching).

3 A subunit of a larger competition which terminates when one side reaches a predetermined score (as in tennis). — see also MATCH, SET

4 A statistical unit to measure the relative position of a team in league standings in relation to other teams in the standings. To compute the numbers of games one team may be ahead of or behind another, add the difference in the number of victories by each team and the difference in the number of losses and divide this resulting number by 2. Example: if team A has a 26–22 record and team B has a 23–25 record, the difference in the number of games won (3) plus the difference in the number of games lost (3) divided by 2 is 3 meaning that team A has a 3-game lead in the standings over team B. If team A loses 3 straight games (26–25) and team B wins 3 straight games (26–25) the teams will then be even in the standings.

5 An individual's or a team's manner, quality, or style of play. ⟨he is off his *game* today⟩ ⟨had to go with their passing *game* today⟩ ⟨a strong baseline *game*⟩

6 An animal sought or taken in hunting for sport. — see also GAME FISH

game ball 1 A ball that is used in playing a game.

2 A game ball that is presented by the members of a football team to a player or coach in recognition of his outstanding contribution to a victory.

3 see GAME POINT

game bird 1 A game point in badminton.

2 A fowl such as an upland game bird sought as game.

game clock *basketball* A clock which shows the total amount of playing time remaining in a period of a game as distinguished from a shooting clock.

gamecock A domestic cock specially bred and trained for cockfighting.

game fish Any fish that is sought for sport with a hook and line and that is valued for its eating qualities or for the fight it puts up when hooked. Though the term is sometimes applied to marine fish it is generally used of freshwater fish. Occasionally its use is restricted to such fish as trout, salmon, bass, and pike as distinguished from panfish. In legal use, a game fish is one that is reserved for sport and may not be taken by commercial fisherman.

game fowl A domestic fowl of a strain developed for the production of gamecocks.

game misconduct penalty A misconduct penalty in ice hockey and box lacrosse that results in the suspension of the penalized player for the remainder of the game while allowing immediate substitution for him. A total of 10 minutes is charged in the records of the offending player for a game misconduct.

game plan The basic strategy that a team intends to follow for a particular game. It includes the selection of starting players and normal and special offensive and defensive tactics designed to take advantage of the opponent's known or supposed weaknesses.

game point A situation (as in tennis or volleyball) in which the side that is leading can win the game by winning the next point; the point that is being played. (also called *game ball*)

games *football* The stunting of defensive linemen.

Games An Olympic Games competition; Olympiad.

gang hitch *dogsled racing* A hitch by which the dogs are attached to the sled and which is arranged with a single lead dog and the other dogs teamed in pairs behind the leader.

gang hook *fishing* Two or 3 fishhooks with their shanks joined together. — see TREBLE HOOK

gangline *dogsled racing* A trace used with a gang hitch. (also called *tow line*)

gang-tackle *football* To bring down a ballcarrier with several tacklers.

gap 1 *archery* The apparent distance the archer sees between the point of aim and the target.

garbage

2 *fishing* The distance between the shank of a fishhook and the point. — see illustration at FISH-HOOK

3 *football* A space between offensive or defensive linemen. — often used in the phrase *shoot the gap*

garbage 1 *basketball* An easy goal scored from under the basket (as on an offensive rebound).

2 *ice hockey* An easy goal scored by a player who knocks in a rebound or deflects another player's shot.

3 *tennis* A soft shot (as a dink or lob).

garbage collector or **garbage man** *ice hockey* A player noted for getting garbage goals.

gardening *mountain climbing* The act or action of clearing away vegetation from a pitch in order to find suitable handholds and footholds.

garland *skiing* A movement in which a skier momentarily sideslips while traversing a slope and then returns to the straight traverse. Garlands are usually performed in a series and are commonly called *parallel garlands.* When begun by a hop they are known as *hop garlands.*

Garrison finish A contest in which the winner comes from behind to win at the very end; a last minute or unexpected victory. The term comes from a nineteenth century jockey Edward ''Snapper'' Garrison who was famous for bringing horses from behind to win at the wire.

Garryowen *rugby* A high lofted punt used as an offensive tactic to gain ground especially when the forwards are charging down the field. The term comes from an Irish rugby club, Garryowen, noted for its use of this kick.

gas *surfing* A wipeout. — usually used in the phrase *take gas*

gas balloon A sport balloon filled with a lighter-than-air gas (as helium).

gas-out see WIPEOUT

gasser *drag racing* A dragster that is run on gasoline. — compare FUELER

gate 1 A starting gate.

2 A pair of markers (as poles or buoys) or the space between them through which a competitor must pass in the course of a slalom race (as in skiing, water skiing, or whitewater racing). There are numerous arrangements of gates to provide a variety of challenges to the competitors. An *open gate* is one that has both markers set in a line perpendicular to the course line; a *closed gate,* also known as a *blind gate,* has the markers set in a line parallel to the course line. A series of 3 gates placed in open, closed, open sequence is called an *open H;* a series of 3 gates

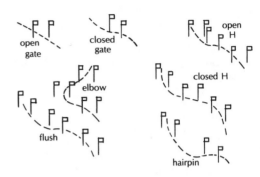

in closed, open, closed sequence is a *closed H.* Other series include the *hairpin,* a series of 2 closed gates; the *flush,* a series of 3 or more closed gates; the *elbow,* a series of 3 open gates with the center gate offset to one side; and a *corridor,* a series of open gates set in line.

3 The spring-hinged part of a carabiner that can be pushed open to allow the carabiner to be inserted into the eye of a piton or to permit a rope to be passed through the ring. — see illustration at CARABINER

4 *equitation* An obstacle for show jumping which resembles a wooden farm gate.

gather shot *billiards* A shot in carom billiards by which a player brings the object balls together so that he may score consecutive caroms with relative ease.

gauge The size of a shotgun expressed as a number equal to the number of round lead balls of the same size as the bore that weigh one pound. — compare CALIBER

gauge pressure *scuba diving* The pressure of a given depth of water indicated on a pressure gauge calibrated to register zero at sea level. — compare ABSOLUTE PRESSURE

gazehound *hunting* A dog that hunts by sight rather than by scent.

geländeläufer see LANGLAUFER

geländesprung *skiing* A jump usually over an obstacle typically made from a crouching position by pushing off with the poles.

gelding A castrated male horse.

general manager A professional club official who is responsible among other things for acquiring players and negotiating player contracts.

General Prudential Rule see LAST CHANCE RULE

genoa A large jib sail that overlaps the mainsail and that is typically used in racing.

German giant swing *gymnastics* A giant swing performed on the horizontal bar with the arms grasping the bar behind the gymnast with the palms turned away.

get A good return of a difficult shot (as in handball, tennis, or squash racquets).

get the axe *surfing* To be wiped out by a breaking wave.

gi A lightweight 2-piece cotton garment worn for judo and karate practice or exhibitions that consists of loose-fitting pants and a loose jacket held closed by a belt which is tied in front with a square knot.

giant roll *gymnastics* A forward or backward roll performed on the parallel bars by swinging the legs up over the head and continuing around in a circle in a layout position rolling on the shoulders. (also called *shoulder roll*)

giant slalom *skiing* A ski race that is essentially a combination of a slalom and a downhill held on a long course having a vertical drop of at least 1000 feet and having only about half the number of gates as a slalom but set farther apart.

giant swing *gymnastics* A full forward or backward swing of the body (as on the horizontal bar or the rings) from a handstand position down and back up to another handstand with the body and arms extended throughout the swing.

gig *fishing* A pronged spear used for catching fish.

gimme *golf* A putt conceded to one's opponent. ⟨you play defense on these greens. You got no *gimmes,* even on a one-footer — Lee Trevino⟩

girdle traverse *mountain climbing* A route that leads from one side of a cliff to the other often requiring the climber to move higher in some places or lower in others but not to reach the top or the bottom of the cliff at any time during the traverse.

girth A strap of a saddle which encircles the horse's body and by means of which it is held in place.

give British term meaning to make a call. ⟨the referee is *giving* offside⟩ ⟨*gave* him out leg before wicket⟩

give a catch *cricket* To hit a ball that may be caught in the air.

give-and-go A play (as in basketball, hockey, lacrosse, or soccer) in which a player passes to a teammate and immediately cuts around his defender toward the goal for a return pass.

give and go To execute a give-and-go.

giveaway *box lacrosse* The act or an instance of a team's losing possession of the ball through error.

give away weight see GIVE WEIGHT

give oneself up *of a baseball batter* To hit the ball to the right side of the infield with a runner on first in order to reduce the likelihood of a play at second. The runner is thereby moved into scoring position although the batter will likely be put out at first.

give rein *equitation* To permit a horse to move freely without exerting control through the reins.

give tongue *of a hound* To bark indicating the scent of the quarry has been found.

give up *of a baseball pitcher* To allow the opposing player or team to get a walk, a hit, or a run.

give weight or **give away weight** *of a racehorse* To carry more weight in a handicap race than another or a particular rival.

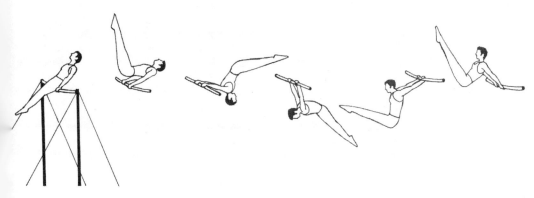

German giant swing

glacis *mountain climbing* A rock face with a slope of up to 30 degrees. — compare OVER-HAND, SLAB, WALL

gladiator A boxer.

glass arm *baseball* A pitching arm that is easily injured or that becomes sore easily; a weak or easily injured throwing arm.

glass ball *basketball* A shot that does not hit the rim but strikes the glass backboard and rebounds. — compare AIR BALL

glass jaw Susceptibility of a boxer to being knocked out easily.

glide **1** *cricket* see LEG GLANCE

2 *fencing* An attack in which a fencer slides his blade along that of his opponent while making a thrust. (also called *coulé*)

3 *gymnastics* A forward swing at arm's length from an overhead bar with the body extended fully as the gymnast reaches the end of the swing.

4 *track and field* The period in the middle of a race when a runner is settled in a relaxed pace before the final kick.

glider An aircraft that resembles an airplane but has no engine for sustained flight. The term *glider* is used generally to include sailplanes though enthusiasts make the distinction that gliders are not designed to be able to gain altitude as sailplanes can do.

glide ratio *soaring* The ratio of the distance a sailplane or glider will fly forward for every foot of altitude it drops.

¹glissade To slide down a snow-covered slope on the feet in a standing or squatting position without the use of skis.

glissade

²glissade The action or an instance of glissading.

GLM *skiing* A method of teaching skiing that involves starting adults on extremely short skis about 3 feet long and teaching parallel turns from the beginning. The GLM, abbreviated from *graduated length method,* is widely used in the United States.

¹glove **1** A covering for the hand that normally has a separate section for each finger and that is worn to protect the hand, to aid the wearer in catching a ball, or to provide a secure grip of a ball or a club handle. The gloves worn in ice hockey and lacrosse and by the batsmen in cricket are padded on the back to protect the back of the hands, and yet they are flexible to enable the player to grip the stick or bat. An ice hockey goalkeeper's stick glove has a flat board along the back for deflecting shots, but his catching glove resembles a baseball first baseman's mitt. A cricket wicketkeeper wears a padded glove on each hand to protect his hands and wrists. A baseball glove has separate sections for each finger, in contrast to a mitt. It is padded in front of the thumb and finger sections and at the heel but has an unpadded pocket in the palm. It normally has the fingers laced together and has leather webbing between the thumb and index finger sections. Though a baseball glove does offer protection for the hand, it is primarily used to increase the effective area of the hand for catching the ball. A golf glove, often worn only on one hand, helps the golfer get a more secure grip on the club handle. A bowling glove normally consists of a covering for the palm of the bowling hand with holes for the fingers. A pad in the palm takes up the space between the palm and the ball to provide a more secure grip. Boxing gloves are really mitts that have one section for the fingers and one for the thumb. They are padded on the back and lace up at the inside of the wrist and they are worn in pairs to cushion the blows to the opponent as well as protect the boxer's hands. An archer's shooting glove is little more than leather coverings for the tips of the fingers of the shooting hand held in place by straps running down the back of the hand to a wrist band. The leather tips protect the fingers from abrasions when the string is released.

2 *baseball* Fielding ability. ⟨he's got a good *glove* at three positions and can pinch-hit — Casey Stengel⟩

²glove **1** *baseball* To catch the ball in one's glove.

2 *ice hockey* To bat the puck with the hand. The puck may be knocked down but may not be

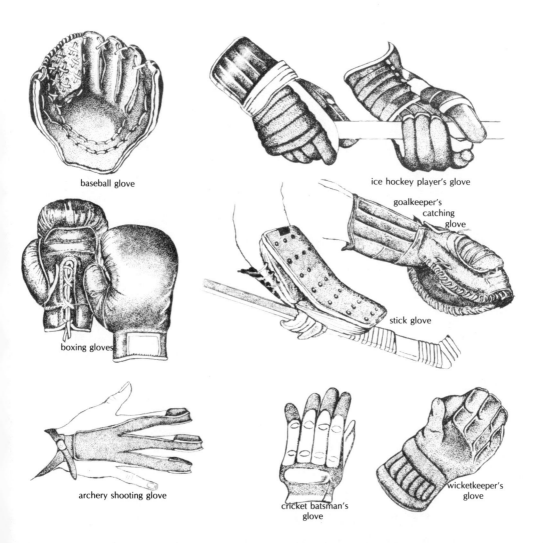

baseball glove

ice hockey player's glove

goalkeeper's catching glove

boxing gloves

stick glove

archery shooting glove

cricket batsman's glove

wicketkeeper's glove

caught or directed to a teammate or at the goal with the hand by a player other than the goalkeeper.

glove man   *baseball*   A fielder.

glove save   *ice hockey*   A save made by the goalkeeper by stopping the puck with the catching glove.

go   A fly pattern in football.

go about   see TACK

go-ahead   Being a score (as a run, touchdown, or goal) that gives a team the lead in a game. ⟨batted in the *go-ahead* run with a sacrifice fly — Parton Keese, *New York Times*⟩

goal   1 An area or structure into or through which a ball or puck must be played for a score:

a *Australian Rules football*   An arrangement of 4 upright posts each 7 yards apart at each end of the field. The 2 inner posts are *goalposts* and the other 2 posts are *behind posts*. The goalposts are at least 20 feet high and more often 25 or 30 feet high while the behind posts are usually somewhat shorter.

b *basketball*   A horizontal metal ring 18 inches in diameter which is mounted to a backboard and supported 10 feet above the floor at each end of the court and from which is suspended

183

goal

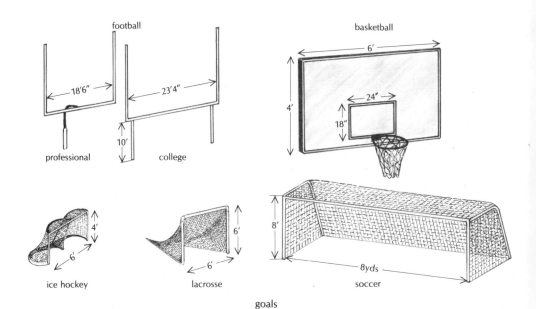

football

professional   college

basketball

18'6"   23'4"

10'

6'

4'

24"

18"

ice hockey   lacrosse   soccer

4'   6'   8'

6'   6'   8yds

goals

a 15-to-18-inch net open at the bottom. The backboard is a rectangle 6 feet wide and 4 feet high and is solid white or transparent. On a transparent board a 24-by-18-inch rectangle is painted just above the basket. For high school play, a 54-inch fan-shaped backboard is approved.

c *box lacrosse* A frame located at each end of the playing area and consisting of 2 goalposts 4 feet high and 4½ feet apart connected by a crossbar at the top and backed with a net enclosing the top, sides, and back.

d *Canadian football* A structure of the same design and size as for American professional football that is centered on each goal line.

e *field hockey* A rectangular frame 4 yards wide and 7 feet high that is centered on each goal line and that is backed by a net enclosing the top, sides, and back. The net extends 4 to 6 feet back of the goal line.

f *football* A structure that consists of 2 upright goalposts at least 20 feet high connected by a 10-foot-high crossbar and that is centered on each end line. The goal is 23 feet 4 inches wide for college play and 18½ feet wide for professional play. College goals are typically H-shaped while for professional play they are usually in the shape of a squared Y. (also called *goalpost*)

g *Gaelic football* An H-shaped structure consisting of 2 upright goalposts 16 feet high and 21 feet apart connected by an 8-foot-high crossbar and centered on each goal line. The lower half of the goal is backed by a net enclosing the top, sides, and back.

h *hurling* Same as for *Gaelic football*.

i *ice hockey* A rectangular metal frame that is centered on each goal line and that consists of 2 upright goalposts 4 feet high and 6 feet apart connected at the top by a crossbar and backed by a net. The net is supported at the top and bottom by a frame consisting of 2 curving sections that resemble the number 3. The back of the goal extends 22 inches from the goal line at the bottom.

j *lacrosse* A square frame at each end of the field that consists of 2 goalposts 6 feet high and 6 feet apart connected by a crossbar at the top and backed by a net in the shape of a pyramid which converges to a single point 6 to 7 feet back of the goalposts.

k *polo* A structure consisting of 2 goalposts at least 10 feet high and 8 yards apart centered on each back line. The posts must be constructed so that they will fall if hit by a horse and rider.

l *rugby* An H-shaped structure consisting of 2 upright goalposts 18½ feet apart connected by a crossbar 10 feet high that is centered on each goal line. The rules require that the posts be over 11 feet high and in practice they are usually 25 to 30 feet high.

184

m *soccer* A rectangular usually wooden frame that is centered on each goal line and that consists of 2 goalposts 8 feet high and 8 yards apart that are connected at the top by a crossbar and backed by a net which encloses the top, sides, and back.

n *speed-a-way* Same as for *field hockey.*

o *speedball* Same as for college *football.*

p *team handball* A rectangular frame that is centered on each goal line and that consists of 2 goalposts 2 meters (6 feet 6¾ inches) high and 3 meters (9 feet 10¼ inches) apart connected by a crossbar at the top and backed by a net which encloses the top, sides, and back.

q *water polo* A rectangular frame of wood or metal at each end of the playing area which consists of 2 goalposts 10 feet apart connected at the top by a crossbar and backed by a net that encloses the top, sides, and back and which extends back from the goalposts about 18 inches. The goal is constructed so that the crossbar will be 3 feet above the surface of the water if the water is 5 or more feet deep and 8 feet above the bottom if the water is less than 5 feet deep.

2 A score made by driving or throwing a ball or puck into a goal:

a *Australian Rules football* A score worth 6 points made when the ball is kicked by an attacking player through the goalposts without touching the posts or without being touched by a defending player. — see also BEHIND

b *basketball* A field goal or a free throw.

c *field hockey* A score made by an attacking player driving the ball over the goal line into the goal. — see also PENALTY GOAL

d *Gaelic football* A score of 3 points made when the ball is driven over the goal line into the goal under the crossbar by an attacking player. — see also POINT

e *hurling* Same as *Gaelic football.*

f *ice hockey* A score made when the puck is driven over the goal line into the goal with the stick by an attacking player or is knocked in by a defending player. If the puck is knocked into the goal by a defending player, the attacking player who last played the puck is given credit for the goal. A goal is not allowed if the shooter is in the crease or if the puck is kicked into the goal except, in professional hockey, in the case of a kicked puck's being deflected into the goal off a defending player other than the goalkeeper.

g *lacrosse* A score made when the ball is thrown with the stick or kicked into the goal by an attacking player who is outside the crease.

h *polo* A score made when the ball is knocked over the goal line between the goalposts by an attacking player. — see also PENALTY GOAL

i *rugby* A score of 3 points made when the ball is kicked through the goalposts over the crossbar from a free kick, dropkick, or penalty kick or a score of 6 points (5 in Rugby League) made as a result of a try and a successful conversion. In Rugby League all goals are 2 points except for a dropped goal, which scores one point.

j *soccer* A score made when the ball is kicked or knocked over the goal line into the goal with any part of the body other than the hands or arms.

k *team handball* A score made when the ball is thrown or driven over the goal line into the goal by an attacking player with any part of the body except the foot or lower leg.

l *water polo* A score made when the ball is thrown or knocked into the goal by an attacking player or a defending player.

3 The basic unit of scoring in several team games such as field hockey, ice hockey, lacrosse, polo, soccer, team handball, and water polo. — compare POINT, RUN

4 *polo* A number from 0 to 10 (from minus 2 to 10 in England) given to a player as a measure of his skill and estimated worth to a team and used in computing the team's handicap. The term *goal* is arbitrary and in no way reflects the number of goals a particular player is expected to score in a game. Ten goals is the highest rating but players of this caliber are extremely rare. — see also HANDICAP

— **in goal** *ice hockey* Playing as goalkeeper.

goal area 1 *lacrosse* A rectangular area 40 yards wide surrounding the goal that extends from the end line to a parallel line 20 yards in front of the goal at each end of the field and that serves as a restraining area in which a team's goalkeeper and close defense and the opposing team's close attack must remain until the ball is put in play on a face-off.

2 *soccer* A rectangular area 20 yards wide and 6 yards deep which is just in front of and centered on each goal and from which goal kicks are taken.

3 *team handball* A D-shaped area that extends 6 meters in front of and on each side of the goals.

goal-area line The line on a playing field or court that marks the limits of a goal area.

goal average *soccer* The difference between the number of goals scored by a team and the number of goals that team has given up during a

goal crease

particular period that is used to break a tie between 2 teams with identical won-lost records and determine which team will get a berth in a tournament or advance to the next round.

goal crease 1 *box lacrosse* An arc with a 10-foot radius that surrounds each goal and that ends with a straight line parallel to the front of the goal and 6 feet back of the goal. Attacking players are prohibited from entering the goal crease, from playing the ball when it is in the crease, or from interfering with the goalkeeper or any other opposing player who is inside the crease.

2 *ice hockey* A rectangular area 8 feet wide and 4 feet deep in Canadian and American play or a semicircle with a 6-foot radius in international play that is marked on the ice in front of each goal. Attacking players are not permitted within the crease unless the puck is in it or unless the goalkeeper has left the crease.

3 *lacrosse* A circular area 18 feet in diameter (19 feet in women's play) that surrounds each goal. No attacking player and no defending player in possession of the ball except the goalkeeper is permitted within the crease.

goaler 1 Canadian term for *goalie.*

2 A polo player with a handicap rating of a specified number of goals. ⟨a 6-*goaler*⟩

goal game A game (as football, basketball, or hockey) in which the object is put the ball or puck into a goal or over a goal line. — compare NET GAME, WALL GAME

goalie Short for *goalkeeper.*

goal judge 1 Either of 2 officials in ice hockey or box lacrosse who are seated in screened cages in the stands immediately behind the goals and who assist the referee by signaling when the ball or puck crosses the goal line between the goalposts. The referee, however, has the final decision on allowing goals and deciding on disputed goals.

2 *water polo* Either of 2 officials located on the side of the pool in line with the goal lines to signal goals and to signal to the referee when a team is to take a goal throw or a corner throw and when the players are in position for the start of play.

goalkeeper or **goaltender 1** The defensive player in various goal games who normally plays in front of the goal he is defending to keep the ball or puck from going in for a score. The goalkeeper is the team's last line of defense and he often is allowed to use special equipment and is accorded certain privileges while in his normal position that are denied his teammates. The

goalkeeper in soccer is the only player who is permitted to play the ball with his hands but only while he is within the penalty area. The lacrosse goalkeeper is not permitted to handle the ball, but he may legally bat it down with the hand while he is within the crease. In addition to wearing a thick body pad, the goalkeeper is permitted to use a stick with a head 12 inches wide. The goalkeeper in field hockey normally wears shin pads and is permitted to kick the ball in clearing it. In ice hockey, the goalkeeper differs markedly from his teammates in appearance because of the additional safety equipment such as shin pads and a face mask. His stick is considerably different, having a wider blade and a wide section at the lower end of the handle. His gloves also are different from those of his teammates; on one hand he wears a catching glove and on the other hand a glove with a flat pad on the back. The goalkeeper is the only player who is permitted to catch the puck in his glove, and while he is in the crease he may not be checked by an opposing player.

2 The position played by a goalkeeper.

goalkeeping The action of guarding a goal (as in hockey, soccer, or lacrosse); the manner in which a goalkeeper plays his position.

goal kick 1 *rugby* A kick at the goal.

2 *soccer* An indirect free kick awarded to a defensive player when the ball is driven out of bounds over the goal line by an attacking player. The kick is taken from within the goal area and must clear the penalty area. (also called *defense kick*)

goalless Without a goal being scored; scoreless ⟨a *goalless* draw in their championship final⟩

goal light A red light set up behind each goal and lit by a goal judge to indicate a score in ice hockey or box lacrosse.

goal line 1 A line at each end of and running the width of the playing field (as in soccer and field hockey) which marks the boundary of the playing area and in the center of which is located the goal. A ball driven over the goal line but not into the goal is out of bounds.

2 A line at each end of and running the width of the playing field in football and rugby over which the ball must be carried or passed to score a touchdown or a try. The goal line does not mark the boundary of the playing area since a ball in the end zone or the in-goal may still be in play. In rugby the goals are centered on the goal lines.

3 A line at each end of an ice hockey rink which

extends across the rink and in the center of which the goal is located. The goal line is normally located 10 to 15 feet in front of the endboards and a puck behind the goal line but not in the goal is still in play.

4 *lacrosse* A straight line between goalposts.

5 *polo* The portion of the back line between the goalposts.

6 *Ultimate Frisbee* A line at each end of the playing area over which the Frisbee must be passed for a score.

7 *water polo* A straight line between markers on either side of the pool at each end of the pool on which the goal is centered and which marks the boundary of the playing area.

goal-line stand *football* A defensive effort involving the turning back of successive attempts by the opposing team to score from very near the goal line.

goalmouth The opening of a goal (as in soccer, hockey, or lacrosse) between the goalposts and under the crossbar.

goalpost **1** Either of the 2 upright poles that with or without a crossbar constitute the goal in various games. — see GOAL

2 A football goal.

goal square *Australian Rules football* A 7-yard by 10-yard rectangular area in front of the goal formed by the goal line and the kickoff lines. After a behind has been scored the ball is put in play by a kickoff from within the area. (also called *kickoff area*)

goaltender see GOALKEEPER

goaltending **1** The action of guarding the goal (as in hockey, lacrosse, or soccer); the manner in which a goalkeeper plays his position.

2 *basketball* The act or an instance of interfering with a shot while the ball is on its downward flight to the basket or of touching the rim or the ball while it is over, on, or within the rim of the basket. Goaltending is a violation which results in loss of the ball and the disallowing of the basket made if committed by an offensive player; if by a defensive player, an automatic field goal is credited to the shooter. Once the ball has hit the backboard or the rim and is not on or inside the rim, touching it does not constitute goaltending. If the ball is caromed against the backboard as part of the upward flight of a shot (as a lay-up), pinning the ball against the backboard is goaltending.

goal throw **1** *team handball* An unhindered throw made by a goalkeeper from within the goal area after the ball crosses the goal line outside the goal when last touched by a member of the attacking team or by the defending goalkeeper. The ball must be thrown out of the goal area and cannot be again played by the goalkeeper until touched by another player. Opposing players must be outside the free throw area during the goal throw. (also called *throw-off*)

2 *water polo* A free throw by the goalkeeper from within his 4-yard line to put the ball in play after an opponent has thrown or knocked it over the goal line out of bounds.

goal umpire An umpire (as in hockey, lacrosse, water polo, or Australian Rules football) who is positioned behind or near each goal to signal when a goal has been scored.

go backdoor *basketball* To make or attempt a backdoor play.

go baseline *of a basketball player* To move along the baseline especially behind the defensive players to receive a quick pass under or near the basket.

go-behind **1** *surfing* A maneuver in which a surfer passes another surfer on the same wave by gliding around behind the other surfer.

2 *wrestling* Any maneuver by which a wrestler is able to move around behind his opponent where he has a better opportunity for a takedown.

godille *skiing* French term for *wedeln*.

go for the fences *of a batter in baseball* To attempt to hit a home run during a turn at bat. ⟨see little guys who don't have the strength to swing a quick bat *go for the fences* — Don Drysdale⟩

going away With an ever increasing lead. ⟨won his 100-mile qualifying race *going away,* at a speed of 190.617 mph — Robert F. Jones, *Sports Illustrated*⟩

gold **1** The gold or yellow center of an archery target; bull's-eye.

2 Short for *gold medal.*

golden gate *bowling* A split that leaves the 4, 6, 7, and 10 pins standing; double pinochle. — see illustration of pin arrangement at BOWLING

Golden Glove An award given to a major league baseball player voted the best fielder at his position.

Golden Gloves A series of amateur boxing tournaments originated in the 1920s by the Chicago Tribune and held in major cities throughout the United States.

gold medal A gold-colored medal awarded for first place in a competition.

gold-shyness see ARCHER'S PARALYSIS

golf

golf **1** A game of Scottish origin in which each participant, using a variety of clubs, attempts to drive a small ball into a succession of 9 or 18 holes on a specially laid out course in as few strokes as possible. Play is usually in groups of 2 to 4 people who move around the course together each taking turns playing his ball. Each person plays his own ball, and all strokes must be made with one of the maximum 14 clubs that a player is permitted to carry. The ball must be played as it lies except in unusual circumstances where the rules provide for improving the lie of the ball. The total number of strokes taken to drive the ball from the tee into the hole, plus any penalty strokes incurred by the player, are recorded as the player's score for that hole. Competition is either stroke play or match play. In stroke play each player's score is the total number of strokes taken to get around the course and the player with the lowest total is the winner. In match play the scores are compared at every hole, and a player wins, loses, or halves each hole. The player or side winning the most holes wins the round. The game is commonly played with each participant playing against every other participant, with one playing against the best score of a partnership, or with one partnership playing its best score for each hole against that of another partnership — see also CLUB, GOLF COURSE; BEST-BALL, FOURBALL, FOURSOME

2 A variation of pocket billiards played with a cue ball and a single object ball. The object of the game is for each player to drive the object ball successively into the 6 pockets on the table in the fewest strokes possible.

golf bag A large bag for carrying golf clubs and accessories.

golf cart **1** or **golf car** A battery-powered electric vehicle designed to carry usually 2 golfers and their clubs around a golf course.

2 A small 2-wheel vehicle to which a golfer attaches his bag of clubs and which he pulls behind him as he walks around the golf course.

golf club see CLUB

golf course An area of grassy land that is laid out and specially constructed for golf with 9 or 18 holes, each of which includes a teeing area, fairway, putting green, one or more natural or artificial hazards such as a body of water or a sand trap, and usually an untrimmed area called the

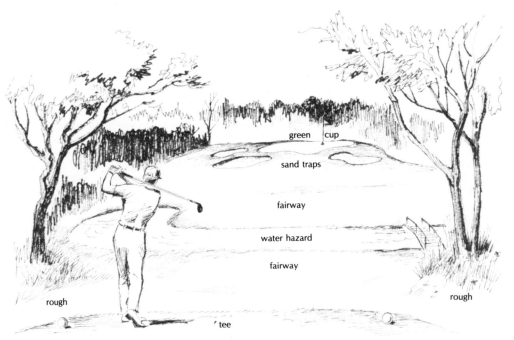

green   cup

sand traps

fairway

water hazard

fairway

rough

rough

tee

golf course

rough. There are no standard specifications for a golf course. Each course is laid out uniquely, often following the natural contours of the land, and each provides a different set of challenges to the golfer. The distance from the tee to the hole is usually from 300 to 500 yards for each hole and a typical 18-hole course may cover as much as 200 acres and have a total yardage of 6500 to 7000 yards. — see also PAR

golfdom The world of golf and golfers; the golf scene. ⟨stamped as the favorite to win this 71-year-old championship, most prestigious in *golfdom* — Lincoln A. Werden, *New York Times*⟩

golfer Someone who plays golf.

golfing The sport or practice of playing golf.

golf widow A woman whose husband spends much time on the golf course.

go long *football* To attempt a long forward pass.

gondola 1 A usually metal frame that is suspended from the envelope of a balloon and that carries the passengers, instruments, and burners. 2 An enclosed car suspended from an overhead cable leading up a mountain and used for transporting passengers especially for sight-seeing or as a ski lift.

gone away *of a fox* Having been driven from the covert by the hounds.

gong buoy see BUOY

good 1 *of a ball in a court game* Inbounds and in play.
2 *of a dirt racetrack* Having some moisture remaining after a rain but affording firm footing so that running times are only slightly slower than on a fast track. — compare FAST, HEAVY, MUDDY, SLOPPY, SLOW

good wood *baseball* Good contact between the bat and the pitched ball which drives the ball solidly. — usually used in the phrase *get good wood on the ball* ⟨when you've shortened up and quickened up, you can wait longer, you get fooled less, you become more consistent getting *good wood* on the ball — Ted Williams⟩

goofy foot A surfer who rides the board with his right foot forward instead of in the usual manner with the left foot forward.

googly *cricket* A ball which is bowled by a right-handed bowler and released with the same wrist action as a leg-break but which spins like an off break upon striking the ground. — compare CHINAMAN

gooseneck 1 A fitting (as a hook and eye or a universal joint) by which a boom or spar is attached to a mast.

2 The curved portion of the handle of a curling stone.

gopher ball *baseball* A pitch that is hit for a home run.

gore An individual panel in a balloon envelope.

go-round *rodeo* A round in which each contestant in a particular event (as bull riding) has a turn.

goshawk Any of several short-winged hawks that are kept and trained for use in falconry.

go the distance or **go the route** *of a baseball pitcher* To pitch a complete game.

go to ground *of a fox* To take refuge in an earth or drain when pursued.

go with the pitch *of a baseball batter* To hit an outside pitch to the opposite field or toward center rather than try to pull it. ⟨all he's got to do is *go with the pitch* to right field or through the middle and occasionally pull an off-speed pitch — *Sporting News*⟩

grab a rail *surfing* To pull out of a wave by grasping the rail of the board on the side opposite the crest of the wave and pulling the front of the board around so that the wave moves past the surfer.

grabbling The act or practice of catching fish (as catfish) by hand. This may involve enticing the fish to strike at the hand whereupon the fingers are poked through the gill openings and the fish pulled out of the water. It may involve tickling the fish on the belly while moving the hand slowly to the gill openings. The fish is then grabbed by the gills and pulled out of the water. (also called *noodling, tickling*)

Granby roll *wrestling* An escape maneuver in which a wrestler who is sitting on the mat with his back to his opponent grasps his opponent's arm on one side and rolls in the opposite direction completely over on his shoulders in a move that resembles a cartwheel. This rolling maneuver while holding the opponent's arm causes the opponent's arm to be twisted and forces him to the mat where the wrestler can gain control.

Grand National 1 A series of races of from 250 to 600 miles for stock cars run mostly on oval tracks in the southern United States.
2 A steeplechase for horses held annually over the 4 mile 856 yard course at Aintree, England, since 1839. The Grand National, which requires the horses to take 30 jumps, is the most famous and most prestigious steeplechase in the world.

Grand Prix 1 One of a series of international auto races for Formula One cars. The term, French for *grand prize,* was first used of the Grand Prix de

grand slam

Granby roll

Paris, a horse race of 1 mile 7 furlongs for 3-year-olds that has been run annually since 1863. Recently, numerous promoters have used the term for many of their own contests ranging from ski races to a series of professional tennis tournaments.

2 *equitation* The expert level of national or international dressage and jumping competition. Grand Prix jumping is both team and individual competition with the competitors making 2 rounds of a course up to 1000 meters long with from 12 to 15 obstacles. The obstacles vary from 1.3 to 1.6 meters (about 4 to 5 feet) high with a spread of 1.5 to 2.2 meters (5 to 7 feet) for the first round. The course must have a water jump at least 4.5 meters (about 14½ feet) wide. The first round for team and individual competition is the same. In the second round, there are 10 obstacles in the individual competition and 6 in the team competition. These range from 1.4 to 1.8 meters (4½ to 6 feet) high.

grand slam 1 or **grandslammer** *baseball* A home run hit with the bases loaded.

2 The winning of the 4 most prestigious tournaments (as in golf or tennis) in one year by the same player. In tennis the 4 tournaments are the French Open, Australian Open, Wimbledon, and the United States Open singles championships. In 1930, Bobby Jones won the grand slam of golf by winning the United States Amateur, the United States Open, the British Amateur, and the British Open championships. Since the second world war, however, professional golf has gained more prominence and today the grand slam of golf consists of the United States Open,

the British Open, the Masters, and the PGA championships.

grandstand A usually roofed section of permanent stands serving as the principal spectator accommodations at an outdoor sports site (as a ball park or racecourse). — see also STANDS; compare BLEACHERS

grandstand play A spectacular play that is often more crowd-pleasing than strategically effective.

grandstand quarterback A football spectator who constantly second-guesses the quarterback. — compare MONDAY MORNING QUARTERBACK

grand touring car or **grand tourer** or **gran turismo** A usually 2-passenger sports coupe. — compare TOURING CAR, SPORTS CAR

granite A curling stone.

granular snow Frozen snow that has large coarse crystals.

grapefruit league *baseball* The major league teams that hold their spring training in Florida and that play exhibition games against each other. — compare CACTUS LEAGUE

grapevine *wrestling* A hold in which one wrestler intertwines his leg around his opponent's leg usually by crossing his leg over his opponent's thigh and hooking his instep around his opponent's ankle. If both legs are entwined, it is a double grapevine.

grapnel A small anchor with several hooklike arms that is used especially for recovering lost objects or retrieving a fouled anchor.

grappling The aspect of wrestling or judo in which opponents attempt to secure holds on each other while on the mat as distinguished from throwing or takedown techniques.

grasp The manner of holding an implement; grip.

grass A running or playing surface covered with grass as opposed to dirt, clay, or a synthetic surface:
1 *horse racing* A turf racetrack.
2 *tennis* A grass court.

grass cutter *baseball* A hard grounder that skims along the ground.

grass skiing The sport of coasting down a grassy slope on specially made skis with rollers on the bottom; turf skiing.

grasstrack racing *motorcycle racing* Racing on a course laid out on a grassy field and often incorporating various types of races such as speedway or sprint races.

graveyard *bowling* A lane on which it is difficult to get good scores.

graze see FROISSEMENT

grease ball *baseball* A spitball in which the offending moisture is supplied by a greasy substance (as hair cream) applied to the ball or fingers.

Greco-Roman *wrestling* Competition in which wrestlers are not permitted to use their legs in any active manner (as in tripping an opponent or in applying a scissors hold or grapevine) and are not permitted to use any holds that involve the opponent's hips or legs. — see also WRESTLING; compare FREESTYLE, SAMBO

¹green 1 *archery* An outdoor shooting range.
2 *golf* A smooth area of close-cut grass at the end of the fairway that contains the hole into which the ball must be played. All strokes on the green are made with the putter. (also called *putting green*)
3 *lawn bowling* A level grassy area approximately 125 feet square that is surrounded by a shallow ditch and that is divided into a number of rinks.

²green *of a racehorse* Not yet raced.

green air *soaring* A rising current of air (*thermal*) on which a sailplane can climb that is indicated by the rise of the green pellet in the sailplane's variometer.

green fee see GREENS FEE

green flag *motor racing* A solid green flag that indicates that the track is clear and that racing may start or resume.

greenie 1 A green pep pill.
2 *golf* A tee shot in which the player reaches the green thereby winning a bet in informal play. — compare SANDIE, CHIPPIE

greens fee or **green fee** *golf* A fee paid for the privilege of playing on a golf course.

greenside At or to the side of or adjacent to a green on a golf course.

gremmie *surfing* An inexperienced surfer; an obnoxious surfer.

Grey Cup The championship game and trophy of the Canadian Football League. The cup is named after Albert Henry George Grey, former Governor General of Canada, who donated the cup in 1909.

¹greyhound A tall slender smooth-coated dog noted for swiftness and keen sight. The greyhound does not have a good sense of smell but is a natural runner and will generally chase anything that runs away from it. The greyhound is popularly used for racing and its poor sense of smell coupled with its natural instinct to chase are factors in the successful use of a mechanical rabbit as a lure.

²greyhound *of a hooked sailfish* To make a spectacular leap or a series of leaps.

¹grid 1 *auto racing* The starting positions of cars on a racecourse before the start of a race; the field of competitors before the start of a race.
2 A network of perpendicular lines that divide a map into equal squares for easy reference.
3 see GRIDIRON

²grid *auto racing* To line up racing cars on a grid.

gridder A football player.

gridiron or **grid** A football field; the game of football. ⟨interesting development on the college *gridiron* scene — *Playboy*⟩

grid start *auto racing* A start of a race in which all cars move off at once from the grid at the starting signal. — compare FLYING START

griff fifi *mountain climbing* A large fifi-hook that incorporates a handle.

grille *court tennis* A 3-foot-square opening at one side of the end wall on the hazard side of the court. A ball driven into the grille in play automatically wins the point.

grind out *football* To gain short yardage chiefly by a number of carries into the line.

grip 1 The part of an implement that is grasped by the hand. The grip in certain instances may be the same as the handle (as the grip of a canoe paddle) or may be part of a handle (as the portion of the handle of a fencing foil that is actually held in the hand as distinguished from the pommel). The grip of a golf club or a racket is the portion of the shaft that is covered with a material such as rubber or leather and is gripped by the hand. The grip of a javelin is a section approximately 6½ inches long near the middle of the shaft that is wrapped usually with cord to provide a secure hold. Attached to the end of the handle of a hammer is a grip which consists of a cable or solid metal loop which is held by the thrower. **2** The manner of gripping a ball, club, paddle, or racket. In throwing a baseball, the player usually grips it with the thumb on one side and 2 fingers on the opposite side. A bowling ball is usually held with one of 3 principal grips, the *conventional grip,* in which the thumb and fingers are inserted in their holes up to the second joint, the *finger-tip grip,* in which the thumb is

inserted fully but the fingers only to the first joint, and the *semi-finger-tip grip* which is midway between the other two, with the fingers inserted in the holes midway between the first and second joints. The *span,* or distance between the thumb hole and the finger holes on a custom-drilled ball, is determined by the grip employed by the bowler. The span is greater for a semi-finger-tip grip than for a conventional grip and greater still for a finger-tip grip.

Three major grips are used in golf. The *over-*

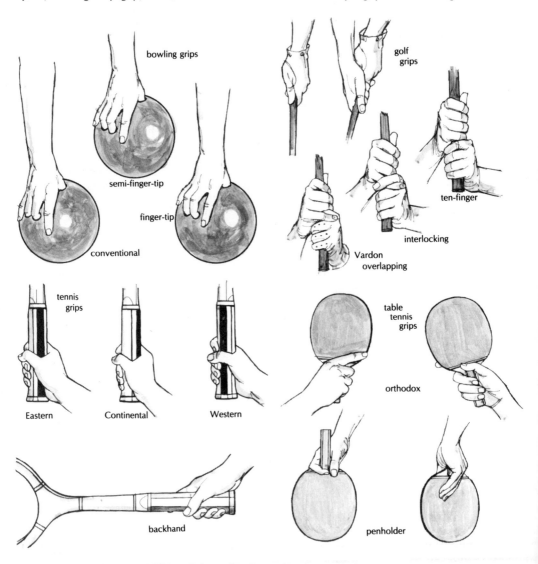

bowling grips

semi-finger-tip

finger-tip

conventional

golf grips

ten-finger

interlocking

Vardon overlapping

tennis grips

Eastern

Continental

Western

backhand

table tennis grips

orthodox

penholder

lapping grip or *Vardon grip* is used by the overwhelming majority of top players while the *interlocking grip* and the *ten-finger grip* or *baseball grip* each has its advocates. In each of the 3 grips, the hands are placed on the club in the same position with the differences being in how the little finger of the lower hand (the right hand for a right-handed golfer) meets the forefinger of the other hand. In the overlapping grip, the little finger nestles between the forefinger and the middle finger of the left hand. In the interlocking grip, the forefinger and the little finger interlock while in the baseball grip the 2 hands meet as in gripping a baseball bat with no overlap.

There are 3 principal grips employed in tennis, the *Eastern, Continental,* and *Western* grips. With the Eastern grip, the palm of the hand is to the side of the handle (when the face of the racket is held vertical) so that the V between the thumb and the forefinger is at the top of the handle. For a backhand stroke with the Eastern grip, the hand is shifted forward so that the V of the hand is toward the front edge of the handle. The Continental grip is between the Eastern forehand and backhand grips with the palm near the top of the handle. For the Western grip, the palm is more toward the bottom of the handle. There is usually no shifting of the hand for a backhand stroke when using the Continental and Western grips. Though both the Western and Continental have supporters, the Eastern grip is favored by the vast majority of players especially in the United States and Australia.

The conventional forehand and backhand grips used for badminton and racquetball are like the Eastern grip in tennis with the thumb and forefinger pointed more toward the head of the racket. The grip used in paddleball and squash racquets resembles the Continental grip. Paddle tennis and platform tennis grips are the same as in tennis.

Table tennis paddles are gripped with one of 2 principal grips, the *orthodox grip* or *tennis grip* in which the paddle is held close to the head with the thumb along the base of the face and the forefinger extended against the back, and the *penholder grip* or *Oriental grip* in which the paddle is held with the head down and the handle extending up between the thumb and forefinger which are curled over the front while the other 3 fingers brace against the back. The orthodox grip is favored by players in the United States and Europe, while the penholder is popular among players from the Orient. With the penholder, all strokes, forehand and backhand, are made with the same side of the paddle; with the orthodox grip, one side is used for forehand shots, and the other side for backhand shots just as in tennis.

3 *gymnastics* The position of the hands on an apparatus. The 2 principal grips used on the horizontal bar are the *regular grip, front grip,* or *overgrip* in which the palms are on the near side of the bar and turned outward, the *reverse grip* or *undergrip* in which the palms are on the far side of the bar and turned toward the body. — see also FALSE GRIP

¹groom A stable hand who is generally charged with the care of a horse and who normally rubs him down after exercise.

²groom To prepare a slope for skiing especially by packing the snow or breaking up crust.

¹groove **1** A rhythm or pattern of play at which a player is most effective. ⟨he hasn't found his *groove* yet⟩
2 One of the spiral cuts in the inside of a rifle barrel. — compare LAND
3 *auto racing* The quickest and most efficient route around a racecourse. In road racing the term *line* may also be used.
4 *baseball* The middle of the strike zone; the area over the middle of home plate where it is generally easiest for a batter to connect with the ball.
5 *bowling* A slightly worn path on a lane as a result of numerous balls following the same route to the pocket. A ball may tend to follow the groove with the result that scoring is easier than on a perfectly flat lane.
6 *mountain climbing* The place on a cliff where 2 walls meet at an angle. In a shallow groove the angle is greater than 90 degrees; in a V-groove, it is less than 90 degrees. If the walls meet at right angles, the groove is usually called a *corner.*

²groove *baseball* To throw a pitch right over the middle of the plate where the batter has a good chance of knocking it out of the park.

grooved *of a swing* Practiced to the point that it can be repeated in practically the same way each time as if following a groove.

gross *golf* The actual number of strokes taken to play a hole or a round before a handicap is deducted.

¹ground **1** *cricket* **a** The playing field. **b** The area behind the popping crease in which a batsman must be standing or be touching with his bat to avoid being out if the wicket is broken. This is analogous to a base in baseball.

2 *football* An offense or the part of an offense utilizing running plays. ⟨were stopped on the *ground* and were forced to take to the air⟩

— **out of one's ground** *of a cricket batsman* Forward of the popping crease and subject to being put out.

²ground **1** *baseball* To hit a ground ball. ⟨*grounded* to short for the second out⟩

2 *football* To throw a football ostensibly for a forward pass but so that it hits the ground in an area away from defensive players. A quarterback may be guilty of intentionally grounding the ball to avoid being caught with the ball and thrown for a loss. — see INTENTIONAL GROUNDING

3 *golf* To touch the head of the club to the ground behind the ball when addressing the ball. The club may be grounded at any time except when the ball is being played from a hazard. For grounding the club in a hazard the penalty is loss of the hole in match play or 2 strokes in stroke play.

4 *rugby* To touch the ball to the ground in the in-goal or to touch the ball while it is in the in-goal to stop play. If a defensive player grounds the ball in his own in-goal, his team is awarded a touchdown, an opportunity to put the ball in play from within their own 25-yard line by a drop kick. This is analogous to football's touchback. If an offensive player grounds the ball in his opponent's in-goal, his team is awarded a try worth 3 points.

ground ball A ball that is on the ground and in play:

1 or **grounder** *baseball* A batted ball that is rolling or bounding. — compare FLY BALL

2 *speedball* A ball that is stationary or rolling or bouncing along the ground and that may be played only with the feet. Once a ground ball has been kicked up and has been caught before it again touches the ground, it is an aerial ball and may be carried or played with the hands.

ground cloth see GROUNDSHEET

grounder see GROUND BALL

ground-gainer *football* An offensive player who gains yardage rushing; running back. ⟨he is their leading *ground-gainer*⟩

ground game *football* Play or strategy utilizing running plays.

ground judge *fencing* One of 2 judges who watch for touches on the piste in competition with electric foil or épée when the piste is not wired to the control box. When a wired metal piste is used, touches on it are registered separately on the recording equipment.

groundout *baseball* A play in which the batter is thrown out at first base after hitting a ground ball to an infielder.

ground out *baseball* To hit into a groundout. ⟨*grounded out* to second⟩

ground quiver see QUIVER

ground rule *baseball* A rule that is adopted to modify play on a particular field because of conditions such as unusually high or unusually close outfield fences or obstructions in the field of play and that normally specifies, except in the case of automatic home runs, that the ball is dead and that base runners may advance only a designated number of bases.

ground rule double *baseball* An automatic double awarded a batter when a batted ball bounces over an outfield fence.

groundsheet or **ground cloth** *hiking* A piece of waterproof material (as canvas, nylon, or plastic) that is spread on the ground to protect a sleeping bag from soil moisture.

groundskeeper Someone employed to maintain the condition of the playing surface in a ball park or stadium.

ground stroke *tennis* A stroke made by hitting the ball after it bounces. — compare HALF VOLLEY, VOLLEY

ground tackle Equipment used in anchoring a boat.

ground wrestling *sambo* Wrestling while one or both wrestlers are on the mat rather than in a standing position.

group **1** A number of arrows or bullet holes in a target shot together or from a single point or position.

2 A group of dives performed from the same position or in the same manner: forward dives make up group one; group two is backward dives; group three, reverse dives; inward dives are in group four; twist dives comprise group five; and armstand dives, group six.

3 An international classification of racing automobiles having similar production, design, or modification characteristics or restrictions: group one consists of unmodified production touring cars (regular passenger cars); group two, modified touring cars; group three, unmodified production grand touring cars (sports cars and GTs); group four, modified grand touring cars; group five, special limited production endurance racing sports cars; group six, experimental competition prototype sports cars; group seven, sports/racing cars; group eight, international formula cars. Group nine is a classification (called *formula libra*) which gives local race promoters and organizations authority to set the requirements for the cars to be raced in a particular race or series and includes most American racing cars such as stock cars, Indy cars, and dragsters.

grudge Being a contest between individuals or teams that have a real or supposed animosity toward each other or one in which one side seeks to avenge an earlier defeat.

¹guard **1** A defensive position, stance, or attitude (as in fencing or boxing).

2 A stone or bowl that is delivered in curling or lawn bowling so as to stop in front of a teammate's stone or bowl to protect it from being knocked out of the scoring area by an opponent's play.

3 *basketball* Either of 2 players who normally play farthest from the basket and who are primarily responsible for bringing the ball into the frontcourt and for starting planned offensive plays. Guards are usually smaller and are better ball handlers than the forwards and centers.

4 *fencing* The somewhat bowl-shaped shield between the blade of a sword and the handle which curves toward the handle to protect the fencer's hand. The guard of a foil is relatively shallow while that of the épée is quite deep. One side of the saber guard curves around to the pommel to protect the knuckles of the sword hand. (also called *bell*) — see illustration at FENCING

5 *football* Either of 2 offensive linemen who normally play on either side of the center. Guards are primarily responsible for blocking to create holes in the interior of the line for the ballcarrier to run through but they occasionally pull out of the line to lead the blocking on sweeps. — see also MIDDLE GUARD

6 *lacrosse* A piece of gut or rawhide along one side of the head of a stick from the throat to the tip which encloses the head and to which the netting is attached. — see illustration at STICK

7 *speedball* Either of 2 defensive players who normally play near the goal and whose duties are analogous to those of soccer fullbacks.

8 *water polo* Any of the 3 players other than the goalkeeper who play close to the goal; back.

9 The position played by a guard.

²guard **1** To attempt to prevent an opponent from playing effectively or from scoring in a team game. Guarding usually involves attempting to prevent an opponent from receiving a pass or to keep the opponent from effectively maneuvering so as to be able to make a shot. It may involve checking or tackling or attempting to knock the ball or puck out of the player's control.

2 To defend oneself from attack in boxing or fencing.

guard line *fencing* A line across the piste 2 meters on either side of the center line that marks where the fencers must assume an on guard position at the beginning of a bout.

guard weight *curling* The momentum required to move a stone into position to be a guard.

gudgeons The eye fittings on the stearn post of a boat into which the pintles of the rudder fit.

guernsey Australian term for a football jersey.

guess hitter *baseball* A batter who likes to anticipate the pitch a pitcher will throw in a particular situation.

guide **1** A person who is familiar with the hunting or fishing in a particular area and who is employed to escort a hunter or fisherman or a party on a hunting or fishing trip.

2 One of a series of metal rings or loops on a fishing rod through which the line passes. Spinning and casting rods commonly have rings braced just off the rod while a fly rod normally uses small loops of wire (called *snake guides*) which hold the line very close to the rod. Big game rods normally have guides that consist of rollers mounted on a frame fixed to the rod. — see also TIP-TOP

guillotine *wrestling* A fall gained from a cross-body ride in which the wrestler holds his opponent's shoulders to the mat with a reverse half nelson and applies a grapevine or scissors hold

guillotine

guinea

on the opponent's far leg. (also called *crucifix*)

guinea *horse racing* A boy who does odd jobs around a stable; groom. The term comes from the wages formerly given such helpers in England.

gully 1 *cricket* **a** The area of the field on the off side somewhat between point and third man and slightly to the rear of the striker's wicket. **b** The fieldsman who plays in this area.

2 *mountain climbing* A cleft in a rock face that is wide enough for a climber to walk around inside and not be able to touch both sides at the same time.

gumbo *horse racing* Heavy sticky mud on the track.

gun 1 The firing of a pistol as a starting signal (as in track and field or swimming) or to signal the end of a period of play (as in football).

2 A large heavy surfboard used especially for riding heavy surf.

gun dog *hunting* A dog (as a pointer, setter, or retriever) that has been trained to accompany a hunter and to flush and retrieve game. (also called *bird dog*)

gun down *baseball* To throw out a player especially when he is attempting to steal, take an extra base, or score on a hit.

gunkholer Someone who enjoys or engages in gunkholing.

gunkholing *sailing* The practice of sailing a small boat in shallow-water areas along a coastline (as in and around small inlets).

gun lap *track and field* The last lap of a race signaled by the firing of a pistol, or sometimes by the ringing of a bell, as the leader begins the last lap. — see also BELL LAP

gunner 1 **a** Someone who hunts game with a gun. **b** A skeet shooter or trapshooter.

2 A basketball player who tends to shoot more frequently than he should, often when a teammate is in a better position to score.

gunning 1 The act or practice of hunting or shooting with a gun.

2 *basketball* The practice of shooting frequently, often without having a good shot or when a teammate is in better position to score.

gunwale The upper edge of the side of a boat; the area where the side and deck meet.

gut 1 The stretched and dried fluid from the silk sacks of silkworms and moth caterpillers that was formerly much used to make leaders for fly fishing. Gut has been almost entirely replaced today by monofilament.

2 Catgut used in stringing rackets.

3 Rawhide, cord, or catgut used in the netting of a lacrosse stick.

4 *football* The middle of the line. ⟨carried the ball right up the *gut*⟩

gutter *bowling* A narrow trough with a rounded bottom that runs along each side of a lane and that catches balls that leave the lane and guides them past the pins. (also called *channel*)

gutter ball *bowling* A ball that rolls into the gutter. A gutter ball is dead and counts as a turn for the bowler but does not score pins. (also called *channel ball*)

gybe see JIBE

gym 1 A room equipped with punching bags and a boxing ring that is used for the training of boxers.

2 Short for *gymnasium*.

gymkhana 1 A riding competition which consists of games and contests designed to demonstrate the skill of both the horse and rider. The gymkhana may include such things as contests in which riders on horseback must spear potatoes and races in which riders are required to change horses and exchange saddles and bridles at various points during the race.

2 An automobile competition often held on an empty parking lot in which drivers take their cars one at a time around a twisting course designed to test driving skill. The gymkhana is usually run with handicaps, and the competitor with the lowest elapsed time and fewest penalty points is the winner.

gymnasium 1 A large room that is typically designed with a permanent basketball court and with spectator accomodations and that may also be used for various other indoor sports (as boxing, wrestling, or volleyball). — compare FIELD HOUSE

2 A building (as on a college campus) that usually contains areas for a variety of sports as well as shower and dressing rooms and administrative offices. A representative gymnasium may have basketball, tennis, and squash courts, a swimming pool, a rowing tank, and rooms for gymnastics, boxing, wrestling, fencing, and weight lifting.

gymnast A person who engages in gymnastics especially in competition.

gymnastic Of or relating to gymnastics. ⟨*gymnastic* apparatus⟩

gymnastic chalk *gymnastics* Magnesium carbonate that is applied to the hands to absorb excessive moisture and to reduce friction between the hands and the apparatus.

gymnastics A sport in which individuals perform optional and prescribed acrobatic feats which demonstrate strength, balance, and body control. Gymnastics encompasses calisthenics and tumbling as well as work on apparatus; it grew out of calisthenic exercises developed in Sweden in the 19th century and exercises on apparatus developed at about the same time in Europe. In competition, individuals are judged on the basis of an abstract standard; the individual having the highest score for a particular event is the winner of that event. A program of competition consists of the horizontal bar, parallel bars, pommel horse, vaulting horse, rings, and floor exercise events for men and the balance beam, uneven parallel bars, vaulting horse, and floor exercise events for women. Men and women compete in separate competitions. Though competitors normally specialize in a single event, they must be good in all events. In international competition, performers are required to compete in all events, and the individual with the highest overall score is the all-around champion.

H

H   see GATE

¹hack   1 *curling* A foothold cut in the ice at each end of the rink 12 feet behind the tee line.
2 The act or an instance of hacking an opponent.
3 *cockfighting* A single match.
— **at hack** *of a hawk or falcon* Allowed to fly free between the time of capture and the beginning of training but regularly fed at an established place by the handler. Newly captured birds are normally fitted with bells and jesses when kept at hack. This period is important for the bird to overcome its natural fear of the handler and his home.

²hack   1 *basketball* To strike the arm of an opponent with the hand.
2 *cockfighting* To enter a cock in a match.
3 *rugby* To deliberately kick the shins of an opponent.
4 *tennis* To make a poor swing at the ball.
5 To ride a horse at leisure as distinct from riding in a hunt or race.

hacker   *tennis* A poor player.

hacking   1 *basketball* A personal foul that results when a player strikes an opponent's arm with his hand.
2 The practice of riding a horse along roads, on bridle paths, or in parks for pleasure.

hackle   A long narrow feather from the neck of a bird (as a domestic fowl) that is commonly used in tying flies for fishing. For dry flies the hackle feathers are wound around the shaft of the hook so as to stand out at right angles. In this way they support the fly above the surface of the water. The hackles on wet flys are normally tied lying toward the rear.

hack line   *curling* A line 18 inches long that is centered on and perpendicular to the center line 12 feet back of the tee. The hack is cut in the ice at the hack line. (also called *foot score*)

haggard   A wild falcon caught when it is an adult.
— compare EYAS, PASSAGER

Haines spin   see SIT SPIN

hairpin   1 A sharp turn in a road course that may change direction by as much as 180 degrees.

2 see GATE

hairpin net shot   or   **hairpin net stroke**   *badminton* A soft shot made almost directly upward at the net so as just to clear the net and fall straight down on the other side.

¹half   1 Either of 2 equal divisions of a game or contest that is played on the basis of time. A half may be made up of 2 quarters.
2 The end of the first half of a game. ⟨leading 27–23 at the *half.*⟩
3 A half-mile race; the half-mile point in a longer race. ⟨ahead by 2 lengths at the *half*⟩
4 Short for *halfback.*

²half   Done or performed with a half revolution of the body. ⟨*half* flip⟩ ⟨*half* twist⟩

halfback   1 A primarily defensive player in team games such as soccer, field hockey, speedball, and Australian Rules football who normally plays in his own defensive half of the field between his forward line and his goal and who has responsibility for guarding opposing forwards. Halfbacks are designated by the part of the field they normally occupy as the left, right, and center halfbacks. Though the halfback is responsible for stopping an attack by the opposing team, he is not restricted to defense and may often initiate an attack.
2 *football* **a** An offensive back who plays to one side of the fullback. Halfbacks tend to be smaller and faster than fullbacks and are used chiefly to run the ball or receive passes. In the straight T formation 2 halfbacks flank the fullback while in the standard pro formation there is only one halfback to the side of the fullback. **b** A cornerback.
3 *rugby* A back who lines up behind the scrum but in front of the threequarter backs and who is responsible for getting the ball from the scrum and initiating his team's attack. There are normally 2 halfbacks on a team.
4 The position played by a halfback.

halfback option   see OPTION (*football*)

half bow   *archery* The second circle out from the center of a clout target.

half-century   *cricket* A score of 50 or more runs

that are made by a batsman during an innings.

half circle *gymnastics* A maneuver performed on the pommel horse in which the gymnast, supporting himself at one side of the horse with his hands on the pommels, swings one leg over the end of the horse, lifts the near hand to allow the leg to pass under, and then grasps the pommel again to end up straddling the horse with one hand holding a pommel in front and the other hand holding the pommel at the rear.

half court A service court (as in badminton or tennis).

half-court line *tennis* A line on each side of the court parallel to the sidelines that extends from the net to the service line and that divides the front part of the court into 2 service courts. (also called *center service line*)

half forward 1 Any of 3 offensive players who play between the center line players and the full forwards in Australian Rules football or Gaelic football.

2 The position played by a half forward.

half hitch A hitch usually tied twice that is used in securing a rope to an object temporarily, in tying flies, or in forming a more complex knot and that consists of making a single turn around the object and bringing the end around the standing part and then back inside the loop. — see illustration at KNOT

half-in half-out or **half-in half-out fliffis** *gymnastics* A double backward somersault with a half twist in the first somersault and another half twist in the second somersault.

half knot An overlapping of the ends of 2 lines or the 2 ends of one line that is usually used in forming a knot (as the square knot). — see illustration at KNOT

half loop see EULER

half-mile *track and field* A middle distance race one half mile in length.

half-miler An athlete who competes in the half-mile.

half nelson see NELSON

half rounder *rounders* A score worth half a rounder made when a batter is able to run around all of the bases without having hit the ball.

half-shaft *auto racing* An axle shaft that leads from the differential or the transaxle to the drive wheel of a racing car.

half sidestep *skiing* A technique of climbing a slope on skis which is essentially the same as a sidestep but in which the uphill ski is placed above and ahead of the weighted ski on each

step with the result that the skier climbs the slope at an angle instead of straight up.

halftime The time between halves of a sports contest during which the players rest. In most major American sports the halftime is 15 minutes long.

half volley 1 A stroke that is made immediately after the ball strikes the playing surface (as in tennis, handball, or squash).

2 *cricket* A delivery that bounces so close to the batsman that he can hit it just as it leaves the ground without having to stride forward.

half volley kick *soccer* A kick of the ball just as it rebounds from the ground.

halfway line A line that is marked across a rugby or soccer field midway between and parallel to the goal lines to divide the field into 2 equal sections.

half Worcester *bowling* A leave in which only the 3 and 9 pins or the 2 and 8 pins remain standing. — see illustration of pin arrangement at BOWLING

halliard see HALYARD

halve *golf* To play a hole or a round in match play in the same number of strokes as one's opponent.

halyard or **halliard** *sailing* A line used to hoist or lower a sail or flag. — compare SHEET

Hambletonian A 1-mile race for 3-year-old trotters that has been run annually since 1930 and that is one of the races in the trotting Triple Crown. It is named for a stallion that from 1851 to 1874 sired 1331 horses. Better than 9 out of 10 outstanding trotters and pacers can trace their lineage back to Hambletonian.

¹hammer 1 The part of the action of a firearm that drives the firing pin into the cartridge.

2 *track and field* **a** The implement used in the hammer throw that consists of a heavy metal ball connected by a steel wire to a grip. The hammer weighs 16 pounds and is approximately 4 feet long overall. **b** Short for *hammer throw*.

²hammer To hit a ball forcefully. ⟨*hammered* out five straight hits and drove in four runs — United Press International⟩ ⟨I don't use the strike zone much. I'm looking for something to *hammer* — Dick Allen⟩

hammer axe *mountain climbing* A relatively short-handled tool with a hammer at one side of the head and a pick at the other that is typically used on climbs where both pitoning and climbing on ice are involved. (also called *North Wall axe*)

hammerlock *wrestling* A hold in which an op-

hammer throw

ponent's arm is bent behind his back. The hold is legal so long as the arm is not bent beyond a 90-degree angle.

hammerlock

hammer throw *track and field* A field event in which the hammer is hurled for distance with 2 hands from within a throwing circle 7 feet in diameter. In order to qualify as a legal throw, the hammer must land in the throwing sector formed by 2 lines extending at a 60-degree angle from the center of the throwing circle and the competitor must not step on or over the throwing circle during the throw.

hammer thrower An athlete who competes in the hammer throw.

hamstring pull A strain or severe pull of any of the 3 hamstring muscles at the back of the thigh. (also called *pulled hamstring*)

¹hand **1** A turn of play in a game (as squash racquets) in which there is an opportunity for a particular side to score; the period between hand-in and hand-out.
2 *archery* A group of 4 arrows shot and scored as a group in field archery.
3 *billiards* A situation (as after an opponent has scratched) in which the shooter may place the cue ball anywhere within a limited area on the table to make his next shot.
— in hand **1** *of a billiard ball* To be placed anywhere within a limited area for the next shot.
2 *ice hockey* Being a game that remains on the schedule at the end of the season for one team but not for a rival team in the league or conference standing. By winning a game a team has in hand, it can pick up 2 points in the standings that the rival team cannot match and may thereby overtake the rival team or increase its own lead in the standings. **3** *of a racehorse* Winning a race with something left in reserve. **4** *of a cricket wicket* Not taken by the opposing team at the time a side wins the match or declares its innings closed. ⟨declared with 166 runs and 4 wickets *in hand*⟩

²hand To illegally touch or play the ball with the hand in soccer.

hand balance see HANDSTAND

¹handball **1 a** A singles or doubles game played on a 1-, 3-, or 4-wall court in which opposing players alternately hit a 2-ounce black rubber ball with the hands, directing it to the front wall with the object of making a shot that the opposition is unable to return to the wall. Play is started with one player or side serving to the opponent by hitting the ball against the front wall. The ball

hammer throw

is then alternately hit before bouncing twice back to the front wall in any combination with the side walls, back wall, and ceiling until one side fails to make a legal return. Points are scored only by the serving side; if the serving side fails to make a good return, the serve goes to the other side. Games are played until one side scores 21 points. **b** The ball used in handball. — see BALL **2** *soccer* A foul which results when a player illegally handles the ball and which is penalized by awarding a free kick to the other team. (also called *hands*)

nent or a disadvantage imposed on a strong opponent for the purpose of allowing competitors of different abilities to compete on a more nearly even footing or with the outcome more unpredictable. Handicaps take many forms but commonly consist of points added to or deducted from one competitor's score or of a time, distance, or weight advantage in a race. In tennis, badminton, and bowling the weaker player may have an agreed upon number of points added to his score, while in golf the handicap is a number of strokes the weaker player may sub-

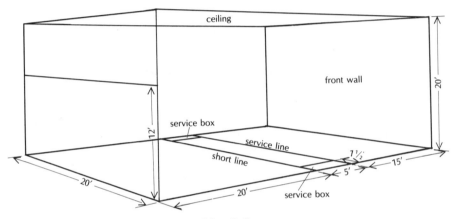

4-wall handball court

²handball *Australian Rules football* To pass the ball by holding it in one hand and punching it with the fist.

handballer Someone who plays handball.

hand bow *archery* A bow that is held in the hand for shooting. — compare FOOT BOW

handcuff *baseball* **1** *of a batted ball* To be hard for a fielder to handle. ⟨his sharp grounder *handcuffed* the shortstop⟩
2 *of a pitcher* To hold an opposing batter or team to relatively few hits. ⟨*handcuffed* Cleveland on three hits — Associated Press⟩

handgrip or **handguard** *gymnastics* A narrow strip of leather that is held to the palm of the hand by finger loops and a wrist strap and that is designed to protect the hands from blisters when gripping or swinging on an apparatus. (also called *lampwick*)

handhold *mountain climbing* Something to hold onto; a place to grasp with the hand for support.

¹handicap **1** An advantage given to a weak oppo-

tract from his score. In match play one or more strokes may be deducted at every hole or at alternate or designated holes. In stroke play, the handicap may be deducted at the end of the round or at individual holes listed on the scorecard in the order in which handicap strokes are to be used. A golfer's handicap is based on the number of strokes he regularly plays over the course handicap rating (not the course par) and is computed as 85 percent of the average difference between the rating and the player's 10 lowest rounds in the last 20 rounds.

Though racing is normally done in classes which group competitors according to ability or type of equipment, where handicaps are used they normally consist of time, distance, or weight advantages. In sailing, when boats of different types or sizes are competing together, an individual allowance based on such factors as length, width, sail area, and past performances is subtracted from each boat's elapsed time. The boat finishing the race with the fastest corrected

handicap

time is the winner regardless of which boat actually was first to finish. When cars of different classes are racing against one another in drag racing, the weaker competitor is usually given the starting signal before the stronger. Handicaps are based on national records of elapsed times for each class, and the difference between the best elapsed times of the 2 classes is the handicap used. In track, the runner with the advantage usually starts from a position ahead of other competitors. Handicaps in horse racing involve adjustments to the weight a horse must carry. This weight includes the weight of the jockey, the saddle, and lead bars carried in pockets in special saddle bags. The weight is normally adjusted by adding lead bars to make up the difference between the weight of the jockey and saddle and that required for the race. Weight requirements are established by a scale of weights for age or by the racing secretary, who handicaps the horses on the basis of his judgment of their respective chances, paying particular attention to past performances. The horses deemed to have the best chance of winning are given highest weight on the premise that additional weight will slow them down somewhat. The weights may vary as much as 15 pounds or more between the highest weighted and lowest weighted horses in a race.

Polo games are generally played with a number of points added to the weaker team's score. Each player is assigned a handicap rating of from 0 to 10 goals, a somewhat arbitrary figure which represents his skill and value to his team. A rating of 7 or 8 indicates an outstanding player; a 10-goal player is extremely rare. For a match, the handicap ratings of the 4 players of one team are added and compared with those of the other team. The team having the lower total has the difference added to its score at the beginning of the match.

In trapshooting, the handicap consists of a distance allowance, with weaker competitors standing closer to the target than more skilled shooters.

2 *horse racing* A race for top horses in which the racing secretary assigns weights to the horses in the field on the basis of their past performances. — compare ALLOWANCE RACE, CLAIMING RACE, STAKES RACE

3 *harness racing* A race in which an allowance (as an inside post position) is made on the basis of past performance or sex.

²handicap 1 To assign handicaps (as to racehorses).

2 To attempt to predict the winner of a contest (as a horse race or a football game) by analyzing the records of participants and other factors the handicapper deems important. The handicapper of a horse race may include the ability of the jockey, the weight to be carried, and the estimated physical condition or form of each horse as well as its past performances in his analysis.

handicapper 1 Someone who engages in handicapping; a person (as a racing secretary) who assigns handicaps.

2 A golfer with a specific handicap. 〈an 18 *handicapper*〉

handicapping The act or practice of trying to predict a winner especially on the basis of published data.

handicap stake *horse racing* A stakes race in which the horses are handicapped by the track handicapper or racing secretary.

handily *of a horse race or a workout* With the racehorse having something left in reserve; with the horse not running all out at the finish.

hand-in The serving side in some court games (as badminton or squash racquets) in which the serve passes to the opponents if the serving side fails to win the point.

hand-in-hand position *skating* A dance position in which the partners stand side by side facing the same direction with their near hands clasped. (also called *extended hold*)

¹handle 1 The part of an implement (as a stick, racket, or bat) that is held in the hand. The handle of an archer's bow is the thick part in the middle between the 2 limbs. The handle of a fencing sword is the part that extends to the rear of the guard and ends in the pommel. The handle of a racket or a hockey or lacrosse stick is the shaft to which the head or blade is attached. Hockey and lacrosse sticks may be grasped anywhere along their length but a racket is normally held at the end on the grip. The handle of a baseball bat is the narrow part; the rules do not specify how long the handle is other than to limit tape, twine, or plastic material, put on for a better grip, to no more than 18 inches above the end.

2 *pari-mutuel betting* The total amount of money bet during a given period (as on a single race or in a day).

3 *track and field* The wire connecting the head and the grip of a hammer.

²handle **1** *baseball* To throw, catch, or catch and throw the ball.

2 *boxing* To train and act as second for a fighter.

3 *soccer* To touch the ball with the hands in violation of the rules. — see HANDBALL

handler **1** Someone who helps train a boxer and who acts as his second during a fight.

2 Someone who raises, trains, and incites a gamecock to fight.

handle the ball *of a cricket batsman* To touch the ball in play with the hands except at the specific request of the fielding side and thereby cause oneself to be out.

¹handline *fishing* A line that is used without a rod and reel. (also called *drop line*)

²handline To fish with a handline.

handling The act or an instance of touching, holding, or playing the ball or puck in some games (as soccer or ice hockey) in violation of the rules.

handoff

handoff **1** The act or an instance of handing the ball to a teammate (as in football). In football, the player handing off normally places the ball firmly against the teammate's abdomen where the teammate holds it in place with both arms rather than having the teammate take it from his hands.

2 *track and field* The act or an instance of exchanging the baton in a relay race.

hand off **1** *football* To hand the ball to a teammate instead of throwing, kicking, or passing it to him.

2 *of the ballcarrier in rugby* To ward off a tackler by pushing him away with the open hand.

hand-out **1** The loss of serve (as in badminton, handball, or squash racquets) by a player in singles play or by the first server of a pair in doubles play. — compare SIDE-OUT

2 The receiving side (as in squash racquets or badminton).

hand pass *Australian Rules football* A pass made by holding the ball in one hand and punching it with the other fist.

hand ride *horse racing* To ride a horse in a race without resorting to a whip or spurs; to ride with a regular rhythmic moving of the hands up the horse's neck to gently urge the horse to the finish line.

hands **1** Catching or fielding ability; skill in maintaining control when catching or fielding a ball. ⟨has good *hands*⟩

2 see HANDBALL (*soccer*)

handspring A somersault in which only the feet and hands touch the floor and in which the performer on passing through a momentary handstand position pushes up with his arms to complete the somersault.

handstand or **hand balance** An acrobatic or gymnastic stunt in which the performer balances upside down on his hands with his body held vertically.

handtrap *trapshooting* A hand-held trap.

hand traverse *mountain climbing* A short traverse usually of no more than 3 or 4 moves where there are no footholds, and the body must be supported solely by the hands.

hand twist retrieve *fishing* A method of retrieving the line in fly fishing in which it is pulled in

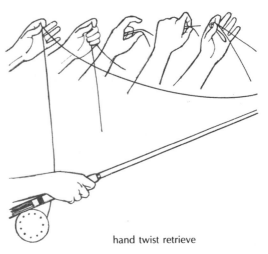

hand twist retrieve

hang

by alternately turning the hand first one way and then the other. The line is taken between the thumb and forefinger, and the hand is turned over so that the other fingers can catch another part of the line. The hand is then turned back and a new section taken between the thumb and forefinger so that a small loop is formed. The process is repeated for as long as the fisherman desires, and when it is properly executed the fly can in this way be retrieved without any perceptible jerking.

¹hang **1** *gymnastics* A position on an apparatus in which the gymnast's body is below the point of support. The gymnast usually but not invariably hangs by his hands. — compare SUPPORT
2 *track and field* A style of long jumping in which the jumper brings both legs and arms back after the takeoff and remains suspended in this position until just before landing when the legs are kicked forward. — compare HITCH KICK

²hang **1** *of a hit or kicked ball* To go high in the air and appear to stay up a long time.
2 To hit or kick a ball high in the air so that it takes a relatively long time to come down; to hit a ball high enough to be carried or affected by the wind. ⟨*hang* a punt so that the defense can get downfield to cover the receiver⟩
3 *baseball* **a** *of a pitch* To fail to break. **b** *of a pitcher* To throw a pitch that fails to break. ⟨*hang* a curve⟩
4 *of a golf ball* To lie on a downslope.
5 *of a racehorse* To run slower than expected especially in the stretch.

hang a rope or **hang out a rope** *baseball* To hit a line drive.

hanger **1** *baseball* A pitch that fails to break.

2 *ice hockey* A player who hangs back in the neutral zone when his team is on defense so that he will be in better position for scoring if his team gets the puck. (also called *floater, sleeper*)
3 *mountain climbing* A small angled plate that is fastened to a bolt to permit a carabiner to be attached.

hang five *surfing* To ride the board with the weight of the body forward and the 5 toes of one foot draped over the front end of the board.

hang glider A small glider made usually in the style of a kite from which the rider hangs for soaring. The rider is held to the glider by a harness, and he holds onto a bar and rolls or shifts his weight to steer the glider, which is launched usually by a run downhill or by jumping off a cliff. — see also ROGALLO WING

hang gliding The sport of soaring in a hang glider. (also called *self soaring, sky surfing*)

hanging arrow *archery* An arrow that hangs on the target face because only the point has penetrated.

hanging glacier *mountain climbing* A large body of ice that overhangs a precipice or steep slope.

hang off *scuba diving* To pause at a predetermined depth for a decompression stop during the ascent from a dive.

hang out the laundry *drag racing* To release the parachute when crossing the finish line.

hang ten *surfing* To ride with all 10 toes draped over the front end of the surfboard. For this to be done it is necessary for the back end of the board to be in the wave so that the water will hold it down.

hang time *football* The length of time a punt

hang technique of long jumping

hangs in the air. The longer a punt stays up the more time tacklers have to get downfield to cover the receiver.

hank *sailing* A fitting that is used to attach a sail to a stay.

hard **1** With force; with speed. ⟨throw the ball *hard*⟩

2 *boating* All the way in the desired or indicated direction. ⟨rudder *hard* alee⟩

hardball A baseball or the game of baseball.

hard-charge *auto racing* To drive as hard and as fast as possible or practical in order to lead the race or catch other drivers often without regard for the strain on the car. — compare STROKE

hardship case A college basketball player who claims a financial hardship so as to be eligible for a special professional draft before his senior year.

harness **1** The straps that fit around and over a horse by means of which a sulky or jog cart is attached to the horse.

2 *mountain climbing* An arrangement of ropes or webbing that is worn over the shoulders and around the chest and sometimes also around the waist and crotch instead of a waistband so that

the shock of an accidental fall will be distributed over a larger area of the body.

3 A snowshoe binding.

harness horse A standardbred that is run in harness racing.

harness race A single race in harness racing.

harness racing The sport of racing standardbred horses harnessed to 2-wheeled sulkies. Harness racing differs from flat racing chiefly in two respects: the horse runs at a different gait, and the driver rides behind in the sulky instead of on the horse's back. Since the sulky eliminates weight as a crucial factor in the race, small persons are not required as drivers, and many trainers drive their own horses in the race. The absence of a weight factor means that horses cannot be handicapped with weight. Instead, horses are normally run in classes based on yearly winnings or in claiming races. Harness races are normally run at a distance of one mile on oval dirt tracks of one half mile or one mile in length. The horses start the race moving at their gait behind a mobile starting gate which consists of barriers that extend out to either side of an automobile. The starter is located in the rear of the car facing the

blinkers

shadow roll

knee boot

hobbles

scalper

bell boot

harness horse (pacer) pulling a sulky

competitors, and he ensures that they are all moving at a steady rate as they reach the starting line. It is the starter who controls the speed of the automobile; the driver only steers. As they approach the starting line, the vehicle speeds up and pulls away from the horses and off the track. Many races are run as single events (*dashes*), but major events are more commonly heat races, with the winning horse the one that wins 2 out of 3 heats, all run on the same day. Where there is no winner after 3 heats, another race among the individual heat winners is sometimes run to determine a final winner. Other horses are placed according to their overall standing in the 3 heats. — see also PACE, TROT; SCORE; HAMBLETONIAN, LITTLE BROWN JUG

harrier A runner on a cross-country team.

Har-Tru A trademark used for a composition surface for tennis courts.

hash mark *football* One of the sections of an inbounds line marked on the ground where it crosses a yard line.

hatch A covered opening in a boat deck for access to a cabin or storage space below.

hatchetman see HEADHUNTER

hat trick Three successive performances of a feat by the same individual in a contest. The oldest use is probably in cricket, where a hat trick is the dismissal by the bowler of 3 batsmen with 3 consecutive balls, for which the bowler apparently received a bonus of a new hat. The term is widely used in hockey and soccer to indicate the scoring of 3 goals by one individual in a single game. Originally the hat trick was the scoring of 3 consecutive unanswered goals, but they need not be consecutive or unanswered to qualify as a hat trick today. The term has also been used of a jockey's riding a winner in 3 consecutive races or winners in an annual race for 3 consecutive years. A notable exception to the 3 successive performances which characterize a hat trick in other sports is its occasional use in baseball to mean that a player has hit for the cycle—a single, double, triple, and home run in one game.

haul *sailing* To change the course of a boat especially so as to sail closer to the wind.

haute école The method of training a horse and the techniques of horsemanship in their most demanding and expert form.

have an angle *of a defensive player in football* To chase a ballcarrier in the open field in a path which will intersect the path of the ballcarrier at some point downfield.

hawking see FALCONRY

Hayes Jenkins spiral see SPIRAL

hazard **1** *billiards* A scoring play in English billiards in which an object ball or the cue ball is pocketed. Whenever an object ball is pocketed, it is called a *winning hazard*; the pocketing of the cue ball after it strikes an object ball is called a *losing hazard*. A winning hazard is worth 2 points if the white object ball is pocketed (*white hazard*) and 3 points if the red ball is pocketed (*red hazard*). If the cue ball is pocketed after first striking the white object ball, 2 points are scored; if it is pocketed off the red ball, 3 points are scored.
2 *golf* A part of the course that is not covered with grass and that is designed to offer an unusual challenge to the golfer. Hazards normally consist of bodies of water (as streams or ponds) and sand traps. A player is not permitted to ground the club head prior to hitting the ball out of a hazard.

hazard side *court tennis* The side of the court on which the receiver stands to receive the serve.

hazer *rodeo* Someone who rides alongside the steer on the side opposite the competing cowboy in steer wrestling competition to keep the steer running in a straight line so the cowboy will have a better chance of jumping onto the steer from his horse.

¹head **1** The principal part of a club, racket, stick, or paddle that actually makes contact with a ball. The head of a lacrosse stick is the triangular section at one end which is strung with rawhide and gut and with which the ball is caught, thrown, and carried. The head of a field hockey stick or a golf club is the thickened part at the end of the shaft. A racket head is the round or oval part holding the strings.
2 The top part of a sail.
3 The pile of an arrow. — see ARROW
4 A toilet on board a boat.
5 The end of a billiard table which is marked by the manufacturer's nameplate and from which the player shoots on the break.
6 *curling* **a** The stones that are within the house at the conclusion of an end. **b** The rings that make up the house.
7 *horse racing* The approximate length of a horse's head used to express a margin of victory or advantage in a race. — compare LENGTH, NECK, NOSE
8 *lawn bowling* The jack and all bowls surrounding it during an end.
— **by the head** *of a boat* Having the bow

sitting lower in the water than the stern.

²head **1** To take the lead over a competitor in a race.

2 *soccer* To propel the ball by striking it with the head.

head back spin see LAY-BACK SPIN

head balance see HEADSTAND

head boat see PARTY BOAT

head butt *football* The act or an instance of butting an opponent especially just under the chin with the helmet.

head-coach To serve as head coach for a club or team. ⟨he *head-coached* the Eagles for awhile — Dan Jenkins, *Sports Illustrated*⟩

head coach The principal coach of a staff who has overall control of the team and its strategy. — see COACH

head court *shuffleboard* The end of the court toward which players shoot in the first half of a round.

head dip *surfing* A stunt performed while surfing by squatting and dipping one's head into the wall of the wave.

head down or **head off** *sailing* To turn the bow of a boat away from the wind.

header **1** A shot or pass in soccer made by hitting the ball with the head.

2 A head-first dive.

3 One of a set of exhaust pipes of equal diameter that run directly from each cylinder of an internal-combustion engine. The pipes are normally the same length so that exhaust gases escape

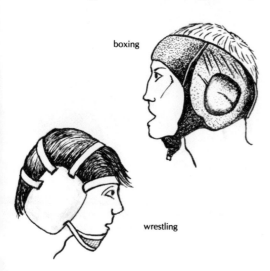

boxing

wrestling

headgear

from each cylinder under the same pressure. An engine equipped with headers runs more efficiently than one equipped with a conventional manifold. (also called *stack*)

headgear **1** or **headguard** or **headharness** *boxing* A padded covering for the head that fits low over the forehead and over the ears and that protects the ears and temples of a boxer during sparring practice.

2 *wrestling* A protective covering for the ears held in place by straps that pass over the head and under the chin.

headhunter A player who engages in unusually rough and violent play for the sake of being violent. In ice hockey, such a player may also be called a *hatchetman*.

headhunting The play or actions of a headhunter.

heading **1** The direction, with respect to a compass, in which a boat or airplane is traveling.

2 *soccer* The act or technique of playing the ball with one's head.

head linesman A football official who takes a position at the sideline on the line of scrimmage and who is primarily responsible for supervising the chain crew, watching for players offside, marking where the ball is out of bounds on his side, and looking for illegal receivers downfield.

headlock *wrestling* A hold in which a wrestler encircles an opponent's head with his arm. Because of the potential danger to the opponent's neck, the headlock is generally illegal unless one of the opponent's arms is included in the lock. (also called *chancery*)

head-man *ice hockey* To pass the puck to a teammate who is closer to the opponent's goal during a rush.

head off see HEAD DOWN

head of the river race or **head race** *rowing* A race held on a river in which shells start at intervals with the boat that traverses the course in the shortest elapsed time winning. — compare REGATTA

headpin *bowling* The number one pin. — see illustration at BOWLING

head pole *harness racing* A pole that runs over the horse's back and by his head on one side to keep the horse from turning his head to that side and bearing in or out.

head race see HEAD OF THE RIVER RACE

heads *bowling* The maple boards that make up the first 16 feet of a lane.

head sail *sailing* A sail (as a jib) carried forward of the mast.

head spot A spot midway between the center spot and the middle of the head cushion on a carom or pocket billiards table. — see also CENTER SPOT, FOOT SPOT

headspring *tumbling* A stunt that is done like a handspring but with the hands and the head in contact with the surface instead of just the hands alone.

headstand or **head balance** An acrobatic or gymnastic stunt similar to a handstand but with the body supported on the hands and the top of the head instead of on the hands alone.

head start An advantage granted or achieved at the beginning of a race. ⟨a 10-minute *head start*⟩

headstay A stay that is attached to the bow and that helps support the mast of a sailboat.

head string *billiards* An imaginary line across the table midway between the middle of the table and the head rail behind which the cue ball is placed when shooting from hand.

heads-up **1** Characterized by alert and resourceful play. ⟨played *heads-up* football⟩ — sometimes used as a warning cry
2 *of drag racers* Competing against each other without a handicap. ⟨will race *heads-up*⟩

head to head **1** In direct competition against another competitor (as in professional skiing) instead of against the clock or against an arbitrary standard.
2 or **head up** In direct opposition to an opposing player. Two opposing linemen in football who face each other across the line of scrimmage and who are blocking and shoving each other on every play are playing head to head.

head trap see TRAP

¹head up *sailing* To turn the bow of a boat into the wind; luff.

²head up see HEAD TO HEAD

headwork *soccer* The use of the head in propelling the ball; heading.

hear footsteps *football* To be distracted from one's assignment (as receiving a pass) by sensing an opponent closing in to make a block or tackle.

heat **1** One of 2 or more short races that make up a single competition in which the competitor that wins the most heats or compiles the best overall record wins.
2 Any of several preliminary contests held to eliminate the less competent competitors from the final contest when there are too many competitors to compete at one time (as in track and field or swimming).
3 see SMOKE

¹heavy **1** *of a pitch in baseball* Tending to drop sharply on nearing the plate.
2 *of a curling delivery* Made with more draw weight than necessary or desired.
3 *of a shot in ice hockey* Traveling through the air very fast and tending to drop on nearing the goal. ⟨a swift skater whose shot is among the . . . *heaviest* in hockey — Mark Mulvoy, *Sports Illustrated*⟩
4 *of a dirt racetrack* Consisting of sticky mud which causes horses to have a hard time running and causes running times to be slow. — compare FAST, GOOD, MUDDY, SLOPPY, SLOW

²heavy **1** *surfing* A large wave.
2 Short for *heavyweight*.

heavy and light system *weight training* A method of training which consists of reducing the amount of weight with successive sets but performing the maximum number of repetitions in each set. — compare LIGHT AND HEAVY SYSTEM

heavy bag A large stuffed canvas or leather bag that is suspended usually from the ceiling of a gym and that is hit by a boxer in training in order to develop punching power. The bag is approximately 3 feet high and one foot in diameter and is supported at the approximate height of a man's torso. (also called *big bag*) — compare SPEED BAG

heavy bag

heavy ice *curling* Ice which requires a stone to be thrown with more than usual draw weight in order to reach the tee line (as because of frost, water, or too much pebble on the surface).

heavyweight Someone who competes in competition for the biggest and strongest competitors;

Hecht dismount

a boxer or weight lifter who competes in a heavyweight division. — see DIVISION

Hecht dismount *gymnastics* A dismount (as from a horizontal bar) in which the gymnast releases the bar at the top of a backward swing or a wraparound and continues forward over the bar with his arms and legs outstretched to land on his feet. (also called *bird dismount*)

Hecht vault *gymnastics* A vault over a vaulting horse with the body and legs straight.

¹heel 1 The part of the head or blade of a club or stick where it joins the shaft. — see illustration at CLUB
2 The upper part of the butt of a rifle or shotgun stock when the weapon is held in firing position.
3 The act or an instance of heeling the ball in rugby.
4 a The rear part of the keel of a boat. **b** The act of a boat's heeling; the degree to which a boat is heeling.

²heel 1 *of a boat* To lean or tilt to one side especially because of the force of the wind on the sails. — compare LIST
2 *rugby* To kick the ball with the heel to a teammate standing behind by a backward swing of the foot. Heeling the ball is the normal method by which a player in Rugby League puts the ball in play after being tackled, and it is the only way in which to pass the ball back to one's teammates in a scrum.

heel and toe 1 *auto racing* A technique of working the pedals of a racing car which consists of controlling the throttle with the heel of one foot (as the right) and the brake pedal with the toe of the same foot while using the other foot only for the clutch pedal. This technique allows the driver to rock the foot forward or back from one pedal to the other and takes much less time than shifting the entire foot back and forth.
2 *skating* A spin in roller skating that is performed on the toe wheels of one skate and on the heel wheels of the other with the feet held together.

heel cup *track and field* A usually soft plastic cup that fits around the heel inside the shoe to protect the heel from becoming bruised as it hits the ground on takeoffs in jumping events.

heel kick A kick (as in soccer) made by kicking the ball backward with the heel.

heel raise SEE TOE RAISE

heel thrust *skiing* Outward movement of the rear part of a ski in preparation for certain maneuvers (as turns).

Heisman Trophy An award made to the outstanding college football player of the year that is named for John Heisman, who was a football player and coach at the turn of the century.

held ball *basketball* **1** A situation in which 2 opponents have their hands on the ball at the same time so that neither can gain control without undue roughness and which results in play being stopped for a jump ball between the 2 players. (also called *tie ball*)
2 A situation in amateur play in which a closely

helicopter

guarded player holds the ball for more than 5 seconds while in his frontcourt which results in a jump ball. (also called *jump ball*)

helicopter *freestyle skiing* An aerial stunt in which the performer makes a full twist while in the air.

helm 1 The rudder or tiller of a boat; the entire steering apparatus.

2 The angle of the rudder away from the fore-and-aft line of the boat. ⟨15-degree *helm*⟩

3 The tendency of a sailboat to drift to one side or the other of its proper course especially when close-hauled thereby requiring that the rudder be constantly adjusted. A boat that drifts to windward and that must be kept on course by holding the tiller to the weather side (the rudder to the lee side) is said to carry *weather helm*. One drifting to the lee side and requiring that the tiller be held to the lee side (the rudder to the weather side) carries *lee helm*.

helmet A protective covering for the head that is worn while participating in or practicing many sports (as football, lacrosse, or ice hockey). Helmets are usually made of plastic, have webbing or foam padding inside to serve as a cushion, and generally protect the head and ears of the player.

baseball batting helmet

football helmet

ice hockey helmet

lacrosse helmet

polo helmet

auto racing crash helmet

helmsman The person who steers a boat.

hemi 1 or **hemi head** A cylinder head in an internal-combustion engine that provides a hemispherical combustion chamber.

2 A car having an engine with hemi heads.

hen hawk *lacrosse* An underhand shot.

Hereford round *archery* A target round in women's competition in which each competitor shoots 72 arrows at a distance of 80 yards, 48 at 60 yards, and 24 at 50 yards.

¹herringbone *skiing* To climb a hill or slope by using the herringbone step.

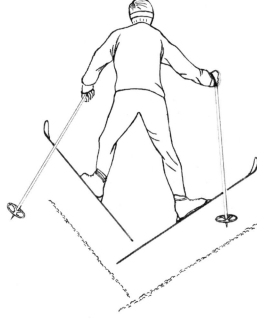

herringbone step

²herringbone or **herringbone step** *skiing* A method of climbing a hill or slope which consists of taking alternate steps forward while keeping the tips of the skis pointed outward and while weighting the inside edges of the skis.

hesitation pitch *baseball* A pitch made with a slight hesitation or pause between the windup and the throw.

Hickok Belt A jewel-studded belt awarded to the professional athlete of the year and named for Stephen Rae Hickok, former manufacturer of belts and jewelry.

high **1** *of a pitch in baseball* Above the strike zone.

2 *of a delivery in bowling* Hitting close to the headpin. — compare THIN

high bar see HORIZONTAL BAR

high board *diving* A diving board placed 3 meters (9.8 feet) above the water.

high goal polo Polo played between teams each of whose total handicap is 19 or more.

high house *skeet* The taller of the two trap houses which is located on the left side of the range and from which targets are propelled in a nearly horizontal trajectory at a height of 10 feet.

high hurdle *track and field* A 42-inch-high hurdle (39 inches high in high school competition) that is used in the high hurdles. — compare INTERMEDIATE HURDLE, LOW HURDLE

high hurdles *track and field* A short race run over high hurdles placed at regular intervals on the course. Each competitor must attempt to clear every hurdle but is not penalized for accidentally knocking down any hurdles. Common outdoor distances are 120 yards and 110 meters, both of which have 10 hurdles. Common indoor distances are 50 yards (4 hurdles), 60 yards (5 hurdles), and 70 yards (6 hurdles).

high-jump To attain a specified height in the high jump. ⟨he *high-jumped* 7 feet⟩

high jump *track and field* A field event in which each competitor attempts to clear a crossbar supported in a horizontal position between 2 upright standards. The bar is raised to a higher position when each contestant has had 3 attempts to clear a given height. A jumper may at any time decline to jump at a given height in order to wait for the bar to be moved higher. The high jump is essentially an elimination contest with 3 successive unsuccessful attempts, whether at a single height or different heights, eliminating the jumper. The winner is the last remaining competitor to clear the bar at its greatest height. (also called *running high jump*) — see also FLOP, SCISSORS, WESTERN ROLL; TIE

high jumper An athlete who competes in the high jump.

Highland Games A traditional Scottish festival that is held in Scotland and other parts of the world and that consists of athletic contests, games, and competition in highland dancing and bagpipe playing. Among the athletic contests are track and field events (as the high jump, pole vault, hammer throw, shot put, and races and hurdles events) as well as the traditional competition in tossing the caber.

high-low-jack *bowling* A leave in which the headpin, the 7 pin, and the 10 pin remain standing. — see illustration of pin arrangement at BOWLING

high pheasant A form of clay pigeon shooting popular in Britain in which targets are propelled in pairs from a 90-foot tower. — compare DRIVEN PARTRIDGE, RUNNING RABBIT, SPRINGING TEAL

high-power Being a big bore military or big game rifle typically firing a bullet with a muzzle velocity of at least 2000 feet per second. ⟨a *high-power* rifle⟩

high run *billiards* The most points made by one player in an inning. The high run for each game is normally listed in scoring summaries.

high-stick *ice hockey* To hit an opposing player with a high stick.

high stick *ice hockey* A stick held with the blade above a permissible maximum height (as 4 feet in amateur hockey or shoulder level in professional hockey) in violation of the rules.

high sticking **1** *box lacrosse* A foul that results when a player injures an opponent on the head, neck, or face with a stick held above shoulder level for which he receives a minor or major penalty.

2 *ice hockey* The act of carrying a high stick or of injuring an opposing player with a high stick that may result in a minor or major penalty.

highway surfer Someone who drives to a surfing beach with a surfboard on or in his car but who does not surf.

highweight *horse racing* A racehorse carrying the highest weight especially in a handicap race. The race need not be a highweight handicap race.

highweight handicap *horse racing* A handicap race in which the top weight is at least 140 pounds.

¹hike A long rather strenuous journey on foot over rough terrain for pleasure. A hike can be only a journey of a few hours duration or may involve overnight camping for several days.

²hike **1** To make a hike.

2 *football* To snap the ball to begin a scrimmage down.

3 *of an iceboat* To be tilted over slightly by the force of the wind on the sails so that the windward runner is off the ice. Hiking is analogous to heeling in a sailboat.

4 or **hike out** *sailing* To lean or hang over the side of a sailboat in order to use body weight to counterbalance the heeling of the boat.

211

hiking board or **hiking seat** *sailing* A board that can be placed over the windward rail to support a person hiking.

hiking stick *sailing* An extension of the tiller that permits the skipper to steer the boat even when he is hiking out.

hiking strap *sailing* A strap fastened usually to the centerboard box that holds down the feet of a person who is hiking out.

hill The pitcher's mound on a baseball field.

hill climb *motor sports* A race against the clock on a trail or road that runs up a hill. Hill climbs normally run over short courses (less than 15 miles) but the climb is usually quite steep with numerous sharp turns. Competitors run one at a time with the winner being the one with the fastest time.

¹hinder **1** Interference with the normal flight of the ball hit by an opponent or obstruction of an opponent who is attempting to return the ball in handball and paddleball. An unavoidable hinder results in the replaying of the point while an avoidable hinder may result in the loss of a point or of the serve. A hinder is also called whenever the ball is deflected by an obstacle in the court (as a door hinge or a lighting fixture). This is called a *court hinder* and results in a replay of the point. **2** Interference (as in squash racquets) which results in the inability of a player to return the ball without risking injury to his opponent. A hinder results in the replaying of the point.

²hinder To interfere with the flight of the ball or to obstruct an opponent thereby causing the replay of the point or loss of the point or the serve.

hinder point *handball* A point or the serve won because one's opponent has committed an avoidable hinder.

hip boot *fishing* A waterproof boot reaching to the tops of the thighs or to the hips. — compare WADER

hip check *ice hockey* A body check in which a player bumps his opponent with his hip.

hip circle or **hip pullover** or **hip swing** *gymnastics* A movement in which the gymnast swings his body around a horizontal bar with his arms straight and his hips held against the bar. (also called *belly grind, merry-go-round*)

hiplock *wrestling* A throw in which a wrestler secures a headlock on his opponent then steps across in front of him and pulls him over his hip. (also called *cross buttocks*)

hip pullover or **hip swing** see HIP CIRCLE

hip throw *judo* A basic throw in which the de-

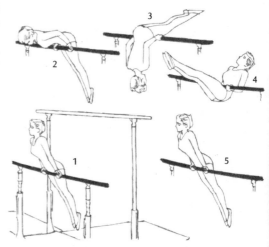

hip circle on uneven parallel bars

fender grabs the attacker usually around the waist, steps across in front of him, and pulls him over the hip.

¹hit **1** To strike and drive an object with a quick blow. **2 a** To make contact with an opponent in giving a body check or in attempting to make a tackle. ⟨was *hit* on the 5-yard line but managed to gain another 4 yards⟩ **b** *boxing* To strike a blow at an opponent; punch. ⟨*hit* him repeatedly with his left jab⟩ **3 a** *of a thrown or propelled object* To strike a target or goal. ⟨his arrow *hit* the bull's-eye⟩ **b** To cause a propelled object to reach an intended target or goal especially for a score. ⟨couldn't *hit* the basket⟩ **c** To score by shooting. ⟨*hit* on 6 of 11 attempts⟩ **4** *baseball* **a** To serve as batter; bat. ⟨will *hit* for the pitcher⟩ **b** To get a base hit. ⟨has *hit* safely in 15 consecutive games⟩ **c** To gain as a result of hitting the ball. ⟨*hit* a home run⟩ **d** To be successful as a batter; to have batting ability. ⟨a good fielder but just couldn't *hit*⟩ **e** To get a hit against a particular pitcher or against a particular type of pitch. ⟨couldn't *hit* his fastball⟩ **5** *of a fish* To take bait or a lure; strike. **6** *football* To complete a pass to a receiver. ⟨*hit* the tight end for a first down⟩

²hit **1** The act, instance, or result of hitting; a hit or stroked ball and especially a base hit in baseball. **2** *fencing* Contact of the point of a foil or épée or of the point or cutting edge of a saber with a valid target which scores for the fencer. (also called *touch*)

3 *fishing* The striking of a fish at a lure or bait.

4 *ice hockey* A body check given to an opponent to take him out of the play.

hit-and-run *baseball* To execute a hit and run play.

hit and run *baseball* A play in which the runner on first base breaks for second on the pitch and the batter tries to hit the pitch toward the position vacated by the infielder who is forced to cover second base to prevent the steal. The batter is obligated to swing at the pitch to protect the runner. With a right-handed batter, the second baseman normally covers the base, so a successful hit and run would have the right-handed batter hitting behind the runner. — compare RUN AND HIT

hit a six *cricket* To hit the ball over the boundary on the fly for a score of 6 runs.

hit batsman *baseball* A batter who is hit by a pitched ball and is consequently awarded first base.

hit behind the runner *of a baseball batter* To hit the ball on the first base side of the diamond so that a runner moving from first base to second base cannot be thrown out easily.

¹hitch **1** A knot that forms a loop in a line or that secures a line to an object (as a pole). — compare BEND

2 *baseball* A tendency to lower or draw back the bat slightly just before beginning the swing that is often considered a defect in the swing.

3 *football* A pass pattern in which the receiver runs a short way downfield then makes a quick turn to the outside to receive a pass.

²hitch *baseball* To lower or draw back the bat slightly just prior to beginning a swing.

hitch and go *football* A pass pattern in which a receiver runs a short way downfield, makes an abrupt turn as if to catch a short pass, and then continues downfield.

hitch kick **1** A kick (as in soccer or gymnastics) made by kicking up first one leg and then the other as the first leg is quickly brought back. The result is a scissors movement of the legs which takes the performer into the air to land on the foot that kicked first.

2 *track and field* A style of long jumping in which the jumper takes 2 full strides in the air after the takeoff and then brings both legs together just prior to landing. — compare HANG

hit for distance *baseball* To hit a long ball.

hit for the cycle *of a baseball player* To hit a single, double, triple, and a home run during a single game.

hit for the distance To try to hit a home run in baseball.

hitless *of a baseball player or team* Without a base hit. ⟨*hitless* in all 30 trips to the plate — Sam Goldaper, *New York Times*⟩ ⟨held the Dodgers *hitless* through the first 6 innings⟩

hit-out see BALL UP (*Australian Rules football*)

hittable *of a pitch in baseball* Easy to hit; likely to be hit whenever thrown.

hitter *baseball* **1** A batter.

2 A game or portion of a game in which a pitcher allows the opposing team to gain only a certain number of base hits. ⟨pitched a 4-*hitter*⟩

hit the dirt *baseball* **1** *of a batter* To fall to the ground to avoid being hit by a pitched ball.

2 *of a base runner* To slide when approaching

hitch kick technique of long jumping

a base to avoid being tagged out with the ball.

hit the hole *of the ballcarrier in football* To move through a hole in the line created by blockers.

hitting weight *curling* The momentum required for one stone to knock an opponent's stone out of the house. — compare DRAW WEIGHT

hit wicket *cricket* A wicket broken by the batsman while making a stroke with the result that he is out. — used in the phrase *out, hit wicket*

hob The peg or stake used as a target in quoits.

hobber A quoit that is touching the hob and that counts 2 points.

hobble or **hopple** *harness racing* A leg harness designed to prevent the horse from using any but the desired gait. Hobbles are normally used on pacers to prevent their lapsing into a trot or gallop. — see illustration at HARNESS HORSE

hobby car *auto racing* An old typically 2-door coupe that is highly modified for stock car racing.

hockey Short for *field hockey, ice hockey.*

hockey stop A method of stopping abruptly when ice skating that is commonly used by hockey players and that involves a quick turning of both feet perpendicular to the line of travel so that the skate blades scrape the ice and stop the skater.

hockey stop

hodad or **hodaddy** A nonsurfer who frequents surfing beaches pretending to be a surfer; a poor surfer.

hog *curling* A stone that fails to cross the far hog line and that is consequently removed from the ice.

hog back *equitation* An obstacle for show jumping which consists of 3 parallel rails one behind the other with the middle rail higher than the other 2.

hog dress *hunting* To bleed and gut fresh killed game leaving the head and skin intact.

hog line or **hog score** *curling* A line across each end of the rink 7 yards in front of the tee beyond which a stone must pass or be removed from play. A stone that has touched a stone in play remains in play even though it rests on the hog line.

hoick *fox hunting* A cry by the master of hounds to call attention to a hound that has picked up the scent and to bring the pack together. (also spelled *yoick*)

¹hold **1** *archery* The pause between the drawing of the string and the release during which the archer takes aim.
2 *billiards* Motion (as drag or draw) imparted to a cue ball to keep it from following a normal course after hitting an object ball.
3 *canoeing* A stroke that is used to stop the forward motion of a canoe and that usually involves holding the paddle in the water with the blade perpendicular to the line of movement or paddling in the reverse direction.
4 *mountain climbing* A portion of a rock face (as a small ledge, crack, or knob) on which a boot or a portion of a boot sole may be placed or which may be grasped or pushed against with the hand for support. — see INCUT, UNDERCUT, JUG HANDLE; compare JAM
5 *wrestling* A grip taken on an opponent; the manner of gripping an opponent. — see BAR ARM, CHICKEN WING, GRAPEVINE, HAMMERLOCK, NELSON, SCISSORS

²hold **1 a** To keep an opposing team or player to a level of performance that is less than usual or expected. ⟨were *held* to 23 points in the first half⟩ **b** *football* To prevent the opposing team from advancing beyond a certain point or from scoring. ⟨*held* them at the 2-yard line⟩
2 To grab or use the hands or arms to restrict the movement of an opponent in violation of the rules of various team sports.
3 *archery* To pause momentarily with the arrow at full draw to steady the bow and take aim.
4 *baseball* **a** To keep a base runner from taking a big lead. The first baseman holds the runner by playing on the base ready to take a throw

from the pitcher and make a tag on the runner. The pitcher holds the runner by keeping close watch on him and occasionally throwing to the base forcing the runner to return and to stay close. **b** *of a base runner* To stop at a base and not try to advance farther (as on a base hit to the outfield). ⟨the runner *held* at second⟩

5 *canoeing* To keep a canoe from moving forward by holding the paddle in the water perpendicular to the line of the keel or by pushing the paddle forward.

hold down *sambo* A situation in which a wrestler holds his opponent to the mat on his back by the weight of his body. If the wrestler succeeds in holding his opponent down for 10 seconds he scores 2 points; for 20 seconds, 4 points.

¹holding 1 A violation of the rules of most team games in which a player impedes the movement of an opposing player by using his hands or arms or (in hockey or lacrosse) his stick. Holding is penalized as a personal foul in basketball and water polo and as a technical foul in lacrosse. In football it is illegal for an offensive player other than the ballcarrier to use his hands or arms to ward off or impede a defensive player, and it is illegal for a defensive player to hold or tackle anyone but the ballcarrier. Offensive holding is penalized by a 10-yard penalty in professional play and a 15-yard penalty in college play. Defensive holding results in the loss of 15 yards in college play and 5 yards in professional play. In rugby a penalty kick is awarded as a penalty for holding; in soccer holding is penalized by a direct free kick or by a penalty kick. A player draws a minor penalty for holding in ice hockey or box lacrosse, and in field hockey the other team is awarded a free hit. **2** *volleyball* The act of allowing the ball to rest momentarily on the hands or arms in violation of the rules.

²holding *of a bowling lane* Having a finish which permits the ball to skid farther than usual before hooking; fast. — compare RUNNING

holdless *of a rock surface* Offering no handholds or footholds by which a climber may ascend.

¹hole 1 A space or opening between 2 players or competitors: **a** *baseball* A space between 2 infielders and especially between the third baseman and the shortstop. ⟨made the throw to first from deep in the *hole*⟩ **b** *football* A space between players in the line through which the ballcarrier can run that is created by one or more players moving or being blocked out of position.

c *horse racing* A space between 2 horses through which another horse can pass. **2** *bowling* The pocket. **3** *drag racing* The starting position for a race. **4** *golf* **a** A circular depression in the ground 4½ inches in diameter and usually 4 inches deep into which the ball is driven; cup. **b** A unit of play from the tee to the hole; the part of the course between one tee and the next hole. ⟨played the *hole* in 3 strokes⟩ **5** *lacrosse* The area directly in front of the goal. — compare SLOT

— in the hole 1 Due to bat or to compete after the competitor who is on deck (as in baseball or track and field). **2** *baseball* **a** *of the pitcher* Having thrown more balls than strikes to the batter. **b** *of the batter* Having the count at 2 strikes.

²hole 1 *drag racing* To defeat another competitor by getting a better start. **2** *golf* To stroke the ball into the hole. ⟨*holed* his putt⟩

holeable *of a golf putt* Relatively easy to make. ⟨had missed three very *holeable* putts . . . and they made all the difference — Herbert Warren Wind, *New Yorker*⟩

hole high *of an approach shot in golf* Stopping or resting to one side of the hole roughly even with it. (also *pin high*)

¹hole in one *golf* A ball hit from the tee that rolls into the hole; a score of one stroke for a particular hole. (also called *ace*)

²hole in one *golf* To make a hole in one. ⟨he was one of a threesome . . . two of whom *holed in one* in the course of the same round — *Glasgow (Scotland) Sunday Post*⟩

hole job or **hole shot** *drag racing* The act or an instance of defeating another competitor by getting a faster start.

hole out *golf* To play the ball into the hole. ⟨*holed out* from eight feet . . . for three birdies in a row — *Washington Post*⟩

hole shot see HOLE JOB

holler guy *baseball* A player or coach noted for constantly shouting encouragement to the other players.

hollow *of a surfing wave* Having a pronounced curl.

¹home 1 The base of operations of a sports team. ⟨sold out all *home* games⟩ ⟨will open the season at *home* on Friday⟩ **2** *baseball* Short for *home plate*. **3** *lacrosse* Either of 2 attacking players (3 in women's lacrosse) who play nearest the goal

215

they are attacking. **b** The positions played by these players. — see also IN HOME, OUT HOME; FIRST HOME, SECOND HOME, THIRD HOME

²home **1** To the ultimate objective (as a goal, finish line, or end of a course). ⟨drove the puck *home*⟩ ⟨came *home* the winner by 3 lengths⟩ **2** To home plate. ⟨made a perfect throw *home*⟩ **3** *archery* To full draw. ⟨draw an arrow *home*⟩

home-and-home or **home-and-away** Having one game played at the home court or field of one team and another game played at the home court or field of the other team. ⟨a *home-and-home* series⟩

homebred or **homebrew** A competitor or player who competes or plays in the area or country in which he was raised. — compare IM-PORT

home court advantage *basketball* **1** The advantage a team feels it has in playing before a home crowd. **2** The right of a team with the better regular season record to play the majority of the games of a play-off series on its home court.

home hole *golf* The last hole on a course or of a round.

homeling A player on the home team.

home plate *baseball* A 5-sided slab of white rubber that is set in the ground at one corner of the infield, that serves as the final base to be touched by a base runner in order to score a run, and that marks the lateral limits of the strike zone. The widest side — 17 inches — is in front facing the pitcher. At the back it tapers to a point which rests on the intersection of the first and third base lines. — see also BATTER'S BOX, STRIKE ZONE

home position A spot on the court in court games from which a player has the best chance of reaching an opponent's shot. In singles play the home position is near the middle of the court, from which point a player can effectively move to either side to return a shot.

¹homer **1** A home run in baseball. **2** An official in a game who appears to favor the home team in conducting the game and especially in calling fouls.

²homer *baseball* To hit a home run. ⟨*homered* in the seventh and tied a National League record — United Press International⟩

view of home plate and surrounding area

home run **1** A base hit in baseball that enables the batter to run around all of the bases and score a run. A home run is usually made by hitting the ball out of the park although an inside-the-park home run is occasionally made.
2 A spectacular scoring play (as a long touchdown pass in football or a 3-point field goal in basketball).
3 British term for *homestretch.*

home stand *baseball* A series of consecutive games played at a team's home field.

homestretch The part of a racing track between the final turn and the finish line.

home whistle A real or fancied advantage given the home team by the officials in a contest.

homing pigeon A pigeon that will return to its home loft when released at distances up to 500 miles and that is used in pigeon racing.

homologate **1** To confirm officially a record performance of an airplane or sailplane.
2 *motor racing* To approve officially a particular vehicle or engine for use in a given class of racing. Most sanctioning bodies require production vehicles to meet certain minimum production or sales requirements before being approved for a class. In auto racing, for example, a manufacturer may be required to prove that 500 identical cars were manufactured during a 12-month period in order for that car to be homologated.

honker *drag racing* An especially fast car.

honor *golf* The privilege of being first to drive the ball from the tee normally accorded the player or side winning the preceding hole or the one using the fewest strokes on the preceding hole. Once a player has the honor, he retains it until another player plays a hole in fewer strokes. The order of play for the first hole is usually decided by lot.

hood *horse racing* A covering for a horse's face that contains blinkers and that is normally the color of a stable's racing silks.

¹hook **1 a** A propelled ball that deviates from its intended course in the direction opposite to the dominant hand of the player propelling it (as to the left when rolled, thrown, or hit by a right-handed player). **b** *bowling* A bowled ball that is released with an upward snap of the fingers and that skids down the alley on one side curving in just as it nears the pins. — compare BACK-UP, CURVE
2 *baseball* **a** The tendency of a manager to go to his bullpen rather than waiting for a pitcher to work himself out of trouble. — used in the phrases *has a quick hook* or *has a fast hook*

b The removal of a pitcher from a game. — used in the phrase *got the hook*
3 *boxing* A short blow delivered with a circular motion while the elbow is bent and kept rigid.
4 *cricket* A stroke that is made by stepping across in front of the wicket with the rear foot and swinging up at the ball to drive it to the leg side. — compare PULL SHOT
5 *handball* see HOP
6 *surfing* The concave part of a breaking wave; curl.
7 Short for *buttonhook, fishhook, hook shot.*

²hook **1 a** To hit or deliver a hook (as in golf, bowling, boxing, or cricket). ⟨*hooked* into the trees⟩ **b** *of a propelled ball* To swerve to the side opposite the dominant hand of the player.
2 To illegally impede the progress of an opposing player in ice hockey or box lacrosse by holding him with one's stick.
3 *fishing* To snare a fish with a hook. The fish is only considered caught when it has been successfully landed.
4 *football* **a** To cut back toward the line of scrimmage after running a short way downfield on a pass pattern. **b** To drive an opposing player to one side by means of a hook block.
5 *rugby* To hook one foot around the ball in the scrum and heel it back to be put in play by a halfback.

hook block *football* A block executed by an offensive lineman who moves to the side of the defender then turns back into him so as to stay between the defender and the ballcarrier.

hook-check *ice hockey* To execute a hook check.

hook check *ice hockey* A stick check executed usually from a position behind the puck carrier

hook check

in which the stick is laid nearly flat on the ice and is swept toward the puck in such a way as to trap the puck in the hook where the blade meets the shaft of the stick.

hooker **1** A golfer who is prone to hook the ball. **2** An ice hockey player noted for hooking.
3 A rugby forward who plays in the middle of the front line in a scrum and who is the only player of the side permitted to use his foot to hook the ball out of the scrum.

hooking The act of using the stick to impede the progress of an opponent in ice hockey or box lacrosse which results in a minor or a major penalty. Hooking an opponent's stick with one's own stick is legal.

hook pass *basketball* A pass made in the manner of a hook shot by swinging the arm through an arc while jumping.

hook shot *basketball* A shot made usually with the body sideways to the basket by bringing the ball up through an arc with the outstretched far arm and releasing the ball when the arm is overhead. Since the shooter's body is usually between the defender and the ball, the hook shot is extremely difficult to block. The ball is often released at the top of a jump.

hook shot

hook slide *baseball* A slide made to the side of a base with one leg bent and stretched back to hook the base as the player passes it. — see illustration at SLIDE

hook tackle *soccer* A tackle made by dropping to one knee and extending the other leg to hook the ball away from the opponent. (also called *sliding tackle*)

hooligan *auto racing* A consolation race in dirt track racing for cars that fail to qualify for the feature race.

hoop **1** *basketball* **a** The rim of the basket or the basket itself. ⟨he always picks you up when you drive to the *hoop* — Don Chaney⟩ **b** A field goal. ⟨hit some really big *hoops* for us down the stretch — Walt Frazier⟩
2 A croquet wicket.

hop **1** A bounce of a ball. ⟨fielded the grounder on the second *hop*⟩
2 *handball* A shot that because of applied spin bounces left or right after hitting the floor. (also called *hook*)
3 *skating* A short jump in which the skater lands on the takeoff foot usually with a change of edge. — compare JUMP, LEAP

hop garland see GARLAND

hopper A bouncing batted baseball. ⟨hit a high *hopper* to second⟩

hopple see HOBBLE

hop-step *track and field* A style of approach in throwing the javelin in which at a predetermined point near the end of the runway the thrower brings the javelin back to a throwing position and turns his body toward the javelin as he steps with his right foot (for a right-handed thrower), takes a low hop on the right foot, and strides forward with the left foot as the javelin is thrown. The hop-step is also employed in the basketball throw and the baseball throw. (also called *American style*) — compare CROSSOVER

hop, step, and jump see TRIPLE JUMP

horizontal bar *gymnastics* **1** A steel bar 2400 millimeters (approximately 8 feet) long and 28 millimeters (one inch) in diameter supported in a horizontal position 2500 millimeters (8 feet) above the floor and used for swinging feats in gymnastic competition.
2 An event in men's competition in which the horizontal bar is used.

horizontal rappel see PENDULUM

horn **1** An arm of a cleat.
2 A knob which projects from the pommel of a stock saddle.
— **around the horn** *baseball* From third base to second base to first base; to each infielder in turn starting at third base.

¹horse **1** An uncastrated male racehorse: **a** A thoroughbred of age 5 or older. **b** A standardbred of age 4 or older.
— compare MARE; COLT, FILLY, GELDING

hop step

2 Short for *pommel horse, vaulting horse.*

3 see TRAVELER

²horse *fishing* To yank a hooked fish out of the water by force rather than play the fish until it can be landed.

horseback archer Someone who engages in horseback archery.

horseback archery A sport combining horseback riding and target archery in which competitors ride horses past targets placed at various spots around a large field and attempt to hit the target while riding at a full gallop.

horse-collar *of a baseball pitcher* To hold an opposing batter hitless; to hold an opposing team runless.

horse collar *baseball* A zero (as in the column for base hits in a box score). — used in the phrases *go for the horse collar* or *wear the horse collar*

horsehide A baseball. — compare PIGSKIN

horsemanship The art of horseback riding; ability to control and guide a horse with great effectiveness and little effort.

horseplayer Someone who regularly bets on horse races.

horse race A race for horses and especially a flat race.

horse racing The sport of racing specially bred horses against one another over a usually oval track. In broad use, the term covers all forms of racing between horses including flat racing, steeplechasing, and harness racing, though in common usage harness racing is usually excluded. The races are normally run over distances from ½ to 1½ miles with the more important races usually being a mile or longer. In the United States, most races are held on dirt with the horses running counterclockwise. In England, grass races are more popular, and at some tracks the horses run counterclockwise and at other tracks, clockwise. The finish line for all races is always at the same point; the starting line varies with the length of the race. Races in the United States are started with the horses in a starting gate which consists of a number of stalls all opened at the same time. In England, the horses often begin the race at a standing start from behind a wire across the track which is lifted out of the way as a starting signal. The thoroughbreds are ridden by small jockeys who usually weigh around 100 to 115 pounds. To equalize the chances of the horses in a race, each horse is given a weight assignment which is usually keyed to the horse's past record and its sex. Horses with better records normally carry more weight. Fillies or mares, when competing against colts and horses, regularly carry 3 to 5 pounds less than the males. The weights of the horses are adjusted by putting lead bars in special pockets in saddle bags to make up the difference between the required weight and the weight of the jockey and his saddle. Horse racing is popular throughout the world. Its major attraction is parimutuel betting and this, along with the fact that races are often run 6 or 7 days a week throughout the season (which may be 12 months long in some areas), accounts for horse racing's position as the number one spectator sport in the United States. — see also STEEPLECHASE; ALLOWANCE RACE, CLAIMING RACE, HANDICAP, STAKES RACE; HORSE, MARE; PARI-MUTUEL BETTING; TRIPLE CROWN

219

horses Players who are responsible for the success of a team's offense. ⟨a coach can't win if he doesn't have the *horses*⟩

horseshoe **1** A shoe for a horse usually consisting of a narrow strip of metal (as steel or aluminum) shaped to fit the outline of the hoof and nailed to the bottom of the hoof. — see PLATE
2 A horseshoe or a U-shaped piece of metal approximately 7½ inches long and 7 inches wide weighing no more than 2½ pounds that is pitched in the game of horseshoes.

horseshoes or **horseshoe pitching** A game for 2 or 4 players in which each in turn tosses 2 horseshoes underhand to a metal stake 40 feet away (30 feet in women's play) in an attempt to ring the stake or to come closer to it than one's opponent. A side scores one point for each shoe closer to the stake than an opponent's and 3 points for a ringer — a horseshoe that encircles the stake. Matches are normally played to 50 points in singles games and 21 points in doubles.

which the balloon drifts, the pilot is able, by heating the air in the balloon or letting it cool, to control the rate of ascent and descent and is thereby able to climb or descend to a level at which winds may be blowing in a favorable direction. (also called *thermal balloon*)

hot corner *baseball* The third base position. ⟨moving over to the *hot corner,* a player with a strong, accurate arm is sought. . . . He's got to be able to knock down the hot ones and still recover in time to get the out — Bobby Richardson⟩

hotdog To perform fancy stunts and maneuvers. ⟨neophytes determined to prove they can *hotdog* their first day on a surfboard—*Newsweek*⟩

hot dog **1** An outstanding athlete; expert. ⟨in order to win the championship, a driver must compete in virtually every race. Due to the preponderance of smaller tracks, the points leader perennially is also the short track *hot dog*—*Motor Trend*⟩

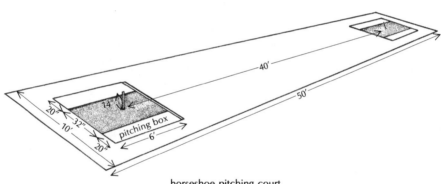

horseshoe pitching court

hosel The socket in the head of a golf club into which the shaft is fitted.

host To provide the facilities for a sports event; to be the home team.

hot **1 a** At the top of one's form; temporarily capable of an unusual performance. **b** Unusually successful or productive. ⟨a *hot* fishing spot⟩ ⟨a *hot* apprectice jockey⟩
2 Hard hit. ⟨a *hot* grounder to third⟩

hot-air balloon A sport balloon that consists of an envelope in the shape of an inverted pear that is open at the bottom and a suspended gondola. Propane burners in the gondola heat the air in the balloon; as the air warms it rises. Although he is unable to directly control the direction in

2 A performer or player who performs unusual or fancy stunts especially for show. (also called *hotdogger*) ⟨could hit nine out of ten from the foul line with his back to the basket. He was a real *hot dog* — *Atlantic*⟩ ⟨*hot dog* passes⟩

hotdogging The practice of performing showy stunts.

hotdogging board A relatively short surfboard used for hotdogging.

hot dog skier A skier who engages in freestyle skiing.

hot dog skiing see FREESTYLE SKIING

hot hand *basketball* The ability to shoot well above one's average for a relatively short period of time. The player who has the hot hand may have it for a part of a season or for only a single game or for only a part of a game.

hot shoe   *auto racing*   A top driver.

hot stove league   Discussion among fans (as of baseball) during the off-season.

hotwalker   A person employed by a stable to walk a horse after it has been worked and rubbed down until the horse has had time to cool off and is ready to be returned to the barn.

hound   A hunting dog that is used to chase game (as a fox or deer).

house   *curling*   A circular area 12 feet in diameter at each end of the rink which consists of the tee circle and 3 concentric rings and toward which the stones are delivered. A stone must be within the house in order to score. — see illustration at CURLING

¹huddle   *football*   A brief gathering together of the players before lining up for the snap in order to receive assignments and signals (as from the quarterback or defensive captain) for the next down. Teams normally line up in a tight circle or in a group facing the player giving the instructions.

²huddle   *football*   To gather together in a huddle.

hug the rail   *of a cue ball in billiards*   To roll or bounce along a rail as a result of English imparted to the ball.

hull   The body of a boat from the keel to the deck exclusive of the cabin, mast, spars, and rigging.

hull speed   The theoretical maximum speed of a boat based on its hull design.

hummer   A fastball in baseball.

hunch player   A bettor (as on horse races) who backs a particular competitor on the basis of a hunch rather than on the basis of handicapping.

hundred   *track and field*   A dash run over a distance of 100 yards or 100 meters. ⟨ran the *hundred* in 9.4 seconds⟩

¹hunt   **1** The act or practice or an instance of hunting or riding to hounds; a session of fox hunting. **2** An association of huntsmen; a group of people with horses and dogs engaged in riding to hounds.

²hunt   **1** To seek game with a weapon or to follow on horseback a pack of hounds in pursuit of game (as a fox); to engage in hunting. **2** To manage the hounds in a hunt.

hunt club   An organization that conducts hunt meetings.

hunter   **1** Someone who engages in hunting or gunning. **2** A horse (as a thoroughbred) that is trained to carry a rider over the countryside in riding to

hounds and especially to jump various obstacles (as ditches or fences) smoothly. **3** A dog used or trained for hunting.

hunter's round   *archery*   A round in field archery competition in which each contestant shoots an average of 2 arrows from different positions at each of 28 targets at distances from 15 to 50 yards on a field roving course.

hunting   The pursuing of game with the means and intention of killing it. Though the meat is usually kept for food, it is the lure of the outdoors, the chase, and the killing that provides the principal attraction. Hunting typically refers to the active searching for and pursuit of game with a weapon (as a rifle, shotgun, or bow and arrow), or sometimes the following of hounds that do the actual pursuing and killing, as distinct from trapping. In England, pursuit of game with a weapon is usually called gunning or shooting while hunting refers to following the hounds.

hunting bow   *archery*   A bow with a relatively high draw weight that is used in hunting game.

hunting horn   *fox hunting*   A small horn consisting of a conical tube with a cup-shaped mouthpiece and flared bell that is used to signal to members of the hunt.

hunting seat   see FORWARD SEAT

hunt meeting   A program of steeplechases and flat races often engaged in by amateur riders and horsemen.

huntsman   The member of the hunt staff who manages or hunts the hounds. Sometimes the master of hounds may hunt the hounds, but more commonly the huntsman is a professional who is employed by and who works under the direction of the master.

¹hurdle   **1 a** *horse racing*   A wooden barrier which consists of several horizontal bars with the highest 3½ feet above the ground and over which horses must jump in hurdles races. **b** *track and field*   A wooden or metal barrier over which athletes must jump in hurdles races or steeplechases. Those used in hurdles races are 44 inches wide and have L-shaped supports so that they will fall forward if hit by the runner. They range from 30 inches high (*low hurdle*) to 42 inches high (*high hurdle*). Hurdles used in steeplechases are beams 13 feet long and 5 inches wide that are supported 3 feet high. They are fixed to the track so that they will not fall if hit or stepped on by the runners. **2 or hurdle step**   A short spring on one foot usually made on the last step of an approach run-up (as at the beginning of a dive or vault) to

hurdle

hurdle

allow the individual to move smoothly from a run to a takeoff on both feet.

²hurdle To jump over an object (as a hurdle) while running; to compete in a hurdles event.

hurdler A runner or racehorse that competes in a hurdles race.

hurdles race or **hurdles** **1** *horse racing* A turf race at least one mile in length (1½ miles in Britain) with 4 hurdles in the first mile (6 in the first 1½ miles in Britain) and one hurdle every quarter mile thereafter.

2 *track and field* A race up to 400 meters (440 yards) long run over hurdles. — see HIGH HUR-DLES, INTERMEDIATE HURDLES, LOW HURDLES

hurdle step — see HURDLE

hurdling **1** The act of jumping over an obstacle while running.

2 Running in hurdles races.

3 *football* The act of a ballcarrier's jumping feet-first over an opponent who is still on his feet. This is violation of the rules which results in a 15-yard penalty.

hurl **1 a** To play hurling. **b** To propel the ball with the stick in hurling.

2 To pitch in a baseball game; to pitch the ball. ⟨*hurled* scoreless ball for five innings — *Los Angeles Examiner*⟩

hurler **1** A hurling player.

2 A baseball pitcher.

hurley **1** The stick used in hurling which resembles a field hockey stick but has a flatter and wider blade.

2 The game of hurling.

hurling An Irish game that resembles field hockey or lacrosse and that is played on a large rectangular field between 2 teams of 15 players each using a broad-bladed stick (*hurley*) to catch and balance the ball while running. The object of the game is to drive the ball between the goalposts for a score and to prevent the opponents from scoring. A goal worth 3 points is scored when the ball is driven under the crossbar of the goal, and a point is scored when it passes over the

hurdle step

crossbar. Players are not permitted to use their hands to pick up or to hurl the ball, and they may not run with the ball in their hands; they may catch the ball in their hands and pick the ball off the hurley to hit it fungo style. It is permissible to charge an opponent as in soccer, but players may not hit, trip, or shove opponents or hit opponents with the hurley. Play is started with the referee throwing the ball between 2 players; a game consists of two 30-minute halves.

¹hustle To play a game in an alert aggressive manner.

²hustle Alert aggressive play.

¹hydroplane A powerboat with a hull designed to plane over the water when running at speed rather than to cut through the water. This is possible because as the speed of the boat increases the resistance of the water increases and forces the boat to ride progressively higher until it is supported on the surface. Hydroplanes are sometimes designed with a bottom like a trough or inverted V so that as the boat rides on the surface a cushion of air under the boat helps to support it, allowing less of the hull to be in contact with the water and further reducing friction.

²hydroplane **1** To ride in or drive a hydroplane. **2** *of an automobile* To ride on a thin film of water covering the roadway or track when traveling at speed in a manner analogous to the principle of the hydroplane with the result that there is little or no directional control or stopping ability.

hyong see KATA

hyperventilate *skin diving* To take a number of quick deep breaths before holding the breath in order to reduce the level of carbon dioxide in the blood and thereby delay the urge to breathe and prolong a dive. The technique is dangerous, however, since a decrease in the carbon dioxide level is followed by a drop in blood pressure which can possibly lead to dizziness, mental confusion, or even unconsciousness.

I

I Short for *I formation.*

¹ice A surface of ice used for ice skating, ice hockey, or curling.

— **on ice** With every likelihood of being won. ⟨two second-half touchdowns put the game *on ice*⟩

²ice 1 To make a score or build a lead that assures victory. ⟨sank a free throw . . . to *ice* the victory — *Spokane Spokesman-Review*⟩

2 *ice hockey* To shoot the puck from one's defensive half of the rink (defensive zone in amateur hockey) across the goal line at the other end of the rink. — see ICING

ice axe *mountain climbing* A combination pick and adze with the handle having a spike at the other end. The ice axe is commonly used in cutting steps in the ice, as a staff for support in climbing or walking on ice, and as a belay anchor.

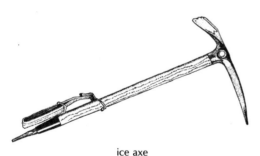

ice axe

iceboat A vehicle designed to be sailed over frozen lakes and rivers that typically consists of a light-weight fuselage supported by a steel steering runner in front or behind and 2 runners outrigged on either side and that carries a fore-and-aft rig. Iceboats are capable of moving over the ice at nearly 4 times the speed of the wind and some have reached 100 miles per hour.

iceboater Someone who engages in iceboating.

iceboating or **ice sailing** The sport or practice of sailing and especially racing iceboats.

ice bollard *mountain climbing* A short column of ice that is carved out of a slope and that is used as a belay anchor in ice climbing.

ice dagger *mountain climbing* A short piton-like device with a strap at one end which allows the climber to secure it to the hand and use it like an ice pick in place of an extra ice axe when climbing a slope.

ice dancing *skating* Competition in which each couple is required to perform ballroom dances (as the waltz, tango, or samba) to music on ice skates utilizing basic skating figures such as the three turn, bracket, and rocker.

ice fall *mountain climbing* A mass of jumbled blocks of ice broken from a glacier or a steep slope of ice with many crevasses formed as a glacier moves over steep ground, around a sharp bend, or between mountain walls that presents a potential hazard to a party of climbers.

ice fishing The sport of fishing through a hole in the ice of a frozen lake or river. Ice fishing requires no more than a baited hand line or a very short fiberglass pole, but fishermen normally set up a number of tip-ups in several holes.

ice hammer *mountain climbing* A piton hammer with a relatively long pick opposite the hammer face. It is more useful than an ordinary piton hammer on climbs that may require some step cutting in ice.

ice hockey A game played on an enclosed rink between 2 teams of 6 players wearing ice skates and using a thin-bladed stick to propel a hard rubber puck up and down the ice with the object to drive the puck past the opposing goalkeeper into the goal for a score and to prevent the opposing team from scoring. A team consists of a goalkeeper who normally plays right in front of his goal to block shots by opponents, 2 defensemen who pursue attacking players to try to disrupt their attack, and 3 forwards (a center and 2 wings) who are primarily offensive players. Players are not permitted to propel the puck with their hands or with any part of the body, but they may use the hands to knock the puck down to

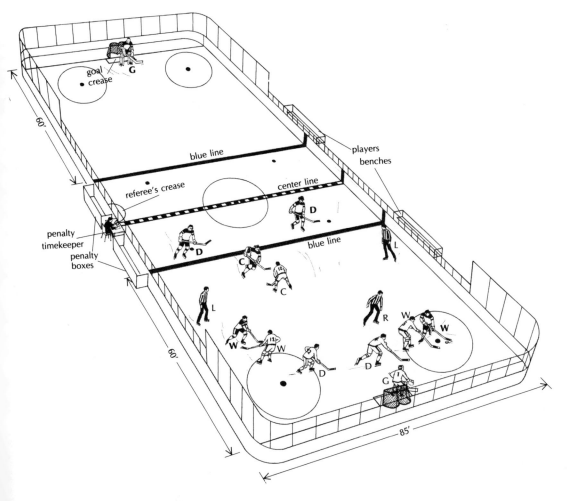

ice hockey: G goalkeeper; D defenseman; W wing; C center; R referee; L linesman

the ice where it is then played with the stick. Body checking of an opponent who has the puck or who is going for the puck is permitted, but players may not hold, trip, or charge an opposing player. For fouls such as charging, holding, or tripping, a player is penalized by being sent off the ice for 2 or 5 minutes, during which time he must sit in a penalty box and his team must play shorthanded. For misconduct a player may be suspended for 10 minutes or for the duration of the game, but his team may replace him immediately with another player. Play is continuous ex-

cept when infractions, fouls, or time-outs occur and whenever the puck is unplayable (as when hit into the seats). A team may substitute freely without stopping play so long as a team has no more than 6 players on the ice at any one time. The game is played in three 20-minute periods. Each period is started with a face-off at the center of the ice. A face-off is also used to resume play after a goal is scored and after play is stopped for a time-out, infraction, or penalty. An attacking player is not allowed to enter the attacking zone ahead of the puck. If he does, he

icekhana

is offside and play is stopped for a face-off. — see also ICING, MAJOR PENALTY, MINOR PENALTY, OFFSIDE

icekhana An automobile gymkhana held on a frozen lake.

iceman An ice hockey player.

ice piton see PITON

ice racing **1** The sport of racing automobiles on a surface of ice (as a frozen lake). **2** Speed skating on ice.

ice sailing see ICEBOATING

ice screw *mountain climbing* A metal spike with screw threads on one end that is screwed into the ice and used in place of an ice piton.

ice skate see SKATE

ice time *ice hockey* Playing time accumulated by a player (as during a game or during a season).

icing *ice hockey* An infraction which results when a player hits the puck from his own defensive half of the ice (his defensive zone in college play) across the opponent's goal line and it is then played by a member of the opposing team other than the goalkeeper. Play is restarted by a face-off in the offending team's defensive zone. Icing is not called if the puck is driven to the opposite end of the ice from a face-off, if it is played by an opposing player before it crosses the goal line (or in the judgment of the officials could have been played), if it is first touched by the opposing goalkeeper, or if it is played first by a teammate of the player hitting the puck down the ice who is onside. If the puck is shot the length of the ice and enters the goal, it is scored a goal. In college and in most professional play, icing is not called when the team icing the puck is playing shorthanded.

Idaho see COLORADO

idle Not scheduled to compete. ⟨the team will be *idle* tomorrow⟩

I formation **1** *football* An offensive formation in which the set backs line up in a line directly behind the quarterback. In the common version of the I formation, 2 set backs line up behind the quarterback and the other back plays wide as a receiver. On occasion, the fourth back will line up as a running back to the side of the other backs, in what is known as a *power I,* or in line with the other backs in a *stack I.* — compare SINGLE WING, T FORMATION, WISHBONE **2** *tennis* see AUSTRALIAN DOUBLES

igniter *motor racing* A highly volatile liquid (as ether or acetone) added to a slow-burning fuel blend to enable it to explode.

illegal Being an act or action not permitted by the

basic
I formation

power I

stack I

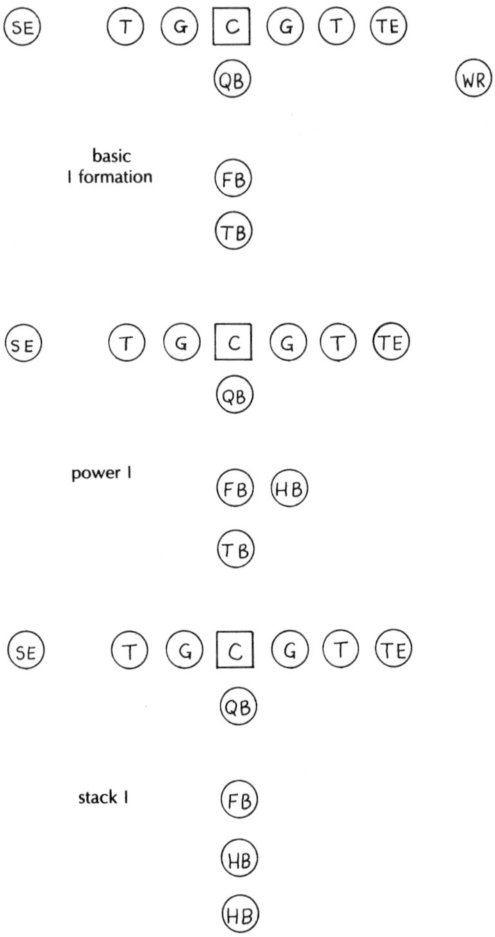

I formation: C center; FB fullback; G guard; HB halfback; QB quarterback; SE split end; T tackle; TB tailback; TE tight end; WR wide receiver

rules of the game being played which usually results in the imposition of a penalty on the guilty player or team.

illegal motion *football* An infraction in which an offensive player is moving forward or more than one offensive player is moving backward or laterally at the snap and which results in a 5-yard penalty.

illegal procedure **1** *football* An infraction in which the offensive team is guilty of any of several rule violations including a false start, having fewer than 7 players on the line at the snap, and illegally handing the ball forward and which results in a 5-yard penalty and sometimes loss of down.

2 *lacrosse* A technical foul in which a team is guilty of any of several rule violations including having a substitute enter the game improperly, delaying the game, violating of a restraining line restriction, or having too many men on the field and which results in loss of the ball or a 30-second suspension for the guilty player.

illusion *gymnastics* A maneuver in which the gymnast rotates the body in a full circle in a manner suggesting a cartwheel while keeping the body supported on one leg.

illusion

impeding *water polo* A personal foul charged against a player who impedes the movement of an opponent not in possession of the ball which results in a free throw for the opposing team.

import A player (as in Canadian football) who is not a native of the country in which he is playing. — compare HOMEBRED

impost or **impost weight** *horse racing* The amount of weight a horse must carry during a race. The impost consists of the weight of the jockey, the saddle, and any lead bars added to the saddlebags to bring the weight up to that required for the race.

improved cylinder The degree of choke on a shotgun which produces the widest pattern and the smallest effective range. — see CHOKE

in **1** Of, relating to, or being the serving side in a game; being hand-in. ⟨at the beginning of each game and each time a side becomes *in* the ball shall be served from whichever service box the first server for the side elects — *U.S. Squash Racquets Association Rules*⟩ ⟨advantage *in*⟩

2 *of a ball* Within the boundary lines of a court

or field; into play. ⟨will throw the ball *in* from the sideline⟩

3 For a score; over the goal line; home. ⟨drove *in* 3 runs⟩ ⟨ran the ball *in* from the 3-yard line⟩

inboard A powerboat that has the engine located within the hull and that transmits power to the propeller by a shaft that extends through the hull below the waterline. The inboard is steered by a rudder. — compare INBOARD-OUTBOARD, OUTBOARD

inboard-outboard A powerboat that has the engine located within the hull as does an inboard but that has a horizontal drive shaft that extends through the hull above the waterline and connects to a vertical propeller housing like that of an outboard motor. The boat is steered by turning the propeller housing. (also called *sterndrive*) — compare INBOARD, OUTBOARD

inbound *basketball* To throw the ball onto the court from out of bounds to put it in play; to make an inbounds pass. ⟨will *inbound* the ball at midcourt⟩

inbounds **1** Into or within the playing area; inside the boundary lines. ⟨a player who jumps to make a catch, interception, or recovery must have the ball in his possession when he first returns to the ground *inbounds* — *NCAA Football Rules*⟩

2 *basketball* Of or relating to putting the ball in play (as after a time-out or after it has been knocked out of bounds) by passing it onto the court from out of bounds. ⟨*inbounds* pass⟩ ⟨*inbounds* play⟩

inbounds line or **inbounds marker** *football* Either of 2 broken lines which run the length of the field parallel to the sidelines, which divide the field into 3 parts lengthwise, and to which the ball is brought to be put in play when it goes out of bounds or when it is dead between an inbounds line and the sideline. On a field marked for college play the inbounds lines are marked 53 feet 4 inches from the sidelines; on a professional field the inbounds lines are 70 feet 9 inches from the sidelines.

incline bench *weight lifting* A board or a portion of a bench supported usually at a 45-degree angle on which the lifter rests and which gives the lifter an angle between supine and standing for pressing the weight. The incline bench is often used for other exercises (as curls) where a different angle is desired.

inclined board A flat board that is inclined from the floor usually 10 or 15 degrees, that normally has a strap at the upper end under which the feet can be hooked, and that is used for doing sit-ups.

By placing the exerciser's head below a horizontal plane, the board increases the magnitude of the work and the distance through which the exerciser must move to overcome the force of gravity.

incomplete *of a forward pass in football* Not caught or intercepted. When a pass is incomplete, the ball is dead and the next down begins from the same line of scrimmage.

incompletion *football* A forward pass that is incomplete.

incut *mountain climbing* A small hold that projects up so that the fingers can be hooked over the edge for support.

independent A school or college that is not a member of an athletic conference.

Indiana *fishing* A spinner with a long somewhat teardrop-shaped blade.

Indiana pants *harness racing* An old term for *hobbles.*

Indianapolis car see INDY CAR

Indianapolis 500 A 500-mile race for open-wheel racing cars (popularly called *Indy cars*) run annually since 1911 at the Indianapolis Motor Speedway that is one of the principal automobile races in the United States.

Indian check *lacrosse* A check made by reaching the stick over the opponent's head with one hand to hit the opponent's stick and knock the ball loose. When successful, the Indian check can be effective, but it is a gambling maneuver for if the player accidentally hits his opponent in the head with his stick, he will be called for a personal foul.

Indian club A usually wooden club shaped like a tenpin that is swung for exercise.

Indian pendants The end strings on the head of a lacrosse stick that can be tightened or loosened to adjust the depth of the pocket. — see illustration at STICK

Indian pool see RUSSIAN POOL

Indian-wrestle To engage in Indian wrestling.

Indian wrestling 1 Wrestling in which 2 people lie on their backs side by side and head to foot, locking near arms and raising and locking their corresponding legs and attempt to force each other's leg down and turn the other wrestler over his head.
2 Wrestling in which 2 wrestlers stand face to face gripping usually their right hands and setting the outside edges of the corresponding feet together and attempt to force each other off balance.
3 see ARM WRESTLING

indirect *fencing* Being a simple attack, parry, or riposte made in a line other than the original line of engagement.

indirect cannon see CANNON

indirect free kick *soccer* A free kick awarded to a team when an opposing player commits a foul such as obstructing an opponent, charging the goalkeeper, or dangerous play or a minor violation such as offsides. A goal cannot be scored directly from an indirect free kick. — compare DIRECT FREE KICK, PENALTY KICK.

individual foul A personal foul in women's play in certain sports (as basketball and speedball).

individual medley *swimming* A race in which each competitor is required to swim each leg with a different stroke. The strokes are normally swum in the following order: butterfly, backstroke, breaststroke, and freestyle. The distances most commonly competed at are 200 and 400 meters and 200 and 400 yards.

individual medleyist A swimmer who competes in individual medleys.

individual pursuit A pursuit race between 2 individuals. — see PURSUIT

indoor polo A version of polo played usually with 3 men on a side in an indoor arena with a playing area approximately 100 yards long and 50 yards wide that is bounded by a wall to keep the ball in play and that has goals 10 feet wide. The game is played with a leather-covered inflated ball about 4½ inches in diameter.

indoor soccer A version of soccer played indoors in a hockey arena with a floor in place of the ice surface and with walls surrounding the playing area to keep the ball from going out of bounds. Each team is composed of 6 players, including a goalkeeper. The goals are 4 feet high and 16 feet wide. The game is played in three 20-minute periods, and fouls are penalized by suspension of the guilty player for 2 or 5 minutes, during which time his team plays shorthanded as in ice hockey or box lacrosse.

indoor track see TRACK AND FIELD

Indy car *auto racing* An open-wheel rear-engine racing car run on a fuel blend (as methanol and nitromethane) and powered usually by a turbocharged racing engine of up to 161 cubic inches displacement which develops up to 700 horsepower. The regulations also permit the use of a supercharged (turbocharged) stock-block engine of up to 203 cubic inches, a nonsupercharged racing engine of up to 256 cubic inches, or a nonsupercharged stock-block engine of up to 320 cubic inches; but in practice only the turbocharged racing engine is competitive. The Indy car is a low essentially wedge-shaped car in which the driver reclines in a single-seat open cockpit ahead of the engine. The radiators are normally located on the sides of the car, and the fuel tank is on the left beside the driver. The car weighs a minimum of 1350 pounds and runs on extremely wide treadless tires mounted on 15-inch wheels. Across the rear behind the engine is an airfoil to increase traction. The Indy car is designed for a series of American oval-track races of which the Indianapolis 500, from which the car gets its name, is the premier event. (also called *championship car, Indianapolis car*) — compare FORMULA ONE

ineligible receiver *football* An offensive player who is not permitted to catch a forward pass and who is restricted to the neutral zone on a pass play — unless he is in continuous contact with the defensive player he is blocking — until the pass has been caught or touched. The players in the interior of the offensive line (normally the center, guards, and tackles) are ineligible receivers; the offensive backs and offensive ends are all eligible to catch a forward pass. Once a pass has been touched by a defender, all offensive players are eligible to catch it.

infield **1** The area enclosed by a racetrack or a running track.
2 *baseball* **a** The part of the playing field enclosed by the 3 bases and home plate. Though the rules specify a 90-foot square, in common usage the part of the field occupied by the infielders when in their normal positions is also included. **b** The defensive positions comprising first base, second base, shortstop, and third base. ⟨wants to play in the *infield*⟩ **c** The players who play the infield positions. ⟨the best defensive *infield* in the league⟩
3 *cricket* **a** The area of the playing field relatively close to the wickets. **b** The fielding positions covering the infield including slips, gully, point, mid-off, mid-wicket, and square leg. **c** The players who occupy the infield positions.

infielder *baseball* A player who plays in the infield.

infield fly *baseball* A fair fly ball that is hit when less than 2 are out with first and second or first, second, and third bases occupied and that in the judgment of the umpire can be caught by an infielder with normal effort. The batter is declared out, and the base runners are therefore not forced to run if the ball is not caught. The rule exists to prevent a situation in which an

infielder deliberately does not catch the ball in order to get a double play on the runners who are forced to remain close to their bases in order to avoid being trapped off base when the ball is caught. The rule does not apply when there is no runner at first base because then no force exists. With only first base occupied, the rule does not apply because if the ball were not caught, the batter would still presumably have time to reach first base and only one out would result when the runner was forced at second.

infield hit *baseball* A base hit on a ball that does not leave the infield.

infielding *baseball* The art or technique of playing in the infield.

infield out *baseball* A batted ball that results in the batter's being put out by an infielder.

infighting Fencing or boxing at close quarters.

infraction A breach of the playing rules; play or conduct that violates a rule and results in a penalty's being imposed on a player or his team. In common usage an infraction may be a foul as well as a technical infringement (as offsides). — see FOUL, VIOLATION

in-goal *rugby* The 25-yard-deep area (6–12 yards in Rugby League) at each end of the field just beyond the goal line which corresponds to the end zone of a football field.

in home *lacrosse* **1** A primarily attacking player who is a member of the close attack.
2 The position played by an in home.

injury time Extra time added to the end of a game (as in rugby or soccer) when much of the playing time has been taken up with treating or removing an injured player.

inlocate *gymnastics* A movement performed on the rings which is essentially the reverse of a dislocate and in which from a hanging position the gymnast swings his legs back and up, swings his arms out and rotates them so that the palms face out, and moves through a handstand position to finish in an inverted pike position.

inner **1** One of 2 forwards in speedball or field hockey who normally play between the center forward and the wings.
2 The position played by an inner.

inning A period in a contest during which all competitors have a turn or an equal number of turns:
1 *badminton* A period of play during which one side has had and subsequently lost the serve.
2 *baseball* **a** A division of a game consisting of a turn at bat for each team. **b** A turn at bat for one team that ends when 3 players have been

put out. When the term *inning,* sometimes also called a *half inning,* is used in reference to the work of a pitcher, the reference is to the opposing team's inning. For the purpose of determining how many innings or parts of innings a certain pitcher was pitching, the inning is divided into thirds corresponding to the 3 outs regardless of the length of time between outs. Example: if a pitcher has worked 5 full innings and retired one batter in the sixth inning, he has pitched 5$\frac{1}{3}$ innings.

3 *billiards* A turn by one player who may shoot as long as he continues to make successful shots that ends when he fouls, misses, scores the maximum number of points allowed, or ends the game.

4 *bowling* A frame.

5 *croquet* An opportunity for all players to have one turn.

6 *curling* The play of all stones from one end of the rink to the opposite house.

7 *handball* A period of play during which each side has had and subsequently lost the serve.

8 *horseshoes* The play of all horseshoes from one end of the court to the opposite stake.

9 *trapshooting* An opportunity for all shooters on a squad to shoot at the same number of targets from a single station.

innings *cricket* **1** A turn at bat for a batsman which continues until he is declared out.
2 A division of a game during which one side bats. The innings continues until 10 players have been declared out or until the captain declares the innings closed. — see DECLARE

in-off A losing hazard in English billiards.

inrun The ramp down which a ski jumper moves to build momentum for the jump.

inshoot An old name for a baseball pitch that breaks toward the batter.

¹inside An area nearest a specified or implied point of reference:
1 a The part of a playing area midway between the sides. **b** *basketball* The area near the basket. **c** *football* The middle of an offensive line; the area of the line between the tackles.
2 a The part or lane of a racecourse or track nearest the infield. **b** The area nearest the center of a turn.
3 a The side of a skier's or skater's body toward which a turn is being made. **b** The side or edge of a ski or skate nearest the other ski or skate.
4 The side of a wave nearest the shore.
5 *baseball* **a** The side of home plate nearest the batter. **b** The area between the batter and home

plate. ⟨the pitch was on the *inside* for a ball⟩
6 *volleyball* The area nearest the center of the net.

²inside **1** To, toward, or on the inside. ⟨ran the fullback *inside*⟩ ⟨weight the *inside* ski⟩ ⟨the pitch was high and *inside*⟩ ⟨drove *inside* for a lay-up⟩
2 *boxing* Within arm's length of an opponent. ⟨destroyed him *inside* with short blows to the body⟩

in side The serving side in certain court games (as badminton, handball, or squash racquets).

inside forward *soccer* Either of 2 forwards who normally play between the wings and the center forward.

inside lines *fencing* Lines of attack leading to the side of a fencer's body opposite the sword hand.

inside-of-the-foot kick A kick made in soccer or speedball by hitting the ball with the inside edge of the foot to drive it to the side or diagonally forward.

inside-out swing *baseball* A swing in which the hands are ahead of the barrel of the bat at the time the bat hits the ball so that the ball will be hit to the opposite field.

inside pass *track and field* A baton exchange in which the incoming runner approaches the outgoing runner on the inside of the lane and passes the baton from his right hand to the left hand of his teammate.

inspector *track and field* A meet official whose duties include the detection and the reporting of all violations occuring in races.

instep kick A kick in soccer or speedball in which the ball is hit with the top of the foot.

instinctive shooting *archery* Aiming and shooting without the assistance of bowsights or point-of-aim technique which is often practiced and developed to a high degree of accuracy especially by field archers and bow hunters.

instructional league *baseball* A league sponsored by major league baseball and operated during the winter for the instruction of prospective players and for veteran players who want to work on some aspect of their game during the off-season or to regain previous form (as after an injury).

insurance **1** *of a score* Increasing the winning team's lead while making it impossible for the other team's next score to tie the game. ⟨an *insurance* run⟩
2 *of a player* Being a reserve but capable of being a starter if a regular is unable to play (as because of injury). ⟨will be earning over $100,-

000 in salary. Not bad for an *insurance* guard — *Sport*⟩

inswinger *cricket* A bowled ball that swerves toward the batsman while in the air rather than after bouncing. When delivered by a right-handed bowler to a right-handed batsman it is analogous to baseball's screwball. If bowled to a left-handed batsman by a right-handed bowler it is similar to a baseball curve.

intentional foul *basketball* A personal or technical foul committed deliberately by a member of the defensive team (as when trailing late in the game) in order to stop the clock and have an opportunity to regain possession of the ball to try to score. The strategy involves giving up one or more free throws in the hope that they will be missed. In college play, an intentional foul is penalized by 2 free throws. Even if these are successful, the tactic may still be resorted to more than once especially to keep the opposing team from freezing the ball. If the free throws are missed or if only one is made the team may have an opportunity to tie or even win the game. In professional play the tactic is sometimes employed as a gamble even though the shooting clock prevents freezing the ball.

intentional grounding *football* An infraction in which the passer deliberately throws the ball to the ground, out of bounds, or to an area where there is no receiver in order to avoid being tackled with the ball for a loss. This is a judgment call by the officials, and when it is called the passer's team is penalized 15 yards (5 in college play) with loss of the down. Intentional grounding is seldom called, however, when there is an eligible receiver in the vicinity of the pass.

intentional walk *baseball* A base on balls purposely given to an opposing batter for purposes of game strategy. The principal reasons for giving an intentional walk are to avoid pitching to a strong or hot batter and to set up a force play when first base (or sometimes first and second) is unoccupied. (also called *intentional pass*)

intercept **1** To gain possession of an opponent's pass before it reaches the player for whom it was intended. ⟨*intercepted* the pass and returned it 43 yards⟩ ⟨three passes were *intercepted* and turned into baskets — *Boy's Life*⟩
2 *football* To have one's pass intercepted. ⟨was *intercepted* three times, one of them leading to the clinching . . . touchdown — Dave Anderson, *New York Times*⟩

interception The act or an instance of intercepting a pass; a forward pass in football that is intercepted and that is charged against the passer and credited to the intercepting player in statistical records. — compare COMPLETION

interceptor *football* A player noted for intercepting opponent's passes.

interchange The act or an instance of changing position with a teammate (as to permit a specific player to make a play or to cover for a player who is out of position).

interfere **1** To obstruct or hinder an opponent illegally.
2 *of a race horse* To strike one leg with the hoof of another leg.

interference **1** Illegal hampering of an opponent:
a A hinder (as in handball or squash racquets).
b *baseball* The act or action or an instance of a batter or base runner hampering a fielder who is trying to field a ball or to make a play on a runner, or a member of the offensive team trying to confuse the opponents (as a third-base coach who runs toward home plate trying to get the defensive team to make a throw home), or a catcher hampering a batter's swing. A batter or base runner who interferes with a defensive player will be called out. If the third base coach causes interference, the runner otherwise entitled to third base will be called out. For catcher's interference, the batter will be automatically advanced to first base. — compare OBSTRUCTION
c *football* The act or action or an instance of hampering an opponent who is attempting to catch a kick or a forward pass. On a kick, members of the kicking team must allow the receiving team to catch the ball. On a kickoff, the ball may be recovered by either side after it has traveled 10 yards, but members of the kicking team may not prevent the opponents from catching the ball. On a forward pass, each side has an equal right to the ball, and neither side may interfere with the other's attempt to catch the pass. If 2 opponents are both trying for a pass, incidental body contact is not considered interference. Interference on a kick is penalized by 15 yards from the spot of the foul. For offensive pass interference, the passing team is penalized by a loss of 15 yards from the previous line of scrimmage (plus a loss of the down in college play); for defensive interference, the passing team is awarded a first down at the spot of the foul.
d *ice hockey* Checking or hampering an opponent who does not have possession of the puck or who is not attempting to gain possession which is a minor penalty.
e *lacrosse* Checking or hampering an opponent

who does not have possession of the ball or who is not attempting to gain possession which is a technical foul resulting in a 30-second suspension for the guilty player.

f *rowing* Impeding the progress of another shell which may result in the disqualification of the guilty crew, the restart of the race, or both.

g *track and field* Hampering or impeding the movement of another runner during a race (as by bumping or shoving) which usually results in disqualification of the guilty runner.

2 *football* **a** The act or action of legally blocking opponents to create a hole for the ballcarrier. **b** The players who block on running plays. — compare PROTECTION

interior line *football* The part of a line between the ends.

interior lineman *football* Any of the offensive or defensive players (as tackles, guards, center, and middle guard) who play in the interior line.

interleague Between or among professional sports leagues. ⟨*interleague* play⟩ ⟨*interleague* trading⟩

interlocking grip see GRIP(*golf*)

intermediate hurdle *track and field* A 36-inch-high hurdle used in the intermediate hurdles. — see HURDLE

intermediate hurdler *track and field* A hurdler who competes in the intermediate hurdles.

intermediate hurdles *track and field* A race run over intermediate hurdles placed at regular intervals on the course. Each competitor must attempt to clear every hurdle successfully but is not penalized for knocking them down accidentally. Common distances are 440 yards or 400 meters, both of which have 10 hurdles, and 330 yards, which has 8 hurdles.

intermediates Short for *intermediate hurdles.*

international A player who competes in international competition.

international formula one see FORMULA ONE
international formula two see FORMULA TWO

interval *track and field* One of a series of runs over a set distance at a predetermined pace that are broken up by periods of walking or jogging and that are part of interval training.

interval trailing *track and field* A training technique which involves alternately running and walking or jogging over a set distance. The set distance is usually less than the distance to be covered in competition so that the runner can cover it a number of times at a fast pace and have the period of walking or jogging between each

for recovery. This training builds endurance and conditions the runner's body to the fast pace and to the strain of having to put on more than one burst of speed during the race.

intimidator *ice hockey* A player known for rough play and fighting who intimidates opposing players with the threat of a fight or unusually rough body checks or some other act of deliberate roughness in order to make them less aggressive in playing the game and especially in chasing the puck into the corners.

in-turn *curling* A delivery in which the hand is turned outward as the stone is delivered so that the stone curls toward the same side as the propelling hand (to the right for a right-handed curler) as it nears the house.

inverted *of a position in gymnastics* Having the feet and legs higher than the body; upside down. ⟨*inverted* hang⟩ ⟨*inverted* pike position⟩ ⟨*inverted* cross⟩

inverted camel *skating* A spin resembling the camel but performed with the free leg held straight out in front and the body leaning back facing upwards.

invitation 1 or **invitational** A contest (as a horse race, track and field meet, or basketball tournament) open to invited participants.
2 *fencing* The intentional opening of a line of attack for the purpose of inducing an opponent to attack.

inward dive *diving* Any of a group of competitive dives which are started from a position facing toward the diving board and in which the diver jumps up and out from the board but rotates forward toward the board and enters the water either headfirst (facing away from the board) or feetfirst (facing toward the board). — compare ARMSTAND DIVE, BACKWARD DIVE, FORWARD DIVE, REVERSE DIVE, TWIST DIVE

inwick *curling* A shot in which the player's stone caroms off the inner edge of an opponent's stone and moves toward the tee to displace another stone.

I-100 *auto racing* A small formula car that is powered by any of numerous engines that develop approximately 100 horsepower.

iron *golf* A club with a relatively thin head made of steel that is usually used in making shots from the fairway or from the rough. Included in the group of irons are clubs numbered 2 (having the least loft) through 9 plus the pitching wedge and the sand wedge. A number one iron, sometimes referred to as a driving iron, is seldom used to-

inward dive in tuck position

Iron Mike A pitching machine used for batting practice in baseball.

island pullout *surfing* A pullout made by moving to the front of the board, squatting and grabbing the rails, and turning the body so that the rear of the board lifts out of the water and swings around toward the front to allow the wave to pass the surfer.

isokinetic exercise A form of conditioning or strength-building exercise in which the muscles strain against a constant resistance throughout the entire range of movement. This form of exercise requires the use of a device which limits the speed with which the muscles can move and at the same time exerts a constant resistance such as would be experienced in pulling or pushing against an automobile shock absorber. Isokinetic exercise is claimed to have the advantage of building the muscle strength through its full range of movement in less time than is required by isometric or isotonic exercises because the muscle is under maximum stress at all points of its movement during each exercise. — compare ISOMETRIC EXERCISE, ISOTONIC EXERCISE

isometric exercise or **isometrics** A form of conditioning or strength-building exercise in which the muscles strain against an unmoving resistance (such as a wall or a door frame). In such an exercise the muscles are subjected to stress yet do not move. This form of exercise tends to build strength at only a single point in the range of movement of the muscle at one time. — compare ISOKINETIC EXERCISE, ISOTONIC EXERCISE

isotonic exercise or **isotonics** A form of conditioning or strength-building exercise in which the muscles strain against a movable resistance (as a barbell). In such an exercise the muscles are subjected to stress while moving through all or part of their range of movement. Once the resistance weight is in motion, however, momentum rather than muscle power plays the major role in the continuation of the movement. The muscle undergoes an unusually great strain at the beginning of the movement to get the weight in motion but then needs to exert only enough force to keep the weight moving. — compare ISOKINETIC EXERCISE, ISOMETRIC EXERCISE

Italian pursuit *cycling* A team pursuit race between 2 or more teams of up to 5 riders each with one rider for each team dropping out at the end of each lap and with the finishing times of the last riders determining the winning team.

day. Though it is made with a steel head, the putter is not regarded as an iron. — see CLUB; compare WOOD
2 A curling stone.
— in irons *of a sailing boat* Having failed to complete a tack with the result that the boat stops moving forward and starts to drift backward. **— in the irons** *horse racing* Riding a particular horse as jockey.

iron boot *weight training* A metal plate in the shape of the sole of a shoe that has straps by which it can be attached to the foot and a hole in each side through which the bar of a dumbbell may pass so that the weight may be attached to the foot for exercises designed to strengthen the legs.

iron cross see CROSS (*gymnastics*)

ironman A durable player who plays every game or who has played in every game for a team for a number of successive seasons.

J

¹**jab** **1** *boxing* A quick straight punch usually to the head normally made with the lead hand (as the left hand of a right-handed boxer) but without the force of the body behind it.

2 *field hockey* A tackle made by thrusting the stick at the ball with the stick close to the ground and the blade up and lifting the ball from in front of the opponent's stick.

²**jab** *boxing* To make or throw a jab.

jab checking *box lacrosse* The act of spearing an opponent which results in a minor or major penalty.

jab kick see FLICK KICK

¹**jack** **1** *lawn bowling* A small white ball rolled to the far end of the rink at the beginning of an end to serve as the target. It is about 2½ inches in diameter and is usually made of a ceramic or rubber composition material.

2 *see* PALLINO

²**jack** To hunt or fish with a jacklight.

jackknife **1** A body position (as in diving or gymnastics) which is similar to a pike but in which the hands are held near or touching the ankles.

2 *diving* A forward or backward dive with the body in a pike or jackknife position and with a headfirst entry. — see illustration at REVERSE DIVE

¹**jacklight** A powerful flashlight or spotlight used in fishing or in illegally hunting game at night. The animal is usually momentarily blinded by the beam of light and freezes with fear long enough to be shot by the poacher.

²**jacklight** To hunt or fish illegally with a jacklight.

Jackson Haines spin A sit spin. It is so named because it was introduced by a former American skater Jackson Haines.

Jacob's ladder *boating* A rope ladder with wooden steps.

jai alai A game similar to handball in which the players catch and throw a hard ball with a curved wicker basket (*cesta*) strapped to one hand. It is played on a 3-walled court (*cancha*) that is 176 feet long and 40 feet wide and is open to spectators on one of the long sides. The object of the game is to serve and return the ball with

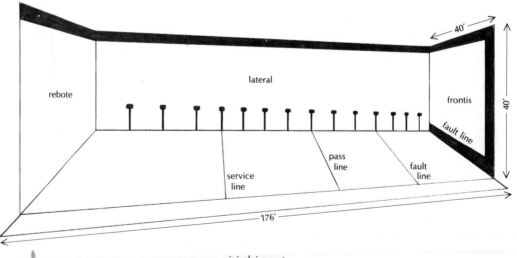

jai alai court

the cesta to the front wall until one side wins the point. The ball may be played off the front, side, or back wall, and the game may be played as either singles or doubles. To be a legal return, the ball must be caught and thrown with a single motion. In a common form of competition, 8 players or sides take part in a game, although only 2 are on the court at any one time. The side winning a point stays on the court to meet the next side while the losing side sits down. The game continues round-robin style until one side has won a predetermined number of points. An important aspect of jai alai is pari-mutuel betting on the outcome of the game. The sides are designated by post position numbers, and betting is for win, place, and show as in horse racing. — see also FRONTON; PARTIDO

¹jam 1 *baseball* To pitch inside to a batter in the hope of preventing him from getting good wood on the ball.
2 *football* To block, crowd, or bump a pass receiver especially as he comes over the line of scrimmage in order to interrupt his concentration or to throw off his timing.
3 *mountain climbing* To employ a jam in climbing.

²jam 1 *gymnastics* see STOOP THROUGH
2 *mountain climbing* A hold that consists of wedging a finger, hand, or foot in a crack.
3 *Roller Derby* A 60-second period during which one or more jammers from a team try to lap members of the opposing team in order to score points.

jam cleat *boating* A cleat that holds the line in position either through the action of one or 2 cams that grip the line when tension is in one direction but open when the line is pulled in the opposite direction or by a pinching action when the line is jammed into a narrow cleft.

jammer *Roller Derby* A player who attempts to lap members of the opposing team to score points for his own team.

jamming *mountain climbing* The technique or practice of employing jams in climbing.

Japanese cross *gymnastics* An inverted cross.

Japanese set *volleyball* A set that gets the ball up just high enough to clear the top of the net. The spiker will usually begin his jump before the setter hits the ball so that he will be at the peak of his jump just as the ball reaches its highest point in order to spike the ball before the other team's blockers expect it.

javelin *track and field* A long metal-tipped wooden or metal shaft that has a cord grip at the middle, tapers to a point at each end, and is thrown for distance in the javelin throw. The taper is somewhat sharper in the front, and the center of gravity is toward the front for stability in flight and so that the javelin will stick in the ground when it lands.

JAVELIN

for high school, college, and international competition

	men	women
length	260–270 cm (8 ft, 6⅜ in– 8 ft, 10¼ in)	220–230 cm (7 ft, 2⅝ in– 7 ft, 6½ in)
weight	800 g (1 lb, 12¼ oz)	600 g (1 lb, 5¼ oz)
diameter (thickest)	25–30 mm (1–1⅙ in)	20–25 mm (¹³/₁₆–1 in)
grip width	15–16 cm (6–6⁵/₁₆ in)	14–15 cm (5½–5⅞ in)

javelin throw *track and field* A field event in which the javelin is thrown with one hand for distance. The throwing of the javelin is preceded by a running approach along a 13-foot-wide runway at the end of which is a scratch line. To qualify as a legal throw, the javelin must land point first within a throwing sector formed by 2 lines extending out at a 30-degree angle from a point approximately 26 feet behind the scratch line. — see CROSSOVER, HOP-STEP

javelin thrower Someone who competes in the javelin throw.

jaw *billiards* 1 A corner of a carom billiards table.
2 The opening to a pocket on a pocket billiards table.

jaw shot *billiards* A shot in carom billiards at object balls in a corner of the table.

jayvee 1 Junior varsity.
2 A member of a junior varsity team.

J-bar lift A ski lift which consists of a series of J-shaped bars suspended from a moving overhead cable. Each bar is intended to pull one skier.

jellyfish float A facedown float in which the swimmer's legs and arms hang down.

¹jerk 1 *cricket* To bowl the ball illegally (as by having the arm bent when the ball is released).

jerk

2 *weight lifting* To heave the weight overhead from shoulder height usually by lunging or squatting under it.

²jerk 1 *cricket* The act or an instance of jerking the ball.

2 *weight lifting* A lift in which the weight is heaved overhead from shoulder height usually as the second part of the clean and jerk. There is no restriction on the movement of the lifter's legs, and he usually squats or lunges under the bar while heaving the weight. — compare PRESS

jersey A short-sleeve, long-sleeve, or sometimes sleeveless pullover shirt worn as part of an athletic uniform. Jerseys normally have numerals on one or both sides and sometimes also have the team name on the front and the player's name on the back.

Jersey see BROOKLYN

jess *falconry* A short leather strap secured to the leg of a falcon or hawk and usually equipped with a ring or swivel to which a leash may be fastened.

jet A boat engine that functions like a high-speed water pump and propels the boat by taking in water at one end and forcing it out the other in a powerful stream.

jet turn *skiing* A parallel turn initiated by pushing the skis forward so that the body weight is farther back than normal and by down unweighting.

jib *sailing* A triangular sail set forward of the mast.

¹jibe *sailing* **1** To change directions when sailing with the wind by turning the bow farther away from the wind and swinging the boom to the opposite side. (also spelled *gybe*) — compare TACK

2 To move the sail to the opposite side when jibing.

²jibe *sailing* The act or an instance of jibing; the movement of the boat in changing direction either in an intentional or accidental jibe (as when the wind shifts and blows over the mainsail).

jibstay *sailing* The headstay of a sloop-rigged boat on which the jib is hoisted. — see illustration at SAILBOAT

¹jig *fishing* A lure consisting of a hook with a usually decorated lead head and a tail of bucktail or feather that is used in jigging.

²jig *fishing* To fish with a jig.

jigger see MIZZEN

jigging *fishing* The action or practice of moving a lure or baited hook by alternately jerking it up and letting it sink.

jink British term for *fake*. ⟨likes to shimmy up to defenders, showing the ball, *jinking* and swaying until he suddenly darts clear — Rob Hughes, *London Times*⟩

jitterbug see STUNT

jiujitsu see JUJITSU

jock 1 An athlete and especially a college athlete. ⟨my classmates expected me to be a *jock*, inarticulate, unintelligent, and interested only in sports — Don Schollander⟩ ⟨you can still be a woman if you're an athlete, just like you can be a woman doing anything else. We don't mind being called *jocks* now — Irene Shea⟩

2 Short for *jockey*. ⟨there's more prestige in winning a Derby than anything else a *jock* can do — Eddie Arcaro⟩

3 see ATHLETIC SUPPORTER

jockette A female jockey. The term was popular for a short while when female jockeys first began riding at major tracks.

¹jockey 1 *horse racing* A professional rider who rides, controls, and rates a throughbred in a race. A jockey's weight is important because it is included in the amount of weight a horse is required to carry during the race. Jockeys usually weigh between 100 and 120 pounds.

2 Short for *bench jockey*.

²jockey 1 To ride a horse in a race as a jockey.

2 To maneuver an opponent, a craft, or oneself into a position that can be used to one's advantage.

Jockey Club *horse racing* The governing body of flat and steeplechase racing in England. The Jockey Club, originally formed about 1750 by leading horsemen and noblemen to regulate and promote horse racing, is presently the lawmaking body of the sport, controlling both the racing calendar and the stud book. There are similar governing organizations in other countries, some of which have taken the name *Jockey Club*.

jockey room A building or portion of a building at a race track for use by jockeys that normally contains dressing and shower rooms and often a steam room and recreation room.

jockstrap see ATHLETIC SUPPORTER

¹jog To run at a steady leisurely pace by taking short strides.

²jog *harness racing* A slow gait similar to a trot that is used for workouts of trotters.

jog cart or **jogging cart** *harness racing* A sulky used in training that is longer and heavier that the sulky used in racing.

jogger Someone who jogs.

jogging The action or practice of jogging especially as a conditioning or warming-up exercise.

joint *horse racing* A small battery-powered device that can be concealed in the palm of a jockey's hand and applied illegally to the horse's neck during a race to give the horse a shock in an attempt to make it run faster. (also called *battery, buzzer, Edison*)

journeyman An experienced reliable performer or player as distinguished from one who is brilliant or colorful. ⟨a *journeyman* infielder⟩ ⟨the public image . . . was of an easygoing guy who didn't let his profession, hockey of the *journeyman* variety, interfere with his fun — Neil Offen, *Sport*⟩

J-stroke *canoeing* A stroke used to correct the trim of the canoe or to counteract sideways drift caused by wind that consists of moving the paddle back through the water as in a normal stroke and, as it reaches a point even with the canoeist's hips, turning the blade out and continuing the stroke outward to the side.

judge An official in any of several sports who is responsible for watching the contest for infractions of the rules, for evaluating the performance of competitors and awarding points, or for determining the order of finish at the end of a race. In many sports, the judge or judges assist a referee who actually conducts the contest.

judo An Oriental form of wrestling originally developed from jujitsu as an art of self-defense. Participants wear a 2-piece garment called a *gi* and are normally referred to as *players*. A player wins the match by making a clean throw, by pinning his opponent to the mat and keeping him under control for 30 seconds, or by applying a submission hold such as a twisting lock on the arm or elbow or a choke hold, which cuts off the flow of blood — not air — and eventually causes temporary unconsciousness. The opponent signals defeat by tapping out, that is, tapping the mat or his opponent twice. A match, which normally has a time limit of from 3 to 10 minutes, is supervised by a referee assisted by 2 judges. The referee, who is on the mat with the players, decides whether or not a throw is clean and awards a point or (if the throw is imperfect) a half point or no point, watches for illegal or dangerous holds, and signals for timing to begin in case of a pin. If in grappling the contestants move off the edge of the mat, they are ordered to freeze their positions and are dragged back to the center of the mat to resume wrestling. Matches, which are conducted in weight classes like intercollegiate wrestling or boxing, begin and end with contestants bowing to the referee and to each other.

judoka or **judoist** A judo student or player. — compare DAN

Judy see PUNCH HITTER

jug fishing or **jugging** Float fishing in which an unattended line is fastened to an empty jug.

¹juggle *speedball* To toss the ball in the air (as past an opposing player) and run and catch it; to make an overhead dribble.

²juggle see OVERHEAD DRIBBLE

jug handle *mountain climbing* A rock, knob, or crack large enough to be grasped with the whole hand as a handhold.

jug handle curve *baseball* A wide sweeping curve.

jujitsu or **jujutsu** or **jiujitsu** An Oriental art of weaponless self-defense that is characterized by striking and throwing techniques and by the use of chokes and nerve pinches designed to cripple or paralyze an adversary.

¹juke *football* To fake an opponent out of position. ⟨I get my chance to *juke* them and go — O. J. Simpson⟩

²juke The act or an instance of juking; fake.

¹jump **1** The action or an instance of jumping; an attempt in jumping or vaulting competition.
2 An obstacle over which competitors must jump in a steeplechase.
3 *fencing* An attacking movement in which both feet leave the floor together. — compare LUNGE, MARCH
4 *skating* A movement in which the skater leaves the surface with both feet and usually performs a turn or a half turn in the air. — compare HOP, LEAP
5 *skydiving* A descent by parachute.

²jump To make a jump.

jump ball *basketball* **1** A method of putting the ball in play (as at the beginning of a period of play, when a held ball is called, or when the referee is unable to determine which side last touched a ball before it went out of bounds) that consists of the referee's tossing the ball up between 2 opposing players who jump and attempt to tap the ball to a teammate. Other players must remain outside a restraining circle until the ball has been touched. — compare FACE-OFF
2 A held ball.

jumper **1** A competitor in a jumping event (as in track and field or ski jumping); a horse used in hunting, steeplechases, or show jumping.
2 A jump shot in basketball.

jump fishing A method of fishing that involves

jumping event

cruising a body of water looking for signs of a school of game fish feeding on bait fish and then casting lures into the area in hopes of a strike.

jumping event *track and field* Any of several field events in which competitors must jump or vault for height or distance including the pole vault, high jump, long jump, and triple jump. — compare THROWING EVENT

jumping hill The hill on which competitors land in ski jumping or ski flying.

jumping jack see SIDE-STRADDLE HOP

jumping seat see FORWARD SEAT

jump kick *soccer* A kick made by jumping and kicking the ball while it is in the air 2 or 3 feet off the ground.

jumpmaster *skydiving* An instructor or other individual supervising a group of skydivers.

jump-off A jumping competition to determine the winner when several competitors are tied at the end of regular competition (as in show jumping or track and field). In track and field, the jump-off is used only to determine first place when other tie-breaking methods (as fewest misses) have failed.

jump pass A pass (as in football or basketball) made by a player while jumping.

jump racing Competition for horses ridden over obstacles in a steeplechase or hurdles race. — compare FLAT RACING

jump rider Someone who rides, controls, and rates a horse in steeplechase events. The weight carried by horses in jumping events is considerably greater than that carried in flat races so that riders as small and light as jockeys are not necessary.

jump set *volleyball* A set made when the ball is passed close to the net in which the setter jumps. If an opposing blocker jumps with him he sets the ball to another spiker; if a blocker does not jump he spikes the ball himself.

jump shooter *basketball* A player who normally shoots a jump shot.

jump shooting A method of hunting waterfowl which involves creeping up to a pond or creek on foot or floating up to an area of birds in a boat and shooting at the birds when they flush. — compare PASS SHOOTING

jump shot *basketball* A shot made by releasing the ball at the top of a jump. Since the ball is released often at a point as high as or higher than the defender can reach when jumping, it is difficult to defend against and is the most common shot used in modern basketball. — compare HOOK SHOT, SET SHOT

jump spin *skating* A spin that is begun with a jump.

jump start *waterskiing* A start made from a dock by jumping up and forward as the tow line becomes taut.

jump stop A hockey stop made by jumping and turning sideways so that on landing the skate blades are perpendicular to the line of movement.

jump the gun To start a race before the starting signal is given; to make a false start. (also *beat the gun*)

jump turn *skiing* A turn made while skiing by placing one or both poles near the ski tips, jumping and pivoting on the poles, and landing so as to face in a new direction with the skis edged uphill.

June bug *fishing* A spinner that consists of a teardrop-shaped blade attached directly to the shaft at the small end and braced at an angle from the shaft by a thin strip, usually a cutout part of the blade, which can be bent or straightened to vary the angle of the blade.

junior **1** Competition for competitors who are too young for senior competition (as in weight lifting) or open to those who have not won a championship in junior or senior competition (as in track and field).

2 A competitor who competes in junior competition.

Junior Columbia round *archery* A target round usually for children under 12 in which each com-

jump shot

petitor shoots 24 arrows at a distance of 40 yards, 24 at 30 yards, and 24 at 20 yards.

junior lightweight A boxer in the junior lightweight division. — see DIVISION

junior middleweight A boxer in the junior middleweight division. — see DIVISION

junior varsity A school or college team composed of members lacking the experience or qualifications required for the varsity.

junior welterweight A boxer in the junior welterweight division. — see DIVISION.

junk *baseball* Pitches consisting chiefly of relatively slow breaking balls.

junkball *baseball* A slow usually breaking pitch.

junk surf *surfing* Small choppy waves that are not consistent and that do not afford a pleasant ride.

jury *fencing* The officials at a bout consisting of the president and 4 judges who watch for valid hits.

juvenile A 2-year-old racehorse. (also called *youngster*)

J valve *scuba diving* A valve on an air tank that has an automatic shutoff when pressure in the tank is reduced to 300 psi. The diver can then pull a lever to release the remaining air, which is usually sufficient for 5 to 15 minutes depending upon the depth. The automatic shutoff serves as a warning to the diver that his air is nearly exhausted and yet permits him to swim deeper if necessary to free himself from an entanglement or to leave a cave or sunken wreck before heading to the surface. — compare K VALVE

K

¹K A strikeout in baseball. Its use comes from the traditional use of the letter K on a scorecard to indicate a strikeout.

²K *baseball* **1** *of a pitcher* To strike out a batter. **2** *of a batter* To strike out.

kaboom *trampolining* A stunt performed on the trampoline which consists of a backward somersault in a tuck position from a back drop position.

kamikaze *surfing* An intentional wipeout.

kamikaze corps or **kamikaze squad** see SPECIAL TEAM

karabiner see CARABINER

karate An Oriental art of self-defense that is characterized by disabling an attacker with crippling kicks and punches and that is widely practiced as a sport. The participants, commonly called *players,* wear a 2-piece costume called a *gi.* Matches, in which players are normally paired according to weight, are usually limited to 2 to 7 minutes, during which time each player directs kicks and punches at his opponent and tries to block his opponent's blows. The blows need not actually land on target to score, and they are normally pulled at the last instant to avoid injuring the opponent. The valid target area is the torso, and blows landing on the head, arms, and legs are not counted. Players customarily wear protective mitts on their hands to soften blows that accidentally hit the opponent. A match is held on a 26-foot-square mat and begins and ends with the players bowing to each other and to the officials. The match is supervised by a referee on the mat who is assisted by up to 4 judges at the corners. They watch for punches and kicks that are not blocked and that, had they not been pulled back, would have landed. Points are awarded for a likely hit, and a player may win a match by accumulating a stipulated number of points for effective blows or half points for scoring less effective blows or by delivering a single killing blow — one that would have landed in one of the more than 20 vital points on the opponent's body and would have been lethal if not pulled back.

karateka or **karateist** A karate student or player.

kart A miniature automobile used especially for racing that has a typically tubular chassis without a suspension system, has a maximum wheelbase of 50 inches, is normally equipped with 4-wheel disc brakes, and is powered by one or more 2-stroke engines with a total maximum displace-

kart

ment of 16.5 cubic inches. Karts have reached speeds in excess of 130 mph. Sprint karts, used for short races, normally do not have bodies; their drivers sit in an upright position. Enduro karts, for endurance races of one hour or longer, often have a fiberglass body enclosing the driver, who is in a reclining position.

karter Someone who drives or races a kart.

karting The sport of racing karts. The sport includes both sprint racing and endurance racing, and competitors compete in any of several categories based on the driver's age, on engine type or size, or on modifications permitted to the engine.

kata A formal exercise in which an individual performs the various movements of an art of self-defense (as karate or judo) usually by himself according to one of numerous prescribed patterns·as if simultaneously combating a number of attackers from several directions. Katas are practiced as an essential part of training, and a student is normally required to show competence at katas as well as in sparring matches before being promoted. (also called *form, hyong*)

kayak

kayak A light narrow boat that is pointed at both ends, is completely covered except for an opening in which the paddler or paddlers sit, and that is propelled by a double-bladed paddle. A tight-fitting skirt goes around the waist of the paddler and over the hole in the top of the kayak to make a waterproof covering. Kayaks are commonly made of molded fiberglass, and a 1-man kayak may be anywhere from 11 to 15 feet long. For competition there are 1-, 2-, and 4-man kayaks. (also called *Alaskan canoe, slalom canoe*) — see also CANOE

kayaker or **kayakist** Someone who paddles a kayak or who engages in kayaking.

kayaking Canoeing competition for singles, tandems, and fours kayaks. — see CANOEING

¹kayo *boxing* To knock out an opponent. ⟨was *kayoed* nine times in 11 fights — Martin Kane, *Sports Illustrated*⟩

²kayo A knockout in boxing.

keel The main structural member running fore and aft along the bottom of a boat. In larger sailboats, the keel is extended downward from the hull as a relatively broad flat vertical surface which resists sideways movement of the boat and enables the boat to move forward even when sailing at an angle to the wind. — compare BILGE BOARD, CENTERBOARD

keelboat A sailboat that has a permanent keel for stability instead of a centerboard or bilge boards.

keeper 1 A small string attached to the upper limb of a bow and to the bowstring to keep the string near the nock whenever the bow is unstrung.

2 A leather loop on a rifle sling that can be adjusted to hold the sling tight on the arm when shooting.

3 *fishing* **a** A fish large enough to be legally kept when caught. **b** or **keep net** A net or cage that is underwater to hold fish that have been caught by a fisherman so that they may be released alive at a later time (as at the end of a contest) or so that they will be fresher when killed at the end of a day of fishing.

4 *football* An offensive play in which the quarterback runs with the ball usually after faking a handoff.

5 Short for *goalkeeper, wicketkeeper*.

keep goal To play the position of goalkeeper.

kegler A bowler.

kegling The game of bowling.

Kelly pool see PILL POOL

kempo see KUNG FU

kendo A Japanese sport of fencing with bamboo staves which are held with both hands. The participants wear traditional costumes and protective coverings for the torso and face protectors resembling fencing masks. A match is conducted by a chief judge assisted by 3 other judges within the 33-by-36-foot competition area and normally lasts for 3 to 5 minutes or until one competitor scores 2 points by landing successful blows.

Kentucky Derby A 1¼-mile stakes race for 3-year-old thoroughbred racehorses that has been held annually at Churchill Downs, Louisville, Kentucky, since 1875 and that is the first race in horse racing's Triple Crown. — see also BELMONT STAKES, PREAKNESS STAKES

Kentucky Futurity A 1-mile stakes race for 3-year-old trotters that is one of the races in the trotting Triple Crown. — see also HAMBLETONIAN, YONKERS TROT

kermesse *cycling* A race run over a course 3 to 5 miles long usually through both urban and rural areas.

kernmantel see ROPE

ketch A 2-masted fore-and-aft-rigged sailboat that has the mizzenmast ahead of the rudderpost. — compare YAWL; SCHOONER

ketch

¹key **1** *basketball* Short for *keyhole*.
2 *football* A clue (as the position or movement of an opposing player) that helps a player read the offensive or defensive alignment or the type of play to be run and to react accordingly. ⟨zones are disguised these days. Usually you'll pick up the *key* by watching the tight safety — Joe Namath⟩

²key *football* To observe the position or movement of a particular opposing player in order to anticipate the play. ⟨when the middle linebacker *keys* on the halfback, he has to watch the half-

back's moves to determine which way he, the middle linebacker, will fill on a running play — either up the middle or outside his tackle's shoulder — Jerry Tubbs⟩

keyhole *basketball* The area at each end of the court marked by the free throw lane and the restraining circle. Before the 1950s, the free throw lane was 6 feet wide, and the 12-foot restraining circle with a 6-foot-wide lane extending from one end of it resembled a keyhole.

keystone *baseball* Second base. (also called *keystone sack*)

kiai *karate* A yell intended to startle one's opponent and to aid one in concentrating muscle energy to deliver a blow with greater than normal power.

¹kick **1** **a** To drive a ball by hitting it with the foot. **b** To score by kicking. ⟨*kicked* the extra point⟩
2 *football* To block a defensive player to the outside so the ballcarrier can run to the inside.
3 *swimming* To propel oneself by moving the feet and legs up and down or back and forth through the water.
4 *track and field* To put on a burst of speed near the end of a race. ⟨when I *kick,* all I do is concentrate on driving with my arms — Dave Wottle⟩

²kick **1** **a** The act, an instance, or the manner of kicking a ball. **b** *football* A punt, field goal, or extra point attempt.
2 The recoil of a gun.
3 *swimming* The propelling movement of the legs in coordination with an arm stroke.
4 *track and field* A burst of speed near the end of a race after a steady pace of less than all-out speed throughout most of the race.

kickable Relatively easy to make or score by kicking. ⟨missed several *kickable* penalties last Saturday — *Wolverhampton (England) Express & Star*⟩

kickback *bowling* A side partition between lanes at the pit.

kickball A variation of baseball played with a soccer ball or playground ball by kicking instead of batting it and by tagging the player or hitting him with the ball while he is off base to put him out.

kickboard *swimming* A buoyant board approximately 30 inches long that is grasped by a beginning swimmer to help support the upper body while practicing kicking. (also called *flutterboard*)

kick boxer Someone who engages in kick boxing.

kick boxing An Oriental form of boxing in which the boxers are permitted to throw punches with gloved hands as in boxing and to kick with bare feet as in karate.

kicker 1 A player who kicks or who is designated to kick the ball; a football player who normally makes placekicks. — compare PUNTER

2 *tennis* see KICK SERVE

3 *track and field* A runner who is noted for a closing kick. A kicker may run a race just off the pace intending to pass the leaders with his kick near the end.

¹kick-in *soccer* A free kick in women's play at a stationary ball on the touchline awarded a team as a method of putting the ball in play after an opponent has driven it into touch.

²kick-in *Australian Rules football* To make a kickoff.

kicking *basketball* A violation that results when a player hits the ball with his knee, leg, or foot.

kicking tee *football* A small rubber or plastic device that supports the ball on one end for a placekick.

kickoff An unhindered kick usually of a stationary ball as a means of putting the ball in play at the beginning of a half or after a score in various games:

1 *Australian Rules football* A kick of the ball up the field from the goal square made by the defending team after the opposing team has scored a behind.

2 *football* A placekick made from the kicking team's 35-yard line in professional play or the 40-yard line in college play that must travel forward 10 yards and must be inbounds. All members of the kicking team must be behind the yard line the ball is on until it is kicked. The receiving team must be behind a restraining line 10 yards in front of the ball and must have at least 5 players within 5 yards of that restraining line. The kickoff is normally made to give the opposing team possession of the ball, and the ball is normally kicked as far down the field as possible. Once the ball has traveled forward 10 yards, members of the kicking team are eligible to catch or recover the ball, providing they do not interfere with an opposing player's attempt to catch the kick.

3 *rugby* A kick of a stationary ball from the halfway line that must travel forward at least 10 yards. The opposing team must be behind a restraining line 10 yards from the ball, and once the ball travels 10 yards, it is recoverable by either team.

4 *soccer* A kick of a stationary ball from the middle of the field normally to a teammate of the kicker. The ball must roll at least the length of its own circumference and may not be touched again by the kicker until played by another player. All members of the kicking team must be behind the ball when it is kicked, and opponents may stand no closer than 10 yards.

5 *speedball* A kick of a stationary ball from the middle of the field to the opposing team in men's play (as in rugby) or to a teammate in women's play (as in soccer).

kick off To kick the ball for a kickoff.

kickoff area see GOAL SQUARE

kickoff circle *soccer* The 20-yard circle in the middle of the field in which the kickoff is made at the beginning of a half.

kickoff lines *Australian Rules football* Two lines that extend into the field from the goalposts for 10 yards and another line between the ends of these 2 lines that with the goal line form the rectangular area known as the goal square.

kickout 1 *Gaelic football* A kick of the ball up the field from the parallelogram or from within the 21-yard line to put it in play (as after a goal has been scored).

2 *surfing* A pullout made by twisting the board around so that it faces toward the wave.

kick out *surfing* To shift the weight to the rear of the board, raise its nose, and twist the board around so as to ride back over the top of the wave, ending a ride.

kickout block *football* A block intended to drive a defensive lineman to the outside.

kickover *gymnastics* 1 A walkover initiated by a kick.

2 A circle swing initiated by a kick.

kick save A save made by a goalkeeper in which the ball or puck is deflected with the foot or leg.

kick serve or **kicker** *tennis* A serve made with a lot of spin so as to bounce unusually high or wide.

kick shot *ice hockey* An illegal shot in which the foot is used to drive the blade of the stick to propel the puck.

kick turn *skiing* A turnaround movement made while standing on skis in a relatively flat area by lifting one leg up until only the tail of the ski touches the ground, swinging the leg out and placing the ski near its original position but facing in the opposite direction, and then lifting the other ski and turning the body to face in the new direction.

kick-up 1 *gymnastics* A rise to a handstand or a headstand initiated by a kick.

2 *speedball* A method of converting a ground

kidney punch

kick turn

ball into an aerial ball by kicking it up to oneself (as by placing the foot on the top of the ball and pulling back quickly to cause the ball to hop or by catching the ball between the feet and jumping, grabbing the ball when it is in the air).

kidney punch   *boxing*   An illegal blow to the small of the back.

Kilian position   *skating*   A position in dance competition in which the couple stand side by side with the girl to the man's right. The man's right hand is placed on the girl's right hip, and he holds her left hand out in front of him. When the girl stands to the man's left and the hand positions are reversed, the position is called the *Kilian position reversed.*

¹kill   1 To use up the playing time of a penalty (as in hockey) while one's team is shorthanded especially by sacrificing most offensive play and playing strong defense. ⟨*kill* a penalty⟩
2 To make a kill shot (as in handball).

²kill or **kill shot   1** A shot in handball or paddleball that rebounds from the front wall so close to the floor that it is extremely difficult to return.
2 A shot in a racquet game (as tennis, badminton, or squash racquets) that is hit so hard that it is virtually unreturnable. (also called *smash, putaway*)

kill off   *track and field*   To set an unusually fast pace in a middle distance or distance race in order to tire out other competitors early in the race.

kill spring   *trampolining*   A landing in which the performer absorbs the rebound action of the trampoline bed by bending his knees so that he does not bounce. The kill spring may be necessary to avoid injury in the event of a poor or awkward landing.

kill the clock   SEE RUN OUT THE CLOCK

kingpin   *bowling*   The number 5 pin. — see illustration at BOWLING; compare HEADPIN

King's round   *archery*   A round in crossbow competition in which each competitor shoots 6 bolts at a special target from a distance of 40 yards. The target has a standard 48-inch face but is marked with 6 circular gold areas placed around the target as on a clock face at the 12, 2, 4, 6, 8, and 10 o'clock positions. Each scoring area is 18 inches from the center of the target and is 4¾ inches in diameter and has a 1-inch black bull's-eye in its center.

¹kip or **kip-up**   *gymnastics*   A quick straightening of the body from an inverted pike position by thrusting the legs out and back and snapping the hips forward to drive the body in a desired direction. When performed as part of a backswing, the kip has the effect of increasing the momentum of the swing so that the gymnast can pull himself up over the apparatus. When done on a forward swing, the kip shoots the gymnast up above the point of support. The kip is a basic movement of gymnastics and is commonly employed as a means of moving from a hang to a support position. The kip can also be performed to snap forward from the floor to a standing position.

²kip To perform a kip; to move up by means of a kip.

kirbed point A point on a fishhook that is set to the left of the line of the shank when viewed from the top of the shank with the point up. — compare REVERSED POINT; see illustration at FISHHOOK

¹kiss *of a billiard ball* To touch another ball very lightly.

²kiss A carom in billiards.

kisser or **kisser button** or **kissing button** *archery* A bump or knot on the bowstring that is positioned to touch the archer's lips when the arrow is at full draw when the archer is using an anchor point under the chin.

kissoff *archery* An arrow that glances off another arrow already stuck in the target and sticks in a lower scoring part of the target or misses the target altogether.

kitchen *shuffleboard* The 10-off part of the scoring area which reduces the score by 10 points for each disk landing in it.

kite **1** *sailing* A spinnaker.
2 *soaring* **a** A hang glider. **b** A glider that remains attached to a ground towrope.

kite soaring see KITING

kite track A harness-racing track designed in the shape of a teardrop with a single large turn and 2 straightaways that come together at a point. Kite tracks were built during the 1890s because with only a single turn, they produced faster racing times than a conventional track and because the old sulkies had a hard time rounding the relatively small turns of the conventional tracks. They were not greatly popular, however, because for most of the race the horses were far from the grandstand, and these tracks gradually disappeared with the development of the modern bicycle-wheel sulky, which has no difficulty with the tight turns of a conventional half-mile track.

kiting or **kite soaring** The sport of hang gliding.

kletterschuh A rock-climbing boot that is lighter and more flexible than a regular climbing boot. — compare PA

klister *skiing* A sticky running wax used when skiing on crust and granular snow if temperatures are above freezing.

knapsack A small backpack.

knee boot see BOOT (*harness racing*)

knee drop *trampolining* A drop to the bed in which the performer lands simultaneously on the knees and shins and rebounds to the feet.

knee flexion and extension machine A piece of weight training equipment that consists of a table which has a pair of bars mounted at different heights on a pivoting frame at one end and that is used in leg exercises. Weights are fitted to the lower bar in the same manner as to a barbell. The user can sit on the edge hooking his legs under the lower bar and lift the weights by extending the legs, or he can lie prone hooking the heels behind the upper bar and pull the bar toward him by bending the knees.

kneeing The act of body-checking an opponent with the knee in ice hockey or box lacrosse which results in a major or minor penalty.

knee paddling *surfing* Paddling the surfboard while kneeling rather than while lying prone on the board.

knee scale *gymnastics* A position of balance in which the gymnast rests on the knee, shin, and instep of one leg with the upper body brought over parallel to the floor and the other leg extended to the rear usually in a graceful upward arch.

knife edge *karate* The edge of the hand oppo-

kip

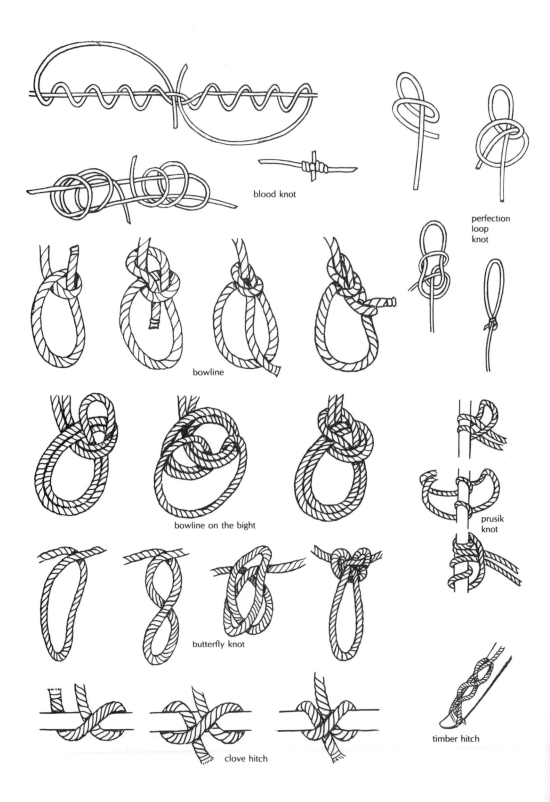

blood knot

perfection loop knot

bowline

prusik knot

bowline on the bight

butterfly knot

clove hitch

timber hitch

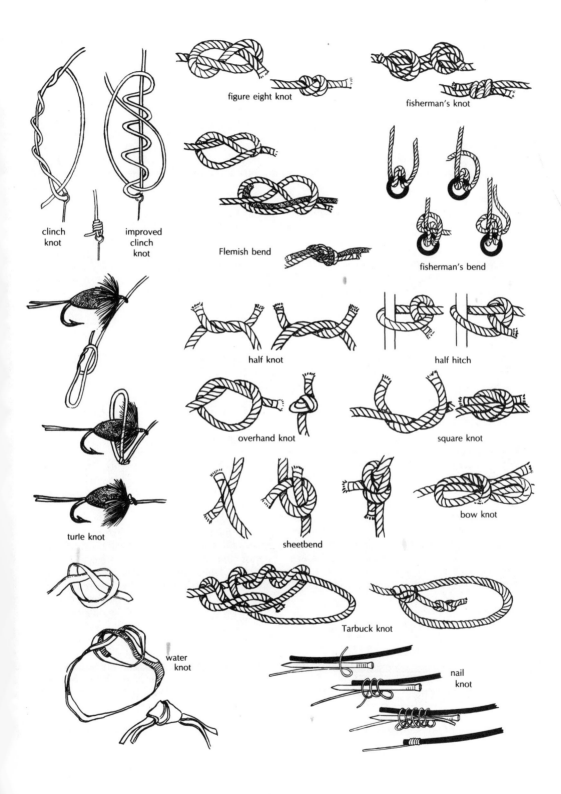

clinch knot

improved clinch knot

figure eight knot

fisherman's knot

Flemish bend

fisherman's bend

turle knot

half knot

half hitch

overhand knot

square knot

sheetbend

bow knot

water knot

Tarbuck knot

nail knot

site the thumb or the edge of the foot opposite the big toe used in striking a blow.

knife hand *karate* A blow made with the knife edge of a hand; chop.

knob **1** *baseball* A small rounded projection at the handle end of a bat.

2 *mountain climbing* A small rounded projection on a rock face that can be used as a handhold or foothold.

knockdown *boxing* The act or an instance of knocking an opponent down but not necessarily knocking him out. Normally during a knockdown the fight is momentarily halted until the boxer can regain his feet. In most cases the referee will count to 8 to give the boxer time to recover somewhat.

knock down *boxing* To strike an opponent with such force that he falls to the floor.

knock-on *rugby* The action or an instance of a ball's bouncing forward (toward the goal) off a player's hand or arm. Once the ball touches the ground from a knock-on, it may not be played again by the player or any member of his team until it has first been played by an opposing player. If the player or a teammate does play the ball illegally after a knock-on, play is stopped and a scrum is formed at the spot of the infraction. A ball knocked forward by a player who blocks an opponent's kick is not a knock-on; if the ball bounces off a player's arm or hand and falls straight down to the ground or is caught again before it reaches the ground, a knock-on has not occured and play is not stopped. A knock-on that in the judgment of the referee is intentional is penalized by a penalty kick. — compare RE-BOUND, THROW-FORWARD

knockout **1** *boxing* **a** The act of knocking an opponent out; the termination of a match when one boxer has been knocked unconscious or has been knocked down and is unable to rise and resume boxing within 10 seconds. **b** see TECHNICAL KNOCKOUT **c** A blow that results in a knockout.

2 Knockout competition.

knock out **1** or **knock out of the box** *baseball* To cause an opposing pitcher to be removed from the game because of a batting rally.

2 *boxing* To knock an opponent unconscious; to defeat an opponent by a knockout.

knockout competition **1** Competition (as in ski racing) in which individuals are paired for a round of competition (as in an elimination tournament) with the winner of the round advancing

to meet other winners and the loser being dropped from competition.

2 British term for an *elimination tournament.*

knot **1** One nautical mile (6,080 feet) per hour. **2** An interlacement of parts of one or more lines or ropes to form a loop or knob, to secure 2 or more lines or ropes together, or to secure a rope to an object (as a ring or spar). Some knots, especially those used to fasten a rope to an object temporarily, are called *hitches,* while others are called *bends.* Distinctions are not common today nor are they consistent. The use of *hitch* and *bend* is generally limited to the names of particular knots.

knuckleball or **knuckler** *baseball* A pitch thrown with little or no rotation that hops, dives, or swerves suddenly and usually unpredictably as it nears home plate. The ball is normally gripped with the fingernails or with the tips of the fingers. The knuckleball is a specialty pitch that is hard for the pitcher to master and harder for a batter to hit. In order to stop the ball, catchers often use abnormally large mitts. (also called *flutterball*)

knuckleballer *baseball* A pitcher whose chief pitch is the knuckleball.

knuckleballing Being a knuckleballer ⟨a *knuckleballing* right-hander⟩

knuckle curve *baseball* A curve thrown from a knuckleball grip.

knuckler see KNUCKLEBALL

¹KO *boxing* A knockout.

²KO *boxing* To knock out an opponent; kayo.

korfball A game of Dutch origin similar to basketball that is played outdoors on a rectangular field 90 meters (295 feet) long and 40 meters (131 feet) wide that is divided into 3 equal zones. At each end of the field is a horizontal goal which resembles a basketball goal without a backboard mounted to a goalpost 3.5 meters (11 feet 6 inches) high. Each team consists of 6 men and 6 women with 2 men and 2 women of each team restricted to each of the 3 playing zones. The ball, similar to a soccer ball, is passed between players by hand; players are not permitted to run with or dribble the ball, and they may not kick the ball or hit it with the fist. Play stops anytime a player allows the ball to hit the ground and is restarted with an unhindered throw by the opposing team. The object of the game is to shoot the ball into the basket for a score and to prevent the opposing team from scoring. Players may guard opponents and may attempt to block shots and passes, but they may not knock the ball out of an opponent's hands, hit, hold, or shove opponents, or guard an opponent of the opposite sex or one who is already guarded. Players are not permitted to shoot the ball while closely guarded. A player who is fouled is awarded a penalty throw at the goal from a spot 4 meters (13 feet) in front of the goal. This throw is analogous to basketball's free throw. The game is played in two 45-minute halves, and players change zones every time 2 goals have been scored.

kumite *karate* A sparring match.

kung fu A Chinese art of self-defense which resembles karate and from which karate developed. (also called *kempo*)

K valve *scuba diving* A simple valve without a reserve supply provision that is used on an air tank. — compare J VALVE

L

lace To hit a ball with notable power or force. ⟨started lobbing effectively and *lacing* shots down both sides — *New York Times*⟩

lacrosse A game played on a rectangular field between 2 teams of 10 players (12 in women's play) using a long-handled stick (*crosse*) having a triangular head with a rawhide-strung pocket by means of which the ball is picked up, caught, and thrown. The object of the game is to move the ball down the field by running with it in the crosse and by passing it and to throw or kick it past the opposing goalkeeper into the goal for a

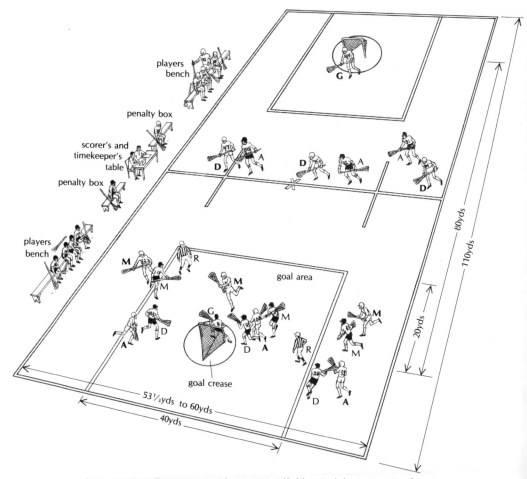

players bench

penalty box

scorer's and timekeeper's table

penalty box

players bench

G

D A   D   A   A   D

M   R

M   M   M

goal area

A   D   M

G   M

D A   R   M

goal crease

D   A

80yds

110yds

20yds

53⅓yds to 60yds

40yds

lacrosse: G goalkeeper; A attackman; M midfielder; D defenseman; R referee

score and to prevent the opponents from scoring. The goalkeeper is permitted to bat the ball down with his hands, but otherwise the hands may not be used. A ball on the ground may be kicked with the foot, but it may be picked up and passed only with the stick. Body-checking is permitted, and players may strike the opponent's stick in an attempt to dislodge the ball; striking an opponent with the stick or pushing, tripping, or holding an opponent is a foul penalized by suspension of the player for one to 3 minutes, during which time his team must play shorthanded. In women's play, a free position is awarded when a foul is committed. Each team consists of a goalkeeper, 3 defensive players (traditionally called point, cover point, and first defense), 3 midfielders (second defense, center, and second attack), and 3 attackmen (first attack, in home, and out home). A women's team is composed of a goalkeeper, point, cover point, and third man, 5 midfielders (a center, 2 attack wings, and 2 defense wings), and 3 attacking players (first home, second home, and third home). The players normally play either offensive or defensive positions with the midfielders helping out on both offense and defense. A team must have at least 3 attacking players and 4 defensive players, including the goalkeeper, in their respective halves of the field at all times, even when playing shorthanded. If a player steps out of an area leaving fewer than the required minimum, that player is offside and is charged with a technical foul, which means loss of the ball if his team has possession or a 30-second suspension for that player if the other team has possession. The ball is put in play at the beginning of a period and after each goal by a face-off in the middle of the field, and play is continuous except for goals, fouls, and time-outs. — see also FIELD, PERSONAL FOUL, TECHNICAL FOUL

ladder A flight of stairs on board a boat.

ladder tournament A tournament arrangement whereby participants are ranked in order of estimated strength with the best one at the top of the ranking and with any participant permitted to challenge either of the 2 participants immediately above him. If the challenger wins, he moves up to occupy the place held by the one he defeated. The defeated player takes the place in the ranking occupied by the player who challenged and defeated him. Often, when a challenger defeats another participant 2 rungs above, he will take the defeated player's place, and then both the defeated player and the player in between drop a rung. After several contests with the winners moving up and losers moving down, the rankings will reflect the true strengths of the participants. The ladder tournament is best suited to long-term play (as in tennis) as a method of maintaining a continuous ranking of participants.

lady paramount *archery* The woman who presides over a woman's tournament. In Britain the term is used of a lady who sponsors an archery tournament.

¹lag 1 *billiards* To shoot the cue ball from within the head string so that it rebounds from the foot cushion and returns to the head cushion. Lagging is a traditional method of determining the order of play. The player whose ball comes to rest nearest the head cushion has his choice of whether to break or to require his opponent to break.
2 *croquet* To hit the ball usually from the middle of the court to a boundary line as a method of determining the order of play.

²lag The act or action of lagging for opening shot (as in billiards or croquet).

lampwick see HANDGRIP

¹land The surface of the inside of a rifle barrel between consecutive grooves.

²land 1 *boxing* To reach the target with a punch. ⟨*landed* a hard right⟩
2 *fishing* To bring a hooked fish to shore or to a net.

landing 1 The act or manner of alighting or coming to rest on the ground or floor after a jump or after dismounting from an apparatus.
2 A boat dock.

landing hill *skiing* The hill on which competitors land in ski jumping competition.

landing net *fishing* A net with a short or long handle that is used to lift a hooked fish from the water after it has been played out and brought in close to the angler.

land sailing see SAND YACHTING

land sailor Someone who engages in sand yachting.

land yacht see SAND YACHT

land yachting see SAND YACHTING

lane 1 Any of several marked or unmarked parallel courses into which a racecourse is divided and within which individual competitors must stay during a race: **a** *swimming* A course at least 6 feet wide marked out by a buoyed rope or a string of buoyant objects (as foam or plastic cylinders). The bottom of the pool may have black lines which run along the middle of each

lane to aid the swimmers in staying on course.
b *track and field* A course usually 4 feet wide marked out on a running track in which a competitor is required to run for the duration of a hurdles or sprint race and for a specified distance in middle distance races which begin with a staggered start.

2 An imaginary lengthwise division of a playing area which serves to define the primary playing zone of a particular player (as a wing or center in ice hockey or soccer).

3 A free throw lane in basketball.

4 *bowling* A narrow wooden surface at the end of which pins are set up and along which the ball is rolled. The lane is 60 feet long from the foul line to the center of the head pin and is 41 inches wide. It is constructed of boards that are set on their side. The first 16 feet of the lane and the area directly under the pins is contructed of maple boards and the remainder is of pine. Along each side of the lane is a channel (*gutter*) which guides errant balls past the pins into the pit. In front of the foul line is a 16-foot-long approach.

langlauf Cross-country skiing.

langlaufer A cross-country skier.

lanyard *boating* A line attached to an object (as a pail or jackknife) to secure it.

¹lap 1 One complete circuit of a closed racecourse; the length of a swimming pool or course from one end to the other. ⟨had one *lap* to go⟩
2 The act or an instance of traversing a lap. ⟨had a very fast first *lap*⟩

²lap 1 To traverse a racecourse; to cover a lap. ⟨was able to *lap* fast enough to have been among the first three on the grid — Karl Ludvigsen, *Motor Trend*⟩
2 To overtake and thereby lead or increase one's lead over another competitor by a full circuit of a racecourse. ⟨at this point the two leaders had *lapped* the entire field — John Bentley, *Sports Illustrated*⟩

lap chart *motor racing* A chart listing the time taken by a competitor to complete each lap of a course (as during a race).

lap money *motor racing* Prize money paid to a competitor for each lap of a race in which he was in the lead.

lapped on *of a harness horse* Being within one length of another horse at a given point during a race.

Last Chance Rule *boating* A provision of the Rules of the Road which sanctions taking whatever action is necessary, including violation of the Rules, in order to avoid a collision between

boats. (also called *General Prudential Rule*)

last gallery see WINNING GALLERY

late closing race *horse racing* A race for which the horses are entered less than 6 weeks but more than 3 days before the race. — compare EARLY CLOSING RACE, OVERNIGHT

late cut *cricket* A stroke which drives the ball almost straight back behind the batsman just to the off side. — compare LEG GLANCE; SQUARE CUT

lateen rig *sailing* A rig consisting of a triangular sail bent on a yard which is set to the mast at an oblique angle.

late model *of a stock car* Manufactured during one of the last 3 production years.

late model sportsman *auto racing* A racing car built from a production car manufactured during a 10-year period before the past 3 years that is typically limited to a non-supercharged engine with a maximum of 430 cubic inches displacement. — compare MODIFIED

¹lateral 1 or **lateral pass** *football* A pass thrown in any direction other than toward the opponent's goal line — the direction in which the team is advancing. A lateral may be thrown either overhand or underhand, and there is no restriction as to the number that may be thrown in a single down or to the players that may catch a lateral. On a lateral pass, the ball remains in play if it is not caught. (also called *backward pass*) — compare FORWARD PASS
2 *jai alai* The side wall of the court.

²lateral *football* To make a lateral pass.

lateral moraine see MORAINE

lateral pass see LATERAL (*football*)

lateral raise *weight training* An exercise for developing the back and shoulder muscles in which the lifter raises dumbbells out to the side and up to shoulder height and lowers them while keeping the arms straight and while standing upright or bent forward at the waist.

lateral water hazard *golf* A water hazard that runs approximately parallel to the line of play. When a ball is hit into such a hazard and it is not possible to drop the ball behind the point of entry, a drop within 2 club lengths from the hazard, but not nearer the hole than the point of entry, is permitted with a one stroke penalty.

lat machine A piece of weight training equipment which normally consists of a bar connected by cables to adjustable weights through a series of overhead pulleys. The lifter normally kneels under the bar and pulls it down with both arms, thereby lifting the weights to exercise the latissimus dorsi muscles.

laugher A game that a team wins by a wide margin; an easy win.

lava tube *caving* A cave that is formed in molten lava when the surface of a flow cools and hardens but the inside continues to flow and leaves a hollow tube.

lawn bowling A sport in which 2 individuals or 2 teams of 2, 3, or 4 players roll bowls over a grass surface (*rink*) toward a smaller white ball (*jack*) with the object for a team to score points for each bowl it has placed nearer the jack at the end of a round of play (*end*) than the opposing team has. The jack is rolled to the opposite end of the rink to start play, and it becomes the target wherever it comes to rest. Opponents alternate bowling toward the jack until all bowls have been bowled. In singles games, the players bowl 4 bowls each. In team games, it is 4 each in doubles matches, 3 each in triples matches, and 2 each in fours matches. This constitutes an *end* for which the score is tallied. The next end is started in the opposite direction with the bowling of the jack. The bowls are not perfectly spherical but have a bias on one side which tends to make them curve when bowled. The jack is always the target, even if its position is changed by being struck by a bowl during play. Strategy, therefore, often involves knocking the jack away from the opponents' bowls or knocking their bowls away from the jack. Players are not permitted to directly interfere with another player or with the movement of any bowl. A match is normally played until one team scores a designated number of points or until a designated number of ends (as 21) have been played. (also called *bowling on the green, bowls*)

lawn croquet see CROQUET

lawn tennis see TENNIS

laxman A lacrosse player.

¹**layback** *mountain climbing* To walk up a wall alongside a vertical crack by placing the feet flat against the wall and pushing in one direction while pulling in the opposite direction on the back of the crack with the hands.

²**layback** or **lie-back** The act or an instance of laybacking; the technique employed in laybacking.

lay-back spin *skating* A spin performed on one foot in which the skater leans back and often raises the arms and the free leg. (also called *headback spin*)

lay down *baseball* To bunt the ball.

lay-in see LAY-UP

lay line *yacht racing* An imaginary line to a

laybacking

windward mark along which a boat may sail to reach the mark without having to tack again.

layout **1** A body position (as in diving or gymnastics) in which the legs are together and straight, the back is arched, and the arms are held up and back.
2 *diving* A forward or backward dive in a layout position. — see illustration at BACKWARD DIVE
3 *track and field* The part of the high jump between the takeoff and the landing during which the competitor is clearing the crossbar with his body relatively horizontal.

layover *skating* A spin performed in a position somewhat resembling a camel position but with the body turned sideways so that the shoulder line and hip line are perpendicular to the skating surface.

lay to *boating* To bring a boat into the wind and hold it stationary.

lay-up *basketball* A shot made from near the basket at the top of a jump usually by playing the ball off the backboard. (also called *lay-in*)

lay up *golf* To hit a shot (as a fairway shot or approach shot) so that it stops short of a normal distance in order to avoid the risk of the ball's going into a hazard.

leach see LEECH

¹**lead** **1 a** To be first or in front. ⟨*lead* the league in home runs⟩ **b** To have a margin over one's opponent. ⟨*led* by 12 at the half⟩
2 a To aim in front of a moving target in order to ensure that the missile and target arrive at a

lead

lay-up

given point at the same time. **b** To pass a ball or puck just ahead of a moving teammate.

3 a *of a boxer* To begin a series of blows with a specific hand or a specific punch. 〈*led* with a short jab to the head〉 **b** *of a horse* To begin a particular gait on a specific foot. **c** *of a track and field athlete* To jump or hurdle an obstacle with a specific leg in front. 〈most other world-class quarter-mile hurdlers *lead* with their left legs — Kenny Moore, *Sports Illustrated*〉

²lead 1 A margin or measure of advantage; a position in front.

2 The amount by which a shooter leads a moving target.

3 a *boxing* The punch that begins a series of punches. **b** *equitation* The foot on which a horse begins a gait.

4 The player who plays first for his team in curling or lawn bowling.

5 *baseball* A position taken by a base runner off a base toward the next base. The runner normally stays just close enough to the base to be able to return quickly if the other team attempts to pick him off.

6 *caving* A passage that leads to another part of a cave.

leader 1 A competitor who is ahead of the other competitors at a given point in a contest. The leader may be a competitor in front in a race or a team in the lead in league standings.

2 or **lead dog** *dogsled racing* The dog that is harnessed at the front of the team.

3 *fishing* A length of line or wire between the end of the main fishing line and the hook or lure. The leader serves as a nearly invisible link (as in fly fishing) or as a strong line to resist the sharp teeth of some game fish. In fly fishing, the leader is normally monofilament from 7 to 12 feet long. Dry fly leaders are usually tapered to a very small tippet — the part where the fly is tied — to allow the cast to straighten properly and to allow the fly to settle gently on the water. Bait-casting leaders are normally short lengths of wire or stout monofilament that cannot be chewed through.

4 *mountain climbing* The most experienced climber in a party of climbers who normally goes up a pitch first so that he can find the best route and provide a belay from above for the rest of the climbers. The leader is also able to direct the following climbers to the best handholds and footholds from his position above.

lead leg *track and field* The leg lifted first in attempting to clear a hurdle or make a jump (as a high jump or long jump).

leadoff 1 *baseball* Of, being, or made by the first batter in the lineup or in an inning. 〈*leadoff* batter〉 〈*leadoff* single〉

2 *track and field* Of, relating to, or running the first leg of a relay race.

lead off *baseball* To bat first for a team in the lineup or in an inning.

lead official or **leading official** *basketball* The official who moves down the court ahead of the players and who stations himself near the basket just off the court. — compare TRIAL OFFICIAL

lead pass A pass that leads a teammate.

lead pony *horse racing* A horse that escorts a thoroughbred during the post parade.

lead sled *soaring* A sailplane that is comparatively heavy and designed principally for distance flight and that, because of its weight, will remain aloft only with strong lift condition. — compare FLOATER

lead through *of mountain climbers* To alternate in leading successive pitches. This practice, normally followed only by experienced climbers, calls for one climber to lead on one pitch and then belay the second climber, who continues past the first climber to lead the next pitch.

league An association of teams that play against each other in a regular schedule during a season which normally ends in a championship play-off. The league usually is the highest unit of organization and is often divided into conferences or divisions.

leaguer A member of a league. 〈a major-*leaguer*〉

lean-to A usually temporary shelter that consists of a flat sloping roof that is open on three sides. The roof may be made of thatched boughs or of a tarpaulin attached at the upper end to a vertical support or tree limb and at the bottom to the ground. Some national and state parks have permanent lean-tos for use by hikers and campers. These are frame or timber structures that are open on one side and have a flat sloping roof.

leap A spring in skating or gymnastics in which the performer leaves the surface entirely and which involves taking off on one foot and landing on the other. In skating, a leap is sometimes distinguished from a jump in that a leap does not involve a turn.

leaper A basketball player noted for his jumping ability.

leathers *motorcycle racing* Leather clothing required for wear in road racing for protection in the event of a fall.

¹leave *bowling* The pins left standing after the first delivery of a frame.

²leave *of a baseball team* To have a usually specified number of base runners on base when an inning ends. ⟨scored 2 runs on 3 hits and *left* 2 men on⟩

ledger A British term for a lead sinker that has a hole in one end through which the line passes and that is used to hold the baited line near the bottom. The line passes freely through the hole in the sinker so that when a fish takes the bait it will not immediately feel the weight of the sinker.

ledgering A British method of fishing which involves using a ledger on a rig that resembles a fishfinder.

lee The side of a boat away from the wind.

leeboard Either of a pair of boards mounted on opposite sides of a flat-bottom boat with the one on the lee side lowered into the water when the boat is heeling to retard sideways movement in the manner of a centerboard.

leech or **leach** The after edge of a fore-and-aft sail. — see illustration at SAILBOAT

leeward On the side opposite the wind; facing the direction in which the wind is blowing. — compare WEATHER, WINDWARD

leeway The leeward drift or off-course lateral movement of a boat caused by wind or tide.

left 1 A punch delivered with the left hand; ability to punch with the left hand.
2 Short for *left field*.

left center field *baseball* The area of the outfield to the left of dead center field; the area that is between center field and left field.

left field *baseball* **1** The left side of the outfield as viewed from home plate; the part of the outfield past third base.
2 The player position for covering left field.

left fielder *baseball* The player who plays left field.

left-handed or **left-hand 1** With the left hand. ⟨threw the ball *left-handed*⟩
2 Swinging from left to right in striking a ball with a bat or club held in both hands (as in baseball or golf). ⟨a *left-handed* batter⟩

left-hander 1 A player who is left-handed and especially one who throws left-handed as distinguished from batting left-handed.
2 A turn to the left in a road course.

left slide *surfing* Movement on a wave to the left when facing toward shore.

leg 1 A portion of a contest or a series; the portion of a course or the total distance of a relay race that each member of a relay team must cover.
2 *cricket* **a** The leg side of the field. **b** Any of several fielding positions on the leg side. — see FINE LEG, SHORT LEG, SQUARE LEG
3 *sailing* The course or distance sailed by a boat on a single tack. ⟨a windward *leg*⟩
4 A division of a match in skittles consisting of 3 turns for each player after which the scores are tallied.

legal Permitted by the rules of a game or competition.

leg-before *of a cricket batsman* Out leg before wicket.

leg before wicket Illegal interference by the batsman with a bowled ball that, in the judgment of the umpire, would have hit the wicket had it not been deflected by some part of the batsman's body. The batsman is out, leg before wicket. This is a judgment call, for the batsman is only out if he is struck by a bowled ball that has bounced between the wickets or on the off side or that has been bowled full pitch and would have struck the wicket. The batsman is not compensated when hit by a thrown ball as in baseball because he is supposed to defend his wicket with the bat to keep a bowled ball from knocking it down.

leg break *cricket* Movement of a bowled ball that on hitting the ground bounces from the leg side toward or across the wicket away from the batsman. — compare OFF BREAK

leg bye *cricket* A run that is scored when the ball is deflected off any part of the batsman's body except his hands allowing the batsmen to exchange places. A run cannot be scored if the batsman deliberately kicks the ball away or if he is out leg before wicket. — compare BYE, WIDE

leg circle *gymnastics* A horizontal swing of the legs around the hand support (as on a pommel horse). — see CIRCLE

leg glance *cricket* A stroke that drives the ball almost straight back behind the batsman just to the leg side. (also called *glide*) — compare LATE CUT

leg hit **1** *baseball* A ground ball that is beat out for a single.
2 *cricket* A ball hit to the leg side.

leg press *weight training* An exercise for the legs which consists of pushing up with the legs against weights while lying on the back.

leg press machine A piece of weight training equipment which consists of a vertical frame that serves as a guide for a horizontal weight support. The lifter lies on his back between the upright members of the frame and pushes up with his feet against the support, which carries the weights.

leg side *cricket* The side of the field, divided lengthwise by an imaginary line through both wickets, on which the batsman is standing when in his normal batting position, including all the area in an arc from side to side extending around behind the batsman. (also called *on side*) — compare OFF SIDE

leg slip *cricket* **1** A fielding position just behind and to the leg side of the wicketkeeper comparable to the slip position on the off side.
2 A player playing a leg slip position.

leg spin *cricket* Spin which causes a ball to swerve from off to leg but on bouncing to move from leg to off.

leg spinner *cricket* **1** A bowled ball that has leg spin.
2 A bowler who employs leg spin.

leg theory *cricket* An offensive strategy which consists of concentrating fieldsmen on the leg side and bowling the ball at the stump nearest the leg side in an attempt to induce the batsman to make leg hits.

leg trap A trap of a bouncing ball (as in soccer) made by stopping the ball with the leg and letting the leg give slightly on contact to absorb the impact so that the ball falls softly to the ground where it can be played.

LeMans start A starting procedure formerly used at the 24-hour automobile endurance race at LeMans, France, in which the race cars are parked side by side along one edge of the course facing the center of the track and the drivers are lined up on the other edge across from their cars. The drivers dash across the track on the starting signal, climb into their cars, start them, and drive off. The LeMans start was widely copied in auto racing, but LeMans eventually abandoned the start in the interest of safety, and since then it has virtually disappeared from auto racing, though it may still be found in motorcycle racing.

lemon *billiards* **1** To win a game in an amateurish manner.
2 To deliberately lose a game.

length **1** *horse racing* The approximate length of a horse's body used to express a margin of victory or advantage in a race. ⟨won by 4 *lengths*⟩ — compare HEAD, NECK, NOSE
2 *squash racquets* A shot that dies at the back wall.

lepper A horse that competes in steeplechase events; jumper.

lever

let A shot or rally in a racket game (as badminton, squash racquets, or tennis) that does not count and that is replayed. In tennis a let is usually called if a serve is made before the receiver is ready or if the serve strikes the net before landing in the service court. In squash, a let is called when one player accidentally interferes with another or when a player does not stroke the ball because he might hit his opponent. In badminton a let is normally called whenever there is outside interference with play. A let may be called if the shuttlecock gets caught in the net after passing over it or if a server or receiver who is in the wrong court wins the rally.

let point *squash racquets* A point awarded to a player who has been interferred with by an opponent.

¹letter An initial or monogram of a school or college awarded to a student for participation in athletics.

²letter To earn a school or college letter in a sport. ⟨went on to the University of Illinois where he *lettered* in football, basketball and baseball — Al Cummings, *Coach & Athlete*⟩

letterman A player on a school or college team who has earned a letter in a sport. ⟨the basketball team will have 9 returning *lettermen*⟩

letter of intent A letter signed by a schoolboy athlete stating his intention to attend a particular college on athletic scholarship that is recognized by some schools or conferences as sufficient for them to refrain from further recruiting of the player.

letup or **letup ball** or **letup pitch** see CHANGE-UP (*baseball*)

level-wind A device for winding fishing line evenly on a bait casting reel that consists of a small loop that moves back and forth across the face of the reel as the handle is turned.

lever *gymnastics* A position in a hang on the rings in which the body is held straight and parallel to the floor. If the gymnast is facing the point of support, he is in a front lever; if away from the point of support, he is in a back lever. — compare PLANCHE

lever action see ACTION (*firearms*)

lie **1** *fishing* A spot in a stream habitually frequented by fish.
2 *golf* **a** The angle at which the shaft is fitted to the head of the club. — compare LOFT **b** The position in which the ball rests after a stroke. ⟨an unplayable *lie*⟩
3 *ice hockey* The angle between the shaft and the blade of the stick usually expressed as a number between 3 (large angle) and 10 (nearly perpendicular).

lie-back see LAYBACK

liement see BIND

life buoy A ring-shaped life preserver.

¹lifeguard An expert swimmer employed (as at beaches and pools) to safeguard other swimmers.

²lifeguard To serve as a lifeguard.

life jacket or **life vest** A life preserver in the form of a sleeveless jacket or a collar which extends down the chest. A life jacket used by boaters is typically a jacket with buoyant material (as kapok or foam) fitted in the front and back to support the individual with his head out of the water. Scuba divers usually wear an inflatable vest or collar that is normally deflated so as not to interfere with the diving but that can be inflated by the diver's breath or instantly by a carbon dioxide cartridge to support the diver faceup in the water. — see illustration at SCUBA DIVER

life line **1 a** A line attached to a life buoy at one end and to the boat at the other for use in pulling a person to safety. **b** A line strung along the gunwale of a boat to serve as a handrail.
2 British term for the rope used in a dynamic belay. — see BELAY

life lining British term for the action of using a dynamic belay. — see BELAY

life preserver A device that is designed to keep a person from drowning by buoying him up in the water. Life preservers may be in the form of life jackets or buoyant boat cushions. They are typically constructed of fiberglass, foam, cork, or kapok in a waterproof covering but may be inflatable.

lifetime Career. ⟨today there does not seem to be a player in baseball who is going to wind up a *lifetime* .333 hitter — Ted Williams⟩

life vest see LIFE JACKET

lift **1** *bowling* The act of snapping the fingers up quickly as the ball is released to impart a particular roll or spin to the delivery.
2 *skating* The act or an instance of the man lifting the woman off the surface in pairs competition.
3 *soaring* The means by which a sailplane gains altitude while soaring. Though the sailplane can take advantage of the airstream over its elevators for a certain amount of lift, the most common source of lift is a thermal — a rising mass of warm air.
4 *weight lifting* The action or an instance of lifting a weight especially in competition; a particular style of lifting a weight. Competitive lifts normally involve moving a barbell from the floor to a position overhead with the arm straight and elbows locked. — see CLEAN AND JERK, SNATCH

lifter An individual who lifts weights especially in competition; weight lifter.

lifting *volleyball* A foul which results when a player permits the ball to rest momentarily on his hands as they move upward.

lift pass *ice hockey* A long flip pass.

light **1** *curling* A stone delivered with less weight than the skip wanted.

light and heavy system

2 *motor racing* One of a number of colored lights used at some race courses in place of flags to notify drivers of dangerous situations. Yellow lights are normally used for caution (as when there has been an accident on the course) and usually require drivers to reduce speed to a preestablished level. A red light may be used to signal that the race has been stopped; a green light normally means the track is clear for racing. — see also FLAG

light and heavy system *weight training* A method of training which consists of increasing the amount of weight with successive sets and often decreasing the number of repetitions in each set. — compare HEAVY AND LIGHT SYSTEM

light buoy A buoy with a steady or flashing light.

light flyweight A boxer who competes in the light flyweight division. — see DIVISION

light heavyweight A boxer or weight lifter who competes in the light heavyweight division. — see DIVISION

light hit *bowling* A hit just out of the pocket which usually fails to get a strike.

light middleweight A boxer who competes in the light middleweight division. — see DIVISION

lightweight A competitor in a group or division for lighter and weaker competitors; a boxer or weight lifter who competes in the lightweight division. — see DIVISION

light welterweight A boxer who competes in the light welterweight division. — see DIVISION

like as we lie *of golf competitors* Having played the hole or round in the same number of strokes.

lily *bowling* A split that leaves the 5, 7, and 10 pins standing. — see illustration of pin arrangement at BOWLING

limb *archery* Either end of the bow from the handle to the tip.

limit **1** The maximum number of fish, birds, or game animals a hunter or fisherman is permitted by law to take during a given period (as a day or the season).
2 The duration of a contest; distance.

¹line **1 a** A narrow typically white marking (normally 1½ to 2 inches wide) on a field or court to indicate the boundaries of the playing area and the lanes and running, jumping, or throwing areas on a field. Boundary lines for playing areas may be wholly inbounds (as in tennis, badminton, table tennis, and volleyball) or wholly out of bounds (as in basketball and football). **b** The boundary between 2 different scoring areas on a target. Hits on the line normally are scored for the higher scoring area.

2 Information on how to play a particular opponent gained from experience or from scouting reports.
3 Betting odds set by bookmakers and usually used in betting other than through pari-mutuel systems. — compare MORNING LINE
4 The scent of the quarry (as a fox) that is followed by hounds.
5 *auto racing* The route around a racecourse taken by a driver; the most efficient route around a course during a race.
6 *boating* Any rope used in rigging, in securing the boat or equipment, or manipulating sails. — see also HALYARD, SHEET; SHROUD, STAY
7 *bowling* A game consisting of 10 frames; string.
8 *fishing* A part of fishing tackle which consists of a braided string or monofilament by which the bait, fly, or lure may be played out or cast and drawn in. The term *line* may also include an attached leader, baited hook, sinker, and float. The type of line used varies with the method of fishing. Heavy fly line is normally used only in fly fishing. A braided line is used in trolling and bait casting, while spinning normally requires monofilament line.
9 *football* **a** The line of scrimmage. **b** The offensive players or the defensive players who line up on the line of scrimmage. The offensive line must include at least 7 players and normally includes a center flanked by 2 guards, 2 tackles and 2 ends. The defensive line commonly contains 4 or 5 players including 2 defensive tackles and 2 defensive ends and, on a 5-man line, a middle guard. **c** The positions occupied by the players on the line of scrimmage.
10 *golf* The direction in which a player intends to send his ball in playing toward a hole.
11 *skiing* The route down a course taken by a skier in downhill or slalom competition.
12 Short for *forward line, free throw line, line of attack, shooting line.*
— **in line** *of a fencing sword* Threatening the target in one of the lines of attack.

²line *baseball* To hit a line drive. ⟨*lined* a single to left field⟩

linebacker *football* **1** A defensive player who normally lines up a yard or 2 behind the defensive line. On running plays linebackers are expected to fill holes in the line created by blockers and stop the ballcarrier. On pass plays they usually have to defend against short passes especially by covering running backs when they are sent out on pass routes. (also called *backer-up*)

2 The position played by a linebacker.

linebacking *football* The action or skill of playing linebacker; the quality of play of linebackers.

line ball A shot that lands on a line in some court games. A line ball is good in tennis and badminton but not good in squash and handball.

line call A call (as by a linesman in tennis) as to whether a hit ball is inbounds or out of bounds.

line drive *baseball* A ball hit in a nearly straight line not far off the ground.

line hand *fishing* The hand that manipulates the line in fly fishing. — compare ROD HAND

line haul *fishing* A pull of the line with the line hand at the beginning of a forward or back cast in fly casting in order to increase line speed to gain more distance on the cast.

line judge A football official who takes a position at the sideline on the line of scrimmage opposite the head linesman and who is primarily responsible for watching for offside and encroachment, checking to see that the quarterback does not cross the line of scrimmage before throwing a pass, and watching for lateral passes. In addition, the line judge serves as the game's official timekeeper.

lineman 1 *football* Any of the offensive or defensive players who play on the line. — see LINE **2** A forward in soccer.

linemate *ice hockey* A forward who plays on the same line with another player.

line of attack *fencing* The part of a fencer's torso toward which an attack is directed. The torso is conceived of as divided into 4 areas by a vertical line and a horizontal line. Those areas above the normal position of the sword hand are high lines and those below are low lines. To the side leading to the front of the target are the inside lines and on the side leading toward the back are the outside lines.

line of engagement *fencing* The position of the sword with respect to a particular line of attack during engagement.

line of scrimmage *football* **1** An imaginary line parallel to the goal lines and tangent to the most forward point of the ball when it is on the ground in position to be put in play at the beginning of each down. The line is established as the point to which the ball was carried on the last play and is the point used in determining whether or not a team has achieved a first down.
2 Either of 2 imaginary lines that are parallel to the goal lines and tangent to each end of the football and that represent the restraining lines for members of the opposing teams when they line up over the ball. The area between the lines (the length of the ball) is the neutral zone. No player other than the center is permitted to have any part of his body inside this imaginary zone when the ball is snapped. Seven offensive players are required to be on the offensive line of scrimmage — that is with their shoulders parallel to and their heads within 12 inches of the near line at the moment the ball is put in play. There is no restriction on the number of players that may be on the defensive line, but no defensive player may have any part of his body beyond his own line of scrimmage. (also called *scrimmage line*)

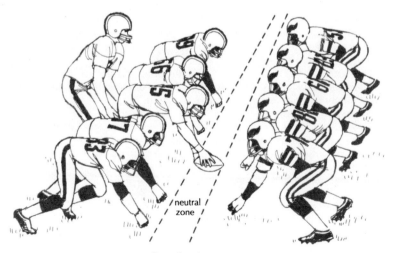

line of scrimmage

line-out

line-out *rugby* A method of putting the ball in play after it has been carried or knocked over the touchline. The forwards of both teams form 2 lines side by side parallel to the goal line and facing the touchline, and a player of the team not responsible for the ball's going out of bounds stands out of bounds and tosses the ball over the heads of the forwards but between the 2 lines where the players jump to try to gain possession of the ball.

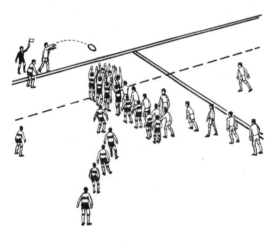

line-out

line out *baseball* To hit a line drive that is caught for an out.

liner A line drive in baseball.

line score **1** A brief printed summary of a baseball game giving the runs, hits, and errors made by each team and sometimes also the batteries for each team and the players hitting home runs. — compare BOX SCORE

2 A brief printed summary of a cricket match giving the total number of runs scored by each team and the number of batsmen for each who made out and sometimes listing the players scoring the most runs for their respective teams.

linesman **1** An official who assists the referee or umpire in certain court and net games (as badminton, tennis, and volleyball) by indicating when a shot is out of bounds.

2 An official (as in soccer) who normally works along each sideline or touchline to assist the referee by indicating when the ball or a player with the ball is out of bounds.

3 *football* An official on the sidelines who assists the referee by marking the progress of the ball, watching for offside and encroachment, and noting when and where the ball goes out of bounds. In a squad of 6 officials the linesman is replaced by a head linesman on one side of the field and a line judge on the other side.

4 *ice hockey* Either of 2 officials who normally work near the sides of the rink and whose duties include calling icing and offside, conducting face-offs, and notifying the referee of fouls.

lineswoman A woman who serves as a linesman (as in tennis).

lineup The players taking part in a game (as baseball or basketball) at a given moment; a list of the players in the lineup.

line-up A pocket billiards game played according to the rules of 14.1 continuous but with all balls scored by a player in an inning being returned to the table and placed in a line extending back from the foot spot. A player must call both the ball and the pocket; he scores one point for each ball legally pocketed. The game is set at an agreed-on number of points.

line up To get into or form in a line; to take one's position in a formation (as in football).

line umpire *Canadian football* An official who is responsible for supervising the play at the line of scrimmage.

linkman A player (as a halfback in soccer) whose position or duties make him a link between primarily offensive and primarily defensive players; one of usually 3 soccer players in modern lineups who play between the strikers and the defenders.

links A golf course. The name comes from the Scottish word for the undulating land along the sea coast on which early courses were often built.

linksman A golfer.

lip *of a golf putt* To hit the rim of the cup and fail to drop.

lipping *archery* A piece of wood set in a bow where a flaw has been cut out.

lip tattooing *horse racing* The practice of tattooing the inside of a racehorse's lip as a means of positive identification.

¹list *of a boat* To incline to one side because of an imbalance in the load. — compare HEEL

²list The degree of inclination of a boat due to imbalance in the load.

little brother *skeet* The second bird of a double target.

longbow

Little Brown Jug A 1-mile stakes race for 3-year-old pacers held annually since 1946 that is the principal American race for pacers and that is one of the races in the pacing Triple Crown. The race is named for Little Brown Jug, a champion pacer from 1881 to 1883. — see also CANE PACE, MESSENGER STAKES

Little League A federally-chartered organization of baseball leagues in individual towns and cities for youths aged 8–12 playing on a diamond two-thirds the size of a standard field.

Little League elbow Injury accompanied by acute pain in the elbow of the pitching arm of a youngster caused by the stress on growing tissues of repeated attempts to throw a baseball hard.

Little League shoulder Injury and pain in the shoulder of the pitching arm of a youngster that is similar to Little League elbow.

livebag A net in which freshly-caught fish may be kept alive underwater until they are to be killed or released.

live ball A ball that is in play and that is under the control of a player or team or that is loose and subject to being recovered or controlled by either side.

live lining A method of fishing especially in streams in which a baited line is allowed to drift with the current, often with no sinker attached.

¹load A charge for a firearm; a cartridge or shell.

²load **1** To insert ammunition into a firearm.
2 *baseball* To place base runners on every base at one time; to cause base runners to occupy every base at one time. ⟨*loaded* the bases with a single and 2 walks⟩ ⟨2 outs and the bases *loaded*⟩ ⟨a walk that *loaded* the bases⟩

¹lob **1** A shot in court games (as handball or squash racquets) hit high off the front wall so as to rebound to a far corner.
2 A stroke (as in tennis or badminton) that lifts the ball over the opponent's head in a high arc so that it comes down near the back of the court.
3 A soft throw (as in baseball).
4 *soccer* A soft high-arching kick.
5 *table tennis* A stroke that sends the ball in a soft high arc and that is usually made at a considerable distance from the table to give a player time to return to position (as after a smash).

²lob **1** To hit, kick, or throw a ball in a soft high arc; to make a lob.
2 To use lobs against an opponent (as in tennis). ⟨If I can't pass her, I can sure *lob* her — Bobby Riggs⟩

lobe *skating* A circle of a school figure.

lob serve A lob hit underhand on the serve (as in badminton, handball, or squash).

lock **1** *wrestling* A hold that prevents any movement of the part of the body that is being held. ⟨arm *lock*⟩ ⟨head *lock*⟩
2 see LOCK FORWARD

locked-in *surfing* Unable to pull out of a wave because it is too steep.

locker room A dressing room adjoining a sports facility that has lockers for use by the players or participants for storing their street clothes while engaged in a sport.

lock forward or **lock** *rugby* Either of 2 second row forwards who are behind and to either side of the hooker.

¹loft **1** *golf* The angle of the face of a club away from vertical. The greater the loft, the higher and shorter the flight of the ball. — compare LIE
2 A stroke that lofts a ball; the height at which a ball is lofted.

²loft **1** To hit or throw a ball in a high arc. ⟨*lofted* a towering drive into the left-field seats — Murray Chass, *New York Times*⟩
2 *bowling* To release a ball on the upswing thereby allowing it to fly through the air and hit hard on the alley.

lofting iron *golf* An old name for a number 8 iron.

log jam *surfing* A tangle of bodies and surfboards resulting from a collision or a mass wipeout. (also called *lumber pile*)

logrolling see BIRLING

lollipop A ball (as a baseball pitch or a tennis serve) that is relatively easy to hit.

long **1** *of a hit ball* **a** Traveling a long distance. ⟨a *long* home run⟩ **b** Going beyond a service court or an end line (as in tennis). ⟨her first serve was *long*⟩
2 *of betting odds* Marked by a large difference in the amount wagered on each side.

long ball **1** *baseball* A batted ball that travels to the back of the outfield; a home run. ⟨a fine fielder and a redoubtable *long ball* hitter — *Sporting News*⟩
2 *box lacrosse* A long shot at the goal.
3 *soccer* A long pass.

longbow A straight bow of the type prominent in medieval England as distinguished from a flat bow or recurved bow. The term *longbow* is sometimes used of straight bows, recurved bows, and flat bows in distinction from crossbows.

longbowman Someone who uses a longbow.

long corner see CORNER (*field hockey*)

long count 1 *baseball* A count in which there are 3 balls and one or 2 strikes on the batter.

2 *boxing* A count over a boxer who is down that is believed to be excessively slow or to last for more than 10 seconds.

long course *swimming* A pool or open course at least 50 yards long.

long distance race see DISTANCE RACE

long gainer *football* A play in which a team makes a long gain. ⟨we were cutting off the *long gainers,* but they were taking the short stuff — Tom Landry⟩

long game *golf* The aspect of play in which placement of long shots (as drives) is of primary importance.

long hop *cricket* A bowled ball that bounces unusually far away from the batsman.

long horse see VAULTING HORSE

Long International *archery* 1 A target round in men's competition in which each competitor shoots 72 arrows at a distance of 90 meters, 48 at 70 meters, and 24 at 50 meters in ends of 3 arrows each.

2 A target round in women's competition in which each competitor shoots 60 arrows at a distance of 70 meters, 48 at 60 meters, and 36 at 50 meters in ends of 3 arrows each.

long iron *golf* An iron with little loft (as a number 1, 2, or 3) that is used for long-distance shots.

long-jump To attain a specific distance in the long jump. ⟨he *long-jumped* 26 feet⟩

long jump *track and field* A field event in which the contestant leaps for distance from a running start. A contestant must jump from behind a scratch line in order to have his attempt qualify as a legal jump. Three jumps are allowed in the finals of a meet, and in a large meet a prior set of 3 jumps is used in a preliminary trial to determine the finalists. The best effort in either the preliminary trial or the finals is credited to the jumper in determining final standings. (also called *broad jump*) — see also TIE

long jumper An athlete who competes in the long jump.

long leg *cricket* 1 A fielding position deep on the leg side behind the striker's wicket.

2 A fielder playing a long leg position.

long line *handball* A line on the floor of a 1-wall court that is 34 feet from and parallel to the wall and that serves as the rear boundary of the court.

long man see LONG RELIEVER

long off *cricket* 1 A fielding position in front of and far distant from the batsman and beyond the far wicket on the off side.

2 The fieldsman who plays the long off position.

long on *cricket* 1 A fielding position in front of and far distant from the batsman and beyond the far wicket on the leg side.

2 The fieldsman who plays the long on position.

long reliever or **long relief man** or **long relief** or **long man** *baseball* A relief pitcher who is brought into a game early and who is expected to pitch more than half the game.

long service line *badminton* A line at each end of a doubles court parallel to and 2½ feet in front of the boundary line which marks the rear limit of the doubles service court.

long shot A competitor deemed to have little chance of winning and especially one with long odds.

long stop *cricket* 1 A fielding position directly behind the wicketkeeper.

2 A fieldsman playing a long stop position.

long string *billiards* An imaginary line from the foot spot to the middle of the foot rail along which balls are spotted in pocket billiard games when the foot spot is occupied.

look at *baseball* To take a pitch; to let a pitch go by without swinging. ⟨*looked at* a called third strike⟩

look for *baseball* To anticipate or hope for a particular pitch or for a base on balls. ⟨was *looking for* a curve⟩ ⟨*looking for* a walk⟩

look-in *football* An offensive pass play in which the quarterback throws a quick pass to a receiver running diagonally across the field.

looking *of a baseball batter* Letting a pitch go by for a called strike and especially a called third strike. — used in the phrase *caught looking*

look off *of a football quarterback* To fool a defender by looking to one side of the field before throwing a pass to the other side.

look the runner back *of a baseball fielder* To check a base runner on second or third base to ensure he will not attempt to advance before throwing the ball to first base for a putout on a routine ground ball.

loom *rowing* The middle portion of an oar from the handle to the blade.

¹loop 1 A closed curve formed in a rope.

2 A sports league or conference.

3 *gymnastics* A flank circle performed on one end of a pommel horse.

4 *skating* **a** A school figure that begins with a

semicircle which leads into a quick rotation in the same direction followed immediately by another semicircle to complete a circle performed on a single edge. **b** A school figure that consists of a figure eight made by 2 consecutive loops.

²loop **1** To hit or drive a ball in a high arc. ⟨*looped* a single to right field⟩

2 *of a defensive lineman in football* To move around another lineman and rush in from a different position on the line in order to frustrate offensive blocking assignments.

loop drive *table tennis* A shot made with a lot of topspin and just enough forward movement to enable it to clear the net so that the ball will rebound very low and when hitting the opponent's paddle will bounce straight up.

looper **1** *football* A short pass thrown in a relatively high arc.

2 *surfing* A large wave that breaks over a surfer putting him in the curl.

loop jump *skating* A full-turn jump in which the skater jumps and lands on the same edge.

loop step *skating* A jump from the outer backward edge of one skate with a half turn in the air and a return to the inner forward edge of the same skate, after a momentary step by the opposite skate on the landing.

¹loose **1** *of a ball or puck* In play but not in possession or under the control of any one team. A shot that rebounds from a backboard or a goalkeeper's stick or pads is loose. A fumble or muff in football results in a loose ball. A ball or puck moving between teammates on a pass is not a loose ball, however, because it remains in continuous possession of one team. If a pass is dropped or fumbled, the ball or puck becomes loose except in the case of an incomplete forward pass in football.

2 *of a return in net or court games* Easily reached by the opponent.

3 *of an offensive player* Not closely guarded or marked.

²loose *archery* To release the bowstring at the anchor point and propel the arrow.

³loose *archery* The act of releasing the bowstring and propelling the arrow.

loose ball foul *basketball* A personal foul in professional play committed by a player attempting to gain possession of a loose ball. The loose ball foul is charged as a team foul, and the ball is put in play with a throw-in by an opposing player. During a bonus situation, the fouled player is awarded 2 free throws.

loose forward *rugby* The lone forward on the back row of a scrum.

loose head *rugby* The front row forward who is nearest the referee in a scrum. The loose head must always be a player of the attacking team, the team not putting the ball into the scrum.

loose impediment *golf* Any natural object (as a loose stone, twig, leaf, or insect) on the course that is not fixed or growing in place and that may be removed from around the ball or from the intended line of play of the ball so long as the ball is not moved and so long as the impediment and the ball are not both in a hazard. Snow or ice on the course may be treated as a loose impediment or as casual water at the option of the player.

loose maul see MAUL

loose scrum see RUCK

lope An easy natural gait of a horse that resembles a canter.

lose **1** To be defeated in a contest.

2 To be defeated in playing for a point in a contest; to fail to win a rally.

losing hazard see HAZARD

losing pitcher *baseball* The pitcher on the losing team who is charged with the loss. A starting pitcher is the losing pitcher if he pitches the entire game or if his team is behind when he is removed from the game and remains behind for the rest of the game. If a relief pitcher takes over when the game is tied or when his team is ahead, he becomes the losing pitcher if his team loses the game while he is pitching.

loss A defeat in a contest or game. Losses are recorded in all team sports for determination of league or tournament standings. In baseball, losses are recorded against losing pitchers and used in determining seasonal and career pitching statistics.

lost ball *golf* A ball not found or identified after 5 minutes' searching; one abandoned as lost by the player who then substitutes a new ball, takes a penalty of one stroke, and plays the shot again.

loss of down *football* Loss of the privilege of repeating a down when a team has been assessed a penalty. The loss of down is a part of certain penalties (as when a forward pass is intentionally grounded or is touched by an ineligible receiver).

lost target A skeet or trapshooting target that is not broken by the shot; a target that is not shot at. For a lost target the shooter has no points credited on his score.

love

love A score of zero for one side in a particular game (as in racquets, badminton, or tennis).

love game *tennis* A game in which the losing player scores no points.

love set *tennis* A set in which the losing player has won no games. In British usage it is a set in which the winner has won 6 straight games, regardless of whether the losing player had previously won a game.

low **1** *of a pitch in baseball* Below the strike zone.

2 *basketball* Close to the basket as distinct from near the free throw line. ⟨*low* post⟩

low blow *boxing* An illegal punch that lands below the belt. For making a low blow, a boxer normally will be penalized by loss of points or disqualification.

low board *diving* A diving board placed one meter above the water.

lowcuts Oxford-style sports shoes as distinguished from ankle-high shoes. In the past 20 years, lowcuts have become the predominant style of shoe for team sports.

low house *skeet* The shorter trap house on a skeet range that is normally located on the right side of the range and from which targets are propelled at an upward angle.

low hurdle *track and field* A 30-inch-high hurdle used in the low hurdles. — see HURDLE

low hurdles *track and field* A race run over low hurdles placed at specified intervals. Each competitor must attempt to clear every hurdle successfully but is not penalized for knocking them down accidentally. Common outdoor distances are 180 yards, run over 8 hurdles, and 220 yards or 200 meters, both run over 10 hurdles.

low tow see TOWING

L support *gymnastics* A position in which the body is supported in an upright position above the hands (as off the floor or above parallel bars) with the legs extended horizontally in front of the body.

lubber's line A mark on a boat's compass that represents the fore-and-aft line of the boat.

¹luff The forward edge of a sail. — see illustration at SAILBOAT

²luff *sailing* **1** To turn a boat into or closer to the wind so that the sails begin to flutter and the boat loses speed.

2 *of a sail* To flutter as a result of the wind passing on both sides when the boat is headed into the wind.

3 To point higher or nearer the wind when racing in order to prevent a windward boat from overtaking.

luge A 1- or 2-man wood and metal or all metal sled that is used for racing. The sled is between 4 and 5 feet long, is slightly wider in the rear than in the front, and has 2 solid metal or metal-faced runners that curve up and in at the front. The rider lies on his back on the sled holding his head up just enough to be able to see the course. He holds onto reins with one hand and a side rail with the other and places his feet just outside the runners. The luge is steered by shifting body weight and by pushing in on one runner while lifting up on the other. In competition the competitors are individually timed on a series of runs down a special course which has numerous high-banked turns and resembles a bobsled run. The competitor with the fastest average time is the winner. (also called *toboggan*)

luge

luger A competitor in luge competition.

lug in *of a racehorse* To tend to move toward the inside during a race rather than run in a straight line. A horse that lugs in may interfere with another horse or may actually bump the rail and go off stride.

lug out *of a racehorse* To tend to move away from the rail when racing. A horse that lugs out may possibly interfere with other horses, or he may put himself wide on a turn so as to lose ground to the other horses.

lumber Baseball bats.

lumber pile see LOG JAM

¹lunge **1** To make a sudden move forward with the body over the forward leg which is bent at the knee while the other leg is stretched out with the back foot remaining in its original position.

2 *fencing* To make an attack by extending the sword arm and lunging.

²lunge 1 The act or action or an instance of lunging; a position in which the body is held above the front leg which is bent at the knee and the rear leg is stretched out behind.

2 *fencing* The basic attacking move toward an opponent which consists of extending the sword arm and stepping forward with the front foot while keeping the rear foot in place.

lunker *fishing* A game fish that is large for its kind. ⟨in this fly-fishing only stream, the fishermen are not taking the real *lunkers,* and the carrying capacity of the water is being used up by these larger and hard-to-catch fish — Harold K. Hagen, *Westways*⟩ ⟨a *lunker* northern pike⟩

lure 1 *dog racing* The mechanical rabbit.

2 *falconry* A padded and often weighted device that may be covered with feathers or that may have a pair of bird's wings attached to it and that is swung at the end of a rope to attract a falcon or hawk back to the handler (as for feeding).

3 *fishing* An artificial device on which one or more hooks are usually fastened that may be designed to represent some natural food of a fish (as a frog, insect, or fish) or that may be designed to attract fish by its color or movement or by the sound it produces.

Lutz *skating* A jump from the outer backward edge of one foot, assisted by a toe pick or toe point from the free foot with a full turn in the air and a return to the outer backward edge of the opposite foot, finishing with a curve in the direction opposite the original curve.

M

Maccabiah Games An international Jewish sports festival similar to the Olympic Games that is held at approximately 4-year intervals. The Maccabiah Games were first held in 1929 in Czechoslovakia and are currently held in Israel.

machine-gun *of a rifle or shotgun* To fire 2 or more consecutive shots because of a malfunction and not because of deliberate action by the shooter.

Madison *cycling* A 6-day endurance race commonly competed in by 2-man teams with riders taking turns on the track. The race takes its name from the 6-day races formerly held in New York's Madison Square Garden.

mag *gymnastics* Magnesium carbonate used on the hands to absorb moisture and reduce friction.

magazine An ammunition holder on or in a rifle or shotgun that feeds the cartridges or shells automatically into the chamber.

magic number A number that represents a combination of wins for a leader (as in league standings) and losses for a runner-up that mathematically guarantees the leader's winning a championship. Example: team A has a 2-game lead in the league standings over team B with 4 games remaining on the schedule. Team A's magic number is then 3, for 3 victories by team A, 3 losses by team B, or any combination of wins by team A and losses by team B that adds up to 3 will mean that team B cannot finish with a record equal to or better than team A's. In ice hockey, where league standings are computed on the basis of points, with a team getting 2 points for a win or one point for a tied game, the magic number will refer to the number of points a team must pick up to be assured a league championship.

magnetic north North as indicated by the north-seeking needle of a compass. Since magnetic north is not at the North Pole, a correction has to be made before the reading given by a compass can be applied to a map. — see BEARING

magneto *motor racing* An ignition device consisting typically of a rotating magnet and stationary coil which, in conjunction with a distributor, supplies a high-voltage spark to the combustion chambers of an internal-combustion engine.

¹magnum **1** *of a cartridge or shell* Containing a larger charge and heavier bullet or shot and usually made with a larger case than a standard cartridge or shell of the same or comparable caliber or gauge.
2 *of a firearm* Chambered to accept magnum ammunition.

²magnum A firearm designed to fire magnum ammunition.

maiden **1** A racehorse of either sex and any age that has never won a race.
2 A racing greyhound that has never won a race.

maiden over *cricket* An over in which no runs have been scored.

maiden race A race (as in horse racing or dog racing) limited to maidens.

mail match *archery* A match in which shooting is conducted at various local ranges with competitors mailing copies of the results to a tournament director who compares them with the results received from other competitors.

main *cockfighting* A program consisting of an odd number of matches.

mainmast *sailing* The principal mast on a boat with two or more masts and the one to which the mainsail is attached.

mainsail *sailing* The principal sail on a boat.

main wall *court tennis* The long wall of the court opposite the penthouse.

major Short for *major penalty*.

major foul *water polo* A deliberate or flagrant violation of the rules (as striking or kicking an opposing player or unsportsmanlike conduct) which results in suspension of the guilty player for the balance of the game and the awarding of a free throw to the opposing team.

major league **1** *baseball* Either of 2 principal professional leagues in the United States.
2 The top level of a sports enterprise or competition.

major leaguer A major league baseball player.

major penalty A penalty in ice hockey or box lacrosse of 5 minutes' duration given to a player for committing certain serious fouls (as fighting or causing injury). The offending player, except the goalkeeper, must go directly to the penalty box and remain there for 5 minutes of playing time while his team plays shorthanded. A major penalty assessed against a goalkeeper likewise leaves the team shorthanded, but the goalkeeper remains while another player serves the penalty. In the event of coincident major penalties, substitutes are permitted to replace the penalized players, and the numerical strength of each team is left unchanged.

majors The major leagues; the top level of competition in a sport.

make weight To have one's weight within the limits of a particular weight division or class. ⟨any contestant failing to *make weight* at the minimum time shall be ineligible for that weight class — *NCAA Wrestling Rules*⟩

Malibu or **Malibu board** *surfing* The basic fiberglass-covered foam surfboard named for one of California's most popular surfing areas where it was first extensively ridden. It is commonly 9 to 10 feet long, approximately 22 inches wide, and weighs from 25 to 35 pounds. It has a deep skeg and a pronounced rocker, and it is rounded at both ends. The length allows the board to be used in moderately heavy surf, while the rounded ends and curved profile make it easily maneuverable.

mallet A hammerlike implement with a cylindrical or barrel-shaped head that is used to strike the ball in various games. A croquet mallet typically has a cylindrical wooden head 6 to 10 inches long and 2½ inches in diameter. A 2-foot-long handle is attached at right angles to the head. The ball is struck with the ends of the mallet and both ends must be alike. The roque mallet is similar to the croquet mallet except that the handle is only 15 inches long, and the ends are not alike. One face is made of hard plastic or aluminun for hard shots, and the other is of rubber for soft shots. The mallet used in polo is made of cane and has a very slender head. The 4-to-4½-foot-long, slightly flexible shaft is set to the head at a slight angle off perpendicular; the ball is struck with the side of the head rather than with the end as in croquet and roque.

maltese cross *gymnastics* A lever performed on the rings.

man A player in a team sport. ⟨she must not allow this player to dodge past her and thus become a free *man,* to be taken on by another member of her team — Margaret Boyd, *Lacrosse Playing and Coaching*⟩

manager **1** The person in charge of a baseball team who directs game strategy, conducts practices, and often instructs players in proper technique. — compare COACH, GENERAL MANAGER
2 A boxer's business manager who arranges fights, sets up training camp, pays expenses, and handles the boxer's finances, usually for a percentage of the fighter's earnings.
3 A school or college student who supervises the equipment and records for a team under the direction of the coach.

mandatory eight count *boxing* A requirement in the rules followed in most bouts that whenever one boxer has been knocked down the fight cannot be resumed until a count of 8 has been reached regardless of whether the boxer has immediately gotten to his feet.

man-down *lacrosse* Played with one player less than the opposing team because of a penalty; shorthanded. ⟨*man-down* defense⟩

maneuvering vent *ballooning* A slit near the top of the envelope of a hot-air balloon that can be opened and closed from the gondola to allow a controlled escape of air for a small degree of maneuverability.

manipulators *fencing* The thumb and index finger of the sword hand which control the movements of the sword.

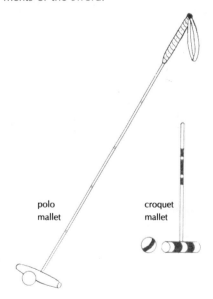

polo
mallet

croquet
mallet

mantel

mantel or **mantelshelf** *mountain climbing* A technique of climbing onto a ledge by pushing the body up with the heels of the hand until one leg can be swung over the ledge. The technique is the same as that often used to climb from a swimming pool.

mantelshelf

man-to-man or **man-for-man** A defense in a team sport characterized by having each player guard a specific opposing player. (also called *man-on-man*) — compare ZONE DEFENSE

man-up *lacrosse* Played with one player more than the opposing team because of a penalty. ⟨*man-up* defense⟩

mapes *skating* A jump that resembles the Salchow but has a toe pick or toe point to assist the takeoff.

maples Bowling pins.

marathon 1 A footrace of 26 miles 385 yards that is normally run over public roads closed to traffic.
2 A point-to-point swimming race of 18 miles normally held in open water.
3 A horse race longer than 1¼ miles.

marathoner A competitor in a marathon.

marbles *auto racing* Dust, dirt, and gravel which create a slippery spot on a racetrack.

¹march *football* To make a sustained drive toward the opponent's goal.

²march 1 *fencing* A forward movement made by advancing first the front foot and then the rear.
2 *football* A sustained drive.

Marconi rig see BERMUDA RIG

mare An older female racehorse:
1 A thoroughbred of age 5 or older.
2 A standardbred of age 4 or older.
— compare HORSE; FILLY

marine ball A variation of water polo played in a shallow pool (not over 3 feet deep) with a playing area of 40 yards by 20 yards. A team scores 2 points for a goal, and fouls are penalized by a free throw worth one point.

¹mark 1 A target. ⟨he hit the *mark*⟩
2 **a** A fair catch in rugby or Australian Rules football. **b** The point at which a fair catch was made and on or behind which the player makes a free kick; the point at which a penalty kick is taken. **c** A shout by a player making a fair catch to inform the referee that he wants to make a free kick.
3 *bowling* A strike or spare given an arbitrary value of 10 points as a rough estimate of an individual's or team's running score in a match.
4 *track and field* **a** The starting line. **b** The position on the starting line assigned to a particular competitor in a race. **c** The spot where an object thrown in a throwing event lands; the point at which a long jumper lands in the pit.
— **on your marks** or **take your marks** A starter's command given to runners and swimmers telling them to assume the starting position in the starting blocks or on the starting platform.

²mark 1 To make a strike or a spare in bowling.
2 To guard an opponent in some team games (as soccer, lacrosse, or field hockey).
3 To make a fair catch in rugby or Australian Rules football and immediately make a mark on the ground (often accompanied by a call of "mark") to notify the referee that a free kick is to be made.
4 To release the target from the low traphouse in skeet. — used as a command by the shooter

marker 1 A score. ⟨assisted on a second goal and went on to clinch the victory with a final *marker* — Soccer News⟩
2 Someone who keeps score (as in golf or court tennis).
3 Something (as a stake or pole) that indicates a boundary area (as on a golf course) or a specified distance (as at a racetrack).
4 A lawn bowling official whose duties include keeping score, aligning the jack, and marking with chalk any bowls touching the jack.

5 A small object (as a flat disk or coin) left on the putting green by a golfer to indicate the position of his ball when it is lifted.

6 A penalty flag thrown by a football official to indicate that a foul has been committed. (also called *penalty marker*)

marksman Someone skilled or practiced at shooting; an accurate shooter.

marlinespike A pointed implement that is used to open the strands of a rope.

Marquis of Queensberry Rules A set of boxing rules devised in 1867 by John Graham Chambers and published under the sponsorship of John Sholto Douglas, 9th marquis of Queensberry, that are the basic rules under which boxing is conducted today. During the early days of London prizefighting, the fighters used practically any means at their disposal, including punching, kicking, wrestling, biting, or gouging, to defeat an opponent. In 1839, London Prize Rules were adopted, which required that the bout take place inside a 24-foot-square ring, specified that a round ends when one fighter is down, required that both fighters be ready to return to the fighting in 30 seconds after the end of a round, and outlawed kicking, biting, butting, low blows, and grappling. The Queensberry rules provided for 3-minute rounds with a 1-minute rest between, required the boxers to wear padded gloves, forbid wrestling or hugging, required a boxer to return to his corner when his opponent went down, and required that the boxer rise unaided and be ready to continue the round within 10 seconds or lose the bout. The fact that the rules were sponsored by the marquis gave them the backing of the nobility, but it remained for such boxers as Jem Mace and John L. Sullivan to adopt the Rules before they became widely accepted.

marshal 1 *auto racing* Any of a number of officials working around a track performing such duties as lining up cars for the start of a race, monitoring work performed in the pits, performing rescue and fire fighting operations, and handling communications and signaling.

2 *track and field* An official whose duty is to ensure that only competitors are permitted on the running track or on the field.

martial artist Someone who engages in one of the martial arts.

martial arts The several arts of combat including karate, judo, kung fu, jujitsu, sumo, and kendo developed in the Orient and widely practiced as sports.

martingale A strap designed to prevent a horse from tossing its head or raising it too high.

Maryland ride see ZONE RIDE

mashie *golf* An old name for the number 5 iron.

mashie-iron *golf* An old name for the number 4 iron.

mashie-niblick *golf* An old name for the number 7 iron.

mask 1 *fencing* A protective covering for the face, head, and neck which has a wire-mesh screen covering the entire face.

2 *fox hunting* The head of the fox taken as a trophy.

3 Short for *face mask.*

massé *billiards* A shot made by striking the cue ball vertically or nearly vertically on one side to drive it around one ball to hit another.

mast *sailing* A vertical pole on which a sail is rigged.

master 1 A classification in some sports for competitors who are older than those normally competing at the top level. In swimming, masters competition is held for swimmers over 25 years old; in track and field, masters competition is for those over 40 years old. — compare SENIOR

2 or **master of hounds** or **master of foxhounds** *fox hunting* The person in overall charge of a hunt. The master usually leads the hunt, and he may hunt the hounds himself or employ a huntsman. Usually the master is a professional who organizes and conducts the hunt.

Masters Tournament An open golf tournament held annually since 1934 at the Augusta (Georgia) National Golf Club among players invited to participate usually on the basis of their having won a major tournament during the preceding 12 months.

master tooth or **master pick** The lowest spike in the series of spikes or teeth at the front of a figure skate blade. The master tooth often serves as a pivot for spins.

mat 1 A pad of soft material (as sponge rubber, kapok, or felt) with a canvas or plastic covering that is spread over the floor to cushion falls in such sports as gymnastics, wrestling, tumbling, and judo. A wrestling mat is normally 2 to 4 inches thick with a cover of soft material. The mat area is typically 42 feet square and provides a 32-foot square or a 32-foot circle as a wrestling area with 5 feet of mat beyond the wrestling area on all sides. In the center of the wrestling area is a 10-foot circle within which the wrestlers begin the match and to which they must return when they go beyond the wrestling area.

2 The sport of wrestling. ⟨expressed a belief that

269

matador

the 11 pinfalls . . . may have established a first in high school *mat* meets in the state — *Trinidad (Colo) Chronicle-News*⟩

3 *lawn bowling* A 24-by-14-inch pad placed on the ground at one end of the rink on which a bowler must have one foot when delivering a bowl.

matador The bullfighter who has the principal role in the bullfight and who ultimately attempts to kill the bull with a thrust of his sword.

match **1** A single game or contest in rugby, cricket, soccer, Australian Rules football, boxing, fencing, shooting, curling, polo, wrestling, judo, or karate.

2 A competition in certain sports for a specific maximum number of games which ends when one side wins a majority of the games (as 2 in a 3-game match or 3 in a 5-game match). A match in shuffleboard, handball, deck tennis, paddleball, volleyball, and badminton consists of a maximum of 3 games. A table tennis match may be 3 or 5 games. In squash racquets, a match is 5 games.

3 A tennis competition of a specified maximum number of sets (as 3 in women's competition and 3 or 5 in men's play) which concludes when one side wins a majority of the sets.

4 a A group of golfers playing against one another and moving from hole to hole as a unit. **b** A single contest between 2 or more players.

mat chairman *wrestling* An official in international competition who has general authority over the conduct of the match and who works with the judge and the referee in awarding points.

match fishing Fishing competition popular especially in England in which competitors fishing in designated sections of a river place all fish caught during an allotted time in individual keep nets so that they can be weighed at the end of the competition and then returned to the river. The fisherman with the largest total weight of catch is the winner.

match foursome *golf* Competition for 2 pairs of partners with one ball for each side and with partners alternating in playing the ball.

matchmaker *boxer* Someone who arranges matches.

match penalty A penalty (as for causing deliberate injury) in ice hockey or box lacrosse which results in the suspension of the offending player for the remainder of the game. A match penalty normally leaves a team shorthanded for a period of 5 or 10 minutes with a substitute permitted to replace the penalized player at the end of this time.

match play **1** *bowling* Competition in which 2 bowlers compete against one another directly (as in a tournament).

2 *golf* Competition in which one individual or side competes directly against another individual or side with the score reckoned after each hole. A side may either win a hole (get down in fewer strokes than the other side), lose a hole (take more strokes), or halve a hole (take the same number of strokes). The side having won the greater number of holes at the end of the round or having a lead in holes greater than the number left to play is the winner. — compare STROKE PLAY

match point A situation (as in tennis, badminton, or squash racquets) in which the side that is leading can win the match by winning the next point; the point that is being played in this situation.

match race A race between 2 competitors.

match-up The assignment of 2 opposing players to guard or play opposite each other in a game; the opposing players who will guard each other.

matinee Races (as in harness racing or dog racing) conducted during the day as distinguished from races normally conducted at night. In harness racing matinee races are usually for amateur drivers with the prizes normally consisting of blankets, trophies, or ribbons instead of money.

matman A wrestler.

mat surfer Someone who surfs using a plastic, foam, or rubber surf mat instead of a surfboard.

matt see BOSS

maturity *horse racing* A race for 4-year-olds in which the horses are entered before they are foaled.

maul **1** A play formerly used in football and rugby in which one or more defending players would attempt to prevent an attacking player who had carried the ball over the goal line from touching the ball to the ground for a score.

2 *rugby* A mob of players of both teams joining around the ballcarrier when he is held in a tackle with all shoving to get into position to play the ball when the ballcarrier releases it. (also called *loose maul*) — compare RUCK, SCRUM

mawashi *sumo* A wide silk belt worn around the waist with a section passed between the legs and up between the buttocks that is the sole costume of a wrestler and is what an opposing wrestler normally grasps during grappling.

mazurka *skating* A jump from an outer backward edge of one foot assisted by a toe pick or toe point from the free foot with the skating foot crossed in front of the other foot and a half turn of the body in the air and a return to the toe of the takeoff foot followed immediately by a glide onto an outer edge of the other foot.

mechanic *gymnastics* The safety belt suspended from the ceiling that may be worn by a gymnast while practicing a new stunt on an apparatus.

mechanical bridge see BRIDGE (*billiards*)

medalist or **medallist** **1** Someone who wins a medal in competition. ⟨an Olympic gold-*medalist*⟩

2 *golf* The low scorer in qualifying medal play in a tournament.

medal play see STROKE PLAY

medial moraine see MORAINE

mediastinal emphysema *scuba diving* A condition in which compressed air escapes from the lungs and lodges in the chest cavity where it interferes with the functioning of the heart and lungs.

medicine ball A heavy leather-covered ball approximately 18 inches in diameter stuffed with several pounds of soft material that is usually tossed between individuals for exercise.

Mediterranean draw *archery* A method of drawing the bowstring by pulling it back with the tips of the first 3 fingers of the string hand. — compare MONGOLIAN DRAW

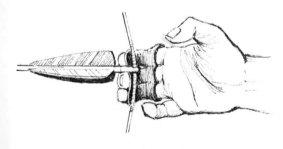

Mediterranean draw

medium-pace bowler or **medium-pacer** *cricket* A bowler who normally bowls straight at the wicket and who is less fast than a fast bowler.

medium start see CROUCH START

medley *swimming* A race in which a different stroke is used for each leg. — see INDIVIDUAL MEDLEY, MEDLEY RELAY

medleyist A swimmer who competes in a medley race.

medley relay **1** *swimming* A relay race (usually

of 400 meters) in which each team member must swim a different stroke. The legs are swum in the following order: backstroke, breaststroke, butterfly, and freestyle.

2 *track and field* A relay race with legs of unequal length. — see also DISTANCE MEDLEY, SPRINT MEDLEY

¹meet To compete or play against a particular competitor or opponent. ⟨the winners of the semifinals will *meet* in the finals on Friday⟩

²meet An athletic competition between 2 or more teams or clubs with participants competing normally on an individual basis but with results counting toward an overall team score. A meet commonly involves a number of teams competing simultaneously, with the team amassing the best overall cumulative score from the scores of individual members being the winner. Sometimes a meet consists of each team competing against every other team with results listed as if they had engaged in several separate competitions. Though the term *meet* is most often employed in competition between schools or colleges, its use with reference to track and field and swimming is so universal that it is employed of nearly all track and field or swimming competition, even invitational meets for individuals as well as for clubs.

meeting A session of horse racing or dog racing that extends over a stated number of days at one track.

mend a cast *fishing* To put a curve in the line in fly fishing by flipping it slightly upstream so as to prevent the fly's being dragged by the line.

Men's National round *archery* A target round in men's competition in which 48 arrows are shot at a distance of 80 yards and 24 arrows are shot at 60 yards.

Men's Western round *archery* A target round in men's competition in which 48 arrows are shot at a distance of 80 yards and 48 arrows are shot at 60 yards.

Mepham *wrestling* A hold in which a wrestler positioned behind and to one side of his opponent grasps the opponent's far arm with both hands by reaching around the opponent from both sides.

merry-go-round see HIP CIRCLE

Messenger Stakes A 1-mile stakes race for 3-year-old pacers that is one of the races in the pacing Triple Crown. The race is named for Messenger, a thoroughbred racehorse who was brought to America in 1788 and who is the direct ancestor of many outstanding thoroughbreds

Mepham

such as Man O'War and Whirlaway and of many outstanding trotting horses, among them his great-grandson Hambletonian.

meter rule A rule regulating the building of certain classes of sailboats by requiring the overall dimensions to conform to a specific formula. The formula allows for individual designs because a modification in one dimension requires an adjustment in another so that the end result in the formula remains the same. The formula for a 12-meter boat takes the length of the boat, plus twice the difference between the skin girth (measurement of the boat's hull under the keel following the precise lines of the hull) and the chain girth (similar measurement that ignores the variations in the shape of the hull), plus the square root of the sail area, minus the freeboard and divides the total by 2.37, an arbitrary number, to arrive at the rating.

methanol An alcohol used in place of gasoline in certain racing engines because it burns cooler than gasoline and permits a higher compression ratio for greater horsepower than gasoline does.

metric mile *track and field* The 1500-meter run. It is so called because it is the metric race that is the nearest equivalent to the mile run.

metric miler An athlete who competes in the metric mile.

M formation *soccer* A formation of a 5-man forward line in which the outside forwards and the center forward play in a line relatively far from the goal and the inside forwards play close to the goal so as to present the appearance of the letter M. — compare W FORMATION

midcourt 1 The area of the court (as in squash

racquets) midway between the front wall and the back wall.

2 The area of the court (as in tennis) midway between the net and the baseline.

3 The area of the basketball court just on either side of the division line.

midcourt line see DIVISION LINE

middle 1 The part of the playing area midway between the side boundaries. ⟨may clear to his crease defenseman breaking up the *middle* — Paul Hartman, *Lacrosse Fundamentals*⟩ ⟨drove down the *middle* on the final hole — Mark Mulvoy, *Sports Illustrated*⟩ ⟨a slick playmaker and an effortless skater . . . No question he can play the *middle* in the pros — Bob Strumm, *Hockey News*⟩ **a** *baseball* (1) The middle of the strike zone. ⟨never throws the ball down the *middle*. He just goes inside and outside — Brooks Robinson⟩ (2) The area of the field between the normal positions of the second baseman and the shortstop. ⟨hit a hard ground ball up the *middle*⟩ **b** *basketball* The area around the free throw lane. ⟨the lane was wide open, they weren't sagging and clogging the *middle* — Don Chaney⟩ **c** *football* The middle of a football line. ⟨on the next play he ran through the *middle* for a touchdown — *New York Times*⟩

2 *Canadian football* **a** A player position analogous to the tackle in American football. **b** A player in this position.

middle distance race *track and field* Any race usually from 800 meters or a half mile to a mile in length. Sometimes a race as short as 400 meters may be considered a middle distance race.

middle guard *football* A defensive lineman who normally plays between the defensive tackles and opposite the offensive center. (also called *nose guard*)

middle heavyweight A weight lifter in the middle heavyweight division. — see DIVISION

middle iron *golf* An iron with medium loft (as a 4, 5, or 6 iron) that is used for medium distance shots.

middle linebacker *football* The linebacker who plays behind the middle of the defensive line.

middleweight A boxer or weight lifter who competes in the middleweight division. — see DIVISION

midfield 1 The middle of a playing field.

2 *lacrosse* The players, including the second defense, center, and the second attack, who normally play both offense and defense and who line up at midfield on face-offs.

midfielder 1 *lacrosse* A player who plays in midfield.

2 *soccer* Any of the 3 players who play near the middle of the field between the forwards and the backs in a 3-3-4 alignment; linkman.

midfield line The halfway line on a soccer field.

midget *auto racing* An open-wheel racing car that is a smaller version of the dirt track car and that is popular for races held indoors. There is a range of midget cars from the standard midget powered by a 155-cubic-inch stock-block engine or a 114-cubic-inch racing engine to three-quarter and quarter midgets, which are scaled down versions of the standard size.

midice *ice hockey* The middle portion of the rink; the neutral zone.

mid iron *golf* An old name for a number 2 iron.

midline *lacrosse* A line across the middle of the field parallel to and equidistant from the end lines that divides the field into 2 halves.

mid-mashie *golf* An old name for a number 3 iron.

mid-off *cricket* 1 A fieldsman stationed just to the off side of the wicket near the bowler.

2 The position played by the mid-off.

mid-on *cricket* 1 A fieldsman stationed just to the leg side of the wicket near the bowler.

2 The position played by the mid-on.

mid-wicket *cricket* 1 A fielding position (as mid-off or mid-on) on either side of the wicket near the bowler.

2 A fieldsman in a mid-wicket position.

mile or **mile run** *track and field* A race one mile in length.

miler A competitor who competes in a one mile race. The term is also used in track and field to designate a runner of a particular race that is a specified fraction or multiple of a mile. ⟨quarter-*miler*⟩ ⟨two-*miler*⟩

mile relay *track and field* A relay race in which each leg is one quarter mile long.

miling Running in footraces of one mile; competing in the mile run.

Military Pentathlon see MODERN PENTATHLON

military press see PRESS (*weight lifting*)

military seat see FORWARD SEAT

mill circle *gymnastics* A forward circle around a horizontal bar or one of a set of uneven parallel bars made with the legs extended and the arms straight and grasping the bar at approximately hip level.

miniski 1 A short ski usually worn by a beginner.

2 A miniature ski worn by a skibobber.

minor league A professional sports league having less status or prestige than a major league and typically made up of clubs owned by or affiliated with major league clubs. When minor league clubs are controlled by major league clubs, the parent club usually supplies the players to the minor league club and handles all transactions involving trading or selling the contracts of the minor league players it controls.

minor penalty A penalty in ice hockey or box lacrosse of 2 minutes' duration given to a player for committing certain minor fouls (as roughing, interference, tripping, or holding). The offending player, except the goalkeeper, must go directly to the penalty box and remain there while his team plays shorthanded. A minor penalty assessed to a goalkeeper likewise leaves the team shorthanded, but the goalkeeper remains while another player serves the penalty.

minors A minor league or the teams in a minor league; minor league baseball.⟨spent most of his career in the *minors*⟩

minus pool *pari-mutuel betting* A situation in which the pool of money available to pay off winning tickets is less than that necessary to make the minimum legal payoff. In such a case the track must supplement the pool to bring it up to the legal minimum.

minute of angle *shooting* The distance of one inch on a target face 100 yards away that is approximately equal to one minute of arc and that is the standard unit of calibration of gun sights.

misconduct penalty A penalty in ice hockey and box lacrosse that results in the suspension of the offending player for 10 minutes but does not affect the numerical strength of his team. A misconduct penalty is assessed for unacceptable behavior (as extended fighting, abusive language, or failure to proceed to the penalty bench or penalty box). In ice hockey a misconduct penalty is automatically given a player who receives a second major penalty in a game. In the case of a penalized goalkeeper, another player serves his penalty.

¹miscue 1 *billiards* A faulty stroke in which the cue slips or glances off the ball.

2 An error (as in baseball).

²miscue *billiards* To make a miscue.

miskick To make a poor kick of the ball (as in soccer or football).

¹mishit To hit the ball poorly (as in cricket).

²mishit A badly hit ball.

mismatch *basketball* A situation in which a small player winds up guarding a tall player usually because a screen has forced a temporary switch in guarding assignments.

¹misplay To play the ball wrongly or unskillfully. ⟨the shortstop *misplayed* the ball⟩

²misplay A wrong or unskillful play; error.

miss 1 *billiards* Failure of a player to accomplish what he intended with a particular stroke which ends his inning and in some games results in loss of one or more points.

2 *bowling* Failure to make a spare when there is no split. (also called *blow, error*)

miss and out *cycling* A race for 3 or more competitors in which the last one to cross the finish line on each lap is eliminated.

mitt A covering for the hand that may be worn in place of a glove by a baseball catcher and first baseman only and that normally consists of a thumb section and another single section for the 4 fingers. The catcher's mitt is normally round with padding in front of the thumb and the finger sections and in front of the heel of the hand but no padding in the pocket. Between the thumb and finger sections is a section of leather or leather webbing laced in place to prevent the ball's passing through. A first baseman's mitt is extremely flat and made in 2 sections somewhat resembling those of a catcher's mitt or in 3 equal sections so as to resemble a scoop.

catcher's mitt first baseman's mitt

mixed doubles Doubles play (as in tennis) with each side made up of a man and a woman.

mixed foursome *golf* Foursome play in which each side consists of a man and a woman.

mixed pairs *skating* Pairs competition with each pair consisting of a man and woman. — compare SIMILAR PAIRS

mixer 1 *bowling* A delivery which strikes the pins in such a way as to cause deflected or spinning pins to knock down other pins.

2 *football* A variation from a normal defensive alignment.

mizzen or **mizzenmast** *sailing* The smaller mast that is aft the mainmast and that is set aft the steering wheel on a yawl and forward of the steering wheel on a ketch. (also called *jigger*)

mizzen sail A sail set on a mizzen.

mizzen staysail A sail set on the stay in front of a mizzen.

modern hunting seat see FORWARD SEAT

Modern Pentathlon A 5-event contest which consists of épée fencing, pistol shooting, a 300-meter swim, a 4000-meter cross-country race, and a 5000-meter equestrian steeplechase on an unfamiliar horse and in which each competitor is judged against an arbitrary point standard. The competitor with the highest point total is the winner. (also called *Military Pentathlon*)

modified A degree of choke on a shotgun that is intermediate between full choke and improved cylinder. — see CHOKE

Modified Eliminator see ELIMINATOR

modified stock car *auto racing* A racing car constructed with an old automobile body (as that of a coupe of the 1930s) but with a new highly modified engine and a sophisticated suspension system.

modify *motor sports* **1** To change the basic components of a stock vehicle especially by substituting different and stronger parts usually in the drive train and suspension and by removing excess weight where possible to make the vehicle better suited for racing.

2 To change the basic design of an internal-combustion engine by substituting different parts and often by changing the valve configuration and enlarging the cylinders for more power. — compare BLUEPRINT

Moebius flip *freestyle skiing* A forward or backward flip with a full twist that is performed in the air during a jump.

mogul *skiing* **1** A bump on a ski slope usually caused by or built up by numerous skiers' turning in the same place on the slope.

2 A competitive event in freestyle skiing in which skiers race one at a time against the clock down a slope consisting of numerous large mounds and bumps.

mohawk *skating* A turn from forward to backward or from backward to forward with a change from one foot to the corresponding edge of the opposite foot (as from a left forward outside edge to a right backward outside edge) but with the curve moving in the opposite direction.

The name comes from its resemblance to a movement in a war dance of a tribe of Mohawk Valley Indians.

mohawk jump *skating* A half-turn jump that involves a mohawk turn with the skater landing on the corresponding edge of the opposite skate and continuing the curve in the opposite direction.

molinello *fencing* A circular cut to the head in saber fencing.

momentum The upper hand in a contest; apparent control of a contest or an advantage gained as a result of superior play.

Monday morning quarterback A football fan who after reflection on the outcome of a game played over the weekend expounds his opinion of how the game should have been played. — compare GRANDSTAND QUARTERBACK

Monday morning quarterbacking The practice of reflecting on and criticizing a team's play or the strategy employed in a football game.

money **1** The first 3 finishers in a race from the standpoint of pari-mutuel payoffs or the first 4 finishers from the standpoint of distribution of the purse. — used in the phrases *finish in the money* or *finish out of the money* **2** Prize money. ⟨took second *money*⟩

money player A player who is at his best in a pressure situation (as in a play-off game).

Mongolian draw *archery* A method of drawing the bowstring by pulling it back between the thumb and bent index finger of the string hand. To help hold the string in place, a thumb ring is normally worn. (also called *Oriental draw*) — compare MEDITERRANEAN DRAW

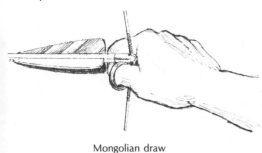

Mongolian draw

monkey see WRENCH

monkey hang *gymnastics* A hang by one arm from the rings after performing a skin the cat stunt.

monkey roll *tumbling* A forward roll in which the legs are kept straight until the performer is on the floor on his back at which time the legs are brought into a tuck position to finish the roll.

monocoque The construction commonly employed in racing cars in which the chassis and strut frame of conventional car construction is replaced by thin metal boxes which bear the stress loads while at the same time housing essential components such as fuel tanks. Monocoque construction, developed originally in aircraft construction, is lighter and stronger than the chassis and frame. — compare SPACEFRAME

monofilament A fishing line made of a single strand of synthetic material (as nylon) and used especially in spinning.

monohull A boat with a single hull. — compare MULTIHULL

monster or **monster man** or **monster back** *football* A roving linebacker who plays wherever he feels he will be needed.

mooch *fishing* To troll for salmon.

Moore *gymnastics* A turning movement performed over one bar of parallel bars or over one pommel of a pommel horse by swinging the legs up above the level of the hands, moving the body in a horizontal circle continuously facing toward the hands, and switching the position of the hands one at a time so as to finish with the body facing in the opposite direction. When the Moore is performed on parallel bars, the performer usually winds up in a handstand facing in the opposite direction. (also called *Czech*)

mooring *boating* A place for boats to tie up in a harbor that typically consists of a permanent anchor on the bottom and a chain or heavy cable leading from it to a buoy on the surface to which the boat is secured.

mooring line The line by means of which a boat is secured to a mooring.

mooring pennant *boating* A short line permanently attached to a mooring buoy which is held on the surface by a small float and by which a boat is connected to a mooring.

moraine *mountain climbing* An accumulation of earth and stones carried by a glacier or eroded from the side of a mountain by the passage of the glacier. A *terminal moraine* is found at the end of a glacier where it was pushed by the moving glacier or exposed when the glacier melted. A *lateral moraine* is found at the edge of a glacier. Where 2 glaciers come together, the lateral moraines unite to form a *medial moraine,* which extends for some distance down the middle of the resulting glacier.

morning glory *horse racing* A racehorse that

Moore

shows great speed in morning workouts but consistently does poorly in races.

morning line *horse racing* The probable odds for a given race estimated by the track handicapper and posted before the start of betting.

Mother Goose Stakes A 1⅛-mile stakes race for 3-year-old thoroughbred fillies that is one of the races in the filly Triple Crown. — see also ACORN, COACHING CLUB AMERICAN OAKS

mother-in-law *bowling* The number 7 pin. — see illustration of pin arrangement at BOWLING

motion Movement of the body (as by a pitcher in baseball or a ballcarrier in football) that is intended to deceive an opponent.
— **in motion** *of an offensive back in football* Running parallel to or back from the line of scrimmage before the ball is snapped.

moto Either of the usually 2 heats that make up a moto-cross.

moto-cross A motorcycle race on a tight closed course over natural terrain featuring steep hills, sharp turns, jumps, and usually mud. A moto-cross is commonly conducted in heats lasting 30 or 45 minutes, with the competitor having the best overall standing being the winner. (also called *scramble*)

motorboat A boat powered by a permanent or detachable motor or engine.

motorboating The pastime of riding in a motorboat.

motorboat racing The sport of racing motorboats. Races are conducted in different classes for stock inboard and outboard boats and for inboard and outboard hydroplanes.

motordrome A racetrack for automobiles or motorcycles.

motor-paced *cycling* Being a time trial in which a motor vehicle (as an automobile or a motorcycle) rides immediately ahead of the cyclist to break the wind for him. Speeds of up to 60 mph have been attained in motor-paced trials.

motor-sailer A sailboat with an engine large enough to permit the boat to be run under power or under sail.

motorsports Any of various activities and especially races or time trials involving automobiles, snowmobiles, airplanes, motorcycles, or powerboats.

moto-scramble A motorcycle contest consisting of a number of short sprint races over a moto-cross course.

mound *baseball* A mound of earth 10 inches high in the center of the diamond which slopes gradually to the level of the playing field and on which the pitcher stands to pitch the ball.

moundsman A baseball pitcher.

¹mount *gymnastics* To move from the floor to a position on an apparatus (as the parallel bars or the pommel horse).

²mount 1 A racehorse ridden by a jockey.

2 *gymnastics* The act or method of mounting an apparatus.

mountain climbing The sport of climbing mountains usually using rock climbing and artificial climbing techniques.

mountaineer Someone who engages in mountaineering.

mountaineering Mountain climbing in its most demanding and rugged form. Mountaineering typically requires skill in rock climbing, artificial climbing techniques, climbing on ice, and, especially on high snow-covered mountains, skiing.

mountain sickness *mountain climbing* Sickness similar in symptoms to seasickness that may affect a climber who is not accustomed to the thin air at altitudes above 10,000 feet. The sickness passes when the climber descends.

mounting *fencing* The part of a fencing sword consisting of the guard, handle, and pommel.

mousetrap see TRAP (*football*)

mouthpiece 1 or **mouthguard** A plastic or rubber device that is worn in the mouth especially by boxers and also by some football or hockey players to protect against broken teeth and cut lips.

2 The part of an air hose or a single-hose regulator that is held in the mouth by a scuba diver for breathing.

move 1 A deceptive move or motion; fake. ⟨gives his guard an inside *move* and goes outside to make the tackle — Vince Lombardi⟩ ⟨put a *move* on his man and lost him⟩

2 The pickoff motion of a pitcher. ⟨has a good *move* to first⟩

3 The maneuvering of a competitor in a race to be in position to challenge or overtake the leader. ⟨began his *move* at the start of the last lap⟩

move list *football* A list on which a team places a player's name when he is being taken off the active roster.

move off the ball *football* To move quickly from a set position when the ball is snapped. (also *come off the ball*)

Mr. and Mrs. A pocket billiards game with a built-in handicap played usually by a man and woman with the woman free to shoot at any ball on the table but the man required to shoot the balls in rotation. Each ball is worth points equal to its number; the first side to score 61 points wins.

mudder *horse racing* A horse that performs well on a wet or muddy track.

muddy *of a racetrack* Thoroughly soaked with rainwater and consisting of soft mud that sticks to the horse's hooves and to the faces and clothing of the jockeys when thrown up by horses ahead. — compare FAST, GOOD, HEAVY, SLOPPY, SLOW

¹muff 1 *baseball* A misplay or dropping of a thrown or batted ball that could have been cleanly caught or fielded. — compare FUMBLE

2 *football* The act or an instance of failing to catch a kicked or thrown ball other than a forward pass. If a member of the defensive team recovers the ball after a muff, the team gains possession of the ball but is not permitted to advance it. — compare FUMBLE; see also FORWARD PASS

3 A leather covering for the spur of a gamecock used in sparring to prevent the cocks from injuring each other.

²muff To drop a ball when attempting to catch, recover, or field it.

mugger A 4-prong nail with a head in the shape of an X that is attached to the soles of certain climbing boots.

mule *auto racing* A backup or practice car.

mule kick *freestyle skiing* A stunt performed in the air during a jump which consists of swinging the legs back so that the tails of the skis come close to or touch the buttocks.

muleta *bullfighting* A cloth spread by a stick attached at one side that is used by the matador to lead the bull through a series of passes during the part of the bullfight just prior to the kill.

mulligan *golf* A free shot sometimes given a golfer in informal play when his last shot was poorly played.

multihull A boat (as a catamaran) having more than one hull. — compare MONOHULL

multiple foul 1 *basketball* A situation in which 2 or more teammates commit personal fouls against the same player at approximately the same time with the result that the fouled player is awarded one free throw for each foul. — compare DOUBLE FOUL

2 *football* A situation in which 2 or more fouls are committed by one team on the same play with the result that the opposing team is permitted its choice of penalties.

multiple offense *football* An offense that employs several different types of plays run from a single formation.

multiplying reel A fishing reel (as a bait casting reel) geared so that the spool revolves several times for each revolution of the handle.

multipoundage system *weight training* A training method in which weight is removed from a barbell at a rate of approximately 20 percent whenever a lifter begins to have trouble completing a set. The weights are removed by fellow lifters so the lifter can continue the exercise with minimum interruption.

mummy bag A sleeping bag designed to fit relatively close to the sleeper's body so that there is very little extra space. The mummy bag normally closes around the sleeper's head so that only his face is exposed, giving the impression of a mummy.

Murphy blind *harness racing* A device consisting of a large piece of stiff leather that is fastened to a horse's bridle in such a way as to obstruct the horse's vision in one eye when the horse turns his head to one side and that is used as a training aid to overcome the tendency to turn to one side.

muscle *gymnastics* The act of muscling up.

muscle up 1 To use all of one's strength in attempting something (as hitting or throwing a ball).
2 *gymnastics* To pull oneself up to a support position using only the muscle strength of the arms (as in a chin-up).

mushing The action or sport of driving dogsleds.

mushroom anchor An anchor shaped like a mushroom. — see illustration at ANCHOR

mutuel or **mutuels** A pari-mutuel system or pari-mutuel machine.

mutuel field see FIELD (*pari-mutuel betting*)

muzzle The open end of the barrel of a firearm.

muzzle energy The force in foot-pounds of a bullet as it leaves the muzzle that is used as a rough estimate of the comparative killing power of the cartridge.

muzzle velocity The speed in feet per second of a bullet as it leaves the muzzle.

N

¹nail A small metal lug once commonly used on the soles of mountain climbing boots to give them gripping power on ledges and slopes. Modern climbing boots normally are made with composition rubber soles having molded lugs which are much less destructive to the rock face of a slope.

²nail **1** *baseball* To throw out a base runner especially when he is trying to steal or reach an extra base on the play. ⟨was *nailed* at the plate — *New York Times*⟩
2 *football* To tackle the ballcarrier or a quarterback with the ball especially at or behind the line of scrimmage. ⟨came right up to the line to blow in and *nail* me in what he must have assumed was going to be another pass play — George Plimpton, *Sports Illustrated*⟩

nail knot A knot used to join a leader to a section of fly line that is formed by laying the 2 lines alongside each other with a nail or similar object between them, wrapping the leader back around itself and the larger line several turns, and passing the end through the space between the lines kept open by the nail. — see illustration at KNOT

Naismith's formula A formula used to estimate the time a hike may take: allow one hour for every 3 miles as measured on the map plus an additional hour for every 2,000 feet climbed.

naked reverse *football* A reverse in which all the blockers move toward one side and the ballcarrier moves toward the other side without any interference in front of him. The play depends for success on the defense's moving with the apparent flow of the play and leaving the field open for the ballcarrier.

¹nap British term for a competitor (as a racehorse) selected as the best bet on a program of racing.

²nap British term meaning to select a particular competitor as a nap.

narrow *of a curling stone* Delivered to the inside of the line of the skip's broom.

Nassau *golf* A system of betting in informal play in which there is a separate wager on the winner of the first 9 holes, one on the winner of the second 9, and one on the overall winner of the entire 18 holes.

natation The action or sport of swimming.

natatorium A building (as on a college campus) housing a swimming pool.

National Invitational Tournament A post-season basketball tournament among specially invited college teams held annually in New York's Madison Square Garden since its inception in 1938.

National round *archery* A target round in women's competition in which all competitors shoot 48 arrows at a distance of 60 yards and 24 arrows at 50 yards.

Nation's Cup *equitation* International jumping competition for 4-man teams consisting of 2 rounds on a course up to 800 meters (872 yards) long with 13 to 14 obstacles. Only the best 3 scores for each team count for each round. The obstacles vary from 1.3 to 1.6 meters (about 4 to 5 feet) high with a spread of from 1.5 to 2.7 meters (5 to 8½ feet). There must be a water jump at least 4 meters (13 feet) wide, and the course must include at least one double and one triple obstacle. (also called *Prix des Nations*)

natural English *billiards* English imparted to a ball to cause it to continue in basically the same direction after striking another ball or a cushion; follow.

natural form *archery* A body position taken when shooting at a target that is characterized by having the feet perpendicular to the line of flight of the arrow. — compare POWER FORM

nautical chart see CHART

Navy ride *wrestling* A hold in which the wrestler secures a waist lock with one arm and with the other reaches across in front of his opponent and secures the opponent's far leg by reaching between the opponent's legs and around the far thigh.

near *wrestling* Relating to or being an arm or leg on the side of the body nearest the opponent.

near fall *wrestling* A situation formerly called *predicament* in college wrestling in which a

needle scale

a position in which the body is supported in the air by the shoulders and hands to a squatting or standing position that is executed by snapping the legs forward and down and pushing up with the hands.

needle scale *gymnastics* A position of balance on one foot with the other foot extended straight or nearly straight up in the opposite direction and the body held parallel to either leg.

nelson *wrestling* A hold in which a wrestler exerts leverage in different directions against an opponent's upper arm and head. In the *full nelson* (sometimes called *double nelson*) the wrestler from a position behind his opponent thrusts his arms under his opponent's arms and places his hands behind the opponent's head in such a manner that as the opponent's head is pushed forward and down, his arms are pulled up. The full nelson is a dangerous hold and is illegal in amateur wrestling. The *half nelson* is applied by placing one arm under the corresponding arm of the opponent and with the same hand reaching up to push against the back of the opponent's head. The *quarter nelson* is similar to the half nelson except that instead of pushing against the head with the same hand, the wrestler pushes down with the opposite hand and grasps his other wrist with his encircling hand. A *three-quarter nelson* is applied by reaching under the opponent's arm from behind with both arms and placing the hands on the back of the opponent's head from both sides. The term *nelson* when used alone commonly refers to a half nelson. When the hold is applied by a wrestler positioned in front of his opponent, it becomes a *reverse nelson.*

nerf *auto racing* To bump another car while racing.

nerf bar or **nerfing bar** *auto racing* A special bumper often attached on the front, back, and sides of a modified stock car to prevent the wheels of the car from touching another car's wheels while racing.

nerved *of a racehorse* Having the nerves leading to a sore foot severed so that pain is not felt when racing.

¹net 1 An open-meshed fabric barricade that divides a court in half and over which a ball or shuttlecock must be hit in playing any of various court games. Nets usually have a white cloth band enclosing the top and some have a cord or wire running along the top for support. The size of the mesh varies with the size of the ball used. — see also COURT

wrestler has his opponent on the mat under control with the opponent's shoulders within 4 inches of the mat or one shoulder on the mat and the other within a 45-degree angle to the mat and which results in an award of 2 points to the controlling wrestler. If the position is held uninterrupted for 5 seconds, the wrestler receives 3 points instead of 2.

near side 1 The left side of a horse.
2 *gymnastics* The side of an apparatus approached by the performer at the beginning of a stunt or routine.

necessary line *football* The yard line to which the offensive team must advance the ball within 4 downs in order to gain a first down.

neck 1 The part of the head of a golf club near the point where it joins the shaft.
2 a The section of a pommel horse to the left of the pommels when viewed from the side on which the gymnast approaches it. — compare CROUP, SADDLE **b** The far end of a vaulting horse.
3 The part of a cartridge case that holds the bullet.
4 *horse racing* The approximate length of a horse's neck and head used to express a margin of victory or advantage in a race. — compare NOSE, LENGTH, HEAD
5 The throat of a lacrosse stick.

neckline *dogsled racing* A line connected to the gangline and fastened to a dog's collar to keep the dog moving in a straight line.

neckspring *gymnastics* A forward spring from

quarter nelson

half nelson

threequarter nelson

full nelson

2a An open-meshed fabric enclosing the back, top, and sides of various goals (as hockey, soccer, or water polo).   **b** The mesh fabric hung from the rim of a basketball goal to slow the ball as it passes through the goal.

3 *golf* A golfer's score after the handicap is deducted from his gross score.

4 A net enclosure in which a cricket batsman takes hitting practice.

²net 1 To hit a ball or shuttlecock into the net for loss of the point or rally.

2 To hit a ball into the goal for a score (as in soccer).

net antenna *volleyball* Either of 2 vertical poles attached at either end of the net and extending 2½ to 3½ feet above the net to assist the officials in determining when the net has been touched during play.

netball 1 A game somewhat resembling basketball that is played in England between 2 teams of 7 players with the object to pass the ball between players and shoot it through a circular ring from within a 16-foot shooting area for a score and to prevent the opponents from scoring.

2 A game which resembles volleyball but in which the ball is caught and thrown instead of hit.

3 *tennis* A ball that touches the net and continues over it to remain in play on any stroke except a serve.

net-cord umpire or **net-cord judge** *tennis* An official who is stationed on the side of the court at the net to detect serves that strike the net.

net game 1 A game (as tennis, badminton, or volleyball) in which an object is played back and forth over a net.

2 *tennis* A style of play in which a player stays in the forecourt close to the net and tries to volley the ball. — compare BASELINE GAME

netkeeper or **netminder** An ice hockey goalkeeper.

netman A tennis player.

net play Play (as in tennis or badminton) from close to the net.

net shot *badminton* A shot (as a smash or push shot) played from close to the net.

netting An interlacing of cords or leather strips (as that forming the head of a lacrosse stick).

neutral corner *boxing* Either of the 2 diagonally opposite corners of the ring not occupied by one of the boxers and his handlers between rounds.

neutral position 1 *skating* The position of a skater when the body is square to the direction of travel and neither shoulder is ahead of the

other in either an open or in a closed position.
2 *wrestling* A position from which the match begins with both wrestlers on their feet in a slight crouch facing each other and holding their arms in front of them at or just above waist level. — compare REFEREE'S POSITION

neutral zone 1 *deck tennis* A 3-foot-wide area on either side of the net which is out of play and in which the ring must not land and players must not step.
2 *football* An imaginary area the width of the football that extends across the field parallel to the goal lines. When the ball is in position to be put into play at the beginning of a down, no player on either side except the center may penetrate the neutral zone without being called for encroachment. In Canadian football the neutral zone is one yard wide. — see illustration at LINE OF SCRIMMAGE
3 *ice hockey* The area of the rink between the 2 blue lines that is neither an attacking zone nor a defensive zone.

névé *mountain climbing* A permanent snowfield at the head of or on either side of a glacier.

ne-waza *judo* The grappling techniques employed after a throw that include pinning holds, choke holds, and joint locks.

niblick *golf* An old name for the number 9 iron.

nick *squash racquets* A shot that hits the crease where the floor and wall meet and is unreturnable.

nickel defense *football* A prevent defense employing 5 defensive backs.

nightcap 1 *baseball* The second game of a doubleheader.
2 *horse racing* The last race on a program.

night watchman *cricket* A batsman at the end of the batting order who takes his turn at the wicket late in the day.

nine 1 A baseball team.
2 *golf* The first or last 9 holes of an 18-hole course. — see BACK NINE, FRONT NINE

nine ball A variation of pocket billiards played with 9 numbered object balls in which the aim is to pocket the nine ball after pocketing the other balls in rotation or in combination shots.

ninepins An early bowling game played with 9 pins arranged as in tenpins but without a headpin.

19th hole A bar or cocktail lounge in the clubhouse of a golf course.

nip-up A neckspring.

nitro see NITROMETHANE

nitrogen narcosis *scuba diving* A condition resembling drunkeness with loss of coordination and judgment that may affect a diver breathing compressed air at depths greater than 130 feet. It results from the anesthetic effect of nitrogen under pressure. The condition becomes more severe as the depth is increased but diminishes with ascent and will vanish completely before the diver reaches the surface. (also called *rapture of the deep*)

nitromethane or **nitro** A combustible liquid fuel used alone or more often mixed with methanol to power race cars.

no-ad game see VAN ALEN SIMPLIFIED SCORING SYSTEM

Noah Australian name for a *shark*.

¹no-ball *cricket* A delivery which in the judgment of either umpire is unfair or not legal because the ball was thrown or because the bowler did not have one foot behind the bowling crease at the time the ball was released. A no-ball cannot take a wicket, and it does not count as one of the 6 good delivers of an over; the batting team is automatically credited with a run unless the batsmen are able to score more by running. A no-ball is not dead, and the batsman may run on a bye or a wide or the batsman may hit the ball without being out if it is caught. When playing the ball, the batsman will be out on a no-ball if he hits the ball twice; either batsman, when running, can be run out or be out by handling the ball or obstructing the field. Any runs gained as a result of hitting the ball are credited to the batsman's total; runs scored without hitting the ball are extras.

²no-ball *of a cricket umpire* To call a particular delivery of a bowler a no-ball.

nobble British term meaning to drug a racehorse.

no block *volleyball* A ball that is set and spiked but that must cross the net at such an angle as to make a return relatively easy and blocking unnecessary.

¹nock *archery* **1** The grooves at the tips of the limbs of a bow to hold the bowstring in place when the bow is braced.
2 The notch in the end of an arrow that fits on the bowstring. — see illustration at ARROW

²nock *archery* To place the arrow against the bowstring so that the string fits into the nock of the arrow. The arrow is nocked so that the cock feather, which is at right angles to the nock, stands away from the bow.

nocking point *archery* The point on the bowstring at which the arrow is nocked.

nod British term meaning to head a soccer ball.

no decompression dive *scuba diving* A dive of such short duration or to so shallow a depth as not to require a decompression stop.

no-hit *baseball* Relating to or being a game or part of a game during which a pitcher gives up no base hits. ⟨pitched 6²/₃ *no-hit* innings⟩

no-hitter *baseball* A game in which a pitcher gets credit for not giving up any base hits to the opposing team.

no-man's land *tennis* The area of the court between the baseline and the service line. Players standing within this area usually have a hard time playing the ball because it will frequently bounce at or near their feet.

Nomex A trademark used for a flame-resistant fabric used to make protective clothing worn by racing drivers.

nominate **1** *horse racing* To designate a horse as a possible entry in a future stakes race by paying the required fee often before the horse is foaled. Of the horses nominated for a particular race, only a small percentage turn out to be good enough or healthy enough to be entered, and fewer still actually start.
2 *snooker* To specify a particular object ball that one is on.

nomination fee *horse racing* A fee required of an owner who nominates a horse for a particular stakes race. The fee is usually relatively small in comparison with entry fees and starting fees which are subsequently paid, and it is forfeited if the horse is not entered or is later withdrawn from the race. All fees paid toward getting horses in the stakes race make up, often along with any added money, the purse for the race.

noncontact sport A sport (as golf, swimming, bowling, or gymnastics) in which individuals compete against each other directly or by trying to approach an arbitrary standard of excellence but in which competitors do not attempt to hinder their opponents and in which there is no necessary or incidental physical contact between competitors.

nonfront serve *racquetball* An illegal serve which strikes a player or another wall before it hits the front wall.

nonstriker **1** British term for a player *(as in billiards or croquet)* who at a given moment is not shooting. — compare STRIKER
2 *cricket* The batsman who is at the wicket from which the bowler is delivering the ball and who is not attempting to hit a ball. The nonstriker is analogous to a base runner in baseball. — compare STRIKER

nontitle Relating to or being a contest in which a title is not at stake. ⟨a *nontitle* fight⟩

nonwinner A competitor who has not won usually during a specified time. ⟨a *nonwinner* in three years on the PGA tour — United Press International⟩

noodling see GRABBLING

Nordic *skiing* A class of skiing competition that includes both cross-country skiing and ski jumping. Nordic competition may also include the Nordic Combined. — compare ALPINE

Nordic Combined *skiing* A competition in which Nordic skiers are rated on the basis of scores made in the cross-country and jumping events. The skier with the highest total wins the Combined regardless of his placing in the individual events. — compare ALPINE COMBINED

normally aspirated *of an internal-combustion racing engine* Designed to take air into the combustion chambers through the normal suction created on the downstroke of the piston and not by means of supercharging or turbocharging.

norm point The point on the landing slope of a ski jumping hill at which the competitors are expected to land. — compare CRITICAL POINT, TABLE POINT

north see MAGNETIC NORTH, TRUE NORTH

Northill A trademark used for a style of anchor. — see illustration at ANCHOR

North Wall axe or **North Wall hammer** see HAMMER AXE

nose **1** *horse racing* The approximate length of a horse's nose used to express a margin of victory or advantage in a race. — compare LENGTH, NECK, HEAD
2 The front end of a surfboard.
— **on the nose** *of a wager* To win.

nose guard see MIDDLE GUARD

nose hit *bowling* A hit full on the headpin.

no set A declaration in badminton or squash racquets that one does not wish to extend the length of the game when the score is tied one or 2 points before the end. — see SET THE SCORE

no side *rugby* The end of the game.

no target *trapshooting* A target that does not count because in the judgment of the official the shooter does not have a fair chance at it (as because of a malfunction of the gun or the trap, because more than one competitor shoots at it, or because the target takes an erratic course).

not out *cricket* **1** *of a batsman* Still batting and not having been put out at the time the team's innings is ended or declared by the captain.
2 *of a team* Still batting with the innings not

yet completed (as at the end of a day's play).

not up *of a ball in court games* Not legally playable usually because of having bounced twice.

novice A competitor (as in swimming or fencing) that has not won or placed among the winners in a particular event.

novillero A novice matador.

number A numeral worn on a player's uniform as an aid to distinguishing a team's players. In most sports, there is little significance to the numbering system used. In football, the numbering system has a special significance in identifying the positions played by the individual players and enabling the officials to determine instantly which players are eligible receivers. The numbers one through 49 are reserved for offensive and defensive backs; offensive centers and defensive linebackers are usually numbered 50 through 59; defensive linemen and offensive linemen other than centers and ends are numbered 60 through 79; offensive ends and wide receivers are numbered 80 through 99. In professional football, the numbers one through 19 are reserved specifically for quarterbacks and kickers and the numbers 90 through 99 may be used only with special permission of the commissioner.

number 8 forward *rugby* The lone forward on the back row of the scrum who is behind the 2 lock forwards of the second row.

nun buoy see BUOY

nunchaku A karate weapon that consists of two 12-to-14-inch-long hardwood sticks joined by a short length of rawhide, cord, or chain. The sticks may be used together as a club, one stick may be held while the other is swung, or they may be used to choke a victim. The nunchaku is illegal in some states.

nurse *billiards* To keep one or more balls in essentially the same position for successive shots (usually in a crotch or along a rail) in carom games by striking them very lightly.

nursery race *horse racing* A race for 2-year-olds; a baby race.

nut *mountain climbing* A metal or plastic block with a hole in the middle that is jammed into a crack in place of a chockstone to provide a secure anchor for a belay. A sling or metal cable is usually passed through the hole; this usually provides more security than passing the sling around a chockstone. — see also WEDGE

nutcracker *football* A strenuous practice drill in which a player is being hit constantly by an opposing player or in which one player is hit simultaneously or alternately by 2 opposing players, one on each side.

nymph *fishing* An artificial fly tied to resemble the larval form of any of numerous aquatic insects such as the dragonfly, caddis fly, or the mayfly.

O

Oaks A 1½-mile stakes race for thoroughbred fillies held annually at Epsom Downs, Surrey, England, that is one of the English Classics. The race was originated in 1779 by the 12th earl of Derby who named it after his nearby estate.

oar **1** A long pole with a flat blade at one end that is pulled against the water to propel a boat. Oars used on a rowboat are generally 7 to 9 feet long and are worked with one in each hand. In sculling, the oars (commonly called *sculls*) are approximately 10 feet long and, like those of a rowboat, are worked with one in each hand. In rowing, the oar is considerable longer, up to about 12 feet, with a 6-to-8-inch-wide blade which is a little over 2 feet long. Each crew member pulls one oar, using 2 hands. About 3½ feet from the handle end of the oar is a small leather sheath with a metal collar which fits into the oarlock to prevent the oar from sliding into the water.
2 An oarsman.

oarlock A usually U-shaped metal frame mounted on the gunwale of a rowboat or fitted on a frame that extends out from the side on a racing shell that serves as a rest for the oar and as a fulcrum point about which the oar turns. (also called *rowlock*)

oarsman *rowing* A member of a racing crew who pulls an oar.

oarswoman *rowing* An female oarsman.

obi The belt of a judo or karate gi.

object ball *billiards* The ball that is to struck by the cue ball.

objection *horse racing* A claim of foul in a race.

observer *golf* Someone appointed by the tournament committee to report infractions of the rules to the referee and to assist the referee in deciding questions of play.

obstruction **1** *baseball* Illegal physical contact with a base runner by an opposing player who does not have the ball and who is not attempting to field or catch the ball which results in the runner's being awarded the base he would have reached, in the judgment of the umpire, had he not been obstructed.

2 *field hockey* A foul caused by a player moving between the ball and an opponent who is going for the ball with the intent to hinder the opponent rather than to play the ball that results in a free hit for the opposing team or, if the foul is committed by the defending team within the striking circle, a penalty bully or penalty flick.
3 *golf* Anything artificial erected, placed, or left on the course which interferes with play and which may be moved from the line of play or away from which the ball may be moved without penalty.
4 *rugby* A foul caused when a player holds, pushes, or charges an opponent who does not have the ball or who is not attempting to gain possession of the ball which results in a penalty kick awarded to the opposing team.
5 *sailing* An object (as a buoy or another boat) large enough to require a boat to make a substantial alteration in course in order to avoid it.
6 A foul in soccer and speedball caused when a player hinders an opponent who is attempting to play the ball or moves between an opponent and the ball in order to prevent his reaching the ball which is penalized by an indirect free kick awarded to the opposing team.

odd *golf* **1** A stroke that when played will be one more than that used for a particular hole by one's opponent.
2 A handicap stroke deducted from a weaker opponent's score for a hole.

odd court *badminton* The left service court. It is so named because the serve is made from the left court when the server's score is an odd number.

odd front or **odd man front** or **odd line** *football* A defensive alignment of a 4-man line in which one defensive tackle lines up directly opposite the center as if there were 5 defensive linemen.

odds **1** The advantage of an unequal wager granted by the person making the bet to the person accepting the bet that is often determined as the ratio of the estimated chance of each bettor's winning and that is intended to make the bet more attractive to accept. The odds normally represent the ratio between the amount that can be won and the amount wagered. A bettor who accepts a wager at 5–1 odds is risking one dollar for a chance to win 5. If he wins, he receives back his own wager plus the amount he wins for a total return of 6 dollars. Should the odds be reversed (1–5), the winner gets back 6 dollars for having put up 5.

2 *pari-mutuel betting* The ratio of the amount a bettor can win to the amount he risks in backing a particular competitor. The odds are listed on a tote board for each competitor, and they are determined by the amount of money wagered by all the bettors. As the betting progresses, the odds are constantly updated to reflect the betting activity. The greater the proportion of money in the pool bet on a particular competitor, the lower the odds will be. Occasionally the odds will be less than even (as 2-3 or 1-10), indicating overwhelming support for the favorite. **3** A handicap.

odds board see TOTE BOARD

oddsmaker A professional who establishes odds for various contests.

odds-on favorite A competitor backed to such an extent that the profit to be made on a winning bet is less than the amount wagered. ⟨an *odds-on favorite* at 4-5⟩

off 1 Being, on, or relating to the off side of a horse or a cricket field. ⟨he must cross his *off-fore* . . . when going to the left — Sheila Willcox, *The Event Horse*⟩ ⟨he bowled Johnson and . . . took Denness's *off-*stump clean out of its hole with the batsman offering no stroke — Robin Mariar, *London Times*⟩ **2** *baseball* At the expense of a particular pitcher. ⟨got a 2-run double *off* the relief pitcher⟩ **3** *football* To the outside of a specified offensive lineman's position. ⟨picks up two yards *off* right tackle — Vince Lombardi⟩ **4** *horse racing* **a** *of a racetrack* Wet or damp and rated less than fast. **b** *of the horses in a race* Out of the starting gate to begin a race.

off break *cricket* Movement of a bowled ball that on hitting the ground bounces from the off side across the wicket toward the batsman. — compare LEG BREAK

off-drive *cricket* To score a specific number of runs on an off drive. ⟨*off-drove* the second four of the innings — *London Times*⟩

off drive *cricket* A drive to the off side. — see DRIVE

offense 1 The act, action, or state of attacking an opponent or of attempting to score points in a

contest while one's opponent is attempting to stop the attack and prevent scoring. ⟨averaged 360.3 yards a game on *offense—New York Times*⟩ **2** The means or method of attacking or of trying to score; a style of play incorporating basic principles of offense. ⟨plays a careful, patterned *offense* — William Leggett, *Sports Illustrated*⟩ **3** An offensive team or members of a team who customarily play offense. ⟨the defense got together and we talked about it. We told each other . . . that the *offense* had played a great game and we couldn't let 'em down — Lee Roy Caffee⟩ **4** Offensive play or ability. ⟨his great personal *offense* continued, but now it was balanced with nearly as much defense — Dolph Schayes⟩ **5** The result of offensive play. ⟨completed 9 out of 19 throws for 109 yards, setting school records for completions and total *offense*— George Minot, Jr., *Washington Post*⟩ **6** *cricket* The act or state of being the bowler and attempting to break the batsman's wicket with bowled balls.

offensive Of or relating to an attempt to score points in a game or contest; relating to or being the team in possession of the ball or puck. ⟨*offensive* lineman⟩ ⟨good rebounding off the *offensive* board⟩ ⟨the *offensive* half of the field⟩ ⟨if one wrestler has the advantage, he will take the *offensive* starting position at the center of the mat — *NCAA Wrestling Rules*⟩

offensive foul *basketball* A personal foul (as charging) committed by a player while his team is on offense that is penalized by loss of possession of the ball.

offhand *shooting* Being or made from a standing position. ⟨an *offhand* shot⟩

off-hand *volleyball* Being a spike made by the hand away from the setter. On an off-hand spike, the spiker must wait for the ball to cross his body before hitting it.

¹official Someone (as a referee or umpire) who administers the rules of a game or sport.

²official 1 Conforming to specifications set forth in the rules of a sport; approved for use. ⟨an *official* Little League baseball⟩ **2** Accepted and recorded by the officials in a contest or by the controlling body in a sport. ⟨*official* results⟩ ⟨holds the *official* world record in the high jump⟩

official scorer *baseball* A person who keeps the official score of a game. In professional baseball the official scorer is usually a baseball writer for a newspaper who regularly covers the home team. For some games (as the All-Star Game) there may be more than one official scorer.

officiate To act as an official in a game or sport.

off-roader Someone who competes in off-road racing.

off-road racing Racing for motorcycles and specially prepared motor vehicles (as dune buggies or jeeps) usually for several hundred miles over rugged terrain that may or may not follow unpaved roads. The races are normally run from one point to another with individual competitors running in one of several classes and starting one at a time at specified intervals. The competitors are required to check in at specified check points along the route which may also serve as stops for resting, eating, taking on fuel, or repairing the vehicle, but they are not required to follow a specific route between check points. The competitor with the best elapsed time is the overall winner; recognition is also given for winners in the various classes.

off-season The period of the year during which a player is not engaged in training, regular season competition, or play-offs.

¹offside or **offsides** **1** *field hockey* Being in the attacking half of the field when there are fewer than 3 defenders nearer the goal when a teammate plays the ball. A player may be called for an infraction if offside when the ball is played by a teammate but not if the player was behind the ball at the moment it was played by a teammate if she subsequently runs ahead of the ball. When a team is called for offside, the opposing team is awarded a free hit.

2 *football* Being over or having any part of the body beyond the scrimmage line on a scrimmage down or beyond the restraining line on a free kick down at the moment the ball is put in play. The only exception to the restrictions of the scrimmage line is that the center is permitted to be in the neutral zone in preparing for the snap so long as he is not beyond the neutral zone and so long as his feet are behind the ball. On a free-kick down, only the kicker or the holder may have any part of his body beyond the restraining line. A team is penalized 5 yards if a player is offside. — compare ENCROACHING

3 *ice hockey* Being in the attacking zone ahead of the puck at the moment the puck is propelled over the blue line by a teammate. A player is considered to be offside if both of his skates are wholly over the blue line at the moment the puck completely crosses the blue line. A potential off-

side situation can occur if a defenseman fails to keep the puck in the attacking zone when his team is on the attack. In this case, all attacking players must come out of the attacking zone before the puck can be carried or passed in again. When a player is offside, play is stopped, and a face-off is held at the spot of the infraction. In professional hockey, a player is also offside if he is in the neutral zone wholly over the red line and receives a pass from a teammate in the defending zone that crossed the blue line and the red line. — see also OFFSIDE PASS

4 *lacrosse* Having fewer than 4 players in the defensive half of the field or fewer than 3 players in the attacking half of the field at any time. When a team is offside, it is charged with a technical foul. If a team scores while offside, the goal is nullified, and the defending goalkeeper is awarded the ball behind his goal. If a goal is scored when the defending team is offside, the goal counts, and the offside is ignored. In women's lacrosse, there is no offside rule.

5 *rugby* Being between the ball and the opponent's goal line at any time the ball is touched, carried, or kicked by a teammate or entering a line-out, scrum, ruck, or maul from the opponent's side or failing to retire behind the appropriate offside line. In ordinary play, a player who is offside will not be called for an infraction if he makes no attempt to play the ball or to obstruct an opponent or if he remains 10 yards from an opponent who catches the ball. When a player attempts to gain an advantage while offside or is offside in a line-out, scrum, ruck, or maul, the opposing team is awarded a penalty kick at the place of the infraction. In ordinary play, a player can get onside by running back behind the teammate who last played the ball or he may be put onside by being passed by the ballcarrier or by another player who was onside. He also will be onside once an opponent kicks or passes the ball or advances it 5 yards.

6 *soccer* Being in the attacking half of the field and between the goal line and the ball when there are fewer than 2 defenders (including the goalkeeper) nearer the goal at the moment the ball is played by a teammate. A player may be offside but not called for an infraction unless he is seeking to gain an advantage from being offside or receives a pass when offside. A player who is behind the ball when it is played cannot be offside even though he may subsequently run ahead of the ball; he is not offside if there are 2 or more defenders nearer the goal, if he receives the ball from a corner kick, a goal kick, or a throw-in, or if the ball was last played by an opposing player. In women's play, a player is offside when in the attacking half of the field with fewer than 3 defenders between her and the goal. When offside is called on a team, the opposing team is awarded an indirect free kick from the point of the infringement.

²offside or **offsides** The act or an instance of being offside; an infraction resulting from a player's being offside.

off side **1** The right side of a horse.

2 *cricket* The side of the field opposite the leg side.

3 *football* The side of an offensive formation opposite the direction of movement of the play. ⟨The *off-side* guard pulled and led the play wide — Nelson Nitchman, *Athletic Journal*⟩

4 *ice hockey* An off wing.

offside line **1** *rugby* An imaginary line across the field parallel to the goal line through the back foot of the rearmost player in a scrum, ruck, or maul or 10 yards from the line of players in a line-out that is a restraining line for players on a team who are not taking part in the scrum, line-out, ruck, or maul and that serves to define the offside area during the play.

2 *soccer* Either of 2 lines parallel to and 35 yards from each goal line formerly used in American professional soccer in place of the halfway line in determining offsides.

offside pass **1** *Canadian football* An illegal forward pass made from in front of the line of scrimmage.

2 *ice hockey* An illegal pass made to a player who is offside; a pass made from the defensive zone to a player who is in the neutral zone across the red line in professional hockey.

off-speed pitch *baseball* A pitch that is slower than normal or expected. ⟨I could pinpoint my *off-speed pitches* and not depend on my fastball all the time — Don Drysdale⟩

off spin *cricket* Spin which causes a ball to swerve from the leg side toward the off side but on bouncing to move from off to leg.

off spinner *cricket* **1** A bowled ball that has off spin.

2 A bowler who employs off spin.

off-target hit *fencing* A touch that lands outside the valid target area and that does not count as a hit.

off time *dog racing* The scheduled starting time for a race.

off wing *ice hockey* The wing position in which

a player, because of the way he normally holds his stick, will have his stick on the side toward the middle of the rink and away from the boards. It is so called from the fact that most wingers play on the wing position in which they hold their stick on the side near the boards. The off wing is for some players a disadvantage because they will have to make many plays backhanded. For others the off wing will be the natural position and an advantage because they will carry the puck nearer the middle of the ice where they can receive and make passes quicker and where they have a better angle to shoot on the goal.

Olympiad A celebration of the Olympic Games.

Olympian Someone who competes in the Olympic Games; a member of an Olympic team.

Olympic Of or relating to the Olympic Games. ⟨an *Olympic* event⟩

Olympic cross *gymnastics* A cross performed on the rings with the body turned to one side so that one arm is holding one ring straight out in front and the other arm is holding the other ring straight out behind the body.

Olympic Games or **Olympics** A program of amateur sports competition held in a different country every 4 years with representatives from more than 120 nations competing. Baron Pierre de Coubertin (1863–1937), a French educator and scholar, was primarily responsible for the establishment of the modern Olympic Games as a revival of the ancient Greek festival held in honor of Zeus. The ancient Olympic Games were held in Olympia every 4 years from 776 B.C. to A.D. 393 and consisted of competition in athletics, horse and chariot racing, music, and literature. The modern Games were first held in 1896 in Greece and, with the exception of 3 Olympiads not held because of wars, have been held in various cities of the world at regular 4-year intervals. Competition in the Games normally includes archery, basketball, boxing, canoeing, cycling, equestrian sports, fencing, field hockey, gymnastics, judo, modern pentathlon, rowing, sailing, shooting, soccer, swimming and diving, team handball, track and field, volleyball, water polo, weightlifting, and wrestling. Since 1924 a separate program of winter sports has been conducted. — see also WINTER OLYMPICS; ASIAN GAMES, COMMONWEALTH GAMES, PAN-AMERICAN GAMES

Olympic lifting Weight lifting competition in which the competitors compete in the snatch and the clean and jerk lifts. — see WEIGHT LIFTING; compare POWERLIFTING

Olympics see OLYMPIC GAMES

Olympic-size pool A swimming pool 50 yards or 50 meters long.

Olympic trench shooting A version of clay pigeon shooting included in the Olympic games in which 6 shooters in turn take 5 shots from each of 5 shooting stations arranged in a line opposite 5 sets of traps. Each set of traps is 15 meters (49 feet 3 inches) from the shooting station and has 3 traps which propel the targets at different angles. Competitors are permitted to use shotguns of 12 gauge or smaller. Competitors leading after a round of 25 shots will compete against each other in a final round of 25 shots.

on 1 At one's peak; hot. ⟨he was *on* and couldn't miss a shot⟩

2 or **on base** *baseball* Having reached base safely. ⟨2 out and 2 men *on*⟩

3 *of an object ball in snooker* To be struck first on the next play. ⟨In attempting a safety, player must drive a red ball *on* or a numbered ball he calls as *on* . . . to a cushion, or cause the cue ball to strike a cushion after hitting ball which is *on* — Billiard Congress of America Snooker Rules⟩

on-deck circle *baseball* A circle marked on each side of the field between the dugout or player's bench and home plate in which the next batter awaits his turn at bat.

on-drive *cricket* To hit an on drive off a particular bowler.

on drive *cricket* A drive to the leg side. — see DRIVE

one and nine balls A pocket billiards game played by 4 players. The balls are shot in rotation, and each ball scores points equal to its number. The player scoring the 9 ball becomes the partner of the player scoring the one ball, and the first partnership to score 61 points wins.

one-and-one or **one-plus-one** *basketball* **1** A situation in amateur play in which a fouled player is given a bonus free throw if his first shot is successful because the fouling team has exceeded the number of personal fouls permitted a team during a period. — see also BONUS

2 A free throw which if successful would result in a bonus. ⟨blew a crucial *one-and-one*⟩

one-bagger or **one-baser** or **one-base hit** A single in baseball.

One Day Event Equestrian competition which is similar to the Three Day Event but in which all events are held on a single day and which includes only the cross-country run of the endurance phase.

one-design A category of racing sailboats or iceboats in which each class has rigid design specifications so that all boats of a given one-design class will be as nearly equal as possible for competition.

one flag A behind scored in Australian Rules football which the umpire signals by raising a flag.

one-hand To catch or grab a moving ball with one hand.

one heel spin *skating* A spin in roller skating performed on the rear wheels of one skate.

100 or **100-meter dash** or **100-yard dash** *track and field* A race run over a distance of 100 meters or 100 yards.

one in the dark *bowling* A pin left standing behind another and therefore hidden from view (as in a 1–5, 2–8, or 3–9 leave).

one old cat or **one o' cat** A ball game developed from rounders and similar to rounders and baseball which is played informally by youngsters and which usually involves 3 players with one at a time being the batter, one pitching, and one playing in the field. The batter stands at a home area and tries to hit the ball pitched by the pitcher and run to a base and back to home to score. He may be put out if he swings at the ball and misses 3 times, if he is touched with the ball or if the ball is returned to the home area before he can return. Each player plays for himself and takes turns batting in a definite order. When one player is put out, the next one becomes the batter. Each player continues to bat for as long as he can continue to score and until he is put out. Often, if a player catches the ball in the air he automatically becomes the next batter regardless of the rotation. The rules are commonly modified to meet the varying demands of the playing situations.

¹one-on-one Playing directly against a single opposing player; defending against or being guarded by a single opponent. When used in reference to basketball, the term often indicates that an offensive player has brilliant individual skills but may not be as good at team play. ⟨got to learn . . . to play together, especially at the end of close games when everyone tends to go *one-on-one* because he thinks he can do it all by himself — Dave Cowens⟩ ⟨if we at least clear enough of their guys out to leave me *one-on-one* with the last tackler, that's cool, because *one-on-one* is my game — O. J. Simpson⟩

²one-on-one An informal playground game of basketball between 2 players with one playing defense when the other is playing offense. The game is normally played at one basket sometimes with the stipulation that a player keeps possession of the ball as long as he continues to score.

one-plus-one see ONE-AND-ONE

one pocket A pocket billiards game played with 15 object balls in which each player attempts to be first to pocket 8 balls in a single pocket of his choice.

1000 or **1000-yard run** *track and field* A race run over a distance of 1000 yards.

One Thousand Guineas A 1-mile stakes race for 3-year-old thoroughbred fillies that has been held annually since 1814 at Newmarket, Cambridgeshire, England, and that is one of the English Classics.

one toe spin *skating* A spin in roller skating performed on the front wheels of one skate.

one-two **1** *boxing* A combination consisting usually of a left lead followed immediately by a right cross.

2 *fencing* An attack that consists of simulating a disengage to draw a parry from the opponent and then following with a thrust in the original line of engagement.

on guard **1** or **en garde** *fencing* The basic starting position in which the fencer stands sideways to the opponent with his front foot facing the opponent and his rear foot perpendicular to the line of his front foot, his sword hand in front with the sword held up, and his other hand up in back for balance.

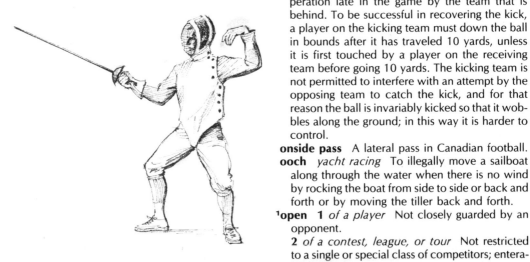

on guard position

2 The basic preparatory stance in such court games as tennis, badminton, and handball in which the player is facing the net or the front wall with his feet apart and knees bent and with one foot usually slightly forward.

on-hand *volleyball* Being a spike made by the hand nearest the setter. For an on-hand spike, the spiker does not have to wait for the ball to cross his body before hitting it.

onside *of a player in certain team sports* In a legal position with respect to the ball or puck or an opposing player; not offside:

1 *football* Being on or behind the team's line of scrimmage when the ball is put in play.

2 *ice hockey* Being behind the puck when it is brought or passed into the attacking zone.

3 *rugby* Being even with or behind the ballcarrier when he is running with the ball or when he kicks the ball forward.

4 *soccer* Being behind the ball when it is driven into the attacking part of the field; having 2 or more defenders nearer the goal when the ball is played by a teammate.

on side **1** *cricket* see LEG SIDE

2 *football* The side of the formation toward which the players move on a running play.

onside kick or **onsides kick** *football* A kickoff in which the ball travels forward just far enough to be legally recoverable by the kicking team. The ball must travel at least 10 yards, but because at least 5 members of the receiving team are positioned within 15 yards from the ball, an onside kick is seldom attempted except in desperation late in the game by the team that is behind. To be successful in recovering the kick, a player on the kicking team must down the ball in bounds after it has traveled 10 yards, unless it is first touched by a player on the receiving team before going 10 yards. The kicking team is not permitted to interfere with an attempt by the opposing team to catch the kick, and for that reason the ball is invariably kicked so that it wobbles along the ground; in this way it is harder to control.

onside pass A lateral pass in Canadian football.

ooch *yacht racing* To illegally move a sailboat along through the water when there is no wind by rocking the boat from side to side or back and forth or by moving the tiller back and forth.

[1]open **1** *of a player* Not closely guarded by an opponent.

2 *of a contest, league, or tour* Not restricted to a single or special class of competitors; enterable by both amateurs and professionals.

3 *of a stance* Having the front foot farther from the line of play of the ball than the rear foot (as in baseball or golf).

4 *of an archery string picture* Having the string appear to one side of rather than immediately behind the limb of the bow.

5 *of a slalom gate* Set up with the 2 poles perpendicular to the line of descent. — see illustration at GATE

6 *of a racket* Held or swung with the face slightly up and the top farther from the front wall or net than the bottom.

7 *of a line in fencing* Not protected from attack by the position of the fencer's arm or sword.

8 a *of a skating position* With an individual's hips or shoulders turned away from the skating foot or with the free leg slightly behind the skating foot; with ice dancing partners facing in the same direction. **b** *of a skating figure* Performed with the individual's body in an open position.

²open An open competition. — used in the name of certain tournaments ⟨the U.S. *Open*⟩

³open **1** To alter one's stance or position from more closed to more open.

2 To increase the distance between oneself and the nearest rival or competitor. ⟨*opened* a lead of 10 games — Peter Carry, *Sports Illustrated*⟩

open boat see PARTY BOAT

open circuit see SCUBA

opener **1** The first contest of a scheduled series; the first game of the season for a team.

2 The first game of a scheduled doubleheader.

3 *cricket* Either of the first two batsmen for a side.

open field *football* The area of the field beyond the defensive line where the defenders are spread apart and where the ballcarrier must dodge and outmaneuver defenders rather than simply follow his blockers.

open frame *bowling* Any frame in which a bowler fails to knock down all of the pins; a frame which is neither a strike nor a spare.

open ice *ice hockey* A part of the ice free of opposing players.

opening **1** *court tennis* An open place in a wall of the court under the penthouse. When a player drives the ball into an opening, he makes either a point or a chase depending on the position of the opening.

2 An opportunity to get through an opponent's defense.

open season The part of the year when it is legal to kill or catch game or fish protected by law.

open water *rowing* A definite space with no overlap between the winning shell and the nearest rival. ⟨his crew went on to win by *open water*, capping an undefeated season — Dan Levin, *Sports Illustrated*⟩

opponent **1** The individual or team that is being opposed directly in a contest.

2 *boxing* A journeyman boxer who is matched with developing contenders to serve as a measure of their skill or as a stepping stone for their advancement.

opposite field *baseball* The part of the field which lies on the other side of home plate from the batter when he takes his stance at the plate and to which he is not normally expected to hit the ball. Right field is the opposite field for a right-handed batter and left field is the opposite field for a left-handed batter. ⟨smashed a 360-foot, *opposite field* double — Joe McGuff, *Sporting News*⟩

opposition *fencing* Movement made while maintaining contact with an opponent's blade.

¹option **1** *baseball* The right of a major league club to send a player to the minors without putting him on waivers. A team normally has a limited number of options before it must waive the player.

2 *football* An offensive play in which the ballcarrier has the choice of running with the ball or of passing it. When a halfback is running the option play, it is commonly called the *halfback option*.

3 The right granted a club by the option clause of some player contracts to the services of a player for an additional year after the expiration of a contract.

²option *baseball* To send a major league player to a minor league team on option.

optional Being a movement, routine, or performance that is left entirely to the discretion of the individual performer (as in skating, gymnastics, or diving competition). — compare COMPULSORY

optional claiming race or **optional claimer** *horse racing* A claiming race in which the owner may take the option of entering his horse without the liability of losing it by a claim.

option clause A clause in certain professional player contracts which gives to the club the option of invoking the terms of an expired contract for one additional season. The option clause enables the club to use a player who has not agreed to a new contract. In some sports (as basketball and football) the player becomes a free agent after the expiration of the option year, and a player who seeks to become a free agent may play during the option year or sit out a season.

Orange Bowl A post-season college football bowl game played in the Orange Bowl stadium in Miami between specially invited teams of which one is often from the Big 8 conference.

ordinal *skating* A number indicating the position in which a judge places a skater in competition on the basis of performance, as 1 for first place, 2 for second, etc.

ordinary foul *water polo* A foul in international play that is equivalent to a technical foul in college play.

ordinary grasp *gymnastics* The grasp taken on a horizontal bar with the palm facing away from the performer; a regular grip.

Oriental draw see MONGOLIAN DRAW

Oriental grip see GRIP (*table tennis*)

orienteer Someone who engages in orienteering.

orienteering A competitive sport in which participants run cross-country using only a map and a compass to find their way between various checkpoints and to the finish line. There is no designated route to be followed; competitors must find the best way of getting to each checkpoint. Individuals leave the starting line at designated intervals and cover the course separately; the competitor with the lowest elapsed time is the winner. Orienteering was begun in 1918 by Major Ernst Killander, a Swedish youth leader.

orthodox grip see GRIP (*table tennis*)

¹out 1 *baseball* Having one's turn as a batter or base runner ended especially through direct defensive action by the opposing team. A batter is out if he hits a fair or foul fly ball that is caught in the air, if he has 3 strikes called on him, if he is tagged with the ball before he reaches base on a fair hit ball or a defensive player touches the base while holding the ball before the batter reaches it, if he hits a fly ball that the umpire calls an infield fly, if he fouls off an attempted bunt for a third strike, or if he in any way interferes with the catcher who is attempting to play the ball. A base runner is out if he is tagged with the ball while off base or before he reaches a base or if a defensive player with the ball touches a base he is forced to advance to, if he runs outside the basepath to avoid being tagged, if he is hit by a batted ball before it passes an infielder, or if he in any way interferes with a fielder who is attempting to play the ball. A team is out when 3 of its players have been put out in one inning. **2** *cricket* Having one's turn as a batsman ended through faulty play or through direct action by the opposing team. A batsman is out if the

bowled ball breaks his wicket (*bowled*), if he knocks down his wicket with his bat or his body (*hit wicket*), if the wicketkeeper knocks down the wicket with the ball while he is out of his crease (*stumped*), if a hit ball is caught in the air (*caught*), if a wicket to which he is running is broken by a thrown ball or by a fieldsman holding the ball (*run out*), if a bowled ball, which in the judgment of the umpire would strike the wicket, hits the batsman who is standing in front of the wicket (*leg before wicket*), if the batsman touches the ball with his hands unless asked to or hits the ball twice, or if he in any way obstructs a player on the opposing team who is attempting to field the ball. A team stays at bat until 10 of its 11 players have made out or until it declares its innings closed. **3** *golf* Relating to or being the first 9 holes of an 18 hole course. ⟨shot a 32 going *out*⟩ ⟨the *out* nine⟩ **4** To, of, or relating to the receiving side; being hand-out or side-out. ⟨advantage *out*⟩ **5** Having one's turn at serving (as in squash racquets, handball, or badminton) ended through failure to serve properly or failure to return the ball properly. **6** *of a hit ball in certain court games* Not bouncing within the boundaries of the court or the service court with the result that the player who hit the ball has committed a fault or loses the rally, the point, or the service.

²out 1 The act or an instance of putting a player out. ⟨got the *out* that retired the side⟩ **2** The act or an instance of being put out. ⟨made an *out* his last 2 times at bat⟩ **3** A player that is put out. ⟨he was the second *out*⟩ **4** A situation in which a player is put out. ⟨hit into an *out*⟩ **5** A ball hit out of bounds in a court game. ⟨In tennis by far the majority of points are made on errors and only a small minority are earned points. Furthermore, most errors are not *outs* but are made at the net — Hollis F. Fait et al., *A Manual of Physical Education Activities*⟩ **6** *football* Short for *square-out*.

out and in *bowling* A wide hook released at about the middle of the foul line that moves toward the gutter before hooking back into the pocket.

outboard A powerboat with an outboard motor.

outboard motor An internal-combustion engine that is mounted on the stern of a boat and that drives an underwater propeller through a vertical drive shaft. The entire engine and drive mechanism is a single unit that fits on the outside of the boat and that can be removed from the boat and carried separately. The engine and drive unit pivots on its mounting, and the boat is steered by turning the motor so that the propeller is turned in the direction opposite that to which the boat will turn. — see also TROLLING MOTOR

outboarder Someone who drives an outboard.

outclass To defeat an opponent or other competitors so decisively as to appear far superior. ⟨he *outclassed* 13 horses from the United States and 9 from France, England, Australia, Scotland, Ireland, and Switzerland — *Southern Living*⟩

outdistance To defeat other competitors by a wide margin.

outduel *baseball* To win a pitcher's duel against an opposing pitcher.

outfield 1 *baseball* **a** The part of the playing field that is beyond the infield and between the foul lines. There is no specific line of demarcation between the infield and outfield though on a traditional dirt and grass field the outfield is considered to begin at the grass line behind the bases. The areas of the outfield are designated left field, center field, and right field as viewed from home plate. **b** The player positions for covering the 3 areas of the outfield. **c** The players who occupy the outfield positions.
2 *cricket* **a** The part of the playing field most distant from the batsman as distinct from the infield. There is no boundary between the outfield and the infield; the distinction is essentially how far from the batsman the fieldsmen play. **b** The player positions for covering the outfield area which may include long on, long off, third man, and fine leg. **c** The players who occupy the outfield positions.
3 The part of the grounds of a racecourse that is outside the track itself; the spectator area in the outfield.

outfielder *baseball* A player who plays one of the positions in the outfield.

outfitter A dealer who sells equipment and supplies for expeditions and hunting or camping trips.

outfoot *yacht racing* To sail faster than a competing boat.

outgun To defeat an opponent with a superior offensive performance; outshoot.

outhaul *sailing* A line that secures the clew of a sail to the end of a boom or spar.

outhit *baseball* To get more base hits than the opposing team.

out home *lacrosse* **1** A primarily attacking player and a member of the close attack.
2 The position played by an out home.

outkick *track and field* To outrun another competitor by having a stronger kick.

Outland Trophy An award for the college football player voted the outstanding interior lineman of the year. It is named in honor of Dr. John Outland, a college All-American in the 1890s.

outlet *basketball* To make an outlet pass. ⟨he *outlets* the ball as well as anyone — John Wooden⟩

outlet pass 1 *basketball* A pass made by the player taking a defensive rebound to a teammate in order to start a fast break.
2 *box lacrosse* A pass made by the goalkeeper after a save to begin the team's fast break.

out of bounds 1 *basketball* On or over the sideline or end line or touching someone or something that is over the line. When a player loses the ball out of bounds, the opposing team puts the ball in play by a throw-in. Whether a player who touches the ball while he is in the air is or is not out of bounds is determined by whether or not he was inbounds when he left the floor.
2 *field hockey* Wholly over the sidelines or goal line but not into the goal. The position of the player in playing the ball is not important as long as the ball is in bounds. When a ball is driven out of bounds over the sideline, the opposing team puts it in play by a roll-in. If the ball is driven over the goal line, it is put in play by a bully or by a corner made by the opposing team.
3 *football* On or over the sideline or end line or touching anyone or anything that is out of bounds other than an official. When the ball goes out of bounds, it is out of play, but it remains in possession of the offensive team and is put in play on the next down from the nearest inbounds line where it crossed the line. If a kickoff goes out of bounds without being touched, it is kicked again after a 5-yard penalty has been assessed against the kicking team. If the ball is knocked out of bounds before it is recovered on a kickoff, it belongs to the receiving team. Once an offensive player steps out of bounds, he cannot legally touch a forward pass until it has been touched by an opposing player. When a player catches a pass near the boundary line, he must touch the ground inbounds (with both feet in some leagues) for the pass to be legally caught unless he is carried out of bounds by a defender while he is still in the air after jumping to catch the pass.
4 *golf* Wholly beyond the vertical plane be-

tween the boundary markers. When a boundary is marked by a line on the ground, the line itself is out of bounds. When a player sends a ball out of bounds, he must replay the stroke from as near as possible to the spot from which the out-of-bounds shot was made and take a one-stroke penalty.

5 *lacrosse* On or over the sideline or end line or in contact with anyone or anything on or outside the boundary lines. When a player throws the ball out of bounds or steps out of bounds with the ball, the ball is out of play and must be put in play by the opposing team with a free play.

6 *polo* Over the sideline or back line and out of play. The ball is put in play by a member of the opposing team at the point at which it crossed the line.

7 *soccer* Wholly over the touchline or end line and out of play. The position of the player in playing the ball does not matter. When the ball is driven over the side boundary line, a member of the opposing team puts it in play by a throw-in. A ball driven out of bounds over the goal line is put in play by the opposing team on a corner kick if driven out by the defending team or a goal kick if driven out by the attacking team.

8 *volleyball* On the floor wholly over the side or back boundary line. The position of the player is not important; the ball must touch the floor or ground to be out of bounds, and when it is out of bounds, the team knocking it out loses the rally.

9 *water polo* Over the boundaries of the playing area; having touched the pool wall above the water line. A ball driven out of bounds is out of play; it is put in play by the opposing team with a free throw or a corner throw.

out-of-bounds play *basketball* A play used by a team getting possession of the ball out of bounds in its own frontcourt that is intended to get a man free to receive the throw-in.

out-of-hand serve *badminton* A serve made by dropping the shuttlecock from the hand just as the racket is about to hit it.

out of shape *of an auto racing driver* Having momentarily lost control of the car so that the car is out of proper position (as off the roadway or skidding) with the result that the driver must interrupt his concentration on the course to straighten the car and get it back on the line.

outpitch *baseball* To pitch a better game than a rival pitcher and by doing so to defeat his team.

outplay To play a better game than an opponent; defeat.

outpoint *boxing* To win a decision over an opponent by points.

outrebound *basketball* To get more rebounds in a game than an opposing player or team.

outrider *horse racing* The person who rides the lead horse in parading the racehorses in front of the stands during the post parade.

outrigger **1** One of usually 2 long poles that extend on either side of a deep-sea fishing boat to hold the lines out to the side during trolling. The outrigger is equipped with a snap catch which will release the line when the fish makes a strike so that the fish can be played directly over the stern of the boat.
2 *rowing* A frame that supports the oarlock out from the side of a racing shell.

outroll *bowling* To defeat another competitor in a series.

¹outrun A relatively flat area at the end of a ski slope or bobsled run on which competitors can slow up and stop.

²outrun To run faster than another competitor; to defeat a specific competitor in a race.

¹outshoot To shoot more often or more accurately than an opponent.

²outshoot An old name for a baseball pitch that breaks away from the batter.

¹outside **1** An area farthest from a specified or implied point of reference:
a *baseball* The side of home plate farthest from the batter; the area to the side of home plate away from the batter.
b (1) The part or lane of a racetrack farthest from the infield. (2) The area farthest from the center of a turn.
c (1) The part of a playing area farthest from the middle or from the goal. (2) *basketball* The area away from the free throw lane and near the division line or near the sideline.
d *football* The outer edges of the offensive line; the flank of the formation.
e The side of a skier's or skater's body away from the direction of a turn; the edge of a ski or skate away from the other ski or skate.
f The side of a wave farthest from shore.
2 *soccer* An outside forward; wing.

²outside To, toward, or on the outside. ⟨the pass reciever ran a short way downfield and cut *outside* for the pass⟩ ⟨pitched him low and *outside*⟩ ⟨forced them to take *outside* shots⟩

out side The receiving side in some court games (as badminton, handball, or squash racquets).

outside agency *golf* A person who is not a player's caddy or partner and who is not permitted to give advice to a golfer during the match.

outside forward *soccer* Either of 2 forwards in a 5-man forward line who normally play along the sides of the field.

outside half *soccer* Either of 2 halfbacks who normally play near the sides of the field.

outside line *handball* A line on the floor to mark the side boundary on the open side of a 3-wall court.

outside lines *fencing* Lines of attack leading to the fencer's body on the sword-hand side.

outside-of-the-foot kick *soccer* A kick made by hitting the ball with the outside edge of the foot.

outside pass *track and field* A baton exchange in which the incoming runner approaches the outgoing runner on the outside of the lane and passes the baton from his left hand to the right hand of his teammate.

outslug *baseball* To defeat the opposing team especially in a high-scoring game.

outswinger *cricket* A bowled ball that swerves away from the batsman while in the air rather than after bouncing. When delivered to a right-handed batsman by a right-handed bowler it is analogous to a curve in baseball; when delivered by a left-handed bowler, it resembles a screwball. (also called *awayswinger*)

out-turn *curling* A delivery in which the hand is turned inward with the knuckles up so that the stone curls toward the side opposite the propelling hand as it nears the house.

outwick *curling* A shot in which the player's stone hits the outside of another stone and drives it toward the tee.

oval A racetrack roughly in the shape of an oval or a rectangle with rounded corners. — compare ROAD COURSE, TRI-OVAL

over *cricket* A series of usually 6 or sometimes 8 balls bowled consecutively by one bowler from one end of the wicket. During the over the bowler may be bowling to different batsmen. The same bowler is not permitted to bowl successive overs so a team must employ at least 2 bowlers who alternate overs.

over and under A shotgun or combination rifle and shotgun having 2 separate chambers and 2 barrels placed one over the other that fire independently.

overarm 1 see OVERHAND
2 *of a swimming stroke* Made with the arm lifted out of the water and stretched forward beyond the head on the recovery.

over-arm drag *wrestling* A movement by a wrestler from a position on the mat facing the opponent in which the opponent is grasped by the arm and pulled forward so that the wrestler can swing his body around behind the opponent.

overdistance *track and field* A training technique in which a runner increases his endurance by running distances greater than that of his usual event. (also called *volume training*)

overdraw *archery* To draw an arrow back too far so that the tip is behind the handle of the bow.

overgrip see GRIP (*gymnastics*)

¹overhand *of a throw or stroke* Made with the hand brought forward and down from above shoulder level. (also called *overarm*)

overhand

²overhand An overhand stroke (as in tennis or handball).

overhand grip An overgrip.

overhand knot A knot often used as a stopper knot or as part of another knot (as the fisherman's knot) that is formed by making a loop in the rope and passing the end over the standing part and back through the loop. — see illustration at KNOT

overhang *mountain climbing* A rock face with a slope of more than 90 degrees that extends back toward the climber. — compare GLACIS, SLAB, WALL

overhaul To overtake an opponent or a competitor who is ahead.

overhead

wrestler applying overscissors to opponent's foot

overhead A stroke (as in tennis or badminton) made during a rally by hitting the ball or shuttlecock while it is in the air above the head.

overhead dribble *speedball* A manuever which consist of throwing the ball into the air (as over the head of an opponent) and running to catch it before it touches the ground. Only one overhead dribble is allowed before a player must pass the ball to a teammate. The overhead dribble is identical to the air dribble of basketball. (also called *juggle*)

overhead kick or **overhead volley** *soccer* A kick made by jumping up and kicking the ball back over one's head with a scissors movement of the legs.

overhead mark *Australian Rules football* A mark taken by catching the ball over the head.

overhead pass A pass (as in speedball or basketball) made by holding the ball above the head with both hands and snapping both hands forward at the same time.

overhead volley see OVERHEAD KICK

overlapping grip see GRIP (*golf*)

overlay *pari-mutuel betting* A situation in which the closing odds on a given competitor are greater than they were in the morning line.

overload To send more offensive players into an area of a zone than there are defenders to cover them thereby creating a weakness in that or in some other area if additional defenders move in to help out.

overmanage *of a baseball manager* To use more strategy in a ball game than is necessary or wise.

overnight or **overnight race** *horse racing* A race for which entries close 72 hours before the race. — compare EARLY CLOSING RACE

overplay To play toward an opponent's favorite or more effective side when guarding him in order to force him to move the other way.

overscissors *wrestling* An illegal hold in which a wrestler who is himself held in a straight body scissors applies a scissors hold or leverage to his opponent's ankles or insteps. The hold may possibly cause injury to the ankles of his opponent.

¹overshift To make an unusual or extreme shift.

²overshift An unusual or extreme shift.

overslide *baseball* To slide beyond a base and thereby be in jeopardy of being put out.

overspin see TOPSPIN

overstand *sailing* To stay too long on a tack and pass an object (as a buoy) at which a turn is to be made.

¹oversteer The tendency of an automobile to turn more sharply than a driver intends.

²oversteer *of an automobile* To tend to turn more sharply on a curve than a driver intends.

over the falls *surfing* Straight over the curl of a breaking wave.

over-the-head check see INDIAN CHECK

¹overthrow 1 To throw the ball beyond the target. 〈*overthrew* second base〉
2 *of a pitcher* To try to throw a pitch too hard.

²overthrow A throw that goes past its target. 〈went to third on the *overthrow*〉

overtime An extension of the playing time or of the normal length of a contest to decide a winner when the score is tied or when 2 or more competitors are tied at the end of regular competition. Though the term is normally used only of extra periods in timed contests, it is sometimes extended to include extra innings in baseball or a shootoff in trapshooting.
1 *basketball* A 5-minute period (3 minutes in high school competition) after the end of regular play. The overtime period is begun with a jump ball and is treated as an extension of the last period of regulation play with respect to fouls. In college play the team fouls situation remains as it was in regulation play, but in professional play the team fouls begin at zero in overtime. Personal fouls, however, remain unchanged and a player who has fouled out during regulation play is not permitted to reenter the game during overtime. If more than one overtime period is needed, there is a 1-minute break between each.
2 *box lacrosse* A 10-minute period played after the end of regulation play in any tied game. The

team scoring the most goals in the overtime period wins, and if the tie remains the game is declared a draw. In play-off games the teams play as many 20-minute periods as needed if a tie remains after the first 10-minute period with the first team to score a goal winning.

3 *football* A 15-minute period played after the end of regulation play of games that are tied in professional football. The overtime period begins with a kickoff decided on the basis of a coin toss, and it ends immediately when one side scores. A regular season game that is still tied at the end of one overtime period is left as a tie game. Championship play-off games may take as many overtime periods as needed to determine a winner. Where more than one extra period is played, there is a 2-minute break between periods.

4 *ice hockey* A 10-minute period played after the end of regulation play in any tied game in certain leagues and only in championship play-off games in other leagues. The overtime is sudden death with the first team to score a goal winning. When the league rules do not permit more than one overtime period (as in college play), the game is left as a tie if the teams are still tied at the end of the extra period.

5 *lacrosse* A 5-minute period played after regulation play. There is a maximum of 2 overtime periods. The first is begun with a 5-minute rest after the end of regulation play, and there is a 2-minute rest before the second period if one is needed. A game tied at the end of the second overtime period remains a tie.

6 *volleyball* An unlimited period of play after the expiration of the time limit for a regulation game. The overtime is played until one side has a 2-point advantage.

7 *wrestling* Three 1-minute periods of wrestling after the end of a match. There is a 1-minute break between the end of the match and the start of overtime, but there is no rest between overtime periods. The overtime is observed by a referee and the judges, who vote for a winner if neither wrestler has a fall or has gained an advantage in points by the end of the overtime.

overtrain To train too hard for an event or a meet with the result that one peaks too soon and is at less than one's best for the competition.

overweight *of a racehorse* Carrying more weight than required for the race because the jockey weighs more than the impost.

own goal *soccer* A goal credited to the opposing team because a defensive player knocks the ball into his own goal.

oxer *equitation* An obstacle for show jumping which consists of a section of brush with a low rail in front.

P

PA *mountain climbing* A lightweight rock climbing shoe with fabric uppers and rubber soles. The letters come from the initials of the designer.

¹pace **1** Speed. The term is used of the speed with which a race is run or the speed of the leader of a race ⟨set the *pace* for the first half mile⟩ ⟨stayed just off the *pace*⟩ or the rate of speed with which a game is played or the speed of players ⟨the four wings . . . all possess blistering *pace* which is so vital on the dry hard grounds — John Dawes, *Sportsworld*⟩ ⟨has lost so much *pace* that he is little more than a sad parody of the player he was — David Lacey, *The (London) Guardian*⟩ or the force or speed of a hit or bowled ball. ⟨a crowd of 45,000 saw the *pace* of Keith Boyce, Van Holder, and Andy Roberts demoralise the Indian batsmen as they collapsed to 118 all out — Peter Laker, *(London) Daily Mirror*⟩ ⟨the only time one can dispense with a wind-up and follow-through is against a very hard ball such as a big serve since a "block" action allows the player to use the opponent's *pace*. To make your own *pace,* a full wind-up and follow-through are necessities — Pancho Segura and Gladys M. Heldman⟩
2a *equitation* A 2-beat gait in which the legs move in lateral pairs supporting the horse alternately on the left and right legs. — compare TROT **b** A harness race in which the horses move at a pace.

²pace **1** To set the pace for a race.
2a *of a horse* To move at a pace. **b** To drive or ride a horse at a pace.
3 To serve as a pacer for another bowler.
4 To compete in such a manner as to conserve some of one's energies for the later stages of a contest.
5 To hit a ball or shuttlecock with a specific controlled force or speed. ⟨it is deemed correctly *paced* if it falls not less than 1 ft. or more than 2 ft. 6 in. short of the other back boundary line — Margaret Varner Bloss, *Badminton*⟩

pace bowler *cricket* A fast bowler.

pace car *auto racing* An automobile that leads the field of competitors through the parade and pace laps and then pulls off the course just before the start of the race.

pace lap *auto racing* A lap of the course taken by the field with all cars keeping the alignment of the grid so that the engines may warm up and so that the field will approach the starting line at high speed for a flying start. The pace lap is usually led by a pace car, though when a pace car is not used or has pulled off the course the pace is maintained by the driver in the pole position.

paceman *cricket* A fast bowler.

pace of the green *lawn bowling* The speed with which the bowl travels from the point of delivery to the other end of the green.

pacer **1** A competitor who sets the pace in a race.
2 A standardbred whose natural or acquired gait is a pace.
3 A bowler who alternates bowling with a tournament competitor who is not matched up with another competitor or team in order to give him a rest between frames and to have him finish his string at the same time other competitors finish. The pacer is not a competitor, and his score is not counted.

pacing **1** Movement of a horse at a pace.
2 Harness racing of pacers.

pack **1** A group of competitors in a bunch behind the leaders in a race.
2 *fox hunting* The group of hounds that run together.
3 *rugby* The group of forwards who line up in a formation for the scrum. Normally the pack has 3 forwards on the front row, 4 on the second row, and one on the third.
4 Short for *backpack.*

packframe A lightweight usually aluminum frame that supports a backpack and is worn on the back by means of 2 padded shoulder straps and usually a padded hip belt. — see illustration at BACKPACK

packsack A backpack.

pad **1** A piece of protective equipment intended

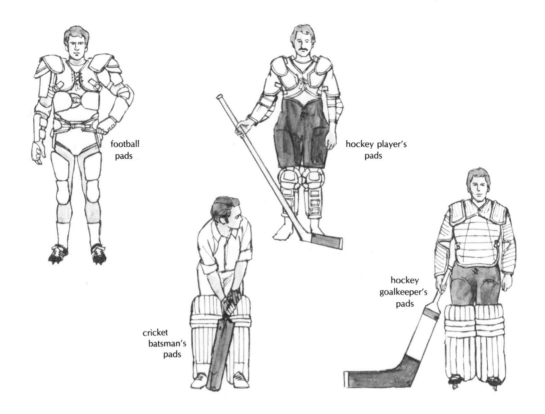

football
pads

hockey player's
pads

cricket
batsman's
pads

hockey
goalkeeper's
pads

to protect various parts of the body (as the shoulders, elbows, hips, or shins) from injury. Pads such as the shoulder pads worn by football or hockey players typically consist of a hard surface (as of molded plastic or leather) backed by a cushioned layer (as of foam rubber). The leg pads worn by the goalkeeper in ice or field hockey or by the batsman in cricket are typically made of tubular rubber encased in a fabric cover. — see also CHEST PROTECTOR, SHIN GUARD

2 *fox hunting* A foot of a fox taken as a trophy.

¹paddle **1** An implement that can be drawn through the water with 2 hands to propel and steer a canoe. It is usually made of wood or aluminum and consists of a broad flat blade approximately 6–8 inches wide and 1½ feet long that narrows to a round shaft about 3 feet long, which serves as the handle. The end of the handle is flared and rounded to fit comfortably in the palm of the hand. A double-ended paddle is used for paddling a kayak. It has a short blade on each end so that the paddler can paddle on each side

without having to switch the paddle from one side to the other. The ends of the blades are slightly bent, and the blades are normally set in planes perpendicular to each other so that as one in pulled through the water, the other is feathered.

2 An implement consisting of a broad flat rounded blade with a short handle that is used in striking the ball in certain games. The paddle tennis and platform tennis paddle is approximately 8 inches wide and 17 inches long and is made of plastic or laminated wood with holes drilled in it to reduce air resistance. The paddle for paddleball is 15 inches long and 8 inches wide and has a leather thong through the end of the handle which is worn around the wrist during play. The table tennis paddle is slightly smaller than the paddleball paddle. It is made of laminated wood, and each side of the blade is usually faced with pebbled rubber. Paddles faced with a layer of sponge topped by a layer of smooth or pebbled rubber have become popular in re-

paddle

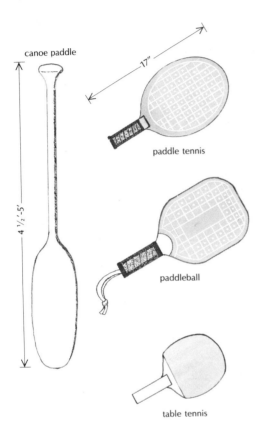

canoe paddle

17"

4 ½'–5'

paddle tennis

paddleball

table tennis

cent years. Paddles faced with plain sponge or with sandpaper are not permitted in formal competition.

3 The game of platform tennis.

²paddle To propel a canoe or kayak by pulling a paddle through the water.

paddleball **1** A singles or doubles game played on a 1-, 3-, or 4-wall handball court under rules identical to handball rules except that the players hit a small gray ball to the front wall with paddles.

2 The ball used in paddleball. — see BALL

paddleboard A relatively long narrow buoyant board that supports a person in the water and is propelled by paddling with the arms and hands. Paddleboards have been used both as aids to nonswimmers and as rescue devices to reach swimmers in trouble.

paddler **1** Someone who paddles a canoe or kayak.

2 A platform tennis player.

paddle tennis A variation of tennis played on a

smaller court using a sponge-rubber ball or a punctured tennis ball and wooden or plastic paddles. When it was first played, paddle tennis employed a court with dimensions exactly half those of the tennis court, and the height of the net was limited to 2 feet 2 inches at the middle. The court was later increased to 20 feet by 44 feet, the net raised, and the service limited to one stroke to correspond with the rules earlier adopted for platform tennis. With the exception of the equipment, the size of the court, and the single serve, paddle tennis is played according to the rules of lawn tennis, and the terminology of both games is the same. (also called *playground paddle tennis*) — see also PLATFORM TENNIS

paddock **1** *horse racing* An area for saddling or harnessing and walking horses before they are brought onto the track for a race.

2 *motor racing* An area where vehicles are parked and prepared for racing before they enter the course. The paddock usually provides space for competitors to park cars and trailers while at the track.

paddock judge *horse racing* An official who supervises the preparing of horses for a race and ensures that the horses are ready on time.

painter *boating* A short line attached usually to the bow with which the boat is secured to a landing.

pairs Competition (as in rowing, lawn bowling, or skating) involving 2 individuals on a side or competing as a unit. In skating, the pair normally consists of a man and a woman.

pair skating or **pairs skating** Free skating in which a man and a woman skate a program of jumps, spins, and lifts to music of their choice.

pallino or **pallina** *boccie* The small ball that is tossed or rolled down the court to begin a round of play and that is the target for the round. (also called *boccino, jack*)

palm ball *baseball* An off-speed pitch that is gripped between the thumb and the palm instead of with the ends of the fingers and that is thrown so that the fingers do not impart rotation to the ball.

palm the ball *basketball* To allow the ball to rest in the upturned palm momentarily while dribbling. Palming the ball is a violation of the rules for which the other team is given possession of the ball out of bounds.

palooka *boxing* An old term for an inept boxer. ⟨anyone who is so inexperienced or stupid that he can be hit by a swing is a *palooka* who can be murdered by straight punches, hooks, or uppercuts — Jack Dempsey⟩

Pan-African Games A program of international athletic competition held in 1965 and again in 1973 among the nations of Africa.

Pan-American Games A program of international sports competition similar to the Olympic Games that has been held every 4 years since 1951 between Olympic Games among the nations of the Western Hemisphere. The events include baseball, basketball, boxing, cycling, equestrian events, judo, Modern Pentathlon, polo, rowing, shooting, soccer, swimming and diving, tennis, track and field, volleyball, water polo, weight lifting, wrestling, and yachting.

pancake *wrestling* A throw in which the wrestler, usually from a position to one side of and facing his opponent, secures an arm lock on the opponent's near arm and reaches across to grasp the far arm or encircle the opponent's waist and then, pulling to the near side, twists the opponent off balance, and pulls him backwards to the mat.

wrestler bringing opponent to the mat with a pancake

panfish *fishing* A freshwater fish (as a sunfish or perch) that is usually smaller and somewhat less of a fighter when hooked than a game fish and that is usually not stocked in rivers and lakes as are many game fish but which is popular especially because of its eating qualities.

pannier *pigeon racing* A large basket in which racing pigeons are carried to the release site.

¹par *golf* **1** A standard score that an expert playing errorless golf under ordinary weather conditions would be expected to make on a given hole. The par for each hole on a course is calculated by the course architect or the greens

committee on the basis of the distance, allowing 2 putts on every hole. If on a given hole, an expert could be expected to routinely reach the green on his tee shot, the allowed 2 putts would make the hole a par 3. Par for a round of golf is the sum of the pars for the individual holes played during the round. — compare BOGEY

2 A score (as for a hole or a round) equal to par. ⟨was 3 strokes behind the leader with an even *par* 72⟩

PAR		
par	men	women
3	up to 250 yds	up to 210 yds
4	251 to 470	211 to 400
5	471 and over	401 to 575
6	——	576 and over

Yardage guidelines of the United States Golf Association

²par *golf* To shoot par for a hole or a round. ⟨*parred* the remaining holes to win by a stroke — Syd King, *Sporting Life*⟩

parachute spinnaker *sailing* An exceptionally large spinnaker used especially in yacht racing.

parachutist A skydiver.

parade lap *auto racing* A lap of the course by the field of cars led by the pace car that precedes and is slower than the pace lap and that is taken both to warm up the cars and to permit the spectators around the course to get a good view of the field before the race starts.

parade ring see WALKING RING

paragraph three *skating* Any of various figure eight patterns (as a bracket, loop, or three turn) skated on one foot with a turn introduced into each circle so that the skater starts a circle facing in one direction and finishes it facing in the other direction.

parakiting or **parasailing** The sport of soaring in a parachute while being towed by a moving vehicle (as a car or motorboat).

¹parallel 1 *of a skiing movement or turn* Made with the skis held relatively parallel throughout. ⟨*parallel* christie⟩

2 *of a stance* Having both feet approximately the same distance from the line of play of the ball. — compare CLOSED, OPEN

²parallel To make a parallel turn in skiing.

parallel bars

parallel bars 1 *equitation* An obstacle in show jumping which consists of posts and rails with a single rail behind them.
2 *gymnastics* **a** A set of wooden bars 3500 millimeters (approximately 11½ feet) long that are supported 420 millimeters (16 inches) apart and 1700 millimeters (5½ feet) above the floor on which such movements as swings, balances, and somersaults are performed.—see illustration at MOORE **b** An event in competition for men in which the parallel bars are used.
parallel garland see GARLAND
parallelogram A rectangular area 15 yards wide and 5 yards deep immediately in front of the goal on a Gaelic football or hurling field. The parallelogram is similar to the goal area of soccer or the striking circle of field hockey in that the goalkeeper may not be charged in the parallelogram and that fouls committed by the defending team within the parallelogram are penalized by a penalty kick.
Paralympics see WHEELCHAIR GAMES
parasailing see PARAKITING
pari-mutuel betting A system of betting used chiefly in horse and dog racing and in jai alai in which all bets are pooled by the track or club management and the winnings distributed after operating expenses and state taxes have been deducted. Pari-mutuel, French for mutual wager, differs from bookmaking principally in 2 respects: 1) the track's commission is taken off the top as a set percentage and is not dependent on the odds or on a particular competitor's winning, and 2) the odds are determined solely by the amount of money that is bet on a given competitor in relation to the total amount in the pool. Throughout the betting, the odds are constantly being updated, and all payoffs are made on the basis of the final odds, which often are not computed until after the beginning of the contest. This system was developed in 1872 by Pierre Oller, a French shopkeeper and bookmaker, as a method of guaranteeing the bookmaker a set commission regardless of the winner of the race. Oller's system gained popularity and was soon taken over by the government as the only legal form of betting on horse racing in France. Pari-mutuel betting gradually gained acceptance throughout the world and has generally replaced bookmaking as the legal form of betting in most of the world. In the United States, betting is usually in 3 separate pools, win, place, and show. In betting a competitor to win, the bettor collects only if the competitor wins. Place betting pays off if the competitor finishes in first or second position; show betting pays for a finish among the top 3. In England, where betting is usually only for win and place, a bet to place is paid if the competitor is among the first 3.

In calculating the payoff, the management first subtracts the taxes and its commission (some of which goes to make up the purses for the races) from the gross amount of the pool and then subtracts the amount wagered on the winning competitor — the amount of the original wager is always returned with the winnings. The remainder is divided among the winning-ticket holders as winnings. Example: in a horse race in which 6 horses are entered, the win pool has a total of $152,000 wagered as follows: on horse A, $70,000; horse B, $40,000; horse C, $20,000; horse D, $12,000; horse E, $8,000; and horse F, $2,000. From the $152,000, the track deducts approximately 15% for its takeout, leaving $129,200 to be redistributed to the backers of the winning horse. If horse A, the favorite, wins the race, the amount wagered on horse A ($70,000) is subtracted from the net pool, leaving $59,200 to be returned as winnings. This is approximately 85 cents profit for every dollar wagered or odds of around 4–5. Tracks, however, round off the dollar odds to the next lowest dime before paying off, keeping the rest as breakage; so the actual profit is only 80 cents on the dollar. For a typical $2 bet on horse A, the bettor would receive $3.60 back — his original $2 plus $1.60 in winnings. If horse F, the long shot, had won, there would have been $127,200 ($129,200 minus $2,000) for winnings or a profit of $63.60 on every dollar bet.

In betting a horse to place, the bettor picks the horse to finish either first or second. The net of the place pool is therefore divided among backers of the first and second place finishers. In the show pool, the money is divided among the backers of the first three finishers. — see also BREAKAGE, MINUS POOL; compare BOOKMAKING
par in *golf* To finish a round by scoring pars on each remaining hole. ⟨shot a couple of bogeys to slip back to even par after 12 holes. I *parred in* from there for a 70 — Frank Beard⟩
parka A hooded typically front-opening jacket that may or may not be insulated and that is worn especially by hikers and mountain climbers for protection from wind and sometimes from rain.
parked out *of a harness horse* Running on the outside with one or more horses nearer the rail.

parlay A series of 2 or more wagers arranged in advance so that if the original wager is successful the wager plus the winnings are risked on successive wagers. If any wager along the way is unsuccessful, the entire amount is lost. (also called *accumulator*)

¹parry *fencing* A defensive maneuver in which the fencer interposes his sword blade to keep the opponent's blade from reaching the target. There are 3 major types of parry: the *blocking parry,*

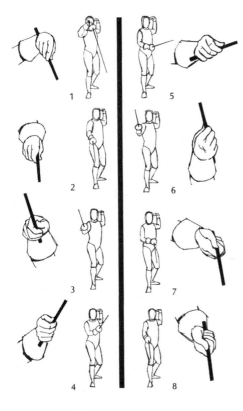

traditional parry positions

in which the blade is moved directly into the line of attack to knock the opponent's blade away; the *semicircular parry,* in which the blade is moved from a high line to a low line or from a low to a high line in a sweeping arc to catch the attacking blade and move it away; and the *circular parry,* in which the blade tip is moved in a small circle to contact the attacking blade from the opposite side and push it away. There are 8 traditional parrying positions covering the 4 quarters into which the target is divided in theory.

²parry To block a thrust or blow by an opponent (as in fencing or boxing).

partido *jai alai* A form of competition in which 2 players or teams play against each other until one player or side scores 15 points. — compare QUINIELA

partner Either of the 2 players who make up a side in a game.

party boat A large seagoing boat that operates on a regular schedule taking groups of customers for full- or half-day trips to off-shore fishing areas. Large party boats may accommodate 100 people or more at a time. (also called *head boat, open boat*)

pase or **pass** *bullfighting* The leading of the bull past the bullfighter on one side with a graceful sweep of the cape or the muleta.

pasgang *ski touring* A technique of striding in which a kick is accompanied with a push with the pole on the same side of the body. This technique is not regularly used because it is less effective than pushing off with the pole in the opposite hand, but it is sometimes employed to rest the arms. — compare DIAGONAL

¹pass 1 A transfer of the ball or puck in a goal game from one player to a teammate who is in better position to advance or score or who can more effectively exploit a weakness in the defense. In making a pass, the player directs the ball or puck to the teammate or the spot where he expects the teammate to arrive.
2 A passing shot (as in tennis).
3 *baseball* A base on balls.
4 *court tennis* A service fault that results when the ball lands beyond the pass line.
5 or **passé** *fencing* Grazing contact of the sword tip with the target which does not count as a hit.
6 *track and field* **a** An election not to compete in a trial at a particular height (as in pole vault or high jump competition) in order to wait for a greater height and avoid the risk of being eliminated at the lower height. **b** The transfer of the baton from one runner to a teammate in a relay race; exchange.
7 *waterskiing* A single run over a course (as a slalom course) in competition.
8 see PASE

²pass 1 To throw, kick, or hit a ball or puck to a teammate.
2 To make a passing shot against a specific opponent (as in tennis).

303

3 *baseball* To give a base on balls to a specific opposing batter.

4 *track and field* **a** To elect not to attempt a trial at a particular height (as in pole vault or high jump competition). **b** To transfer the baton to the next runner in a relay race.

passager *falconry* A wild immature falcon caught while migrating.

pass-block *football* To block for the passer on a pass play. ⟨when I began to *pass-block* in the pros, I realized I had to nullify the size of those big linebackers on a blitz — Matt Snell⟩

passcatcher *football* A pass receiver.

pass-completion average *football* A number between 0 and 1 carried to 3 decimal places that is determined by dividing the number of passes completed by the total number of passes thrown and that is used as a measure of the effectiveness of a passer. Example: a player who has attempted 24 passes and has completed 16 has a pass-completion average of .667.

pass cut *lacrosse* A maneuver in which an attacking player who does not have the ball gets free of his man (as by a fake or screen) to be open for a pass.

passed ball *baseball* A pitched ball not hit by the batter that passes the catcher when in the opinion of the scorekeeper he should have been able with reasonable effort to stop it and that enables a runner to advance. — compare WILD PITCH

passer A player who passes the ball to a teammate. In football, the term denotes the player who makes a forward pass. Because the football passer is protected by the rules from undue roughness, he is considered the passer until the pass is completed or intercepted or until it falls to the ground incomplete.

pass-in see THROW-IN (*basketball*)

passing **1** The act or action of throwing, kicking, or hitting a ball or puck to a teammate in a goal game.

2 *football* The effectiveness of passing; yardage gained by forward passes. ⟨ranked fifth in the league in *passing*⟩

passing game *football* Offense based on use of the forward pass.

passing lane *basketball* The space between 2 teammates through which a pass can be made. ⟨learned a lot more about basketball . . . like overplaying the man, or protecting the *passing lane* — Earl Monroe⟩

passing shot A hard shot in a court game (as handball or tennis) driven to one side of and beyond the reach of the opponent. (also called *pass shot*)

passing zone see EXCHANGE ZONE

pass interference *football* Illegal interference with the opponent's attempt to catch a forward pass. — see INTERFERENCE

pass line *court tennis* A line on the hazard side of the court parallel to and 7 feet 8 inches from the main wall which runs from the last gallery line to the end wall and which serves as the side boundary of the service court.

passout *ice hockey* A pass made from behind the offensive goal to a teammate in front of the goal. ⟨scored on a *passout*⟩

pass over *surfing* To pass behind another surfer on the same wave.

pass pattern *football* A specific route run by the pass receiver in moving downfield to be in position to catch a pass. Some patterns such as the buttonhook, curl, square-in, and square-out involve cutting back upfield or to one side of the field after running a short way across the line of scrimmage. Other patterns, such as the hitch and go, zig-in, or zig-out, require the receiver to fake one way and go another. Still other patterns simply call for the receiver to run in a particular direction at full speed. These include the fly, slant, flag, and post patterns.

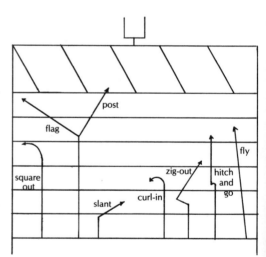

typical pass patterns

pass receiver *football* An eligible receiver and especially one who is used primarily for catching forward passes. — see also END; WIDE RECEIVER

pass rush *football* A rush of the passer by the defensive linemen.

pass rusher *football* A defensive lineman.

pass shooting *hunting* The shooting of wild waterfowl as they pass over the location of the hunters (as in moving from feeding areas to resting areas).

pass shot see PASSING SHOT

pass under *surfing* To pass in front of another surfer on the same wave.

past performance A printed record of the results of one or more of the last races run by a racehorse or dog showing by means of symbols and abbreviations such information as the length and type of race, the post position and position of the competitor at various points during the race, the speed at which the race was run, and the condition of the track.

patch *skating* An area of ice surface about 20 feet by 40 feet that is used by an individual skater in practicing figures.

patent anchor Any of several stockless anchors whose designs are patented.

pat-lid *curling* A stone lying on the tee.

Pat Lowe *skating* A jump from the inner backward edge of one foot with a full turn in the air and a return to the inner backward edge of the opposite foot. On landing, the skater follows a curve in the opposite direction from the rotation of the turn.

patrol judge *horse racing* Any of a number of judges stationed usually in high towers around the track to watch for riding infractions during a race. — compare PLACING JUDGE

pattern 1 or **pattern offense** A style of play characterized by set plays in which each member of a team is assigned a specific position or movement in relation to other team members. **2** The distribution of shot in a 30-inch circle measured 40 yards from the muzzle of a shotgun. **3** *skating* A specific sequence of steps and edges to be skated by a couple in dance skating. **4** Short for *pass pattern*.

pavilion A building at an English cricket ground that serves as the clubhouse. For a cricketer being sent back to the pavilion means being dismissed as a batsman.

pea *billiards* Any of several small numbered balls or counters which are dispensed from a shake bottle for the playing of certain games (as pill pool or forty-one).

peach basket *gymnastics* A stunt performed on the parallel bars in which the performer kips up

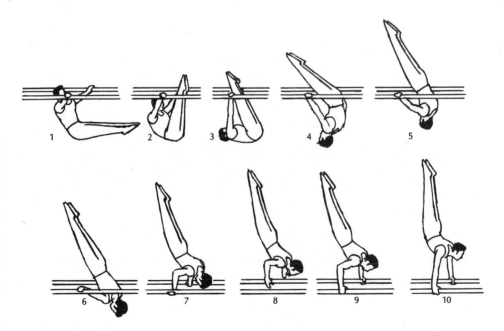

peach basket

PAST PERFORMANCE

Secretariat X — **Ch. h. 5, by Bold Ruler—Somethingroyal, by Princequillo**

Own.—Meadow Stable — **Br.—Meadow Stud Inc (Va)** — **Tr.—Laurin L**

Turf Record	St.	1st	2nd	3rd
	2	2	0	0

	St.	1st	2nd	3rd	Amt.
1973	12	9	2	1	$860,404
1972	9	7	1	0	$456,404

Date-Race-Track	Cond.	Dist.				Race	PP	St			Str	Fin	Jockey	Eq.	Wt.	Odds		Finishers	Comment	Field
28Oct73- 8WO	fm	1⅝	Ⓣ:47⅖	1:11⅗	2:41⅘	3↑Can Intern'l	12	2	21½	15	112	16½	Maple E	b	117	*.20	96–04	Secretariat 1176½ Big Spruce 1261½ Golden Don 117¾	Ridden out	12
8Oct73- 7Bel	fm	1½	Ⓣ:47	1:11⅗	2:24⅘	3↑Man o' War	3	1	13	11½	13	15	Turcotte R	b	121	*.50	103–01	Secretariat 1215 Tentam 1267½ Big Spruce 126½	Ridden out	7
29Sep73- 7Bel	sly	1½	:50	1:13⅖	2:25⅘	3↑Woodward	5	2	2½	1hd	21½	24½	Turcotte R	b	119	*.30	86–15	Prove Out 1264½ Secretariat 11911 Cougar II 126½	Best of rest	5
15Sep73- 7Bel	fst	1⅛	:45⅗	1:09⅕	1:45⅖	3↑Marl Inv. H	7	5	51¼	3½	12	13½	Turcotte R	b	124	*.40e	104–07	Secretariat 1243½ Riva Ridge 1272 Cougar II 1266½	Ridden out	7
4Aug73- 7Sar	fst	1⅛	:47⅘	1:11	1:49⅕	3↑Whitney	3	4	31	2½	2hd	21	Turcotte R	b	119	*.10	94–15	Onion 1191 Secretariat 119½ Rule by Reason 1192	Weakened	5
30Jun73- 8AP	fst	1⅛	:48	1:11⅕	1:47	Invitational	4	1	13	12½	16	19	Turcotte R	b	126	*.05	99–17	Secretariat 1269 My Gallant 120nk Our Native 12017	Easily	4
9Jun73- 8Bel	fst	1½	:46⅕	1:09⅘	2:24	Belmont	1	1	1hd	120	128	131	Turcotte R	b	126	*.10	113–05	Secretariat 12631 Twice A Prince126½MyGallant12613	Ridden out	5
19May73- 8Pim	fst	1 3/16	:48⅕	1:11⅖	1:54⅖	Preakness	3	4	1½	12½	12½	12½	Turcotte R	b	126	*.30	98–13	Secretariat 1262½ Sham 1268 Our Native 1261	Handily	6
19May73-Daily Racing Form Time1:53 2/5.																				
5May73- 9CD	fst	1¼	:47⅖	1:11⅘	1:59⅖	Ky Derby	10	11	69½	2½	1½	12½	Turcotte R	b	126	*1.50e	103–10	Secretariat 1262½ Sham 1268 Our Native 126½	Handily	13
21Apr73- 7Aqu	fst	1⅛	:48⅕	1:12⅕	1:49⅘	Wood Mem	6	7	66	55½	45½	34	Turcotte R	b	126	*.30e	83–17	Angle Light 126hd Sham 1264 Secretariat 126½	Wide, hung	8
7Apr73- 7Aqu	fst	1	:45⅕	1:08⅗	1:33⅖	Gotham	3	3	1hd	12	1½	13	Turcotte R	b	126	*.10	100–08	Secretariat 1263 Champagne Charlie 11710Flush1172½	Ridden out	6
17Mar73- 7Aqu	sly	7f	:22⅕	:44⅘	1:23⅕	Bay Shore	4	5	56	53	1hd	14½	Turcotte R	b	126	*.20	85–17	Secretarit1264½ChmpgneChrlie1182½Impecunious126no	Mild drive	6
18Nov72- 8GS	fst	1 1/16	:47⅖	1:12	1:44⅖	Garden State	6	6	46¼	33	11½	13½	Turcotte R	b	122	*.10e	83–23	Secretariat 1223½ Angle Light 122½ Step Nicely 122¾	Handily	6
28Oct72- 7Lrl	sly	1 1/16	:45⅘	1:11⅖	1:42⅘	Laurel Fut	5	6	510	53	15	18	Turcotte R	b	122	*.10e	99–14	Secretariat 1228 Stop The Music 1228 Angle Light 1221	Easily	6
14Oct72- 7Bel	fst	1	:45⅕	1:09⅘	1:35	Champagne	4	11	98½	53½	1½	12	Turcotte R	b	122	*.70e[D]	97–12	[D]Secretariat 1222 Stop The Music 1222 Step Niiely1221½	Bore in	12
14Oct72-Disqualified and placed second																				
16Sep72- 7Bel	fst	6½f	:22⅗	:45⅗	1:16⅖	Futurity	4	5	65½	53½	12	11¾	Turcotte R	b	122	*.20	98–09	Secretariat 1221¾ Stop The Music 1225SwiftCourier1222½	Handily	7
26Aug72- 7Sar	fst	6½f	:22⅘	:46⅗	1:16⅕	Hopeful	8	8	96½	1hd	14	15	Turcotte R	b	121	*.30	97–12	Secretariat 1215 Flight To Glory 121nk TopTheMusic1212	Handily	9
16Aug72- 7Sar	fst	6f	:22⅘	:46⅕	1:10	Sanford	2	5	54	41	1½	13	Turcotte R	b	121	1.50	96–14	Secretariat1213Linda'sChief1216NorthstarDncer1213½	Ridden out	5
31Jly72- 4Sar	fst	6f	:23⅕	:46⅖	1:10⅘	Allowance	4	7	73¾	3½	1hd	11½	Turcotte R	b	118	*.40	92–13	Secretariat 1181½ Russ Miron 1187 Joe Iz 1182½	Ridden out	7
15Jly72- 4Aqu	fst	6f	:22⅕	:45⅖	1:10⅗	Md Sp Wt	8	11	66½	43	1½	16	Feliciano P5	b	113	*1.30	90–14	Secretariat 1136 Master Achiever 118¾ Be On It 1184	Handily	11
4Jly72- 2Aqu	fst	5½f	:22⅖	:46⅕	1:05	Md Sp Wt	2	11	107	108¾	75½	41¼	Feliciano P5	b	113	*3.10	87–11	Herbull118nkMsterAchiever1181Flet'NRoyl118no	Impeded, rallied	12

Career past performance chart of Triple Crown winner Secretariat. The information at the top of the chart gives the horse's color (chestnut), sex classification (horse), age, and pedigree. It also lists the breeder, owner, and trainer. In this chart, the large X after the name shows the horse to be a good runner in mud. At the top right of the chart is a complete summary of his racing career including his record on turf courses with the total number of starts (St.) and first, second, and third place finishes as well as the amount of money won in each year. The twenty-one lines that follow list the horse's races in reverse order with the last race first. Each line shows the date, a code for the name of the track, the condition of the track, the length of the race (the f stands for furlongs; other races are at a mile or more), and the fractional times of the leader at two points of call and at the finish. Next comes the type or the name of the race and the position of this horse at the starting gate (post position), the starting line, two early calls in the race, the stretch call, and the finish line. The small superior numbers indicate the number of lengths by which this horse was leading or trailing the leader at a particular point. The abbreviations hd, nk, and no stand for head, neck, and nose. Following is the name of the jockey. Any apprentice allowance claimed is indicated by the small superior number after the name. Next comes a notation of the equipment used (blinkers or spurs), the total weight carried by the horse in the race, and the dollar odds. A star in front of the dollar odds indicates that this horse was the betting favorite. The final section contains the names of the first three finishers in the race along with the weight carried by each and the margin of each over the horse behind. Finally there is a comment on how this horse raced, and the number of horses in the race is given.

above the bars from a hang position, releases the bars and turns over, and grasps the bars again to wind up in a handstand position.

peak or **peak up 1** *of an athlete* To reach the peak of physical conditioning and psychological readiness at a predetermined time (as for an important meet) following a careful program of training and conditioning.

2 *of a wave* To reach a peak and begin to break.

¹pearl *of a surfboard* To make a nose dive in the trough of a wave as a result of the nose's being too low in the water.

²pearl *surfing* The act or action or an instance of a surfboard's pearling.

peas *skydiving* Fine gravel spread in the center of the target area to cushion the landing of the jumpers.

pebble *curling* To sprinkle the surface of the ice with hot water so that the drops will form little pebble-like bumps on the surface which increase the friction between the stone and the ice surface and permit the stone to be more precisely controled.

peel 1 *croquet* To drive someone else's ball through a wicket.

2 *lawn bowling* To tie the opponent or the opposing team.

peep sight see SIGHT

¹peg 1 *baseball* A hard throw to a base in an attempt to put out a runner.

2 *croquet* The stake in the middle of an association croquet court.

3 *mountain climbing* A piton.

²peg 1 *baseball* To make a peg.

2 *mountain climbing* To drive a piton into a crack.

pegging *mountain climbing* The practice or art of using artificial climbing aids (as pitons) when climbing; artificial climbing.

pelota The ball used in jai alai. — see BALL

peloton *cycling* The pack of cyclists in a road race.

penalize To assess a penalty against a particular individual or side; to deduct penalty points from an individual's score.

penalty 1 A disadvantage imposed on a player or team or an advantage awarded the opposing player or team when a player is guilty of a breach of the playing rules:

a *Australian Rules football* A free kick is awarded a player when an opponent is guilty of an infraction. During the free kick, no other player is allowed within 10 yards of the kicker.

b *basketball* A team is given possession of the ball out of bounds or a player is awarded one or more free throws when an opponent commits a technical or personal foul. A player is suspended for the remainder of the game if he is charged with 5 personal fouls (6 in professional play) or 2 technical fouls.

c *billiards* For foul strokes, a player loses his turn and may be required to forfeit one or more points. In snooker, the penalty points are added to the opponent's score but are not deducted from the fouling player's score.

d *bowling* A player forfeits the count of pins knocked down on any delivery that is a foul.

e *boxing* For unfair or illegal blows, a boxer may be cautioned and may subsequently lose points in amateur boxing or may be disqualified in amateur or professional boxing.

f *Canadian football* For a foul, a team loses 5, 10, or 15 yards, depending on the seriousness of the foul. When the defensive team is charged with the foul, the yardage is awarded to the offensive team.

g *equestrain events* A horse and rider are charged penalty points for errors, for the horse's disobedience, for knocking down fences in the jumping competition, or for exceeding the time limit in endurance competition.

h *fencing* A fencer is first warned and subsequently charged with a hit for illegal actions such as use of the free hand in defense or stepping over the side or end boundaries of the piste.

i *field hockey* For minor infractions, the opposing team is awarded a free hit at the point of the infraction. For serious fouls, the other team is given a penalty flick in men's play; a penalty bully is held in women's play.

j *football* When a team is charged with a foul, it loses 5, 10, or 15 yards, depending on the nature of the foul. When the foul is charged against the defending team, the offensive team is awarded the appropriate yardage. The spot of enforcement for penalties varies with the type of foul but in most cases penalties for fouls committed on running plays are enforced from the succeeding spot (where the ball is next to be put in play), and fouls on loose ball plays are penalized from the previous spot (where the ball was last put in play). When the offensive team fouls at a point behind either of these spots, the penalty is usually enforced from the spot of the foul. When enforcement of the full penalty would place the ball more than halfway to the goal line, it is moved only half the distance to the goal.

k *Gaelic football* A free kick is awarded the

penalty area

opposing team when a player commits a foul. If the foul is committed by a defending player within the parallelogram, a penalty kick is awarded the attackers from the middle of the 14-yard line.

l *golf* (1) A single stroke is added to a player's score for poor play which results in the player's having to drop his ball from a hazard or having to play a new ball from the spot of the last stroke. (2) A player is penalized with an assessment of 2 strokes in stroke play or loss of the hole in match play for a breach of the playing rules.

m *horse racing* For riding or driving infractions, a horse may be disqualified from a particular position at the finish and moved down one or more places, and the rider or driver may be set down. When a horse is disqualified, it receives only that share of the purse (if any) going to the position in which the horse is officially placed, and betting payoffs are made according to the official placing, regardless of how the horses actually finish.

n *hurling* A player is awarded a free puck for infractions committed by the opposing team. The referee may allow a goal or a point if a foul was committed to prevent the scoring of a goal or point.

o *ice hockey* A player may be suspended for 2, 5, or 10 minutes or for the duration of the game depending on the seriousness of the foul. — see MAJOR PENALTY, MATCH PENALTY, MINOR PENALTY, MISCONDUCT PENALTY; PENALTY SHOT

p *lacrosse* For technical fouls, a player is suspended for 30 seconds, or his team loses possession of the ball. For a personal foul, a player is suspended for one to 3 minutes while his team plays shorthanded.

q *polo* For a foul, the opposing team is awarded a free hit 30, 40, or 60 yards from the goal or from the spot of the foul, depending on the seriousness of the foul.

r *rugby* For minor infractions such as offside, play is stopped, and a scrum is formed at the point of the infraction. For more serious fouls, the fouled team is awarded a penalty kick from anywhere behind the point of the foul.

s *soccer* An indirect free kick or a direct free kick, depending on the seriousness of the foul, is awarded to the other team when a player commits a foul. When a foul which is ordinarily penalized by a direct free kick is committed in the penalty area by a member of the defending team, the offensive team is awarded a penalty kick.

t *speedball* A penalty kick is awarded a team

when an opposing player commits a technical foul; for a personal foul, the opposing team is awarded 2 penalty kicks.

u *team handball* A free throw is awarded the nearest opposing player when a player commits a minor infraction; for serious infractions, the other team is awarded a penalty throw.

v *water polo* For technical and personal fouls committed by a team, the nearest opposing player is awarded a free throw. Each personal foul is charged against the guilty player, and if he is charged with 5 personal fouls during a game, he is suspended for the remainder of the game. If a player is fouled while he is in the penalty zone facing the goal, he is awarded a penalty throw.

w *wrestling* After a warning, one point is deducted from a wrestler's score for such infractions as stalling, unnecessary roughness, and use of illegal holds on the first and second offenses. For a third offense, 2 points are deducted. A further infraction result in the wrestler's disqualification.

2 *ice hockey* A foul for which a player will be assessed a penalty. ⟨they're holding my stick. That's a *penalty,* but the refs aren't calling it — Phil Esposito⟩

3 Short for *penalty goal, penalty kick, penalty shot.*

penalty area **1** *roller hockey* A rectangular area 40 feet 6 inches wide and 18 feet deep in front of each goal that is analogous to the penalty area in soccer.

2 *soccer* A marked area on the field in front of each goal within which a foul by a defending player results in a penalty kick. The penalty area in men's play is a rectangle 44 yards wide by 18 yards deep centered on the goal. An arc 10 yards from the penalty kick mark extends beyond the far end of the area. This arc is a restraining line that serves to extend the penalty area during a penalty kick, since no player except the kicker is permitted to stand within 10 yards of the ball. In women's play the penalty area is a semicircle with a radius of 15 yards centered on the goal.

penalty bench The penalty box in ice hockey and box lacrosse.

penalty box A designated area in ice hockey and lacrosse in which a penalized player must stay for the duration of his penalty. In ice hockey and box lacrosse the penalty box is a bench partitioned off from the stands and the playing area in the neutral zone across the ice from the player's benches. In lacrosse the penalty box is located at the middle of the field on one sideline.

penalty bully *field hockey* A bully in women's play held at a spot 5 yards in front of the goal when a member of the defending team has committed a flagrant foul or a foul which in the judgment of the referee prevented the scoring of a goal. — see also PENALTY FLICK

penalty corner **1** *field hockey* A free hit of a stationary ball placed on the goal line 10 yards from the goalpost that is awarded to a member of the attacking team when a defensive player has deliberately driven the ball over the goal line or in women's play has committed a foul in the striking circle which would not be penalized by a penalty bully. During the penalty corner, 6 members of the defending team must be beyond the goal line while the remaining defenders must be in the opposite half of the field until the ball is played. All attacking players are restrained from being in the striking circle until the ball has been played. (also called *short corner*)

2 *speed-a-way* An opportunity for a member of the attacking team to put the ball in play from the spot where the striking circle meets the goal line when the defending team has fouled inside the striking circle. The ball is put in play by an unhindered throw-in or kick.

penalty flick *field hockey* A free hit at the goal in men's play from a point 8 yards in front of the goal that is awarded a member of the attacking team who is fouled inside the striking circle.

penalty goal **1** A goal scored in rugby or soccer on a penalty kick.

2 *field hockey* A score of one goal awarded the offensive team if a member of the defending team fouls during a penalty bully.

3 *polo* A goal awarded when a foul is deliberately committed by the defending team to prevent a score.

penalty hit *roller hockey* An unhindered shot at the goal defended only by the opposing goalkeeper that is awarded to an attacking player for a serious foul committed by the defense in the penalty area. The player taking the shot is given the ball at a point 18 feet in front of the goal and may not play the ball again unless it is deflected by the goalkeeper or rebounds off the goalposts. During the penalty hit, all other players must be in the opposite half of the rink.

penalty kick **1** *Gaelic football* An unhindered kick at the goal defended only by the opposing goalkeeper taken from the middle of the 14-yard line that is awarded to an offensive player fouled in the parallelogram by a defensive player. During the free kick, all other players must remain behind the 21-yard line.

2 *rugby* A free kick at the goal awarded to a player for certain fouls committed by the opposing team. The dropkick or placekick is taken from the spot of the foul and if successful, scores 3 points (2 points in Rugby League). To be successful, it must pass between the uprights and over the crossbar. During a penalty kick, opposing players are not permitted to charge the kicker. — see also FREE KICK

3 *soccer* A free kick directly at the goal defended only by the goalkeeper that is taken from the penalty kick mark by a player who has been fouled by a defensive player inside the penalty area. All other players are restricted to the area outside the penalty area and the adjoining arc during the attempt. A successful goal scores one point. After the attempt the ball is dead and play is restarted by a kickoff.

4 *speedball* **a** A placekick directly at the goal from the penalty kick mark taken by a player when the opposing team commits a technical foul or when a member of the defending team commits a violation or a personal foul inside his own end zone. In the case of the violation, one attempt is awarded, and the ball remains in play if the goal is missed. For the personal foul, 2 penalty kicks are awarded, with the ball being dead after the first attempt and in play if the second is unsuccessful. A single point is scored for each successful penalty kick. During the penalty kick attempt only the opposing goalkeeper, who is restricted to the center of the end line until the ball is kicked, may attempt to prevent the goal. To score, the ball must pass between the goalposts and under the crossbar. **b** A dropkick from the penalty kick mark awarded in women's play to the attacking team when the defensive team commits a team foul or when a defending player commits an individual foul in her own end zone. For a successful attempt, the ball must pass between the uprights and over the crossbar.

penalty kick mark **1** *soccer* A short line on the field parallel to and 12 yards in front of the goal line which is centered on the goal and on which the ball is placed for a penalty kick. (also called *penalty spot*)

2 *speedball* A spot on the goal line directly in front of the center of the goal on which the ball is placed for a penalty kick.

penalty killer *ice hockey* Any of the players put on the ice to play while his team is playing short-

penalty killing

handed. Penalty killers are usually the available players who are most proficient at controlling the puck or at breaking up the opponent's plays.

penalty killing The process of killing a penalty.

penalty mark *team handball* A spot 7 meters (approximately 23 feet) out from the front of the goal from which a penalty throw is taken.

penalty point 1 A point deducted from a competitor's score as a penalty for poor form, faulty performance, or breach of the rules.
2 *water polo* A point charged against a player in competition under international rules who has committed a major foul. After a player has been charged with 3 major fouls (3 penalty points), he is suspended for the remainder of the game.
3 *wrestling* A point charged against a wrestler in international competition for losing or drawing a match or for winning by less than a fall or evident superiority that is used in determining the final standings of the competitors. Up to 4 points may be charged depending upon the outcome of the match. — see WRESTLING

penalty shot 1 *box lacrosse* An unhindered shot at the goal defended only by the opposing goalkeeper that is awarded to a team when an opposing player is guilty of certain fouls (as throwing the stick or other object at the ball or the ball handler to prevent a goal). The ball is placed at the center face-off circle by the referee, and the player taking the shot plays it from there. Once he has entered the attacking zone, the player must continue his forward movement toward the goal. The play ends once the shot has been taken; a goal cannot be scored on a rebound.
2 *ice hockey* An unhindered shot at the goal defended only by the goalkeeper that is awarded to a player for certain infractions (as interfering with a player from behind on a breakaway in the player's attacking zone) committed by an opponent. The puck is placed at the center face-off spot (at the defending team's blue line in college hockey) and taken there by the fouled player who must continue his forward motion toward the net once he has crossed the blue line. The goalkeeper must stay in his crease until the puck is touched and may stop the puck in any manner short of throwing his stick or some other object at it. The play is complete once the puck is shot or crosses the goal line since no goal may be scored on a rebound. While the penalty shot is being attempted, all other players must remain out of the area. The puck is dead after the shot and play is restarted by a face-off.

penalty situation see BONUS SITUATION

penalty spot see PENALTY KICK MARK

penalty stroke *golf* A stroke added to a player's score as penalty for a breach of the playing rules.

penalty throw 1 *team handball* An unhindered throw at the goal defended only by the goalkeeper from a penalty mark 7 meters (approximately 23 feet) out from the middle of the goal by a player who has been fouled. During the throw, the goalkeeper is permitted to move about in the goal area, but he may not be closer than 3 meters (10 feet) to the player making the throw. The thrower must stay behind the penalty mark and take the throw immediately; all other players must be outside the free throw line and at least 3 meters from the thrower. Play continues if the goalkeeper stops the ball; if the ball rebounds out of the goal area, the defenders restart play with a free throw.
2 *water polo* An unhindered throw at the goal defended only by the goalkeeper that is taken from the 4-yard line and is awarded to a player on the attacking team who is fouled while he is in the penalty throw zone facing the goal and in possession of the ball. The player is given the ball at the 4-yard line and must immediately make a shot on goal without faking or hesitating. If the attempt is unsuccessful, the ball remains in play. During the attempt, all other players are restricted to being outside the 4-yard line, and no one may be within 5 yards of the player taking the penalty throw.

penalty throw zone *water polo* An area at each end of the pool directly in front of the goals that extends from the goalposts out to the 4-yard line and that is 22 feet wide at the 4-yard line. A penalty throw is awarded to an attacking player who is fouled while holding the ball and facing the goal in this zone.

penalty timekeeper *ice hockey* An official whose duties include keeping records of all penalties committed and ensuring that penalized players serve the full duration of their penalties.

pendulum *mountain climbing* A traverse movement from one line of ascent to another (as when there are no longer suitable holds on the first pitch) made by swinging or walking sideways while suspended on a rope from an overhead anchor point. (also called *horizontal rappel*)

penetrate To get around or through the last line of a team's defense.

penholder grip see GRIP (*table tennis*)

pennant *baseball* A large pennant-shaped flag emblematic of a league championship that is awarded to the team that wins a league championship and that is normally flown in the club's ball park through the following season.

pentathlete   An athlete who competes in the pentathlon or in the Modern Pentathlon.

pentathlon   An athletic contest made up of 5 distinct events in which each participant competes in all events with the one having the best overall score being the winner. A pentathlon was a part of the ancient Greek Olympic Games where it consisted of a footrace the length of the stadium, a long jump, javelin and discus throws, and wrestling. A pentathlon consisting of a long jump, javelin throw, 200-meter dash, discus throw, and 1500-meter run was incorporated in the track and field events of the modern Olympics until 1924. It is this pentathlon that Jim Thorpe won (while also winning the decathlon) in the 1912 Olympic Games in Sweden. This pentathlon, for men, is still a part of some meets but has generally given way to the decathlon. The women's pentathlon is a regular feature of national and international competition. It consists of the 100-meter hurdles, the shot put, the high jump, the long jump, and the 200-meter dash and is staged over 2 days. Still another pentathlon, usually for high school athletes, consists of the long jump, the high jump, the 220-yard run, the discus throw, and the mile run. Scoring for the pentathlon, as for the decathlon, is based on a scale of points relating performance to an arbitrary performance standard for each event. — see also MODERN PENTATHLON

penthouse   *court tennis*   The sloping roof that runs from the lower inner wall up to the outer wall on 3 sides of the court. On the serve and during play, the ball is played off the penthouse.

pepper or **pepper game**   *baseball*   A warming up or loosening up activity in which several players in a semicircle a short distance from a batter field the ball and toss it back to the batter who hits the ball to different fielders in turn usually with a short choppy swing.

¹percentage   The ratio of the number of successful attempts (as shots) to the total number of attempts usually expressed as a 2-place decimal and used as a measure of an individual's or team's effectiveness. ⟨free throw *percentage*⟩ — compare AVERAGE

²percentage   **1** Using techniques or strategy that have been successful most of the time rather than unusual or gambling plays; conservative. ⟨*percentage* baseball⟩
2 Being successful on a high percentage of one's efforts. ⟨a *percentage* shooter⟩

percentages   *baseball*   The likelihood that a strategy believed or known to be successful more often than not will be successful again. ⟨decided to go with the *percentages* and put in a left-handed pinch hitter against a right-handed relief pitcher⟩

perfecta   *pari-mutuel betting*   A betting pool in which the bettor must pick the competitors that will come in first and second in a particular race or contest in the correct order of their finish in order to win. (also called *exacta*) — compare QUINIELA

perfect end   *archery*   An end in which all arrows are in the target center.

perfect game   **1** *baseball*   A no-hitter in which no opposing batter has been allowed to reach base; a game in which all opposing batters are put out in succession.
2 *bowling*   A game in which the bowler rolls 12 consecutive strikes and scores the maximum 300 points.

perfection loop knot   A knot that is used for tying a symmetrical loop in the end of fishing leader and that is formed by making one loop under and another loop over the standing part of the line, passing the end between the 2 loops just formed, and pulling the second loop through the first. — see illustration at KNOT

period   A timed division of a game or match. The term is not commonly used of a game like rugby which is played only in 2 halves, but it is used widely for the divisions of a game or match having 3 or 4 divisions. Ice hockey is played in 3 periods of 20 minutes each. A wrestling match is divided into 3 periods. For games having 4 equal divisions the term *period* is synonymous with *quarter*.

personal foul   **1** *basketball*   A foul (as charging, hacking, blocking, pushing, or elbowing) that involves illegal physical contact with an opponent. If a player is fouled in the act of shooting, he is given one free throw if his field goal was successful or 2 free throws if it was not. At other times when a player fouls, the other team is given possession of the ball out of bounds except during a bonus situation. Then the fouled player is given a free throw on a one-and-one situation in high school or college play or 2 free throws in professional play. Each time a player commits a personal foul, it is charged against him, and if he accumulates 5 personal fouls (6 in professional play) he is suspended for the remainder of the game. In international play, a player is disqualified after being charged with 5 fouls; free throws are awarded the fouled player only if he is fouled in the act of shooting and misses his shot. — compare TECHNICAL FOUL

2 *football* A foul (as striking, kicking, kneeing, or elbowing an opponent or running into or roughing a kicker or passer, hurdling a player on the ground, piling on a tackled player after the ball is dead, or clipping) that constitutes dangerous and unsportsmanlike play and that is normally penalized by loss of 15 yards and, if the foul is considered flagrant, disqualification of the offending player.

3 *lacrosse* A foul (as tripping, pushing, slashing an opponent, making an illegal body check on an opponent who does not have the ball, or unnecessary roughness) that is penalized by suspension of the offending player for from one to 3 minutes at the discretion of the referee and the awarding of the ball to the other team. — compare TECHNICAL FOUL

4 *speedball* A foul (as kicking, tripping, or holding an opponent or any unnecessarily rough play) that is penalized by awarding the fouled player a free kick at the spot of the infraction. If the personal foul is committed by a defending player in his own end zone, it is penalized by awarding the fouled player 2 penalty kicks. The ball is dead after the first but in play if the second is unsuccessful. — compare TECHNICAL FOUL

5 *water polo* A foul (as holding or dunking an opponent who does not have possession of the ball, striking or kicking an opponent, or committing a technical foul deliberately to prevent a goal) that is penalized by awarding a free throw to the other side. A personal foul is recorded against the guilty player, and he is disqualified if he commits 5 fouls during the game. — compare TECHNICAL FOUL

petticoat *archery* The part of the target face outside the largest ring which has no scoring value.

photo finish A finish of a race that is so close that the officials must examine a photograph of the finish to determine which competitor finished ahead of another. In many types of racing and especially horse racing, photographs are routinely taken of the finish of races but generally examined only when the placing judges are unable to decide a finish.

phrase or **phrase d'armes** *fencing* A period of continuous action by one or both combatants which usually includes attacks and ripostes. The phrase ends whenever there is a pause in the action.

physical Marked by or employing much physical contact and rough play. ⟨the women's game, admittedly, is not as *physical* as the men's — New York Times⟩ ⟨they're *physical* along with it. We've got a big, strong team but they pushed us around as much as anybody we've played — Eddie Sutton⟩

piaffe *equitation* A dressage movement consisting of a collected trot executed in place with the horse making a smooth up and down movement.

pic *bullfighting* A picador's lance.

picador *bullfighting* A mounted member of the cuadrilla who prods the bull with a lance to weaken its neck and shoulder muscles.

pick **1** see SCREEN

2 Short for *toe pick.*

pick a cherry *bowling* To fail to knock down all the pins of a simple leave; make a cherry.

pick-and-roll *basketball* A maneuver in which a player sets a screen (pick) for a teammate with the ball and then cuts away from the defenders toward the goal for a pass.

picket *football* A wall of blockers for the ball-carrier on a kickoff or punt return.

picket fence *bowling* A leave of the 1, 2, 4, and 7 pins or of the 1, 3, 6, and 10 pins. — see illustration of pin arrangement at BOWLING

pickle *baseball* A situation in which a player is caught in a rundown between bases. ⟨was caught between third and home. . . . He managed to get out of the *pickle* and score — Tom Shea, Springfield (Mass) Daily News⟩

pickoff **1** *baseball* The act or an instance of picking a runner off base.

2 *football* An interception.

pick off **1** *auto racing* To pass another driver during a race.

2 *baseball* To put out a base runner who is off base with a quick throw from the pitcher or catcher.

3 *football* To intercept a forward pass.

¹pickup **1** *fishing* The backcast in fly fishing made to lift the line and fly from the water.

2 *wrestling* A maneuver in which the opponent or some part of the opponent's body is lifted off the mat in order to take the opponent down or to unbalance him so that he will fall to the mat. (also called *tackle*)

²pickup Utilizing or made up of local or available players without formal organization and usually without prior planning or practice. ⟨*pickup* game⟩ ⟨*pickup* team⟩

pick up **1** To assume responsibility for guarding an opponent (as in basketball or lacrosse) who is momentarily unguarded (as because of a screen). **2** *bowling* To convert a spare.

pickup man *rodeo* A mounted horseman who rides alongside the competitor to help him dismount from a bronc in the bronc riding competition. Because bulls may attack the horses, the pickup men are not used in the bull riding competition. Clowns are used instead to distract the bulls from a dismounted or thrown rider.

picture or **picture-book** Having or made with nearly perfect form or technique. ⟨a *picture* header — *North American Soccer News*⟩ ⟨worked too much at setting up *picture-book* plays from his center position, too little on addressing the puck to the . . . net — Jerry Kirshenbaum, *Sports Illustrated*⟩

pie alley *bowling* An alley on which it is relatively easy to make strikes.

pied ferme *fencing* A movement made while keeping the feet stationary. — compare PROGRESSIVE ATTACK

pig board A small surfboard for use on small surf or for hotdogging.

pigeon racing The sport of racing homing pigeons which involves transporting the pigeons to a release point sometimes up to 500 miles from the loft and releasing them at an appointed time. As the pigeons gradually return to the home lofts, they are recorded in. The pigeon covering the distance in the shortest elapsed time is the winner. The racing is quite leisurely from the standpoint of the owners, since on long races it may take several days for the pigeons to return. As they return the report of the elapsed time is forwarded to the officials, often by mail, so there may be quite a delay in learning the results of a race. In seeking to coax more speed from his birds in short races, a trainer may send the birds out at their normal feeding time so that hunger will augment each bird's normal ability to find its way home.

pigskin **1** A football. — compare HORSEHIDE **2** A jockey's saddle.

¹pike A body position (as in gymnastics or diving) in which the body is bent at the waist with the legs held straight and the back bowed so that the body is in the shape of a V. The hands may touch the feet or grasp the backs of the knees or the arms may be extended straight out to the sides. — see illustration at FORWARD DIVE

²pike To move the body into a pike.

pile The point of an arrow. — see ARROW

pile driver An aggressive action in professional wrestling in which one wrestler picks up his adversary, turns him upside down, and slams his head to the floor of the ring.

piling on *football* The act of illegally jumping on a ballcarrier after he has been tackled. The offending team will be penalized 15 yards.

pillow *canoeing* A large rock that lies just far enough under the water to allow the water to pass over it in a smooth swell.

pillowball A softball 16 inches in circumference.

pill pool A pocket billiards game in which each player before starting play draws little numbered balls or pills from a shake bottle and tries during the game to pocket the balls corresponding to the numbered pills he holds. There are 15 object balls and 16 pills with the player drawing the number 16 pill shooting on the opening break. Any balls that are legally pocketed during the game by any player are credited to the player holding that pill. The first player to have all of his balls pocketed wins. (also called *Kelly pool*)

¹pilot **1** Someone who flies an aircraft. The term has also been used in reference to the person who controls any of a number of other vehicles, such as racing cars or ice boats. **2** *baseball* The manager of a professional team. **3** or **pilot shot** *shuffleboard* A shot in which a disk is placed near the tip of the scoring area so that another disk can be hidden behind it in the scoring area or so that the opponent will have to waste a shot to knock it away. — see also CROSS PILOT, TAMPA PILOT

²pilot **1** To control a vehicle as pilot. ⟨*pilot* a sailplane⟩ ⟨chosen to *pilot* the new Ferrari 712 Can-Am car — *Watkins Glen Racing News*⟩ **2** To manage a professional baseball club. ⟨when his father *piloted* the Red Sox to their remarkable pennant — Roger Angell, *New Yorker*⟩

¹pin **1** *bowling* A distinctively shaped target object consisting usually of solid hardwood with a plastic covering or of solid plastic. For specifications, see *candlepin, duckpin, tenpin.* **2** *golf* see FLAGSTICK **3** *judo* The act or an instance of holding an opponent to the mat on his back for 30 seconds while maintaining control so that he cannot escape. It is not necessary for the opponent's back to be in constant contact with the mat so long as he is unable to escape or to gain a counter hold. A successful pin scores one point and wins the match. **4** *mountain climbing* see PITON **5** *wrestling* The act or an instance of holding an opponent to the mat on his back with his shoulder blades in contact with the mat for a full second. A pin, which is officially called a *fall*, immediately wins the match. In dual meet scoring in college competition, a fall is worth 6 points to the wrestler; in tournament scoring, one point. In international competition, a win by a fall means no penalty points for the winner and 4 penalty points for the loser.

²**pin** To secure a pin on an opponent in judo or wrestling.

pin bowler *bowling* A bowler who regularly aims at the pins when delivering the ball. — compare SPOT BOWLER

¹**pinch** **1** *bowling* To grip the ball unusually tight and thereby affect the delivery adversely.

2 *of a racehorse* To be forced to slow slightly because the space between horses or between another horse and the rail is not sufficient to pass.

3 *sailing* To sail a boat too close to the wind with the result that the sails luff and the boat loses forward speed.

²**pinch** or **pinch-hit** *baseball* Made by a pinch hitter. ⟨a *pinch* single⟩ ⟨ a *pinch-hit* home run⟩

pinch-hit *baseball* **1** To take another player's turn at bat as a pinch hitter. ⟨sent up to *pinch-hit* for the pitcher — *Scholastic Coach*⟩

2 To make a base hit while pinch hitting. ⟨*pinch-hit* a double against the right field screen — John Wilson, *Sporting News*⟩

pinch hit *baseball* A base hit made while pinch-hitting. ⟨holds the major league record for *pinch hits* — *Sporting News*⟩

pinch hitter *baseball* A player who is sent in to bat in place of another player. The pinch hitter is typically used when the team especially needs a hit, and he usually replaces a weaker hitter (as the pitcher) or one who bats from the opposite side of the plate. The pinch hitter bats only once, and the player in whose place he batted is removed from the game. When another player takes the place in the field of the removed player, the pinch hitter is officially out of the game. If the pinch hitter remains in the game and takes a position in the field, he is no longer considered a pinch hitter but a substitute. — compare DESIGNATED HITTER

pinch-out *caving* A passage that tapers down and becomes too small to pass through.

pinch-run *baseball* To act as a pinch runner. ⟨does nothing for the A's but *pinch-run* — Ron Fimrite, *Sports Illustrated*⟩

pinch runner *baseball* A player who enters the game to run for another player who is consequently removed from the game. The pinch runner is used only for one assignment. When an-

other player takes the removed player's place in the field, the pinch runner is officially out of the game. If the pinch runner remains in the game and takes a position in the field, he is no longer considered a pinch runner but a substitute. — compare COURTESY RUNNER

pin deck *bowling* The section of the alley under the pins that is made of maple boards.

pinfall **1** *bowling* The number of pins that are knocked down by one ball; the total number of pins scored by a bowler (as during a game or series).

2 *wrestling* A fall achieved by pinning an opponent's shoulders to the mat.

Ping-Pong A trademark used for table tennis.

pin high see HOLE HIGH

pinning combination *wrestling* A combination of holds and maneuvers which result in the securing of a fall.

pinsetter or **pinspotter** *bowling* A person or device that sets up the pins on a bowling lane.

pintle The upright pin of a rudder which fits into the gudgeon on the boat when the rudder is installed and on which the rudder pivots.

pinwheel *gymnastics* A sideways circle around a horizontal bar performed while straddling the bar with the hands in front of the body holding the bar.

piolet *mountain climbing* An ice ax.

pipe *ice hockey* A goalpost.

— **between the pipes** *ice hockey* Playing as goalkeeper.

pirouette **1** A full turn of the body made while balancing on one foot or while in the air on a jump.

2 *gymnastics* A turn performed on the parallel bars while in a handstand.

piste **1** *fencing* The surface on which the fencers move during the course of a bout. The strip is between 1.8 and 2 meters (5 feet 11 inches and 6 feet 7 inches) wide and 14 meters (46 feet) long. The saber piste is 24 meters (78 feet 9 inches) long. The strip is marked with 7 parallel lines. Bisecting the strip is a center line. Two meters on either side of the center line are guard lines behind which the fencers assume the on guard position at the beginning of the bout. At the end of the piste are end lines, and 2 meters (one meter in foil competition) from the end lines are warning lines. When a competitor crosses a warning line, he is warned that he is nearing the end of the strip. If, after a warning, the fencer is driven over the end line, he is penalized with a hit. — see illustration at FENCING

2 *skiing* A long trail prepared for skiing. ⟨when the *piste* gets rough I let my feet separate to the extent that I feel secure — Jean-Claude Killy⟩

¹pit **1** *bowling* The sunken area behind the pin deck into which the pins fall when they are knocked down.

2 *caving* A vertical hole or crevice.

3 *cockfighting* A circular area approximately 20 feet in diameter with an enclosing barrier in which fights are held.

4 *football* The area comprising the middle of the offensive and defensive lines. ⟨like animals, trying to claw one another apart in there. It is very hard in the *pit* — Merlin Olsen⟩ (also called *trenches*)

5 *motor racing* An area off the course where vehicles are refueled and repaired and tires are changed during a race. In auto racing, the pits are usually located on a road that parallels the main straightaway. Drag racing pits are mainly parking areas where competitors can work on their vehicles between races.

6 *track and field* The landing area for any of the jumping events constructed to cushion the impact of landing. The long jump and triple jump pits are long rectangular excavations filled with a soft loose material (as a mixture of sand and sawdust) that allows the landing spot of the jumper to be clearly marked for measuring. The pole vault and high jump pits may consist of an excavation filled with a soft material (as loose foam rubber) or may be a portable 1-piece air-filled or foam rubber mattress several feet thick.

7 *water polo* The area directly in front of the goal.

²pit **1** *cockfighting* To match cocks together in a pit.

2 *of a racing driver* To come into one's pit while the race is in progress. ⟨started out looking like a winner by taking the lead on the first lap and continued picking up the lap money . . . until he *pitted* on the 50th lap — Mike Anson, *Road & Track*⟩

pit board *motor racing* A portable blackboard on which pit crews communicate information to their drivers.

¹pitch **1** Up and down movement of the front or nose of a vehicle (as a boat or airplane). — compare ROLL, YAW

2 British term for *playing field*. Though its use is unambiguous in reference to the playing area for soccer or rugby, the term is used in cricket not only to mean the entire playing ground but also that 22-yard-long stretch, more commonly

called the *wicket*, in the center of the ground at opposite ends of which the 2 wickets are set.

3 *baseball* **a** The delivery of the ball by the pitcher to the batter. ⟨a fast *pitch*⟩ **b** The ball delivered by the pitcher. ⟨fouled off the *pitch*⟩

4 *bowling* The angle at which the finger holes are drilled in a bowling ball. — compare SPAN

5 *football* Short for *pitchout.*

6 or **pitch shot** *golf* A shot made by pitching the ball. — compare CHIP SHOT

7 *horseshoe pitching* The court on which horseshoes are pitched. — see COURT

8 *mountain climbing* The stretch of a climb traversed between belay points. For obvious reasons, climbers avoid extending the pitch beyond the length of the safety rope connecting them.

²pitch **1** *baseball* **a** To deliver the ball to the batter. The ball is generally thrown overhand; and for the pitch to be legal the pitcher must have his foot in contact with the pitcher's rubber and the delivery must be with a single uninterrupted motion except when the stretch or set position is used. The term is sometimes used broadly as a synonym for *throw.* **b** To play in a game as the pitcher. ⟨*pitched* 6²/₃ innings today⟩ ⟨*pitched* them to a 1–0 victory⟩ **c** To use a particular starting pitcher in a game. ⟨hadn't decided whether to *pitch* his righthander or go with the lefty⟩ **d** To pitch in a particular way to a batter. ⟨knew he had to *pitch* him high and away⟩

2 a *of a bowled ball in cricket* To bounce on the pitch before reaching the batsman. **b** To cause the ball to pitch. ⟨the ideal bumper is one which will rise without being *pitched* too short — Sir Donald Bradman⟩

3 *golf* To hit the ball, usually with a wedge, in a high arc with backspin so that it stops abruptly after striking the green.

4 *softball* To deliver the ball to the batter. To be a legal delivery, the ball must be thrown underhand with a single continuous motion while the pitcher's foot is in contact with the pitcher's rubber. Slow pitch softball requires, in addition, that the ball travel in an arc between 3 feet and 10 feet high on its way to the batter.

5 *of a boat or plane* To undergo pitch.

pitch-and-run see CHIP SHOT

pitch around *baseball* To give a batter an intentional walk or pitch to a batter in such a way as to risk a walk rather than give him anything good to hit.

pitcher **1** *baseball* **a** The player who takes a position in the middle of the diamond and delivers the ball to the batter. **b** The position of pitcher.

2 *horseshoe pitching* The player who is tossing the horseshoes at a given moment.

pitcher of record *baseball* The pitcher of either team who at a given point in the game will be the winning pitcher or the losing pitcher (depending on whether his team is winning or losing at that time) if the situation does not change before the end of the game. — see also LOSING PITCHER, WINNING PITCHER

pitcher's box see PITCHING BOX

pitcher's duel *baseball* A close low-scoring game in which both pitchers are effective.

pitcher's mound *baseball* An elevated portion of the playing field in a line between home plate and second base that rises to a height of 10 inches and is 9 feet in diameter. The front of the mound has a slope of one inch per foot for a distance of 6 feet out from the center. At the top of the mound is a level area 5 feet by 3 feet. The rest of the mound slopes gradually to the level of the surrounding playing area. In the center of the mound is the pitcher's rubber — a 24-inch-long, 6-inch-wide slab of white rubber — set in the ground with the long side facing home plate and the front edge exactly 60 feet 6 inches from the rear corner of home plate.

pitcher's plate or **pitcher's rubber** see RUBBER (*baseball*)

¹pitching *baseball* **1** The action of pitching.

2 The overall effectiveness of a team's pitchers. ⟨their trouble is in their *pitching*⟩

3 A number of good pitchers. ⟨a team with speed and *pitching*⟩

²pitching *baseball* Of, relating to, or being the pitchers on a team. ⟨*pitching* staff⟩ ⟨*pitching* coach⟩

pitching box or **pitcher's box** *horseshoe pitching* Either of two 6-foot-square areas surrounding the stakes from which the shoes are pitched.

pitching chart *baseball* A chart kept by a teammate of a pitcher that gives a detailed description of every pitch he throws to every opposing batter including the type of pitch, whether it was high or low, whether it was a ball or a strike, and to what part of the field it was hit. The pitching chart enables the pitcher to review which pitches were most successful against each batter before he faces the same club again.

pitching niblick *golf* An old name for the number 8 iron.

pitching wedge see WEDGE (*golf*)

pitchout 1 *baseball* A pitch that is intentionally

thrown wide of the plate to prevent the batter from hitting it and to enable the catcher to throw out a runner who is stealing or to prevent one from stealing.

2 *football* A lateral pass usually made underhanded from one back to another behind the line of scrimmage. The pitchout is normally made by the quarterback just after the snap to a running back who is moving toward the side of the formation (as on a sweep).

pitch out To make a pitchout in football or baseball.

pitchpole *of a boat or an iceboat* To flip end over end.

pitch shot see PITCH (*golf*)

pit crew *motor racing* The people who work in a driver's pit. ⟨he races for fun, with friends and neighbors as a *pit crew* — Ross R. Olney, *Auto Racing*⟩

pit lane see PIT ROAD

pitman A member of a pit crew.

¹piton *mountain climbing* A metal spike, wedge, or peg that is driven into a crack in a rock face or into an ice surface to serve as an aid in climbing or to support a climber in place or while descending. Pitons, which are commonly made of aluminum alloy or chrome-molybdenum, have either a hole — called an *eye* — or a ring in one end through which a carabiner is inserted. There is a variety of sizes and shapes of pitons

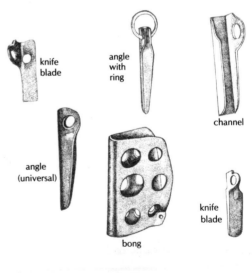

knife blade

angle with ring

channel

angle (universal)

bong

knife blade

rock pitons

to conform to the different shapes of the cracks into which they are inserted. Many of those used on rock have a U or V cross section which allows them to be used in cracks too wide for a flat piton. Rock pitons are made of relatively soft metal which conforms to the shape of the crack when it is driven in. Ice pitons are essentially identical to those used on rock except that they are made of a harder metal. (also called *pin*)

²piton *mountain climbing* To drive a piton into a crack or into ice.

piton hammer *mountain climbing* A short-handled hammer that is used to drive pitons.

pit road or **pit lane** *motor racing* The road usually parallel to the racecourse that leads to and from the pits. In auto racing, the pits are normally located along the side of the pit road.

¹pivot **1** A central player position: **a** *Australian Rules football* The position of the center. **b** *basketball* A position to the side of or at the top of the free throw lane taken by a player (as the center) who stands usually with his back to his own basket and serves as the hub of the offense relaying passes, providing screens for teammates, and shooting. **c** *ice hockey* The position on offense in front of the opponent's goal taken by the center; slot.
2 or **pivotman** The player who occupies the pivot; center.
3 *baseball* The action of the second baseman in taking the throw from the shortstop or the third baseman, stepping on second base for a force-out, and throwing the ball to first base in an attempt to make a double play.
4 *basketball* The act or action of keeping the pivot foot in place while stepping with the other foot.
5 *canoeing* A rotation of a canoe about its center with the bow and stern moving in opposite directions.

²pivot To make a pivot:
1 *of a baseball pitcher* To keep one foot in contact with the pitcher's rubber when turning sideways to the batter in the normal preliminary movement to pitching the ball.
2 *basketball* To keep one foot in place while moving the other foot one or more times. A player is permitted to take only one step while holding the ball; so long as the pivot foot remains in contact with the floor, any number of steps with the other foot is considered only one step.

pivot dodge *lacrosse* A dodge made by planting one foot close to the opponent and, while pivoting on that foot, turning away from the opponent

in a full circle, keeping the back to the opponent at all times.

pivot foot The foot on which a player pivots; the foot that a basketball player must keep in contact with the floor when holding the ball in order to avoid being charged with traveling. If a player receives a pass while running or stops a moving dribble, the pivot foot is the first one to touch the floor after the ball is caught or the dribble is stopped or the second foot to touch the floor if both feet were off the floor when the ball was caught. If the player lands on both feet simultaneously, he may pivot on either foot. A player is permitted to jump in the air after establishing a pivot foot (as to make a pass or a shot) but he must release the ball before either foot again touches the floor.

pivot instep kick *soccer* A kick of a ball made by swinging the leg around in front of the body and hitting the ball with the instep to drive it to one side instead of straight ahead.

pivotman see PIVOT

¹place *pari-mutuel betting* Second place or better at the finish. When a bet is made on a competitor for place, the bettor collects if the competitor finishes first or second. In British usage, place may be any of the first 3 positions at the finish. — see also PARI-MUTUEL BETTING

²place **1** To finish second or at least second in competition involving betting. In British usage, to finish third or better. ⟨bet him to *place*⟩ — compare SHOW, WIN
2 To hit or stroke a ball, puck, or shuttlecock so that it goes precisely where aimed.

placed man *Australian Rules football* Any of the 15 players on a side who have relatively fixed positions on the field. — compare RUCKMAN

¹placekick The kicking of a ball (as in football, rugby, or soccer) that is placed in a stationary position on the ground. The placekick is normally used to put the ball in play to begin the game or after a goal has been scored. In rugby and football, the ball is usually held on end by a teammate of the kicker or placed in a small depression in the ground or on a special tee which holds the ball upright. The placekick is normally used for kickoffs and for field goal and conversion attempts.

²placekick **1** To make a placekick.
2 To score a field goal or conversion by means of a placekick.

placekicker *football* A player who specializes in placekicking the ball.

placement

placement **1** An accurately hit ball (as in tennis or handball) which cannot be returned by the opponent.
2 *football* **a** The position of the ball for a place-kick. **b** A placekick.

placer One of the top finishers in a competition.

placing judge *horse racing* Any of a number of judges stationed above the track at the finish line to decide the order of finish of a race.

planche *gymnastics* A position in which the body is supported horizontally above the hands (as on the floor or on rings or parallel bars). — compare LEVER

planing hull *boating* A hull of a boat designed to rise partially out of the water at high speed so that a portion of the hull is planing on the water. With the planing portion of the hull supported by the surface of the water, the displacement and with it the resistance of the water on the hull is reduced so that higher speeds can be attained. — compare DISPLACEMENT HULL

plant *track and field* The act of placing the pole in the box just before initiating the upward motion of a pole vault.

planting pit see BOX (*track and field*)

plastron *fencing* A quilted pad worn under the jacket to protect the fencer's chest, waist, and side during a bout.

plate **1** A horseshoe worn by a racehorse.
2 Short for *home plate*.

plater *horse racing* A horse that runs in claiming races. The term is a carryover from the days when the winners of non-stakes races were awarded a silver plate or tray.

plate umpire *baseball* The umpire stationed behind home plate; umpire-in-chief. — see UMPIRE

platform **1** *diving* A flat level rigid surface at least 20 feet long and 6½ feet wide which is covered with a nonslip material and from which divers leap in competition. For national and international competition, the platform is 10 meters above the water level. The structure supporting the platform will often have additional platforms at the 5- and 7½-meter heights for use by younger divers. — compare SPRINGBOARD
2 *platform tennis* A floor of wood which is surrounded by a 12-foot-high chicken-wire fence and which is used as the platform tennis court. The standard platform is 60 feet long and 30 feet wide leaving 8 feet between the end lines of the court and the backstops and 5 feet between the sidelines and the sidestops.

platform tennis A variation of tennis played on a wooden platform enclosed by a high chicken-wire fence using a sponge-rubber ball and wooden or plastic paddles. The game was originated in 1928 by Fessenden Blanchard and James Cogswell, who began playing paddle tennis on a wooden platform they has constructed for playing deck tennis and badminton during the winter. They found the 44-foot-by-20-foot dimensions of the badminton court more suitable than what was then the standard 39-foot-by-18-foot dimensions of the paddle tennis court. They enclosed the court with chicken wire to keep from losing the ball, but because of the short distance between the boundaries of the court and the fence, they found it expedient to permit the playing of the ball off the sidestop and backstop. This playing of the rebounds has become one of the principal features of the game. As in paddle tennis, the rules of tennis are followed in playing and scoring except that balls may be played off the fence and only one serve is permitted. Originally taking the name *paddle tennis,* the game later became known as *platform paddle tennis* to distinguish it from its sister, playground paddle tennis. Today it is officially referred to as *platform tennis* but often called simply *paddle.*

¹platoon **1** *baseball* Two or more players who alternate at the same position. The players who make up a particular platoon are usually average players who are adequate fielders but who are not outstanding hitters. Typically one player will bat right-handed and the other left-handed. The right-handed player will be started in a game in which a left-hander is pitching and vice-versa.
2 *football* A group of players who specialize in offense or defense and who are inserted in or taken out of the game as a unit. Before a rule change in 1958 made unlimited substitution possible, players had to play both offense and defense.

²platoon *baseball* **1** To alternate players in the same position in different games.
2 To use one player in place of another in a platoon system.

¹play **1** The action, conduct, or progress of a game or contest. ⟨*play* begins with the serve⟩ ⟨the referee stopped *play*⟩
2 The manner, style, or quality of playing. ⟨combined with the pressure of a championship game it caused loose and ragged *play*— Mark Baicker & Bob Berney, *Student Life*⟩
3 Participation in a sport or in an individual contest. ⟨the injury kept him out of *play* for 3 months⟩

4 A particular strategic action which is usually planned and practiced before a game and which involves specific duties and assignments for some, most, or all of the players on the team. ⟨the hit-and-run *play*⟩ ⟨the quarterback called a new *play* at the line of scrimmage⟩

5 The act or action of hitting or stroking a ball, puck, or shuttlecock. ⟨simultaneous contact by 2 players is considered only one *play* in volleyball⟩

6 A particular action in a game or contest. ⟨he made the big *play* of the series⟩ **a** *baseball* The action between pitches which is usually initiated by a member of the offensive team (as by attempting to steal or by hitting a pitch) and which includes the action of the offense in trying to reach base, advance, or score and the action of the defense in trying to put out one or more offensive players. ⟨reached second on the *play*⟩ ⟨a double *play*⟩ **b** *baseball* A putout. ⟨made the *play* at first base to retire the side⟩ **c** *football* The action that occurs during a free kick or scrimmage down and that includes the initial impetus to the ball (as by a kick or the snap) and the interplay between the teams as the offense attempts to advance the ball and the defense seeks to prevent the advance or gain possession for itself. ⟨gained 6 yards on the *play*⟩ ⟨the second *play* from scrimmage⟩

7 Short for *swordplay*.

— **in play** *of a ball, puck, or shuttlecock* Subject to or in the process of being thrown, hit, kicked, or handled in accordance with the rules of a game. Any action between the time the ball or puck is put in play and the time play is stopped constitutes the actual progress of a game, and it is during this time that scoring is possible and the clock, if used, is running. In racket games such as tennis, squash, or badminton, the ball or shuttlecock is in play only from the moment it is served until the point is decided or a fault or let occurs. In golf, the ball is in play from the time it is teed up until it is holed out, and it may not be touched by the golfer except to be picked up once on the putting green to avoid interfering with the putt of another player. In baseball, the ball is in play from the time the umpire calls "play ball" or delivers a new ball to the pitcher or catcher until he calls "time" or until some action (as a batter's being hit by a pitched ball) causes the ball to be dead. In goal games (as rugby, basketball, or hockey) the ball is put in play (as by a jump ball, kickoff, throw-in, face-off, corner kick, bully, or scrum), and it remains in play until it goes out of bounds, a violation or foul is called, or, in some games, a goal is scored. In football, the ball is only in play during the course of a free kick or scrimmage down. It is put in play by a free kick or by the snap from center and remains in play until the down ends (as by the ballcarrier's being tackled or his stepping out of bounds, by an incompleted pass, or by a score). The clock normally continues to run between downs except when there is a violation, an incompleted pass, a score, or a time-out.

— **out of play 1** *of a ball, puck, or shuttlecock* Not in play; dead. **2** *of a foul ball in baseball* In the stands or over a wall and beyond the reach of a fielder. **3** Not a legal part of the playing area. ⟨the ceiling of a squash court is *out of play*⟩

²play 1 To engage or participate in a sport or in an individual contest. ⟨*play* football⟩ ⟨*played* a round of golf⟩

2 To contend against a particular opponent in a contest. ⟨will get a chance to *play* the defending champion⟩

3 To use in a game or sport. ⟨complained that the coach didn't *play* him enough⟩ ⟨a new ball that can be *played* on any surface⟩

4 a To perform the duties of a specific position. ⟨*plays* quarterback⟩ **b** To play one's position in a specific manner or area. ⟨the outfielders were *playing* deep⟩ **c** To direct one's players to play in a specific manner or area. ⟨*played* his linebackers close to the line⟩

5 a To hit, kick, or stroke a ball. ⟨*play* the ball where it lies⟩ **b** To direct the course of a ball or puck. ⟨*played* a wedge shot to the green⟩ **c** To cause a ball or puck to rebound from a surface. ⟨*play* the shot off the backboard⟩

6 To guard or move into position to guard an opponent in a specified manner. ⟨*played* his man loose so that he could drop off to help out the rookie on defense⟩

7 To direct one's offense toward a particular aspect of the opponent's game. ⟨tennis players have always had lines on opponents — *play* to his backhand, lob him, those obvious basics — Frank Deford, *Sports Illustrated*⟩

8 To bet on a sport or on a particular competitor. ⟨*plays* the horses⟩ ⟨*played* 5 losing favorites in a row⟩

9 *baseball* **a** To pick up or catch a ball or move into position to catch a ball. ⟨*played* the ball bare-handed⟩ ⟨knows just how to *play* the ball off the left field wall⟩ **b** *of a batted ball* To cause a fielder to have difficulty in handling. ⟨the ball hit right at the infielder seems to give the

playable

most difficulty, for you don't know whether to go in or wait, and sometimes the ball *plays* you — Bobby Richardson⟩

10 *fishing* To work a hooked fish in carefully by allowing it to move or run with the line until tired or by alternately pumping and reeling or by a combination of both methods.

11 To conduct oneself in a specific manner while engaging in a game or sport. ⟨he always *plays* hard and always *plays* fair⟩

12 *of a hole on a golf course* To be longer or shorter than at some other time because of the position of the cup on the green. ⟨the hole *plays* longer today⟩

playable 1 In play. ⟨a ball that rebounds from the backstop is still *playable*⟩
2 *of a lie in golf* Affording an opportunity to hit the ball.

play-action pass *football* A pass play in which the quarterback fakes a handoff to one or more backs before throwing the ball. For the play-action pass to be successful, the linemen must carry out blocking assignments like those of a running play to keep the defensive players from rushing across the line.

play ball *baseball* The traditional call of the umpire to signal for play to commence or restart after a time-out.

playbook *football* A notebook which contains diagrams of all of a team's plays and which is issued to each member of the team in training camp.

play-by-play A broadcast description of the action of a game; a running commentary on a sports event.

playdown A play-off series (as in basketball).

player 1 Someone who participates or engages in a competitive sport (as baseball, football, handball, jai alai, karate, soccer, or tennis).
2 Short for *registered player.*

player control foul *basketball* A personal foul committed by a player while he or his team has possession of the ball; an offensive foul.

play for one *basketball* To work the ball around in order to run down the clock near the end of a period of play so that after the team takes a shot, the opposing team will not have sufficient time remaining to get the ball to the other end of the court for a good shot.

playground ball An inflated rubber ball of any of various sizes but commonly the size of a soccer ball or a basketball that is used especially by children in informal ball games in playgrounds or school yards.

playground paddle tennis see PADDLE TENNIS

playing area The area within the boundary lines of a field or court on which a game is played.

playing coach or **player coach** A coach who is on the roster of active players and who usually participates in the games as a member of the team he is coaching; a player who coaches his team.

playing field A field on which a game is played. — see FIELD

playing time 1 The total amount of time involved in the actual progress of a game or contest exclusive of time-outs or intervals between periods; the time during which a game clock is running.
2 The amount of time a particular player is in a game. ⟨hasn't had much *playing time* this year⟩

play line 1 *court tennis* A line on the side and end walls of the court marking the upper limits of the playing area. On the end walls the line is 23 feet above the floor and on the side walls it is 18 feet high.
2 *racquets* A line on the front wall of the court 27 inches above the floor above which the ball must hit the wall to be in play. — compare TELL-TALE

playmaker A player in a goal game who generally leads the team's offense (as by calling for and initiating set plays). ⟨a slick *playmaker* and an effortless skater, who is murder in the slot — Bob Strumm, *Hockey News*⟩

playmaking Offensive action (as of a player) which usually involves calling for set plays, trying to create situations in which a teammate may get open for a shot, and making assists.

¹play-off An extra contest or an extension of a contest to determine a winner when 2 or more competitors or sides are tied at the end of regular play.

²play-off Of or relating to a play-off or to play-offs. ⟨*play-off* schedule⟩

play-offs A series of post-season contests, usually in an elimination-tournament format, among the teams that have finished the regular season at or near the top of their league, conference, or division standings that is held to determine a champion or to determine competitors for a championship contest or series of contests.

play on *Australian Rules football* A call of the field umpire to indicate that the ball is in play and that play will not be stopped for a mark or a penalty.

play out *fishing* To play a hooked fish until it is exhausted.

play out one's option *of a professional player*

To play for a team under the provisions of the option clause of an earlier contract without signing a new contract after the old one has expired.

play-the-ball *rugby* A method of putting the ball in play after a tackle in Rugby League play in which the tackled player is released and permitted to stand and face the opponent's goal line and drop or place the ball on the ground where it is to be kicked or heeled back to a teammate to start play. One opposing player is permitted to stand immediately in front of the tackled player and either of these players may play the ball, but in practice it is the tackled player who usually plays it. During the play, one player of each side is permitted to stand directly behind his teammate who is participating in the play-the-ball to receive the ball when it is heeled back, but all other players may be no nearer than 5 yards.

play the ball To attempt to gain control of the ball in a game (as soccer or football) rather than to stop the opponent in possession. In most goal games the object is to play the ball and avoid any but incidental contact with the opponent. In football, however, where the normal procedure is to attempt to tackle the ballcarrier, aggressive players sometimes seek to snatch the ball from the grasp of the ballcarrier for a fumble with the risk of winding up with neither the ball nor the runner. When 2 football players who are both trying to catch a forward pass make contact, pass interference is not called so long as both were playing the ball.

play the field To bet on every competitor in a race in the hope that a winning long shot will eventually produce a profit.

play through *of a golfer or a group of golfers playing together* To move ahead of a slower party which is in front with permission of the slower party.

plinking Casual shooting with a rifle or handgun at small objects such as tin cans, sticks, or table tennis balls.

pluck *archery* To jerk the string hand away on releasing the arrow thereby causing the bow to tilt and the arrow to fly off target.

plug **1** *fishing* A lure which consists chiefly of a solid wood, plastic, or cork body with one or more treble hooks. Plugs are commonly made in a variety of shapes, some of which may resemble small fish and others which resemble nothing in particular. There are plugs designed to float on the surface of the water (*surface plugs*), plugs designed to sink to the bottom and rise when pulled in (*sinking plugs*), and plugs designed to float but dive when pulled through the water (*semi-surface plugs*).

2 *horse racing* An inferior and often aged or unsound racehorse.

¹plunge *football* To run headlong or dive into the line for a short gain (as when only a few yards are needed for a first down or touchdown).

²plunge *football* A run into the line which is designed to gain short yardage.

plunger *surfing* A wave that collapses suddenly rather than gradually. — compare SPILLER

pneumothorax *scuba diving* A condition in which compressed air from a ruptured lung lodges in the chest cavity and expands as the diver ascends causing pain and possibly interfering with the function of the heart and lungs.

poach **1** To take game or fish illegally.

2 To hit a ball which normally would be played by one's partner in doubles play of a racket game (as tennis). The term usually applies to play of the ball at the net.

¹pocket **1** A position in which a competitor in a race is hemmed in and cannot move around other competitors.

2 *baseball* The part of a glove or mitt extending from the center of the palm to the area at the base of the index finger which is the deepest and most secure part of the glove in which to catch the ball.

3 *billiards* Any of the 6 holes at the sides and corners of an English billiards, pocket billiards, or snooker table or either of the 2 openings at the ends of a bumper pool table into which the balls are driven. — see also BILLIARD TABLE

4 *bowling* The space between the headpin and the number 3 pin for a right-handed bowler or between the headpin and the number 2 pin for a left-handed bowler which is the most effective place for a ball to hit in order to produce a strike.

5 *curling* A group of stones resting usually behind the tee line in a semicircle concentric with the rings.

6 *football* An area a few yards behind the line of scrimmage for which protection is created by blockers and from which the quarterback passes. On a usual pass play, the quarterback drops back from the line with the snap, and the blockers pull back, closing to the inside to force the onrushing linemen to move to the outside to get to the quarterback. As the defensive linemen move around to the outside, the quarterback can step forward into the pocket.

7 *lacrosse* The area of the head of the stick near

the throat which is slightly deeper than the rest of the head and in which the ball rests. It is somewhat analogous to the pocket of a baseball glove. Rules do not permit a pocket so deep that the ball will not fall out.

²pocket *billiards* To drive a ball into a pocket.

pocket billiards An American form of billiards played on a table with 6 pockets into which the balls are driven in scoring. (also called *pool*) — see BILLIARDS

pocket split *bowling* A split left after hitting the pocket which includes the 5 pin and a pin from the back row (as the 5–7 or 5–9). — see illustration of pin arrangement at BOWLING

¹point **1** The basic scoring unit in most games: — compare GOAL, RUN

a *archery* From one to 9 points are scored for each arrow in the target depending on the values of the scoring rings. The outer ring has the lowest value, one, with the other rings worth 3, 5, 7, and 9 points respectively.

b *association croquet* One point is scored by a team for each ball that has been played through a wicket and for hitting the center peg. The team that first scores 26 points wins the game.

c *Australian Rules football* Six points are scored for a goal and one for a behind.

d *badminton* One point is scored by the serving side when an opponent fails to make a good return during a rally. If the receiver wins the rally, he gains the right to serve but not the point.

e *basketball* One point is scored for a successful free throw and 2 points for a field goal. In one

league, a field goal from more than 26 feet from the basket is worth 3 points.

f *billiards* In English billiards, 2 points are scored for a cannon, 2 points for a winning or losing hazard off the white ball, and 3 points for a winning or losing hazard off the red ball. In American carom billiards games, a player scores a point for each carom. In pocket billiards games and in snooker, points are scored (depending on the particular rules of the game being played) for driving the object ball into a pocket. For certain balls or in certain games, a player gets one point for each ball pocketed. In other games, each ball has a designated value.

g *boxing* A number of points, usually the maximum permitted by the scoring system (as 5, 10, or 20), are awarded to the boxer judged to have won the round with a lesser number going to the loser of the round. When a round is judged even, the boxers receive the same number of points.

h *Canadian football* Point values are the same as in American football except that one point may be scored for a rouge.

i *court tennis* Same as for tennis.

j *curling* One point is scored by a team for each stone it has nearer the tee than the opponent has at the conclusion of an end.

k *darts* Points are scored by the player according to the value of the scoring section in which the dart lands, and these points are subtracted from the player's total. The first player to reach exactly zero wins the game.

l *deck tennis* One point is scored by the serving side when the opponent fails to make a good return.

m *diving* Points are awarded to a diver on the basis of the execution of the dive, including the approach, takeoff, movements in the air, and entry into the water. The style points, from 0–10, are adjusted by a degree of difficulty factor for each dive.

n *fencing* Each hit is scored as a point. When simultaneous hits occur in épée, a point is awarded to each fencer.

o *fives* One point is scored by the receiving side whenever the serving side fails to make a good return or when the serving side makes 3 consecutive unreturned blackguards.

p *football* Six points are scored for a touchdown, 3 for a field goal, 2 for a safety, and usually one for a conversion after a touchdown. In college play, it is possible to score 2 points on a conversion by running or passing the ball over the goal line.

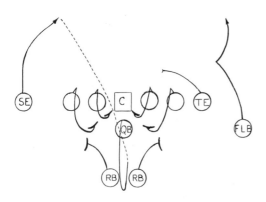

pass play with pocket forming for the quarterback: C center; FLB flankerback; QB quarterback; RB running back; SE split end; TE tight end

q *Gaelic football* Three points are scored for a goal — putting the ball into the goal under the crossbar — and one point for putting the ball over the crossbar.

r *gymnastics* Points from 0–10, usually in gradations of $^1/_{10}$ or $^1/_{100}$ point, are awarded on the basis of the execution of the routine.

s *handball* One point is scored by the serving side when the opponent fails to make a good return. Paddleball and racquetball are scored in the same way.

t *horseshoes* One point is scored by a player or side for each shoe it has closer to the stake than its opponent has; three points are scored for every ringer. If at the end of an inning each side has the same number of ringers and neither has a shoe nearer the stake, neither side scores.

u *hurling* Same as Gaelic football.

v *jai alai* A point is scored by either side when the opponent fails to make a good return.

w *lawn bowling* A point is scored for each bowl a team has nearer the jack than its opponent has at the conclusion of an end.

x *paddleball* Same as for handball.

y *paddle tennis, platform tennis* Same as for tennis.

z *racquetball* Same as for handball.

aa *racquets* Same as for squash racquets.

bb *rugby* A try is worth 4 points (3 in Rugby League), a conversion adds 2 points, a free kick or penalty goal is worth 3 points (2 points in Rugby League), and a dropped goal 3 points (2 points in Rugby League).

cc *shuffleboard* Points are scored on the basis of the values of the scoring sections in which the disks rest. To be scored, a disk must be wholly within the scoring area and not on the line.

dd *shooting* Points are scored in target shooting on the basis of the values of the rings of the target. A typical rifle target has a scoring value of 10 for the inner ring with each successive ring worth one point less than the one inside. In skeet and trapshooting, the shooter gets one point for each broken target.

ee *ski jumping* Points for style, usually from 0–20 in half-point steps, are added to the points given for distance jumped in determining the competitor's score. The longest distance jumped is given a value (as 60 points) and lesser distances are graded on a scale down from that.

ff *speedball* Three points are scored for a field goal, 2 for a dropkick, and one each for a touchdown, penalty kick, and end kick (when used). In women's play, a field goal is worth 2 points, a dropkick 3 points, a touchdown 2 points, and a penalty kick one point.

gg *squash racquets* One point is scored by a player or side when the opponent fails to make a good return. In the British version, only the serving side can score points. Racquets is scored like British squash racquets, but squash tennis is scored like American squash racquets.

hh *swimming* Points are awarded to finishers to determine the overall team standings in a meet. The number of points awarded and the number of positions through which the points are awarded depend on the number of lanes being used. Example: in a large meet where 8 lanes are used in a final heat, the scoring would be 9–7–6–5–4–3–2–1 from the first through the eighth-place finisher.

ii *table tennis* A point is scored by either player when his opponent fails to make a good return during a rally.

jj *tennis* A point is scored by a player when his opponent fails to make a good return. In traditional scoring, the points have individual names: *15* (or *5*) for the first point won, *30* for the second, *40* for the third point, and the last, simply *game*. If both sides reach 40, the situation is known as *deuce,* and the next point won by either side is their *advantage*. To win a game from deuce, a side must win 2 consecutive points. Court tennis, paddle tennis, and platform tennis are scored in the same way.

kk *track and field* Points are awarded to competitors in meets in the order of their finish to determine overall team standings. A usual arrangement is 5 points for a first-place finish, 3 points for second, and one point for third. In cross-country running, the scoring is usually according to actual finish (1 for first, 2 for second) with the team having the lowest cumulative total winning. Scoring for the pentathlon and decathlon is based on an arbitrary standard of achievement for each event which is worth a stated maximum number of points (as 1200) with lesser performances being graded on a scale down from the standard.

ll *volleyball* A point is scored by the serving side when the opponent fails to make a good return during a rally. If the receiving side wins the rally, it gets to serve but does not get a point.

mm *wrestling* Points are awarded to wrestlers for certain actions during a match. These include 2 points for a takedown, one for an escape, 2 for a reversal, 2(or 3) for a near fall, and one for having accumulated a margin of one minute or

point

more of riding time. In dual meets, wrestlers are awarded points for their finish to determine the team's overall score. A wrestler is awarded 6 points for winning a match by a fall, forfeit, default, or disqualification, 4 points for a decision in which he has a margin of 10 or more points, 3 points for a decision with a margin of less than 10 points, and 2 points if the match ends in a draw. In international competition, wrestlers are given penalty points for losing a match or for winning by anything less than a fall or a total victory, and these determine the team's overall standing in the competition.
2 A rally in court games which begins with the serve and ends when one side scores a point or wins the right to serve the next rally or both. ⟨the surface on which a match is played has a great deal to do with the tenor and length of the *points* — Tony Verna, *Playback*⟩
3 A player position: **a** *basketball* A player position in the frontcourt in the area roughly between the division line and the free throw circle which is occupied by a guard who directs the team's offense. **b** *cricket* A fielding position several yards to the off side and more or less in line with the batsman. **c** *ice hockey* Either of 2 offensive positions on either side of the rink just inside the attacking zone that are usually taken by the defensemen who back up the forwards and help keep the puck in the attacking zone. **d** *lacrosse* A defensive position in the close defense usually to the right of the goal. **e** A player occupying a point position.
4 *fishing* The sharp end of a fishhook that penetrates the mouth of a fish.
5 *fox hunting* The distance between the most widely separated points covered by a hunt. — compare DISTANCE
6 *hunting* The rigid attitude of a hunting dog that has its head and gaze intently directed toward scented or sighted game.
7 a A unit of credit (as in hockey or soccer) for each goal and for each assist that is used in evaluating an individual player's performance for a season. ⟨has 93 *points* on 48 goals and 45 assists⟩ **b** *ice hockey* A unit of credit awarded a team for each victory or tie that is used in determining the team's standing in relation to other teams in the league or division. A team is given 2 points for a victory, one point for a tied game, and no points for a loss.
8 The game of 14.1 continuous pocket billiards.
²point 1 *of a hunting dog* To assume a point.
2 *sailing* To sail a boat into the wind.

point after touchdown *football* A single point added to a team's score by making a successful placekick over the crossbar after scoring a touchdown; one of 2 points which can be added to a team's score after a touchdown in college play by running or passing the ball over the goal line from the 3-yard line. (also called *extra point, conversion*)
point-blank range 1 *archery* The distance from the target at which the point of aim coincides with the center of the target. — see illustration at POINT OF AIM
2 *shooting* The distance from the target at which a bullet or slug will travel in a straight line to the target.
point break *surfing* Waves which approach the shore at an angle after appearing to bend around a pier, jetty, or submerged point of land extending out from shore. Such an approach causes the portion of the wave nearest the point to break before the rest of the wave. The break gradually progresses along the wave out from the point. With the waves approaching the shore at an angle, the surfer can ride from one end of the wave to the other moving steadily toward the shoulder.
point d'arret *fencing* A serrated or three-pronged point on certain foils and épées intended to help the point catch in the clothing so that hits will be accurately recorded.
point dogs *dogsled racing* The pair of dogs hitched just behind the leader. — compare SWING DOGS, WHEEL DOGS
pointer A hunting dog that hunts out game by scent and points on finding the game.
point fund An amount of money which is distributed among individual competitors (as in auto racing) at the end of the season on the basis of points earned throughout the season for victories or high finishes.
point guard *basketball* A guard who plays the point where he can direct the team's offense.
point man 1 *box lacrosse* A player (as a defenseman) who occupies a position near the middle of the attacking zone when the team is on offense.
2 *ice hockey* A player (as a defenseman) occupying the point position especially during a power play.
point of aim *archery* A point with which the archer lines up the pile of the arrow in aiming at known distances. The point of aim will vary for different distances and will be between the archer and the target for distances shorter than

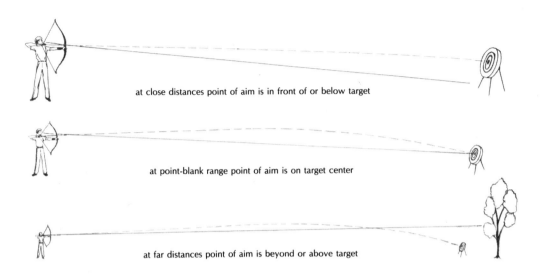

at close distances point of aim is in front of or below target

at point-blank range point of aim is on target center

at far distances point of aim is beyond or above target

point of aim

point-blank range and beyond the target for distances greater than point-blank range. When the arrow is held at the anchor point, the archer's eye is several inches above the level of the arrow; if the pile were lined up directly with the target at all distances, the arrow would fly over the target at short distances and would fail to reach the target at long distances.

point of goal *lacrosse* The point 6 to 7 feet behind the front of the goal where the nets from the side and top of the goal meet.

point race *cycling* A long race in which several laps are designated for sprints before the race with the first rider crossing the finish line on the designated sprint laps receiving a specified number of points. In order to accumulate points, a rider must be on the same lap with the race leaders. The rider with the highest point total at the end of the race is the winner.

point spread The number of points by which a stronger opponent can be expected to defeat a weaker opponent. Point spreads are set by oddsmakers in order to make a contest (as a football game) between 2 unevenly matched opponents attractive to bettors without having to set specific odds. If the bettor backs the favorite, he collects only if the favorite wins by a margin greater than the spread. A backer of the underdog can win his bet if the underdog wins the contest or loses by a margin less than the point spread. If the

contest ends with the favorite winning by exactly the number of the point spread, the bet may be lost or cancelled.

point system A system of betting in which a point spread is established for a contest (as a football game).

poke-check To make a poke check.

poke check **1** *ice hockey* A stick check in which the blade of the stick is pushed at the puck to knock it away from the opponent.
2 *lacrosse* A stick check in which the head of the stick is jabbed or shoved at the handle end of the opponent's stick or at the opponent's gloved hand to dislodge the ball from the opponent's stick.

poke checker A player in lacrosse or ice hockey who poke-checks and especially one who is skillful at poke-checking.

poker pocket billiards A variation of pocket billiards played between 2 or more players using a cue ball and a set of 16 specially marked object balls. Fifteen of the object balls are numbered 1–15. The 16th ball and 3 of the numbered balls are marked on 2 sides with a J while 4 of the other numbered balls are marked with a K, 4 with a Q, and 4 with an A, representing the jack, king, queen, and ace of a deck of cards. Players are limited to pocketing 5 balls in an inning. The object of the game is to have the best "poker hand" when all the balls are off the table.

pole

¹pole 1 The position on the inside of the front row at the beginning of a race on a closed course. Because the inside portion of the track offers the shortest distance around it, this position is usually most advantageous and in auto racing, for example, is awarded the car with the fastest qualifying time.

2 *horse racing* Any of a number of vertical posts placed around the inside of a racetrack at specific distances from the finish line which are used especially by a caller to indicate the distance remaining in the race. A typical one-mile track has poles every $^{1}/_{16}$ of a mile with the following designations: $^{15}/_{16}$ pole (7½ furlongs from the finish), $^{7}/_{8}$ pole, 6½ furlong pole, ¾ pole, 5½ furlong pole, 5 furlong pole, 4½ furlong pole, half-mile pole, 3½ furlong pole, $^{3}/_{8}$ pole, $^{5}/_{16}$ pole, quarter pole (¼ mile from the finish line), $^{3}/_{16}$ pole, eighth pole, sixteenth pole, and finish pole. The poles are of different sizes and are sometimes painted with different colors to help distinguish them. The largest poles are the ¾, half-mile, quarter, and finish-line poles; the poles marking the odd sixteenths of a mile are the smallest.

3 *track and field* **a** The inside lane of a track. **b** A long flexible pole with which a pole vaulter springs into the air and over the crossbar in the pole vault. There is no restriction on the length, diameter, or composition of the pole, but most modern poles are of fiberglass and are from 14 to 18 feet long.

4 Short for *ski pole.*

²pole 1 *baseball* To hit the ball hard. ⟨*poled* a two-run homer⟩

2 *skiing* To assist oneself in moving by pushing with the ski poles.

pole horse *harness racing* The horse starting next to the inside rail.

pole sitter *auto racing* A driver who has won the pole position for a given race. ⟨the difference between the *pole sitter* and the 20th fastest qualifier was 0.65 of a second — John S. Radosta, *New York Times*⟩

pole-vault To attain a specific height in the pole vault. ⟨*pole-vaulted* 18 feet⟩

pole vault *track and field* A field event in which each contestant uses a long pole to vault over a horizontal bar that rests between 2 upright standards. The bar is raised to a higher position when each contestant has had 3 opportunities to clear a given height or has elected to pass at the height. The pole vault is essentially an elimination contest with 3 successive unsuccessful at-

tempts at any height eliminating the vaulter. The winner is the last man remaining to have cleared the bar at its highest position. — see also TIE (*track and field*)

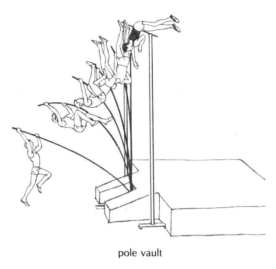

pole vault

pole vaulter An athlete who competes in the pole vault.

policeman see ENFORCER

polo A game played on horseback on a large field between 2 teams of 4 players each with the object to drive a small wooden ball down the field with a long-handled mallet and into the opponent's goal for a score and to prevent the opponents from scoring. The ball is played with the side of the mallet head, and all strokes must be made from horseback. Polo is believed to have originated in Persia, and it is known to have been played as early as 500 B.C. A match consists of 6 or 8 7½-minute periods of play (*chukkers*). Because of the strain on the horses, traditionally called *ponies,* the same horse is not used in successive chukkers. A polo player normally has 3 ponies which he alternates. Two of the 4 players on the team play forward of their teammates and are referred to as *forwards.* The other 2 players, who have primarily defensive duties, are the *backs.* Polo is played using a handicap system in which each player is rated at a certain number of points according to his skill and relative value to his team. The sum of the handicaps of the individual team members equals the team's handicap. The team with the lower total is given the difference in points at the beginning of the game. The game is controlled by 2 mounted umpires positioned at each end of the field who watch for riding infractions. Because of the obvious danger to both horse and rider from collisions and rough play, the rules of polo have to do principally with safe riding. It is generally illegal for one rider to cut across in front of an opponent to play the ball though a rider may move in front from a slight angle if he continues in the same direction as the opponent. Contact between horses is permitted so long as the pace is slow or the angle at which one rider approaches another from the rear is slight. A player may ride an opponent off the ball by veering his horse into the opponent's, but his horse may not have its shoulders in front of the opposing horse. It is permissible to hook an opponent's mallet with one's own, but it must be done only on the same side of the horse while the other player is attempting to play the ball. Violations of these rules and any playing of the mallet into a horse's legs are fouls which are penalized by the awarding of a goal (if the foul was intended to prevent a goal) or a free hit to the other team at the spot of the foul or at a spot 30, 40, or 60 yards in front of the goal, depending on the seriousness of the foul.

poloist A polo or water polo player.

Poma lift A ski lift consisting of a seat connected by a bar to an overhead moving cable. The skier straddles the bar and leans against the seat to be towed uphill.

pommel **1** The raised front portion of a stock saddle. — see illustration at SADDLE

2 *fencing* A relatively heavy metal part screwed to the back of the handle of a sword to hold the blade to the handle and to serve as a counterbalance.

3 *gymnastics* Either of the 2 rounded hand grips which extend from the top of the pommel horse and which are grasped in doing maneuvers on the horse.

pommel horse or **pommeled horse** *gymnastics* **1** An apparatus which consists of a padded leather-covered rectangular or cylindrical form 1600 to 1630 millimeters (about 5 feet 3 inches) long and 350 millimeters (13½ inches) wide with 2 pommels on the top 400 to 450 millimeters (15½ to 17½ inches) apart. The horse is supported in a horizontal position 1100 millimeters (3 feet 6 ⁷/₈ inches) high. The pommel horse is used in men's competition for swinging and balancing feats. (also called *side horse*) — see illustration at FLANK CIRCLE

2 A competitive event in which the pommel horse is used.

poncho A lightweight waterproof garment which is made in a large rectangular shape with a hooded opening in the center for the head.

pony **1** *horse racing* A horse used for work around a stable or track and not for racing. A horse ridden by a member of a stable that escorts a racehorse in the post parade is referred to as a *lead pony.*

2 *polo* Any horse ridden in playing the game. At one time, there was a limitation on the height of the mounts used (a pony is less than 14.2 hands), but today the horses are generally 15 to 15.2 hands high and are predominately thoroughbreds or a mixture of thoroughbred and quarter horse or other local breeds. The prime requisites for a polo pony are speed, stamina, gentleness, and maneuverability.

pony car *auto racing* Any of a group of American-made high-performance 2-door hardtops of different makes including and patterned after the original Mustang. For racing, major modifications to the body and engine are made, though the engine displacement may not exceed 305 cubic inches (5000 cc).

ponying *horse racing* The practice of sending a racehorse out accompanied by a stable pony for exercise and limbering up especially after a long layoff from racing.

Pony League see BOY'S BASEBALL

pony trekking A British pastime which consists of taking an organized mounted excursion into the hills or country (as for a trip of one or several days).

pool **1** *fencing* A group of fencers who compete against each other in a tournament for the right to advance to the next round.

2 *pari-mutuel betting* The aggregate stake of persons betting on the outcome of a contest which, after deduction of taxes and the management's commission, is returned to the winning bettors. There are separate pools for win, place, and show betting and for the daily double and other exotic forms of betting like the perfecta or superfecta; a separate ticket is purchased for each pool. — see also PARI-MUTUEL BETTING

3 *swimming* A chiefly rectangular tank filled with water. For competition, the pool is divided into separate lanes approximately 6 feet wide. The standard sizes for competition pools are 25 yards long (short course) and 50 or 55 yards or 50 meters long (long course).

4 see POCKET BILLIARDS

pool ball *billiards* Any of the colored object balls other than the red balls used in snooker.

¹pop 1 A hit or shot; the act or an instance of hitting or shooting. 〈the traditional move of the pass-blocking lineman is the forearm *pop,* catching his man in the center of the body — Paul Zimmerman, *A Thinking Man's Guide to Pro Football*〉

2 *auto racing* A fuel blend of methanol and nitromethane.

3 *baseball* Short for *pop fly, pop-up.*

4 *football* A short pass.

²pop 1 To make a hit or a shot. 〈*popped* ten home runs last year — Bob Hunter, *Sporting News*〉 〈put in all kinds of inside stuff while his fellow forward . . . *popped* away outside — Barry McDermott, *Sports Illustrated*〉

2 or **pop up** *baseball* To hit a pop fly. 〈*popped* to the second baseman〉 〈*popped up* to the catcher〉

3 *lacrosse* To flip the ball into the air and toward a teammate from a face-off.

Pope Young round *archery* A kind of informal competition in which archers shoot one arrow at each of 6 targets set up at distances from 20 to 80 yards away within a 45-second time limit. There are 6 separate shooting stations, and the archers shoot from each station in turn.

pop fly or **pop-up** *baseball* A short very high fly ball.

pop foul *baseball* A pop fly hit foul.

popinjay shooting *archery* The practice of shooting special blunt arrows at artificial birds of various sizes and scoring values fixed to perches high overhead.

¹pop-out 1 *baseball* An out made on a pop fly.

2 *surfing* A mass-produced surfboard.

²pop-out *baseball* To hit a pop fly which is caught for an out.

popper or **popping plug** *fishing* A floating lure with a single or double hook that is made of cork or lightweight wood and that has a slightly concave face which catches air bubbles when pulled over the water creating a sound to attract the attention of fish.

popping crease *cricket* A line at least 8 feet long at each end of the wicket and parallel to and 4 feet in front of each bowling crease which marks the forward limit of the batsman's ground. While batting, the batsman stands with one foot behind the crease. The nonstriker normally rests the tip of his bat behind the other popping crease. While either batsman is behind the crease or has his bat touching the ground behind the line, he is not subject to being run out or stumped. This area is somewhat analogous to both the batter's box and a base in baseball.

pop-up 1 *baseball* see POP FLY

2 *tennis* A high lob to the baseline made from close to the net.

3 *track and field* A practice jump in training (as for the long jump) in which the jumper strives chiefly for height in the takeoff after a short run-up.

pop up see POP (*baseball*)

Pop Warner Junior League Football A commercially sponsored football league for boys aged 9 to 15 who compete in separate age and weight groups. The league is named for Glenn Scobie "Pop" Warner, a college football coach who developed the single wing offense while coaching at the University of Pittsburgh and at Stanford University from 1915 to 1932.

¹port 1 *boating* The left side of a boat. — compare STARBOARD

2 *curling* A space between 2 stones that is large enough for another stone to pass through.

²port *motor racing* To enlarge the intake and exhaust passages of an internal-combustion engine.

¹portage To transport a canoe overland between bodies of water or around a treacherous area in a river.

²portage The act or an instance of transporting a canoe overland.

position 1 A station on the playing field or a particular duty assumed by a member of a team. In some cases, the only distinguishing characteristic between positions is the physical place of the player in relation to the other members of his team (as in the case of football linemen or infielders on a baseball team) since their principal duties are essentially the same. On the other hand, the difference between the position of center and quarterback on a football team or that of pitcher and catcher on a baseball team involves the duties of each rather than simply the position on the field. In addition, the rules of certain sports specify the location of certain players either throughout the game or in special instances. A baseball pitcher is required to have one foot on the pitcher's rubber to be in the legal position to pitch; the catcher must stand within the catcher's box until the pitch is made. The other members of the team are free to take up any position on the field, but except in rare situations, they occupy fairly set positions. In football, the rules require that an offensive team have at least 7 players on the line of scrimmage and that backfield players other than the quarterback must be at least one yard behind the line. On the kickoff, no member of the kicking team may be in advance of the ball, and five members of the receiving team must be between 10 and 15 yards from the ball. In cricket, only the bowler is limited to a particular position with the other members of the fielding team placed around the field usually as the captain directs.

2 The location of a player or of a played ball with respect to the opponent or the playing area itself. ⟨got good *position* on his man and took down the rebound⟩ ⟨*position* is the key to all billiard games. . . . You've got to know at all times not only where the cue ball's going, you've got to know where the object ball's going; and you gotta know where some of the other balls are going — Minnesota Fats⟩

3 *basketball* The right of a defensive player to occupy a particular position on the court as a result of his having reached the spot ahead of the offensive player he is guarding. Any contact between a moving offensive player and the defensive player who has established position is charging.

position of advantage see ADVANTAGE (*wrestling*)

possession Control of the ball or puck by an individual or team. An individual has possession of a ball when holding or dribbling it. A team has possession when one of its players is controlling the ball or puck or when it will have the ball or puck when it is next put in play. The concept of team possession normally extends to passes where an individual gives up possession in making the pass, but the team retains possession until the pass is intercepted by an opponent or goes out of bounds. In football, on an unsuccessful forward pass, the ball remains in the possession of the passing team unless it is intercepted.

¹post 1 A shooting station in skeet, trapshooting, or archery.

2 *basketball* An offensive position occupied usually by the center near the free throw lane either close to the basket (*low post*) or out near the free throw line (*high post*) where he serves as the focal point of the team's offense. The term is usually synonymous with *pivot,* though on occasion a team may employ an offense built around 2 posts, usually with one player on the high post and the other on the low post.

3 *football* A pass pattern in which the receiver runs downfield and cuts toward the goalpost.

4 *horse racing* A pole. The term is most commonly used in reference to the starting pole, or more precisely the starting gate which is usually placed several yards behind the starting pole, but it sometimes is used in reference to the pole at the finish line. ⟨there is no true stimulus in following racing, except as a mental exercise, when there was no bookmaker in Loitokitok and the paper arrived, sometimes, a week or a month after the horses had gone to the *post* — Ernest Hemingway⟩ ⟨as though they were whipping up their horse on the last straight before the winning *post* — Graham Greene⟩

5 Short for *goalpost.*

²post 1 To rise from the saddle, supporting ones weight chiefly on the knees and thighs, when one diagonal pair of a horse's legs strikes the ground on a trot and to return to the saddle as the other pair of legs hit the ground.

2 To achieve a specified score or result in competition. ⟨*posted* his second straight shutout⟩ ⟨slashed four strokes off par on the first four holes . . . and went on to *post* a 67–138 that gave him a one-stroke lead — *Las Vegas Sun*⟩

postal match *shooting* A competition in which each competitor shoots on his local range and mails his targets and scores to judges who compare them with the results received from other competitors.

post and rails *equitation* An obstacle for show jumping which consists of usually 4 horizontal rails between 2 upright posts.

postboy *horse racing* A jockey.

post man *basketball* A player who plays the post.

post parade *horse racing* A parade of the racehorses that will run in the next race up the front stretch in front of the grandstand on their way to the starting gate.

post position 1 *horse racing* The position in which a given racehorse will start his race. Post positions are numbered from the rail out with the lowest numbered position on the rail and the highest on the outside.

2 *jai alai* Numbers assigned to players or teams on the analogy of horse racing positions for the purpose of identifying the teams in the betting.

post race *horse racing* A race in which an owner or trainer is permitted to list a number of horses he may enter in the race provided, at a stipulated time before the race, he specifies which horse or horses he will actually run.

postseason Occuring or to occur after the end of the regular season. ⟨*postseason* play-offs⟩ ⟨*postseason* bowl games⟩

post time *horse racing* The time at which a given race starts or is to start.

postward *horse racing* To the post for the start of a race.

pot **1** *auto racing* A carburetor.

2 *billiards* A winning hazard in English billiards.

potentially dangerous hold *wrestling* A legal hold (as the double wristlock, chicken wing, or guillotine) which could result in injury to a wrestler if forced beyond the normal range of body movement. If such forcing is attempted, the hold becomes illegal.

¹pothole A deep cave opening upward to the surface.

²pothole To engage in caving; to explore caves and potholes.

potholer Someone who engages in caving, potholing, or spelunking.

powder *skiing* Light, fluffy, usually new fallen or newly made snow.

powder puff Women's competition (as in auto racing) often held as a supplementary event on a program where the usual events are competed in almost exclusively by men. Occasionally powder puff events may be the principal or sole attraction on a program.

power **1** *baseball* The ability to hit the long ball. ⟨they have a lot of guys who can hit the ball out, so I think you have to respect their *power* — Jim Palmer⟩ ⟨hits with *power* to all fields⟩

2 *rowing* A short burst of maximum effort.

power alley *baseball* Either of the areas of the outfield between center field and right field and between center field and left field. They are so called because home runs are more frequently hit to these areas rather than to straightaway center, left, or right fields.

power block *football* A block in which the offensive lineman attempts to drive the defensive lineman straight back or to one side as distinguished from a trap or pass block.

powerboat A pleasure boat or fishing boat powered by an inboard or outboard engine; motorboat.

powerboating The sport of operating a motorboat in competition or for pleasure.

powerboat racing The sport of racing inboard and outboard motorboats and inboard and outboard hydroplanes.

power form *archery* A stance in target shooting in which the feet are turned more toward the target than usual so that the archer twists his upper body somewhat away from the target in taking aim. The stance is supposed to create greater than usual muscle tension in the body during the aiming.

power forward *basketball* A forward who is strong and who is responsible primarily for physically preventing opposing players from driving toward the basket or from getting near the basket to get rebounds instead of for gaining a lot of points or for being a playmaker.

power game *tennis* Play characterized by hard serves and smashes designed to overpower one's opponent.

power head *skin diving* The point of a spear gun equipped with an explosive charge (as a shotgun shell or bullet) designed to explode on contact and drive the barbed point into the fish.

power hitter *baseball* A batter noted for home-run hitting.

powerhouse A strong team or ball club.

power I *football* An I formation which employes three running backs in the backfield. — see I FORMATION

powerlifting Weight lifting competition in which competitors compete in the squat, bench press, and dead lift. — compare OLYMPIC LIFTING

power play **1** *football* A running play in which one or more blockers run ahead of the ballcarrier to clear the way for him.

2 *ice hockey* **a** A situation in which a team has a numerical advantage on the ice over the opposing team (usually 6 men to 5 or 4) because of players in the penalty box. During a power play, the team with the advantage plays usually with its 4 best offensive players and a defenseman and concentrates on attacking the opposing goal usually by trying to set up a free man for the score. **b** A concentrated attack by a team with the advantage during a power play situation. ⟨and when the *power play* is going great, everything is great — Ken Hodge⟩

power-play defense *box lacrosse* A defense in which the ball handler is double-teamed.

power serve *handball* A hard serve made to rebound low usually into the opposite corner.

power slide *auto racing* A somewhat sideways slide through a turn with the engine still driving the rear wheels; drift.

power sweep *football* A sweep in which one or both guards pull out of the line at the snap and lead the ballcarrier around the end of the formation.

power to weight ratio *motor sports* A number obtained by dividing the vehicle's weight (in pounds) by its horsepower that is an approximate measure of the vehicle's potential speed and that is sometimes used in classifying vehicles for racing against one another.

power 20 *rowing* A brief burst of speed in a race during which the crew rows 20 strokes at its maximum rate in order to pick up ground on a leader or extend its lead.

power volleyball Volleyball played at its best with precise setups and hard spikes on nearly every rally.

practice plug *fishing* A small rubber or plastic object somewhat resembling a fishing plug without hooks that weighs $3/8$ or $5/8$ ounce and that is used in casting practice or in tournament casting competition.

pram *boating* A small usually flat-bottomed square-ended boat.

Preakness Stakes A $1\,3/16$-mile stakes race for 3-year-old racehorses that is held annually at Pimlico Race Course in Maryland and that is one of the races in the thoroughbred Triple Crown. The race was originated in 1873 and held at Pimlico until 1889. After being revived at another track, the race has been held regularly at Pimlico since 1909. — see also BELMONT STAKES, KENTUCKY DERBY

predicament see NEAR FALL

predicted log racing *boating* A form of competition for motorboats in which each skipper before the race estimates the amount of time it will take him to reach the end of the course maintaining a set cruising speed and then tries to finish precisely according to his estimate.

preliminary or **prelim** **1** A heat or trial of an event in competition held to eliminate less competent competitors from the final round.
2 *boxing* A bout usually between younger or less skilled boxers that precedes the main event.

prep *horse racing* A trial run; a race that is entered mainly to condition or test a horse in preparation for a longer or more important race.

preparation of attack *fencing* A movement of the body, foot, or sword blade prior to an attack which serves to open a line for the attack.

prepare *motor racing* To modify a stock vehicle for racing.

prescribed exercises *gymnastics* The exercises to be performed during the compulsory portion of competition.

preseason The time immediately prior to the opening of the regular season when competitors are engaged in conditioning and training and when teams are competing against one another in exhibition games.

president see DIRECTOR (*fencing*)

¹press **1** A pressure defensive tactic (as in basketball or lacrosse) in which players guard their opponents more closely than usual in an attempt to disrupt the opposing team's normal pattern of play or as an intensive attempt to gain possession of the ball. The press is often employed as a desperation measure in crucial situations such as in the closing minutes of a game when a team is attempting to protect a small lead or to overtake its opponent. The press may be a tight man-to-man defense or a zone defense where each defensive player has a certain zone of the playing area to cover and applies the press only when the ball is in his zone. Often in the zone press, the player with the ball will be double-teamed.
2 A frame designed to clamp over a wooden racket head when it is not in use to prevent warping.
3 *fencing* A push against the opponent's sword by pressure from the blade of one's own sword.
4 *weight lifting* A lift in which the weight is pushed up from shoulder height to a position straight overhead by the strength of the arms and back alone without movement of the feet or legs. (also called *military press*)

²press **1** To employ a press against a team.
2 To try too hard especially when behind in a game or when not playing well.
3 *weight lifting* To lift a specific weight in a press.

press up **1** *gymnastics* Movement from a headstand position to a handstand by pushing with the arms as distinguished from snapping up with a kick of the legs.
2 British term for *push up.*

prevent defense *football* A defensive formation characterized by the use of an additional pass defender (as an additional linebacker or defensive back). The prevent defense is often employed late in a game by a team that is leading in order to protect itself against a long pass by the opponents which could tie or win the game. The prevent defense sacrifices some protection against the run and short passes, but such plays use up a lot of time and a team that is behind and trying to score quickly usually will not settle for plays that will only result in short gains.

previous spot *football* The spot at which the ball was last put in play (as by a snap or free kick) and that is used in enforcing certain penalties for fouls.

primer An explosive which is set off by the concussion from the firing pin and which ignites the powder charge in a shell or cartridge.

price The dollar odds on a racehorse.

primary receiver *football* The pass receiver who is the primary target on a particular play.

Princeton lock *wrestling* A combination of a threequarter nelson and a leg lock.

prise de fer *fencing* The taking of an opponent's blade and the moving of it out of the line of attack by means of an envelopment, bind, or croisé.

privileged *of a boat* Permitted by the Rules of the Road to hold course and speed when meeting or being overtaken by another boat. — compare BURDENED

Prix des Nations see NATION'S CUP

prizefight A boxing match in which the fighters are paid; a professional boxing match. Boxers originally competed for a stake put up by backers of the opposing fighters. Today the boxers are usually guaranteed a certain sum by the promoters of the match.

prizefighter A professional boxer.

prizefighting Professional boxing.

pro Short for *professional.*

pro-am *golf* A best-ball competition usually preceding a regular professional tournament in which amateurs are paired with professional players. A pro-am is usually run for the benefit of a charity, which receives the fees paid by the amateurs for the privilege of playing in the competition with the professionals.

Pro Bowl A postseason football game between the all-stars of the National Conference and the all-stars of the American Conference of the National Football League.

prodify *auto racing* To modify a production sports car within the limits set forth by the sanctioning organization.

produce race *horse racing* A race for horses which are not yet foaled at the time their dams are nominated.

production *of a motorcycle or sports car* Built on a manufacturer's production line and sold from regular stock. Production vehicles are usually modified for racing within the limits set forth by the individual sanctioning organization. The term is commonly used in reference to production line sports cars as distinguished from stock cars, which are racing versions of production line passenger sedans.

professional 1 An athlete or sportsman who participates in a sport or contest for financial gain and who is consequently prohibited from competing at the amateur level. The term has almost as many interpretations as there are organizations to interpret it. In the most general interpretation, a person is a professional if he makes his living in a sport whether as a participant, teacher, or coach. Other interpretations range from classifying one a professional who receives a salary or prize money for competing in a sport to a broad classification of anyone who competes with professionals or who capitalizes on his athletic fame, whether by promoting a product or accepting an athletic scholarship.

2 An expert (as in golf, skiing, or tennis) hired to give instructions and run a pro shop at a resort or country club.

professional croquet see CROQUET

professionalism The characteristics, standards, or methods of professionals.

program 1 A combination of movements and stunts (as in gymnastics or figure skating) performed by an individual in competition.

2 *horse racing* The races run at a track in a single day.

progressive *skating* A maneuver like the chassé except that the free foot is placed on the surface ahead of the skating foot instead of beside it.

progressive attack *fencing* The execution of the various movements of a compound attack while progressing toward an opponent. — compare PIED FERME

promoter An individual or organization that organizes a meet, race, or match and that guarantees the purse for professionals or often provides expense money for amateurs.

prone *surfing* To assume a prone position on the surfboard (as when paddling to catch up with the speed of a wave or when riding out a broken wave to the shore).

prone float *swimming* A floating position in which the swimmer lies face down in the water with arms out to the sides or in front of the head. (also called *dead man's float*)

prop forward or **prop** *rugby* Either of the 2 front row forwards in the scrum who stand on either side of the hooker and who place an arm on the shoulder of an opposing forward for support in maintaining the scrum until the ball is thrown in.

pro shop A retail store (as at a country club) run by the club professional that sells equipment and often sportswear.

Pro Stock Eliminator see ELIMINATOR

pro T A variation of the T formation commonly employed by professional teams that is characterized by use of a split end, a flankerback, and 2 running backs. — see T FORMATION

protect a lead *of a team* To play conservatively usually in the later stages of a game in order to avoid giving up possession of the ball or puck unnecessarily and giving the opponent an easy opportunity to score and possibly tie or win the game.

protect a player *of a team or club* To list a player among a number that are exempt from being drafted (as by an expansion team). During an expansion draft, a club is allowed to protect a certain percentage of its roster (usually all of its regulars and a number of substitutes).

protection *football* Blocking designed to keep opposing players away from the quarterback while he is setting up for and making a forward pass. — compare INTERFERENCE

protect the plate *of a baseball batter* To swing at any pitch that is near the strike zone especially when the count is 2 strikes in order to avoid being called out on strikes.

protect the runner *of a baseball batter* To swing at any pitch when a base runner is attempting to steal or when a hit and run play is being executed in order to hit the ball or at least force the catcher to wait to receive the ball before moving to throw out the runner. At times, it may be necessary for a batter to swing at a bad pitch in order to protect the runner.

protest A formal objection to the status or conduct of a competitor or to a ruling made by an official in a contest that is made to the officials or to the league or association headquarters. Protests against officials may be made only to decisions which involve interpretations of the rules and which are believed to be in conflict with the rules, not to decisions (such as whether a baseball player is safe or out) which are judgment calls. When a protest is made and cannot be immediately resolved, the protesting individual or club commonly continues the competition under protest. Rarely does a club let a protest stand if it eventually wins the contest.

protest flag *yacht racing* A small red signal flag which is hoisted to signal that the skipper is making a protest.

prototype *auto racing* A specially-built racing sports car in a class which does not require that a certain minimum number be built in order for it to qualify for racing.

provisional ball **1** *bowling* A ball that is rolled when the pinfall from a previous delivery is protested or a foul on the previous delivery is claimed and a ruling cannot be made immediately.

2 *golf* A ball that is put is play immediately when a golfer assumes his regular ball may be lost or out of bounds. The provisional ball is hit from as close as possible to the spot from which the regular ball was last hit. If, before a second stroke is made with the provisional ball, the original ball is found and is playable, the provisional ball may be removed from play without penalty. If the original ball is declared lost, the provisional ball becomes the player's regular ball and he is charged a penalty stroke for the lost ball.

provisional driver *harness racing* A novice driver; a driver who has not driven in 25 races. — compare APPRENTICE JOCKEY

provisional frame *bowling* A frame that is rolled by a bowler when the results of a previous frame are protested and a ruling cannot be made immediately.

prusik **1** To climb a rope by using foot loops attached to the rope by prusik knots.

2 To climb a rope by mechanical ascenders.

prusik knot A sliding friction knot that is commonly used by mountain climbers for tying ropes and slings to vertical ropes used in climbing out of crevasses and holes that is formed by making a bight in a rope or sling and passing it twice around the standing rope, each time passing the free ends through the bight. The prusik knot will hold its place on the standing rope when the climber's weight is on it, but with the tension off, can be slid up the rope. In that way a person can climb his way out of a crevasse. — see illustration at KNOT

prusik loop A loop of rope or sling material that is attached to another rope by means of a prusik knot.

psych or **psyche** **1** or **psych out** or **psyche out** To make an opponent psychologically uneasy. ⟨pressure doesn't *psych* me — Jerry Quarry⟩ ⟨tried to *psych* him *out*⟩

2 or **psych up** or **psyche up** To make oneself psychologically ready for a performance. ⟨you rebel against a manager trying to *psych* you *up*. It's an insult to your intelligence. It's as if he's trying to hustle you into performing better than you are — Al Downing⟩

puck *ice hockey* A vulcanized rubber disk 3 inches in diameter and one inch thick that weighs approximately 6 ounces and that is used as the object to be driven into the goal.

puck carrier *ice hockey* The player who is in possession of the puck.

puck-out *hurling* A free hit of the ball by a member of the defending team from within the parallelogram to put the ball in play after the offensive team has driven it over the end line.

puckstopper An ice hockey goalkeeper.

pudding A British term for a playing ground thoroughly soaked by rain.

pug Short for *pugilist*.

pugilism The sport of boxing.

pugilist A boxer.

puissance *equitation* Jumping competition consisting of several rounds in which competitors are eliminated on every round and the number of fences is reduced and the height of the fences increased until a single winner emerges.

¹pull 1 To take a player out of a game; to remove a goalkeeper (as in soccer or ice hockey) when trailing late in the game and replace him with an additional offensive player in order to increase the chance of scoring.
2 To release the target from the trap in trapshooting or from the high house in skeet. — used as a command by the shooter
3 *baseball* To hit the ball to the field on the same side of the plate as the batter stands when he takes his normal position in the batter's box. A righthanded batter stands on the left side of home plate and will pull the ball to left field.
4 *football* **a** or **pull out** *of an offensive guard or tackle* To move back from the line of scrimmage at the snap and run around the end of the formation to block for the ballcarrier. **b** To direct one's guards or tackles to pull on a running play.
5 *golf* To hit the ball so that it will curve toward the side opposite to the dominant hand of the golfer (as to the left when hit by a right-handed golfer). The ball is intentionally made to curve in order to avoid obstacles on the course. — compare FADE
6 *horse racing* To restrain a horse intentionally during a race so that it does not win.

²pull 1 *curling* The amount a stone will deviate from a straight line during the delivery.
2 *swimming* The part of a stroke in which the arm is moving through the water propelling the body forward.

pull a punch To hold back on a punch (as in boxing or karate) so that the punch ends just before reaching the target or so that it strikes the target with less than full force. Pulling one's punches in boxing is not considered sporting, for it generally means that a superior boxer is avoiding an inevitable victory or is attempting to prolong the match; in karate competition, it is absolutely necessary if the players are to avoid injuring each other.

pull down a mark *Australian Rules football* To make a successful overhead mark.

pulled hamstring see HAMSTRING PULL

pull hitter *baseball* A batter who normally pulls the ball.

pulling guard *football* An offensive guard who is designated to pull and lead the blocking for the ballcarrier.

pull it out To gain victory by overcoming a deficit in the last moments of a contest.

pullout *surfing* The act or an instance of pulling out of a wave.

pull out 1 *football* see PULL
2 *surfing* To get out of a wave by slowing the board to let the wave pass or by turning the board and riding up over the top of the wave.

pullover 1 *gymnastics* A maneuver in which a gymnast kicks up from a hang on a bar and swings his legs up above the bar and pulls with his arms so that he swings around the bar winding up in a support position with his hips against the bar.
2 *weight training* An exercise performed while lying supine on a bench in which the weight is pulled from behind the head up and over the head to the chest and then returned.

pull shot *cricket* A shot made by stepping in front of the wicket with the rear foot, stepping to the leg side with the other foot, and hitting the ball to the leg side with the bat swung in a nearly horizontal arc.

pull the pace *cycling* To ride in front of one or more other bikers thereby creating a slipstream behind for the other riders.

pull the string *of a baseball pitcher* To throw a change-up.

pull-up see CHIN-UP

pull up *horse racing* To slow a horse to a stop before the end of the race (as because of lameness).

¹pump 1 To fake a pass or a shot with the ball (as in football or basketball).
2 *baseball* To swing the arms back and then forward over the head as part of a windup.
3 *fishing* To pull back on the rod when playing a hooked fish in order to bring the fish closer. The pump is usually followed by reeling in the line as the rod is again lowered. In this way a fish is gradually brought in without overstraining the line.

²pump 1 The act or an action of pumping.
2 A supercharger.

pump action see ACTION

pump gun or **pump** A pump action shotgun.

pumpkin *bowling* A delivery that results in a small pinfall.

pumpkin ball *hunting* A solid metal ball or rifled slug fired from a shotgun and used in hunting big game.

¹punch **1** To strike something with the fist. The term is used of one person punching another (as in boxing or karate) or of a person punching a ball (as in volleyball).
2 To hit a ball with a short chopping motion rather than with a full swing.

²punch A blow made by punching. ⟨was telegraphing his *punches*⟩

punchball A version of baseball played with an inflated rubber ball that is punched with the fist instead of hit with a bat. — compare KICKBALL

puncher *boxing* A fighter noted more for his punching strength than for his speed and skill in boxing. (also called *slugger*) — compare BOXER

punch hitter *baseball* A player who hits a lot of singles especially because he punches the ball. The term has gradually developed into *Punch and Judy hitter,* and ultimately simply *Judy.*

punching bag *boxing* A speed bag or a heavy bag used to develop strength or coordination in punching.

¹punt A kick (as in football, soccer, or rugby) in which the ball is dropped from the hands and kicked with the instep before it reaches the ground.

²punt To make a punt; to kick the ball with the instep before it reaches the ground.

punter **1** Someone who bets on horse races; a horseplayer.
2 A football player who is a specialist at punting the ball.

punt pass *Australian Rules football* A pass made by punting the ball.

purge valve A one-way valve in a skin diver's face mask which allows the diver to purge water from the mask merely by exhaling through his nose into the mask.

purse The prize money to be won or shared by the winner or top finishers in a contest (as a race). In most cases, the purse is put up by the promoter; in horse racing, the purse for most races is provided by the track. For stakes races, however, it is made up of the entry, nomination, and starting fees paid by the owners of the horses competing often with money added by the track.

pursuit **1** *cycling* A race in which individuals or teams start on opposite ends of the track with the object for each to overtake the opposing side. In top competition, it is rare for one individual or team to catch up with the other, so the winner is the one covering the prescribed distance in the shortest elapsed time. In team pursuit races, each team rides around the track in single file so that the teammates of the leader can take advantage of the leader's slipstream. At regular intervals the leader will pull out and let his teammates pass him and then fall in behind them so that each teammate in turn leads his team.
2 *football* Movement by a defensive player in pursuit of the ballcarrier often after being blocked out of the play or from the other side of the formation. Pursuit is usually relatively parallel to the line of scrimmage.

pursuit relay A relay race (as in track and field) in which all members of the team move in the same direction and each runner approaches the succeeding runner from behind in the same lane. — compare SHUTTLE RELAY

¹push **1** To hit the ball (as in golf or baseball) to the same side as the dominant hand of the player hitting it (as to the right side by a right-hander).

punt

push

2 To stroke a ball or shuttlecock (as in tennis, table tennis, or badminton) with a pushing motion and with the face of a racket or paddle held flat so that no spin is imparted.

3 *billiards* To drive a ball illegally by shoving it with the cue instead of stroking it; to move a ball that is touching the cue ball in snooker when stroking the cue ball.

²**push** 1 A situation in which a bettor neither wins nor loses a wager (as when the outcome of a game equals the point spread).

2 *golf* A stroke in which the ball is hit in a straight line but off at an angle to the intended line of flight to the same side as the dominant hand of the player.

pushaway 1 *bowling* The moving of the ball forward from a position just in front of the body by extending the arm so that the arm can freely begin the backswing at the start of the approach.

2 *canoeing* A stroke in which the blade of the paddle is pushed away from the canoe and which is used to keep the canoe from hitting obstacles.

pushball 1 A game played informally between 2 sides composed of an agreed-on number of players with each side attempting to push an inflated ball 6 feet in diameter across the opponent's goal line for a score and to prevent the opposing team from scoring.

2 The ball used in this game.

push-button reel see SPIN CASTING REEL

push-in *field hockey* A method of putting the ball in play after the opposing team has driven it over the sideline in which a player standing outside the sideline pushes or taps the ball into the field of play with his stick where it is played by another player. The player making the push-in may not play the ball or come within playing distance of the ball until it is touched by another player. During the push-in no player may be within 5 yards of the ball.

pushing A foul in basketball, lacrosse, or soccer that results when one player shoves an opponent. In lacrosse, it is permissible for an attacking player to push off from an opponent to get free when carrying the ball. An attacking player who is carrying the ball may be pushed or checked but if the player being pushed is not holding the ball or within 5 yards of the ball, it is a technical foul.

push off To shove an opponent with the hands in violation of the rules (as in basketball or lacrosse).

push pass A pass in field hockey or soccer which

is made by shoving the ball with the foot or stick instead of hitting or kicking the ball.

push-pull method *archery* A method of stringing the bow in which the lower nock is placed against the inside of one foot while one hand pulls at the handle and the other hand pushes the upper limb while working the string up over the nock. — compare STEP-THROUGH METHOD

push shot 1 A shot in racket games in which the ball or shuttlecock is pushed rather than stroked.

2 *basketball* A shot made by extending the arm up and out to push the ball rather than by snapping the wrist forward. Except for its occasional use for shooting free throws, the push shot has been almost entirely replaced by the jump shot.

3 *billiards* An illegal shot in which the cue ball is pushed rather than stroked.

push-up An exercise in which a person is supported off the floor in a relatively prone position on the outstretched hands and on the balls of the feet and which consists of lowering the body to the floor by bending the elbows and then straightening the arms to return to the original position.

¹**put** *track and field* To propel the shot in the shot put event by extending the arm quickly so that the shot is pushed away from the shoulder.

²**put** *track and field* The act or action or an instance of putting the shot.

put-and-take fishing The practice of stocking lakes, streams, and ponds with fish raised in hatcheries so that they will be available for fishermen during the fishing season.

put-away see KILL

put away 1 To hit a kill shot in a racket game.

2 *boxing* To knock out an opponent who has been hurt by one's earlier punches.

put down To humanely kill a racehorse that has suffered a permanent injury or that is old and terminally ill.

putout *baseball* The act or an instance of putting a player out. Putouts are credited in permanent statistical records to the player who makes them. The player who catches a ball in the air, tags out a base runner, or tags a base for a force-out is credited with the putout. The catcher is credited with a putout if the batter strikes out, bunts foul on the third strike, or is called out for improper batting or interference with the catcher. The nearest defensive player or the one who would have made the play is credited with the putout when a base runner is hit by a batted ball or called out for interference with a fielder. — compare ASSIST

put out **1** To defeat an opponent in an elimination tournament.

2 To cause an opposing player to be out in baseball or cricket.

¹putt *golf* A stroke made on the putting green or from just off the green in which the ball is struck with a putter and made to roll along the surface of the grass toward the hole.

²putt *golf* **1** To stroke the ball with the putter causing it to roll over the surface of the green.

2 To make a putt on a particular green.

¹putter *golf* **1** An iron club that has a flat face with no loft and a relatively short shaft and that is used in rolling the ball over the putting green toward the hole.

2 A player who is putting; a player noted for his putting.

²putter Short for *shot putter.*

put the ball on the floor **1** *basketball* To dribble.

2 *cricket* To drop a batted ball that should have been caught in the air.

putting green *golf* An area of extremely close-cut grass which surrounds the hole and on which the ball is putted; green.

pyramid spot A spot on an English billiards or snooker table midway between the center spot and the middle of the top cushion. The first of the racked balls is located on the pyramid spot at the beginning of a game of snooker in American play. In British snooker, the pink ball is placed on the pyramid spot. The pyramid spot is the British equivalent to the foot spot on an American carom or pocket billiards table. — see also BALKLINE SPOT, BILLIARD SPOT, CENTER SPOT

pyrometer *ballooning* An instrument that measures the temperature of the air inside a hot-air balloon.

Q

quad Short for *quadruple sculls.*

quadrangular meet A meet (as in track and field, swimming, or wrestling) in which 4 teams compete together but which is scored as if each team were competing against each of the other teams simultaneously. Each team's score is the sum of the scores of the individual members. The team with the highest point total is credited with 3 victories, the team with the next highest total is credited with 2 victories and one loss, the next highest team with one victory and 2 losses, and the team with the lowest total is charged with 3 losses.

quadruple sculls *rowing* Competition for 4-man sculls.

qualifier A competitor who qualifies for the final stages of a competition.

qualify **1** To earn the right to compete in the semifinal or final stage of a competition by defeating other competitors in a preliminary heat (as in track and field or swimming) or by attaining a position above the cutoff point in a field of competitors (as in golf).
2 *motor racing* To become eligible for a specific place at the start of a race by virtue of the lap time achieved during a time trial. ⟨*qualified* on the pole⟩

qualifying The process of determining which competitors will be in a contest or in the final stage of competition on the basis of preliminary heats or time trials.

quarry The object of a hunt; a game animal or bird hunted by hawks or falcons.

quarter **1** Any of the 4 equal divisions of a game or contest that is played on a time basis.
2 *sailing* The after part of a boat's side; the part of a boat from stern to beam on one side.
3 or **quarter mile** *track and field* A race ¼ mile in length.

¹quarterback **1** *football* An offensive back who lines up just behind the center in the T formation to receive the ball directly on the snap and initiate the team's offensive action on a play from the line of scrimmage. The quarterback is responsible for calling signals and directing the team's offense. The quarterback is usually a good passer and may often be adept at running with the ball as well.
2 The position played by a quarterback.
3 A player (as in basketball) who is primarily responsible for handling the ball and directing the team's offense.

²quarterback **1** To play the position of quarterback.
2 To direct the offensive play of a team.

quarterback draw *football* An offensive play in which the quarterback drops back as if to pass and then breaks quickly forward past the pass rushers.

quarterbacking The play of a team's quarterback or quarterbacks.

quarterback sneak *football* An offensive play in which the quarterback runs directly forward with the ball immediately after receiving the snap. (also called *sneak*)

quarter boot see BOOT (*harness racing*)

quarterfinal Of or relating to the quarterfinals of a tournament.

quarterfinalist A competitor in the quarterfinals of competition.

quarterfinals The round of an elimination tournament which precedes the semifinal round and in which 4 contests remain to be played.

quarter horse A relatively small horse developed originally by the pioneers of the American colonies for short races and later extensively used in the western United States as a range horse. The quarter horse is rather stocky and muscular and extremely fast over short distances. Its responsiveness and quick reaction make it popular as a range and rodeo horse for cowboys and as a polo pony. Quarter horse racing is usually conducted on tracks which permit races of approximately ¼ mile in a straight line with the horses running all out the entire distance. They are timed to the nearest $1/100$ of a second.

quartering *of a wind* Blowing toward something at an oblique angle; coming over a boat's quarter.

quarter mile see QUARTER

quarter-miler *track and field* An athlete who competes in the quarter mile race.

quarter nelson see NELSON

quarter pole see POLE (*horse racing*)

quarters The quarterfinal round of a tournament.

Queensberry Rules see MARQUIS OF QUEENSBERRY RULES

Queen's Plate A 1¼-mile stakes race for 3-year-old Canadian-bred thoroughbred racehorses that was inaugurated in 1860 and that is the oldest and most important horse race in Canada.

quick count *football* A shortening of the signals called by a quarterback at the line of scrimmage that is intended to catch the defensive team by surprise.

quick kick *football* A punt attempted on first, second, or third down from a passing or running formation that is intended to take the opposing team by surprise and ultimately to gain better field position. Because of the surprise nature of the quick kick, it may not be an obvious kicking play; and defensive players will not necessarily be charged with roughing the kicker if they run into or tackle him.

quick opener *football* An offensive play in which a back takes a direct handoff from the quarterback and runs straight to a hole in the line created by blockers with little or no attempt at deception.

quick out *football* A pass pattern in which the receiver runs a short distance downfield then cuts toward the sideline to receive a quick pass.

quick-pitch *of a baseball pitcher* To make a quick pitch.

quick pitch *baseball* **1** A pitch made before the batter is set that is intended to catch the batter off guard. The quick pitch is illegal and, if the bases are empty, will be called a ball unless the batter reaches first base. If there are runners on base, a quick pitch will be called a balk unless the batter reaches first base.
2 A legal pitch made by merely pivoting on the rubber and throwing without first making a windup.

quiniela **1** *jai alai* A form of competition in which several teams play each other one at a time with the team that wins a point staying on the court to meet the next team. The winning team is the one that first reaches a designated number of points.
2 or **quinella** *pari-mutuel betting* A betting pool in which bettors must pick the first and second place finishers of a race but need not designate the order of finish in order to win.

quintet A basketball team.

quiver *archery* A case or a device to hold arrows. A common quiver is a long leather container that is open at one end and that is worn usually over the shoulder or at the waist. A ground quiver usually consists of a wire or wood stand or frame which is placed on or inserted in the ground to hold several arrows upright. A bow quiver consists of a frame attached to a hunting bow that has several clips to hold arrows and a small case that covers the piles of the arrows.

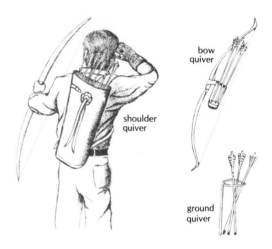

bow quiver

shoulder quiver

ground quiver

quoit A metal, plastic, or rope ring used in the game of quoits.

quoits A game similar to horseshoe pitching in which a ring is tossed at a stake with the object of ringing the stake or having one or more rings nearer the stake than one's opponent has. The game is old, having originally been played with iron rings approximately 8 inches in diameter that were rounded on one side and that had a 4- or 5-inch hole. The playing area consisted of 2 stakes or *hobs* 18 feet apart that extended from the ground one inch. The rings were thrown so that they would ring the hob or stick in the ground near the hob. Each player threw 2 rings and a side scored one point for each ring it had nearer the hob, 2 points for one that touched the hob (a *hobber*), and 3 points for a ringer. When playing with metal hobs, it was sometimes possible to knock an opposing ring away from the hob with a toss. Quoits came to be played on board ocean liners using a taller stake and rings made of heavy rope. Today the game is mostly played by children using rope or rubber rings.

R

¹rabbit 1 *dog racing* A mechanical lure sometimes in the shape of a rabbit that is mounted on an arm which extends onto the racetrack and is moved along an electrified track by an operator who keeps the rabbit just ahead and out of reach of the dogs. The greyhounds run after the rabbit because they chase by sight rather than by scent and because they will generally chase anything that runs away from them.
2 A competitor in a race who sets a fast pace often to enable a teammate to set a record or to attempt to burn out a particularly dangerous rival so that a teammate will have a better chance to win; a pacesetter.
3 *golf* A professional touring golfer who is not an exempt player and who must play one or more qualifying rounds at the beginning of the week in order to have a chance to enter a tour event.

²rabbit *hunting* To hunt rabbits.

rabbit ball A ball that is livelier and capable of being hit farther than another. The present-day baseball is sometimes considered to be a rabbit ball in comparison with the ball used in the era before World War II.

rabbit ears An extreme sensitivity to criticism.

rabbiter *hunting* Someone who hunts rabbits.

rabbit punch *boxing* An illegal short chopping blow delivered to the back of the neck or to the base of the skull with the back of the fist.

¹race 1 A contest of speed in which the participants either compete directly against one another (as in auto racing, horse racing, swimming, or track and field) or attempt to record the fastest time made on a course (as in skiing or bobsledding).
2 Competition for a league or conference title. ⟨the pennant *race*⟩
3 A particular style of racing. ⟨run your own *race,* not your opponent's⟩

²race 1 To compete is a race.
2 To enter (as a racehorse) in a race; to use in a race. ⟨*raced* his new car⟩

race chart see CHART (*horse racing*)

race committee *yacht racing* A committee usually from the yacht club sponsoring a race that is responsible for conducting the race and ruling on all aspects of the race and on all protests.

racecourse A course used for racing.

racedriver Someone who drives a racing car.

racegoer Someone who frequently attends races (as horse races or dog races).

¹racehorse A thoroughbred trained for steeplechase or flat racing.

²racehorse *basketball* Being a style of basketball characterized by a lot of running and fast breaks with little use of set plays and minimal attention to defense.

racehorse start *air racing* A start in which all competitors are on the ground and stationary when the starter drops a flag. On the signal the competitors take off and make a lap of the course before timing for the race begins.

racer 1 Someone who races.
2 A vehicle (as an automobile, boat, bicycle, or canoe) used for racing.

racer's edge *auto racing* The maximum speed at which a driver can negotiate a turn and maintain control of his car.

racetrack A closed course on which races are run. — often used for courses for horse racing or auto racing as distinguished from *running track*

racetracker A racegoer.

¹race-walk see WALK (*track and field*)

²race-walk *track and field* To compete in a competitive walk.

race-walker Someone who competes in racewalks.

race-walking *track and field* The competitive walk; competing in a walk.

raceway A course for racing and especially a racetrack for harness racing.

racing The sport or profession of engaging in or holding races.

racing backstroke see BACKSTROKE (*swimming*)

racing commission The controlling body of horse racing in each state.

racing dive A flat shallow dive made from the

racing dive

starting platform for the beginning of a race or a leg of a relay race to be swum in the crawl, breaststroke, or butterfly.

racing form see FORM

racing plate A horseshoe worn by a racehorse.

racing secretary *horse racing* An official at a track who determines entry requirements (as sex, age, and racing record) for each race and who assigns weight in handicap races.

racing sound *of a racehorse* Considered able to race though not necessarily fit or in good health.

¹rack **1** *billiards* **a** A triangular frame used to set up the balls for a break shot in pocket billiards. **b** The triangular arrangement of balls set up at the beginning of a game. **2** *equitation* **a** A moderately fast 4-beat gait in which the feet hit the ground one at a time in the same sequence as in the walk but with each leg raised unusually high and with the horse supported alternately on one or 2 legs. (also called *single foot*) **b** A pace.

²rack *billiards* To arrange the balls in a rack for a break shot.

racket **1** An implement usually made of hardwood or lightweight metal that is used to hit a ball or shuttlecock in a racket game and that consists of a handle with a round or oval frame at the end which is strung with nylon or catgut to provide a surface for striking. The size, shape, or weight of a tennis racket is not set by tennis rules, but manufacturers have standardized the racket at 27 inches in overall length with a head 9 inches wide and 12 inches long. The head is oval, and the overall weight usually varies from 12 to 14 ounces. The badminton racket is also not set by the rules of the game but is typically 26 inches overall in length with an oval head approximately 8 inches wide and 10 inches long. The weight usually varies between 3½ and 5 ounces. A squash-racquets racket is 27 inches

long, weighs approximately 9½ ounces, and has a round head no more than 9 inches in diameter. The racket used in racquets is similar to a squash racket; that used in squash tennis is similar to a tennis racket. The court-tennis racket is normally 26 to 27 inches long with a pear-shaped head that is somewhat straighter on one side than on the other. The head is 7 to 8 inches wide at the widest part, and the racket weighs between 13 and 18 ounces. That used in racquetball has a somewhat oval head no more than 9 inches wide and 11 inches long and a handle about 7 inches long. The rules specify that the sum of the overall length and width of the racket cannot exceed 27 inches.

2 A table tennis paddle.

tennis racket

squash racket

badminton racket

racquetball racket

racket game Any of numerous games (as tennis, badminton, or squash racquets) in which a ball or shuttlecock is driven over a net or against a wall with a racket.

rackets British spelling of *racquets.*

rack up To score. ⟨*racked up* 30 points in the first half⟩

racquetball A game played on a 4-wall handball court in which all the rules of handball apply except that an 18-inch-long strung racquet is used to strike a slightly larger and softer ball.

racquets A game which is similar to squash racquets and from which squash racquets devel-

rag

oped that is played on a large 4-wall court with rackets and a small, hard, leather-covered ball. Racquets is played as a singles or doubles game and differs from squash basically in that only the serving side may score points. Because of the unusually large size of the court and the hardness of the ball, racquets is considered to be the fastest of all racket games. Because of the great expense of constructing courts and the cost of the balls, however, racquets is also a relatively rare game.

rag To maintain possession of the puck or ball in ice hockey or box lacrosse (as when trying to kill a penalty) especially by adroit stickhandling.

rail **1 a** A fence bounding the edge of a racetrack (as for horse racing or dog racing). **b** A position close to the inside rail and especially the inside post position at the start of a race.
2 The rim around the outside of a billiard table to which the cushions are attached.
3 The edge of the topsides or the deck of a boat; the edges of a surfboard.
4 see SLINGSHOT (*drag racing*)

railbird A racing enthusiast who sits on or near the track rail to watch a race or workout.

rail job see SLINGSHOT (*drag racing*)

rail lugger *horse racing* A horse that usually runs close to the inside rail in a race.

railroad **1** *bowling* A difficult split (as the 7–10, 8–10, or 4–6). — see illustration of pin arrangement at BOWLING
2 *court tennis* An overhead serve made with spin on the ball so that it moves along the penthouse, hits the grille wall, and twists back toward the penthouse wall instead of bouncing out into the court.

rail shot see ALLEY SHOT

rain check A ticket stub that is good for admission to another contest (as a baseball game) when the scheduled one is rained out.

rainout *baseball* A game suspended or postponed because of rain. (also called *washout*)

rain out To rain to such an extent that a particular game is postponed. (also *wash out*)

raise *curling* To hit another stone and knock it closer to the tee.

raise one flag *Australian Rules football* To kick a behind.

raise two flags *Australian Rules football* To kick a goal.

rake *sailing* The fore-and-aft inclination of a mast.

¹rally **1** A series of strokes in a court game (as tennis, badminton, handball, squash racquets, or volleyball) with sides alternately playing a ball or shuttlecock over a net or against a wall from the time it is served until one side fails to make a good return. In some games (as tennis, table tennis, and squash racquets) the rally ends in a let or with one side scoring a point; in other games (as badminton, handball, or volleyball) the rally ends in a let or with the serving side scoring the point or losing the right to serve.
2 a or **rallye** A competitive motor sports event for automobiles or motorcycles that is run usually over public roads under ordinary traffic conditions and traffic rules with the object of maintaining a specified schedule between checkpoints on a route unknown to the competitors before the start of the run. In the United States, rallies are primarily local club-sponsored TSD (time-speed-distance) competitions which are basically tests of navigation skill with competitors following a set of written instructions to find the route and maintain a specified average speed between checkpoints. Competitors are not required to exceed the posted speed limits for any stretch of road. An automobile requires a team of 2, a driver and a navigator to read and interpret the instructions and make the necessary calculations. The competitors are penalized for arriving early or late at a checkpoint, and the team with the fewest penalty points is the winner. International rallies, in contrast, are essentially long-distance endurance races which may be held on major public roads or on off-road areas or on logging roads. These are highly competitive events usually run at high speeds that are a severe test of both the driver's and the navigator's skills. Most successful competitors are factory teams with highly modified vehicles and with crews of mechanics and supplies of spare parts at each checkpoint. The rallies are often run in various stages with designated rest stops where competitors may sleep while their crews repair their vehicles. **b** An informal motor sports contest (as for automobiles, motorcycles, or snowmobiles) intended essentially to be a test of driving and maneuvering skill.
3 A renewed, sustained, or abrupt offensive or scoring action. Often, but not invariably, the term is used of an offensive action by the trailing team which ties the game or gives the team a lead. ⟨four-run *rally* in the first inning⟩ ⟨staved off two . . . *rallies* in the game's closing minutes to stop the Steelers, 21–17 — Dick Treglown, *Palm Beach Post*⟩

²rally **1 a** To engage in a rally (as in tennis). **b** To practice or warm up for a court game by playing the ball or shuttlecock over the net or against the wall with one's opponent.

2 To compete in a rally.

3 To produce a rally in a game; make a comeback.

rallycross A competitive event for automobiles in which small groups of drivers at a time race for a number of laps around a small closed course that includes paved and unpaved portions and often grass and mud. The winning times for each heat are recorded, and the competitor with the overall fastest time is the winner.

rallye see RALLY

rallying The sport or practice of driving in rallies.

rallyist Someone who competes in a rally.

rallymaster A person who organizes and conducts a rally and who is responsible for selecting the route to be taken and publishing the instructions.

Randolph *trampolining* A stunt performed on the trampoline which consists of a one and a half forward somersault with 2 full twists of the body.

randori *judo* Free play or sparring between 2 players.

range **1** The total horizontal distance a bullet or arrow travels.

2 The distance between a target and a weapon.

3 A place specially designed for shooting competition or practice.

4 *baseball* The ability of a fielder to move to the left or right to reach a batted ball in practically any area of his position in time to make an effective play.

5 Short for *driving range.*

range finder *archery* A device that enables an archer to find the proper point of aim for a target a given distance away. The range finder is typically a small strip of wood that has a hole in one end to fit over the arrow point, a target mark, and marks indicating the point of aim for standard distances. The range finder is slipped on the point of the arrow, and the arrow is held in position for shooting. By lining up the target mark with the bull's-eye and noting the background behind the proper distance mark, the archer is able to locate the proper point of aim for that particular target distance. — see also POINT OF AIM

range officer *shooting* The official who has sole authority for conducting a match, for starting and ending the shooting, and for ensuring the safety of the participants.

rapid fire *shooting* **1** Rifle competition in which

each competitor is required to fire 10 rounds a minute.

2 Pistol competition in which each competitor is given 10 seconds to fire 5 rounds. — compare SLOW FIRE, TIMED FIRE

¹rappel *mountain climbing* Descent of a steep cliff by sliding down a fixed rope which runs through the legs, across the chest, and over the shoulder or through a tension device attached to a climber's waist line. (also called *abseil*)

rappel

²rappel To make a rappel; to descend a cliff by means of a rappel. (also *rope down*)

rappel point *mountain climbing* The point to which a rappel rope is secured at the top of a cliff.

rapture of the deep or **rapture of the depths** see NITROGEN NARCOSIS

raspberry A Bronx cheer.

rassling see WRESTLING

rat catcher *fox hunting* A tweed suit worn as informal attire for cub hunting.

rate *horse racing* To run a racehorse at less than full speed in the early part of a race so that it will stay in contention but will not tire before the stretch run.

rat tail *skating* A short scratch mark made on the ice by a figure skating blade as the skater pushes off from one foot to glide backward on the other foot.

rattle **1** To cause a competitor to lose composure and concentration (as by heckling).

2 *hunting* To beat a cover for game.

razorhead *archery* **1** An arrow pile used on hunting arrows that consists of 2 perpendicular triangular blades of different sizes with the shorter blade projecting from the middle of the longer blade.

2 A hunting arrow equipped with a razorhead.

razzle-dazzle Tricky plays or maneuvers intended to confuse the opposition.

RBI *baseball* A run batted in.

¹reach *sailing* A course that is approximately at right angles to the wind. When at a 90-degree angle, a boat is said to be sailing a *beam reach.* When the course is less than a 90-degree angle, it is called a *close reach;* when more than 90 degrees, it is a *broad reach.* — compare BEAT, RUN

²reach To sail on a reach.

reach base *baseball* To be successful in getting to first base. ⟨*reached base* on a throwing error⟩

read To correctly anticipate the action (as the defensive coverage or offensive blocking) of an opponent by observing the opponent's position or movement. ⟨*read* a defense⟩ ⟨*read* a blitz⟩

read the green *golf* To analyze the slope of a putting green to determine how much and in what direction a putt will break.

real tennis see COURT TENNIS

reaping throw *judo* A method of throwing one's opponent from a standing position by sweeping a leg into the opponent's leg to upset his balance.

rearguard An ice hockey defenseman.

rebote *jai alai* **1** The back wall of a jai alai court.

2 A shot played off the back wall.

¹rebound **1** A shot (as in basketball, ice hockey, or lacrosse) that hits the goal or the goalkeeper and bounces away. In ice hockey a shot that bounces off the boards may also be called a rebound.

2 A goal scored by knocking in a rebound (as in ice hockey).

3 *archery* An arrow that hits the target and bounces off and that is given an arbitrary value of 5 or 7 points.

4 *basketball* The act or an instance of gaining possession of a rebound. ⟨leads the league in *rebounds*⟩

5 *rugby* A ball that hits a part of a player other than his hand, arm, or lower leg and bounces forward but that is not a knock-on and that may be played again by that player.

²rebound To gain possession of a rebound.

rebounder *basketball* A player skilled at rebounding.

rebound tumbling see TRAMPOLINING

rebreather see SCUBA

recall The act of calling back the competitors just after the start of a race (as by repeating the starting signal) because of a false start.

receive **1** To catch or gain possession of a kickoff or punt.

2 To return or attempt to return an opponent's serve in a court game.

receiver **1** The player in a court game who receives the serve. — compare SERVER

2 A player who catches a pass; an offensive player in football eligible to catch a forward pass.

3 The metal frame in which the action of a firearm is fitted and to which the breech end of the barrel is attached.

4 *football* A player who receives a kickoff or punt; safety.

5 *track and field* The runner who receives the baton during an exchange in a relay race.

6 A baseball catcher.

receiving barn *horse racing* A barn at a racetrack in which horses that have been stabled at another track and shipped in for a race are held prior to the race.

receiving line *racquetball* An imaginary line 5 feet behind the short line behind which the receiver must stand until the ball is served. On a court marked for racquetball play, the receiving line is indicated by a 3-inch-long line that extends up from the floor on each side wall 5 feet back of the short line.

receiving zone *handball* The floor area of the court between the short line and the rear of the court in which a player receives the serve.

reception *football* An act of catching a forward pass; a forward pass that is caught by a receiver and credited to him in statistical records. — compare COMPLETION

recheat *fox hunting* A call sounded on a horn to assemble the hounds.

record **1** An attested top performance or prominent achievement. ⟨the *record* for the mile run⟩ ⟨the *record* for most errors in one game⟩

2 A competitor's or team's cumulative statistics over a specified period of time. ⟨a pitcher's season *record* of 25–12⟩

recover **1** To make a recovery.

2 To gain possession of a loose ball (as after a fumble or muffed kick) in football.

recovery **1** or **recovery to guard** *fencing* The return to the on guard position after a lunge.

2 *golf* A golf stroke played from the rough or a sand trap onto the green or fairway.

3 *rowing* The action following the completion of a stroke in which the blade is raised, feathered, and brought toward the bow of the boat into position for the next stroke.

4 *swimming* The action following the completion of an arm or leg stroke in which the arm or leg is brought back into position for the next stroke.

recruiting The practice of seeking to get certain high school athletes to attend a particular college or university so that they can play on the school's varsity team.

recurved bow An archery bow that is constructed so that the tips of the limbs curve toward the back when the bow is unstrung.

red or **red ball** *billiards* **1** The solid red object ball in English billiards and carom billiards games.

2 Any of the 15 solid red balls used in snooker.

red card A red card shown by the referee (as in international soccer) to indicate that a player is being sent off.

red-dog *football* To rush a passer from a linebacker or defensive back position; blitz.

red dog see BLITZ (*football*)

red-dogger *football* A linebacker or defensive back who blitzes.

red-flag *motor racing* To stop a race by signaling with a red flag.

red flag *motor racing* A solid red flag that is used to indicate that a race is being stopped and that competitors are to come to an immediate and complete stop.

red hazard *billiards* A winning hazard in English billiards in which the red ball is pocketed and which counts 3 points.

red light *ice hockey* A red light behind the goal that is lit by the goal judge to indicate that a puck has entered the goal.

red line *ice hockey* A 1-foot-wide red line across the middle of a rink used for professional play that is parallel to the goal lines and that divides the rink in half. The red line serves as a reference line for calling icing and offside passes.

redoublement *fencing* Any attack made after the opponent parries the original attack but does not follow immediately with a riposte.

¹redshirt A college athlete who remains out of intercollegiate competition for a year while attending school in order to recover from an injury or in order to extend his eligibility for an additional year and in the meantime gain experience practicing but not playing with the team.

²redshirt **1** To become a redshirt and remain out of varsity competition for a year while attending school.

2 To keep a player out of varsity competition by making him a redshirt.

¹reef *sailing* To reduce the area of a sail by rolling or folding a portion at the foot and securing it to the mast or a spar.

²reef *sailing* **1** A part of a sail that is reefed.

2 The reduction in area of a sail by reefing.

reef break *surfing* Waves that begin to break over an underwater reef. Because there is usually a stretch of deeper water between a reef and the shore, the waves tend to hold up and give a relatively long ride.

reefing point see REEF POINT

reef knot see SQUARE KNOT

reef point or **reefing point** *sailing* One of a number of short ropes or strips of material usually sewn in a row to a sail by means of which the sail is secured to the mast when reefed. (also called *stop*)

reel *fishing* A flared metal spool and supporting frame that is attached to the butt of a fishing rod for winding in and storing fishing line. There are 2 principal types of reels in common use. One is designed with the spool axis at right angles to the rod. The spool takes up the line directly as the handle is turned. The handle may be connected directly to the spool as in a single-action fly-fishing reel, where the spool turns once for every turn of the handle, or it may be connected by means of a series of gears, as in a bait casting reel, so that the spool turns 3 or 4 times for every turn of the handle. The other style of reel is designed with the axis of the spool in line with the rod. With this design, used for spinning or spin casting reels, the spool remains stationary, and the line is picked up by a revolving arm or cup which winds it on the spool as the handle is turned. During casting, the cup or arm is moved out of the way, and the line spirals off the free end of the spool. These reels employ a set of gears between the handle and the spool which causes the spool to turn faster than the handle. They also have the advantage of freedom from backlash, a common problem on bait casting reels; but they are not suited to bait casting or fly casting because the line tends to remain in tiny coils after it is cast.

reel seat *fishing* The part of the butt of a fishing rod designed to hold the reel.

reeve *boating* To pass the end of a line through

345

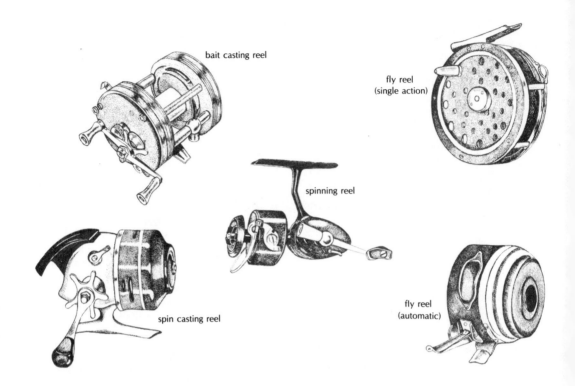

bait casting reel

fly reel
(single action)

spinning reel

spin casting reel

fly reel
(automatic)

the hole or opening in a fitting (such as a block).

¹ref Short for *referee.*

²ref To serve as a referee.

re-face *of an ice hockey official* To face the puck again after calling a violation in the previous face-off.

referee **1** *aikido* An official on the mat with the players who conducts the mock fighting part of the competition and who awards points and penalizes fouls.

2 *badminton* An official whose duties are identical to those of a tennis referee.

3 *basketball* One of 2 officials who have equal responsibility in conducting the game, indicating successful goals, and calling violations and fouls. In professional play, both officials are called *referees,* while in high school and college play, one is officially called the *referee* and the other the *umpire;* in practice however, both are generally referred to as *referees.*

4 *billiards* An official in formal competition who is responsible for conducting the match, racking the balls for a break, marking the positions of the balls if there is an interruption in the play, and

noting infractions of the playing rules and imposing penalties.

5 *boxing* An official in the ring with the boxers who conducts the bout and enforces the rules, who separates the boxers from a clinch, conducts the count when one boxer is down, notes infractions of the rules and imposes cautions and warnings, and has sole authority for stopping a bout if one boxer is unable to continue.

6 *box lacrosse* Either of 2 officials who have equal responsibility for the conduct of the game, including conducting face-offs, calling infractions and assessing penalties, and awarding goals.

7 *Canadian football* An official on the field whose duties are identical to those of an American football referee.

8 *diving* An official in charge of the competition who enforces the rules and certifies the scores awarded by the judges.

9 *football* The principal official on the field who takes a position in the offensive backfield on scrimmage plays and who is primarily responsible for running the game, putting the ball in play, starting the clock, and watching for lateral passes, illegal moves by the offensive players, and roughing of the kicker or passer.

10 *Gaelic football* An official on the field of play who is solely responsible for the conduct of the game and who watches for and penalizes infractions and fouls.

11 *golf* A tournament official who follows the competitors around the course and who is responsible for dealing with questions regarding the rules and for enforcing penalties for breach of the rules.

12 *handball* An official who conducts the match by deciding on proper serves, hinders, and infractions, keeping a record of the score and of the order of serve, and ruling on questions of interpretations of the rules.

13 *hurling* An official on the field who has sole responsibility for conducting the game and for noting and penalizing infractions and fouls.

14 *ice hockey* A single official on the ice in Canadian and American professional hockey who is assisted by 2 linesmen or either of 2 officials in amateur and international hockey who have equal responsibility for conducting the game. The referee is responsible for conducting face-offs, awarding goals, and noting fouls and assessing penalties.

15 *judo* An official on the mat who is responsible for conducting the match and for awarding points for good throws and for successful submission holds and pins. When the competitors move off the mat, the referee halts the match and drags them back to the center of the mat.

16 *karate* An official on the mat who conducts the match and awards points, notes fouls, and issues warnings and in the event of a tie, casts the deciding vote.

17 *lacrosse* An official on the field who has equal responsibility with the umpire for the conduct of the game and for noting infractions and fouls and assessing penalties. Often both officials are called *referees*.

18 *paddleball* Same as for handball.

19 *racquetball* Same as for handball.

20 *rugby* An official on the field who is assisted by 2 touch judges and who is responsible for conducting the match, noting infractions and fouls, cautioning, warning, or sending off offending players, keeping the time of the match and the official score, and interpreting the laws of the game.

21 *skating* **a** An official in figure skating competition who is responsible for the overall conduct

of the competition and who certifies the scores awarded by the judges. **b** Either of 2 officials who are responsible for the conduct of speed skating competition, for enforcement of the rules, and for noting and penalizing infractions.

22 *skeet* Same as for trapshooting.

23 *soccer* An official on the field who is assisted by 2 linesmen and who is responsible for the conduct of the game, for awarding scores, and for watching for and penalizing infractions and fouls by awarding direct and indirect free kicks and penalty kicks.

24 *speedball* An official on the field who is assisted by 2 linesmen and who is responsible for the conduct of the game, for awarding scores, for noting and penalizing infractions and fouls, and for interpreting the playing rules.

25 *squash racquets* An official who has sole control of the match and who decides on faults, hinders, and general interpretations of the rules.

26 *sumo* An official in the ring who conducts the match, announces the names of the competitors before the bout, indicates to the wrestlers when the preliminary ritual should end and the wrestling should begin, and judges the winner of the bout.

27 *swimming* An official who has overall responsibility for the conduct of the meet, for enforcing and interpreting the rules, and for supervising the starters, timers, and judges.

28 *team handball* Either of 2 officials on the field who have equal responsibility for the conduct of the game, for awarding goals, and for noting and penalizing infractions and fouls.

29 *tennis* An official who has overall authority for a match but who is not involved in the actual conduct of the match until appealed to on a ruling made by the umpire. The referee has the ultimate authority for postponing a match.

30 *track and field* An official with overall authority for the conduct of a meet who is responsible for enforcing the rules and disqualifying offenders, deciding on questions of interpretations of the rules, and certifying record performances.

31 *trapshooting* An official who is responsible for the conduct of the individual competition, deciding when a target is broken or lost, calling no-targets, ensuring that competitors shoot in the proper order, and enforcing the rules of the sport.

32 *volleyball* The principal official in a game who is seated at one end of the net with his head at least 2 feet above the level of the top of the net and who has responsibility for the conduct of a game, for enforcing the rules, for permitting time-outs and substitutions, and for penalizing infractions.

33 *water polo* Either of 2 officials who have equal control of a game in college play or a single official with sole control of the game in international play with responsibility for starting and stopping play, awarding goals, noting and penalizing infractions and fouls, and deciding matters involving interpretation of the rules.

34 *weight lifting* Any of 3 officials who ensure that the weights are accurate and that competitors are competing in the proper weight division, and who observe and rule (by majority vote) on the legality of each lift.

35 *wrestling* An official who is on the mat with the wrestlers to conduct the match and ensure that all holds used are legal and that potentially dangerous holds are not pushed beyond the legal limits, to issue warnings, to award points for aggressive actions, to halt the match when a wrestler is off the mat, and to signal when one wrestler has secured a fall.

referee's crease A semicircle with a radius of 10 feet marked on the surface of an ice hockey rink or a box lacrosse box directly in front of the penalty timekeeper in which no one is permitted while the referee is in discussion with the penalty timekeeper (as when handing out penalties).

referee's position *wrestling* A position assumed by both competitors at the center of the mat in which one wrestler gets down on his hands and knees on the mat and the other kneels beside him with one arm around the opponent's waist and the other hand on the opponent's near elbow. The referee's position is used to start the

referee's position

second and third periods of a match and to resume action during a period after the competitors go off the mat while one competitor has an advantage. — compare NEUTRAL POSITION

referee's throw *team handball* A method of restarting play after an unusual interruption or after both teams commit an infraction simultaneously in which the referee rolls the ball along the ground or bounces the ball in the air with both teams seeking to gain possession. All players must be at least 3 meters (10 feet) from the ball until it leaves the referee's hand, and no attacking player may be inside the free throw line.

reflex bow A recurved bow.

refusal *equitation* The act or an instance of a horse's refusing to make a jump in show jumping or steeplechase competition.

regatta A rowing, speedboat, or sailing race or series of races. In rowing, a regatta is distinguished by the fact that a number of boats start together and cover the course in adjacent lanes.

registered player *tennis* A player permitted by a governing body to keep all prize money won in an open tournament but still be eligible to compete in amateur competition.

regular A player who is on the starting team as distinguished from one who is a substitute. ⟨will have size and so much depth that pro scouts, as in years past, will be watching third and fourth stringers just as much as the *regulars* — Gib Landell, *Coach & Athlete*⟩

regular grip see GRIP (*gymnastics*)

regulation croquet see CROQUET

regulator *scuba diving* A device that provides a diver with a constant supply of air at the same pressure as the surrounding water. The regulator, in one, 2, or sometimes 3 stages, reduces the pressure of the air in the tank from over 1000 pounds per square inch to that of the surrounding water (approximately 44 psi at a depth of 66 feet) so that all the diver has to do is inhale to receive air. A simplified form of regulator consists basically of 2 chambers, one an air chamber connected directly to the air-tank valve and leading by a rubber hose to the mouthpiece, and the other a chamber open to the sea and separated from the air chamber by a flexible rubber diaphragm. As the diver inhales, he creates a slight vacuum in the air chamber allowing the water pressure to push in the diaphragm. As the diaphragm is depressed, it pushes a spring-activitated lever which opens the air-tank valve to supply air to the diver's lungs. When the diver's lungs are full, the air stops flowing, and with the air pressure on one side of the diaphragm equalling the water pressure on the other side, the valves are closed. Nearly all modern regulators employ at least one intermediate stage which reduces the pressure of the air from the tank to approximately 100 psi before it is reduced to that of the water in order to provide a smoother flow of air and less abrupt opening and closing of the valves. Regulators come in 2 styles: the double-hose type which has both step-down stages at the rear of the tank and which supplies air to the mouthpiece at the pressure of the surrounding water through one hose and carries exhaled air around behind the diver through the other hose, and the single-hose type which has one reduction stage on the air tank that supplies air at 100 psi through a small high-pressure hose to the second step-down stage at the mouthpiece. With this type of regulator, the exhaled air escapes from the mouthpiece on either side of the chin. (also called *demand regulator*)

rein or **reins** The lines connected to a bit in a horse's mouth by which the horse is controlled.

relative work see SKYDIVING

relay or **relay race** A race (as in swimming or track and field) between teams that consists usually of 4 stages (*legs*) with only a single team member competing at a time and a different team member competing on each leg. In swimming, the swimmer completing one leg normally has to touch the wall before his teammate is permitted to start the next leg. In track and field, the runner finishing one leg is usually required to pass a baton to the next runner, but the outgoing runner normally begins running before the actual pass some distance before the end of the exchange zone so that he is moving when he receives the baton. In swimming, the relay events commonly include the 400 meter medley relay (4 × 100 — 4 swimmers each swimming 100 meters), and the 400 meter and 800 meter (4 × 100 and 4 × 200) freestyle relays. In track and field, relay races with all team members running the same distance include the 400 meter (4 × 100) or 440 yard (4 × 110) relay, the 1600 meter (4 × 400) or the mile (4 × 440) relay, and the 2 mile (4 × 880) relay. — see also EXCHANGE, EXCHANGE ZONE; DISTANCE MEDLEY, SPRINT MEDLEY; SHUTTLE RELAY

¹release To move from one's normal position in order to assume another position or to perform a second assignment. ⟨the defender who *re-*

leases and double teams the ball is determined by the direction which the dribbler takes — Jack Kaminer, *Coach & Athlete*⟩ ⟨*releases* from his tight-end spot and comes across and . . . blocks him — Vince Lombardi⟩

²release 1 *archery* The act of releasing the bowstring to loose an arrow; the manner of releasing a bowstring.
2 *football* The action or manner of throwing a ball. ⟨he has a quick set-up, a quick *release* and the ability to unload the ball into wide-open spaces when his receivers are covered — Tex Maule, *Sports Illustrated*⟩
3 *gymnastics* The act of momentarily taking one's hands off an apparatus while performing a stunt (as a twist).

release binding A ski binding designed to release the boot when a predetermined amount of forward or upward pull or twisting force is applied at any of numerous angles. The amount of force required to release the binding can be adjusted so that the binding will release in the event of a fall but will not release during normal turning maneuvers.

relief 1 *baseball* The pitching done by a relief pitcher. ⟨4 innings of one-hit *relief*⟩ ⟨his best *relief* performance of the season⟩
2 *golf* The opportunity for a golfer to move without penalty a ball that lies in casual water or near an obstruction on the course which is not a course hazard.

relief pitcher or **reliever** *baseball* A pitcher who replaces another pitcher during a game and especially one who relieves regularly instead of starting.

relieve *of a baseball pitcher* To take over for another pitcher during a game; to serve as a relief pitcher.

reliever see RELIEF PITCHER

remaining back see SET BACK

rematch A second match between the same 2 competitors and especially a boxing match that gives a defeated champion a chance to win back the title.

¹remise *fencing* A second thrust at the target while still in the lunge position and with the arm still extended after an initial attack has missed that is made immediately after the opponent has parried the initial attack but before he makes a riposte or before he is able to complete the movements of a complex riposte.

²remise *fencing* To make a remise.

renewed attack *fencing* Any of the 3 attacks of redoublement, remise, and reprise.

renvers *equitation* A dressage maneuver in which the horse is guided beside a wall with his hind quarters near the wall and his body angled away from the wall at an angle of about 30 degrees and with his head facing in the direction of movement. — compare TRAVERS

repechage A second-chance heat in cycling or rowing in which losers of the first round of competition are matched against each other for another chance to qualify for the final heat.

repetitive dive *scuba diving* A second dive performed within 12 hours of a previous dive. Because excess nitrogen absorbed by the body during a dive requires 12 full hours to pass out of the body tissues, before any repetitive dive the diver must take into consideration special decompression requirements.

reprise *fencing* A second attack made after returning momentarily to the on guard position.

reserve A substitute player.

reserve clause A clause formerly in a professional baseball contract that gave the club the right to invoke the terms of a player's expired contract for one additional year if a new contract was not agreed to by a specified date. Since the reserve clause was one of the terms of the old contract, it was traditionally interpreted as being self-perpetuating, binding a player to one club for his entire playing career. Legal challenges to the reserve clause eventually resulted in its being dropped in favor of a universal contract provision that specifies a certain period of professional experience before a player can become a free agent. — compare OPTION CLAUSE

resin bag see ROSIN BAG

rest 1 see SUPPORT

2 British term for a mechanical *bridge* in billiards.

restraining circle Any of the five 12- or 15-foot circles surrounding the face-off spots on an ice hockey rink, or the five 12-foot circles surrounding the face-off circles on a box lacrosse box, or the three 12-foot circles in which a jump ball is held on a basketball court which serve to restrain all players not taking part in a face-off or jump ball.

restraining line Any of numerous real or imaginary lines on a playing field or court (as in football, rugby, soccer, or lacrosse) behind which certain players must remain until the ball is in play (as in a face-off or free kick).

rest step *hiking* A method of conserving energy while maintaining a steady climbing pace that involves pausing momentarily as each leg is advanced but before the weight is shifted to it.

retaining wall *auto racing* The wall constructed on the outside of the track of a speedway to keep race cars from leaving the track in the event the driver loses control.

retire 1 To put out an opposing batter, batsman, or side in baseball or cricket.

2 To voluntarily withdraw from competition usually because of illness, injury, or failure of one's equipment.

3 *fencing* To step back to avoid an attack; give ground; retreat.

¹retreat *fencing* To move back from an opponent by first stepping back with the rear foot and then bringing the front foot back the same distance.

²retreat The act or an instance of retreating.

¹retrieve 1 To return a difficult shot in a court game.

2 *fishing* To reel in the line or a lure.

3 *of a hunting dog* To seek out and bring in game shot by the hunter.

²retrieve The act or process of retrieving.

retriever Any of several medium-sized hunting dogs with a thick water-resistant coat used especially for retrieving game.

¹return 1 To hit a ball or shuttlecock back to the front wall or back over the net in a court game.

2 *football* To advance the ball after receiving a kickoff or punt or after intercepting a pass.

²return 1 The action of returning a shot; a ball or shuttlecock that is returned.

2 *football* An advance of the ball made by the team receiving a kick or intercepting a pass. ⟨a 40-yard punt and a 45-yard *return*⟩

return crease *cricket* Either of 2 lines of unspecified length that extend back from the ends of the bowling crease. The bowler is required to have one foot touching the ground behind the bowling crease and inside the return crease when delivering the ball to the batsman. — see illustration at WICKET; see also BOWLING CREASE, POPPING CREASE

returner *football* A player who returns a punt or kickoff.

return kick A kick made in football or rugby by a player immediately after his team gains possession of the ball on a play (as immediately after receiving a kick). A return kick is legal in American professional football but not in college football, where it draws a 5-yard penalty.

return to guard *fencing* To return to the on guard position after making a lunge.

reversal *wrestling* A maneuver in which a wrestler goes from a position of disadvantage to a position of advantage and for which he is awarded 2 points.

¹reverse 1 *football* An offensive play in which a back moving laterally in one direction gives the ball to a teammate moving in the opposite direction.

2 *track and field* The action of reversing the position of the feet just after releasing an object in a throwing event (as the javelin throw or shot put).

²reverse *wrestling* To perform a reversal against one's opponent.

reverse corner A crosscorner shot in squash racquets.

reverse cradle *wrestling* A cradle hold taken by a wrestler on an opponent who is behind him by looping one arm under the opponent's leg and getting a headlock and then joining hands.

reverse curl *weight training* A curl performed with the palms turned down rather than up.

reverse dive *diving* Any of a group of competitive dives started from a position facing away from the diving board in which the diver springs up and rotates backward to enter the water headfirst facing toward the board or feetfirst facing away from the board. (also called *gainer*) — compare ARMSTAND DIVE, BACKWARD DIVE, FORWARD DIVE, INWARD DIVE, TWIST DIVE

reverse dive in pike position (jackknife)

reversed point The point of a fishhook that is set to the right of the line of the shank when viewed from above with the point up. — see illustration at FISHHOOK; compare KIRBED POINT

reverse dunk *basketball* A dunk shot made by approaching the basket backwards or by driving underneath the basket and dunking the ball back over the head or over the shoulder.

reverse English *billiards* English which causes a ball to spin in the opposite direction to that in which it is traveling so that when it strikes a cushion or another ball it tends to stop or come back or rebound at much less of an angle than it would if it had no English; draw.

reverse grip see GRIP (*gymnastics*)

reverse hook see BACK-UP (*bowling*)

reverse kickout *surfing* A fancy kickout in which the board is turned one way and the surfer turns the other way.

reverse nelson see NELSON

reverse shoulder see COUNTERROTATION

reverse start *motor racing* A method of lining up competitors for the start of a race in which the fastest qualifiers start at the rear.

reverse stick *field hockey* The stick turned around and held with the toe pointing toward the player so that it may be swung from left to right to hit a ball with the flat part, which is the only part with which the ball may be legally played.

rhubarb A heated dispute on the field during a baseball game.

rib A metal ridge running the length of a shotgun barrel to assist in sighting.

ribby *baseball* A run batted in; RBI.

ridden out *of a racehorse* Winning a race under moderate urging so as to maintain a comfortable lead. — compare DRIVING

¹ride 1 *auto racing* A job or assignment driving a racing car for the car owner.

2 *cycling* A single heat.

3 *lacrosse* **a** A legal charge into an opponent who is playing the ball or seeking to gain possession of the ball; body check. **b** A pressing defense used to prevent the opposing team from clearing the ball into their own attacking half of the field.

4 *wrestling* **a** The maintaining of control over an opponent while one has a position of advantage. **b** A particular hold employed during a ride. ⟨an inside crotch *ride*⟩

²ride 1 To tease, annoy, or harass an opponent or an official during a contest.

2 *lacrosse* To charge an opposing player or to employ a pressing defense against a particular opponent.

3 *wrestling* To maintain control over one's opponent on the mat.

ride off To physically force an opponent off the

ride the bench

line to the ball or puck (as in polo or ice hockey).

ride the bench *of a player in a team game* To spend most of one's time on the bench as a substitute rather than playing as a regular.

ride the nose *surfing* To ride the surfboard with one or both feet on the front; to hang five or hang ten.

ride to hounds To ride a horse following foxhounds; to engage in foxhunting.

ridgeling or **ridgling** *horse racing* A partially castrated horse.

riding time see TIME ADVANTAGE

¹rifle A shoulder weapon that has a stock and a long barrel with spiral grooves on the inside and that is designed to shoot a bullet. Rifles are made in single shot, manually operated multiple shot, semi-automatic, and fully automatic models. Target rifles are normally made for .22 or .30 caliber cartridges. Hunting rifles may be made for any of a number of different size cartridges including .22, .25, .30, .308, .32, and .35 calibers.

²rifle **1** To throw or propel a ball or puck with great speed. ⟨*rifled* a throw to third base⟩
2 To cut spiral grooves into the barrel of a firearm.

rifled slug A shotgun slug typically having a round nose, a hollow base, and sides cut with a series of spiral grooves that increase the accuracy of the slug by causing it to rotate as it passes through the smooth bore of the shotgun. With a rifled slug, a shotgun has an effective range of only about 75 yards, but it has enormous killing power. The slug for a 12 gauge shotgun is comparable to a .73 caliber bullet.

riflescope A telescopic sight used on a rifle.

rifling The spiral grooves cut in the inside of a rifle barrel.

¹rig *sailing* **1** To fit out a boat with the proper tackle.
2 To fit shrouds and stays to a mast or spar.
3 To move a boom in a desired direction.

²rig **1** *fishing* The terminal tackle on a line including the lure or baited hook, leader, and sinkers.
2 Short for *rigging*.

rigger Short for *outrigger* (*rowing*).

rigging The lines on a sailboat used for supporting the mast or for trimming sails. The headstay, backstay, and shrouds which support the mast are known as *standing rigging* because they stand more or less permanently in place. The sheets, halyards, and downhauls used for setting or trimming sails are referred to as *running rigging*.

right **1** A punch delivered with the right hand; ability to punch with the right hand.
2 Short for *right field*.

right center field *baseball* The area of the outfield to the right of dead center field or between center field and right field.

right field *baseball* **1** The right side of the outfield as viewed from home plate; the part of the outfield past first base.
2 The player position for covering right field.

right fielder *baseball* The player who plays right field.

right-handed or **right-hand** **1** With the right hand. ⟨throws *right-handed*⟩
2 Swinging from right to left in striking a ball with a bat or club held in both hands (as in baseball or golf). ⟨a *right-handed* batter⟩

right-hander **1** A player who is right-handed and especially one who throws right-handed as distinguished from batting right-handed.
2 A turn to the right in a road course.

right of way *fencing* The right to attack in foil and saber fencing gained by the fencer who first extends the arm or initiates an attack or who parries an opponent's attack. The fencer has the right to continue with his attack until it has been parried by the opponent, at which time the opponent has the right of way with a riposte until that is parried, giving the original fencer the right of way again for a counter riposte. This series of attacks, parries, and counterattacks constitutes a fencing phrase. It is possible for a fencer to score on an attack made without first parrying the opponent's attack if he manages to land a hit (a *stop hit*) before the opponent begins his last movement of a complex attack or a simple attack which is preceded by a number of feints.

right slide *surfing* Movement on a wave toward the right when facing the shore.

righty A player who is right-handed.

¹rim **1** *basketball* The circular metal frame of the basket from which the net is suspended. — see GOAL
2 *golf* The edge of the cup.

²rim *of a golf putt* To hit or run around a portion of the rim of the cup but not drop in.

rimfire **1** *of a cartridge* Having the primer in a rim surrounding the base.
2 *of a firearm* Designed for rimfire cartridges. — compare CENTER-FIRE

ring **1** One of the scoring areas of a circular target or of a curling house.
2 *boxing* An area which is typically 20 feet square and surrounded usually by 3 parallel

ropes and in which a match is conducted. The ring is normally raised on a platform 3 to 4 feet high. The ropes are at 2-, 3-, and 4-foot heights and are connected to a post at each corner of the ring by means of padded turnbuckles. The floor of the ring consists of a layer of felt or rubber covered with taut canvas, and it extends generally 2 feet beyond the ropes on all sides. — see also ROPE

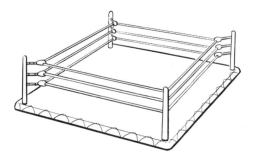

boxing ring

3 *sumo* A circular area 15 feet in diameter in which a match is conducted. The ring is formed of packed earth 2 feet high with a flat top. The circular area for the competition is defined by a heavy rope half imbedded in the top of the mound.
4 A 6-inch ring of rope or rubber tossed back and forth over the net in deck tennis.
5 A throwing circle.
6 Short for *snowring*.
ringer **1** A superior racehorse that is fraudulently entered in a race under another horse's name or a ficticious name to obtain better odds in the betting. The term is also applied to racing vehicles (as race cars) that are illegally substituted for qualifying vehicles.
2 A horseshoe or quoit that encircles the stake or hob and is worth 3 points.
rings *gymnastics* **1** A pair of metal or wooden rings 236 millimeters (approximately 9¼ inches) in diameter suspended 500 millimeters (19½ inches) apart and 2500 millimeters (approximately 8 feet) high that are used in gymnastic competition.—see illustration at DISLOCATE
2 An event in men's competition in which swinging and balancing movements are performed on rings held as motionless as possible.

ringside The area just outside a boxing ring. ⟨has *ringside* seats⟩
ringsider Someone who watches a boxing match from ringside.
rink **1 a** *curling* A rectangular playing area 14 feet wide and at least 138 feet long that is marked on a flat ice surface. The rink has a series of concentric rings (a *house*) at each end. These houses are centered on lines 114 feet apart. Twenty-one feet in front of the center of each house is a hog line across the rink. Twelve feet back of the house is a foothold (*hack*) cut in the ice. **b** *ice hockey* A rectangular playing area with rounded corners that consists of a floor of ice surrounded by a wooden wall (*boards*) 3 to 4 feet high. These boards are topped by a section of plate glass, plastic, or screen designed to keep the puck from flying into the spectators. The optimum size of a hockey rink is 200 feet long and 85 feet wide. There is a goal at each end centered on a red goal line 10 feet from the end of the rink. In front of each goal is a rectangular goal crease 8 feet wide and 4 feet deep. For international play the crease is a semicircle with a 6-foot radius. The rink is divided by two 12-inch-wide blue lines, each 60 feet from a goal line. In addition, a rink for professional play has a 12-inch-wide red line — actually more commonly a line of alternate red and white squares — across the middle dividing the rink in half. There are 9 face-off spots on the surface and 5 of these — the center spot and the face-off spots in both end zones — are surrounded by 15-foot (12 feet in amateur hockey) face-off circles. **c** *lawn bowling* A flat section of closely cut grass 14 to 21 feet wide and 110 to 125 feet long that has a ditch 6 to 8 inches deep and 8 to 11 inches wide at each end backed by a bank at least 9 inches high.
2 A team composed of 4 players in curling or lawn bowling.
3 A surface for skating. Ice skating competition is typically conducted on a hockey rink or outdoors in an area of comparable size. Roller skating competition is conducted usually on an asphalt, concrete, or hardwood surface in an area approximately the same size as for ice skating.
rinkside Located at or near the side of a rink. ⟨the *rinkside* officials⟩
rip cord *skydiving* A cord or wire which when pulled releases the fasteners on a parachute pack allowing the pilot chute to pop out and pull out the main parachute.

rip current A strong seaward rush of water piled up on the shore by successive breaking waves that usually flows along the surface in a relatively narrow channel. The rip is often fed by water flowing relatively parallel to the shore which is pushed along by the waves until it finds an area of static water where it runs out to sea often for a hundred yards or more. The rip current can be dangerous to inexperienced swimmers caught in it and pulled out to sea, but it is often used by scuba divers as the source of a free ride to the deeper water beyond the line of breakers. (also called *riptide, sea puss*)

¹riposte *fencing* A counterattack immediately following a successful parry.

²riposte *fencing* To make a riposte.

rip panel *ballooning* A panel in the top of a balloon that can be opened by a pull of a control line that hangs into the gondola in order to deflate the balloon quickly (as to avoid being dragged along the ground when landing in high winds).

riptide SEE RIP CURRENT

rise *fishing* A disturbance in the surface of a body of water caused by a fish moving upward to take food or bait.

rise ball or **riser** *softball* A pitch that rises on the way to the plate.

roach *sailing* The outward curve in the leech of a sail.

road Being or relating to a game or a series of games played on an opponent's home field, court, or rink. ⟨a 10-day *road* trip⟩ ⟨seventh consecutive *road* loss⟩
— **on the road** On a trip made away from one's home playing area to play at an opponent's home field, court, or rink. ⟨will be *on the road* for the rest of the season⟩

road course A closed racecourse usually from 1½ to 3 miles long laid out over public roads or designed to simulate public roads with hills, sharp curves, and right- and left-hand turns.

road race **1** A race (as for automobiles or motorcycles) held on a road course.
2 *cycling* A race of usually from 10 to 100 miles in length held on public roads under normal traffic conditions that usually begins at one point and ends at another (often in another town).
3 *track and field* A race (as the marathon or some cross-country races) held over public roads.

road racer **1** Someone who competes in road races.
2 A vehicle designed for road racing.

road racing Racing conducted on a road course. In cycling, road racing is the principal form of long-distance racing. The competitors use lightweight 10- or 15-speed bicycles that resemble those used for pleasure cycling. The scoring in road racing is individual, but competition usually involves teams of riders who assist their own star rider by riding ahead of him for long distances to provide him with a slipstream so that he will not exhaust himself early in the race or by letting him get out in front of the pack and then attempting to block off or slow down the rest of the competitors. In motorcycle and auto racing, road racing may be limited to a fixed distance with the winning competitor covering the distance or a specified number of laps first, or it may have a fixed time limit (as 6, 12, or 24 hours) with the winning competitor the one to cover the greatest distance (most laps) in that time. Competition is normally conducted for a specific class of vehicle, according to the type or engine size. Occasionally (as in endurance races) vehicles of different classes will compete together. In such an event, there will be an overall winner plus several individual class winners. Road racing is the principal form of auto racing in Europe and constitutes the competition for formula cars and sports cars. In the United States, road racing competes with oval track racing for a share of the audience. Road races are usually run clockwise, and the racing is usually not stopped for rain.

roadrunner *racquetball* A player who specializes in making defensive shots.

roadster **1** An open or convertible sports car.
2 An old open-wheel racing car having the engine in front and offset slightly so that the drive shaft is beside, rather than under, the driver's seat.

roadwork A part of an athlete's (as a boxer's) training and conditioning program which consists of long-distance running usually along public roads before normal traffic hours.

roan A horse with a black, red, gray, or brown coat muted with an admixture of white hairs.

rob the cradle *bowling* To make only one of the pins of a baby split.

rock A curling stone.

rock climbing The aspect of mountain climbing which involves climbing up rock cliffs by means of available footholds and handholds as distinguished from climbing on ice or hiking up a trail. Rock climbing normally involves the use of such techniques as bridging, laybacking, and jamming and often such artificial aids as chockstones, pitons, and bolts.

rocker **1** The curve or the amount of curve on the bottom of an ice-skate blade, a surfboard, or a kayak.

2 *skating* **a** A half turn from forward to backward or from backward to forward on the same foot made by rotating the body away from the curve being skated and continuing on with a new curve in the opposite direction. **b** A school figure which consists of 3 connecting circles formed by making a rocker when ending one circle and beginning another so that both cusps lie in the middle circle.

rod Short for *fishing rod.*

rode Short for *anchor rode.*

rodeo A contest of basic cowboy skills that is indigenous to the ranges of the western United States and Canada. The term *rodeo* comes from a Spanish word meaning "roundup", and the sport developed from the natural competitive urges of cowboys involved in mass roundups on the western plains. The principal events of rodeos today are bull riding, saddle bronc riding, bareback riding, calf roping, and steer wrestling, with steer roping and team roping contests often added to the list. Many rodeos add some other popular events such as barrel riding (a slalom-like race for women on horseback around a number of barrels), wild-horse racing, and wild-cow milking contests essentially for the amusement of the audiences. Organized rodeos go back to the 19th century; the principal feature of Buffalo Bill Cody's famous Wild West show, which began in 1883, was the rodeo. — see BAREBACK RIDING, BULL RIDING, CALF ROPING, SADDLE BRONC RIDING, STEER ROPING, STEER WRESTLING, TEAM ROPING

rod hand *fishing* The hand holding and manipulating the fishing rod as distinguished from the line hand.

Rogallo wing A triangular hang glider which consists of lightweight polyester fabric connected to 3 struts that are joined at the front and held apart at about an 80-degree angle at the rear. The glider, named for its inventor Francis M. Rogallo, is shaped by the air much the way a parachute is and holds a rider in a harness suspended beneath it. The rider controls the glider by shifting his weight. (also called *delta wing kite*)

rogue's badge see BLINKERS

¹roll **1** To turn and move toward the goal (as after setting a screen in basketball or lacrosse). ⟨one minute he's standing in front of you and the next he's gone, *rolling* in toward the basket or straight

up in the air shooting his jumper — Jerry Lucas⟩

2 or **roll out** *of a football quarterback* To receive the snap and run to one side of the formation usually parallel to the line before turning upfield, pitching the ball out to a back, or throwing a pass.

3 *of an airplane* To undergo roll.

²roll **1** *curling* The movement of a stone after striking another stone.

2 *gymnastics* A somersault performed on the floor.

3 *skating* A half circle skated on one outside edge followed usually by another half circle skated on the other outside edge.

4 Rotation about a fore-and-aft axis (as of a plane). — compare PITCH, YAW

roll back dodge *lacrosse* A dodge made by stopping in front of the opponent, turning away from him as in a pivot dodge, and then as he reacts returning to the original position and continuing around him.

roll bar *auto racing* A heavy bar of usually tubular steel that is built into a racing car and that extends above the driver's head to protect him in the event his car overturns.

roll block A cut block in football.

roll cage *auto racing* A cage of usually tubular steel that is built into a racing car and that surrounds the driver to protect him in the event his car overturns.

roll cast *fishing* A cast in dry-fly fishing made with the line out on the water in front of the fisherman in which the rod tip is raised and brought back until it is just past vertical and then snapped forward so that it creates a loop in the line which rolls forward picking up the line from the water and straightening it out to settle again on the water in a new place.

roll dodge *lacrosse* A dodge similar to the pivot dodge in which the attacker leans into the defender and rolls around him.

roller *baseball* A ground ball that rolls rather than bounces along the ground.

Roller Derby A service mark used for an entertainment of roller speed skating that is conducted on a banked oval track approximately 200 feet around between 2 professional teams of 5 men or 5 women skaters. A match consists of eight 12-minute periods with men and women alternating periods on the track. During a period, the officials will designate specific 60-second spans (*jams*) during which designated skaters (*jammers*) from each team break away from the pack, circle the track, and attempt to lap opposing skaters to score points. A team is awarded one point for each opposing skater passed by a jammer. Players are permitted to assist their own jammers around the pack by pulling them or blocking opposing skaters out of the way and to prevent the opposing jammers from passing by blocking, jostling, or shoving. Violent play such as tripping, elbowing, or slugging opposing skaters is barred but in practice it is generally overlooked and it provides Roller Derby with its principal spectator attraction.

roller hockey A game similar to ice hockey and field hockey that is played between 2 teams of 5 players wearing roller skates on a rink approximately 120 to 140 feet long and 60 to 70 feet wide with a goal 4 feet wide and 3 feet high at each end. In front of each goal is a penalty area 18 feet deep and 40½ feet wide which is similar to the penalty area of soccer. A ball about the size of a field hockey ball is played with a stick of the same general size and shape of a field hockey stick but which is flat on both sides. A team consists of a goalkeeper, 2 backs, and 2 forwards. Play is started at the beginning of a half and after a goal with a strike-off, which is similar to a face-off or a bully. The ball is played only with the blade of the stick, but within the penalty area the goalkeeper is permitted to stop or knock down the ball with his hands. The game is conducted by a referee assisted by 2 goal judges. Infractions are penalized by awarding a free hit to the other team. Fouls committed by the defending team inside the penalty area result in a penalty hit for the other team. The game is played in two 15- or 20-minute halves.

roller-skate To skate on roller skates.

roller skate see SKATE

roller skater Someone who roller-skates.

roll-in *field hockey* A method of putting the ball in play after it has gone out of bounds across a sideline in which a member of the non-offending team rolls the ball back across the line to a teammate.

rolling start A start of a race (as in auto racing) in which the competitors are moving toward the starting line usually at less than racing speeds as the starting signal is given; flying start.

roll-off A play-off match in bowling.

rollout *football* A play in which the quarterback rolls to his left or right after receiving the snap but before handing off or passing.

roll out see ROLL (*football*)

Roman cross see CROSS (*gymnastics*)

rookie A first-year player in professional sports.

roostertail An arching spray of water thrown up behind a racing hydroplane.

rope **1** *boxing* Any of the 3 or 4 strands of rope surrounding a ring. The ropes are between one and 2 inches thick and are covered with a soft material. When 3 ropes are used on a ring, they are placed at heights of 2, 3, and 4 feet from the ring floor (40, 80, and 130 centimeters in international amateur boxing). When 4 ropes are used, they are at heights of 18, 30, 42, and 54 inches.

2 *mountain climbing* **a** A length of rope used for connecting climbers, belaying a moving climber, or in rappelling. The most common rope is made of nylon because of its strength and resistance to rotting, and its ability to stretch to absorb some of the force of a fall. A typical rope would be 120 or 150 feet long and 7/16 inch in diameter. Rope is made in either of 2 different styles, *cable-laid*, which is formed of 3 smaller strands twisted together, or *kermantel*, which consists of a number of straight fibers with a braided covering. **b** A group of climbers roped together and climbing as a group. Usually no more than 4 climbers will move together on one rope.

rope down see RAPPEL

rope tow see SKI TOW

roque A variation of croquet played with short-handled mallets on a hard-surfaced court that has 10 wickets and that is bounded by a concrete wall which is frequently used in making bank shots. Each side plays 2 balls through each of the wickets. When the game is played with 2 players on a side, partners start from opposite ends of the court. A side scores one point for each ball that passes through a wicket. Each ball can score a total of 16 points (6 of the wickets must be played twice, once in each direction), and the first side scoring 32 points is the winner. Games may also be played to a time limit or for a designated number of innings.

¹roquet *croquet* A stroke in which one's ball strikes another ball during play. A roquet gives the player making it the option of making a croquet or a roquet-croquet on the other ball and taking an additional stroke, of moving his ball one mallet-head length away from the other ball and playing 2 additional strokes, or of playing one additional stroke from where his ball lies.

²roquet *croquet* To make a roquet.

roquet-croquet *croquet* The driving of a player's ball into a previously roqueted ball which is against it without holding the first ball in place with the foot as in a croquet so that both balls will move off in desired directions.

Rose Bowl A postseason college football bowl game played in the Rose Bowl stadium in Pasadena, California, between a team representing the Pacific 8 Conference and one representing the Big 10 Conference. The first game was held in 1902, but the event has been held annually only since the second game in 1916.

rosin bag *baseball* A small cloth bag or pouch filled with powdered rosin used by a pitcher to improve his grip on the ball. (also called *resin bag*)

roster The members of a team; a list of these members. — compare LINEUP

rotate **1** *of a defensive player or the defensive backs in football* To move in a circular pattern to cover a weakness in the formation or to protect against a particular type of offensive play.
2 *of a volleyball team* To move in a clockwise direction when regaining the serve so that the player originally on the right side of the front row winds up on the right side of the back row in position to serve.

rotation **1** *baseball* The schedule by which a team's starting pitchers regularly start games; the starting pitchers for a team who regularly start successive games or games in turn.
2 *billiards* **a** The order of shooting at the object balls in certain games in which the lowest-numbered ball on the table is the next one to be played. **b** A pocket billiards game in which the balls are shot in rotation. — see BILLIARDS
3 *football* A movement by the defensive backs and sometimes by the linebackers in a somewhat circular direction with one or more players moving into an area to protect against a particular offensive play or to fill a gap in the defensive coverage and with other players shifting toward the area vacated so that no area is left totally unprotected.
4 *volleyball* The act or an instance of rotating.

rouge *Canadian football* A score of one point awarded to the kicking team when a member of the receiving team fails to run a kickoff or a punt out of his own end zone.

rough *golf* An area of rough ground usually having tall grass that borders the fairway.

roughing see UNNECESSARY ROUGHNESS (*ice hockey*)

roughing the kicker *football* A personal foul that results when a defensive player runs into or knocks down the kicker on a scrimmage kick without first touching or deflecting the ball. The defensive player, in attempting to block a kick, has the responsibility for avoiding all but incidental contact with the kicker unless he touches the ball or unless the kicker's own momentum causes the contact, in which case the defensive player is no longer responsible. What constitutes roughing the kicker is usually a matter of the force of the contact and is left to the judgment of the official. When it is called, the penalty is 15 yards from the previous spot.

roughing the passer *football* A personal foul in professional play that results when a defensive player runs into or tackles a passer after a forward pass has been thrown. The foul is largely dependent on the judgment of the official as to whether the defensive player started his action before the pass was thrown and had reasonable time in which to avoid contact. When it is called, the penalty is 15 yards from the previous spot.

rough play *Canadian football* A foul comparable to unnecessary roughness in American football that results in a 15-yard penalty.

round **1** A stage in an elimination tournament in which competitors are paired and only the winners advance to the next stage.
2 A series of 25 shots in which each competitor shoots from all the stations on the range in trapshooting or skeet.
3 A single cartridge for a firearm.
4 *aikido* A unit of mock fighting competition lasting one minute.
5 *archery* An event in which each competitor must shoot a specified number of arrows at the target from specified distances. — see AMERICAN ROUND, COLUMBIA ROUND, HEREFORD ROUND, LONG INTERNATIONAL, MEN'S NATIONAL ROUND, MEN'S WESTERN ROUND, NATIONAL ROUND, SHORT INTERNATIONAL, WESTERN ROUND, WINDSOR ROUND, YORK ROUND
6 *boxing* One of the periods of actual boxing into which a match is divided. In professional and international amateur boxing, a round lasts for 3 minutes with a 1-minute rest between rounds. Amateur competition in the United States may be conducted in 2- or 3-minute rounds.
7 *golf* A circuit of the course during which the player plays each of the holes in turn. A round normally consists of 18 holes.
8 *shuffleboard* A unit of play which consists of the playing of all disks to the head court and the scoring followed by the playing of the disks back to the foot court and the scoring.

roundball The game of basketball.

rounder

rounder **1** *boxing* A match lasting a specified number of rounds. ⟨won a dull 10-*rounder*⟩
2 *rounders* A unit of scoring in the game that is analogous to a run in baseball.

rounders A game similar to baseball and softball and from which baseball developed that is played with a ball and a bat and is especially popular in Britain. The game is played on a field somewhat resembling a softball field with 4-foot-high posts in place of bases set out around a figure similar to the diamond but with the fourth post off to the left side of the batter instead of by the batter. There are 9 players on a team, a bowler who bowls the ball (tosses it underhand) to the batter, a backstop (catcher), a fielder at each of the posts, and 3 fielders in the playing area deep behind the posts (outfielders). A team scores one rounder each time a player is able to hit the ball and circle the outside of the posts and touch the fourth post before another ball is bowled. A player scores a half rounder if he rounds the posts at a single run without having hit the ball. If a player stops at any post to avoid being put out, he cannot score a rounder or half rounder when he reaches the fourth post, but he must attempt to do so safely to avoid being put out. The bowler is required to make at least one good delivery to the batter on which the batter must try for the first post whether or not he hits the ball. The game has most of the basic elements of baseball with a backward hit (analogous to a foul ball) out of play, with putouts made as in baseball, with a batter required to run on hitting the ball and with other players forced to advance, and with a player at a post able to "steal" if the bowler is in the bowling square without the ball. It also has many elements of cricket with no-balls called if the bowled ball is too wide of the batter, with the awarding of a penalty half rounder if the bowler delivers 3 consecutive no-balls, with a team's inning lasting until all 9 players have been put out, and with a team leading by 10 or more rounders able to require the other team to follow on. A game consists of 2 full innings with the team leading at the end being the winner.

roundhouse **1** *baseball* A wide slow curve.
2 *bowling* A wide sweeping curve.
3 *boxing* A hook delivered with a wide swing.

roundhouse kick *karate* A kick started with the leg held out at the side of the body and snapped forward in a relatively horizontal arc while pivoting on the other foot.

roundoff *gymnastics* A movement to change from forward tumbling to backward tumbling without interrupting the body's momentum which consists of a forward flip or handspring combined with a half twist so that the performer lands facing in the opposite direction.

round robin **1** A tournament in which every contestant meets every other contestant in turn with the overall won-lost records determining final standings.
2 *pari-mutuel betting* A system in which the bettor places parlay bets on all possible combinations of several horses.

round-the-head shot *badminton* An overhead shot in which contact with the shuttlecock is made above the left shoulder of a right-handed player or above the right shoulder of a left-handed player.

round-the-houses *motor sports* British term for racing on a road course set up on city streets.

round-tripper A home run in baseball.

¹rout To defeat decisively.

²rout A one-sided contest; decisive defeat.

roundoff

route 1 *football* A pass pattern.

2 *horse racing* A race one mile in length or longer.

router *horse racing* A horse trained for routes or that runs best in routes.

routine *gymnastics* A series of movements and stunts performed as a unit on an apparatus or in floor exercises.

rover 1 *Australian Rules football* A member of the ruck who generally is smaller and faster than the followers and who is responsible for receiving the ball from the followers on a ball up or throw-in and initiating the team's offense, playing the ball to open forwards, and making kicks at the goal.

2 *croquet* A ball that has been played through all of the wickets but has not hit the final stake or peg and that can be played around the course to assist the other ball of the side or to interfere with the opponents by hitting and driving their balls out of play.

3 Short for *roverback*.

roverback *football* A defensive player whose duties are a combination of those of a linebacker and a cornerback.

rovers or **roving** or **roving archery** *archery* A shooting session in which 2 or more archers wander around an area shooting at random targets such as trees, stumps, a piece of paper, or a clump of grass with the archers alternating in choosing targets or with the archer closest to one target choosing the next.

row To propel a boat as a member of a crew by pulling a single oar with both hands. — compare SCULL

rowing The sport of racing long narrow shells propelled by oars. As a sport, rowing encompasses both rowing and sculling competition. A shell is a long, narrow, extremely lightweight boat designed exclusively for racing. A shell for a crew of eight may be up to 60 feet long, but it is no more than 2 feet wide; the oarsmen sit in line, and there is little space in the boat not taken up by a crew member. The oars in both rowing and sculling are set in oarlocks about 2 feet out from the side of the shell on outriggers.

rowing: an 8-oared shell

The outrigger allows the use of long oars. The oarsman braces his legs against a cross strut (*stretcher*) and sits in a sliding seat so that he can push himself back with his legs on each stroke. The sliding seat combined with the outrigger, which sets the pivot point of the oar out from the side of the shell, gives the oar a long sweep and allows the oarsman to use his back and his legs as well as his arms in pulling the oar.

Major international races are usually held for single, double, and quadruple sculls, pairs, fours (both with and without coxswain), and eights. A regatta, or *sprint* as it is sometimes called, is a race in which several competitors compete side by side on a straight course and is typically held on a lake or a still stretch of a river over a course 2000 meters (1.2 miles) long. For boys under 18, the course is 1500 meters and for women, 1000 meters. A course is usually laid out with 6 lanes marked by buoys. Each boat is required to stay in its lane but will not necessarily be disqualified for drifting out of its lane during the race provided it does not interfere with another boat or create a wake or disturbance in the water which affects the timing, balance, or rhythm of another boat. Regattas are usually conducted in heats, with boats not placing high enough in preliminary heats to qualify automatically for the final allowed to compete again in a repechage or second-chance heat, from which the field for the final is filled out. In addition to regattas, there are other forms of rowing competition, notably the head of the river race in which competitors start at intervals and are individually timed over a course laid out on a river that is not wide enough to accommodate all the competitors at one time.

Because of the strength required for rowing, crews made up of bigger oarsmen have an advantage over smaller crews. Many regattas have separate competition for heavyweight and lightweight crews (as those having an average weight of no more than 150 pounds). Oarsmen under 18 generally engage in junior competition; all others compete in the senior division. A senior who has won 6 races, or one who has rowed in an elite crew is required to compete only in elite (the highest classification) events. (also called *crew*)

rowing tank   *rowing*   A large tank of water containing a mock-up of a shell in which an oarsman or sculler can practice his stroke and work on technique. The effectiveness of a stroke is indicated by a meter which measures the turbulence of the water.

rowlock   see OARLOCK

royal tennis   see COURT TENNIS

Rozelle Rule   A rule in professional football which requires a team that signs a free agent who has played out his option with another team to give the other team mutually agreeable compensation or the compensation for the player will be set by the commissioner of the league. The rule is named for the Commissioner of the National Football League who instituted it.

ruade or **ruade christie**   *skiing*   A parallel turn made by unweighting both skis and pivoting on the tips of the skis to swing the tails around to a new line.

rub   see CHIP (*curling*)

rubber   **1** A 3-game match or series; a series or match in which one side must win 2 out of 3 games. The term in general is found chiefly in British usage ⟨they beat Cambridge by three *rubbers* to nil without losing a set — *London Times*⟩ though it is often used attributively in the United States to refer to a final game or match played between 2 individuals or teams that have previously split an even number of games or matches. ⟨scarcity of second-string starting pitchers, the craftsmen who win the *rubber* games in three-game series, the games that win pennants — Robert Creamer, *Sports Illustrated*⟩ **2** *baseball* A rectangular slab of white rubber measuring 6 inches by 24 inches set crosswise on the pitcher's mound with the front edge 60 feet 6 inches from home plate. The pitcher must maintain contact with the rubber during a pitch and must step off the rubber before throwing to a base when attempting to pick off a runner. (also called *pitcher's plate, pitcher's rubber*) — see illustration at WINDUP **3** A hockey puck. **4** Tires for an automobile, motorcycle, or bicycle.

rubber arm   *baseball*   The ability of a pitcher to pitch frequently and for long periods without suffering from soreness or stiffness.

rub of the green   *golf*   A situation in which a ball in motion is affected by someone on the course other than a player or caddie and must be played where it comes to rest.

¹ruck   **1** A group of competitors trailing the leaders in a race. ⟨came up from the *ruck* to win⟩ **2** *Australian Rules football* A group of 3 players on a team including the rover and 2 followers who are free to follow the play all over the field. The term is sometimes used of the followers alone.

3 *rugby* A mob of players of both teams closing around the ball when it is loose on the ground after being dropped by the ballcarrier when tackled with each player shoving and struggling to play the ball to a teammate with his feet to restart play. To join in a ruck, a player must bind at least one arm around a teammate who is already in the ruck. (also called *loose scrum*) — compare MAUL, SCRUM

²ruck 1 *Australian Rules football* To play in the ruck.
2 *rugby* To struggle to gain possession of the ball in a ruck.

ruckman *Australian Rules football* **1** Any of the 3 players in the ruck.
2 Either of the 2 followers.

ruck-rover *Australian Rules football* A player in the ruck who plays like a follower or like a rover as the play dictates. A ruck-rover is usually employed only where the lone follower is large enough to be able to gain possession of the ball most of the time by himself on ball ups or throw-ins.

rucksack A large backpack that typically has 2 or more outside pockets and that is designed to be worn without a packframe. — see illustration at BACKPACK

rudder 1 A flat piece of wood or metal that is attached to the stern of a boat and extends into the water or that is attached to the rear of a keel to offer resistance to the water when it is turned to one side or the other forcing the bow of the boat to turn in the same direction.
2 A movable vertical airfoil at the rear end of an airplane that serves to control the direction of flight in the horizontal plane.

rudderpost The vertical frame on which a rudder pivots.

Rudolph *trampolining* A stunt performed on the trampoline which consists of a one and a half somersault with a full twist in which the body moves from a pike position at the start of the somersault to a layout position during the twist and back to a pike position just before the finish.

rugby A game played with an inflated oval ball on a large rectangular field with H-shaped goals at each end between 2 teams of 15 players with the object to kick or carry the ball toward the opponent's goal line and to kick it through the goal or carry it over the goal line for a score and to keep the opposing team from scoring. Defensive players are permitted to tackle the ballcarrier as in football, but teammates are not permitted to block or interfere with opponents

seeking to get to the ballcarrier or to a loose ball. Forward passing is not permitted, but a team is permitted to recover its own kick. Consequently, lateral passing and kicking play as much a part in the game as running with the ball. For common infractions during play, a scrum is formed at the spot of the infraction. This is suggestive of a face-off except that usually 8 players (forwards) from each team take part, pushing and shoving against the opposing forwards so that one of their players can heel the ball back out of the scrum to the halfbacks and threequarter backs to start the team's offense. For serious fouls, a penalty kick is awarded to the fouled player.

A player is offside if he is at anytime nearer the opponent's goal line than the ball when his team is in possession, and he is prohibited from taking part in the play (as by attempting to assist the ballcarrier, recover a loose ball, or tackle an opponent who has recovered a loose ball) until he has been put onside. If he drops the ball or knocks it forward off his arms or hands (a *knock-on*), he may not play the ball again until it has been touched by an opponent. If a player catches a kick or a knock-on before it strikes the ground, he may call for and be awarded a free kick on which he can score a goal. When a player is tackled, he is required to release the ball immediately and roll away from it so that another player, either a teammate or an opposing player, may kick it to put it back in play. The mass of players attempting to get into position to play the ball after a tackle is aptly named a *maul*. A similar situation in which players are attempting to play a loose ball on the ground is known as a *ruck*. A player scores 3 points for a dropkick or a placekick in which the ball passes through the goal over the crossbar (*goal*). For carrying the ball over the opponent's goal line and grounding it there, a player is awarded a *try* (for a goal). The try itself is worth 4 points and gives the player an opportunity for a free kick which can score another 2 points. The game is usually played in two 40-minute halves with no time-outs. A maximum of 2 substitutions may be made during a game but only for players injured too seriously to continue. The game is under the control of a referee on the field who calls infractions and orders a scrum or awards free kicks or penalty kicks. He is assisted by 2 touch judges who note when and where the ball goes out of bounds and who signal when a goal or a try is made.

The game of rugby, which resembles Ameri-

Rugby fives

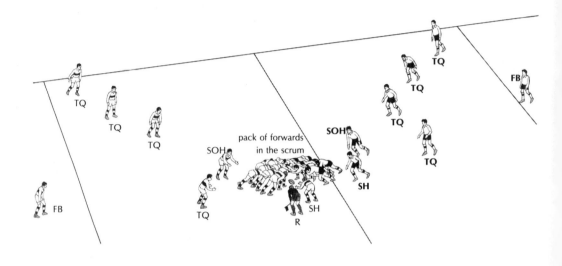

rugby: SH scrum half; SOH standoff half; TQ threequarter back; FB fullback; R referee

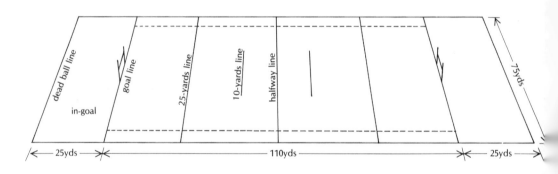

can football and from which football developed, is named for Rugby School in England where it developed near the middle of the 19th century. Legend has it that the game grew out of an incident in which a student, apparently in a fit of frustration during a soccer game, ran with the ball. He is immortalized by a plaque on the school grounds which reads: "This stone commemorates the exploit of William Webb Ellis, who, with a fine disregard for the rules of football as played in his time, first took the ball in his arms and ran with it, thus originating the distinctive feature of the Rugby game, A.D. 1823." Little is known of the actual beginnings of the game aside

from the fact that early games played at Rugby may have included as many as 300 players and that such actions as tripping and hacking (kicking an opponent in the shins) as well as tackling were permitted. — see also FIELD, LINE-OUT, OFFSIDE, SCRUM

Rugby fives see FIVES

Rugby League A form of rugby played as an amateur or professional sport especially in Britain, Australia, New Zealand, and France. The rules are essentially the same as for rugby with the following notable exceptions: (1) The game is played with 13 rather than 15 players on a side. A team normally has only 6 forwards. (2)

The in-goal area on the field is only 6 to 12 yards deep instead of 25 yards. (3) When a player is tackled, a maul is not formed. The tackled player is released and permitted to stand and kick the ball or heel it back to a teammate (a *play-the-ball*) to begin another attack. The team may thus in effect retain possession of the ball for 5 successive tackles. On the sixth tackle, a scrum takes place at the point of the tackle. (4) A ball that is driven out of bounds is returned to play with a scrum instead of with a line-out. (5) A try is worth 3 points, and a goal from a free kick, penalty kick, or kick after a try is worth 2. A goal from a dropkick is worth one point.

Rugby Union The amateur form of rugby played in Britain under the authority of the Rugby Football Union.

rugger 1 The game of rugby.

2 A rugby player.

rule off *horse racing* To bar an individual from racing or from entering the tracks controlled by a particular racing authority.

Rules Short for *Australian Rules football.*

Rules of the Road Local or international rules regulating the movements of traffic on water. The Rules specify which vessels have the right of way (are *privileged*) and which do not (are *burdened*) when 2 crafts meet in a situation which could result in a collision.

¹run 1 a A special course constructed down a slope for skiing or for bobsled or luge competition. b A pass down or through a special course (as a ski or bobsled run or a slalom course).

2 A running approach taken before jumping, diving, or throwing something (as a javelin).

3 *baseball* The basic scoring unit of the game made each time a base runner reaches home plate safely and credited to that player and to his team in statistical records.

4 *billiards* A series of consecutive scoring shots.

5 *canoeing* A stretch of fast rough water.

6 *cricket* The basic scoring unit of the game made each time the batsmen are able to exchange places. It often is possible for the batsmen to exchange places several times on one play scoring a run each time they do so. When runs are scored directly as a result of a batted ball, they are credited to the batsman in statistical records. If the batsmen score one or more runs other than by hitting the ball, these are added to the team's score as extras but are not credited to the batsmen. For long hits over the boundary, 4 or 6 runs may be added to the score and credited to the batsman without the bats-

men's having to run. It is also possible for a team to be awarded runs as a penalty for improper play by the fielding side or for improper bowling.

7 *curling* An imperfection in the ice surface which slightly alters the direction of movement of a stone passing over it.

8 *football* a A play in which the ball is carried rather than passed. b A gain of usually a specific number of yards made on a running play. ⟨scored on an 8-yard *run*⟩

9 *golf* The distance a ball rolls forward after landing.

10 *sailing* A course sailed in the same or nearly the same direction as the wind is blowing. — compare BEAT, REACH

11 *track and field* A race other than a relay or steeplechase which is usually more than 440 yards in length. — compare DASH

12 British term for *progressive.*

— **on the run** While running. ⟨caught the ball *on the run*⟩

²run 1 a To compete in a race; to compete in a particular event. ⟨he will *run* the 220 and the high hurdles⟩ b To be in a particular position during a race. ⟨*running* second after only 12 laps⟩

2 or **run off** To make a series of consecutive scores or victories. ⟨*ran* 125 balls before scratching⟩ ⟨in the second set, the 5-foot-7-inch, 140-pound Australian *ran off* nine straight games — New York Times⟩

3 *of a hooked fish* To swim quickly away from the fisherman.

4 *football* To conduct the offense out of a particular type of offensive formation. ⟨*ran* out of a variety of offensive formations including the so-called pro set — Ron Fimrite, *Sports Illustrated*⟩

5 *golf* To hit the ball on an approach shot so that it rolls after landing. ⟨on the next hole the intelligent approach might be to *run* the ball into the green, but on the next you'd be required to fly it in high and drop it down dead — Jack Nicklaus⟩

6 *sailing* To sail with the wind; to sail in the direction toward which the wind is blowing.

run a coup *billiards* To scratch the cue ball into a pocket after missing the object ball in English billiards.

run and gun *basketball* To employ a fast freewheeling style of play without emphasis on set plays or defense.

run and hit *baseball* A situation in which a base runner on first base breaks for second on the pitch and the batter has the option of swinging or not swinging at the pitch as he chooses. On such a play, the batter is not required to protect the runner. If the ball is hit, the runner usually has enough of a jump to prevent a double play or to reach an extra base on a base hit beyond the infield; if the ball is not swung at, the runner may still come up with a stolen base. — compare HIT AND RUN

runaway A one-sided or overwhelming victory.

run away and hide *of a competitor in a race or contest* To take such a commanding lead that the opposition is unable to catch up.

runback *football* A run made to advance the ball after catching a kick or punt or after intercepting a forward pass.

run back *football* To return the ball after a free kick, punt, or intercepted pass.

run batted in *baseball* A run that scores as a direct result of an offensive action by the batter and that is credited to the batter in statistical records. A run batted in is credited for a base hit (including the batter on a home run) or a forced advance (as when the batter gets a base on balls or is hit by a pitch). A run batted in may also be credited on a fielding error if there are less than 2 out and the runner on third base could have scored had there been no error.

rundown *baseball* A situation in which a base runner is caught between bases and is forced to run back and forth along a basepath between opposing players while they toss the ball back and forth between them in an attempt to tag the runner off base. Though the rundown is usually a result of overzealousness on the part of the base runner, it sometimes can be employed as a strategic measure in a double steal so that while the defensive team is concentrating on the player in the rundown, another baserunner can attempt to score.

run down **1** *baseball* To put out a base runner in a rundown.
2 *of a racehorse* To scrape the flesh of the heels on the track surface while racing, causing strained tendons and ligaments.

Run for the Roses The Kentucky Derby, so called from the horseshoe-shaped garland of roses presented to the winner.

run free To sail before the wind; sail on a run.

runless *of a baseball team* Without having scored a run. ⟨held them *runless* for 7 innings⟩

runner **1** *baseball* Short for *base runner*.
2 *curling* A fast moving stone.
3 *football* The ballcarrier. ⟨a defensive player

may not tackle or hold any opponent other than a *runner* — *National Football League Rules*⟩
4 *track and field* An athlete who competes in a race rather than in a field event.

¹running **1** *of a ball team or a style of play* Characterized by the use of running plays, fast breaks, or much base stealing.
2 *of a bowling alley* Having a surface that tends to make a ball hook sooner than normal or curve more than normal. — compare HOLDING

²running An occurence of an annual horse race. ⟨the 100th *running* of the Kentucky Derby⟩

running back *football* An offensive back who is used primarily to carry the ball on running plays.

running belay see BELAY

running English *billiards* English which causes a ball to spin in the same direction it is traveling so that when it strikes a cushion or another ball it tends to come off at the same or a greater angle than it would if it had no English; follow.

running game *football* Offense based on use of running rather than passing plays.

running high jump *track and field* A high jump in which each competitor is permitted to run up to the takeoff point. The term is used to distinguish the popular event from a less common variation in which competitors jump from a standing position.

running long jump or **running broad jump** *track and field* A long jump in which each competitor is permitted to run up to the takeoff point. The term is used to distinguish the popular event from a less common variation in which competitors jump from a standing position.

running rabbit A form of clay pigeon shooting popular in Britain in which the target is bowled along the ground. — compare DRIVEN PARTRIDGE, HIGH PHEASANT, SPRINGING TEAL

running rigging *sailing* The part of the rigging that is used to control the position of sails, booms, and spars and that includes sheets, halyards, and downhauls.

running start see FLYING START

running track A track used for footraces in track and field competition.

running wax *skiing* A wax applied to the bottom of touring skis which has the property of holding the ski in position when it is placed and yet letting it slide forward when gliding.

runoff A final contest or series of contests serving as a tiebreaker or matching competitors who have won preliminary or elimination competitions.

runout 1 *mountain climbing* A pitch.

2 *surfing* A rip current.

run out *cricket* To put out a batsman by knocking down the wicket he has just left (if the batsmen have not yet crossed) or the wicket toward which he is running (if they have already crossed) with the ball. For a batsman to be out, he must not have any part of his body or his bat touching the ground behind the popping crease when the wicket is broken.

runout bit *horse racing* A bit with an extension on one side to give the jockey more leverage on that side to prevent the horse from lugging in or bearing out.

run out the clock To use up as much as possible of the playing time remaining in a game while retaining possession of the ball or puck especially in order to protect a lead late in a game. (also *kill the clock*)

run-up A run made to gain momentum for throwing a ball or javelin, bowling a cricket ball, or making a jump.

runway 1 *bowling* The approach area.

2 *track and field* A special area or path for use in the run-up (as for the high jump, pole vault, or javelin throw).

¹rush 1 *football* **a** To carry the ball in a running play; to accumulate yardage by rushing. ⟨*rushed* for 1000 yards in one season⟩ **b** To move in quickly on a passer or kicker to hinder, prevent, or block a pass or kick.

2 *ice hockey* To advance the puck into the attacking zone.

²rush 1 *football* **a** The action or an instance of carrying the ball on a running play. The total number of rushes by a team or player is noted in statistical records. **b** The action or an instance of charging in on an opposing passer or kicker.

2 *ice hockey* An effort to advance the puck into the attacking zone; the action of moving the puck up the ice for an attack.

rusher A player who rushes. ⟨a fine pass *rusher*⟩

rush line The defensive line of a football team.

rush the net *tennis* To charge to the net immediately after making a stroke in order to be close to the net in position to volley the opponent's return.

Russian *gymnastics* A stunt performed on the pommel horse which consists of a Moore performed first over one pommel and then over the other with the body held relatively horizontal throughout.

Russian pool A variation of English billiards using a white cue ball and 4 object balls — yellow, green, blue, and black — in which players score points for winning and losing hazards and for cannons. A cannon is worth 2 points and winning and losing hazards score according to the color value of the ball off which they are made: black 9 points, blue 7, green 5, and yellow 3. Winning and losing hazards off the black ball may be made only in the 2 top pockets; hazards off the blue ball may be made only in the 2 side pockets, and off the green or the yellow ball only in the 2 bottom pockets. Each time a ball is pocketed, it is replaced on the table on its designated spot, and the appropriate number of points is added to the player's score. As in English billiards, there is a limitation on the number of consecutive hazards which may be made off the same object ball and on the number of consecutive direct cannons which may be made using the same 2 object balls. (also called *Indian pool, slosh, toad-in-the-hole*)

Russian split jump *skating* A leap in which the skater performs a straddle split with his legs slightly forward and with his hands reaching to his feet.

Russian split jump

Ryder Cup International match-play golf competition held every 2 years between 8-man teams of professional golfers from the United States and Great Britain which includes foursome, singles, and fourball competition. The competition, named for Samuel Ryder who donated the trophy, began in 1927 and is held alternately in the United States and Britain.

saber

S

saber or **sabre** **1** A fencing sword with an arched guard that covers the back of the hand and a relatively rigid blade of V-shaped cross section that tapers to a blunted point. The saber is derived from the old calvary sword, which had a cutting edge along all of one side of the blade and on the lower third of the back of the blade. The saber is therefore used as both a cutting and thrusting weapon. Its overall length is about 41 inches, somewhat shorter than the foil or épée, and it weighs up to 17 ounces. — compare ÉPÉE, FOIL

2 The art or sport of fencing with a saber; competition in which a saber is used. Saber fencing is governed by the same rules of attack and defense as foil fencing. The target in saber is the body above the top of the hips including the arms, hands, and head. — see illustration at FENCING

sabreur Someone who fences with a saber.

¹sack *football* To tackle the opposing quarterback behind the line of scrimmage before he can throw a pass.

²sack **1** *baseball* A base.

2 or **sacking** *football* The act or an instance of sacking an opposing quarterback.

sacker *baseball* A first, second, or third baseman. ⟨an outstanding third *sacker*⟩

¹sacrifice or **sacrifice hit** *baseball* A bunt made with less than 2 out which advances a base runner and on which the batter is put out or would have been put out had an error not been made. A sacrifice does not count as a time at bat for the batter and does not affect his batting average, but the batter is credited with an RBI.

²sacrifice *baseball* To make a sacrifice.

sacrifice fly *baseball* A fair or foul fly ball hit with less than 2 out that is caught for an out but that is long enough to permit a base runner to tag up and score. A sacrifice fly does not count as a time at bat for the batter, but the batter is credited with an RBI.

sacrifice hit see SACRIFICE

¹saddle **1** A shaped leather seat constructed over

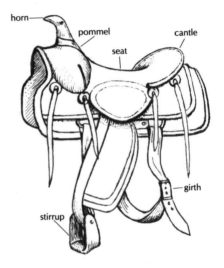

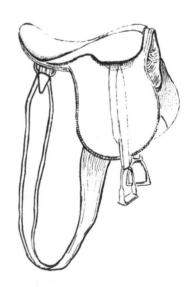

saddle: top, stock (Western) saddle; bottom, English (Eastern) saddle

366

safety valve

a wooden frame that is designed to fit the contours of the buttocks of the rider and is padded to rest on the back of a horse. It consists essentially of the seat, cantle, pommel, and stirrups, and a girth which passes under the belly of the horse.

2 The seat of a bicycle or motorcycle that is designed to be straddled and that is similar to a riding saddle.

3 The part of a pommel horse between the pommels. — compare CROUP, NECK

4 *mountain climbing* A shallow depression on the ridge of a mountain that suggests the curve of a saddle.

²saddle To fasten a saddle to a horse in preparation for riding.

saddle bronc *rodeo* A bronco that is ridden with a saddle.

saddle bronc riding *rodeo* An event in which contestants are required to ride a saddled wild horse for 10 seconds while it is bucking. The rider is permitted to hold on with only one hand to a strap attached to the saddle; he may not touch the horse, saddle, or the strap with the free hand. During his ride, the cowboy must spur the horse with blunted spurs and swing his legs forward of the horse's front legs on every jump. The horse and the rider are rated by 2 judges with each awarded up to 25 points from each judge for a ride. In this way no competitor has an advantage because his horse is not as active as those of his rivals.

saddle cloth *horse racing* A cloth that is placed over or under a saddle and that bears the racehorse's number.

saddling The action or process of putting a saddle on a horse; an instance of saddling a horse.

safari A hunting expedition for big game.

safe *baseball* Successful in reaching base.

safety **1** *baseball* A base hit.

2 *billiards* A defensive play in which a player makes a stroke that is not a foul but that ends his inning with the intent of sacrificing an opportunity to try to score in order to leave his opponent with a difficult shot.

3 *football* **a** A score of 2 points awarded the defensive team when the offensive team gives impetus to the ball causing it to go into the team's own end zone and the ballcarrier is tackled or downs the ball in the end zone or steps out of bounds or loses the ball out of bounds from the end zone. If the receiver of a kickoff catches the kick in his own end zone and downs the ball there, no safety results, since the other team has

given impetus to the ball. If he catches the ball in the field of play and runs into his end zone to avoid tacklers, a safety results if he is tackled there. A receiver in the end zone who muffs a kick which goes out of bounds does not give up a safety since he never had possession; if he catches the kick and while running in the end zone fumbles the ball and loses it out of bounds, a safety results since he did have possession and had given impetus to the ball. A defensive player who intercepts a pass near the goal line and is carried into the end zone by his momentum would not give up a safety if tackled there. After a safety, the ball is next put in play by a free kick made by the team giving up the safety from its own 20-yard line. — compare TOUCHBACK **b** or

safetyman Either of 2 defensive backs who normally line up farthest from the line of scrimmage and who are primarily responsible for covering the downfield area on pass plays and breakaway runs. Occasionally in professional football an offensive team will have a player, also called a *safety,* line up several yards behind the running backs, especially near the end of a close game, to be in position to prevent the opposing team's running a fumble back for a touchdown to win the game. **c** or **safetyman** Any player on the receiving team who is positioned several yards behind his teammates in position to receive a kick (as a punt or a kickoff) from the opposing team.

4 A mechanism on a firearm that locks the trigger or the hammer so that the weapon cannot be fired accidentally.

safety belt *gymnastics* A belt with ropes attached to swivels at either side worn by a gymnast in practicing certain stunts. The ropes are attached to overhead supports or are held by assistants to safeguard the gymnast. (also called *spotting belt*)

safety blitz *football* A blitz by a safety and usually by the free safety.

safety hinder *racquetball* A let that results when a player cannot play a ball for fear of possibly hitting his opponent.

safetyman see SAFETY (*football*)

safety squeeze see SQUEEZE PLAY

safety strap see ARLBERG STRAP

safety touch *Canadian football* A situation identical to a safety in American football.

safety valve *football* A short pass thrown to a back in the flat when downfield receivers are covered. The safety valve is usually used as a way for the quarterback to get rid of the ball for little or no loss or a short gain rather than risk a sack or interception.

safety zone *polo* An unobstructed area surrounding the field of play which extends 10 yards beyond the sideline and 30 yards beyond the back line so that a pony will not run into a wall or spectators immediately if ridden out of bounds while chasing the ball.

sag *basketball* To pull back from the player one is guarding in order to stop another player driving for the basket or to double-team the player with the ball.

sag wagon *cycling* A vehicle that follows the competitors in a road race to pick up those that drop out of the race.

¹sail **1** An extent of cotton or more commonly polyester fabric used to catch the wind and propel a wind-driven vessel (as a sailboat, an iceboat, or a sand yacht). Most sails used on modern pleasure and racing sailboats are triangular

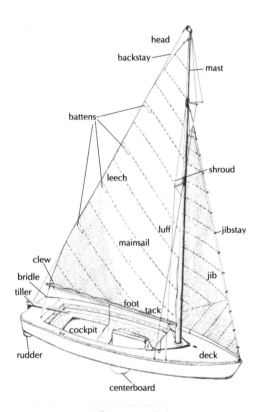

sailboat: a small sloop

because most boats are fore-and-aft rigged. A small sloop typically carries a mainsail and a jib, and sometimes a spinnaker for reaching and running with the wind. Yawls and ketches, which have a mizzenmast, will also carry a mizzen sail and often a mizzen staysail.

2 An excursion or trip in a sailboat. ⟨go for a *sail*⟩

— under sail *of a boat* In motion driven by the force of wind on the sails.

²sail To travel by means of the force of the wind upon sails. ⟨on windy days I could take off my life jacket, hoist my parka on my ski poles, and *sail* downwind across the lake — John D. Casey, *Harper's Magazine*⟩

sail area The surface area of the sails of a vessel normally measured in square feet or square meters.

sailboard or **sailing board** A small sailboat with a flat hull and usually a single sail.

sailboat A boat that is powered by the force of the wind upon sails.

sailing The sport or pastime of handling or riding in a sailboat.

sailplane An aircraft that resembles an airplane but has no engine for sustained flight and that is used in the sport of soaring. Sailplanes are classed as gliders by the FAA though soaring enthusiasts make the distinction that sailplanes are so designed that they can gain altitude with rising warm air or with air that rises as it is deflected over a hill or ridge. The gliding efficiency of sailplanes is expressed as a glide ratio — the ratio of the distance it moves forward to the distance it moves down. Some sailplanes have a glide ratio of 40 to one or better: meaning the plane will move forward 40 feet for each foot it descends while sinking at an average rate of 2 feet per second. Depending on the design of the sailplane, it may soar at a rate of 100 to 500 feet per minute in an average thermal, though rates of over 2500 feet per minute can be achieved in unusual conditions.

sailplaner Someone who pilots a sailplane.

sailplaning see SOARING

St. George round *archery* A target round in men's competition in which each competitor shoots 36 arrows at a distance of 100 yards, 36 at 80 yards, and 36 at 60 yards.

St. Leger A 1¾-mile stakes race for 3-year-old thoroughbred racehorses that is held annually at Doncaster, Yorkshire, England, and that is one of the English Classics and one of the races in the English Triple Crown. The race is named for

Colonel Barry St. Leger, who originated the race in 1776. It was originally run at a distance of 2 miles.

saker An Old World falcon used in falconry.

Salchow *skating* A jump from the inner backward edge of one foot with a full turn in the air and a return to the outer backward edge of the opposite foot. The jump is named for the Swedish skater Ulrich Salchow who first performed it.

saliva test *horse racing* An examination of the saliva of a racehorse usually just after a race for an indication of the presence of illegal drugs or medications.

salle d'armes A fencing room; a fencing club.

salto *gymnastics* A forward or backward somersault performed in the air (as during floor exercises).

salute A traditional gesture of acknowledgment and respect toward one's opponent or the officials at the beginning or at the end of a contest. In such sports as judo and karate, the competitors bow to each other and to the officials. In fencing the traditional salute is made with the feet together, the sword pointing diagonally down to the floor, and the mask held under the other arm. The sword is then brought up until it is pointing straight up and the guard is at chin level, after which it is lowered to the original position.

sambo A version of judo originally developed in the Soviet Union and now competed in internationally. The wrestlers wear a special costume which consists of a judo-style jacket, shorts, wrestling shoes, and a wraparound belt. Opponents wear different colored belts as a means of identification. A wrestler can win the match outright by making a perfect throw from a standing position so that his opponent lands on his back or by securing a painful submission hold which forces the opponent to give up. Failing this, the wrestler can win by scoring more points than his opponent during the 6-minute match. The bout is supervised by a referee on the mat and a judge and mat chairman off the mat. The referee has primary responsibility for conducting the bout, allocating points, issuing warnings and cautions, and preventing illegal holds. Sambo is conducted with the same weight classes as the other forms of international wrestling. — see also EVIDENT SUPERIORITY, TOTAL VICTORY; compare FREESTYLE, GRECO-ROMAN WRESTLING, JUDO

sanction To give formal recognition as the governing body of a sport or of a branch of a sport to an event or an achievement. ⟨has had 42

sanctioned 700 series and in four of the last eight years has led all women bowlers in the nation — Herman Weiskopf, *Sports Illustrated* ⟩

sandbag To put forth less than one's utmost effort in the early stages of competition or in preliminary trials or practice in order to lull the opposition into a false sense of security.

sandbagger Someone who sandbags.

sandie *golf* A shot in which a player gets out of a sand trap on his first attempt and sinks his putt on his next shot to win a bet in informal play. — compare CHIPPIE, GREENIE

sandlot Played informally (as by boys) on whatever area is available. ⟨*sandlot* baseball⟩

sandlotter Someone who plays sandlot ball.

sand sailing see SAND YACHTING

sandshifter An old derogatory term for a pacer.

sand trap *golf* A hazard on the course usually located near or around the green that consists of a depression filled with loose sand; bunker. — see illustration at GOLF

sand wedge see WEDGE (*golf*)

sand yacht A 3-wheeled vehicle with a single seat, a steering wheel, and a mast and sails that is driven by the wind over sandy areas (as beaches or deserts). (also called *land yacht*)

sand yachting or **sand sailing** The sport of racing sand yachts. (also called *land yachting*)

sand yachtsman Someone who races sand yachts.

sanitary 1 Free from accidents or unsportsmanlike tactics; clean. ⟨a *sanitary* race⟩
2 Well engineered and well constructed. ⟨a racing car with a *sanitary* engine⟩

sault Short for *somersault*.

savate A French form of kick boxing.

¹save 1 To keep a goal from being scored by stopping the ball or puck before it can enter the goal.
2 To hold onto a lead; to prevent the opposing team from tying or winning a game.

²save 1 The act or an instance of a goalkeeper's blocking or stopping a ball or puck to prevent the scoring of a goal. Sometimes in statistical records, the goalkeeper is credited with the number of saves he makes during a game or the season.
2 *baseball* Credit for a game the team wins given a relief pitcher when he is able to preserve his team's lead with the potential tying or winning run at the plate or on base or when he is able to maintain the team's lead for at least 3 innings of relief.

saving *horse racing* The practice whereby certain jockeys agree to guarantee each other a sum of money if either of the jockeys wins a particular race (as a major stakes race). Saving is generally disapproved of by racing commissions except where the jockeys involved are riding for the same owner.

saw-off Canadian term for *tie, draw.*

¹scale *gymnastics* A position of balance in which the gymnast stands on one foot with his free leg stretched out and up to the rear or side. In the *front scale* the gymnast leans in the direction in which his supporting foot is pointing and usually arches his back, stretching his arms up or out and extending the free leg to the rear. In the *side scale,* the gymnast leans to one side holding his upper body parallel to the floor and extends his raised leg to the opposite side. — see also KNEE SCALE, NEEDLE SCALE, SWAN SCALE

²scale To remove the scales from a fish in cleaning it.

scale of weights *horse racing* A chart that lists the weights to be carried for racehorses depending upon the distance of the race, the age and sex of the horses, and the month in which the race is run.

scale weight *horse racing* Weight which each horse must carry based on the scale of weights without modifications or handicaps for individual horses. In races run with scale weights, all the horses carry the same weight except for any allowance given to fillies or mares running against males.

scalp *of a trotter* To hit the hoof of the hind foot with the toe of the forefoot while trotting.

scalper *harness racing* A boot worn on the hind hooves of trotters to protect against scalping. — see BOOT

scarf hold *judo* A hold in which a wrestler sitting on the mat to one side of his supine opponent traps the opponent's near arm under his armpit and with the other arm encircles the opponent's neck grasping the collar of the gi so as to hold the opponent to the mat.

scatback *football* A fast elusive ballcarrier.

scatter *of a baseball pitcher* To give up a stated number of hits distributed throughout the game so that little or no scoring is permitted. ⟨scattered nine hits, walked two and struck out seven in hurling City to victory — *New York Times*⟩

scatter arm Inability of a player to make consistently accurate throws or passes.

scattergun A shotgun.

scattershield *auto racing* A protective housing for the clutch and flywheel assembly of a racing car designed to prevent parts from flying onto the track in the event the assembly breaks apart.

school To train a horse to race or to jump or to be obedient and responsive to the rider's commands.

school figures **1** *equitation* A series of movements performed in competition which involve riding the horse through turns, changes of lead, and tight circles.
2 *skating* A group of 69 distinct figures involving various skating movements (as changes of edge, rockers, three turns, counters, brackets, and loops) skated in 2- or 3-lobe figure-eight patterns. In competition, each skater is normally required to skate each of 6 prescribed figures in place 3 times. He is judged not only on the movement but also on his precision in making the circles and in following the trace or the outline on the surface.

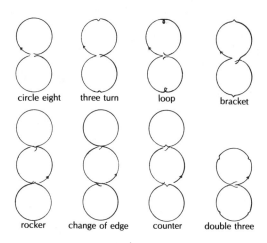

circle eight   three turn   loop   bracket

rocker   change of edge   counter   double three

skating school figures

schooling The training of a horse to be obedient and responsive to the rider's commands.

schooner A fore-and-aft rigged sailboat characteristically having 2 or more masts with a smaller foremast ahead of the main and the mainmast approximately amidships. — compare KETCH; YAWL

¹schuss or **schussboom** *skiing* To ski freely down the fall line at high speed without turning and often without proper control.

²schuss *skiing* The action or an instance of schussing.

schussboom see SCHUSS

schussboomer *skiing* A skier who schusses.

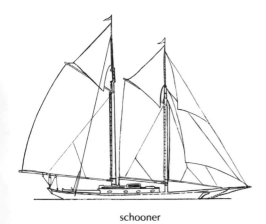

schooner

scissor-kick To execute a scissors kick.

scissors 1 *gymnastics* **a** A movement on the pommel horse in which the gymnast swings his body back and forth from one end of the horse to the other while straddling the horse and supporting himself on the pommels. As his legs swing down, he momentarily lifts each hand in turn to allow his legs to pass under. As his legs reach the end of the horse, he switches the position of his legs so that on the next pass, the leg that was originally in front is now to the rear of the horse and the other leg is in front. **b** or **scissors vault** A straddle vault in which the gymnast makes a half twist after pushing off so that he lands facing toward the horse. **c** A mount (as on a balance beam) in which one leg is kicked high and then the other leg is brought up as the first is snapped down to stand on the apparatus. **2** or **scissor jump** A variation of the mazurka in which the skating foot is crossed behind the free foot at the top of the jump.
3 *track and field* A method of high jumping in which the jumper leads with the leg nearest the bar, crosses the bar in a sitting position, and then brings the trailing leg up over the bar as the lead leg is brought down on the other side. — see also EASTERN CUT-OFF; compare FLOP, STRADDLE, WESTERN ROLL
4 *wrestling* A hold in which a wrestler locks his legs around an opponent's head or body. In applying a body scissors, the wrestler is permitted

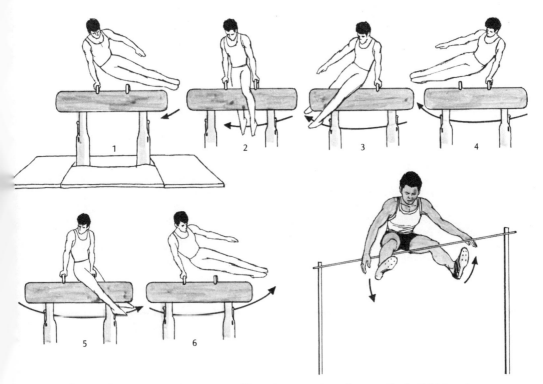

scissors: scissors movement on a pommel horse in gymnastics; scissors method of high jumping

scissors kick

wrestler holding his opponent in a straight body scissors

to have both legs relatively straight with one foot hooked under the other ankle. Only a figure 4 scissors is permitted as a head scissors. — see also FIGURE 4 SCISSORS

5 Short for *scissors kick*.

scissors kick 1 *soccer* A kick of the ball made by a player who jumps up kicking first one leg into the air and then the other, striking the ball above the head on the second kick usually driving it to the rear.

2 *swimming* The kick used especially in the sidestroke in which the legs are moved apart and then brought together forcefully in a manner resembling the movement of scissors blades. — see illustration at SIDESTROKE

scissors vault see SCISSORS

¹sclaff *golf* A stroke in which the clubhead strikes the ground and bounces into the ball instead of striking the ball cleanly.

²sclaff *golf* To make a sclaff.

scoop 1 *basketball* An underhand swing of the ball up to the basket in attempting a lay-up as distinguished from the more common pushing movement.

2 *field hockey* A pass or shot made by placing the head of the stick against the ball and flipping the ball forward and into the air with a snap of the wrists.

3 *lacrosse* The act or action of scooping a ball off the ground with the head of the stick.

scope 1 *boating* The length of the anchor rode that is played out.

2 Short for *riflescope*.

¹score 1 A count showing the achievement of each side in a game or contest; the count achieved by one individual or side. ⟨the *score* is 4–3 at the end of seven innings⟩ ⟨the server's

score is always called first, even if he is losing at the time — Margaret Varner & J. Rufford Harrison, *Table Tennis*⟩

2 An act (as a goal, run, or touchdown) which adds to a team's score. ⟨returned an interception 50 yards for the third *score* — Tex Maule, *Sports Illustrated*⟩

3 Any of the lines marked across a curling surface.

4 A hit in fencing.

5 *rodeo* The distance from the chute to the score line which serves as a head start for the steer or calf in steer wrestling or calf roping contests.

²score 1 To make a score in a game or contest. ⟨a bad throw from the catcher is almost sure to allow the runner to *score* — W. L. Myers, *Athletic Journal*⟩ ⟨*score* a touchdown⟩

2 To count towards a team's score. ⟨a touchdown *scores* 6 points⟩ ⟨no run may *score* on any play when the third out is a force out — *NCAA Baseball Rules*⟩

3 To gain or achieve. ⟨*scored* the most spectacular of all his victories — Jack Altman, *Playboy*⟩

4 To keep score; to act as scorer or scorekeeper.

5 *baseball* To drive in a base runner for a score. ⟨*scored* the runner from second with a base hit to right field⟩

6 *harness racing* To warm up a horse during the parade before the start of a race by driving the horse a short way up the stretch at speed.

scoreboard A large board for displaying the score of a contest and often the remaining playing time and other information.

scorecard 1 *boxing* A card or sheet of paper on which an individual or judge keeps his own record of the round-by-round progress of a fight.

2 *golf* A card on which a golfer keeps his own score for each hole; a card on which is kept the score of each player in a group (as a foursome). **3** A program containing the names and numbers of the players and often a form on which to keep score. ⟨you can't tell the players without a *scorecard*⟩

scorekeeper The scorer in various sports.

scoreless Having no score; involving no points. ⟨played to a *scoreless* tie⟩

scoreline *rodeo* A line several feet in front of the chute to mark the amount of head start a calf or steer gets in calf roping and steer wrestling events.

scorer **1** A player or competitor who scores. ⟨leading *scorer* in the school's history⟩ **2** Someone who records the score of a game or contest as an official or under the direction of the chief official. The scorer may simply keep track of the points accumulated by each individual or team (as in archery or handball) or record points awarded to individual competitors by judges (as in gymnastics or diving), or he may keep an account of the progress of the contest by recording goals scored, who scored them, which players have been charged with fouls, and when and for how long substitutes were in the game (as in basketball or lacrosse). In baseball the scorer, usually called the *official scorer,* is charged with recording not only the score and the activities of each player such as base hits, balls and strikes, putouts, and bases on balls, but also with keeping statistics and deciding on whether to record a base hit or an error, determining wild pitches, passed balls, assists, earned runs, and the winning and losing pitcher of the game.

scoring area The triangular area at each end of a shuffleboard court which is marked off with sections having different scoring values.

scoring position *baseball* Second or third base from which a base runner is normally able to score on a routine base hit to the outfield. — used with *in*

Scotch foursome see FOURSOME

scotch serve A serve in handball or racquetball in which the ball is made to rebound from the front wall at a height of about 5 feet, strike the side wall near the corner, and travel crosscourt to strike the back wall and then the other side wall at the opposite corner.

¹scout **1** To observe the practice or play of an eventual opponent so that strategy may be formulated on the basis of the opponent's strengths and weaknesses.

2 To observe an individual in order to evaluate his ability or potential.

²scout Someone who scouts a rival or opposing team or a prospective player or recruit; an individual employed by a professional club to regularly scout and evaluate amateur players.

scow A relatively flat-bottom boat with square ends. A sailing scow typically has bilge boards instead of a centerboard.

¹scramble **1** To climb a steep, rocky, or muddy slope on all fours. **2** *of a football quarterback* To run around behind the line of scrimmage dodging would-be tacklers after initial pass protection has broken down before passing or running.

²scramble **1** The act of climbing a slope on all fours. **2** The act or an instance of scrambling by a quarterback. **3** see MOTOCROSS

scrambler *football* A quarterback who is noted for scrambling.

scrambles tournament An informal or club tournament in which weaker players are paired or grouped with a stronger player so that there is no side of strong players to dominate. In golf, each of the players in a group will play from the same spot, normally the spot where the ball of the player with the best stroke (as the longest drive or the nearest approach shot) landed. Each player plays his own ball, and the best score for a hole counts as the side's score.

scrappy Characterized by sharp and aggressive play and a determined spirit. ⟨a *scrappy* basketball team⟩

¹scratch **1** To withdraw from a contest after being listed officially as an entrant but before competition actually begins. **2** *billiards* To make an error (as driving the cue ball into a pocket or failing to make a legal safety shot) that results in a player's losing his turn but that may or may not result in a penalty. **3** *surfing* To paddle hard especially to pick up sufficient speed to be able to catch a wave. **4** *track and field* To foul on a jumping or throwing attempt.

²scratch **1** A competitor that is scratched from competition. **2** The act or an instance of scratching from competition; the act or an instance of scratching in billiards. **3** The condition in which the actual results of competition are recognized and no handicap or allowance is given. ⟨converted 12-meter sloop

scratch

. . . sailed at *scratch* and was first to finish — New York Times⟩

4 A foul in a field event.

³scratch 1 a Equal for all competitors; without handicaps or allowances. ⟨*scratch* competition⟩ **b** Good enough to compete at scratch in competition in which others are given handicaps. ⟨a *scratch* golfer⟩

2 *baseball* Being a scratch hit. ⟨a *scratch* single⟩

scratch hit *baseball* A batted ball that enables a batter to reach base safely but that is neither an error nor a clean base hit.

scratch line *track and field* **1** The starting line for a race.

2 A line over which a contestant in a field event must not step while competing in order to have his throw or jump qualify for measurement. In events (as the long jump and triple jump) in which a takeoff board is used, the scratch line is the edge of the board nearest the pit. Where a stopboard is used on a throwing circle (as in the shot put), the inside edge of the stopboard is the scratch line.

scratch sheet *horse racing* A publication listing entries, scratches, probable odds, and other information (as jockeys and weights) for the day's races at one or more tracks.

scratch spin *skating* A spin performed on the forward part of the blade of an ice skate just behind the lowest toe pick. The spin is characterized by two lines on the ice, as the toe pick scratches its own fine line. (also called *toe spin*)

scratchy *baseball* Being or resulting from scratch hits. ⟨three of the hits off him were *scratchy* grounders — Jack McDonald, *Sporting News*⟩

scree Stones and rocky debris covering a slope.

scree collar The padded top of a hiking boot that fits snugly around the leg or ankle to keep small stones from getting inside the boot.

¹screen 1 A maneuver in various sports by which an opponent is legally cut off from the play: **a** A maneuver in basketball and lacrosse in which an offensive player stations himself in such a position as to momentarily impede the movement of a defender trying to keep up with another man. The other player runs close past his stationary teammate so that the defender is forced to stop and move around the screen thereby momentarily freeing the moving player to take a shot or to receive a pass or giving him one or 2 steps advantage to move in to the goal to score. The screen is a legal maneuver only if the player is stationary and has positioned himself far enough from the defensive player to give the defender time to stop or alter direction to avoid a collision. (also called *pick*) **b** A maneuver (as in soccer, ice hockey, or lacrosse) in which an offensive player positions himself between the goalkeeper and the player with the ball or puck so as to keep the goalkeeper from having a clear view of the attacking player or the ball or puck.

2 The body used as as a shield to free one's teammate from a defender momentarily. (also called *pick*) ⟨set a *screen*⟩

3 see SCREEN PASS

²screen 1 To station oneself so as to momentarily impede the movement of an opponent trying to keep up with his man or to prevent an opposing goalkeeper from having a clear view of the ball or puck.

2 To momentarily impede the progress of a particular opponent with a screen.

3 To hide the action of a shot (as in squash) from one's opponent by keeping the body between the opponent and the racket.

4 *of a football team* To employ a screen pass.

screen ball see SHADOW BALL

screen out see BOX OUT

screen pass or **screen** *football* A short forward pass to a back in the flat in front of whom a wall of interference has been formed by linemen who have moved over after the snap.

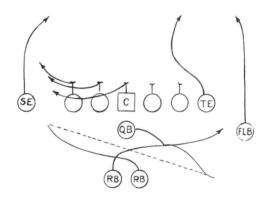

screen pass: C center; QB quarterback; TE tight end; SE split end; RB running back; FLB flankerback

screen shot *ice hockey* A shot made while one or more players are screening the goalkeeper.

screwball *baseball* A pitch thrown with spin that makes it swerve to the right when thrown with the right hand or to the left when thrown with the left hand. — compare CURVE, FASTBALL

scrimmage **1** A practice game often between squads formed from the same team.

2 *Australian Rules football* Disorganized scrambling for a loose ball.

3 *football* The play during a down that begins with a snap at the line of scrimmage as distinguished from that which begins with a free kick. ⟨gained 27 yards on the first play from *scrimmage*⟩ ⟨a *scrimmage* down⟩

scrimmage kick *football* A kick (as a field goal attempt or a punt) that is made on a play that begins with a snap from the line of scrimmage. A scrimmage kick differs from a free kick in that members of the receiving team are permitted to rush the kicker in an attempt to block the kick and members of the kicking team are not permitted to recover a kick that travels beyond the neutral zone unless it is first touched by a member of the receiving team.

scrimmage line see LINE OF SCRIMMAGE

scrub A second- or third-string player who usually does not get a chance to play in a game until the outcome is no longer in doubt.

scrum or **scrummage** *rugby* A formation in which the forwards of each side come together in 2 packs forming a tunnel between them into which the ball is tossed to restart play (as after an infraction). The scrum half of the defending side tosses the ball into the tunnel, where the hookers for each team attempt to heel the ball back to their own halfbacks to begin an attack while the other forwards try to push the opposing pack away from the ball. During the scrum, all backs are required to be behind their forwards until the ball is heeled out of the scrum; after tossing the ball into the tunnel, the scrum half has to run around to the rear of his own pack of forwards to get onside. While the ball is in the scrum, it is illegal for any player to handle it before it has been heeled out behind the first line of forwards. Only the designated hooker for each side is permitted to try to play the ball with his feet. The *set scrum* or *tight scrum,* as this formation is sometimes called, is somewhat analogous to the face-off in hockey or lacrosse or to the jump ball in basketball since each side has an equal chance to get the ball.

scrum half or **scrum halfback** *rugby* The halfback who normally takes a position just to the rear of the scrum to be in position to pick up the ball as it is heeled out to begin his team's attack. If the scrum is formed for an infraction by one side, the opposing scrum half normally tosses the ball into the scrum. — compare STANDOFF HALF

scrummage see SCRUM

scrutineer *motor sports* To make a technical inspection of a vehicle or craft.

scrutineering *motor sports* The practice of inspecting a vehicle or craft before or after a race to ensure that it complies with restrictions and safety specifications for the class in which it is competing.

scuba An apparatus designed to permit a swimmer to breathe air or an oxygen mixture while swimming underwater. *Scuba,* an acronym for

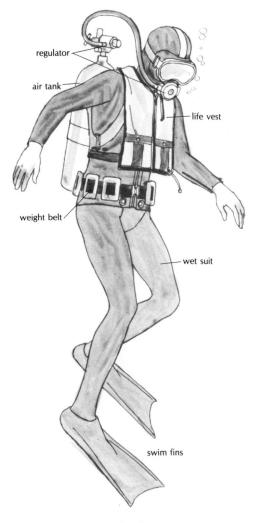

scuba diver

scuba dive

self-contained underwater breathing apparatus, includes closed-circuit oxygen-rebreathing systems developed for military use and the open-circuit compressed-air systems used almost universally for sport and research diving. The closed-circuit system, sometimes called a *rebreather,* normally uses pure oxygen and employs a filter to remove carbon dioxide and add fresh oxygen so that the gas can be recirculated with no escaping bubbles. Because pure oxygen becomes toxic when breathed at pressure greater than one atmosphere (*gauge pressure*), the rebreather cannot be used at depths greater than 25 or 30 feet. In its most common use, *scuba* means the open-circuit system, developed in 1942 by Jacques-Yves Cousteau and Emile Gagnan, which uses a compressed-air tank and a demand regulator. The diver carries one or more tanks of compressed air — sometimes research divers use a helium and oxygen mixture for unusually deep or extended dives — on his back and breathes through a mouthpiece connected to the regulator by an air hose. The regulator provides the diver with a constant source of air at the right pressure to fill his lungs. Exhaled air is allowed to escape into the water. The amount of time a diver can remain underwater depends upon the amount of air in his tank and the depth of his dive. A tank that would last one hour at the surface would last only 35 minutes at 20 feet and only 20 minutes at 60 feet. — see also J-VALVE, REGULATOR

scuba dive To engage in scuba diving.

scuba diver Someone who engages in scuba diving.

scuba diving The activity of diving with scuba equipment as distinguished from skin diving or free diving without an air supply.

¹scull **1** An oar mounted in the stern of a boat to propel it by a back and forth sculling motion.
2 One of a pair of oars usually less than 10 feet in length that are mounted on opposite sides of a boat directly across from each other and pulled by one person.
3 A racing shell propelled by one, 2, or 4 persons using sculls.

²scull or **skull** **1** To move a paddle, oar, or the hand back and forth through the water in a figure-eight pattern turning it in such a way as to be constantly pulling or pushing in the same direction: **a** To propel a boat forward by moving an oar mounted in the stern of the boat from side to side in a sculling motion. **b** To move a canoe sideways toward or away from the paddle by using a sculling motion. **c** To maintain position in the water or to move forward or backward by moving the hands in a sculling motion.
2 To propel a boat by simultaneously pulling 2 oars mounted on opposite sides of the boat. — compare ROW

sculling

3 *skating* To propel oneself forward or backward by alternately moving the heels or the toes apart and together changing from an outer edge on the outward movement to an inner edge on the inward movement.

sculler Someone who competes in sculling.

sculling The sport of racing single, double, or quadruple sculls.

sea anchor A drag typically made of canvas in the shape of a cone or parachute that is trailed from the stern of a boat to retard drifting and to keep its head to the wind.

sealskin *skiing* A strip of sealskin tied to the bottom of a ski with the hairs pointing toward the rear to prevent the ski from sliding back when climbing a slope. Sealskins were formerly much used for cross-country skiing, but today they have been largely replaced by special waxes.

seam A relatively open area between 2 zones of coverage in a zone defense.

seamanship The art or skill of handling or navigating a boat.

seam bowler or **seamer** *cricket* A bowler who grips the ball so that the position of the seams with respect to the line of flight of the bowled ball and not sideways spin will cause the ball to swerve to one side; a swing bowler.

sea puss see RIP CURRENT

sear A catch in the action of a firearm that holds the hammer in a cocked position.

sea skiff A medium-size inboard powerboat typically having a cabin and a flying bridge.

season **1 a** The time of year during which a particular sport is normally played or engaged in. ⟨*football* season⟩ **b** The total schedule of games played by a team during one season exclusive of exhibition, play-off, or bowl games. ⟨trying to get through the *season* undefeated⟩

2 The open season. ⟨no special bow *season* for moose in the state — Charles J. Farmer, *Archery World*⟩

seat **1** The relatively flat portion of a saddle. — see illustration at SADDLE

2 The posture of a rider or the manner of sitting in a saddle.

3 *gymnastics* A position on an apparatus in which the body is supported on the buttocks or on the back of the thighs.

seat-of-the-pants Using intuitive knowledge or ability and experience instead of relying on mechanical aids. ⟨not every karter is going to rush out and buy special electronic tuning instruments . . . only a few are going to be this zealous, the rest are going to rely on good old *seat-of-the-*

pants adjustments to go fast — Leroi Smith, *Karting*⟩

second **1** *baseball* Short for *second base.*

2 *boxing* A boxer's aid who is permitted to enter the ring during the rest period between rounds to advise and aid the boxer.

3 *curling* The player who follows the lead during play in an end; the second player to deliver a stone for his team.

4 *mountain climbing* The second climber on a rope. The second is always responsible for belaying the leader when the leader is climbing and he is normally responsible for removing artificial aids such as pitons placed by the leader.

secondary *football* The defensive backfield; the cornerbacks and safeties.

secondary receiver *football* A pass receiver who runs a pattern so as to be open in case the primary receiver is covered.

second attack *lacrosse* **1** A player stationed near the middle of the field who plays both offense and defense and who is a member of the midfield.

2 The position played by a second attack.

second base *baseball* **1** The base that is positioned on the diagonally opposite corner of the diamond from home plate and that is to be touched second by a base runner.

2 The player position for covering the area to the right of second base.

second baseman *baseball* A player who is stationed usually to the right of second base and who is responsible for making plays at second base and for covering the area between second base and first base.

second defense *lacrosse* **1** A player stationed near the middle of the field who plays both offense and defense and who is a member of the midfield.

2 The position played by a second defense.

second home *lacrosse* **1** A chiefly offensive player and a member of the close attack in women's play.

2 The position played by a second home.

second sacker A second baseman in baseball.

second-string Of or being a substitute as distinguished from a regular on a ball team. ⟨a *second-string* forward⟩

second wind A condition of regular breathing during strenuous exercise that is attained after an initial period of exhaustion and that is due to the adjustment of the body to the increased waste production (as of carbon dioxide and lactic acid) by improved circulation.

section or **section out** *of a surfing wave* To break unevenly with some parts breaking ahead of others.

sedan *auto racing* A production touring car that may or may not be modified for racing and that is classified for road racing in the United States in one of 4 classes on the basis of engine displacement: Class A: 2500–5000cc; Class B: 1300–2500cc; Class C: 1000–1300cc; Class D: under 1000cc.

¹seed **1** To schedule tournament players or teams so that superior ones will not meet in early rounds.
2 To rank tournament players or teams on the basis of their demonstrated or estimated abilities. ⟨top-*seeded* player in the tournament⟩

²seed A player who has been seeded in a tournament. ⟨she beat the sixth, third, and second *seeds* to reach the final — Robert H. Boyle, *Sports Illustrated*⟩

seeding The process or result of seeding players for competition.

seeing-eye single *baseball* A single that is hit just hard enough to get between 2 infielders. The phrase is derived from the trademark Seeing Eye used for guide dogs trained to lead the blind.

Seelos *skiing* An H gate. — see GATE

seize *of an internal-combustion engine* To stop running abruptly when a piston sticks in the cylinder because of expansion from overheating.

sekitori A sumo wrestler.

self *of an archery bow or arrow* Made from a single piece of wood.

self-arrest *mountain climbing* A method of stopping one's own slide down a slope by turning over to a prone position, jamming the pick of an ice axe into the slope, and spreading the legs and digging in with the toes.

self soaring see HANG GLIDING

sell a dummy British term meaning to make a fake.

selling plater *horse racing* A racehorse entered in a claiming race.

selling race or **seller** *horse racing* A claiming race. At one time selling races were races in which the winning horse was put up for auction, but these have disappeared and have been replaced by the claiming race which has inherited the name.

semi see SEMIFINAL

¹semiautomatic *of a firearm* Employing the force of recoil or gas pressure and mechanical spring action to eject the empty cartridge case after the shot is fired, to load a new cartridge from the magazine, and to cock the hammer so that it can be fired when the trigger is again pulled.

²semiautomatic A semiautomatic firearm.

semicircular parry *fencing* A parry in which the blade is moved in a semicircle from a high line to a low line.

semifinal or **semi** The next-to-last round of a tournament.

semifinalist A competitor in the semifinal round of competition.

semi-finger-tip grip see GRIP (*bowling*)

semipro or **semiprofessional** Of or being an activity or a sport for which a player is compensated for playing (as a stipulated amount per game or travel expenses) but which does not constitute the player's profession.

semi-roller or **semi-spinner** *bowling* A delivery in which the ball is held with the fingers on the side near the rear and released with a forward and upward lift and a snap of the wrist which causes the ball to slide down the alley with rotation somewhat between that of a full roller and that of a full spinner. This is the most popular and most effective delivery for a hook. — compare FULL ROLLER, FULL SPINNER, STRAIGHT BALL

semi-surface plug see PLUG

send down *cricket* To bowl the ball at the wicket defended by the batsman.

send in To put a player into a game.

send off **1** *of the referee in soccer and rugby* To dismiss or disqualify a player for the remainder of the game for foul play or misconduct. When a player is sent off, his team has to play the remainder of the game shorthanded. — see also BOOK
2 *horse racing* To send the horses from the starting gate to start a race. ⟨*sent off* at 15–1 odds⟩

senior **1** Competition (as in track and field) unrestricted by age and typically being the highest level of competition. — compare JUNIOR, MASTER
2 Competition (as in bowling, tennis, or golf) for players over a specified age (as 55).
3 Someone who competes in senior competition.

sensei A teacher of karate or judo.

sérac *mountain climbing* A tower or wall of ice standing in an ice fall. Climbers must be careful because of the danger that a sérac may collapse at any time because of melting or movement of the glacier.

series **1** A number of games played between 2

teams (as during a championship play-off).

2 *bowling* Three games bowled in succession with the total score counting toward the team's score in league competition.

3 *football* A group of 4 downs in which a team must advance the ball 10 yards.

serpentine **1** *equitation* A school figure in which the horse is ridden the length of the arena in a series of turns in opposite directions.

2 *skating* A 3-lobed school figure that consists of 2 figure eights that have one lobe in common.

¹serve **1** To put a ball or shuttlecock in play at the beginning of a rally by dropping it, tossing it up, or bouncing it and then hitting or throwing it over a net or against a wall.

2 *archery* To wrap the bowstring with string or thread at the ends and at the nocking point to protect it from chafing.

²serve **1** The act of putting a ball or shuttlecock in play in various games by hitting it over a net (as in tennis, badminton, or volleyball) or by hitting or throwing it against the front wall of the court (as in handball, squash racquets, or jai alai) usually from a designated area on the court.

2 The turn or right of a player or side to serve which is maintained for a stipulated number of serves, for the duration of the game, or for as long as the side continues to score points. In tennis, one player maintains service throughout a game making his serves alternately from the right and left side of the court. Opponents serve alternate games throughout the match. In doubles play, only one partner serves at a time before the service goes over to the opposing side. On the next service by a side, the partner of the original server will serve; turns alternate throughout the game. The server stands behind the baseline to the right or left of the center mark, depending on which side he is serving from, tosses the ball into the air, and hits it in the diagonally opposite service court. The player has two opportunities to make a good serve; if both fail to land in the designated court, the player has double-faulted and loses the point.

In badminton, the player serves as long as he or his side is scoring points. Since only the serving side can win a point, the loss of a rally by the serving side means loss of service. In doubles, after the first player has served, each partner on a side serves in turn; after the second partner has lost his service, the service goes to the opposing side. The server is required to stand within the service court and hit the ball with an underhand stroke over the net into the diago-

nally opposite service court. The server gets only one opportunity to make a good serve for each rally; after winning the point, he serves for the next rally from the other service court, alternating between left and right courts. He is required to serve from the right court whenever his or his side's score is zero or an even number.

The server in volleyball is required to stand behind the baseline within 10 feet of the sideline until the ball has been served. The only restriction on how he may hit the ball specifies that he must hit it with his hand, fist, or arm. Only the serving side can score points, and the player continues to serve as long as his team continues to score points. On regaining service, the team rotates clockwise with the last server moving to his left and the player on the right of the front row moving back to become the server.

Each player in table tennis is permitted to make 5 consecutive serves, regardless of which side wins the points; if the score reaches 20–20, the sides alternate serves on every point until the end of the game. The ball is tossed up from the open palm — the fingers may not touch the ball — and is hit so that it bounces on both sides of the net. In singles play, the ball may be hit to any part of the table, but in doubles play, the serve must first hit in the server's righthand court and then in the diagonally opposite court to be legal. The player who was the receiver for the first 5 serves then serves to the partner of the original server. During a rally, each partner alternates in returning the ball.

The service rules for platform tennis are identical with those of lawn tennis except that only one serve is allowed and a single fault results in loss of the point.

Service in court tennis differs from that in other net games in that it is always from the same side of the net. One player serves for the entire game (as in lawn tennis), but then the players change courts and the former receiver serves from the service side. The players also change sides to play off a chase. The server stands anywhere on the service side and hits the ball over the net so that it strikes the penthouse roof on the hazard side and hits the floor within the service court. The server has 2 opportunities to make a legal serve; if he makes 2 consecutive faults, he loses the point.

In games played on walled courts without a net, the serve is directed to the front wall, usually from a designated spot on the court.

In handball, the server stands inside the service zone, bounces the ball and hits it to the front wall so that it rebounds past the short line. Failure to hit the front wall first on the serve loses the serve. If the serve fails to pass the short line or if it strikes more than one side wall or the back wall before hitting the floor, it is a fault and the serve is replayed. Two consecutive faults result in loss of service. In doubles play, the server's partner is required to stand in one of the service boxes with his back against the wall until the ball has passed the short line. Except after the first service of the game, each partner will take his turn serving before the service goes over to the opposing side.

The server in squash racquets is required to have one foot in the service box when he serves the ball. In serving, he hits the ball directly to the front wall so that it hits the wall above the service line and rebounds beyond the service line on the floor in the opposite service court. The server may begin his service from either service box, but he alternates sides each time he wins a point. The server has 2 opportunities to make a good serve, but if he makes 2 consecutive faults he loses the point and the serve. In doubles play, after the first player has lost service, each opponent has a turn serving before his side gets the service again.

The serve in paddleball, racquetball, and jai alai is made in the same way as in handball except that in jai alai the ball is thrown against the front wall with the cesta, and in paddleball and racquetball the ball is hit with the paddle or racket instead of with the hand.

3 A stroke made on the service. ⟨an underhand *serve*⟩

server The player in a court game who is serving.
— compare RECEIVER; STRIKER OUT

service The act or an instance of serving; the opportunity or a turn to serve.

service ace *tennis* A serve that lands in the proper service court but out of reach of the receiver so that it scores a point for the server; ace.

service area The area in which a server stands in making a serve; the area just behind the baseline of a volleyball court and within 10 feet of the sideline.

service box **1** A 1½-foot-wide rectangular area at each end of the service zone within which the server's partner must remain until the serve passes the short line in handball, paddleball, or racquetball.
2 *squash racquets* A quarter circle with a 4½-foot radius on each side of the court within

which the server must have one foot when making a serve.

service break *tennis* An instance of a player's winning a game against the opponent's service.

service court A portion of the court into which the ball or shuttlecock must be hit for a valid serve:
1 *badminton* Either of 2 areas on each side of the net located between the center line and the sideline and extending from the short service line to the back boundary line (in singles) or to the long service line (in doubles). The shuttlecock must be hit so that it would land in the proper court if it were not returned. If it is not returned and lands outside the service court, the server loses the serve.
2 *court tennis* The area between the galleries wall and the pass line behind the last gallery line on the hazard side of the court within which a serve must land to be good.
3 *deck tennis* Either of 2 areas on each side of the net between the center line and the sideline extending from the foul line to the baseline. The ring must be tossed so that it would land in the service court if it were not returned.
4 *platform tennis* Either of 2 areas on each side of the court between the half court line and the service sideline extending from the net back to the service line.
5 *squash racquets* Either of 2 areas at the back of the court between the half court line and the side wall extending from the service line back to the back wall.
6 *table tennis* The right-hand side of a player's side of the table between the center line and the edge of the table on which a serve must bounce in doubles play.
7 *tennis* Either of 2 areas on each side of the court between the half court line and service sideline extending from the net back to the service line.

service line A line on a court marking the boundary of a service court or service zone:
1 *badminton* see LONG SERVICE LINE, SHORT SERVICE LINE
2 *court tennis* The last gallery line on the hazard side of the court that is parallel to the net and that marks the front boundary of the service court.
3 A line across the court parallel to and 5 feet in front of the short line in handball, paddleball, and racquetball which marks the front boundary of the service zone.
4 *racquets* A line on the front wall parallel to

and 9 feet 7½ inches from the floor above which a serve must hit the wall to be in play. (also called *cut line*)

5 *squash racquets* **a** A line on the front wall parallel to and 6½ feet from the floor (8 feet 2 inches on a doubles court) above which a serve must hit the wall to be in play. (also called *cut line*) **b** The line on the floor parallel to and 10 feet in front of the back wall (15 feet on a doubles court) which defines the forward limits of the service courts.

6 *tennis* A line on each side of the court parallel to and 21 feet from the net which marks the rear limit of the service court.

service over *badminton* The loss of service by a side; side-out.

service side *court tennis* The side of the court on which the server stands. — compare HAZARD SIDE

service sideline *tennis* The portion of the sideline of a singles court lying between the net and the service line which defines the side limit of the service court in both singles and doubles play.

service zone The area between the service line and the short line on a handball, paddleball, or racquetball court within which the server must be standing when serving the ball.

serving **1** The act or process of putting the ball or shuttlecock in play in a court or racket game. **2** *archery* A wrapping of thread or twine around parts of a bowstring (as the loops and the nocking point) to protect it from chafing.

serving zone *jai alai* The area on the court within which the serve must land to be good.

¹set **1** *cockfighting* To place a gamecock in the pit for a bout.

2 *fencing* To make a slight permanent bend in the blade of a sword before it is used for fencing so that the blade will always flex in the same direction thereby reducing the chance of injury or a broken blade.

3 *fishing* To drive the point of a fishhook into the fish's mouth by pulling the line taut when the fish strikes.

4 *of a hunting dog* To point out the position of game by crouching or pointing.

5 *volleyball* To hit the ball approximately straight up close to the net so that it can be spiked over the net.

²set *of a track athlete* In the starting position ready for the starting signal. In dashes, the runner is usually in a crouch start with his hands on the ground behind the starting line, his hips raised,

and his body leaning forward. — usually used as a command in the phrase *get set*

³set **1** A unit of a match: **a** A division of a match (as in tennis, deck tennis, and platform tennis) that is won by the side that wins at least 6 games by a margin of 2 games or that is won by the side that wins a tiebreaker. **b** A division of a match in tennis played in a 21- or 31-point scoring system that is won by the side that scores at least 21 (or 31) points and leads the opponent by at least 2 points. **c** *court tennis* A division of a match won by the side that first wins 6 games. **d** *table tennis* A match.

2 *archery* A group of 6 arrows having identical or very similar flight characteristics.

3 *boating* The direction of the tide or current or of the leeway of a boat.

4 *football* see FORMATION

5 *hunting* A large group of decoys arranged together.

6 *surfing* A series of 3 or 4 waves that move toward the shore in a group. There is usually a noticeable lull between the sets during which the wave action appears milder; this is usually the best time for paddling out to get into position to catch a wave from the next set.

7 or **setup** *volleyball* The act or an instance of setting the ball to a teammate; the manner of setting the ball. When the setter is at the net, he normally sets the ball forward or backward to the spiker. When he is in the back row, the set is normally made crosscourt to give the spiker a better angle to approach the ball.

8 *weight training* A number of repetitions of one exercise performed as a group.

— in straight sets *tennis* Without losing a single set in the match. ⟨won the match *in straight sets*⟩

set back *football* An offensive back who usually lines up behind the quarterback. In the standard pro T formation, the fullback and one halfback line up as set backs. (also called *remaining back*)

set down **1a** To defeat an opponent. **b** *baseball* To put out a batter; retire. ⟨they were *set down* in order⟩

2 *horse racing* To suspend a jockey or a driver for a riding or driving infraction.

set line *fishing* A baited line fastened to an object (as a tree) and left unattended. A set line is illegal in some states.

set point A situation in certain racket games (as tennis) in which the player or side that is leading will win the game and with it the set by winning the next point; the point being played in this

set position

situation. — compare GAME POINT, MATCH POINT

set position *baseball* The position of a pitcher after a stretch with one foot on the pitcher's rubber and the ball held in front of his body while he checks the baserunner. The pitcher is required to come to a complete stop in the set position before pitching, throwing to a base, or stepping off the rubber.

set scrum or **set scrummage** see SCRUM

set shot *basketball* A shot made typically with 2 hands from long range in much the same manner as the chest pass by thrusting both arms forward and releasing the ball with the fingers. The set shot is seldom seen in modern basketball play, having generally been replaced by the jump shot.

setter **1** *hunting* A gun dog that indicates the position of game by crouching.
2 *tennis* A match of a stated number of sets. ⟨one must remember that a tough five-*setter* on any hot day would hurt a man of his age — Parton Keese, *New York Times*⟩
3 *volleyball* The player who is responsible for setting the ball up in the air close to the net so that it can be spiked by a teammate.

set the score or **set the game** To extend the length of the game (as in badminton or squash) by exercising the option of naming a new total to be played to when the score is tied at a predetermined total. The first player to have reached the designated total (as 13 or 14 points in a 15-point game) has the option of setting the game to 5 points, if the score is tied at 13, or to 3 points if the score is tied at 14. If the score is not set, then the game is played to 15 points. If it is set, it is then played until one player has gained the specified number of points (as 5).

setting The method of setting the score in a racket game (as badminton or squash).

setup **1** A shot that is easily returned (as in handball or badminton).
2 *billiards* A situation in which the positions of the balls on the table makes it relatively easy to score.
3 *bowling* The arrangement of pins to be knocked down.
4 *volleyball* The act or manner of setting the ball for the spiker.

set up **1** To maneuver one's opponent or another competitor into such a position or situation as to be able to take advantage of him or of his subsequent action (as by passing him in a race or by getting free to score or to receive a pass).
2 To make a pass of the ball or puck to a team-

mate who is in better position to try to score.
3 *football* **a** To make a particular play or a particular style of play successful by effective use of contrasting plays or styles of play or by moving the ball into a strategic position. ⟨relied on a strong defense and ground game to *set up* his passing — Paul Zimmerman, *A Thinking Man's Guide to Pro Football*⟩ **b** *of a passer* To get into position (as in a pocket) to pass.
4 *motor racing* **a** To prepare a racing car for a particular track or course by making adjustments in such things as the suspension system and tire pressure. **b** To be in position when coming out of a corner to be able to take the proper line through the next corner or to move properly into the next straight.
5 *volleyball* To provide a spiker with a set.

seventh-inning stretch *baseball* A brief period before the start of the first or second half of the seventh inning during which spectators stand and stretch. It is a custom dating from the 19th century which is still observed today.

sextet An ice hockey team.

shade *baseball* To defend against a particular opponent by playing slightly to one side of a straightaway position so as to be a step or two closer to the area in which he is expected to hit the ball. ⟨the outfield is *shading* him to the left⟩

shadow *ice hockey* To stay close to one's man; to guard a particular opponent closely even when he does not have the puck.

shadow ball **1** A ball which rebounds from the front wall in handball, paddleball, or racquetball close to the side of the player who hit it and on the opposite side from his opponent so that the opponent cannot get to the ball and which results in an unintentional hinder. (also called *screen ball*)
2 *bowling* A ball rolled for practice of one's delivery down a lane on which there are no pins set up.

shadow box To engage in shadow boxing.

shadow boxing *boxing* Practice at moving and punching by going through the motions of sparring with an imaginary opponent.

shadow roll *horse racing* A thick roll of lamb's wool fitted across the face of a racehorse or a harness horse between the eyes and the nostrils to prevent his looking at the ground directly in front and getting confused by his own shadow or the shadows of other horses. — see illustration at HARNESS HORSE

shadow serve A serve which is a shadow ball.

shaft **1** or **shaftment** The hollow or solid cylindrical body of an arrow extending from the nock to the pile. — see ARROW

2 The relatively thin or narrow portion of a club, mallet, or implement: **a** The flexible cylindrical part of a golf club that connects the head and the handle. **b** The handle of a canoe paddle. **c** The narrow part of a hockey or lacrosse stick by which it is held and manipulated.

shag **1** To chase after a ball hit or knocked out of play and return it.

2 *baseball* To catch fly balls in practice.

shake bottle *billiards* A small leather or plastic bottle open at the small end which holds and serves as a shaker for tiny numbered balls or counters used in certain games and which may be used as a secondary object of the cue ball in other games. — see BOTTLE POCKET BILLIARDS, FORTY-ONE, PILL POOL

shake off *of a baseball pitcher* To reject a sign given by the catcher by making a negative gesture (as shaking the head or waving or flicking the glove).

shallow *baseball* In or into the portion of a player's normal fielding area that is closest to home plate; closer to home plate than usual or normal. ⟨a fly ball to *shallow* right field⟩ ⟨had the outfielders playing *shallow*⟩

shallow-water blackout *skin diving* Loss of consciousness by a diver who is holding his breath and resisting the urge to breathe. The longer the breath is held, the greater the amount of oxygen absorbed by the body resulting in a change in the proportion of carbon dioxide in the blood. The excess of carbon dioxide results in oxygen starvation and blackout.

shamateur An athlete or player who is classified as an amateur but who receives illegal payments under the practice of shamateurism.

shamateurism The practice of treating athletes as amateurs so that they will be eligible for amateur competition but at the same time subsidizing them with illegal payments or with payments officially referred to as expense money. ⟨men who for years were responsible for the hypocrisy of *shamateurism,* with one hand pointing pious fingers at the professional promoters who would sully their game, and with the other hand paying off the amateur stars under the table — Herbert Warren Wind, *New Yorker*⟩

¹shank **1** The part of an anchor which extends up from the arms roughly parallel to the flukes and to which the anchor rode is attached. — see illustration at ANCHOR

2 The part of a fishhook that is between the eye and the bend. — see illustration at FISHHOOK

²shank **1** *golf* To hit the ball with the heel of the clubhead or with the shaft rather than with the face of the club causing it to go off in an unintended direction.

2 *of a punter in football* To kick the ball with the ankle or with the side of the foot instead of with the instep causing it to go off to one side and only a short distance.

sharking **1** The sport of fishing for sharks.

2 *Australian Rules football* **a** The act or practice of intercepting the ball when it is knocked from an opposing ruckman to his own rover during a ball up or throw-in. **b** The act or practice of scouting opponents or prospective players.

shave down *of a swimmer* To shave off body hair before competition in order to cut down on resistance in the water.

sheet **1** The expanse of ice approximately 140 feet long by 14 feet wide that is used for curling.

2 A line attached to a boom or the clew of a sail that is used to adjust the sail with respect to the wind. — compare HALYARD

sheet bend A knot used to join 2 lines temporarily that is formed by making a loop in the end of one line with the end passing over the standing part and then passing the end of the other line up through the loop, around the other standing part, and back through the loop in the opposite direction. (also called *becket bend*) — see illustration at KNOT

sheet down *sailing* To fasten a sheet to a cleat so that the sail (as a jib) stays in a fixed position with respect to the wind (as when tacking).

¹shell **1** A light extremely narrow racing boat propelled by oars. The shell, which consists of a thin skin of cedar or sometimes fiberglass on a wooden and metal framework, has a sliding seat and a footrest (*stretcher*) for each oarsman and oarlocks set out from the sides of the shell on outriggers. In rowing competition the outriggers are staggered on alternate sides of the boat because each oarsman handles a single oar. In sculling, where 2 oars are used by each sculler, the outriggers are set directly opposite each other. The outrigger, by setting the fulcrum point about 2 feet beyond the side of the boat, increases the arc through which the oarsman pulls the oar. By so doing, it spreads over a greater distance the amount of work required to pull the oar while at the same time allowing the oarsman to push with his legs as he pulls with his arms and back and thus put more muscle power into each stroke. In both rowing and sculling the oarsmen sit facing the stern. The oarsmen are usually numbered from the bow with the last one (number 8 on an 8-oared shell) called *stroke*. The stroke is in effect the captain of the crew, determining strategy and setting the beat. The other members of the crew adjust their strokes to his. When a coxswain is used, on some 4-oared and on all 8-oared shells, he sits in the stern facing forward, steers the shell by means of tiller ropes attached to the rudder, and keeps the stroke informed on the progress of the race. A typical 8-oared shell is approximately 62 feet long and 2 feet wide with a covered bow and stern section and a 38-foot cockpit for the crew. The depth of the shell is around 9–11 inches.

2 a A cartridge. **b** A metal and paper or plastic case for holding primer, powder, and shot or a rifle slug used as ammunition for a shotgun.

3 A lightweight usually water-repellent jacket worn by a hiker or mountain climber over a sweater or parka for protection from wind and rain.

²shell *baseball* To score a large number of runs at one time off an opposing pitcher. ⟨was *shelled* for 11 runs in five innings in his first two starts — *Sporting News*⟩

shepherd *Australian Rules football* To push, shoulder, or block an opposing player in order to prevent his reaching and tackling the ballcarrier. Shepherding is legal only so long as the opponent is not more than 5 yards from the ballcarrier.

shiai A judo tournament.

¹shift **1** The act of switching from the guarding of one opponent to another who is a greater offensive threat or who has eluded his defender (as in basketball or lacrosse).

2 *baseball* A realignment of certain fielders in order to cover more effectively the area of the field that a particular batter most often hits to.

3 *football* A simultaneous change of position by one or more offensive players after they have lined up for the snap. The shift is legal so long as the players are motionless one full second before the snap.

4 *ice hockey* **a** The period during which a player or a particular line is on the ice. **b** A quick change of direction by the puck carrier in order to get around a defender.

²shift **1** *of one or more offensive players in football* To change position or move to a new position after lining up for the snap.

2 To leave the man that one has been guarding to cover an opponent who has gotten free

from his defender (as in basketball or lacrosse).

shinai The bamboo staff used in kendo.

shin boot see BOOT (*harness racing*)

shine ball *baseball* A ball that is unnaturally smooth (as from rubbing against the glove or uniform) and that is prohibited by the rules from being pitched.

shinguard A protective covering (as of plastic, fiber, or hard leather) for the shin. Lightweight shinguards are worn under the stockings by soccer players to protect them from kicks. A baseball catcher wears fiber or plastic shinguards over his uniform to protect his shins, knees, and insteps from foul balls when catching. — see also PAD

shining The practice of finding big game at night by means of a spotlight.

shinny **1 a** A variation of field hockey played informally (as in streets or fields) with curved sticks and a ball, piece of wood, or a can. **b** The stick used in shinny.

2 *ice hockey* Play that is disorganized or of poor quality.

shin splints Pain and swelling in the shins as a result of inflammation of the tibial and toe extensor muscles that is caused by overexertion (as in running on a hard surface).

shin trap *soccer* A trap of the ball made against the shin.

ship water *of a boat* To take in water over the side or through a hole in the hull.

shiver *football* A hard upward shove usually with the heels of the hands or the forearms made by a defensive lineman against an opposing lineman to neutralize the effectiveness of the offensive lineman's block.

shoe **1** A covering for the feet that is worn while participating in most sports for protection for the feet or to provide secure footing. Most sports shoes are constructed of either leather or canvas uppers with a leather or rubber sole. The shoe worn by players in most field sports (such as football, soccer, and lacrosse) is usually of leather with a fairly rigid leather sole studded with blunt cleats. The pattern of the cleats traditionally differs from sport to sport, but there is little practical difference. Shoes designed for wear on synthetic surfaces may have molded lugs or cleats or may even have ripple soles.

Tennis shoes usually have soft leather or fabric uppers and a flat rubber sole. Boating shoes, or *deck shoes* as they are sometimes called, are similar to tennis shoes, but the sole normally has wavy or zig-zag creases which help grip wet boat decks. Basketball shoes are also similar to tennis shoes but the sole has a molded design which keeps the player from slipping. This type of shoe is most often worn for indoor court games.

The shoe designed for wear by boxers and wrestlers typically has a lightweight leather sole and light leather uppers that lace up above the ankle. Bowling shoes also are of lightweight leather with soft leather or rubber soles. One shoe normally has a rubber sole with a small leather tip while the other sole is all leather to permit sliding.

Baseball shoes are usually of leather with a set of 3 short, wide spikes on the sole and 3 spikes on the heel. Golf shoes resemble ordinary dress or casual shoes but have a number of small thin spikes on the sole and heel. The spikes are small and thin enough that they do not tear up the surface of the putting green. Track and field shoes normally are lightweight leather shoes with a one-piece leather or rubber sole. Shoes used for outdoor running and jumping events normally have leather soles with sharp spikes which dig into cinder or dirt for traction. For indoor running events and for use on synthetic surfaces, a shoe with very short spikes, which just catch on the boards or in the surface, is worn. The shoes worn by competitors in field events normally have flat rubber soles, since most of the throwing circles are of concrete or asphalt.

2 *auto racing* A tire.

3 Short for *horseshoe.*

shoe board *horse racing* A sign that informs the bettors of the kinds of horseshoes worn by the horses in a race.

shoestring catch *baseball* A running catch of a fly ball or a line drive just before it hits the ground made by bending forward and stretching the glove hand as far forward and as low as possible. The term is sometimes used of a similar catch in other sports (as football).

¹shoot 1 a To discharge a weapon at a target or at game. ⟨*shot* the rifle a few times⟩ ⟨*shot* the arrow⟩ **b** To wound or kill game with a missile from a weapon. ⟨*shot* a deer⟩

2 To propel or drive a ball or puck toward a goal by striking, punching, or throwing it with the hands or with an implement. ⟨he *shoots* with his left hand⟩

3 To attempt to make a kill shot (as in handball).

4 To steer a canoe or kayak through rapids.

5 To achieve a particular score or mark by shooting. ⟨*shot* a 66 on the final day of the tourna-

ment⟩ ⟨*shooting* 63 percent from the floor⟩

6 To play a game or a portion of a game in which a ball is driven toward a hole. ⟨*shoot* pool⟩ ⟨*shot* a round of golf⟩

7 *of a bowled ball in cricket* To move close to the ground after bouncing.

8 *fishing* To allow additional fly line to be drawn out by the momentum of the moving line in fly casting in order to extend the length of the cast.

9 *football* **a** To rush the passer from a linebacker or safety position; blitz. **b** To direct one's linebackers or safeties to rush the passer.

10 *gymnastics* To pike the body and then thrust the legs forward and out or up in a new direction by quickly straightening the body.

11 *ice hockey* To drive the puck to the opposite end of the ice in a clearing action.

12 *sailing* To approach an object (as a mooring or dock) to windward with sails luffing by utilizing the boat's momentum.

²shoot 1 A shooting match or contest.

2 *football* A rush made by a linebacker or safety; blitz.

shooter 1 a Someone who shoots a weapon. **b** A player who is making a shot.

2 A handball or racquetball player noted for making kill shots.

3 A player who takes an inordinate number of shots or who is noted for his ability to make goals.

shooting 1 The action of discharging a weapon at a target or at game; the sport of shooting a rifle or pistol at a target and scoring points for each round that lands within specified scoring areas of the target.

Rifle competition is divided into 2 categories: small-bore (.22-caliber rifle) and big-bore (.30-caliber military rifle). In small-bore competition, the targets have a 10-point bull's-eye within which is a smaller "X-ring" used to break ties; the targets are placed at distances of 50 yards, 50 meters, and 100 yards (50 feet in indoor competition). Competitors shoot from standing, sitting, kneeling, and prone positions using slow-fire (up to one minute per round) procedure. Both standard metal and telescopic sights are used.

Big-bore matches are held on ranges of 200, 300, 600, and 1000 yards and include both slow-fire and rapid-fire (10 rounds per minute) procedure. Competitors fire from all positions, but at the longer distances the prone position is normally used at slow fire. Targets in big-bore competition have a 5-point bull's-eye with a smaller "X-ring" for tie breaking.

In pistol shooting, targets have 10-point bull's-eyes and are placed at 25 and 50 yards. The .22-caliber pistol, the .38-caliber revolver, and the .45-caliber pistol are used. Indoor competition involves only the .22-caliber pistol at 50 feet. Competitors fire from the standing position and fire 30 rounds at slow fire, 30 rounds at timed fire (5 rounds in 20 seconds), and 30 rounds at rapid fire (5 rounds in 10 seconds). — compare TRAPSHOOTING, SKEET SHOOTING; ARCHERY

2 The action of attempting to drive or throw a ball or puck into a goal as a method of scoring in various games.

3 British term for hunting with a rifle or shotgun.

shooting clock or **shot clock** *basketball* A clock that shows the players how much time remains in which to make a shot in a game played under a 24- or 30-second rule.

shooting glove see GLOVE

shooting head A weight-forward fly line; the belly of a weight-forward line. — see FLY LINE

shooting line *archery* A line parallel to the target which is straddled by all archers when shooting.

shootoff Additional competition to determine the winner when several competitors are tied at the end of regular shooting or archery competition.

shoot set *volleyball* A low fast set made to a spiker near the sideline.

shoot the curl see SHOOT THE TUBE

shoot-the-duck *skating* A position in which the skater is moving forward or backward in a squat with one leg extended forward.

shoot the gap *football* To charge between opposing linemen to get at the ballcarrier or the passer.

shoot the tube or **shoot the curl** *surfing* To ride a surfboard into the hollow part of the curl of a wave.

shoot through *gymnastics* A stunt performed from a position with the body leaning forward and supported off the floor on the feet and hands (with the body and arms straight as for the beginning of a push-up) in which the gymnast thrusts his hips in the air, swings his legs forward, and as the body starts back down slides the legs between the arms to wind up in a sitting position or in an L support.

shore break *surfing* Waves that break close to shore. — compare POINT BREAK, REEF BREAK

¹short 1 In or into the portion of a player's normal fielding area that is closest to home plate; shallow. ⟨the third baseman was playing *short* expecting a bunt⟩ ⟨a fly ball to *short* right field⟩

2 *of a thrown or hit ball* Failing to reach the intended position or goal. ⟨his throw to first was *short*⟩

3 Near the front part of a playing area or near the net. ⟨the serve was *short*⟩

4 *of betting odds* Marked by little difference in the amount wagered on each side.

²short 1 A serve (as in handball or paddleball) that fails to pass the short line or that hits the server's partner before passing the short line and that is charged as a fault against the server.

2 *curling* A stone that stops short of the desired position.

3 Short for *shortstop.*

short-arm *baseball* To throw or pitch a ball with the arm held relatively close to the body and not fully extended.

short corner see PENALTY CORNER

short course *swimming* A course at least 25 yards long but not more than 50 yards.

short fielder *softball* **1** An extra outfielder who takes up a position just beyond the infield in slow pitch softball.

2 The position played by a short fielder.

short game *golf* The aspect of play in which control of relatively short shots (as approach shots or putts) is of primary importance.

shorthanded Having fewer players on the ice or playing area than the opposing team has because one or more players have been suspended from the game for rule infractions; scored by a team that is playing shorthanded. ⟨the team has to play *shorthanded* when a player is sent off⟩ ⟨scored a *shorthanded* goal⟩

short-hop *baseball* To catch a short hop; to catch a ball on the short hop.

short hop *baseball* A batted ball caught immediately after it bounces. — often used in the phrase *on the short hop*

Short International *archery* A target round in which each competitor shoots 30 arrows at a distance of 50 meters, 30 at 35 meters, and 30 at 25 meters.

short iron *golf* An iron with great loft (as a 7, 8, or 9 iron) that is used for short approach shots.

short leg *cricket* **1** A fieldsman stationed just to the leg side about midway between the 2 wickets.

2 The position played by a short leg.

short line A line on the court beyond which a served ball must bounce to be in play:

1 A line midway between and parallel to the front and back walls of a 4-wall handball, paddleball, or racquetball court.

2 A line 16 feet from and parallel to the wall on a 1-wall handball or paddleball court.

3 A line on the floor 35 feet 10 inches from and parallel to the front wall of a racquets court which marks the forward boundary of the service courts.

short man   see SHORT RELIEVER

short pin   *bowling*   A pin which is rolling on the alley but which fails to knock down a standing pin.

short reliever or **short man**   *baseball*   A relief pitcher who is usually brought in late in the game especially to protect the team's lead.

short serve   A serve (as in handball, racquetball, or paddleball) that fails to bounce beyond the short line or that hits 2 side walls before bouncing and is charged as a fault.

short service line   *badminton*   A line parallel to and 6½ feet from the net on each side that marks the forward boundary of the service courts. (also called *front service line, service line*)

short set   *platform tennis*   A set that is won by the first side to win 6 games regardless of whether it has a 2-game margin. The short set is sometimes employed in a tournament to speed up play.

short side   **1** The side of the goalmouth in ice hockey or box lacrosse on which there is less space between the goalkeeper and a goalpost when the goalkeeper is playing toward one side. **2** *football*   The side of an unbalanced line that has the fewer linemen; weak side.

short ski   *skiing*   A ski usually less than 4 feet long designed for use by adults.

shortstop   *baseball*   **1** An infielder who normally plays to the left of second base and who is responsible for making plays at second base and for covering the area between second and third base. **2** The position played by a shortstop; the area normally covered by a shortstop.

short swing   *skiing*   A maneuver similar to the wedeln but made by edging the skis instead of keeping them flat.

shot   **1** The act or action or an instance of shooting: **a** The discharging of a weapon. **b** The throwing or propelling of a ball or puck toward a goal. **2** A stroke in which a ball is hit with an implement (as in tennis or billiards). **3** A hard blow. ⟨gave him a *shot* to the head⟩

4 Someone noted for shooting. ⟨he was a good outside *shot*⟩ ⟨she is a good *shot* with a pistol⟩

5 *baseball*   A hard-hit ball and especially a home run. ⟨hit a three-run *shot* over the left field wall⟩

6 *fishing*   A lead pellet partially cut through that can be pinched on a fishing line to cause it to sink. (also called *split shot*)

7 *golf*   A stroke. ⟨a 4-*shot* lead on the field — Gwilym S. Brown, *Sports Illustrated*⟩

8 Small lead or steel pellets used as ammunition for a shotgun. Shot ranges in size from approximately .05 inches in diameter to buckshot at .30 inches and larger.

9 *track and field*   A smooth metal sphere approximately 5 inches in diameter that is used in the shot put. For men's competition, the shot, which may be solid metal (as steel, iron, or brass) or a shell of metal or plastic filled with shot, weighs 16 pounds. In women's competition, the shot weighs 8 pounds 13 ounces. High school boys put a 12-pound shot.

shotgun   **1** A breech-loading smoothbore shoulder weapon for firing shot at short ranges. The shotgun is often made with 2 barrels located either side by side or one over the other that can be fired independently. Because of the short range and the wide dispersal of the shot, the shotgun does not have an aiming sight as does the rifle, but it does have a ridge along the top of the barrel to aid in pointing it. **2** *football*   An offensive formation primarily used for passing in which the quarterback stands a few yards behind the center to receive a direct snap, and the other backs are spread out as flankers and slotbacks.

shotgunner   Someone who hunts with or shoots a shotgun.

shotmaker   A good shooter; someone noted for making accurate shots or for shotmaking.

shotmaking   **1** The stroking or hitting of the ball in making a shot. **2** Success in making shots; the making of accurate placements. ⟨the most spectacular exhibition of *shotmaking* so far on the . . . tour — Grace Lichtenstein, *New York Times Magazine*⟩

shot on goal   A shot (as in ice hockey or soccer) that enters the goal for a score or that would have entered the goal had it not been stopped by the goalkeeper. Shots on goal are often recorded in statistical records for reference in determining a goalkeeper's effectiveness or the effectiveness of a team's offense.

shot put

shotput

shot put *track and field* A field event in which a shot is heaved for distance. The shot is held in the palm at shoulder level and heaved with a pushing motion using one arm. The competitor must remain in a 7-foot throwing circle, and the shot must land within a throwing sector formed by lines extending from the circle at a 45 degree angle. Each competitor is allowed 3 trials in the finals; in a large meet a prior set of 3 trials is used to determine the finalists. The best effort of the competitor in either the trial or the finals is credited to the athlete in determining final standings.

shot-putter An athlete who competes in the shot put.

shot rock *curling* The stone lying closest to the center of the house.

shot string The elongated mass of shot pellets fired from a shotgun.

shoulder *surfing* The unbroken portion of a wave to one side of the curl.

shoulder balance *gymnastics* A position of balance with the legs and body extended upwards and supported on the back of the shoulders, neck, and head and with the arms sometimes placed on the floor for additional support.

shoulder block *football* A block made by hitting the opponent with the shoulder.

shoulder check see BODY CHECK

shoulder roll *tumbling* A forward or backward roll over one shoulder. (also called *football roll*)

shovel The upturned front part of a ski.

shovel pass An underhand pass (as in basketball or lacrosse) made by swinging the arms or the stick forward in a shoveling motion.

¹show *pari-mutuel betting* Third place or better at the finish. When a bet is made on a competitor for show, the bettor collects the amount specified in the show pool if the competitor finishes first, second, or third. — see also PARI-MUTUEL BETTING

²show To finish third or at least third in competition involving betting. ⟨bet him to *show*⟩ — compare WIN

showboat A player or performer who makes a showy display of skill; hotdog.

showboating Indulgence by a player or performer in showy displays of skill; hotdogging.

show jumping *equitation* Competition for horse and rider in which each horse is required to jump a series of fences in a prescribed order within a time limit. The fences are not over 4 feet high, but many of them are placed in difficult combinations allowing only one or 2 strides between each. In show jumping, the course is set up in an arena as distinct from the cross-country course set up in the countryside. — see also GRAND PRIX, NATIONS CUP

shroud *sailing* A line that leads from the mast to the deck or rail and that gives lateral support to the mast. — compare BACKSTAY, HEADSTAY

shuffle The moving of one foot in the desired direction and then the bringing of the other foot up to but not beyond the first when advancing or moving sideways (as in guarding a player). — compare CROSSOVER

shuffleboard A game played on a long, narrow court with triangular scoring areas at each end between 2 sides that alternate in shoving red and black disks down the court toward the far scoring area with the object of placing disks in the scoring area and knocking opposing disks out of play. The disks are pushed with a long-handle implement called a *cue,* and they must be played from the "ten-off" area at the base of the near scoring triangle. Three feet in front of each scoring area is a dead line beyond which disks must travel to remain in play. Each side plays 4 disks from one end of the court toward the opposite scoring area after which the score is tallied and the disks are then played from the other end to complete the round. In singles play, players

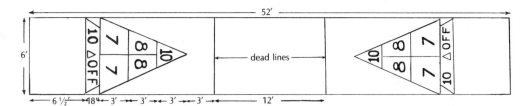

52'

10 △ OFF 7 8 8 7 8 10 10 △ OFF

6'

dead lines

△ 10 8 8 7 10

6½' 18" 3' 3' 3' 3' 12'

shuffleboard court

move to the opposite end of the court to play the next round in the opposite direction. In doubles play, one member of each side is at each end. After the round is scored, the partners of the previous shooters then play the disks in the opposite direction. In the scoring, only those disks wholly within the particular scoring areas are counted. Any disks in the ten-off area result in 10 points being deducted from the side's score. A game usually consists of 75 points and a match consists of 3 games.

shunt *auto racing* A collision.

shut down *drag racing* To defeat a competitor.

shutdown strip *drag racing* The part of the course beyond the finish line on which the competitors decelerate.

shuto see KNIFE HAND

shut off **1** To prevent the execution of a planned play or strategy. ⟨they *shut off* the long pass⟩
2 *auto racing* To slow down just before entering a turn.

shutout A victory in which the opponent was prevented from scoring.

¹shut out To prevent an opponent from scoring in a game.

²shut out *of a pari-mutuel bettor* Unable to place a bet because the machine has been shut off at the start of the race.

shuttlecock or **shuttle** A lightweight conical object that is volleyed over the net in badminton. The shuttlecock consists of a 1-inch cork rounded at one end and having 14 to 16 feathers fixed in the other end. The feathers are approximately 2½ inches long, are fastened together with thread, and have a 2½-inch spread at the top. The total weight of the shuttlecock must be between 73 and 85 grains (approximately ¹/₅ ounce). For informal play, molded plastic or nylon shuttlecocks with rubber-covered heads are commonly used. (also called *bird*)

shuttle relay or **shuttle hurdles** *track and field* A relay race which is run back and forth over

hurdles on a straight course with the first and third runners of a team running in one direction and the second and fourth runners running in the opposite direction in adjacent lanes. The outgoing runner starts his leg when the incoming runner either passes a predetermined point or touches him on the shoulder.

side **1** An individual, a pair, or a team for which a single score is kept and which may as a unit win, lose, or tie in competition.
2 *gymnastics* A position in which the breadth axis of the performer is parallel to the length axis of the apparatus. — compare CROSS

sidearm *of a throw or stroke* Made with the hand brought forward relatively parallel to the ground and the wrist even with or slightly below the level of the hand.

sideboards The boards along the sides of a hockey rink.

side cast *fishing* A cast made by swinging the rod through a relatively horizontal arc.

shuttlecock

389

side-foot

side-foot *soccer* To make a shot or a pass by kicking the ball with the side of the foot.

sidehiller *golf* A putt that must roll across the slope of the green rather than up or down the slope to reach the cup.

side horse see POMMEL HORSE

side kick *Gaelic football* A free kick of the ball to put it in play after an opponent has driven it over the sideline.

¹sideline **1** A line on each side of a playing field or court which is at right angles to the goal line, end line, or baseline and which marks a side boundary of the playing area.
2 *football* A pass pattern in which the receiver runs straight downfield and then cuts sharply toward the sideline to catch the pass. The receiver can then turn downfield or continue out of bounds to stop the clock.

²sideline To put a player out of action; to cause a player to be unable to play. ⟨a victim of an errant pitch that *sidelined* him 30 days — Gary Ronberg, *Sports Illustrated*⟩

sidelines The area immediately outside the sidelines of a playing field or court. ⟨allowed to watch from the *sidelines*⟩

side-out Loss of service by a side in a court or net game (as badminton, handball, or volleyball) in which only the serving side can score points and loss of the rally by the serving side means loss of service. In volleyball and in singles play of other games, one player serves until he or his side loses the rally. The serve then goes to the other side. In doubles play, when one player is serving and his side loses the rally, his partner becomes the server until the side loses another rally. Then the serve goes over to the other side.

side puck *hurling* A free puck taken by a player to put the ball in play after an opponent has driven it over the sideline.

side scale see SCALE

¹sideslip *skiing* To slide sideways down a slope or a section of a slope by holding the skis relatively flat with respect to the surface of the snow and by edging just enough to control the rate of slide.

²sideslip *skiing* The act or process of sideslipping; an instance of sideslipping.

sidespin Spin imparted to a ball causing it to rotate from side to side and to bounce to one side. — compare TOPSPIN, UNDERSPIN

¹sidestep *skiing* A method of climbing a slope on skis by standing with the skis pointed across the slope and stepping up with the uphill ski and then bringing the downhill ski up to it and continuing the procedure up the slope. In stepping up, it is necessary for the skis to be edged to prevent sideslipping. It is also important that the skis are pointing directly across the fall line so that they will not slide downhill.

²sidestep *skiing* To climb a slope by employing a sidestep.

sidestep

sidestep traverse *skiing* A variation of the sidestep in which the skier places the uphill ski up and forward or to the rear of the lower ski so that he climbs the slope at an angle.

sidestop *platform tennis* The wire wall that bounds the court on either side. The ball may be played on the rebound from this wall. — see also BACKSTOP

side-straddle hop A conditioning exercise which consists of jumping from a normal standing position with the hands at the sides to a position with the feet spread apart and the hands together often at arm's length over the head and then back to the original position. (also called *jumping jack*)

sidestroke *swimming* A stroke executed on the side by combining a scissors kick with a glide made with the lower arm extended straight ahead and the upper arm swept sideways. During the recovery, the lower arm is swept down toward the waist and then extended for the glide on the next stroke.

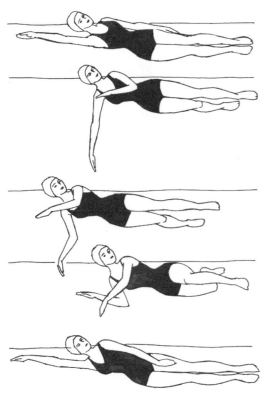

sidestroke with scissors kick

sidewheeler A pacing horse so called because of the side-to-side rocking motion it exhibits in shifting weight back and forth from one side to the other.

side zone *football* The part of a playing field between the inbounds line and the sideline. Whenever the ball is downed in a side zone, it is put in play on the next down at the nearest inbounds line.

¹sight A device used for aiming a bow or a rifle. The bow sight typically consists of a vertical plate attached to the upper limb of the bow and having a movable horizontal bar. The bar is adjusted until the archer is able to hit the target when the bar and the target are in line. The bar must be adjusted anytime the archer shoots from a different distance. There are 3 principal types of sights on rifles. The simplest and most common is the open rear sight, which consists of a vertical plate with a notch in the top mounted on a track at the back of the rifle. The shooter lines up the notch and a vertical post on the front of the barrel with the target. The track permits the rear sight to be moved forward, backward, or to the side to adjust for windage and elevation. The peep sight is similar to the open sight. It too is mounted on an adjustable track. The peep, however, employs a tiny hole through which the shooter views the target. The shooter's eye is very close to the hole so that he has a wide field of view. It is necessary, then, for the shooter merely to line up the front sight with the target instead of 3 points as with the open sight. The telescopic sight is the easiest to use because it is basically a telescope mounted on top of the rifle in place of the metal sight. The telescopic sight not only magnifies the image but improves visibility in low-light situations. The telescopic sight usually has cross hairs for precise aiming which the shooter lines up with the target.

²sight **1** To point or aim a weapon.
2 To adjust the sights of a weapon.

sight-in To adjust the sights of a rifle so that the shots will hit the target at a predetermined distance. The rifle is normally sighted-in at the most common distance at which the shooter expects to use the rifle.

sightscreen *cricket* A fence or wall erected at each end of a playing ground in line with the 2 wickets to provide a plain background behind the bowler so that the batsman can better follow the flight of the bowled ball.

sight window A section of the upper limb of a bow that has been cut away to permit the arrow to rest closer to the center line of the bow and to give the archer a better view of the target.

sign *baseball* A prearranged gesture or word by which a coach or a player can secretly relay instructions to other members of the team. The catcher gives the pitcher a sign in calling for a specific pitch. The base coaches give signs to the batter and base runners calling for certain plays (as a bunt, steal, or hit and run).

signal caller A football quarterback.

signals *football* A sequence of code words, sounds, or gestures by which a player (as the quarterback) informs the other players on the team what play and formation to use for the next down. The quarterback normally calls the play in the huddle and at the line merely uses signals to inform the players when the ball is to be snapped. Occasionally a quarterback will change a call at the line of scrimmage, in which case his signals indicate what kind of play is to be run, who will be the ballcarrier or pass receiver, what special blocking assignments are to be followed, and when the ball is to be snapped.

silks *horse racing* The distinctly patterned and colored silk or nylon jacket and cap worn by a jockey or harness driver during the race to identify the owner of the horse. Each owner has his own distinctive colors and pattern registered with the state racing authority so that the particular pattern and color combination is reserved exclusively for his horses. It is the color and pattern of the silks that the caller uses to distinguish the different horses. (also called *colors*)

silly *of a cricket fieldsman or fielding position* Extremely close to the batsman. ⟨*silly* point⟩ ⟨*silly* mid-off⟩

similar pairs *skating* Competition in which pairs consist of 2 men or 2 women.

simple attack *fencing* An attack made directly (as by a thrust) or indirectly (as by a cutover) with a single action.

simple parry *fencing* A direct block or beat of the opponent's blade to deflect it.

simultaneous fouls *lacrosse* Fouls committed simultaneously by opposing players with the result that the 2 players are suspended and each team plays below normal strength.

sin bin The penalty box in ice hockey.

¹single **1** A single target thrown at a time in skeet or trapshooting.
2 A contest or match (as in golf) in which one individual competes directly against another.
3 *baseball* A base hit that allows the batter to reach first base.
4 *Canadian football* see ROUGE
5 *cricket* A hit on which the batsmen are able to change places once and score one run.
6 *rowing* A shell designed for a single sculler.

²single *baseball* **1** To hit a single.
2 To advance or score a base runner by hitting a single. ⟨*singled* him to third⟩
3 To bring about the scoring of a run by hitting a single. ⟨*singled* in the winning run⟩

single action **1** see ACTION
2 *of a fishing reel* Revolving once for every revolution of the handle. A single action reel is used today chiefly on fly rods.

single foot see RACK

single leg balance *gymnastics* A position of balance on one leg in which the gymnast raises the other leg as high as possible, grasps it with the hand, and stretches the other arm up in the opposite direction so as to resemble the letter Y.

single-pole *ski touring* To move oneself forward by pushing off with the pole on the side opposite the ski that is gliding.

singles A form of play in court games (as tennis, badminton, table tennis, or handball) in which one player competes directly against one other player.

singleton *baseball* A single run scored in a given inning.

single wing *football* An offensive formation in which an unbalanced line is used and in which one back lines up just outside the end of the strong side of the line as a wingback, the quarterback lines up behind the strong side of the line as a blocking back, and the fullback and tailback line up 4 or 5 yards behind the line in position to receive a direct snap from the center. In the single wing, the fullback or the tailback gets the snap directly and initiates a passing or running play.

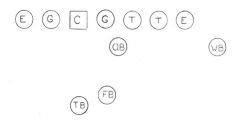

single wing formation with an unbalanced line: C center; E end; FB fullback; G guard; QB quarterback; T tackle; TB tailback; WB wingback

¹sink **1** *of a pitched baseball* To drop on nearing home plate. ⟨has a fastball that *sinks*⟩
2 To make a successful shot or stroke in which a ball is directed to a hole. ⟨*sink* a free throw⟩ ⟨*sank* a 40-foot putt⟩

²sink or **sink hole** *caving* A hole in the ground often caused by the collapse of a subterranean passage that usually affords access to a cavern.

sinker **1** or **sinker ball** *baseball* A pitch that drops down as it nears the plate but usually does not break to the right or left.
2 *fishing* A lead weight attached to the line to sink the lure or bait.

sink hole see SINK.

sinking line *fishing* A fly line designed to sink.

siphon *caving* A part of a cave that leads underwater and that requires swimming and sometimes the use of scuba equipment.

sissy bar or **sissy rail** *karting* A horizontal rail on each side of the seat to keep the driver from sliding to the side during hard cornering.

sit on a lead or **sit on the ball** To play conservatively (as in football) when in the lead in order to avoid turning over the ball and giving the opponents an easy opportunity to score.

sit-out *wrestling* An escape movement in which a wrestler who is on his knees and is held from behind places one foot on the mat and steps through with the other foot to a sitting position from which he quickly rolls over to face his opponent thereby getting out of the hold.

wrestler escaping from a hold by means of a sit-out

sit out **1** *of a professional athlete* To refuse to play during the last season or the option year of a contract with one club in order to be able to sign with another club for the following season.
2 *wrestling* To get out of a hold by means of a sit-out.

sit spin *skating* A spin on one skate made in a squatting position usually with the free leg stretched out in front of the body. The spin is often called the *Haines spin* or the *Jackson Haines spin* after the American skater and instructor who made it popular.

sit-up A conditioning exercise performed in a supine position by raising the trunk to a sitting position usually while keeping the legs straight and then returning to the original position.

sitzmark *skiing* A hole in the snow made by a skier who falls backward and sits in the snow.

six **1** A boundary worth 6 runs in cricket.
2 An ice hockey team.

600 or **600-yard run** *track and field* A race run over a distance of 600 yards.

six-man football A variation of football played with 6 players on a side on a field 80 yards long by 40 yards wide. Six-man football differs from the regular game essentially in that the team in possession must advance the ball 15 yards during a series of downs and the ball must be passed by a lateral or a forward pass before it can cross the line of scrimmage. — compare TOUCH FOOTBALL

six-man lacrosse A variation of lacrosse played with 6 players on a side on a field 80 yards long by 53 yards wide. — see also BOX LACROSSE

sixth man *basketball* The player who is regularly used as the first of a team's substitutes in a game. For many teams the sixth man is as important as any of the starting players, for he is regularly and frequently sent into the game not only to give a starting player a short rest but also to spark the team with his own offensive play.

60 or **60-yard dash** *track and field* A race run over a distance of 60 yards.

skag see SKEG

¹skate **1** A metal runner or a set of wheels attached

sit spin

skate

to the sole of a boot that is used in gliding over ice or a smooth flat surface. Ice skates are made in 3 principal styles. The figure skate, used in skating competition and in general pleasure skating, has a relatively short blade with tooth-like picks at the front. The toe picks are used in making stops, spins, and jumps. The bottom of the blade has a pronounced curve so that little more than one inch is in contact with the surface at a time. This permits the skater to make sharp turns and spins. The ice hockey skate has a flatter blade which allows the skater to skate faster. Since the hockey player does not have to make tight turns and circles or jumps, the picks are not needed. The hockey boot extends high in the back to protect the lower calf muscles. The speed skate is similar in appearance to the hockey skate except that is has an extremely long (16 to 19 inches) virtually flat blade which allows

hockey skate

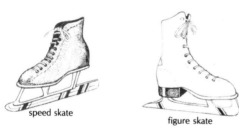

speed skate

figure skate

roller skate

the skater to achieve maximum straight-line speed. Ice skates actually move over the ice on a thin film of water formed as the ice momentarily melts from the weight of the skater. To prevent the blade's skidding sideways and to give the skater precise control, the bottom of the

blade of an ice skate is ground with a slight hollow running the length of the blade. This hollow creates 2 distinct edges for control. In turning, it is only necessary for the skater to lean to one side for the skate to turn toward that side.

The roller skate, used on surfaces other than ice and particularly on hardwood-floored skating rinks, has 2 pairs of rollers or wheels fitted to the sole in tandem. The wheels are so designed that whenever pressure is applied over one wheel, the wheel assembly turns in the direction of the pressure. Therefore, by leaning to the right or left, the skater makes the wheels turn toward the right or left; the greater the lean, the sharper the turn.

2 A period of skating.

²skate **1** To glide on skates; to go skating.

2 To play ice hockey; to play hockey in an aggressive manner.

3 To glide over a surface (as in skiing) by sliding first on one foot and then on the other in the manner of skating.

skateboard A short board 1½ to 2 feet long and 5 to 6 inches wide equipped with 2 pairs of roller skate wheels mounted in tandem that is ridden by balancing on the board and shifting the weight to one side or the other to turn.

skateboarder Someone who rides a skateboard. (also called *skurfer*)

skateboarding The act or practice of riding on a skateboard. (also called *skurfing*)

skate guard A device that fits over the blade of an ice skate to protect the blade whenever the skater is not on the ice.

skate off *ice hockey* **1** To skate against an opposing player making continuous body contact in order to drive him away from the puck and out of the play.

2 To kill a penalty with good defensive play.

skater Someone who engages in skating as a pastime or in competition.

skate sailer Someone who engages in skate sailing.

skate sailing The sport of gliding over an ice surface on ice skates being propelled by the force of the wind on a 50-to-60-square-foot sail set on a frame that is held in the hands.

¹skating The sport of gliding on skates for pleasure or in competition. — see FIGURE SKATING, SPEED SKATING

²skating Of or relating to the foot that supports the body when the skater is on one foot. ⟨*skating* foot⟩ ⟨*skating* leg⟩ — compare FREE

skating turn see STEP TURN

skeet or **skeet shooting** The sport of shooting at clay pigeons with a shotgun from 8 positions around a half-circle range. The targets are thrown from 2 trap houses, a high house located on the left of the range from which the targets are thrown on a nearly horizontal trajectory, and a low house located on the right from which the targets are thrown on a rising trajectory. A round at skeet consists of 25 shots. The shooter fires at a target thrown from each house from each of the 8 positions and then from 4 of the positions takes 2 shots at targets thrown from both houses simultaneously. The 25th shot is essentially a make-up shot to be taken at any position at which the shooter missed earlier. Because the targets are always thrown at the same angle, the shooter is not permitted to have his shotgun in shooting position before the target is thrown. Competition is conducted in classes made up according to the type of shotgun used and the past record of the individual. — compare TRAP-SHOOTING

skeet gun A typically small-gauge shotgun used in skeet. The skeet gun usually has a relatively short barrel and wide choke since the skeet shooter gets a wide variety of angles and because he is not permitted to raise and point the gun before the target is released. It must be capable of firing 2 shots from a single loading.

skeg or **skag** 1 The stern of the keel of a boat; the part of the keel where the rudder is attached.

2 A fin attached to the rear bottom of a surfboard for directional stability.

skein A string of consecutive victories; winning streak.

¹ski 1 A long narrow thin strip of wood, metal, plastic, or fiberglass curved up at the front that is worn in pairs attached to the soles of boots for gliding over snow. Along the bottom of a ski is a shallow groove that runs most of the length of the ski and helps to keep it tracking in a straight line. Skis for adults generally range from 5½ to 6 feet in length, although shorter skis 3 to 4 feet long have become popular in recent years for downhill skiing. Cross-country skis are generally a bit longer than downhill skis and have a pronounced upturn at the front that is especially useful in moving through deep fresh snow. Downhill skis have less of an upturn and have sharp metal edges on the bottom to help the ski bite into the hard crust on turns. To distribute the skier's weight over the entire length of the ski, it is built with a slight upward curve in the middle; the ski is slightly flexible to help absorb bumps. — see also BINDING

2 A short flat runner turned up in front like a ski that is used to support and steer a vehicle (as a snowmobile).

3 Short for *water ski.*

²ski 1 To glide over snow on skis; to engage in skiing.

2 To ski on a particular area or slope. ⟨*skiing* the

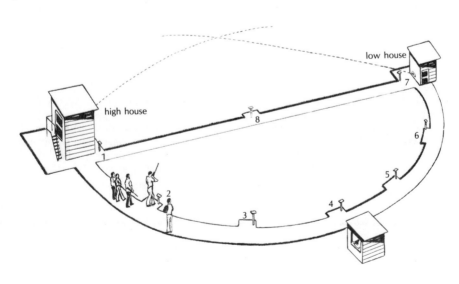

skeet range

skiable

frosted mountains one day and swimming in the warm sea the next — Robin Wright, *Christian Science Monitor*⟩

skiable *of a slope or hill* Suitable for skiing.

skibob A vehicle with 2 short skis one behind the other, a steering handle attached to the forward ski, and a low upholstered seat over the rear ski that is used for gliding downhill over snow by a rider who wears miniature skis for balance.

skibobber Someone who rides a skibob.

skibobbing The sport of riding a skibob.

skid pad A large usually circular area of asphalt that is often oiled to make it slick and is used for testing automobiles and motorcycles with turns, controlled skids, and spins.

skier Someone who engages in skiing.

ski flying Ski jumping competition in which the distance to be jumped is greater than 90 meters (295 feet).

skiing The sport of gliding over snow and especially down a snow-covered slope on skis. Skiing originated as a means of everyday winter transportation in Scandanavian countries and involves moving over level ground and climbing as well as sliding down slopes. As a sport, skiing encompasses downhill skiing, ski touring, and cross-country ski racing. Skiing for sport did not become widely popular in this country until ski lifts to transport skiers to the top of slopes became commonplace. The development of lifts brought enormous growth in downhill skiing and consequent development of sophisticated ski equipment such as safety release bindings and lightweight metal skis with plastic running surfaces which enable the skier to maneuver and make sharp turns as he skis down a slope.

A number of different techniques or methods of skiing have come in vogue during the last half century. Most of the techniques have been national systems and often developed as a result of improvements in equipment which permitted more maneuverability on the slope. In the early 1900s in Austria, Hannes Schneider developed the Arlberg technique which emphasized a crouched position over the skis and the making of turns by stemming one ski and turning the entire body in the direction of the turn. Later the Austrian system taught stem turns and counterrotation (leaning the inside shoulder forward in making a turn instead of the outside shoulder as in the Arlberg system). The French taught beginners to make all turns parallel and to keep the shoulders in line with the skis. After the second World War, American ski schools took what was

believed to be the best aspects of the other schools and standardized an American Ski Technique which included stem turns, counterrotation, and sideslipping. Today in the United States, skiers are typically started on very short skis (from 3 to 5 feet long) and instructed in making parallel or only slightly stemmed turns from the beginning and in maintaining a relaxed straightforward position over the skis without exaggerated movements of the upper body. — see also SKI TOURING; CROSS-COUNTRY; DOWNHILL SKIING, FREESTYLE SKIING; GLM

skijoring A sport in which a person wearing skis and holding a rope is pulled over the snow by a horse or a vehicle.

ski jump **1** A jump made by someone on skis. **2** A course or hill prepared for ski jumping.

ski jumping *skiing* A competitive event in which individuals jump for distance after skiing down a long sloping hill. The inrun down which the competitors ski to gain momentum may be a natural hill or a scaffold structure. The competitors, competing one at a time, ski down the inrun in a crouch to lessen air resistance, jump up on reaching the end of the inrun, attempt to keep the body and skis relatively parallel during the flight, and land on a steep slope some distance beyond and below the point of takeoff. By landing on a steep slope, the competitors are able to convert the force of the landing into forward skiing momentum. The most common distances in international competition are 70 meters (approximately 76 yards) and 90 meters (approximately 98 yards) measured from the point of takeoff to the nearest likely point of landing. Competitors make 2 jumps and are judged on both distance and style during the jump. The highest and lowest scores from 5 judges are discarded and the remaining 3 scores added.

ski lift or **ski tow** A device for transporting skiers up to the top of a ski slope which typically consists of a system of bars or chairs suspended from a moving overhead cable. — see also CHAIR LIFT, GONDOLA, J-BAR, POMALIFT, SKI TOW, T-BAR

skim board A small round or rectangular plywood board that is used to ride over the shallow water that rushes up onto the beach and then back to the sea just after a wave breaks on the beach. The rider typically tosses the board ahead of him onto the water, jumps onto the board, and rides it a few yards as he would ride a surfboard.

skim boarder Someone who rides a skim board.

skim boarding The sport of riding a skim board.

skimeister A skier having the best overall scores in the downhill, slalom, cross-country, and ski jumping competition at a single meet.

skimming The sport of planing on one's stomach over the shallow water on the beach after a wave breaks. Skimming is to skim boarding what body surfing is to board surfing.

skimobile see SNOWMOBILE

skin see SEALSKIN

skin-dive To engage in skin diving.

skin diver Someone who engages in skin diving.

skin diving The sport of swimming or diving underwater with swim fins and a face mask as dis-

performer from a hang position swings his legs up and over his back, between his arms, and under the bar so that his legs wind up pointing toward the floor. To return to the original position, the performer reverses the movement.

skip **1** The captain of a curling or lawn bowling rink. The skip directs the team's strategy and usually is the last member of the rink to play the stone or bowls.

2 Short for *skipper.*

ski patrol A group of expert skiers who are on the mountain whenever ski slopes are open to ensure that conditions are safe and to be ready

skin diver carrying a spear gun

tinguished from ordinary swimming and from deep sea diving with special equipment and an air supply coming from the surface. In broad use, the term skin diving may be used of both free diving and scuba diving as distinguished from deep sea diving or of free diving alone as distinguished from scuba diving. Because underwater exploration is the primary reason for skin diving, the diver usually wears a snorkel which enables him to breath while swimming at the surface with his face down. It is necessary to hold the breath on diving and to exhale through the snorkel upon surfacing in order to clear it of water that gets in during the dive. The face mask, a necessary part of the equipment, gives an undistorted view of the underwater scene and the swim fins provide extra propulsion relieving the diver of the necessity of using his hands and arms for swimming. — see also SCUBA DIVING

skin the cat *gymnastics* A stunt performed on the horizontal bar or on the rings in which the

to provide rescue and first aid assistance to skiers.

ski patrolman A member of a ski patrol.

skip ball or **skip-in** *racquetball* An illegally returned ball that strikes the floor before hitting the front wall.

skip breathing *scuba diving* The practice of holding every breath or every other breath an unusually long time in order to conserve air and extend a dive. Skip breathing can be dangerous if done to excess, for then the body has an insufficient supply of oxygen.

skip-in see SKIP BALL

ski pole *skiing* A long tapering pole with a point at the smaller end and a hand grip at the other end that is used to assist the skier in maintaining balance while skiing, in climbing and walking, and in beginning turns. To prevent the pole's going into the snow too deep, there is a ring (*basket*) fastened to the pole by straps about 5 or 6 inches above the point.

skipper

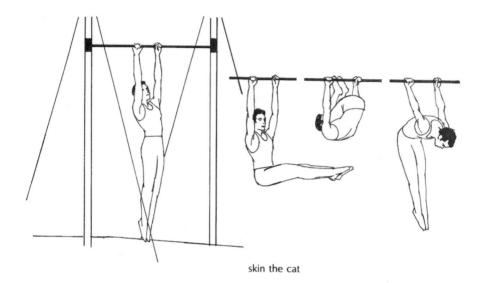

skin the cat

skipper **1** A person in charge of piloting or sailing a boat.
2 The manager of a professional baseball team.
3 A manager, coach, or captain of a British sports team.

skip step *gymnastics* A short hop on one foot followed by a step that is used to move from a run into a tumbling movement (as a cartwheel or a handspring).

ski racer A skier who competes in ski racing.

ski racing Competitive skiing usually in Alpine events.

skirt **1** The fabric that fits around the kayaker and over the cockpit opening to keep water out of a kayak. (also called *spray sheet*)
2 The part of the face of an archery target outside the largest ring that is used in pinning the face to the boss.

skish Tournament casting events similar to regular bait casting and fly casting but scored differently. Skish was originally developed as a separate group of events for regular fishing tackle since expert tournament casters generally used highly specialized equipment in the regular casting

skip step

events. Today, developments in fishing tackle have resulted in the same equipment's being suitable for both regular events and skish. There are 3 different skish events: skish bait, skish spinning, and skish fly casting.

In skish bait competition, each competitor uses bait casting equipment to cast a ⅜- or ⅝-ounce practice plug at 10 targets at distances of from 40 to 80 feet from the caster. Each competitor makes 2 casts at each target and scores 6 points for a perfect cast (one in which the plug lands on or within the 30-inch target ring) on the first cast and 4 points for a perfect second cast. The event is won by the competitor having the highest total after 20 casts.

Skish spinning competition is conducted in the same manner as skish bait, but the competitors use spinning equipment and only a ⅜-ounce practice plug.

Skish fly casting is made up of 3 separate phases: dry fly casting, roll casting, and wet fly casting. The competitors are not restricted in the type of fly casting equipment they may use, but the same tackle must be used in all 3 phases. In the dry fly phase, each competitor has 2½ minutes to make his casts at 5 target rings placed at distances of from 20 to 40 feet away. He makes 3 casts at each target scoring 5 points for a perfect first cast, 3 points for a perfect second cast, and 2 points for a perfect third cast. He must start his casting with the fly in the hand and anytime the fly touches the water, the caster is charged with having made a cast. In the roll casting phase, he moves to the next station, leaving the fly on the water from his last dry fly cast, and makes roll casts to the next 5 targets. He casts to each target until he has made a perfect cast before moving to the next target or until the 1½-minute time limit expires. For each perfect cast, the competitor scores 5 points. The wet fly phase has a 1½-minute time limit in which the caster has to make 2 casts to each of the 5 target rings. For a perfect first cast he scores 3 points and for a perfect second cast 2 points. — see also BAIT CASTING, FLY CASTING

ski sled see SNOWMOBILE

ski tourer Someone who engages in ski touring.

ski touring The sport of skiing for pleasure over the countryside (as through woods and fields) as distinguished from downhill skiing. Ski touring, which is more akin to hiking or showshoeing than to downhill skiing, is essentially what skiing was in its beginnings before the proliferation of resorts and ski lifts. Its recent growth in popularity is partly a result of the cost and overcrowding of downhill skiing areas and partly related to the growth of interest in hiking and backpacking as a way of getting out into the woods. The equipment used in ski touring is not so sophisticated or complicated as that used in downhill skiing. Only the toe of the boot is held in place so that the heel may rise when the ski tourer is striding. This allows more comfort in moving over the countryside, but such a simple binding does not allow the tourer to perform the quick turns and leaps normally associated with downhill skiing. Since an integral part of ski touring is climbing the slope as well as sliding down, climbing waxes which hold the ski in place for steps but allow it to glide when sliding are a necessary part of the ski tourer's equipment. (also called *cross-country, tour skiing*) — see also SKIING; compare DOWNHILL SKIING

ski tow 1 A motor-driven conveyor used for pulling skiers up a slope that usually consists of an endless moving rope which the skier grasps. (also called *rope tow, tow lift*)

2 see SKI LIFT

skittering *fishing* A method of fishing in which a lure or bait is suspended from a long pole by a line approximately the same length as the pole and is pulled or jerked back and forth along the surface. — compare DAPPING

¹skittle A wooden object of any of various shapes that is knocked down by a ball or cheese in skittles. The skittle normally has a 3-inch diameter base and stands approximately a foot high.

²skittle *cricket* To put out a number of successive batsmen relatively quickly and easily. — often used with *out*

skittles A bowling game popular especially in England in which 2 individuals or 2 sides of up to 5 players each take turns tossing or bowling a ball or a round disk (*cheese*) at 9 wooden skittles set up in a diamond arrangement at the opposite end of an alley. The alley is 3 feet wide and 21 feet long from the throwing position to the nearest skittle. Each player has a turn of 3 throws (a *chalk*) in which he seeks to knock down as many skittles as possible and score one point for each. If he knocks down all of the skittles before making his third throw, they are set up again. When each player has played 3 chalks, the scores are compared and the side with the higher score wins the *leg*. A match is won by the side first winning 2 legs.

skull 1 see SCULL

2 *of a player or a ball* To hit a player in the

head. ⟨almost *skulled* by a pitch in batting practice — George Vecsey, *New York Times*⟩

skuller A baseball batting helmet.

skull session or **skull practice** A training class
held by a coach at which he discusses strategy
and diagrams plays. (also called *chalk talk*)

skurfer see SKATEBOARDER

skurfing see SKATEBOARDING

sky To hit the ball high in the air and often almost
straight up.

skydive To jump from an airplane with a parachute and perform maneuvers during free fall
before pulling the rip cord; to engage in skydiving.

skydiver Someone who engages in skydiving.

skydiving The sport of jumping from an airplane
with a parachute and delaying the opening of the
chute for a free-fall period during which the diver
floats or glides through the air or performs various stunts and maneuvers. The sport parachute
is designed with panels missing at strategic
places to facilitate maneuvering. The air rushes
through the openings in a stream pushing the
parachutist in the opposite direction. By turning
the chute, the skydiver is able to maneuver with
a high degree of accuracy and often land exactly
on target. There are 3 distinct events in competition. In style competition, the competitors are
required to perform a number of stunts and maneuvers during a timed interval of free fall and
are judged solely on form. Where or how they
land is immaterial. In accuracy competition, the
diver is judged only on how close he is able to
come to the center of a target, a small disk in the
center of a 6½-yard circle. The third event
(*relative work*) is essentially team competition in
which teams of up to 20 or more divers attempt
to pass a baton or form a star pattern by joining
hands during free fall. (also called *sport parachuting*) — see also FREE FALL

sky surfer Someone who engages in hang gliding
or sky surfing as it is sometimes called.

sky surfing see HANG GLIDING

slab 1 *baseball* The plate on the pitcher's
mound; the rubber.
2 *mountain climbing* A rock face that slopes
at an angle of between 30 and 60 degrees. —
compare GLACIS, OVERHANG, WALL

slalom 1 A race against the clock in which each
competitor individually traverses a zigzag course
around markers. In skiing competition, the skier
must pass between pairs of poles (*gates*) set in
various combinations and at various angles to
the fall line. Certain combinations may allow the

skier to make easy turns while other combinations may require a series of very tight turns; the
skier may be required to go through a gate by
going across the fall line or even slightly uphill.
In international competition, there may be as
many as 75 gates on a course that has a vertical
drop of 650 to 975 feet.

In waterskiing and in motor sports, the slalom
course typically consists of markers (as buoys or
traffic cones) placed in a straight line, and the
competitor has to swing around each, passing
one on the left and the other on the right. Water-
skiers usually use a single slalom ski rather than
the 2 conventional skis. — see also GATE; GIANT
SLALOM, DOWNHILL (*skiing*)
2 An automobile gymkhana.

slalom canoe see KAYAK

slalomist A skier who competes in slalom races.

slalom ski *waterskiing* A special water ski that
is tapered at the back, has a deep metal fin on
the bottom near the rear, has bindings for both
feet, and is used mostly in slalom racing.

slam *wrestling* An illegal action in which an opponent is lifted and dropped or thrown to the
mat so that his upper body makes contact first.

slam dunk *basketball* An unusually forceful
dunk shot.

slant *football* An offensive play in which a particular player moves in a straight line at an angle
to the goal line:
1 A running play in which the ballcarrier moves
into the line at an oblique angle.
2 or **slant-in** A pass pattern in which the receiver runs across the line of scrimmage and then
cuts toward the goal line at about a 30-degree
angle.

slap check *lacrosse* A check made by hitting the
opponent's stick sideways.

slap pass *ice hockey* A pass that a player deflects on to another player without gaining full
control of the puck.

slap shot or **slapper** *ice hockey* A hard shot
made with a swinging stroke in which the stick
blade hits the ice just behind the puck usually
causing the puck to leave the ice.

slash To swing the stick at an opponent in ice
hockey and lacrosse.

slashing The act of swinging the stick at an opponent (as in ice hockey or lacrosse) which results
in a penalty. Slashing is penalized by a minor or
major penalty (at the discretion of the referee)
in ice hockey and box lacrosse and by a suspension of from one to 3 minutes (at the discretion
of the referee) in lacrosse.

slide

sled 1 A vehicle for transportation over snow and ice which consists essentially of a platform on parallel runners. A sled pulled by a team of dogs typically has a wooden platform, wooden rails that extend up in back to form handlebars, and long wooden runners with fiberglass or steel on the bottom. A child's coasting sled usually consists of a wooden platform mounted on steerable steel runners.

2 *football* A device used for blocking practice which consists of a steel framework with one or more large pads on the front that slides along the ground when a player hits and pushes against the pad.

3 Short for *bobsled*.

sledding The use of a sled; the pastime of coasting down a snow-covered slope on a sled.

sled dog A dog (as a husky or malamute) trained to draw a sled.

sled dogger Someone who drives a dogsled team; a dogsled racer.

sleeper 1 *bowling* A pin that is hidden behind another pin in a leave. (also called *barmaid*)

2 *horse racing* A horse that wins after a series of poor performances.

3 *ice hockey* see HANGER

4 *shuffleboard* A disk that is placed near the front part of the scoring area to serve as a blocker for one later placed behind it.

sleeping bag An insulated bag in which a person can sleep outdoors. Sleeping bags used by climbers and backpackers usually consist of 2 layers of a lightweight material (as nylon) filled with insulating material (as goose down). To prevent loss of warmth at the seams, the better bags are constructed with partitions which have the dual function of holding the outer and inner layers together without the necessity of their being sewn directly together and of holding the insulation in place.

¹slice 1 A propelled ball that deviates from its intended course in the direction of the dominant hand of the player propelling it (as to the right when hit by a right-handed player). — compare HOOK

2 A stroke (as in tennis) made by hitting down on the ball with a slicing motion with the racket face open so as to impart backspin.

²slice To hit a slice; to hit a ball with a slicing motion imparting backspin.

slicks *auto racing* Tires with no tread pattern. Slicks are used in virtually all racing on paved courses today because they allow more rubber to be in contact with the road for better traction

and cooler temperatures. The lack of grooves, however, makes them useless in the rain; road racers, who race in the rain, must switch to a more conventional grooved tire for wet tracks.

¹slide 1 *baseball* To approach a base by gliding along the ground headfirst or feetfirst. The base runner resorts to sliding in an effort to avoid being tagged. In approaching the base, he dives or leaps toward the base or just to one side of the base, thrusting one arm or leg out to touch or hook the base. When sliding feetfirst, the player is normally turned so that only one thigh and hip is on the ground. — see also HOOK SLIDE

2 *curling* To glide over the ice in delivering the stone and as part of the follow-through.

3 *football* To move sideways.

4 *surfing* To ride down the face of the wave angling to one side.

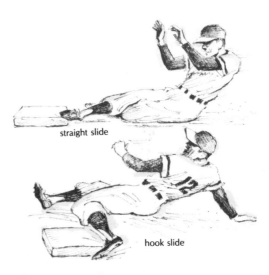

straight slide

hook slide

²slide 1 The action or an instance of sliding: **a** *baseball* A sliding approach to a base made usually feetfirst in order to avoid being tagged. **b** *curling* A sliding follow-through after the delivery of the stone. **c** *surfing* A ride down the face of a wave usually at an angle.

2 The part of a pump-action firearm under the barrel that is slid back to cock the hammer and reload the chamber.

3 *auto racing* A sideways slipping of the car usually under the control of the driver.

4 *sailing* A metal fitting that is attached to the luff of a sail and that slides in a track on the rear of the mast as the sail is hoisted. The use of a slide and track to hold a sail to the mast is not universal. Some boats employ a series of rings on the sail which fit loosely around the mast.

slide chassé *skating* A variation of the chassé in which the original skating foot is lifted and brought forward and held there a moment before being returned to the surface for the new thrust.

slider *baseball* A breaking pitch that is thrown hard like a fastball and breaks in the same direction as a curve but much less sharply and much later than a curve so that it is harder for the batter to detect.

sliding friction arrest see ARREST

sliding seat *rowing* A seat of a racing shell mounted on wheels which move in metal tracks fastened to the frame of the shell. The seat moves about 2 feet and permits the oarsman to use the strength of his legs as well as that of his arms and back in rowing.

sliding tackle *soccer* A tackle which resembles a slide in baseball and is made by leaping forward toward the ball and hooking or kicking the ball while sliding along the ground; hook tackle.

¹sling 1 A length of narrow flat material (as webbing or tubular nylon) sewn or knotted in a loop and used in mountain climbing and caving in making belays, body harnesses, and prusik loops.

2 An adjustable strap attached to a rifle by 2 swivels for use in holding the rifle steady against the shooter's arm while firing.

²sling see CARRY (*badminton*)

slinging *Australian Rules football* A foul that results when a player catches an opponent around the neck or shoulder and attempts to tackle him.

¹slingshot 1 A weapon consisting essentially of a forked or U-shaped stick or frame with an elastic band attached to both prongs that propels small stones or steel balls between the prongs by the sudden release of tension on the band. As a homemade weapon the slingshot typically consists of a forked branch and strips of rubber. Modern slingshots, suitable for target competition as well as small game hunting, often employ steel or aluminum prongs, arm braces for steadiness, archery-type sights for precise aim, and counterbalance weights.

2 *auto racing* A maneuver in which a drafting car pulls out from behind and accelerates past the leading car taking advantage of the reserve power it has as a result of riding in the other car's slipstream. — see DRAFTING

3 *drag racing* A dragster with the engine located in front of the rear wheels and with the driver's seat formed within a narrow roll cage located between or just behind the rear wheels. (also called *rail, rail job*)

²slingshot *auto racing* To pass another car by means of a slingshot. ⟨would try to set up a draft and then *slingshot* past him — John S. Radosta, *New York Times*⟩

¹slip *boxing* To avoid a punch by moving the head to one side.

²slip *cricket* 1 A fielding position just behind and to the off side of the wicketkeeper. The most common slip position is first slip; second and third slips, when used, are progressively farther to the side away from the wicketkeeper.

2 A player occupying a slip position.

slip pitch *baseball* An off-speed pitch gripped with the ball against the palm and the fingertips off the ball and thrown with a fastball motion so that it has little forward rotation and drops as it nears the plate.

¹slipstream An area of reduced air pressure behind a rapidly moving body (as a racing car or a cyclist). By riding in a competitor's slipstream a racer is able to keep up with him without expending the same energy as that competitor, part of whose energy is used to overcome air resistance.

²slipstream To ride in the slipstream of another competitor to take advantage of the reduced air resistance; draft.

slipstreaming see DRAFTING

sloop A fore-and-aft rigged sailboat with a single mast stepped approximately ²/₅ the waterline length back from the bow.

sloop-rigged *of a sailboat* Having a single mast with a triangular mainsail and a triangular jib.

slope soaring *soaring* The practice of soaring on the rising air currents that blow up and over the top of a slope. The pilot generally soars in a figure eight pattern on a course roughly parallel to the ridge. It is of utmost importance that the pilot remain on the windward side of the slope if he intends to stay in the air, for once beyond the crest, the air no longer rises.

slo pitch see SOFTBALL

sloppy *of a dirt racetrack* Having puddles of water after a heavy rain before the water has had time to soak in. A sloppy track is usually not appreciably slower than a fast track. — compare FAST, GOOD, HEAVY, MUDDY, SLOW

slot 1 *football* A gap between an end and tackle in an offensive line.

2 *ice hockey* An area without precise boundaries directly in front of the goal from which an attacking forward has the best opportunity for a successful shot.

slotback *football* A back who lines up just behind the slot between a tackle and end.

slot T or **slot formation** *football* A variation of the T formation employing a slotback.

slough off *of a basketball player* To move away from the opponent one has been guarding or is supposed to be guarding in order to help a teammate guard a more dangerous scorer (as the opposing center) or in order to be in position to get a defensive rebound.

slow *of a playing surface* **1** Relatively soft or yielding so that the movement or bounce of a ball is slowed.

2 *of a bowling lane* Having a finish that slows the ball and causes it to hook relatively early.

3 *of a dirt racetrack* Thoroughly soaked by rain usually without puddles but soft and yielding enough to cause slower running times. — compare FAST, GOOD, HEAVY, MUDDY, SLOPPY

slow ball A slow pitch (as in sandlot baseball).

slowdown see STALL

slow fire *shooting* Competition in which each competitor is allowed usually one minute for each round. — compare RAPID FIRE, TIMED FIRE

slow gait *equitation* A gait that is a variation of the rack and is characterized by a slight swaying from side to side.

slow pill *horse racing* A depressant illegally administered to a horse before a race to slow it down and keep it from winning.

slow pitch see SOFTBALL

slow whistle **1** *ice hockey* see DELAYED WHISTLE **2** *lacrosse* A delay by the official in blowing the whistle to stop play after a foul has been committed by a defending player against an attacking player when the attacking player maintains possession of the ball and continues to move toward a potential score. The foul is signaled, but play is not stopped until the attacking player shoots or passes the ball to a teammate who shoots or until the player breaks off the direct offensive move. The slow whistle is intended to avoid penalizing the attacking team by stopping play when a score appears imminent. If the slow whistle is for a technical foul and a goal is scored, the penalty is not enforced. On a personal foul, the penalty is enforced whether or not a goal was scored.

slugfest **1** *baseball* A game characterized by high scores and many hits.

2 *boxing* A bout between two sluggers with each attempting to knock out the other and neither concentrating on defensive tactics.

slugger **1** *baseball* A long-ball hitter.

2 *boxing* A boxer who depends mostly on the strength of his punch and little on defense and boxing skill. (also called *puncher*)

slugging average *baseball* A number between 0 and 4 carried to 3 decimal places that is obtained by dividing the total bases reached on safe hits by the number of official times at bat and that is used as a measure of the batter's effectiveness at making extra-base hits. Example: A player who has 388 total bases in 458 times at bat has a slugging average of .847.

¹slump A period of poor or losing play by a team or an individual.

²slump *of a team or a player* To be in a slump.

slurve *baseball* A pitch that curves more than a slider but that travels faster than a curve.

small ball *bowling* A delivery that has little action on it and consequently must hit exactly in the pocket for a strike.

small-bore see SHOOTING

small craft warning *boating* A red pennant (during the day) or a red light above a white light (at night) to indicate that winds up to 33 knots (38 mph) and sea conditions dangerous to small craft operations are forecast.

small game Game birds and small animals (as rabbits, squirrels, and woodchucks) hunted for sport that are not classified as big game.

smart money Well-informed bettors; bettors thought to have inside information.

¹smash **1** A hard overhand stroke (as in tennis, badminton, or squash) that drives the ball or shuttlecock down at an angle into the opponent's court or to the front wall.

2 *baseball* A hard-hit ball.

²smash To make a smash; to hit the ball or shuttlecock down with a hard overhand stroke.

smasher A player who smashes; a player noted for his smashes.

¹smoke *baseball* A fastball; fastballs. (also called *heat*) ⟨if a guy's going to hit you . . . he certainly isn't going to throw a spitter — he gives you *smoke* — Tony Conigliaro⟩ ⟨looked for . . . *smoke* and got instead two slow breaking balls — Arnold Hano, *Sport*⟩

²smoke **1** *of a baseball pitcher* To throw fastballs to a particular batter.

2 *skeet* To hit a target with a full pattern of shot so that it bursts in a puff resembling smoke.

¹smoothbore A shotgun.

smoothbore

²smoothbore *of a firearm* Having a smooth-surfaced bore.

smother *of an ice hockey goalkeeper* To fall on the puck to prevent the scoring of a goal.

smother shot *platform tennis* A shot that bounces high and just brushes the backstop as it comes down so that the receiver has very little room in which to swing at the ball as it comes off the backstop.

snaffle see BIT

snakebit *of a team or a player* Having a spell of bad luck; playing as if jinxed.

snake guide see GUIDE

¹snap **1** *football* **a** The method of putting the ball in play from scrimmage to begin a down in which the center hands or passes the ball back between his legs to a back positioned behind him. **b** The act of making a snap; a ball passed back by the center on the snap. ⟨fumbled the center *snap* and lost two yards — Ron Fimrite, *Sports Illustrated*⟩ **2** The name for the center on a Canadian football team. **3** *trapshooting* A shell that misfires.

²snap *football* To hand or pass the ball back between the legs to begin a down.

snap catch *lacrosse* A catch in which the stick is brought toward the ball and at the moment of contact is snapped around to keep the ball from bouncing out.

snapdown *wrestling* A takedown maneuver in which a wrestler from a position facing his opponent jumps back as the opponent dives for his feet, pushes the opponent to the mat, and then jumps around behind the opponent to secure a hold.

snap for goal *Australian Rules football* A hurried kick for a goal.

snapkick *karate* A kick to the front or side made by raising the leg and kicking the foot out and back with a snapping motion, moving only the lower leg.

snaplink see CARABINER

snap pass *ice hockey* A quick pass made by snapping the wrists forward to move the stick instead of taking a backswing and sweeping the stick into the puck. (also called *wrist pass*)

snap ring see CARABINER

snap shooting *hunting* Shooting (as with a shotgun) by bringing the gun to the shoulder and pointing it at the target in a single action and firing almost as soon as the stock touches the shoulder.

snap swivel *fishing* A swivel that has a snap on one end for fastening lures to the end of a line.

¹snatch *weight lifting* A lift in which the lifter raises the weight from the floor to a position directly overhead with the arms straight in a single motion. The lifter is not restricted in the movement of his feet during the lift, and he normally squats or lunges under the bar as it is on its way up; when the bar is at arm's length overhead, he stands. The lift is completed when the lifter has been standing and holding the weight overhead for a specified length of time (as 3 seconds). — compare CLEAN AND JERK, PRESS

snatch

404

²snatch *weight lifting* To lift a specified amount in the snatch.

sneak 1 *football* SEE QUARTERBACK SNEAK

2 *shuffleboard* A disk placed behind a pilot.

sneakboat or **sneakbox** A small flat-bottomed boat that is covered with a deck and that is used for duck hunting. The sneakboat is extremely shallow and has a small cockpit in the middle in which the hunter sits or lies. It may be propelled by oars or by sails on a removable mast.

¹snell *fishing* A short line (as of nylon) that is attached to a fishhook and that has a loop at the end for easy attachment to the fishing line.

²snell *fishing* To attach a snell to a hook.

¹snick *cricket* A hit ball that just glances off the edge of the bat and goes straight back usually to the wicketkeeper or to the slips.

²snick *of a cricket batsman* To hit a snick.

snooker SEE BILLIARDS

snookered *of a snooker player* Unable to shoot directly at the proper object ball because one or more other object balls are in the way. When a player is snookered, he must strike the proper object ball first or he fouls.

snorkel A usually J-shaped rubber or plastic tube that has a mouthpiece at the short end and is used for breathing by a skin diver while swimming facedown on the surface of the water. — see illustration at SKIN DIVER

snorkeler Someone who swims on the surface with a face mask and a snorkel; a skin diver.

snorkeling The use of a snorkel; skin diving.

snout *mountain climbing* The lower end of a glacier.

snowblindness *mountain climbing* Inflammation of the cornea of the eye (comparable to sunburn on the skin) and extreme sensitivity to light caused by the glare of sunlight on snow and ice and reflected ultraviolet light on unprotected eyes.

snow cave *mountain climbing* A cave or burrow dug in a snow bank as a place to bivouac.

snow farming The care and conditioning of the snow on a ski slope.

snow goggles *mountain climbing* Goggles with tinted lenses that are worn to prevent snowblindness.

snow gun or **snow machine** *skiing* A device for spraying water mist into the air to make man-made snow.

¹snowmobile A vehicle designed to travel over snow that is usually powered by a 2-stroke internal-combustion engine, that runs on an endless belt and 2 steerable skis controlled by motorcy-

cle-type handlebars, and that is usually ridden by straddling a long padded seat. (also called *ski mobile, ski sled*)

²snowmobile To drive or ride on a snowmobile.

snowmobiler Someone who drives a snowmobile.

snowmobiling The sport or recreation of driving or riding on a snowmobile. Competition for snowmobile drivers is similar to that for automobile drivers with races and gymkhana events.

snow picket *mountain climbing* An aluminum stake about 4 feet long that is driven into snow to serve as a belay anchor.

¹snowplow 1 *skiing* A stemming of both skis in order to descend slowly, slow down, or stop. The snowplow has traditionally been one of the first movements learned in skiing, and by using it the skier can progress to various simple turns. **2** *skating* A stop made by pushing the heels of ice skates out in opposite directions so that the blades scrape the ice and stop the skater.

snowplow

²snowplow To make a snowplow. ⟨*snowplowed* to a stop⟩

snowplow turn *skiing* A turn made by stemming the skis as in a snowplow and weighting one ski so as to turn in the direction in which the weighted ski is pointing.

snow ring SEE BASKET (*skiing*)

¹snowshoe A lightweight relatively oval wooden

snowshoe

frame (as of hickory or ash) strung with rawhide webbing that can be attached to the boot by a simple leather harness and worn in pairs for walking over snow without sinking. Near the front there is an opening in the webbing for the toe of the wearer's boot to pass through when striding. Snowshoes are made in 2 basic styles: the long narrow trail shoe and the shorter and broader bearpaw. The trail shoe, in which the frame is brought together at the rear to form a tail, is usually used in open country where its length is not an inconvenience and where the tail can drag in the snow on each step to give stability. The bearpaw shoe, which is broader, shorter, and usually has a rounded back is better suited for walking in woods and brush. On many snowshoes, the front is slightly turned up so that is will not catch in the snow when moved forward for each step. Snowshoes are also available with neoprene webbing instead of rawhide and some manufacturers offer snowshoes of molded plastic.

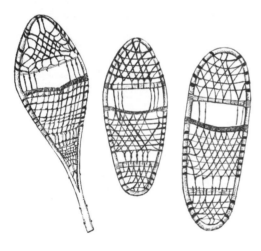

snowshoes: left, trail; center, bearpaw; right, Green Mountain modified bearpaw

²**snowshoe** To walk on snowshoes.

snowshoeing The sport or recreation of walking on snowshoes.

snowshoer Someone who goes snowshoeing.

snub *sailing* To check a line that is playing out by turning it around a cleat, bollard, or post.

Soap Box Derby A service mark for a contest in which youngsters of ages 11 to 15 construct and race coasting cars down a special sloping course. The cars have no propulsion system or brakes. Each car must be designed and built by the youth who races it, and its cost is strictly limited by the rules. Winners from local competitions in United States and Canadian cities compete in the finals, the All-American Soap Box Derby, in Akron, Ohio, for scholarship prizes.

soaring The sport of piloting a sailplane and remaining aloft for extended periods by taking advantage of lift provided by rising air currents. The sailplane is either towed to a suitable height by an airplane or launched from the ground by a tow from an automobile or a huge winch. Soaring is totally dependent on atmospheric conditions, for without rising air the pilot would be able to stay aloft only a very short time. The most common form of soaring is thermal soaring in which the pilot soars over the countryside taking advantage of the rising warm air over fields warmed by sunshine or over cities to regain altitude for additional soaring. It is possible to make cross-country flights by making use of available thermals. Slope soaring, which is basically soaring back and forth just over the face of a slope, is a way of enjoying the sport in areas where there are few thermals. The plane is kept aloft by the air currents that flow up over the crest of the slope. On flights away from the soaring center, a recovery crew normally follows on the ground hauling a trailer to pick up the plane and pilot when he has landed. Though soaring is basically an individual-participation sport, there are competitions for maximum height during a flight and for maximum distance on a one-way flight, and speed contests held on triangular courses. (also called *sailplaning*) — see also SLOPE SOARING; GLIDER, SAILPLANE; TOWING

soccer A game played between 2 teams of 11 players using an inflated ball on a rectangular playing field having a goal at each end with the object to drive the ball past the opposing goalkeeper into the goal for a score and to prevent the opposing team from scoring. The ball is propelled mostly by kicking. While the ball is in play only the goalkeeper within the penalty area is permitted to catch the ball or to touch it with his hands. Players are not permitted to hold, push, or trip an opponent, but they may bump him with a shoulder charge, and are allowed to intercept passes and to attempt to kick the ball away from the opponent. For rule violations (as handling the ball) and for fouls (as tripping, shoving, or kicking an opponent) the offending team is penalized by the awarding of a free kick — an

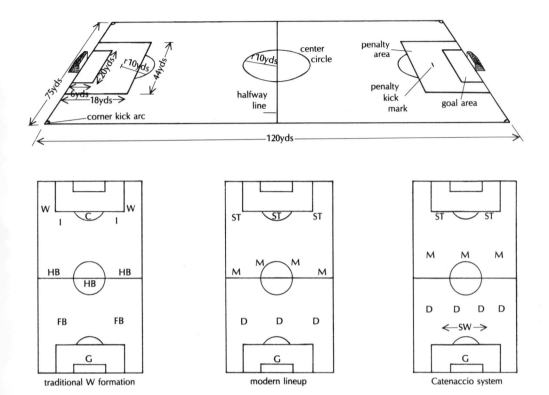

soccer: W wing forward; I inside forward; C center forward; HB halfback; FB fullback; G goalkeeper; ST striker; M midfielder; D defender; SW sweeper

unhindered kick at a stationary ball from the point of the infraction — to the other team. For fouls committed within the penalty area by the defending team, the opposing team is awarded a penalty kick — a free kick directly at the goal. Play is started by a kickoff in which a player kicks the ball to a teammate from the center of the field, and it is continuous, stopping only when a goal is scored, when the ball is driven out of bounds, or when the referee stops play for a violation, foul, or injury. When the ball is driven over the touchline, it is put in play by a throw-in by a member of the opposing side. A ball driven over the goal line but not into the goal by the attacking team is returned to play with a goal kick by the opposing goalkeeper. When it is driven over the goal line by the defending team, the ball is put in play by the attacking team with a corner kick. Soccer is normally played in two 45-minute halves, though school and college games are often played in quarters. (also called *association football*) — see also DIRECT FREE KICK, INDIRECT FREE KICK, PENALTY KICK

soccer ball throw A competitive track and field event in which a soccer ball is thrown for distance.

soft 1 *of a thrown or hit ball* Propelled without great force. ⟨a *soft* shot⟩ ⟨a *soft* stroke will produce more curve than a hard one — Willie Mosconi⟩ ⟨let a *soft* double-play bouncer go right past him — Leonard Koppett, *New York Times*⟩ **2** *of a grass racing course* Wet and yielding with the result that running times are slow.

3 *of a bowling lane* Easy to make a strike on.

softball 1 A game similar to baseball that is played on a smaller field with bases 60 feet apart using a ball larger than a baseball which is pitched underhand. There are 2 basic versions of softball, fast pitch and slow pitch, each of which uses the same equipment and playing area

407

and, except for a few variations, essentially the same rules. Fast pitch softball is played with 9 players as baseball is. A good softball pitcher can throw the ball underhand as fast as a baseball pitcher can throw a baseball overhand and because of this pitchers play a major role in fast pitch. The action is fast and base runners are permitted to steal, provided they do not leave the base before the ball leaves the pitcher's hand.

Slow pitch was created so that older and less athletic players could compete in a game that would have more emphasis on hitting and fielding than on pitching. Slow pitch differs from fast pitch in these essential points: the pitch must be thrown at moderate speed and must travel in an arc from the time it leaves the pitcher's hand (at least 3 feet above the point of release but not more than 10 feet high). There are 10 players on a side with the extra player typically playing a short outfield position. Bunting and base stealing are not permitted, the base runner cannot leave the base until the ball has reached the batter, and a batter who is hit by a pitch is not awarded first base. A variation of regular slow pitch softball is played with a ball 16 inches in circumference. The rules are the same, but the distance between bases is only 55 feet for men and 50 feet for women.

The name softball is a bit of a misnomer since the ball is nearly as hard as a baseball. The game is generally understood to have originated as an indoor game around 1887, was then referred to as indoor baseball, and was probably played with a softer ball.

Baseball terms are common in softball, and in this book separate definitions for softball have not been written when a term applies to both sports.

2 The ball used in the game of softball. — see BALL

softball throw A competitive track and field event in which a softball is thrown for distance.

soft load *trapshooting* A shot that fires with just enough power to propel the wads and load out of the barrel but not to the target. — compare DUD

sole **1** *golf* The bottom of a clubhead.
2 *skiing* The bottom surface of a ski; the part in contact with the snow.

sole kick or **sole of the foot kick** or **sole trap** A kick (as in soccer or speedball) in which the sole of the shoe is placed on top of the ball and the ball is then pushed hard to the rear.

soleplate *skiing* A metal plate attached to the top of a ski to raise the skier's boot just high enough to make proper contact with the binding.

sole trap see SOLE KICK

solid **1** *of a team* Having good players at most or at certain positions. ⟨*solid* on defense but looking for a capable quarterback⟩
2 *of a player* Having won the starting role at a particular position. ⟨he is *solid* at tight end⟩

Soling *sailing* A sloop-rigged keelboat of a one-design class that is 26½ feet long, has a sail area of 233 square feet plus a 350-square-foot spinnaker, and carries a crew of 3.

solo To operate an airplane, sailplane, or balloon by oneself during training.

solocross An automobile gymkhana.

solo home run *baseball* A home run hit with no men on base. — compare GRAND SLAM

somersault **1** A movement in which the body turns forward or backward through a complete revolution with the feet moving up and over the head. In tumbling, the somersault is made completely off the floor. When the body is in contact with the floor, the movement is called a *roll*. In diving, a somersault is any backward or forward rotation of the body. Rotation through a half turn from a standing position to a headfirst entry is a half somersault. A complete revolution with a feetfirst entry is a full somersault. If the diver rotates an additional half turn and enters the water headfirst, it is a 1½ somersault.
2 *track and field* A method of long-jumping in which the jumper turns a forward somersault in the air to gain extra distance.

sommie A somersault in gymnastics.

sooping *curling* The sweeping of the ice ahead of a moving stone.

sorrel A horse with a brown coat that is lighter than chestnut and often with a white mane and tail.

sort or **sort out** *auto racing* To determine precisely what needs to be fixed or improved in a racing car usually by extensive driving over the racecourse before a race.

sounding *boating* A measurement of the depth of the water (as by means of a pole or weighted line).

soup *surfing* The fast-moving white water that rolls shoreward as a wave breaks.

sour apple *bowling* A split which leaves the 5, 7, and 10 pins standing. — see illustration of pin arrangement at BOWLING

southpaw A left-hander. The term originated in baseball in reference to a left-handed pitcher.

Baseball parks are commonly oriented with home plate toward the south or west so that the afternoon sun does not shine in the batter's eyes. A left-handed pitcher, therefore, facing toward the west would be throwing with his south paw.

spaceframe An automobile chassis consisting chiefly of tubular metal bars joined together to form a basic supporting structure on which the body is built. — compare MONOCOQUE

spade mashie *golf* An old name for the number 6 iron.

span The distance between the thumb hole and the finger holes on a bowling ball.

¹spar *sailing* A stout metal or wooden pole (as a mast, boom, or spinnaker pole) that supports rigging.

²spar To engage in a practice or exhibition bout (as in boxing or karate).

spar buoy see BUOY

¹spare *bowling* The knocking down of all 10 pins with the first 2 balls in a frame. For making a spare, the bowler is given a bonus of the number of pins knocked down with the first ball of the next frame which is added to his score for the frame in which he got the spare. — see also BONUS; compare STRIKE

²spare *bowling* To make a spare.

sparring *wrestling* The action before a takedown during which the wrestlers are on their feet grappling with each other.

sparring partner *boxing* Someone who spars with a boxer in training for a bout. The boxer in training usually hires several sparring partners. An established boxer does not usually work as someone else's sparring partner.

spear **1** To catch a ball (as in baseball) with a sudden outward thrust of the arm. ⟨dived to his right to *spear* a hard line drive⟩
2 *box lacrosse* To jab an opponent with the head of the stick.
3 *football* To block an opponent by ramming him in the chest with the helmet.
4 *ice hockey* To jab an opponent with the end of the stick blade.

spear blocking *football* The illegal blocking of an opponent by ramming him with the helmet.

spearfish To engage in spearfishing.

spearfisherman or **spearfisher** Someone who engages in spearfishing.

spearfishing The sport of taking fish with a spear gun while skin diving.

spear gun A pneumatic or elastic band-powered gun that shoots barbed spears and is used in spearfishing. — see illustration at SKIN DIVER

spearhead *Australian Rules football* A full forward who is noted for his ability to kick goals.

spearing The act of jabbing or of attempting to jab an opponent with the point of the stick blade or with the head of the stick in ice hockey or box lacrosse which results in a minor or major penalty.

spearing

Special Olympics An international program of sports competition similar to the Olympic Games held for mentally retarded children and adults.

special team or **specialty team** *football* A team made up chiefly of reserves that is used on kicking plays (as kickoffs, punts, and field goal attempts) in order to rest most of the regulars and spare them the risk of injury which can occur during these plays. The injury risk is generally higher on kickoffs and punts than on scrimmage plays because they usually involve blocking or tackling someone who is running down the field at top speed. (also called *bomb squad*, *Kamikaze corps*, *suicide squad*)

specialty teamer A football player on a specialty team.

special weight race *horse racing* A race in which the weights are assigned without reference to the weight-for-age scale. The assigned weights are even except for allowances for sex and for apprentice jockeys. Special weight races are most often held for the top maidens.

spectator sport A sport (as baseball, football, or auto racing) that appeals to spectators as distinguished from a sport (as hunting, fishing, or scuba diving) which is engaged in principally for the pleasure it affords the participant.

speed

speed **1** The ability to move or to run fast. ⟨if you can keep the ball in the park, their *speed* isn't that good; you can get a lot of double plays — Jim Palmer⟩
2 The ability of a baseball pitcher to throw a fastball; a fastball. ⟨has a good curve but no *speed*⟩
3 *horse racing* The amount of time taken by a particular horse to run a race. ⟨*speed* handicappers⟩
— **at speed** At relatively high speed. ⟨has that deep, raspy idle and the competitive howl *at speed* — Road & Track⟩

speed-a-way A game played between 2 teams of 11 players on a field hockey field with the object to kick the ball past the opposing goalkeeper into the goal or to pass or carry it over the opponent's goal line to score and to prevent the opposing team from scoring. Speed-a-way, like the similar speedball, is based on playing a ground ball — one lying or bouncing on the ground — only with the feet (as in soccer) and an aerial ball — one kicked up and not having bounced more than once — by running with it and passing it with the hands (as in football or rugby). Players may run with the ball and throw it to teammates, but they lose possession of the ball if tagged by an opponent while carrying it. A player about to be tagged may pass the ball to a teammate, or put the ball on the ground and play it with the feet to avoid losing possession. It is permissible to guard an opponent and to seek to take away the ball, but a player may not physically obstruct or interfere with an opponent. The game is conducted much like soccer or field hockey, from which it was derived. Infractions are penalized by awarding the other team a free kick or, if the infraction was committed by the defending team within the striking circle, a penalty corner. A ball driven over the boundary line is put in play by a throw-in. A team scores 3 points for a field goal when the ball is kicked into the goal under the crossbar and 2 points for a touchdown when an aerial ball is carried or passed over the goal line.

speed bag *boxing* An inflated teardrop-shaped leather punching bag that is suspended at head height close to a support so that it bounces back quickly when struck. It is hit repeatedly in training to develop speed and coordination. — compare HEAVY BAG

speedball A game played between 2 teams of 11 players on a football field with the object of kicking a ball between the uprights of the goal or passing the ball over the end line to score and preventing the opposing team from scoring. The ball is moved by kicking or dribbling it along the ground (as in soccer) or passing it (as in basketball) when it has been caught on the fly from a kick. Players are not permitted to run with the ball, but when catching the ball on the run they may juggle it — toss the ball over the head of a defender and run past him to catch it on the other side. This play is similar to the air dribble in basketball. Speedball is played very much like soccer; players take essentially the same positions, and the usual soccer rules regarding tackling and obstruction apply. A ball driven out of bounds may be put in play by the other team by a throw or a kick. Violations, such as improper handling of the ball, result in the opponents' getting the ball out of bounds. Violations committed in a player's own end zone result in a penalty kick. Fouls are penalized by awarding the opposing team one or 2 penalty kicks. A team gets 3 points for kicking the ball under the crossbar (*field goal*) and 2 points for drop-kicking the ball over the crossbar. A touchdown, a successful forward pass over the end line, and a penalty kick count one point each. The game is played in four 10-minute quarters.

speedboat A motorboat designed principally for speed rather than for pleasure cruising.

speedboating The act or sport of driving a speedboat.

speedbag

speed shop A shop that sells custom automotive equipment.

speed skater Someone who competes in speed skating.

speed skating The sport of racing on skates. Speed skating encompasses racing on both ice skates and roller skates. International *ice racing,* as speed skating on ice is sometimes called, is conducted on a closed oval course 400 meters long. It is divided into 2 separate lanes separated by a curb of snow. Two skaters at a time compete against the clock with each staying within his own lane. On the back straight is an area where the skaters change lanes. This is done so that each will have an opportunity to have the shorter inside lane on one turn in each lap. Races are conducted at distances of 500, 1500, 5000, 10,000 meters for men and 500, 1000,1500 and 3000 meters for women. In ice speed skating, competitors compete in several events and are judged on an overall score as well as on each individual race. Speed roller skating is conducted essentially the same as the ice form except that the track has a single lane used by the competitors, and the competitors are judged solely on the individual races, not in an overall category.

speed trap A measured stretch of a racecourse over which electronic timing devices measure the speed of a moving vehicle (as a racing car or a dragster). The trap typically consists of 2 parallel electric eye beams separated by a precisely measured distance. The timer starts when the vehicle breaks the first beam of light and stops when it breaks the second. At a drag strip the speed trap normally has beams 66 feet before and after the finish line. (also called *time trap, trap, traps*)

speedway **1** A usually oval racecourse for automobiles thay may be from ¼ mile to 3 miles long and that usually has banked turns.
2 Motorcycle racing for 4-man teams on a short flat unpaved closed course 350 yards long. A program consists of 20 races with each rider competing in 5 races so that during the course of the competition he has competed against every other competitor. The motorcycles used are lightweight machines with rigid frames and no brakes. The riders normally ride standing up and typically slide the machine sideways through the turns. Individuals are scored according to their overall placing in all races, and team scores are determined from the individual team members' scores.

speed work *track and field* Sprints run in practice as part of training especially for a distance or middle distance runner in order to accustom him to the faster pace required for a kick or for overtaking a leader during the longer race.

speedy cut An injury to the rear of a horse's foreleg just above the hoof as a result of being struck with one of the hind feet when running or trotting.

spelunk To engage in spelunking.

spelunker Someone who engages in spelunking.

spelunking The sport of exploring caves. Mountain climbing techniques and terms are commonly employed in spelunking.

¹spike **1** A sharp nail-like or chisel-like metal projection fixed to the sole of a baseball, track, or golf shoe for traction.
2 *volleyball* The act or an instance of spiking the ball.

²spike **1** To hit or cut someone with the spikes of a baseball or track shoe.
2 *football* To throw the ball down hard especially in the end zone after scoring a touchdown.
3 *volleyball* To drive the ball into the opponent's court at a sharp angle by jumping close to the net and hitting the ball down from above the top of the net.

spiker *volleyball* A player who spikes the ball.
— compare SETTER

spikes A pair of baseball or track shoes with spikes attached.

spiking line see ATTACKING LINE

spiller **1** *bowling* A strike gained on an imperfect delivery as a result of luck.
2 *surfing* A wave that breaks slowly and evenly.
— compare PLUNGER

spill wind *sailing* To luff or slacken the sheet controlling the mainsail of a boat in order to let out the wind to keep the boat from heeling over too far.

¹spin **1** To turn around usually in a complete circle.
2 or **spin out** *of an auto racing driver* To lose control of a car and slide around often in one or more complete circles sometimes leaving the roadway.
3 *fishing* To fish or cast with spinning equipment.
4 *skating* To make several revolutions in place on one or both skates.

²spin **1 a** Rotation imparted to a ball by striking it off center or with a glancing blow so that it bounces or rebounds at more or less of an angle than normal; English. **b** A stroke (as in tennis) made with spin.
2 or **spinout** *auto racing* A loss of control of

a car with the rear swinging out and around so that the car usually makes one or more complete circles.

3 *cricket* see LEG SPIN, OFF SPIN

4 *skating* A series of consecutive turns on one or both skates performed in place. The spin may be slow or quite fast in any of several positions from sitting to upright, and from a camel to a lay-back position.

spin bowler or **spinner** *cricket* A bowler who specializes in bowling balls that have spin that makes them rise sharply to the right or left when bouncing. — see also LEG SPIN, OFF SPIN; compare FAST BOWLER

spin cast *fishing* To cast with spin casting equipment.

spin casting *fishing* The casting of bait or an artificial lure using a spin casting rod and a spin casting reel. — see also SPINNING

spin casting reel *fishing* A reel with a fixed spool that is similar to and functions like a spinning reel but which is enclosed by a hemispherical or cone-like hood with a hole in the front for the line to pass through and which has a push-button control for releasing the winding cup for casting. (also called *push-button reel*) — see also SPINNING REEL; see illustration at REEL

spin casting rod *fishing* a casting rod used with a spin casting reel.

spine *archery* The properties of stiffness, resilience, and elasticity of the shaft of an arrow.

spinnaker *sailing* A large balloon-like triangular sail set forward of the mast on a spinnaker pole on the side opposite the mainsail when sailing before the wind or on a broad reach. Because of its shape, the spinnaker catches a large volume of wind and greatly improves the speed of the boat on a run or reach. The spinnaker is of no use in sailing into the wind and is usually stored in a special box or tube under the deck at the bow of the boat.

spinnaker pole *sailing* A pole that is used to hold the tack of the spinnaker out from the mast. There is a fitting at each end of the pole that allows the end to be attached to the mast fitting and also to each bottom corner of the spinnaker.

spinner **1** *cricket* **a** A spin bowler. **b** A delivery that has off spin or leg spin.

2 *fishing* A lure that consists of an oval or teardrop-shaped blade that whirls around a shaft reflecting light in a series of intermittent flashes as it is pulled through the water. A bare or baited hook or a fly is fastened to the end of the shaft behind the blade.

spinner play *football* A single-wing offensive play in which the fullback receives the snap and makes a full 360-degree turn toward the line making or faking handoffs to the other backs as they cut close by him.

spinning *fishing* The casting of bait or an artificial lure using a spinning rod and spinning reel. In spinning, as in bait casting, the weight of the lure pulls out the line during the cast. Because the fixed-spool reel does not revolve, however, the line and lures used in spinning and in spin casting may be extremely light in contrast with the relatively heavy lures required to turn the spool of a bait casting reel. Casting with spinning equipment is greatly simplified since there is no need to learn to apply thumb control to prevent backlashes as in bait casting. — compare BAIT CASTING, FLY CASTING

spinning reel *fishing* A reel with a fixed spool that is mounted usually underneath the rod with the spool axis in line with the rod. The spool is open at the front and is surrounded on the sides and back by a cup which revolves around the spool as a handle is turned. A pickup bail, which is locked out of the way during the cast, is mounted on the cup so that it snaps into place and catches the line winding it on the spool as the handle is turned. During the winding, the spool moves in and out so that the line is wound evenly. Though the spool normally does not revolve, it is designed with a drag mechanism that allows it to turn when the line is pulled out by a hooked fish. The drag adjustment control is located on the front of the spool. — see illustration at REEL

spinning rod *fishing* A relatively flexible fishing rod commonly made of fiberglass that is characterized by a series of progressively smaller ring guides, from a very large butt guide to the tip top, mounted on the under side of the rod. The rings allow the line to spiral off the reel freely.

spinout see SPIN

spin out see SPIN

spiral **1** *football* **a** The rotation of the ball around the long axis during a well-thrown pass or a well-kicked punt. **b** A punt or a pass in which the ball rotates around its long axis.

2 *skating* A body position assumed chiefly in skating an edge. For women, the spiral is simply an arabesque position. Men normally assume an upright position with the arms out to the sides and the free leg crossed behind the skating leg, stretched out to the opposite side with the foot held close to but not touching the surface. The men's spiral is often called the *Hayes Jenkins spiral* in honor of the American skater who first performed it. Originally the term *spiral* referred to a large edge skated slowly in an ever-decreasing diameter. Today because of crowded programs skaters have no time for the long graceful spiral glide and simply refer to the position as a spiral.

ladies' spiral in arabesque position; men's spiral

spitball or **spitter** *baseball* A pitch thrown much like a fastball but with the ball or fingers moistened with saliva or some other lubricant so that the ball slips from the fingers with little rotation and breaks sharply downward as it nears the plate. The spitball was officially banned in 1920, but practicing spitballers were permitted to continue using it until retirement. Although the last legal spitball was thrown by Burleigh Grimes in 1934, the pitch has reputedly continued in surreptitious use down to the present.

spitballer *baseball* A pitcher noted for throwing the spitball.

spitter see SPITBALL

¹split **1 a** To end a game in a tie. ⟨winning four games and *splitting* one — *New York Times*⟩ **b** To finish a series of games with the same number of victories as the rival team. ⟨they *split* the doubleheader⟩
2 *bowling* To have a split after the first delivery.
3 *of an offensive lineman in football* To line up wide of the formation.

²split **1** *bowling* A situation after the first ball has been delivered in which 2 or more pins — but not the headpin — remain standing with one or more pins down between them or the pin directly ahead of one or both of them down. A leave of the 4 and 6 pins is a split because the 5 pin is missing from between them. A leave of the 9 and 10 pins is a split because the 6 pin in front of them is down. Most splits are referred to by the numbers of the pins remaining (as a 6-7-10 split) but some of them have names. — see BABY SPLIT, BEDPOST, BIG FOUR, DOUBLE PINOCHLE, POCKET SPLIT, SOUR APPLE
2 *football* see GAP
3 *gymnastics* A sitting position in which the legs are extended in opposite directions. In the regular split the gymnast is facing toward one leg and the knee of the front leg is turned up while that of the other leg is toward the floor. In the straddle split, the legs are out to either side with the insides of both legs to the floor.

regular split; straddle split

4 *weight lifting* A lunge used by the lifter to get his body down under the weight in the clean and jerk or the snatch.

split decision *boxing* A decision awarded by a majority but not all of the officials.

split end *football* **1** A pass receiver who lines up on the end of the line several yards wide of the rest of the formation.
2 The position played by split end.

split jump *skating* A jump from a backward edge of one foot assisted by a toe pick or toe point from the free foot, with a half turn in the air during which the performer kicks his legs up and out to each side nearly parallel to the surface in a split, and a return to the forward edge of the same or opposite foot.

split lean *gymnastics* A straddle split in which the body is brought forward until the chest touches the floor.

splits The recorded times for the leader at specific intervals (as every quarter mile) in a distance race in horse racing or track and field.

split shot see SHOT *(fishing)*

split T *football* A variation of the T formation in which there is a normal space between the guards and center, a wider space between the tackles and guards, and a still wider space between the ends and tackles. (also called *spread T*)

split tackle *soccer* A tackle executed by keeping one foot in place and stretching the other out to knock the ball away from the opponent with the result that the tackler winds up in a position similar to a split.

split the defense *ice hockey* To carry the puck between 2 opposing defensemen.

split the uprights *football* To make a successful field goal or point after touchdown.

spoiler 1 A team with no chance of becoming league or conference champion that spoils the chances of a potential championship team by upsetting them.
2 A long narrow plate along the upper surface of an airplane or a sailplane wing that can be raised to increase drag and reduce lift or speed.
3 An air deflector on a racing car which breaks up the flow of air to help increase traction at high speed.

sponge *table tennis* A paddle with a layer of sponge rubber between the wood and the pebbled rubber face. — see PADDLE

spool A cylindrical device (as in a fishing reel) on which fishing line is wound.

spoon 1 *fishing* A metal lure that is shaped like the bowl of a spoon and that wobbles when pulled through the water. (also called *wobbler*)
2 *golf* An old name for the number 3 wood.

spoor *hunting* Signs (as tracks, droppings, or the remains of food) that a wild animal has been in the area.

sport A recreational or competitive activity which involves a degree of physical exertion or which requires skill in the playing of an object (as a ball, disk, or shuttlecock) for scoring. There is a wide divergence of opinion as to what constitutes a sport, but for the purposes of this dictionary the term encompasses races, athletic contests in which the outcome is in doubt, and outdoor physical recreations such as hunting and fishing, hiking, and sailing, but excludes board and card games and children's games.

sport car see SPORTS CAR

sporterize To convert a military rifle into a hunting rifle usually by substituting a new stock and lighter barrel.

Sportface A trademark used for a synthetic playing surface for tennis courts.

sport fish A fish that is sought with hook and line for the sport it affords the angler when hooked. The term is often used of both freshwater and marine fish and is often interchangeable with *game fish*. Some marine fish that are considered sport fish and are caught on rod and reel may also be actively sought by commercial fishermen who catch them with nets.

sportfisherman *fishing* A large inboard powerboat designed for offshore fishing and typically having electronic navigation and fishfinder equipment, a cabin with lounging or living accommodations, a tower, outriggers, and a fighting chair.

sportfishing Fishing with a rod and reel for sport fish and especially for marine sport fish.

sporting dog A dog (as a foxhound, pointer, or retriever) used in hunting.

sport parachuting see SKYDIVING

sports car or **sport car** A usually 2-passenger high-performance production automobile suitable for use as a private passenger car on public roads that is designed to incorporate such features of a racing car as quick response, fast acceleration, and precise handling and maneuverability. A sports car is typically smaller, lower, and more streamlined than a conventional passenger car. To be classified as a sports car for racing, a car is usually required to have head and tail lights, windshield wipers, a self-starter, and other equipment normally required of a car for highway driving. In addition, a specified number of identical cars are commonly required to be produced during a year for the particular model to be eligible to race.

sportsman 1 Someone who is active in sports. In Britain, the term is commonly used in reference to anyone in sports other than track and field sports (athletics) while in the United States the term is often limited to those who engage in hunting and fishing as distinct from competitive sports. Sometimes a professional gambler who bets on sports events is called a sportsman.

2 see LATE MODEL SPORTSMAN.

sportsmanlike   Exhibiting qualities of good sportsmanship.

sportsmanship   The ethical behavior exhibited by a sportsman or athlete. Good sportsmanship is generally considered to involve participation for the pleasure gained from a fair and hard-fought contest, refusal to take unfair advantage of a situation or of an opponent, courtesy toward one's opponent, and graciousness in both winning and losing.

sports medicine   The aspect of medicine concerned with the prevention and treatment of injuries related to or incurred during participation in sports.

sports-racing car or **sports/racing car**   A 2-seat open-cockpit racing car with the engine in the rear and a body that covers the wheels so that it resembles a sports car. Though the cockpit is designed to permit 2 seats abreast, it only has a driver's seat. Normal highway equipment, such as headlights and windshield wipers, are not used. Sports-racing cars compete in one of 4 classes depending on engine displacement: class A, over 2 liters (122 cubic inches); class B, 1300-2000 cc (79-122 cubic inches); class C, 850-1300 cc (51.9-79 cubic inches); class D, under 850 cc (51.9 cubic inches).

a white center that is used in placing object balls in various games. **b** or **spot white**   The white cue ball with a red or black spot that is used in English billiards and in American carom and balkline billiards.

3 *bowling*   Any of several small dots or triangles marked across the lane approximately 16 feet from the foul line for use by a bowler in aiming his delivery.

²spot   **1 a** To concede a certain number of points to an opponent as a handicap.   **b** To allow the opponent to get a lead inadvertently which must be overcome in order to win. ⟨got past a shaky second inning that *spotted* Pittsburgh three runs — Joseph Durso, *New York Times*⟩

2 *billiards*   To place an object ball on one of the spots on a table especially after a foul.

3 *football*   **a** *of an official*   To place the ball officially at a specific spot on the field in preparation for the next down.   **b** To hold the ball at a specific yard line for a placekicker.

4 *gymnastics*   To assist a gymnast or tumbler in practicing a stunt in order to keep him from falling while learning it.

spot ball   *billiards*   An object ball that is placed on one of the spots on the table in accordance with the rules (as when it has been illegally pocketed or driven off the table).

spot bowler   *bowling*   A bowler who regularly

sports-racing car

sports sedan   *auto racing*   A pony car.

¹spot   **1** *archery*   The small round usually black spot in the center of a bull's-eye that is used in aiming but that does not affect scoring.

2 *billiards*   **a** Any of the points on various billiard tables often marked by a small black patch with

aims at one of the spots on the lane instead of at the pins. — compare PIN BOWLER

spot kick   *soccer*   A kick of a stationary ball (as on a free kick or penalty kick).

spot of enforcement   *football*   The spot at which the penalty for a foul is enforced and from which yardage is usually stepped off against the offending team. The spot of enforcement varies with the type of foul and type of play, and it may be the point of the foul, the point at which the ball becomes dead, the spot from which the play began (*previous spot*), or the point at which the next down is to begin (*succeeding spot*).

spot pass A pass (as in football, basketball, or ice hockey) that is made to a particular spot instead of directly to a player so that the player, arriving at the spot at the same time as the pass, can receive it on the move.

spot shot *billiards* A shot at a ball that has been spotted.

spot starter *baseball* A pitcher who is used occasionally as a starting pitcher but who is not part of the regular rotation.

spotter **1** Someone who assists a broadcaster (as at a football game) by identifying the players.
2 *gymnastics* Someone (as a coach or another student) who is engaged in spotting for a gymnast learning a new stunt.

spotting *gymnastics* The practice or technique of assisting a gymnast in practicing various stunts usually by holding him or turning him with the hands but also by holding ropes that control a safety belt.

spotting belt see SAFETY BELT

spotting scope *shooting* A small telescope mounted usually on a tripod that is used to observe the grouping of shots in the target without the shooter's having to leave the firing line.

spot white see SPOT (*billiards*)

spray hitter *baseball* A batter who hits to all fields. ⟨a wily but unsurpassedly powerful *spray hitter* — Roy Blunt, Jr., *Sports Illustrated*⟩

spray sheet or **spray skirt** see SKIRT

¹spread *hunting* The width of a set of antlers.

²spread **1** *of a defensive alignment* Having relatively wide spacing between players; spread out. **2** *football* Split. ⟨a *spread* end⟩

spread eagle **1** *bowling* **a** A leave of the 2, 3, 4, 6, 7, and 10 pins. — see illustration of pin arrangement at BOWLING **b** A Worcester. **2** *skating* A glide executed with the skates held heel-to-heel in a straight line and the arms held out to each side.

spreader *sailing* A horizontal strut that extends on either side of the mast to hold the shrouds out from the mast.

spreader rig *fishing* A device typically consisting of a thin metal bar with loops or rings on the ends to which separate lines can be attached. The spreader rig is used to keep 2 terminal lines

spread eagle

that are attached to one main line from tangling.

spread T see SPLIT T

¹spring *gymnastics* A thrust that is made with a quick push from the hands to flip the body forward or backward usually to complete a somersault. — see HANDSPRING, HEADSPRING, NECKSPRING

²spring To get a teammate open by preventing the defender from reaching him or keeping up with him (as by means of a block or a screen).

springboard **1** *diving* A relatively thin flat board of laminated wood or aluminum 16 feet long and 20 inches wide that is fastened at one end and rests over a fulcrum and that is used to gain height for a dive. The top surface of the springboard is roughened or is covered with a nonslip material, and the end of the board extends 5 to 6 feet beyond the edge of the water. For competitive diving, springboards are mounted one and 3 meters above the water. (also called *diving board*) — compare PLATFORM
2 *gymnastics* A spring device consisting essentially of two rectangular boards fastened together at one end and separated at the other by a spring that is used to gain height for vaulting and for mounting certain apparatus.

springboarder A diver who dives from a springboard.

spring conditions *skiing* A surface of wet sticky snow that is typical of a period of alternate freezing and thawing.

springing teal A form of clay pigeon shooting popular in Britain in which targets are propelled vertically from a hidden trap at ground level.

416

— compare DRIVEN PARTRIDGE, HIGH PHEASANT, RUNNING RABBIT

spring practice *football* A period of training and drilling held during the spring by a school or college team.

spring snow see CORN SNOW

spring training *baseball* A period usually from around the first of March until the first day of the regular season used by professional teams for training camp and exhibition games.

¹sprint To go at top speed usually for a relatively short distance.

²sprint **1** A relatively short race or a part of a race in which the emphasis is usually on all-out speed rather than on pace and tactical maneuvering: **a** *auto racing* A race of usually no more than 200 miles in length. — compare ENDURANCE RACE **b** *cycling* A race of usually 1000 meters (1090 yards) held between 2 competitors on a banked track. During a sprint, which usually involves 3 laps of the track, the competitors circle the track slowly for the first 2 laps jockeying for position to be ready to put on a burst of speed for the final lap. Only the final lap of the race is timed. **c** *horse racing* A race of less than one mile in length. — compare ROUTE **d** *karting* A relatively short race involving several laps of a track no more than half a mile long. — compare ENDURANCE RACE **e** *rowing* A race over a straight course of usually 2000 meters (2180 yards). **f** *speed skating* A race of 500 meters (545 yards). **g** *swimming* A race of 100 meters or 100 yards or less. **h** *track and field* A race of up to 400 meters or 440 yards; dash.

2 The action or an instance of sprinting.

sprint car *auto racing* An open-wheel open-cockpit racing car normally powered by a 305-cubic-inch stock-block engine that is typically run in short races on short paved or dirt tracks. The front-engine version resembles the larger dirt-track car, and the rear-engine version resembles a formula car.

sprinter A competitor trained to compete in sprint races.

sprinting British term for *drag racing.*

sprint medley *track and field* Any of several medley relays in which the individual legs are run at sprint distances. A typical sprint medley consists of legs of 440, 220, 220, and 880 yards respectively for men or 220, 110, 110, 440 yards respectively for women.

sprint out see ROLL OUT

sprint pass *track and field* The nonvisual exchange usually used in sprint relays.

sprint relay *track and field* Any of several relays run in 4 equal legs at sprint distances. Typical sprint relays include the 4x110 yard (4 legs of 110 yards each) and 4x220 yard relays.

sprint start *track and field* A bunch start typically used in sprint races. — see CROUCH START

spud *fishing* A long-handled chisel used for cutting holes in the ice for ice fishing.

spur *cockfighting* A stiff bony projection on the rear of the leg of a gamecock that is used in fighting. In many bouts, a steel or specially hardened bone spur is attached to the cock's leg for use in place of the natural spur.

squad **1** A group of athletes or sportsmen who make up a single unit for competition or practice. The term *squad* is generally synonymous with *team,* though in common usage a team may be divided into squads for practice or a squad may include the entire body of players representing a school or club in a team sport, while only a few make up the team actually engaged in competition at any given time.

2 A group of 5 shooters who move from station to station as a group shooting in turn in skeet and trapshooting competition.

¹square **1** *cricket* Off to one side of the wicket more or less at right angles to the line of the stumps and approximately even with the batsman's crease.

2 *of a golf match* Even; tied.

²square *rowing* To turn the blade from a horizontal position to a vertical one in preparation for entry at the beginning of a stroke. — compare FEATHER

square around *of a baseball batter* To turn from the normal batting stance to one facing the pitcher with the feet side by side. A batter normally squares around to make a bunt.

square ball *soccer* A pass made across the field relatively parallel to the goal line.

square cut *cricket* A stroke made on a bowled ball that is outside the off stump and that sends the ball to the off side toward cover point or gully.

square-gaiter Australian term for *trotter.*

square-in *football* A pass pattern in which the receiver runs downfield for about 15 yards and then cuts inside and runs directly across the field parallel to the line of scrimmage.

square knot A knot that is used to join 2 lines together and that is formed by overlapping the 2 ends and twisting one around the other and then bringing the ends together again and twisting the same end over the other again so that a

square leg

symmetrical knot is formed. Because this knot was used in tying reef points in the days of the square rigger ships, it is also called a *reef knot.* — see illustration at KNOT

square leg *cricket* **1** A player position on the leg side approximately even with the batsman and usually somewhat distant from the batsman.
2 The fieldsman occupying this position.

square-out *football* A pass pattern in which the receiver runs downfield for about 15 yards and then cuts sharply to the outside and runs straight toward the sideline parallel to the line of scrimmage.

squash **1** *bowling* A delivery with little or no action.
2 Short for *squash racquets*

squash racquets A game played on a 4-wall court in which players on each side alternately hit a small black ball to the front wall of the court with rackets with the object to make a shot that the opponent cannot return to the wall. The ball is put in play by a serve which must rebound from the front wall and bounce within a designated service court. On all subsequent play the ball may strike any combination of walls before or after hitting the front wall so long as the ball does not hit the board or telltale near the bottom of the front wall and so long as it is not allowed to bounce twice before being returned. The American version of squash racquets is played as a singles or doubles game in which either side may score and in which a game is played to 15 points. The British version of the game is strictly a singles game in which 9 points by one side constitute a game and in which only the serving side may score. Both versions are played on similar courts, and in each version players are not permitted to interfere with the opponent's opportunity to play a ball. There are provisions for setting the game if the score is tied at a predetermined point. — see also BALL, SET THE SCORE; compare RACQUETS, SQUASH TENNIS; COURT TENNIS

squash tennis A game similar to squash racquets and played on the same court but different from squash racquets chiefly in that only a singles game is played, only the server may score, and the server stands in the service court instead of in a service box and serves the ball so that it lands on the other side of the court in front of the service line. Squash tennis is played with a larger highly pressurized ball that rebounds at high speed. The racket is larger and heavier, more like a lawn tennis racket, because of the larger and harder ball.

squat *weight lifting* A competitive lift or an exercise which consists of squatting all the way down and then rising again to a standing position while holding a barbell behind the head resting on the back of the shoulders.

squat balance see FROG BALANCE

squat jump A conditioning exercise performed from a squatting position usually with one foot in front of the other and the hands together behind the head which consists of jumping up as high as possible so that the feet leave the ground and returning to the squatting position with the other foot in front.

squat rack see STANDARD (*weight lifting*)

squat thrust A conditioning exercise in which a person from a standing position squats and places his hands on the floor, extends his legs to the rear in a quick thrust so as to be supported on his hands and toes, then jumps back to the squatting position, and finally returns to the standing position.

squat vault *gymnastics* A vault over a long horse or between the pommels of a pommel

squash racquets court (singles)

horse made by bringing the legs up in a squatting position between the pushoff with the hands and the landing.

¹squeeze 1 *baseball* To cause to score on a squeeze play. ⟨*squeezed* in the winning run in the 8th inning⟩

2 *football* To block a single defensive lineman simultaneously with 2 blockers; double-team.

²squeeze 1 *caving* An extremely tight passageway.

2 Short for *squeeze play.*

squeeze bunt *baseball* A bunt made on a squeeze play.

squeeze off *shooting* To fire a round or a particular weapon by squeezing the trigger.

squeeze play *baseball* A play in which a runner on third base breaks for home with the pitch and the batter attempts to bunt the ball to give the runner a chance to score. If the runner waits to make sure that the pitch is actually hit on the ground before running home at top speed, the play is called a *safety squeeze.* If the runner runs all out as soon as the pitch is released without regard for whether or not the batter meets the ball, it is called a *suicide squeeze.*

squibbler see DRIBBLER (*baseball*)

squib kick *football* A relatively short kick from a kickoff that is made to bounce along the ground so as to be hard for the receiving team to handle.

squidding *fishing* The casting and retrieving of artificial lures instead of natural bait in surf fishing.

squirrel see FISHTAIL

squirrelly *of a racing car* Difficult to handle on a turn or at high speed. ⟨a little wind had kicked up, making the faster cars just a bit *squirrelly* through the chutes — Robert F. Jones, *Sports Illustrated*⟩

squirrel rifle A small-bore rifle.

stabilizer or **stabilizer bar** *archery* A metal rod with a movable weight near the end that extends from the back of the bow to assist the archer in steadying the bow. — see illustration at BOW

stab kick *Australian Rules football* A short pass to a teammate made by kicking the ball in the same way as for a punt.

stable A group of athletes, horses, or racing cars under a single management.

stablemate A racehorse or a boxer in the same stable as another.

stack 1 *football* An alignment of one or more players in line behind another player that is employed especially in order to hide the intended

direction of movement from the opponents.

2 *motor racing* **a** Short for *velocity stack.* **b** see HEADER

stacked bow *archery* A bow with narrow limbs that are thicker than they are wide.

stack I see I FORMATION

stacks on the mill *Australian Rules football* Confused play in which players of both teams are falling over each other in a struggle for possession of the ball.

stack the defense To align defensive players in such a way as to counter a particular strength of the opponent.

stack-up *of an archery bow* To become progressively harder to draw through the range of the draw.

stadium A structure of permanent usually open stands and the enclosed playing area that is used for games and sports events.

stage *drag racing* To place a car at the starting line in position for the start of the race.

stage race *cycling* A race run in a number of successive stages (as on different days).

stagger *track and field* The starting line for a particular lane when a staggered start is used.

staggered start *track and field* A start of a race in which the starting point for each lane from the inside to the outside is progressively farther ahead of the inside lane. The staggered start is used in races in which runners must stay in their assigned lanes for one or more turns. Because the distance around the turn for the runners in the outer lanes is greater than that for those in the inner lanes, the stagger compensates each runner for this extra distance so that although the runners in the outside lanes appear to have a head start, the distances for all runners are the same.

stag hunting The sport or pastime in which mounted riders chase a deer pursued by a pack of hounds. Stag hunting, which is quite similar to fox hunting, is practiced mostly in Britain.

staging area *drag racing* The area between the pits and the starting line where cars are lined up and prepared for the race. Often the staging area will have separate lanes for the different classes of vehicles. Immediately behind the starting area is the burnout pit.

staging light *drag racing* A light on the Christmas tree that indicates to the driver that his front wheels are in proper position for the start of the race.

stag jump *skating* A jump in which the skater assumes a stag position in the air.

stag leap *gymnastics* A leap in which the performer assumes a stag position in the air.

stag position A body position (as in gymnastics or skating) in which the performer's legs are spread as in the front split but with the forward leg bent so that the knee is foremost and the foot is held up under the body.

stake *horseshoes* A shaft of iron or steel stuck in the ground to serve as the target at which the horseshoes are tossed.

stake boat *sailing* A moored boat that serves as a marker in a race especially at the starting line.

stake horse see STAKES HORSE

stakes or **stakes race** *horse racing* A race other than an overnight race in which the purse is made up of the fees (as entry, nomination, and starting fees) put up by the owners of the horses entered in the race. Usually the track will put up an additional sum (added money) to attract top horses and enhance the prestige of the race. Because the owners have to pay for the privilege of running in stakes races, these races invariably attract the best horses. (also called *sweepstakes*) — compare ALLOWANCE RACE, CLAIMING RACE, HANDICAP

stakes horse or **stake horse** *horse racing* A horse that runs mostly or only in stakes races.

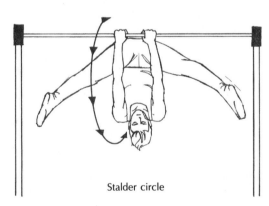

Stalder circle

Stalder circle *gymnastics* A circle performed on the horizontal bar with the arms straight and the legs extended in a straddle split straddling the arms.

stalemate *wrestling* A situation in which the competitors are in a position in which neither can improve his position or move to a position of advantage.

¹stall **1** A tactic (as in basketball or lacrosse) of maintaining possession of the ball for long periods without attempting to score. A stall may be resorted to by a weak team in order to keep the scoring of a powerful opponent low. When resorted to in the later stages of a game to protect a lead, it is often called a *freeze*. (also called *slowdown*)

2 *surfing* The act of momentarily slowing the board while riding a wave.

²stall **1** To hold the ball without attempting to shoot (as in basketball or lacrosse) as part of a strategy of preventing the opposing team from having an opportunity to score; freeze the ball.

2 *surfing* To slow a surfboard often by shifting the weight to the rear in order to pull out of the wave or to move higher on the face of the wave.

stallion *horse racing* A male horse used for breeding. — compare BROODMARE

stall out *surfing* To stall the board so that the wave passes the board. The technique is sometimes used at the end of a ride or as a means of getting out of a wave that is too large or dangerous.

stamp board see TAKEOFF BOARD

stance **1** The manner of standing or the position assumed in addressing a ball, taking one's place as a batter or bowler, or in facing an opponent in fencing or boxing.

2 *mountain climbing* A place on a rock face (as a small ledge) where a climber may stand or sit in relative comfort in order to belay a fellow climber moving ahead of or behind him.

stand **1** A defensive effort of some duration or success. ⟨a goal-line *stand*⟩

2 A place where hunters wait for game that is being driven toward them. ⟨spent four days on *stands* on opposite borders of a 12-acre clearing — Pat Moynahan, *Archery World*⟩

3 *archery* The manner or position in which an archer stands in shooting.

4 *lacrosse* The act of remaining in place when the referee has signaled for play to stop in women's play.

standard **1** *track and field* One of a pair of adjustable upright posts with short horizontal pins or braces to support the crossbar for a pole vault or high jump.

2 *weight lifting* One of a pair of adjustable upright posts with curved rests at the top that support a barbell at a height convenient for the lifter.

standardbred Any of an American breed of trotting or pacing horses bred for speed and endurance and used in harness racing. The standardbred was originally a composite of several strains, most notable the thoroughbred. It differs from the thoroughbred, however, in having a longer and more robust body, shorter and heavier legs, and greater endurance. Trotters and pacers were commonly used to pull wagons and carriages before the age of the automobile, and the natural competitive urges of the owners led to racing and to a desire to improve the breed. The name for the standardbred comes from the rules for registration adopted by the Association of Trotting Horse Breeders in 1879. Originally the rules required that a horse conform to a standard of performance or produce offspring capable of meeting the performance requirements in order to be registered. As performances improved, the rules were updated. Today the requirements for registration are based on blood lines alone. Because of the remarkable ability of the progeny of Hambletonian in trotting and pacing, they were more and more sought after for breeding in the late 19th century. All standardbreds racing today can trace their ancestry in a direct male line back to the great 18th century thoroughbred Messenger, the great-grandsire of Hambletonian.

¹standing   Traversed or to be traversed (as in speed trials) after a standing start. ⟨*standing* kilometer⟩

²standing   The position of a team in the standings.

standing broad jump   A jump for distance without a running start.

standing high jump   A jump for height without a running start.

standing part   The straight part of a rope around which the end or bight is usually turned in making a knot.

standing rigging   *sailing*   The part of the rigging which is in place at all times whenever the mast is up. The standing rigging includes the headstay, backstay, and shrouds.

standings   A listing of individuals in a body or teams in a league, conference, or division in the order of the individual rankings or the records of each individual or team.

standing start   **1** A start of a race in which all competitors are stationary just before the starting signal is given. — compare FLYING START

2 *track and field* A start (as of a middle or long distance race) in which competitors are standing rather than crouched. — compare CROUCH START

standing wave   *soaring*   A wave pattern in the air on the downwind side of a mountain caused by

the air's alternately rising and falling as it flows past the mountain. By staying on the wave the pilot is able to take advantage of the rising air to maintain altitude and stay aloft for long periods.

standoff half or **standoff halfback** or **standoff**   *rugby*   The halfback who normally lines up behind the scrum and off to the side somewhat between the scrum half and the threequarter backs to be in position to receive the ball from the scrum half and either start the offense or pass off to the threequarter backs.

stands   **1** Tiered seats for spectators at a sports event. The word *stands* in general refers to all of the spectator seats for an event including grandstands and bleachers.

2 The spectators in the stands.

standstill   *cycling*   A period during a sprint race in which both competitors come to a complete stop with each waiting for the other to make a tactical error.

stand-up   *wrestling*   An escape maneuver in which a wrestler who is on the mat on his hands and knees places his feet under himself and straightens his legs thereby rising above his opponent and usually escaping the opponent's hold.

standup goalie   *ice hockey*   A goalkeeper who attempts to stop most shots while standing up rather than by dropping to the ice.

Stanley Cup   The championship trophy and playoff series of the National Hockey League. The trophy was originally donated by Frederick Arthur, Lord Stanley of Preston, governor-general of Canada, for competition in 1893 among amateur hockey teams.

stanza   One of the periods of a game. This is sportswriter jargon and is used for everything from an inning in baseball to a period of an ice hockey game.

Star   *sailing*   A sloop-rigged keelboat of a one-design class that is 22½ feet long, has a sail area of 285 square feet, and carries a crew of 2.

starboard   *boating*   The right side of a boat. — compare PORT

starboard tack   *sailing*   A tack made with the wind on the starboard side.

star drag   *fishing*   A drag mechanism on a fishing reel that has a star-shaped adjusting wheel.

¹start   **1** A baseball game in which a particular pitcher was the starting pitcher. ⟨won his first two *starts*⟩

2 A horse race in which a particular horse was entered and started from the starting gate whether or not it finished the race.

start

²**start 1** *baseball* To be the starting pitcher in a game.
2 *horse racing* To leave the starting gate at the beginning of a race.

starter 1 A race official who supervises the lining up of competitors for the start of the race, gives the starting signal, calls false starts, and reports infractions and misconduct to the chief officials. In a track and field meet, the starter is also responsible for signaling the start of the bell or gun lap.
2 a A player in a team game who starts the game. **b** *baseball* see STARTING PITCHER
3 *horse racing* A horse that has left the starting gate with the other horses in a race regardless of whether or not it actually runs the course.

starter's list *horse racing* A list of horses that have been declared ineligible for racing by the starter because of chronic misbehavior at the starting gate. The horses on the list are not permitted to be entered in a race until their bad habits have been corrected.

starter's pistol *track and field* A small-bore pistol designed to fire blanks that is used to signal the start of a race and the start of a gun lap.

starting block 1 or **starting platform** *swimming* One of a series of boxes or low platforms at one end of the pool on which a competitor stands for the start of a race or a leg of a relay.
2 *track and field* A device that provides a runner with a rigid surface against which to brace his feet at the start of a short race and that consists of 2 adjustable pedals or blocks mounted on opposite sides of a frame which is usually anchored to the track. — see illustration at CROUCH START

starting box *dog racing* A set of individual stalls with doors that open simultaneously on signal from the starter that is used to keep individual competitors in place at the starting line until the start of a race. (also called *trap*)

starting fee *horse racing* A fee paid by the owner of a racehorse for the privilege of having his horse start in a stakes race. — compare ENTRY FEE, NOMINATION FEE

starting gate A device which keeps individual competitors behind the starting point of a race until the starting signal is given and which typically consists of a barrier which is swung out of the way at the start of the race (as in downhill skiing) or of separate stalls with individual doors which open simultaneously on a signal from the starter (as in horse racing).

starting line A real or imaginary line across the course beyond which competitors may not go until the starting signal. For most races the starting line is marked on the track. In swimming the line is the edge of the starting block. All lines at a horse racing track are overhead wires with the starting lines for the various distance races usually several yards ahead of the starting gate. The imaginary line between the committee boat and a marker serves as the starting line for yacht racing.

starting pitcher or **starter** *baseball* A pitcher who starts a game for a team and especially one who regularly starts games as distinguished from a relief pitcher.

starting platform see STARTING BLOCK (*swimming*)

station The position on the range occupied by an individual shooter in trapshooting or skeet competition. At a trapshooting range, there are 5 lanes arranged so that all lead to a single point at the trap house. Each lane is divided into 10 stations, each one yard farther from the trap house than the one in front. In competition, there is one shooter in each lane occupying the position appropriate to his handicap.
 On a skeet range, the stations are points around a semicircular layout. There are 7 positions around the outside of the semicircle and an eighth station near the center of the circle. Each shooter advances from station to station shooting at single and double targets from the 2 trap houses.

Statue of Liberty play *football* An offensive play formerly used especially from the single wing formation in which a back raises his arm as if to pass and the ball is taken from his hand by a teammate who circles behind him.

stay *sailing* A guy wire attached directly from the mast to some part of the boat to hold the mast rigidly in place. — see HEADSTAY, BACKSTAY; SHROUD

stayer *horse racing* A horse able to run well at distances greater than a mile; router.

staysail *sailing* A triangular fore-and-aft sail other than a jib that is set on a stay. Staysails are usually named according to their position: forestaysail, spinnaker staysail, mizzen staysail.

¹**steal 1** To take the ball or puck legally from an opponent by wresting or knocking it away and subsequently controlling it.
2 *of a base runner in baseball* **a** To run for a base in an attempt to reach it safely by catching the opposing team off guard. ⟨he was thrown out

stealing⟩ **b** To reach a base safely solely by running, catching the opposing team off guard and not on a force or as a result of a misplay by the opponents. ⟨*stole* second on the play⟩

3 *of cricket batsmen* To take advantage of an opportunity to make a run at a time when a run would not ordinarily be attempted.

4 *of a racehorse* To win a race unexpectedly when leading from the start by setting a pace just fast enough to stay ahead of any horse that moves up to challenge but not fast enough to tire before the end.

²steal 1 The action or an instance of stealing the ball or puck.

2 *baseball* The action or an instance of stealing.

stealer *horse racing* A racehorse that steals a race.

steel elbow *tennis* A stiff-arm style of swinging.

steeplechase or **steeple 1** *equitation* A cross-country endurance race of several miles in which horses must jump a number of fences, hedges, and ditches. — see also THREE DAY EVENT

2 *horse racing* A race usually from 1½ to 4½ miles long on a special steeplechase course that is often located inside an oval flat-racing course. An American steeplechase course must have at least 6 obstacles in every mile. One of these has to be a water jump which is 12 feet wide and 2 feet deep and guarded by a 2-foot-high fence on the approach side. Another obstacle required in every mile is an open ditch 5 feet wide and 2 feet deep that is guarded by a fence 4½ feet high and 3 feet wide. All other fences are at least 4½ feet high and, when constructed of brush or shrubs, 3 feet wide. British steeplechase courses are similar except that they must have at least 12 obstacles in the first 2 miles and 6 obstacles in every succeeding mile. In every mile there must be a water jump 12 feet wide and 2 feet deep that is protected by a fence 3 feet high. In every mile there is also an open ditch 6 feet wide and 2 feet deep, guarded by a fence 4½ feet high and 2 feet wide. All other fences are at least 4½ feet high.

3 *track and field* A race on a ¼ mile track on which are set up 4 hurdles and a water jump. The most common distances for the steeplechase are 3000 meters (1.9 miles), in which the competitors are required to clear each of the hurdles and the water jump 7 times, and 2 miles, in which the obstacles must be cleared 8 times. In running the course, the competitors are required to clear the barriers by hurdling or vaulting over or by jumping onto and then over the hurdles. — see also HURDLE

steeplechaser A track-and-field athlete or a horse that competes in steeplechases.

steeplechase seat *horse racing* A posture of the rider in a steeplechase that is characterized by holding the legs somewhat straighter than in flat racing, well forward, and braced against the stirrups and by being erect or leaning backward during the jumps.

steeplechasing Racing in steeplechases.

steepler A steeplechaser.

steering yoke *motor sports* A frame made roughly in the outline of a butterfly's wings that is used in place of a steering wheel. — see illustration at KART

steer roping *rodeo* A timed event essentially the same as calf roping except that the cowboy must rope a full-grown steer, secure one end of the rope to the saddle horn and stop his horse quickly so that the steer is jerked to the ground, and dismount and quickly tie any three of the steer's legs together.

steer wrestling *rodeo* A timed event in which the cowboy jumps from the back of his horse onto the neck of a running steer and wrestles the steer to the ground by twisting its neck so that it falls. (also called *bulldogging*)

¹stem *skiing* To slide the tail of one ski outward and edge it usually in preparation for making a turn.

²stem 1 *gymnastics* see UPRISE

2 *skiing* The act or an instance of stemming a ski.

stem christie or **stem christiania** *skiing* A turn made by stemming and weighting the uphill ski to initiate the turn and then bringing the other ski beside it so as to finish the turn with the skis parallel. The stem christie is the middle step in the progression from the stem turn to the full christie.

stem turn *skiing* An elementary turn made by stemming and weighting the uphill ski so as to turn in the direction of the stemmed ski and then bringing the unweighted ski beside it at the end of the turn.

¹step 1 *mountain climbing* **a** A sudden sharp rise in a slope. **b** A foothold cut in the face of rock or ice.

2 *sailing* A frame or block into which the foot of a mast fits in being set upright.

²step *sailing* To erect a mast by placing the foot in the step.

step-across

step-across see STEPOVER

step jump *skating* A jump in which the takeoff and landing are made on the same foot with both takeoff and landing assisted by a toe pick or toe point.

stepover or **step-across** *wrestling* A counter maneuver in which a wrestler who is held in a sitting or kneeling position on the mat throws his leg over his opponent and shifts his weight onto that leg thereby escaping from the hold.

step-through method *archery* A method of stringing a bow in which the archer steps between the limb of the bow and the string so that the handle is directly behind the thigh, braces the tip of the lower limb on the instep of the other foot, and pulls the upper limb across the body bending the bow around the leg.

step turn *skiing* A turn made by lifting one ski and placing it out to the side in the direction of the turn, weighting it, and then bringing the other ski alongside. In making wide turns, it is often necessary to make two or more successive step turns. The step turn, because of its slowness, is chiefly used in ski touring and cross-country skiing where the bindings do not permit sharp parallel turns. (also called *skating turn*)

stern The rear of a boat.
— **by the stern** *of a boat* Having the stern lower in the water than the bow.

sterndrive see INBOARD-OUTBOARD

sternman *canoeing* The person paddling in the stern of the canoe. — compare BOWMAN

steroid Short for *anabolic steroid*.

steward One of a group of people who have total charge of a race or a race meeting including authority over other officers at the race or meeting and responsibility for ruling on foul claims and misconduct.

stick **1 a** *field hockey* A wooden implement that is used to hit the ball and that consists of a 3-foot-long shaft or handle that is bent at the end to form a thick blade with which the ball is struck. The blade is flat on one side and rounded on the other; the ball is struck with the flat side only. A stick usually weighs from 16 to 20 ounces. It has a rubber insert in the handle to absorb the shock from hitting the ball.
b *hurling* A wooden implement about 3 feet long that has a 4-inch-wide thin slightly curved blade at one end; hurley.
c *ice hockey* A wooden implement that is used to play the puck and that consists of a thin handle that is joined at one end to a flat blade with which the puck is struck. The blade extends from the handle at an angle of about 130 degrees and is often curved to one side to make controlling the puck easier. In the NHL, the length of the stick may not exceed 55 inches. The handle is 1¼ inches wide and ¾ inch thick. The blade is between 2½ and 3 inches wide. A goalkeeper's stick is slightly larger, having a flat blade up to 15½ inches long and 3½ inches wide and a handle widened for the lower 24 inches to up to 3½ inches.
d *lacrosse* An implement that is used to catch, throw, and carry the ball and that consists of a wooden, plastic, or fiberglass handle with a triangular frame at one end strung with rawhide lacing. The stick is held in both hands, and the ball is played by maneuvering the stick with the hands. The overall length of the stick is between 40 and 72 inches with the width of the head limited to a maximum of 9 inches for fielders and 12 inches for the goalkeeper. The stick averages 16 to 18 ounces in weight. (also called *crosse*)
— compare BAT, CLUB, MALLET, PADDLE, RACKET

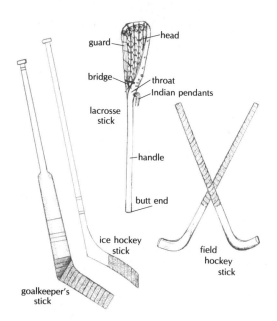

guard head
bridge throat
Indian pendants
lacrosse stick
handle
butt end
ice hockey stick
field hockey stick
goalkeeper's stick

2 *Australian Rules football* A behind post or a goalpost.
3 *baseball* Batting ability. ⟨was said to have a good glove but a weak *stick*⟩
4 *cricket* Any of the 3 stumps of a wicket.
5 *horse racing* A jockey's whip; bat.

6 *skiing* A ski pole.

7 *surfing* A surfboard.

stickball A version of baseball played in small areas (as city streets) with a lightweight ball and a broomstick. Because of the confined area, sides normally have only 4 or 5 players. When it is played in city streets, the length of long hits is commonly measured by sewers — the number of manholes the ball passes in flight.

stickboy *ice hockey* A young boy who is responsible for caring for a team's spare sticks and for providing a player with the proper replacement stick in the event his stick breaks during play.

stick bridge *billiards* A mechanical bridge. — see BRIDGE

stick-check To execute a stick check.

stick check **1** *ice hockey* An act of hitting the puck away from the puck carrier by using the stick to poke, hook, or sweep the puck free.

2 *lacrosse* see CROSSE CHECK

sticker A calk on a horseshoe.

stick glove *ice hockey* A glove with a padded flat rectangular surface on the back that is worn by a goalkeeper on the hand that controls the stick and that is used to block shots at the goal. — see illustration at GLOVE

stickhandler A hockey or lacrosse player who is adept at stickhandling.

stickhandling The art of moving and controlling the puck or ball in hockey or lacrosse by maneuvering the stick.

stickman A lacrosse player.

sticks **1** *field hockey* A foul that results when a player raises the stick above shoulder level in hitting or stopping the ball and that is usually penalized by a penalty corner.

2 *horse racing* The fences over which horses jump in hurdles or steeplechase races.

stick save A save made by a goalkeeper in which the ball or puck is stopped or deflected with the stick.

stickside *ice hockey* The side of a goalkeeper on which he holds his stick.

stickwork *lacrosse* The use and management of the stick in offensive and defensive techniques (as cradling, catching, or checking).

sticky wicket *cricket* A pitch that is drying in the sun after having been soaked with rain and that is temporarily tacky with the result that spin bowlers have a great advantage over batsmen.

¹stiff **1** *of a bowling lane* Having a finish that resists the tendency of the ball to hook; fast, holding. — compare SLOW

2 *of a sailboat* Inherently stable with a tendency to remain upright and not heel in a strong wind.

²stiff *horse racing* A horse entered in a race but not sent out to win.

³stiff *horse racing* To prevent a horse from winning deliberately (as by using drugs to slow it down or by poor riding). It is not uncommon for trainers to keep horses from winning races at low odds in order to build up the odds for subsequent races.

stiff-arm see STRAIGHT-ARM

still fishing A method of fishing in which the baited line is allowed to remain in one place in the water until a fish comes along and takes the bait.

still hunting **1** A method of hunting game by slowly stalking it without the use of a dog.

2 A method of hunting by waiting in one place for the game to pass.

still rings *gymnastics* Rings which must be kept relatively still throughout the performance as distinguished from flying rings.

stirrup One of a pair of small rings or frames suspended from the saddle by straps to support the feet of the rider. — see illustration at SADDLE

¹stock **1** The crosspiece of an anchor located at the top of the shank. — see illustration at ANCHOR

2 The wooden part of a rifle or shotgun to which the barrel and action is fitted and by which the weapon is held for firing.

3 The butt or handle of a fishing rod.

²stock *motor racing* Built on a production line and unmodified; as it comes from the manufacturer's stock or showroom. Though racing modifications are not permitted to engines that are to be raced as stock, most racing organizations do permit blueprinting — rebuilding the engine to exact design specifications in order to improve its performance by removing the minor irregularities inherent in mass production.

³stock To release game fish or game birds that have been raised in captivity in a wild area so that they may be sought by fishermen and hunters during the open season.

stock appearing *of a stock engine or car* Having internal modifications for racing limited usually to the extent that the external appearance is not changed.

stock block *of an internal-combustion engine* Designed originally for use in a passenger car and characterized by having push-rod-activated valves instead of an overhead camshaft.

stock car **1** *auto racing* A racing car which

Stock Eliminator

resembles a commercially produced passenger sedan but which usually has all or most of its components modified or rebuilt for greater strength, better performance, and longer wear. A racing stock car is based on the passenger car of a particular manufacturer, but it resembles the manufacturer's car only in name and model designation and in external appearance. In preparing a car for racing, a team normally obtains a bare body and chassis from the factory and after removing all nonessentials such as upholstry and side windows modifies the car by strengthening the body, installing a safety roll cage, and providing a sturdier suspension system. The engine, though it must retain its original design features such as the configuration of the cylinder head and valve layout, is usually extensively modified or rebuilt to more precise specifications and with sturdier components than the showroom model.

2 or **stocker** *drag racing* A usually unmodified or only slightly modified passenger car.

Stock Eliminator see ELIMINATOR

stocker see STOCK CAR

Stockli *gymnastics* A stunt performed on a pommel horse that consists of a double out followed by a double in or a double in followed by a double out.

stock saddle A saddle of the style used by western cowboys in rounding up stock which is characterized by a high pommel and cantel and a horn which projects up from the pommel around which a rope can be secured. — see illustration at SADDLE

stolen base *baseball* The stealing of a base credited to a base runner in statistical records.

stomach throw *judo* A back sacrifice throw.

stone Short for *curling stone.*

stonewall *of a cricket batsman* To bat in a purely defensive manner with little or no attempt to score runs.

stonewaller *cricket* An excessively cautious batsman who only seeks to protect the wicket without attempting to score runs.

stool *hunting* A group of decoys arranged together.

stoopball A game based on baseball played usually by throwing a rubber ball against the steps of a porch or stoop with the fielders attempting to catch the rebounding ball on the fly to make an out and with the thrower awarded a base hit valued according to the number of times the ball bounces before it is caught.

stoop through *gymnastics* A backward swing from a handstand support on the horizontal bar in which the gymnast pikes his body and tucks his legs inside his arms between the bar and his chest as he starts the downward movement. The gymnast keeps his legs straight throughout the movement. (also called *jam*)

stoop vault *gymnastics* A vault which is made like a squat vault but in which the legs are held straight.

¹stop *boxing* To knock out an opponent. ⟨*stopped* [him] at 2:41 in the third round — *Sports Illustrated*⟩

²stop **1** see SAVE
2 see REEFING POINT

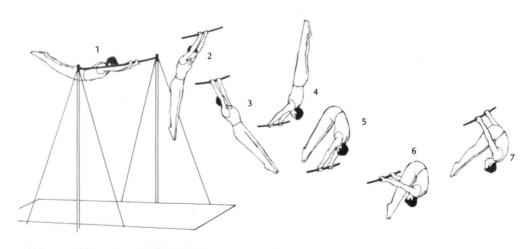

stoop through

426

stop and go *football* A pass pattern in which the receiver runs a short way downfield, stops as if to catch a short pass, and then continues downfield for a long pass.

stopboard *track and field* **1** A 4-foot-long 4-inch-high curved block of wood that is secured to the ground at the front edge of the shot put throwing circle to keep the competitor from overstepping the circle. The competitor is permitted to touch the side of the stopboard, but he may not touch the top.

2 The rectangular somewhat vertical board at the rear of the pole vaulter's planting pit that catches the pole at the beginning of the vault.

stop hit *fencing* A counterattack that is made during the period in which the opponent is making the feints and complex movements of his attack. To be legal, the stop hit must be made before the beginning of the final movement of the opponent's attack; otherwise, the opponent's attack must first be parried before a counterattack is permitted. (also called *stop thrust*)

stopper *baseball* A starting pitcher who is a consistent winner and who can be counted on to stop a losing streak.

stopper knot A single knot (as an overhand or figure eight knot) that is formed in the end of a line to prevent the end from slipping through another knot or through a block.

stop shot *billiards* A shot that is made with backspin so that the cue ball will stop upon striking the object ball.

stop thrust see STOP HIT

stop volley *tennis* A soft volley that places the ball just over the net short of the opponent's reach.

storm warning *boating* A square red flag with a black center (during the day) or 2 red lights (at night) used to indicate that winds of more than 48 knots (55 mph) are forecast.

straddle or **straddle roll** *track and field* A technique of high jumping in which the jumper leads with the leg farthest from the bar, turns to cross the bar on his stomach, and lets his trailing leg follow over the bar after his body. (also called *barrel roll, belly roll*)—compare FLOP, SCISSORS, WESTERN ROLL

straddled ball A ball in handball, paddleball, or racquetball that rebounds from the front wall and passes between the legs of a player on the side that just returned the ball so that the player who must next play the ball does not have a fair opportunity to see or return the ball and that results

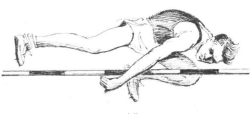

straddle

in an unavoidable hinder.

straddle mount *gymnastics* A method of mounting the balance beam in which the performer leaps up and lands on the beam in a straddle position.

straddle position *gymnastics* A body position in which the performer is standing with his feet spread wide to the side and pointing in the same direction. (also called *straddle stand, straddle stance*)

straddler *track and field* A high jumper who uses the straddle.

straddle roll see STRADDLE

straddle seat *gymnastics* A balance position on the parallel bars in which the performer supports himself above the bars on his hands with his legs straddling the bars.

straddle split *skating* A position in which the feet and legs are split wide to the side. — see illustration at SPLIT

straddle stand or **straddle stance** see STRADDLE POSITION

straddle vault *gymnastics* A vault made with the legs spread wide on either side of the hands.

straight **1** *pari-mutuel betting* First place at the finish. When a straight wager is made, the bettor collects only if the competitor wins. — see also PARI-MUTUEL BETTING

2 or **straightaway** A long straight section of a racecourse.

¹straight-arm *of a ballcarrier in football* To ward off a tackler by placing the palm of the hand against the tackler's body and holding the arm extended from the shoulder with the elbow locked.

²straight-arm *football* The act or an instance of straight-arming a tackler.

¹straightaway see STRAIGHT

²straightaway **1** *baseball* In or into the area of the outfield normally occupied by an outfielder. ⟨hit the ball to *straightaway* center field⟩ ⟨had the outfielders playing *straightaway*⟩

straight ball

2 *basketball* Directly in front of the basket. ⟨hit on a jump shot from *straightaway*⟩

straight ball *bowling* A delivery in which the ball is held with the fingers behind the ball and released so that the ball rolls down the alley rotating in the direction of travel. The straight ball has no sideways rotation and therefore does not hook or curve into the pocket. — compare FULL ROLLER, FULL SPINNER, SEMI-ROLLER

straight bow *archery* A bow that when unstrung is perfectly straight.

straight corner shot *handball* A serve in which the ball rebounds from the front wall and travels to the back of the court close to the wall to bounce near the back wall.

straight off *surfing* Directly toward the shore in front of a wave. ⟨must wait a second, going *straight off* before turning into the curl — Jess Money, *Westways*⟩

straight pool The game of 14.1 continuous pocket billiards. — see BILLIARDS

straight rail see BILLIARDS

straight running *skiing* Gliding virtually straight down the fall line of a hill with the skis parallel.

straight thrust *fencing* A simple attack made by extending the sword arm without changing the line of engagement.

straight up *basketball* Without resorting to special strategies or defenses. ⟨wanted to play them *straight up* . . . but they just did more things good — Norm Sloan⟩

strand *baseball* To leave a base runner on base.

strangle hold *wrestling* Any hold across the throat which would cut off breathing. All possible strangle holds are illegal.

¹streak **1** A series of successive victories or defeats. ⟨the end of her 46-match winning *streak* — Caleb Pirtle, *Southern Living*⟩
2 A brief period of unusually outstanding performance. ⟨a hitting *streak*⟩ ⟨*streak* shooter⟩

²streak To be on a winning streak; be hot. ⟨the *streaking* Cards turned in their 14th triumph in the last 16 games — Sam Goldaper, *New York Times*⟩

streamer *fishing* A wet fly tied on a long-shanked hook and dressed with feathers to resemble a minnow. — compare BUCKTAIL

street hockey A version of ice hockey played on ground or in the streets by players who do not wear skates and who use hockey sticks and a small ball.

strelli *gymnastics* A movement on the parallel bars in which the performer rolls backward from an upper arm support and swings the body down through the bars and up again on the other side to complete a full circle ending in a handstand position at the point at which he started.

stretch **1** The homestretch of a racecourse. The term is used broadly to mean the final stage of a regular season when a few teams may be in a close race for first place in league or conference standings.
2 *baseball* A movement a pitcher uses instead of a windup when there are runners on base. The

stretch

stretch usually consists of raising both hands to about head height and then bringing them down to chest or waist level for a short pause during which the pitcher checks the position of the runner before pitching. During the stretch the pitcher is normally standing sideways to home plate, facing toward third base if he is right-handed and toward first base if left-handed. The stretch, with its integral pause, allows the pitcher to throw to the base to try to pick off the runner or to keep him close to prevent his stealing without interrupting the pitching motion and making a balk.

stretcher 1 *rowing* A footrest against which an oarsman braces his feet.

2 *wrestling* A breakdown maneuver used on an opponent who has assumed a defensive position on his hands and knees in which the wrestler from a position on top of his opponent applies a scissors hold or a grapevine on the opponent's legs and at the same time pulls the opponent's arms out from under him with a double bar arm.

stretch runner *horse racing* A horse that usually makes a strong bid in the homestretch.

¹strike 1 *baseball* A pitched ball that is swung at and missed or hit foul or that is not swung at but which crosses home plate in the strike zone and that is charged against the batter. A batter is out if 3 strikes are called against him during one time at bat. Foul balls which are not caught in the air are treated as strikes when the count is less than 2 strikes; any fouls hit after the batter has 2 strikes, except while attempting to bunt, are not counted as strikes. — compare BALL; see also FOUL TIP

2 A perfectly thrown ball. ⟨backhanded a hot smash . . . deep behind third base . . . wheeled quickly and fired a *strike* to first base for the putout — Earl Lawson, *Sporting News*⟩ ⟨the touchdown *strike* came on a third-and-one play — Bob Broeg, *St. Louis Post-Dispatch*⟩

3 *bowling* The act or an instance of knocking down all the pins with the first ball delivered in a frame. As a bonus for making a strike, the bowler adds to his score for that frame the total pinfall of his next 2 deliveries. To indicate a strike, an X is marked in the frame on the score sheet, but the score is not entered until after the bonus pins have been made. — compare SPARE

4 *cricket* The condition of being the striker. ⟨tried to keep the *strike* as long as possible in order to score more runs⟩

5 *fishing* The act or an instance of a fish's taking bait or a lure being pulled through the water that is characterized by a sharp pull on the line.

6 *skating* The point at which a change from one foot to the other is made.

²strike 1 *bowling* To knock down all the pins with the first ball delivered in a frame.

2 *fishing* **a** To pull the line taut to set the hook. **b** *of a fish* To snatch at the bait or lure; take.

3 *of a hunting dog* To pick up the scent of the quarry.

4 *rowing* **a** To place the oar in the water at the beginning of a stroke. **b** To row at a particular rate. ⟨got off cleanly the next time, *striking* . . . 44 before settling down to a smooth 38 — Hugh D. Whall, *Sports Illustrated*⟩

5 *skating* To begin skating on the other foot by placing it on the surface and shifting the weight to it.

strike-off *roller hockey* A play similar to a face-off in which 2 opposing players stand over the ball facing each other with their backs to their own goals and with their sticks on the floor and at a signal from the referee attempt to hit the ball to a teammate.

strikeout *baseball* An out that results when a batter is charged with 3 strikes and that is charged to the batter and credited to the pitcher in statistical records. The traditional symbol for a strikeout on a scorecard is *K*.

strike out 1 *baseball* **a** *of a batter* To be out on strikes. ⟨*struck out* swinging⟩ **b** *of a pitcher* To put a batter out by getting 3 strikes on him. ⟨*struck* him *out* with a fastball⟩

2 *bowling* To finish the game by rolling 3 successive strikes in the tenth frame.

striker 1 British term for a player (as in billiards or croquet) whose turn it is to shoot. — compare NONSTRIKER

2 *cricket* The batsman who is at a given moment defending the wicket which the bowler is attacking; the batsman who is trying to hit the bowled balls. — compare NONSTRIKER

3 *soccer* Any of the usually 3 forwards in a modern lineup. — compare BACK, LINKMAN

striker out *court tennis* The player on the hazard side of the court who is receiving the serve.

strike zone *baseball* The area over home plate between the level of the batter's knees and his armpits when he is taking his natural stance through which a pitched ball must pass to be called a strike.

striking circle *field hockey* The area enclosed by a nearly semicircular line which extends in an arc from the goal line on either side of the goal to a point 15 feet (16 feet in men's play) in front of the goal. A foul committed in the striking circle is considered more serious than one committed elsewhere on the field of play, and when the foul is committed by a defensive player in his own striking circle the opposing team is awarded a penalty bully.

¹string **1** One of the nylon, gut, or linen cords or steel wires that are woven in the frame of a racket to provide a firm, lightweight surface with which to hit a ball.

2 *billiards* **a** A usually imaginary line across the table parallel to the head and foot rails passing through a spot. **b** A balkline. **c** The act or an instance of stringing for break.

3 *bowling* A complete game consisting of 10 frames; line.

4 a *horse racing* A group of racehorses owned by one stable or trained by a single trainer. **b** *polo* A group of ponies owned and used by one player.

5 *shooting* A group of shots fired successively by an individual shooter.

6 Short for *bowstring.*

²string **1** To weave the strings in a racket head.

2 *archery* To bend the bow and attach the loops of the bowstring over the notches in the ends of the limbs so that the bow will be ready to shoot; brace.

3 *billiards* To drive the cue ball from the head of the table to the foot with the intention of making it rebound from the foot rail, return to the head rail, and stop closer to the head rail than the opponent's ball in order to determine the order of play; lag.

string arm *archery* The arm that pulls the string.

string dampener or **string silencer** *archery* A piece of rubber or plastic that fits on the bowstring to absorb some of the vibrations that result when the arrow is released and the string snaps forward against the bow limbs. The dampener is essential in hunting to cut down the twanging noise that usually accompanies release of the arrow.

stringer **1** *fishing* A string or cord on which a fisherman strings caught fish or a chain equipped with snap hooks on which fish are secured.

2 *surfing* A strip of wood sandwiched in the middle of a fiberglass covered foam board to add longitudinal stiffness.

string fingers *archery* The first three fingers of the string hand which control the string in the Mediterranean draw.

string hand *archery* The hand that pulls the bowstring.

string picture *archery* The relative positions of the bowstring and the upper limb of the bow viewed (as through peripheral vision) when the string is held at the anchor point. In the normal string picture the string will coincide with the far edge of the bow limb. If the string appears nearer the center of the limb of the bow, the window is said to be closed; if outside the limb, open. (also called *bow window*)

string silencer see STRING DAMPENER

string walking *archery* The practice of nocking the arrow at different points on the bowstring for targets at different distances in order to avoid having to readjust the basic aim.

¹strip **1** The surface of a racecourse.

2 The surface on which fencing takes place. — see PISTE

²strip **1** *fishing* To pull line from the reel by hand in preparation for fly casting.

2 *football* To pull or knock the ball out of the grasp of an opposing player for a fumble.

stripe *football* A yard line. ⟨moved the ball across the midfield *stripe*⟩

¹stroke **1 a** A controlled swing with the hand or a paddle, racket, club, or cue intended to hit a ball or shuttlecock in a precise manner and drive it in a definite direction. **b** The particular method of making a stroke at a ball or shuttlecock. ⟨the overhand *stroke*⟩

2 a A propelling push or pull with legs, arms, or a paddle, or an oar (as in skating, swimming, or rowing). **b** The entire movement of the arm or of an oar from the time it enters the water at the beginning of a stroke, through recovery, to the point of starting to enter the water again for the next stroke. **c** *swimming* The distinctive combination of arm and leg movements used in swimming. ⟨the crawl *stroke*⟩

3 *golf* **a** A swing at the ball whether or not it is actually hit that is charged to a golfer as a unit of scoring. **b** A penalty assessment of a stroke added to a golfer's score for a breach of the playing rules.

4 *rowing* The oarsman who sits in the sternmost seat and who sets the pace in rowing which the other oarsmen follow by timing their strokes to his.

5 The distance the piston in an internal-combustion engine travels in compressing the fuel-air mixture.

²stroke **1** To hit a ball or shuttlecock with a controlled stroke of the hand or of a racket, paddle, club, or cue.

2 *auto racing* To drive the car at less than its

maximum speed in order to avoid unnecessary wear on the engine or other mechanical equipment. — often used in the phrase *stroke it* ⟨I'd rather lead one lap and fall out of the race than *stroke it* and finish in the money — Junior Johnson⟩

3 *baseball* To hit the ball. ⟨*stroked* a single past the second baseman⟩

4 *rowing* **a** To row at a particular rate. ⟨with 500 yards to go, the Cairo Police, *stroking* 38, edged past Oxford — Clement Freud, *Sports Illustrated*⟩ **b** To serve as stroke on a crew. ⟨*stroked* his university's rowing eight to a record today — Associated Press⟩

5 *skating* To glide on one skate after pushing off with the other foot.

stroke hole *golf* The hole at which a handicap stroke is given.

stroke play *golf* Competition in which the total number of strokes taken by a player or side to complete a round (as of 9 or 18 holes) is used in determining the winner. Stroke play is common in competition among individuals and between teams and is used in most professional tournaments, where each individual is basically playing against every other individual. (also called *medal play*) — compare MATCH PLAY

strong safety or **strong safetyman** *football* A defensive safetyman who plays on the side directly across from the strong side of the offensive line. (also called *tight safety* or *tight safetyman*) — compare FREE SAFETY

strongside *football* Of, being, or on the strong side of the field. ⟨*strongside* safety⟩ ⟨the *strongside* rotation zone is a defense geared to stopping the deep threat of the flankerback — Paul Zimmerman, *A Thinking Man's Guide to Pro Football*⟩

strong side **1** The side of a court or field on which the ball is being played at a given moment.

2 *football* **a** The side of an unbalanced line having the larger number of players. **b** The side of the line on which the tight end plays.

stud **1 a** A stallion used for breeding. **b** The service or duties of a stallion or broodmare. — used in the phrase *at stud, in stud,* or *to stud* ⟨she was retired to *stud* with total winnings of $25,883.31 — Philip A. Pines, *The Complete Book of Harness Racing*⟩

2 see CLEAT

studbook The official pedigree of a racehorse or dog; the register in which pedigrees are listed.

¹stuff **1** Spin imparted to a thrown or hit ball to make it curve or change course. ⟨they vary their *stuff* until you yield a loose return, which they efficiently kill — Margaret Varner & J. Rufford Harrison, *Table Tennis*⟩

2 *baseball* The liveliness of a pitch; the movement of a fastball or breaking pitch out of its apparent line of flight. ⟨the greatest pitcher of my time . . . had tremendous *stuff* — Ted Williams⟩ ⟨I'd say [he] had pretty good *stuff,* but he didn't have [his] usual fastball — Danny Murtaugh⟩

²stuff **1** *basketball* To throw the ball down into the basket from above the rim; dunk.

2 *ice hockey* To hit the puck into the goal forcefully from close range and especially from the area of the crease.

stuff bag A small nylon bag with a drawstring closure into which a down-filled sleeping bag is stuffed for transporting.

stuffer *drag racing* A supercharger.

stuff shot A dunk shot in basketball.

¹stump *cricket* Any of the 3 upright rods about one inch in diameter that are set in the ground approximately 4 inches apart at each end of the pitch and topped with bails to form a wicket. The top of the stumps is 28 inches high; the stumps are set in the ground so that they may be knocked over by a bowled ball. — see illustration at WICKET

²stump *of a wicketkeeper in cricket* To cause the batsman to be out by knocking down the wicket with the ball in hand while the batsman is beyond the popping crease after a missed swing or a batted ball on which a run is not being attempted. If the batsman were attempting a run, he would be run out, not stumped.

¹stunt **1** *football* An action (as jumping in and out of the line or looping) by a member of the defensive team intended to upset the concentration or blocking assignments of the offensive linemen.

2 *gymnastics* A definite pattern of movements that make up a unit of a routine.

²stunt *of a defensive player or team in football* To move in and out of the defensive line or to loop or make quick changes in position just before the snap of the ball in order to confuse the blocking assignments of the offensive team. (also *jitterbug*)

stutter-step To fake an opponent with a stutter step. ⟨he has inside and outside moves, a bull move where he puts his head down and runs over you, or he'll just *stutter-step* you like a ballet dancer — Doug Van Horn⟩

stutter step A quick feint made while running (as in football) or dribbling (as in basketball) in order

Stutz

to induce the defender to stop or reverse direction. The player steps forward or to one side and quickly shifts his weight back to the other foot for an instant as if to change direction before continuing.

Stutz or **Stützekehre** *gymnastics* A stunt performed from a handstand position above the parallel bars in which the performer swings his legs down through the bars and up on the other side and as the legs come above the bars releases his grasp, performs a half twist, and then regrasps the bars to wind up in a handstand facing in the opposite direction.

in order to get to the passer or ballcarrier. ⟨I was told [he] would *submarine* the blockers and tackle the ballcarrier . . . and that's just what he did do to me when I got the ball. He wormed right in there and nailed me — Leroy Kelly⟩

submariner A baseball pitcher who uses a submarine delivery.

submission hold A painful hold legally applied in judo or sambo wrestling or a legal choke hold applied in judo which is intended to force the opponent to give a submission signal which ends the bout.

¹substitute A player who enters a game in place

Stutz

stymie *golf* A situation in which a ball closer to the cup on the putting green lies directly in the line of play of another ball which is to be putted first. The stymie is no longer a part of the golf scene since a ball on the putting green may be picked up after its position has been marked.

¹sub Short for *substitute*.

²sub To employ substitutes; to put substitutes in a game. ⟨with a large lead the coach began *subbing* early⟩

¹submarine **1** *baseball* A pitcher's delivery in which the arm is brought forward in a slight downward arc with the hand usually just below the level of the waist.

2 *football* A maneuver in which a defensive lineman ducks under the block of an offensive lineman.

3 *surfing* A surfboard that is too small for the rider.

²submarine **1** *baseball* To pitch the ball with a submarine delivery.

2 *of a defensive lineman in football* To dive or crawl under the block of the offensive lineman

of another player because that player is injured or needs an opportunity to rest; a player who is in uniform and ready to replace another player if necessary.

²substitute **1** To enter a game officially in place of another player who is already in the game and who will come out.

2 *of a coach or manager* To replace a player with a substitute.

substitution The replacing of one or more players in the game by other players on the team. Rules for substitution vary with almost every game from relatively free substitution while the game is in progress to no substitution even for injured players who must leave the game:

1 *baseball* A substitute may replace a player whenever time is out. The substitute takes the replaced player's position in the batting order, but he does not necessarily have to take the same position on the field. Once he has been replaced in the lineup, a player may not reenter the game.

2 *basketball* Free substitution is permitted

whenever time is out except that a player who is to shoot a free throw cannot be replaced until after the free throw. Players may leave and reenter the game any number of times. In international play, only the team in possession of the ball may initiate substitution; if it requests to substitute, then the other team may substitute.

3 *cricket* Substitution is permitted only in the event that a player has been injured and is unable to continue playing. The substitute takes the injured player's place on the field, but he may not bat or bowl in his place.

4 *field hockey* A player may be replaced only in cases of injury or disqualification and only at the beginning of the second half. Once a substitute has entered the game, the replaced player may not return. A player who leaves the game temporarily but is not replaced by a substitute may return. During the time between the player's leaving and the substitute's entering, the team must play shorthanded.

5 *football* Unlimited substitution is permitted with players free to enter and leave the game anytime the ball is dead. Consequently, it is possible to use certain players or groups of players only on special plays or for special duties (as on defense or for kicking).

6 *ice hockey* The rules permit unlimited substitution anytime during the game. It is not necessary for play to stop for substitutes to enter the game. The only restriction is that the players being replaced must be at the bench and out of play before the substitutes come onto the ice. It is common for a team to have 3 or 4 lines — groups of players who play together — alternating time on the ice.

7 *lacrosse* Substitution is unlimited with players free to come and go as often as desired when the ball is dead.

8 *rugby* Only 2 substitutions are permitted per game and only for injured players. Formerly no substitution was allowed, and if a player was injured, the team had to play shorthanded.

9 *soccer* Substitution is limited to 3 players per game. Once replaced, a player may not reenter the game.

10 *volleyball* Limited substitution is permitted whenever the ball is dead. A team is limited to 12 substitutions during a game; a player may appear in the game 3 separate times — that is, he may come in 3 times as a substitute or reenter twice if replaced as a starter — and each time he must take up the same position relative to his teammates.

11 *water polo* Free substitution is permitted between periods, after a goal has been scored, or during time-outs.

succeeding spot *football* The spot at which the ball is next to be put in play (as by a snap or a free kick) and which is used in enforcing certain penalties for fouls.

sucker play A deceptive play in which a defensive player is victimized by his own gullibility, inexperience, or even by his quick reaction and anticipation of how the play is going to develop. The most common sucker play in football is one in which an offensive lineman pulls out of the formation hoping to influence a defensive lineman to pursue thus creating a hole through which the ballcarrier can run.

suck wheels *cycling* To ride in another cyclist's slipstream to take advantage of the reduced air pressure behind the cyclist in order to conserve energy; draft.

sudden death A period of extra play to break a tie that terminates when one side scores, gains a lead, or reaches a predetermined number of points. The most common situation is in team games like football, soccer, or ice hockey in which the team that scores first during the sudden death period wins immediately and further play is unnecessary. In golf, when 2 or more competitors are tied at the end of the final round in stroke play, they begin a sudden death round from a designated hole (as the 15th) and play until one plays a hole in fewer strokes. A sudden death period — commonly called a tiebreaker — is played in tennis, with players alternating service, usually until one side reaches a predetermined score (as 9 or 12 points).

sudden victory Euphemism for *sudden death.*

Sugar Bowl A post-season college football game played in the Sugar Bowl stadium in New Orleans between specially invited teams of which one is often from the Southeastern Conference.

suicide pass *box lacrosse* A pass made from directly behind a receiver that requires the receiver to turn his head in order to see the ball and thereby risk being checked from his blind side.

suicide squad see SPECIAL TEAM

suicide squeeze see SQUEEZE PLAY

suit up *of a player in a team sport* To put on the team uniform and join the other players on the bench in order to be able to play in a game. ⟨suffering from a touch of the flu and didn't *suit up* for the contest — Ed Gilooly, *Boston Herald Traveler*⟩

sulky *harness racing* A vehicle pulled by a harness horse during a race that consists of a lightweight frame with a single seat for the driver supported on 2 wheels like those of a bicycle. The sulky commonly has 2 poles that run alongside the horse to a harness where they are attached, though one design uses a single shaft that runs from the middle of the sulky up over the horse to be attached to a harness in the middle of the horse's back. — see illustration at HARNESS HORSE

Sullivan Award An award established in 1930 by the AAU in honor of James E. Sullivan, former president of the AAU, that is given to the person voted Amateur Athlete of the Year.

summit pack *mountain climbing* A small backpack that is used to carry clothing and equipment (as pitons and carabiners) for rock or technical climbing and that typically has a smooth outline without outside pockets, a strap for holding an ice axe, and sometimes a loop by which the pack can be hauled to the top.

sumo A traditional Japanese form of wrestling marked by a great deal of pageantry and ceremony. Sumo originated over 2000 years ago and was associated with early religious practices. The modern customs are essentially remnants of the early religious purification rites. The wrestling is conducted in a circular ring about 15 feet in diameter on a hard dirt floor covered with sand and bounded by a heavy rope embedded in the dirt. The actual wrestling time is usually quite short with many bouts decided in a few seconds. At the beginning of each bout, the 2 combatants spend 3 or 4 minutes alternately throwing salt in a purification ritual and stomping and squatting and glaring at each other, each trying to psych out his opponent. On a signal from the referee, the wrestlers lunge and try to unbalance each other or secure an advantageous hold on the thick belt which is the only garb worn by the wrestlers. To win a bout, a wrestler must drive his opponent out of the ring or trip or throw him to the ground. A wrestler loses if any part of his body except the soles of his feet touches the ground. If both wrestlers fall or go out of the ring, the first one out or the one who lands on the bottom loses. Because sumo is not contested in weight divisions, all top sumo wrestlers are huge men, with many over 6 feet tall and weighing over 300 pounds. The referee supervises the bout and decides the winner in close situations. In addition to the referee, there is a panel of 5 judges who confer and decide contests in which the referee is unable to determine a winner. Sumo retains many ancient feudal customs with the wrestlers having a hierarchy ranging from the grand champions to the novices who must wait on those who outrank them. The bouts, though not following a weight division system, are conducted in classes according to rank with a wrestler being allowed to rise only after first proving himself in the lower ranks. Likewise the referees have a ranking system, and the higher the class of the wrestlers, the higher the rank of the referee conducting the bout.

Sunday punch *boxing* A boxer's hardest and most effective punch.

Super Bowl The championship game of the National Football League played between the teams winning the American and National Conference championships and held usually in a different city each year.

supercharged Equipped with a supercharger.

supercharger *motor sports* A blower that forces more air, and consequently a greater fuel-air mixture, into an internal-combustion engine to produce more horsepower than is possible with a conventional air intake.

superfecta *pari-mutuel betting* A variation of the perfecta in which a bettor must select the first 4 finishers of a race in the correct order of finish in order to win. — compare TRIFECTA

super heavyweight A weight lifter who competes in the super heavyweight division. — see DIVISION

super set *weight lifting* A set of exercises for one group of muscles followed immediately by a set for the opposing muscles.

superspeedway *auto racing* A motor speedway used especially for stock car racing that is typically 2 to 2½ miles long with extremely high-banked turns which allow the cars to go at or near top speed for the entire race.

superstar A big-name athlete who is conspicuous by his outstanding talent, his consistent superior performance, his leadership qualities, and his ability to markedly effect the outcome of a contest. Superstars usually have high salaries or high earnings. In team sports, they are standout members of the team whose contributions to the team are often significantly greater than those of other players. The superstar usually gets more exposure in the media, and as a result he tends to take on the status of a local or national hero in both team and individual sports.

Super Stock see ELIMINATOR

supersub A substitute (as on a basketball team)

who is as good as or nearly as good as the starter he regularly replaces.

supplement *horse racing* To enter a horse in a stakes race after the normal closing date for that race.

support *gymnastics* A position in which the body is supported by the hands pushing down against a surface (as the floor or an apparatus) with the torso above the hands. (also called *rest*) — compare HANG

support money *motor racing* Money paid by a manufacturer to a driver or rider who wins or finishes well in a race while using the manufacturer's vehicle but who is competing independently of the factory team.

surf To ride the surf (as on a surfboard); to engage in surfing.

surface dive *swimming* A dive made while swimming at the surface usually by bending at the waist and submerging the head until the torso is nearly vertical and then raising the legs into the air so as to glide down. From this position, the swimmer can move deeper by pulling with the arms or kicking.

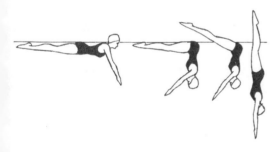

surface dive

surface interval *scuba diving* The interval of time between repetitive dives during which the diver is on the surface. It is an important consideration in computing the time and depth of decompression stops.

surface line *scuba diving* A line that is secured to the diver and to the boat so that the diver can quickly find his way back to the boat when ascending.

surface plug see PLUG

surfari *surfing* A group of surfers traveling together in search of a good surfing area.

surfboard *surfing* A long narrow board of lightweight wood or fiberglass-covered foam that is used for riding the waves. Surfboards vary in size from the big guns 11 feet or more in length, which are heavy and narrow and are used for fast riding through heavy surf, to the small hotdogging or pig boards used only on small shorebreaking waves. A typical example of the modern surfboard is the Malibu board, a medium-size board that is a compromise between the gun and the hotdogging board. — see MALIBU

surf-cast *fishing* To cast bait or a lure in surfcasting.

surfcaster *fishing* Someone who engages in surfcasting.

surfcasting *fishing* The casting of bait or a lure from the seashore into or beyond breaking waves.

surf-casting rod A fishing rod that is 6 to 7 feet long and has a 28-to-32-inch handle with separate grips for both hands and is used for surf casting.

surfer Someone who engages in the sport of surfing.

surfer's knot *surfing* A hard lump just below a surfer's knee or on the top of his foot that is caused by constant friction between the skin and the board in paddling the board out beyond the breakers.

surf fishing *fishing* Saltwater fishing involving the casting of bait or lures into or beyond the breakers for fish that normally feed on sea animals uncovered by the wave action or for larger fish that feed on these fish.

surfing The sport of riding the waves on a surfboard. Born in Hawaii during the reign of the kings, the sport is widely enjoyed today all over the world but especially in Hawaii, in Australia, and on the west coasts of North and South America. The surfboard, which is held constantly at a downward angle, actually slides down the wall of water as the wave moves shoreward, but because the water in front of the board is continuously rising, it somewhat counteracts the gravitational pull on the board making the board and rider appear to remain relatively motionless on a single moving mound of water. The board is normally paddled beyond the line at which the waves are breaking where the surfer waits for a suitable wave. To catch the wave, the surfer must paddle hard in the same direction the wave is moving and try to match the speed of the wave. Once he is caught in the wave, he stands sideways on the board, normally with his left foot forward, and maneuvers the board by shifting his weight. By leaning to one side, he can turn the board to cut diagonally across the wave. By leaning forward, he causes the front of the board to sit lower on the water and move down the wave faster. To pull out of a wave (as when nearing shore), the rider usually shifts his weight to the rear and allows the wave to break over the board or he turns the board and, using the force of the rising swell, rides back over the top of the wave and into the calm water behind. Though it appears relatively simple, surfriding requires stamina and good swimming skills, for even the best of surfers is occasionally knocked off the board. In competition, surfers are required to ride a specified number of waves within a time period (as 3 waves in 30 minutes or, in championship competition, 6 waves in 45 minutes) and are judged on how soon they catch the wave, the length of the ride, and ability in maneuvering the board on the wave. — compare BODY SURFING

surfmanship The art or skill of maneuvering a surfboard safely.

surf mat A rubber-coated inflatable canvas float that is rectangular in shape and is used at a beach for floating in the water or for riding the surf.

surf-off *surfing* The final round or a tie-breaking round in surfing competition.

surfriding The sport of riding the breaking waves (as on a surfboard or in a dory).

surf ski A long narrow shallow boat usually for 2 people that is used in Australia for surfriding.

suspended game *baseball* A called game that will be finished at a later date.

swamp **1** To sink a boat by allowing water to enter over the side.
2 *of a boat* To fill with water from over the side and sink.

swan balance see SWAN SUPPORT

swan dive *diving* A forward header in which the diver extends his legs to the rear and arches his back usually also stretching his arms out and up as he turns toward the water.

swan scale *gymnastics* A scale performed usually on a balance beam in a position that somewhat resembles a split with one leg stretched out in back with the top of the thigh, the knee, and the top of the foot in contact with the beam and the other leg in front but bent so that the shin and top of the foot rest on the beam. In the swan scale the torso is held vertical and the arms are raised.

swan support or **swan balance** *gymnastics* A balancing position assumed usually on one of the

uneven parallel bars in which the gymnast balances on the front of the hips and extends her legs out to the rear and arches her back.

swan vault *gymnastics* A vault in which the gymnast extends his legs to the rear and arches his back after touching the horse but before landing.

¹swat *baseball* A long hit and especially a home run.

²swat *baseball* To hit a ball solidly with the bat.

sway bar A metal bar attached close to and parallel to the axle of a racing car to reduce excessive swaying during turns.

sweats A sweatsuit. ⟨quit in the middle of a race, picked up his *sweats* and went home — Pat Putnam, *Sports Illustrated*⟩

sweatsuit An outfit consisting of a long-sleeve shirt and long pants that usually have elastic cuffs and a drawstring waist that is worn in practice and often during a warm-up period before a contest. The inside of the sweatsuit is typically napped to absorb perspiration. (also called *warm-up suit*)

Swedish box *gymnastics* A vaulting apparatus consisting of a series of rectangular frames graded in size to fit one over the other. — see illustration at THIEF VAULT

Swedish fall *gymnastics* A fall forward from a standing position or from a front scale with the force of the fall absorbed by the arms and with the body finishing in a prone position supported on the hands and one foot with the other leg extended back and up.

Swedish medley *track and field* A sprint medley with legs of 440, 220, 220, and 300 yards respectively in indoor competition.

¹sweep **1** *curling* To brush the ice immediately ahead of a moving stone with the broom in order to remove small bits of dirt or straw that might affect the movement of the stone and also to attempt to increase the distance the stone will travel. Though evidence as to the effect of sweeping on the distance the stone travels is inconclusive, sweeping still plays a major part in keeping all members of a rink actively engaged in the play.
2 *football* To carry the ball on a sweep.

²sweep **1** A winning of all the contests or all the places in a competition. ⟨made a 3-game *sweep* of their series⟩ ⟨helped his team to a *sweep* of the first 3 places in the finals⟩
2 or **sweep stroke** *canoeing* A stroke employed especially for steering in which the stern paddler places his blade in the water out to the

side even with his hip and sweeps it back toward the stern and the bow paddler places his paddle in the water at the bow and sweeps it around to a point even with his hip.

3 *football* A running play in which the ballcarrier runs around the end of the line usually following a number of blockers who try to clear the way for him. — see also POWER SWEEP

4 *rowing* A long oar used to propel a racing shell. The oars used for an 8-man crew are typically 12 to 12½ feet long and have a 2-foot-long blade.

sweep check *ice hockey* A stick check made usually from a position in front of the puck carrier in which the stick is laid nearly flat on the ice and swept toward the puck.

sweeper 1 *bowling* A good hook that clears all or most of the pins.

2 or **sweeper back** *soccer* A lone back who plays between the line of defenders and the goal in the Catenaccio system.

sweeping score see TEE LINE

sweep pass *ice hockey* A pass made by sweeping the puck toward the player who is to receive the pass rather than by hitting the puck.

sweep shot *ice hockey* A shot made by moving the puck with a sweeping motion of the stick.

sweepstakes see STAKES

sweep stroke see SWEEP (*canoeing*)

sweet spot The area surrounding the center of mass of a racket, bat, or clubhead which is the most effective part with which to hit the ball.

¹swim To propel oneself through the water by pulling against the water with the arms and hands and by kicking; to engage in the sport or pastime of swimming.

²swim A period of swimming. ⟨go for a *swim*⟩

swim fin A flat rubber or plastic shoe with a long front expanded into a paddle that is worn in pairs by a swimmer or skin diver to give added thrust to the kick. (also called *fin, flipper*) — see illustration at SCUBA DIVER

swimmable *of a body or stretch of water* Suitable for swimming.

swimmer Someone who swims and especially one who swims well; someone who engages in swimming competition.

swimming The sport of propelling oneself through the water by kicks and arm strokes. Swimming competition, most often conducted in pools, involves 4 basic propulsion strokes: the crawl, the backstroke, the butterfly stroke, and the breaststroke. The most common size for pools is 50 meters or 55 yards. There are smaller pools of 25 yards which are used in competition, but because these pools require the competitors to make twice as many turns which affect their overall time, there is a separate category for short-course records. The pool is divided lengthwise into lanes for the competitors. Each lane is at least 6 feet wide and is separated from the other lanes by a series of floats strung on a rope that runs the length of the pool. For all races except the backstroke, the swimmers start from a platform not more than 2½ feet above the surface of the water and at the starting signal dive into the water. For the start of the backstroke, the swimmers grasp the edge of the pool or a handgrip on the platform and hold themselves in a tuck position against the wall almost out of the water. At the signal they spring backwards to begin the stroke upon hitting the water. A meet normally includes races in each of the 4 basic strokes at distances of 100 and 200 meters or 110 and 220 yards. Freestyle competition, in which the crawl stroke is invariably used, also is contested at 400, 800, and 1500 meters or 440, 880, and 1760 yards. In addition to the individual races, there are usually the individual medley, in which each competitor has to use all 4 strokes; team relay races; and the medley relay, in which each team member has to swim a different stroke. When competition is held in a 50-yard pool, the distances are normally 100, 200, 400, 800, and 1650 yards. — see also BACKSTROKE, BREASTSTROKE, BUTTERFLY, CRAWL; DIVING

¹swing 1 A stroke or blow delivered with one or both arms swept in an arc.

2 *cricket* The sudden sideways movement of a bowled ball just before it bounces that is caused by the smooth surface of the cover when the ball is new and by the angle of the seams with respect to the line of flight instead of by side spin imparted by the bowler. Though not strictly parallel, the swing is to cricket roughly what the knuckleball is to baseball.

3 or **swing pass** *football* A short pass to a back running to the outside; flare.

4 *gymnastics* A movement in which the body is swung forward or backward through an arc around the point of support which is usually overhead.

5 *skating* The uncontrolled rotation of the body in the direction of the edge being skated which sometimes results in the free leg's moving past the skating leg.

6 *skiing* A high-speed parallel turn.

swing

²swing **1** To attempt to strike an object by sweeping the hand or a club, bat, or racket through an arc to meet the object; to make a swing.

2 *basketball* To be able to play effectively in 2 different positions; to be a swingman.

3 *of a back in football* To run to the outside of the formation in anticipation of receiving a swing pass.

4 *gymnastics* To perform a swing.

swing away *baseball* To take a full swing at a pitch rather than attempt to bunt the ball.

swing bar or **swing bell** *weight training* A weight device consisting of a short bar (as from a dumbbell) with weight disks fastened at the center that is gripped with both hands and used for swinging exercises.

swing bowler *cricket* A bowler who bowls inswingers and outswingers.

swing dogs *dogsled racing* The pair of dogs hitched between the point dogs and the wheel dogs.

swing from one's heels To swing as hard as possible (as in baseball or tennis).

swinging bunt *baseball* A ball that is swung at but poorly hit so that it rolls slowly along the ground like a bunt.

swingman A player who is capable of playing effectively in 2 different positions and especially of playing both guard and forward on a basketball team.

swing pass see SWING (*football*)

swing roll *skating* A roll performed with a controlled swing of the free foot past the skating foot and then back alongside it.

swing up *gymnastics* A movement from a prone position or from a hang to a support (as a handstand or a sitting position on a horizontal bar) made by swinging the legs back and up and at the same time pulling or pushing with the arms.

swingweight *golf* The overall balance of a club that is evident when the club is swung.

swingy *of the ice surface in curling* Offering less than usual resistance to the curl of a stone.

swipe *horse racing* A groom.

swish *basketball* To shoot a swisher. ⟨he drove across the lane and *swished* in a hook — Peter Carry, *Sports Illustrated*⟩

swisher *basketball* A successful shot that passes through the cords of the net without touching the rim. ⟨his corner *swisher* gave the Celtics a 101–

100 lead . . . with eight seconds left — Bob Ryan, *Boston Globe*⟩

¹switch **1** A simultaneous exchange by 2 teammates in basketball or lacrosse of the opponents each is guarding. The switch is usually made on a screen with the player whose man set the screen picking up his teammate's man and the teammate switching to guard the player who set the screen.

2 *volleyball* An exchange of places by 2 players after the serve so that a setter who has wound up on the back line because of the rotation can move to the front line to receive the pass and set the ball for the spiker.

3 *wrestling* A reversal maneuver in which a defensive wrestler who is held by an opponent behind him and facing in the same direction reaches back and secures a leg hold on his opponent while at the same time turning toward the arm which secures the hold, often trapping the opponent's arm under his own in the process.

²switch **1** or **switch off** To change from guarding one's own man to guarding a teammate's in basketball or lacrosse; to make a switch.

2 *volleyball* To move from the back line to the front line or from the front line to the back line in a switch.

switchback A hairpin turn.

switch-hit *baseball* To bat from either side of the plate; to be able to hit batting either left-handed or right-handed.

switch-hitter *baseball* A batter who can bat either right-handed or left-handed. A switch hitter usually bats left-handed against right-handed pitchers and vice versa.

switch off see SWITCH

sword Any of the weapons (as the foil, épée, or saber) used in fencing.

sword arm *fencing* The arm holding and maneuvering the sword.

sword hand *fencing* The hand that holds the sword.

swordplay **1** The art or skill of wielding a sword in fencing.

2 A period of fencing. ⟨engage in a little *swordplay*⟩

system *horse racing* A rule or a set of rules of handicapping used as a shortcut to finding potential winners.

T

T **1** *basketball* Technical foul. ⟨When things get a little out of hand, I like to warn players about it. . . . I try to keep it a little jocular, but at the same time they know the first guy who opens his mouth is going to get a *T*— Richie Powers⟩
2 Short for *T formation.*

tab Short for *finger tab.*

table **1** A level platform supported on legs and used for the game of billiards or table tennis. — see BILLIARD TABLE; TABLE TENNIS
2 British term meaning league standings.

table point *skiing* The point on a ski-jumping landing hill that represents the farthest point at which a jumper is expected to land. — compare CRITICAL POINT, NORM POINT

table tennis A singles or doubles game played across a 2½-foot-high table that is 9 feet long and 5 feet wide and divided by a 6-inch-high net across the middle. The players alternately hit a small hollow plastic ball back and forth across the net with rubber-faced wooden paddles. The game is started with one player serving the ball by tossing it up from the open palm and hitting it so that it strikes the server's side of the table and then the opposite side. After the serve the ball is hit so that it strikes the table only on the far side of the net, and play continues until one side fails to make a good return. Either the receiving or serving side can score points. Each side serves 5 consecutive points, and the game is played until one side scores 21 points. The game must be won by a margin of at least 2 points, so if the game is tied at 20, each side alternates serves until one side has a 2-point margin. The table is marked into service courts by a white line around the top edge of the table and one dividing the table lengthwise, but these are not used for singles play. In doubles play, all serves are made from the right-hand court of the server to the right-hand court of the receiver, and all players alternate returning the ball in a definite sequence.

¹tack *sailing* **1** To change the direction of a boat when sailing close-hauled by turning the bow toward the wind and shifting the sails so that the wind strikes the boat from the opposite side at about the same angle as before. By a repetition of this tacking maneuver progress can be made against the wind in a zigzag course where no progress could be made by heading directly into the wind. (also *come about, go about)* — compare JIBE
2 To progress toward the wind by sailing on a series of alternate tacks.

²tack **1** *sailing* **a** The lower forward corner of a fore-and-aft sail. **b** The direction a boat is headed with respect to the direction of the wind. When the wind approaches the boat from the starboard (right) side, the boat is on a starboard tack; when from the port (left) side, the boat is on a port tack. A boat will be on a tack whenever it is not heading directly into or directly away from the wind, whether on a beat, reach, or run; but in common usage a tack refers to a heading toward the direction of the wind. **c** The progress of a boat on one tack. **d** A change of direction when close-hauled from one tack to another; an instance of tacking.
2 The equipment (as saddle, bridle, bit, and reins) used on a horse.

¹tackle **1** To throw or knock the ballcarrier to the ground or to hold him and stop his forward progress in football or rugby.
2 To knock or kick the ball away from the control of the ballhandler in field hockey, soccer, or team handball.
3 *Australian Rules football* To grab and hold on to the ballcarrier so that his progress is stopped, and he is forced to pass the ball. In making a tackle the defenders do not throw the ballcarrier to the ground as in football or rugby, and the defending players may not interfere with his opportunity to pass the ball, though they do not have to allow a teammate of the ballcarrier to catch the pass.
4 *hurling* To charge an opponent shoulder to shoulder when he is playing the ball or attempting to gain possession of the ball.

tackle

5 *lacrosse* To body-check or crosse-check an opponent who has the ball or to try to dislodge the ball from the opponent's stick.

6 *water polo* To make body contact with an opposing player who has the ball.

²**tackle** 1 The act or an instance or method of tackling an opponent or the ball being played by an opponent.

2 **a** The equipment used in a sport (as archery or fishing). **b** A boat's rigging.

3 *football* **a** Either of 2 offensive linemen who normally play just outside the guards. Offensive

tackle: football player tackles the ballcarrier; soccer player tackles the ball

tackles are primarily responsible for blocking to create holes in the interior of the line for the ballcarrier to run through and to protect the quarterback during pass plays. **b** Either of 2 defensive linemen who line up inside the defensive ends. Defensive tackles normally rush the passer and try to contain running plays coming to the inside. **c** The position played by a tackle.

4 *wrestling* see PICKUP

tackle back *field hockey* To tackle a player who has himself just gained possession of the ball on a tackle.

tackle eligible play *football* An offensive play in which one of the tackles becomes eligible to receive a pass by being the outermost player on one side of an unbalanced line. Because the tackle normally wears a uniform number of an ineligible receiver, he is required to inform the officials that he will be playing in the position of an eligible receiver.

tackler A player who makes a tackle.

tackling The action, manner, or quality of making tackles.

tackling dummy *football* A heavy stuffed cylindrical bag used for tackling practice.

¹**tag** *baseball* 1 To put out a runner by touching him with the ball or with the gloved hand holding the ball while he is off base.

2 To get a hit or run off a pitcher. ⟨was *tagged* for 5 runs in the second inning⟩

²**tag** 1 The act or an instance of tagging a player with the ball; a putout made by tagging the player. ⟨made the *tag* on the runner at second⟩

2 *fishing* A small piece of tinsel or other bright material around the shank of the hook at the end of the body of an artificial fly.

tag out *baseball* A putout made by tagging the base runner.

tag team A team of 2 or more professional wrestlers who are supposed to spell each other during a match. The wrestler in the ring must tag his partner before his partner may enter the ring.

tag up *baseball* To remain touching a base on a fly ball with the intention of advancing to the next base after the ball is caught.

¹**tail** The rear part of a ski or a surfboard.

²**tail** *of a fastball in baseball* To deviate from the apparent line of flight in the direction to the same side as the pitcher's throwing hand. ⟨a right-hander whose fastball *tails* away from a left-hand batter and *tails* in to a right-hand batter⟩

tailback *football* The running back who lines up farthest from the line of scrimmage in certain formations (as the single wing or I formation).

tailblock *surfing* The rear area of a surfboard.

tail female *horse racing* The female ancestral line of a racehorse.

tail fly *fishing* A fly that is tied to the end of a leader as distinguished from a dropper fly.

tail football see FLAG FOOTBALL

tail male *horse racing* The male ancestral line of a racehorse.

tape

¹take **1** To win a contest. ⟨*took* the set 6 games to 2⟩
2 *baseball* **a** To refrain from swinging at a pitch. ⟨*took* a called third strike⟩ **b** To field a batted ball. ⟨he *took* the ball on the first hop⟩ **c** To advance to a base. ⟨*took* second on the throw⟩
3 *of a fish* To strike at bait or a lure.
²take **1** *baseball* **a** The act or an instance of taking a pitch. **b** Instruction from a coach or the manager to take a pitch.
2 *pari-mutuel betting* The money deducted from a betting pool for profit and taxes before payoffs are computed. — compare HANDLE
take a dive *of a boxer* To pretend to be knocked out in a fixed fight.
take a wicket *cricket* To cause an opposing batsman to be out.
take croquet *croquet* To croquet a ball.
takedown *wrestling* The act or an instance of gaining control over an opponent and forcing him to the mat. A takedown is worth 2 points.
take down **1** *horse racing* see SET DOWN
2 *wrestling* To force an opponent to the mat; to secure a takedown.
take gas *of a surfer* To lose control and wipe out.
take guard *of a cricket batsman* To assume a defensive position with the bat in front of the wicket.
takeoff **1 a** The act or an instance of leaving a surface (as in diving, figure skating, track and field competition, or ski jumping) to make a dive or jump or to clear an obstacle. **b** The rise from the ground in making an ascent by aircraft or balloon.
2 The point at which a takeoff is made.
take off To make a takeoff.
takeoff board *track and field* A rectangular board set into the ground at the end of the long jump and triple jump runways that assists the jumper in his takeoff. The far edge of the takeoff board serves as a scratch line. The runner may step on the board to begin his takeoff, but if any part of his foot touches the ground beyond the board, he has fouled. (also called *stamp board*)
takeoff fan *track and field* An arc of usually 180 degrees in front of the high jump crossbar in which the competitors make their run-up prior to jumping. The length of the run-up is unlimited, but the area should provide the competitors with at least 18 meters (57 feet 3 inches) of space.
takeoff foot *track and field* The foot on which a takeoff is made.
takeoff leg *track and field* The leg that supplies

the push in attempting a jump (as in the long jump) or in attempting to clear a hurdle. — compare LEAD LEG
take-out *curling* The knocking of an opposing stone out of play.
takeover *track and field* The exchange of the baton in a relay race.
take over *football* To gain possession of the ball on a turnover. ⟨*took over* on downs⟩
takeover zone see EXCHANGE ZONE
take the blade *fencing* To make contact with the opponent's sword in preparation for an attack in order to move it out of the line or to a new line (as by a bind or envelopment).
take the count *of a boxer* To fail to rise before a count of 10 is reached and thereby lose by a knockout; to be counted out.
¹tally A score or point in a competition.
²tally To register a score or point.
tallyho *fox hunting* A cry by a huntsman on sighting a fox breaking from cover.
talus *mountain climbing* **1** A slope covered by small rock debris.
2 Rock debris at the base of a cliff.
tambour *court tennis* A projection of the main wall into the court on the hazard side about 15 feet from the end wall. The tambour reduces the width of the court on the hazard side by about 1½ feet and its sloping surface causes balls to bounce off it at unusual angles.
Tampa pilot *shuffleboard* A pilot disk played near the tip of the scoring area on the shooter's side. — compare CROSS PILOT
¹tandem Being or relating to a competition in which 2 teammates compete as a pair (as in canoeing, surfing, or bicycle racing).
²tandem *bowling* A leave of 2 pins with one directly behind the other.
¹tank **1** A swimming pool.
2 An air tank.
²tank To lose a game or contest intentionally; dump.
tank job The act or an instance of deliberately losing a contest.
tank suit *swimming* A lightweight tight-fitting swim suit worn in competition as distinguished from one worn for casual bathing (as at a beach).
tap **1** *bowling* A solid hit in the pocket that leaves a single pin standing.
2 Short for *tapoff.*
tape **1** A solid narrow band running along the top of the net in certain net games. ⟨a topped backhand hit the top of the *tape* and dribbled over — Neil Amdur, *New York Times*⟩

2 A narrow line used to delineate the boundaries in certain court games (as tennis or badminton). **3** *track and field* A piece of string or yarn stretched across the track 4 to 5 feet above the finish line that aids the officials in determining the winner of a race. (also called *finish tape*)

tape measure job A long home run in baseball.

tapered leader *fishing* A leader used in fly fishing that tapers from a heavy section where it is attached to the line to a very small diameter at the end where the fly is tied.

tapered line SEE FLY LINE

tap-in 1 *basketball* A field goal made by tapping a rebound into the basket.
2 *golf* A putt made from very close to the cup.

tap in 1 *basketball* To tap a rebound into the basket; to make a tip-in.
2 *golf* To tap a ball into the cup.

tap loop jump SEE TOE LOOP JUMP

tapoff SEE TIPOFF

tap out *judo* To tap one's opponent or the mat twice to indicate submission when a choke or twisting hold has been applied by the opponent. The match is immediately stopped when one competitor taps out, and the victory is given to the opponent.

tap weight *curling* The momentum needed to make a stone gently knock an opposing stone out of position or curl in around guard stones.

Tarbuck knot A sliding friction knot that is formed by making a large loop in the end of a rope and twisting the end around the standing part inside the loop 3 or more times, then bringing the end up around the standing part above the loop and then back down through the smaller loop thus formed. — see illustration at KNOT

target The mark at which one aims for scoring in various sports:
1 *archery* A usually circular outline mounted on a straw backing and marked by concentric rings into various scoring areas, with the innermost area (*bull's-eye*) having the highest scoring value. **a** *target archery* A 48-inch circular face marked with a 9.6-inch center spot and 4 concentric rings each 4.8 inches wide. The bull's-eye is gold and has a scoring value of 9 points. It may have a black center aiming spot no larger than 3 inches in diameter. The ring immediately out from the bull's-eye is red and has a scoring value of 7 points. Outside that is a blue 5-point ring, then a black 3-point ring, and finally a white ring worth one point. The target used in interna-

tional competition and for the FITA international rounds is a 48-inch (122 centimeter) target face with the 5 colored scoring rings of a regular target but with each scoring area divided into 2 equal sections and with the scoring value for the inner section worth one point more than for the outer section of the same color. The shot thus can score from one to 10 points in 1-point increments. A smaller (80 centimeter) target is also used with the same scoring values and with the rings in the same proportions as the larger target. **b** *field archery* A circular face 6, 12, 18, or 24 inches in diameter that consists of an inner circle and a surrounding ring. For the field round the inner circle is half the total diameter of the target and is white with a black center spot ¼ the diameter of the circle. The surrounding ring is black. The inner circle has a scoring value of 5 while the ring is worth 3 points. The target face for the hunter's round is the same size and has the same scoring value as that for the field round but is all black with a white center spot and a white line separating the inner circle from the outer ring.
2 *fencing* A part of the body on which a valid hit may be made. The target area differs with the weapon being used. For foil fencing, the target is the torso excluding the head, arms, and legs. For épée fencing, the entire body is a valid target. The saber target includes all of the body above the top of the hips. — see illustration at FENCING
3 *shooting* A sheet of paper or cardboard marked with an inner circle and 9 concentric rings and usually having scoring values of 10 for the inner circle decreasing to one for the outer ring. The innermost rings are normally black while the outer ones are white. The target for the 300-meter distance is one meter in diameter with an inner bull's-eye 600 millimeters (23½ inches) in diameter. For pistol shooting, the target is usually a 5-foot-high 1½-foot-wide silhouette of a man marked with 10 scoring rings valued from 10 (for the inner circle) to one. Several targets are set up at a distance of 25 meters from the shooter and are designed to turn from a side to a front view at a predetermined rate of speed.
4 *skydiving* An area marked on the ground by a cross large enough to be seen from the sky by the divers and which contains a 6-meter (6½-yard) circular landing area of very small gravel or sand with a small disk at the exact center.
5 A clay pigeon.

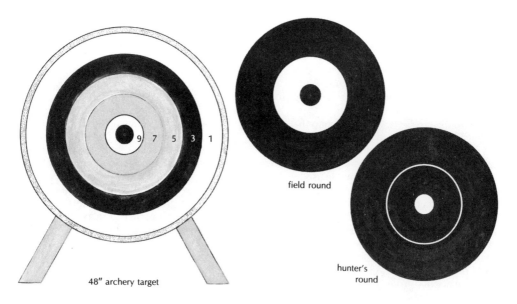

9 7 5 3 1

48″ archery target

field round

hunter's round

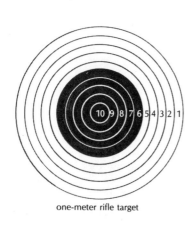

10 9 8 7 6 5 4 3 2 1

one-meter rifle target

4
5
6
7
8
9
10
9
8
7
6
5
4
3
2
1

pistol target

target archery Competition in which archers shoot at a standard target at a fixed distance. — see ARCHERY

target arrow *archery* An arrow used for target shooting that normally has an equal-diameter shaft, a relatively small fletching, and a target point.

target bow *archery* A bow used for target

shooting as distinguished from one used for bow hunting. A target bow normally has a lower draw weight than one used for hunting and frequently has additional equipment such as a bowsight and stabilizer bars attached for improved accuracy.

target captain *archery* A member of a group of usually 4 archers assigned to a particular target who is responsible for ordering the beginning

443

and the end of the shooting, determining the scoring values of each arrow in the target, and deciding minor questions of interpretation of the rules.

target diving The sport of diving for accuracy from a high platform or tower (as 80 feet high) into a target (as a paper circle or a ring of balloons) on the water.

target point *archery* An arrow pile that tapers conically to a point and that is used in competitive shooting. — see illustration at ARROW

target rifle *shooting* A rifle used for target shooting as distinguished from one used for hunting. Target rifles are typically heavier than those used in hunting, and the additional weight adds stability for more precise aiming. There are normally 2 sizes of target rifles used in competition: small-bore (.22 caliber) and big-bore (.32 caliber).

target round *archery* A round in target shooting as distinguished from one in field archery or in flight or clout shooting.

Tartan A trademark used for a synthetic surface used in place of cinder or dirt for running tracks and racetracks.

Tartan Turf A trademark used for a synthetic surface used in place of grass especially on baseball and football fields.

Tasman Series A series of auto races in Australia and New Zealand for formula 5000 cars.

tassel *archery* A piece of cloth used to clean wet or dirty arrows.

taut-line hitch A sliding friction knot used to attach one rope to another or one end of a rope to the standing part that is formed by making 2 turns around the other rope, bringing the end across its own standing part, making another turn in the same direction, and tucking the end under the last turn so that it resembles a clove hitch with an extra turn.

taxi *football* To put a player on a taxi squad; to play on a taxi squad. ⟨ a tight end . . . who may be *taxied* for experience⟩

taxi squad *football* A group of players under contract to a professional ball club who may practice with the team but who are ineligible to play in the team's games. The term comes from the practice of a former professional football club owner of employing extra players as drivers for a taxi company he also owned. In recent years the use of taxi squads has been abandoned. (also called *cab squad*)

taxi-squadder A football player who is a member of a taxi squad.

T-bar lift A ski lift which consists of a series of bars in the shape of an inverted T suspended from a moving overhead cable. Each bar is intended to pull 2 skiers.

T-bone *auto racing* To strike another car broadside or to run head-on into an object (as a pit wall).

team Two or more players or participants that make up a side or a single competitive unit in a sport. The term may be used for the entire body of participants representing a club or school and including the regulars and reserves, or it may mean only those players in action at a given time. The term is also used in some sports to refer to a specific group of participants (as those that participate in a particular relay event in track and field or swimming).

team area *football* An area on the sidelines between the two 35-yard lines on opposite sides of the field in which the players benches are located and which is for the use of the coaches, reserves, and staff members of the clubs.

teamer An athlete who is a member of a team. ⟨a specialty *teamer*⟩

team foul 1 *basketball* A personal foul other than an offensive or player control foul committed by a team member and charged to the team as one of a limited number permitted before the bonus free throw is in effect. In professional play each team is limited to a maximum of 4 team fouls in each quarter (3 in each overtime period). In college play the limit is 6 during a half; in high school play, 4 during a half. The team foul is not a part of basketball played under international rules since international rules award no free throws except when a player is fouled in the act of shooting and the shot is missed.
2 *speedball* A foul such as illegal substitution charged to the team rather than to an individual player in women's play that is identical to a technical foul in men's play.
3 *water polo* A personal or major foul committed by a team member that is charged against the team as one of 10 permitted before a player is suspended from the game for 30 seconds. The suspended player is the one committing the tenth foul. After 10 fouls have been charged against a team and a player has been suspended, the team's total reverts again to one on the next team foul. After 10 more fouls are charged against the team, another player is suspended for 30 seconds.

team game A game (as basketball, football, or soccer) that is played between 2 teams.

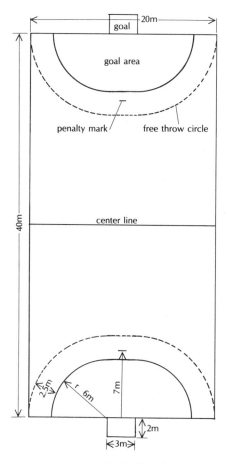

goal —20m—

goal area

penalty mark / free throw circle

40m

center line

2.5m r 6m 7m

2m

3m

team handball court

team handball A game played between 2 teams of 7 players using an inflated ball on a rectangular playing area (*court*) having a goal at each end with the object to move the ball by passing and by dribbling basketball style and to throw it past the opposing goalkeeper into the goal for a score and to prevent the other team from scoring. The game is played only with the hands, and kicking the ball is not permitted. Each team consists of a goalkeeper, who normally plays in the goal area in front of the goal, and 6 field players who move about the court. Players are not permitted to hold, push, or trip opponents, but they may charge opponents in an attempt to gain control of the ball. Play is continuous, stopping only when a goal is scored, when the ball is lost out of bounds, or when the referee stops play for a violation, such as kicking or improper dribbling or failing to pass the ball in the required time, or for a foul or injury. The game is started by one player throwing the ball in from the sideline after winning a coin toss. Any time a player has stopped dribbling, he must pass the ball within 3 seconds, and he may not take more than 3 steps while holding the ball. The game is normally played in two 30-minute halves. — see also FIELDBALL

teammate Someone who plays on the same team as another.

team pursuit *cycling* A pursuit race between 2 or more teams. — see PURSUIT

team roping *rodeo* An event in which 2 cowboys working as a team attempt to rope and immobilize a steer in the shortest time possible. One team member lassoes the steer around the neck while his partner lassoes the steer's 2 hind legs. The timing stops when the steer is standing upright but unable to move.

team tennis Tennis played between teams with a match consisting of 5 sets: men's singles, women's singles, men's doubles, women's doubles, and mixed doubles. Each set is won by the side winning 6 games; a game is won by the side first getting 4 points. The winning team is the one winning the most games during the match.

tech inspection *auto racing* An official prerace inspection of the cars entered in a race to ensure that they meet racing specifications (as for weight, brakes, steering mechanism, and ground clearance).

technical Short for *technical foul.*

technical foul **1** *basketball* An infraction such as delay of the game, illegally calling a time-out, holding onto the basket, or unsportsmanlike conduct that is penalized by awarding a free throw (2 free throws in international play) to the other team. In high school and college play, the team shooting the free throw is awarded the ball out of bounds after the free throw, but in professional play the team in possession of the ball at the time the technical foul was called is awarded the ball out of bounds. In American college and professional basketball, a player is automatically ejected from the game if he receives 2 technical fouls during one game, regardless of the number of personal fouls he has accumulated. In international play, a technical foul counts the same as a personal foul as one of the maximum of 4 fouls a player may accumulate before being ejected. — compare PERSONAL FOUL, VIOLATION

445

2 *lacrosse* A foul such as interference with an opponent, stalling, entering the goal crease illegally, throwing the crosse, or holding or pushing an opponent that is less serious than a personal foul and that is penalized by loss of possession of the ball if the player's team has possession or suspension of the guilty player for 30 seconds if the other team has possession.

3 *speedball* A foul in men's play such as delay of the game, illegal substitution, or unsportsmanlike conduct that results in a penalty kick for the opposing team. — compare PERSONAL FOUL, VIOLATION; TEAM FOUL

4 *water polo* A procedural infraction such as beginning play before the referee's signal, playing the ball while standing on the bottom of the pool, holding the ball underwater, holding onto the goal, or delay of the game that is penalized by awarding a free throw to the nearest opponent. — compare MAJOR FOUL, PERSONAL FOUL

technical knockout *boxing* The termination of a bout when a boxer is unable or unwilling to continue but has not been counted out. The referee may stop a fight when he feels a boxer is unable to defend himself or risks serious injury by continuing.

¹tee **1** *curling* The circular area in the center of the house.

2 *football* A usually plastic device used to support the football in an upright position for a placekick.

3 *golf* **a** A small wooden or plastic peg with a concave top on which the ball is placed prior to being driven. The term is applied occasionally to a small mound of dirt used for the same purpose. **b** The area from which a golf ball is driven at the beginning of play on a hole.

²tee or **tee up** To place a ball on a tee to be hit or kicked.

teeing ground *golf* The area from which a ball is driven at the beginning of play on a hole; tee.

tee line *curling* A line through the middle of the house parallel to the back line. On a sliding delivery, the player is required to release the stone before it passes the near tee line. After an opponent's shot has passed the tee line of the house at which he is aiming, it may be swept by the opposing curlers in an effort to get it to continue out of the scoring area. (also called *sweeping score*)

tee off **1** To hit a ball hard. ⟨*teed off* on the first pitch and drove the ball into the stands⟩

2 *golf* To drive a ball off a tee to start play on a hole.

tee shot *golf* A shot made from the tee. — compare APPROACH SHOT, PUTT

tee up see TEE

telegraph To inadvertently reveal one's intention to do something (as to make a shot or pass or throw a punch) usually by some recognizable preliminary pattern of movement.

telegraphic match see MAIL MATCH

telemark *skiing* **1** A position in which one ski is advanced ahead of the other.

2 A turn made in the telemark position in which the outside ski is advanced considerably ahead of the other ski and turned inward at a steadily widening angle until the turn is completed.

telescopic sight see SIGHT

telltale **1** *sailing* A strip of material that is tied to a shroud to indicate wind direction.

2 *squash racquets* A strip of resonant material (as metal) extending along the base of the front wall to a height of 17 inches. A ball must strike the wall above the telltale to be a legal return. (also called *board, tin*)

Tempest *sailing* A sloop-rigged keelboat of a one-design class that is approximately 22 feet long, has a sail area of 247 square feet plus a 225-square-foot spinnaker, and carries a crew of 2.

tempo see CHRISTIE

tender A small sailboat that is inherently unstable with a tendency to heel in a wind.

tend goal To guard a goal (as in ice hockey); to play as goalkeeper.

tendinitis Inflammation of a tendon that occurs most often in the elbow or shoulder (as of a quarterback or pitcher) or in the knee (as of a runner or basketball player). (also spelled *tendonitis*)

tendon boot see BOOT (*harness racing*)

tendonitis see TENDINITIS

ten-finger grip see GRIP (*golf*)

tennis A singles or doubles game played usually outdoors on a rectangular court in which players using rackets hit a pressurized ball back and forth over a low net with the object of making a stroke that will land within the court boundaries but that the opponent cannot return. Players play on opposite sides of the net and are not permitted to interfere with the movements of their opponents. Play is started with one player, standing behind his own baseline, serving the ball over the net to the opponent so that it lands in the proper service court. A player scores a point whenever the opponent is unable to make a good return (and in the case of the receiver when the server

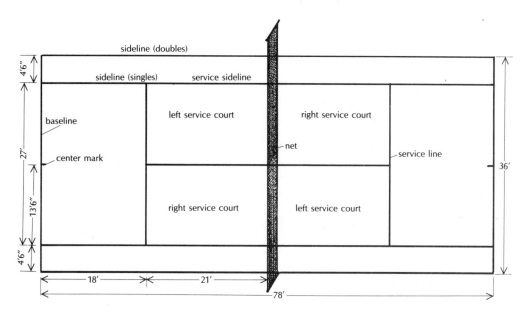

sideline (doubles)

4'6"

sideline (singles)   service sideline

baseline

left service court   right service court

net

center mark

27'

service line

36'

13'6"

right service court   left service court

4'6"

18'   21'

78'

tennis court

fails in 2 attempts to make a legal serve). Both the serving and the receiving sides can score points. Players serve for a game at a time with the serve going to the other player or side in the next game. Serves are alternated on each point first into the right and then into the left service court. A single contest is a *match* which consists of a predetermined maximum number of *sets,* each of which consists of a number of *games.* A game is won by the first side to win 4 points, though it must be by a 2-point margin. The first point in a game is traditionally called *fifteen* or *five,* the next point *thirty,* the next *forty* and the final point *game.* If both sides reach forty so that one side needs to win 2 consecutive points to win the game, the situation is known as *deuce.* From deuce, the next point won is *advantage* (it may be for the server or the receiver). If the side with advantage wins the next point, it wins the game; if the other side wins the next point, the score reverts to deuce. A set is won by the side first winning 6 games (by a 2-game margin). A match in men's competition is normally won by the side winning 2 of 3 or 3 of 5 sets; in women's play and in doubles competition, it is normally the best 2 of 3 sets. In most major competition a tiebreaker is used when a set is tied at 6 games apiece. In a tiebreaker, players alternate serves until one side reaches a predetermined number of points (as 5 or 7) at which point he wins the tiebreaker and with it the set. Other scoring plans have been tried in tennis from a 21- or 31-point game to a "no-ad" game in which there is no deuce and the first player to win 4 points wins the game, but none has become widely used. (also called *lawn tennis*)

tennis elbow Injury of the outer side of the elbow accompanied by inflammation and pain that is due usually to torn muscle fibers from excessive or violent twisting movements of the hand (as when making a topspin stroke in tennis).

tennis grip A grip normally used in holding a tennis racket and especially the Eastern grip. — see GRIP (*tennis*)

tennist A tennis player.

tenpin A bottle-shaped bowling pin used in the game of tenpins. The tenpin is 15 inches tall and has a maximum diameter of 4¾ inches tapering to 2¼ inches at the base. — see illustration at BOWLING

tenpins A bowling game in which a large heavy ball with finger holes is rolled at tenpins. — see BOWLING

10-point must system *boxing* A scoring system in which the winner of a round is given 10 points and the loser any number less than 10. In practice the difference between the 2 scores is seldom more than 2 points. If the round is scored even, each boxer is given 10.

10-second line *basketball* The division line when used in the interpretation or enforcement of the 10-second rule.

10-second rule *basketball* A rule that requires the offensive team to bring the ball across the division line within 10 seconds of inbounding or gaining possession of the ball in its backcourt.

10,000 or **10,000-meter run** *track and field* A race run over a distance of 10,000 meters (6.2 miles).

10-yard line or **10-yards line** *rugby* A broken line across the field on each side of and 10 yards from the halfway line that is parallel to the halfway line and serves as a restraining line for the receiving team on a kickoff.

terminal moraine see MORAINE

terminal tackle or **terminal rig** *fishing* The lure, leader, and sinker attached to the end of a line.

test match An international match in cricket or rugby.

Texas leaguer *baseball* A short fly ball that falls too far out to be caught by an infielder and too close in to be caught by an outfielder.

textbook Having or made with fundamental and nearly perfect form or technique. ⟨a 94-yard *textbook* drive that . . . ended with a 12-yard scoring toss — Ron Reid, *Sports Illustrated*⟩

T formation *football* An offensive formation in which the quarterback lines up close behind the center with the fullback approximately 4 to 5 yards behind the quarterback and the halfbacks on either side of and slightly ahead of the fullback so as to give the appearance of a T. There are several variations of the basic T formation, some of which, though still called T formations, no longer have the characteristic T shape. The basic T is sometimes known as the *tight T* because of the small amount of space between the linemen. In the *split T,* there is the same alignment in the backfield, but greater spacing between the linemen. In the *wing T,* one of the halfbacks plays wide of the line as a flanker (*wing*) and the other halfback and the fullback normally play side by side behind the quarterback as running backs. The *Pro T* or *Pro set,* which is popular today with professional teams, has the 2 running backs behind the quarterback and the other back wide as a flanker just as in the wing T but in addition has the end usually on the side opposite the flanker playing wide (split). In the *Slot T,* the tight end is spread away

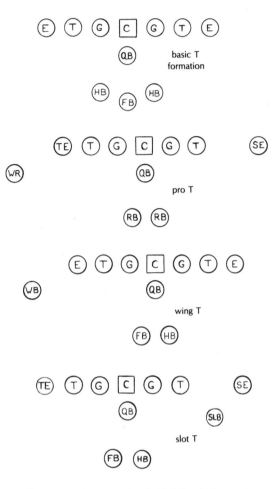

T formation: C center; E end; FB fullback; G guard; HB halfback; QB quarterback; RB running back; SE split end; SLB slot back; T tackle; TE tight end; WB wingback; WR wide receiver

from the tackle and the flankerback moves over to line up behind the slot between the tackle and the tight end. Sometimes the flanker lines up behind the slot between the tackle and split end. — compare I FORMATION, SINGLE WING, WISHBONE

thermal A rising body or current of warm air.

thermal balloon see HOT-AIR BALLOON

thermal soaring see SOARING

thief vault *gymnastics* A vault over a vaulting horse or pommel horse made by hurdling the

thief vault over a Swedish box

horse with one leg forward and one back, then when over the horse, placing the hands on the horse, and as the rear leg is brought forward pushing off with the hands to clear the horse and land on both feet.

thigh trap   *soccer*   A trap made with the thigh.

thin   **1**   *of a team or squad*   Having few talented or experienced players for each position; not deep.
2   **a** Just grazing the ball or curling stone aimed at.   **b** *bowling*   Toward the side of the pocket away from the headpin. ⟨a *thin* hit that left the 7 pin standing⟩

thinclad   A member of a track team.

third   Short for *third base.*

third base   *baseball*   **1** The base that is positioned on the baseline on the left side of the field and that is to be touched third by a base runner.
2 The player position for covering the area around third base.

third baseman   *baseball*   A player stationed usually to the right of third base who is responsible for making plays at third base and covering the area between third base and shortstop.

third home   *lacrosse*   **1** A chiefly offensive player and a member of the close attack in women's play.
2 The position played by a third home.

third man   *cricket*   **1** A fielding position far from the batsman on the off side opposite the batsman and slightly back of the line of the striker's wicket.
2 The player occupying the third man position.

third sacker   A third baseman in baseball.

30 or **thirty**   The second point made by a side in a tennis game.

35-pound weight   *track and field*   The implement used in the 35-pound weight throw that consists of a heavy metal ball attached to a handle by a welded steel link. The 35-pound weight must be 16 inches or less in overall length and 35 pounds in overall weight.

35-pound weight throw   *track and field*   A field event in which the 35-pound weight is hurled for distance with 2 hands from within a throwing circle 7 feet in diameter. In order to qualify as a legal throw the weight must land in the throwing sector formed by 2 lines extending out at a 45-degree angle (60-degree angle for college competition) from the center of the throwing circle. The 35-pound weight throw commonly replaces the hammer throw for indoor meets.

30-second clock   *basketball*   A shooting clock used to indicate the time remaining under the 30-second rule. Once a shot has been made, the timing clock is reset for another 30 seconds, even if the offensive team gains the rebound.

30-second rule   *basketball*   A rule that requires the offensive team to try for a goal within 30 seconds of inbounding or gaining possession of the ball (as after a basket or a turnover).

30-second violation   *basketball*   A violation of the 30-second rule.

.30-30 or **thirty-thirty**   *hunting*   A rifle that fires a .30 caliber cartridge having a 30-grain powder charge.

thoroughbred

thoroughbred Any of a breed of horses bred for speed and used in horse racing. The term *thoroughbred,* in contrast to *purebred,* means that a horse is a direct descendant in the male line from one of 3 English stallions of the late 17th and early 18th centuries: the Byerly Turk, the Darley Arabian, and the Godolphin Barb. The Byerly Turk was a military charger of Captain Robert Byerly in the 1690s; it was supposedly captured from the Turks in the 1686 campaign. The Darley Arabian was a gift from Thomas Darley to his father Richard around 1704. The Godolphin Barb was taken from France to England around 1730 and was eventually acquired by the Earl of Godolphin. English mares were bred to these stallions and produced the beginnings of the Thoroughbred breed. Though these 3 horses are regarded as the foundation sires of the thoroughbreds, the direct line survives only through a single descendant of each: Herod, the great-great-grandson of the Byerly Turk; Eclipse, the great-great-grandson of the Darley Arabian; and Matchem, the grandson of the Godolphin Barb.

thread the needle **1** To make a pass with extreme accuracy between defenders.

2 *of a baseball pitcher* To pitch the ball in a particular area of the strike zone.

three Short for *three turn.*

three-bagger A triple in baseball.

three-ball *golf* A golf match in which 3 players compete against one another with each playing his own ball. — compare THREESOME

three-base hit A triple in baseball.

Three-Day Event Equestrian competition held over 3 consecutive days that includes dressage competition on the first day, cross-country and endurance riding on the second, and stadium show jumping on the third day. The Three-Day Event is held as both team and individual competition; team members are also judged for the individual competition, and their performances are scored for both categories. Team scores are determined by totaling the scores of the best 3 of the 4 team riders. The dressage competition is identical to other dressage events with performers judged on a point system of from 0 to 6 points for each required movement. The endurance test consists of 4 separate phases: the first and third phases are on roads and tracks with the horses required to cover a total distance of from 16 to 20 kilometers (9.9 to 12.4 miles) at an average speed of 240 meters per minute (9 mph). The second phase is over a steeplechase course of 3600 to 4200 meters (2.2 to 2.6 miles) at an average speed of 600 meters per minute (22 mph) with an average of 3 fences to be jumped every 1000 meters. The final phase of the endurance event is a cross-country run for a total distance of 8000 meters (5 miles) at an average speed of 450 meters per minute (17 mph) with an average of 4 obstacles to be jumped every 1000 meters. The competitors are judged separately on all 4 phases with penalty points deducted for failing at obstacles or for failing to finish in the required time. Competitors can gain bonus points for finishing phases 2 and 4 under the time limit. The show jumping competition is a test of the horse's ability to perform creditably after a grueling endurance test. The event consists of 10 to 12 obstacles, including a water jump, spread over a distance of 750 to 900 meters which is to be covered at an average speed of 400 meters per minute (15 mph). One third of the obstacles are at the maximum height of 1.2 meters (4 feet). Competitors are given penalty marks for failing to jump or clear obstacles and for exceeding the time limit.

300 or **300-yard dash** *track and field* A race run over a distance of 300 yards.

.300 hitter or **three hundred hitter** A baseball player with a batting average of at least .300 which is considered exceptionally good.

three jump see WALTZ JUMP

three old cat or **three o' cat** A version of old cat played with 3 batters, and usually with an extra base, in which batters who are unable to return home safely are permitted to occupy the bases while the other player bats.

3-point circle *basketball* Either of 2 arcs marked on the court 26 feet from the baskets in one professional league. A field goal made from beyond a 3-point circle is worth 3 points rather than the usual 2 points.

three-pointer A play or situation (as in wrestling) worth 3 points; a three-point play.

3-point play *basketball* A situation in which a player is fouled as he shoots a field goal and in which he makes the field goal and the free throw for a total of 3 points.

three-point stance *football* A position assumed prior to the snap by linemen and often by running backs in which the player crouches with his feet spread while leaning forward with one hand touching the ground.

three-putt *golf* To take 3 putts to sink a ball. Par for each hole is based on the golfer's taking 2 putts to hole out.

threequarter back *rugby* Any of 4 backs who normally line up between the halfbacks and the fullback for a scrum.

three-quarter midget A scaled-down version of a midget racer that is ¾ the size of a standard midget.

threequarter nelson see NELSON

three-second area or **three-second lane** *basketball* The free throw lane when used in the interpretation or enforcement of the three-second rule.

three-second rule *basketball* A rule prohibiting an offensive player from remaining in the free throw lane for more than 3 consecutive seconds while his team is in possession of the ball in its frontcourt.

three-second violation *basketball* A violation of the three-second rule.

360 or **three-sixty** A full 360-degree revolution of the body around its vertical axis (as in surfing or freestyle skiing).

threesome *golf* 1 A match in which one player plays against 2 players who alternately hit one ball.
2 A group of 3 golfers playing together with each playing his own ball and each competing against the others.

three turn *skating* 1 A turn from forward to backward or backward to forward while changing to the opposite edge with rotation in the direction of the edge being skated.
2 A school figure consisting of a figure eight with a three turn at the outside of each circle.

throat The part of a club, racket, stick, or paddle that connects the head or blade and the shaft.

throttle *motor sports* A control that regulates the flow of fuel to an engine.

through pass *soccer* A lead pass between 2 opponents to a teammate.

through the green *golf* The area of a course in which play is permitted excluding the teeing ground, hazards, and the putting green of the hole being played; the fairway and rough.

¹throw 1 **a** To propel an object (as a ball) through the air by a forward or upward motion of the hand and arm. ⟨*throw* a football⟩ **b** To make a pass by throwing. ⟨*throw* a bomb⟩ **c** To make a pitch in baseball. ⟨*threw* a curve⟩
2 To force an opponent to the floor (as in wrestling and judo).
3 To lose intentionally. ⟨*throw* a fight⟩
4 *football* To tackle a ballcarrier behind the line of scrimmage. ⟨the quarterback was *thrown* for a 5-yard loss⟩

²throw 1 The act or an instance of throwing. ⟨a perfect *throw* from center field⟩
2 An object thrown; a thrown ball. ⟨the catcher dropped the *throw,* allowing the run to score⟩
3 A put of the shot in track and field.
4 The act or an instance of carrying a shuttlecock on the racket in badminton.

thrower Someone who throws something and especially someone who is a participant in a throwing event in track and field.

thrower-in *basketball* The player who inbounds the ball.

throw-forward *rugby* The act or an instance of illegally propelling the ball forward toward the opponent's goal which results in a scrum. If an opposing player catches the ball before it is touched by a teammate of the player throwing it forward, play is not stopped. If the opposing player claims a fair catch, he will be awarded a free kick.

throw-in A method of putting a ball in play in some team sports. In basketball a player is permitted 5 seconds to throw, bounce or roll the ball to a teammate in order to restart play after a score, after a violation or foul for which no foul shot is awarded, or after the ball is knocked or thrown out of bounds. In soccer a throw-in is made by the player nearest the ball who is permitted to throw the ball inbounds to a teammate using only a 2-handed overhead pass after an opposing player has driven the ball out of bounds. In other sports (as lacrosse, polo, and water polo) the referee makes a throw-in (as after a score) by throwing or rolling the ball onto the playing area between 2 opposing players. The throw-in in Australian Rules football, made after the ball bounces over the sideline, differs from that in other sports in that the boundary umpire stands on the sideline with his back to the field and throws the ball back over his head to restart play.

throwing circle *track and field* A circular area in which a competitor in certain field events must remain during his attempt in order to have it qualify for measurement. The throwing circle is 7 feet in diameter for the shot put, weight throws, and hammer throw and 8 feet 2½ inches in diameter for the discus throw. The circle for the shot put has a white curved stopboard at the front that is 4 feet long, 4½ inches wide, and 4 inches high.

throwing event *track and field* Any of the field events in which an object is thrown, hurled, or put for distance including the shot put and the

throwing line

javelin, discus, hammer, and weight throws. Events in which a ball is thrown for distance (as a baseball throw) are also included when they are part of the competition. — compare JUMPING EVENT

throwing line *track and field* The curved line at the end of the approach area for the javelin throw over which the competitor must not step in making a throw.

throwing sector *track and field* The area in which the implement used in a throwing event must land in order to qualify as a legal throw. It is defined by 2 lines extending out from the center of the throwing circle or, in the case of the javelin throw, from a point 26 feet behind the scratch line. The throwing sector for the weight, hammer, and discus throws is a 45-degree arc for international competition and a 60-degree arc for American college and high school competition. For the shot put the arc is 45 degrees and for the javelin throw it is approximately 30 degrees.

throw-off see GOAL THROW (*team handball*)

throw out 1 *baseball* To make a throw usually to a base that enables a teammate to put out a base runner.
2 *cricket* To dismiss a batsman by knocking down the wicket with a direct throw of a fielded ball when he is running between wickets.

thrust 1 *fencing* The quick extension of the sword arm in the line of engagement in either a feint or an attack.
2 *skating* A push onto a skate for a glide in a particular direction.

thunderboat An unlimited hydroplane.

thwart A crosswise seat or brace connecting the gunwales of a canoe or boat.

ticket 1 A card which admits a spectator to an event and often to a designated seat.
2 A card purchased from a seller at a pari-mutuel window which is printed with the contest or race number, the competitor's program number, and amount of the wager and which must be surrendered in cashing a bet.

tickling see GRABBLING

¹tie 1 a Equality of the score of a contest; a situation in which both sides in a contest have the same score. b A contest that ends in a tie. In many team sports (as ice hockey, soccer, and amateur football) a tie usually stands unless it is in a play-off or tournament game. These may be played off with an extra period of sudden death play. In soccer, a tie may be played off with each team taking a designated number of penalty kicks

at the opposing goalkeeper with the team making the most credited with another goal which wins the match. In baseball, a tied game continues into extra innings until one team has a lead at the end of a full inning. Basketball games have one or more 3- or 5-minute overtime periods with the winner being the team leading at the end of an overtime period. In golf, there is normally a sudden death play-off between competitors tied for first place — a head-to-head competition for one or more extra holes — until one golfer plays a hole in fewer strokes than the other. In bowling, ties are commonly played with a roll-off of an additional 3 full games with the player or team having the highest score winning. In races in track and field, tied competitors may compete again or the results may stand. When a tie affects the number of runners that advance to the next heat, normally both tied competitors will advance. In field events, ties stand in jumping events except when they are for first place. These are decided in favor of the competitor with the second-best jump (*for distance*) or with the fewest attempts at the height at which they are tied. If there is still a tie, there is a jump-off at a height at which they both missed or if necessary at higher or lower heights until only one is successful in clearing the bar. Ties in throwing events are decided in favor of the competitor with the next-best throw.
2 A contest between 2 teams in tennis or table tennis.

²tie 1 To make one's score equal to the opponent's score.
2 To cause a contest to be a tie.

tie ball 1 *basketball* see HELD BALL
2 *speedball* A situation in which 2 opposing players simultaneously knock the ball out of bounds, hold the ball, or commit a double foul. When a tie ball occurs, the referee tosses the ball up between the 2 opponents, who attempt to hit it to a teammate as in basketball.

tie-break or **tiebreaker** A method of breaking a tie at the end of competition (as in tennis).

tiercel A male hawk or falcon.

tie up *track and field* To lose the ability to perform at peak effectiveness before or during an activity due to either tension or fatigue.

tiger balance A position (as in gymnastics) in which the body is supported on the forearms, which are kept parallel to one another, with the legs together in the air.

tiger press *gymnastics* A move from a tiger balance to a handstand by shifting the weight to the hands and pressing up to raise the body off the forearms.

¹tight 1 *football* **a** Characterized by relatively little distance between players. ⟨a *tight* defensive formation⟩ ⟨a *tight* T⟩ **b** In the tight end position. ⟨lines up *tight* on the left side⟩
2 a Unusually close or near. ⟨brought the infield in *tight*⟩ **b** With the score relatively even. ⟨a *tight* match⟩

²tight Short for *tight scrum*.

tight end *football* **1** An offensive end who usually lines up within 2 yards of the tackle and who is responsible for both blocking and pass receiving.
2 The position played by a tight end.

tight safety or **tight safetyman** see STRONG SAFETY

tight scrum see SCRUM

tight T *football* The basic T formation. — see illustration at T FORMATION; compare SPLIT T

tight waist *wrestling* A waist lock.

tigna *gymnastics* A stunt which consists of forward somersault in a half tuck position followed by a tinsica.

tiller *sailing* A horizontal handle used to turn the rudder of a boat.

tilt see TIP-UP

timber hitch A hitch that is commonly used to secure the bowstring to the nock at the lower limb of a bow and that is formed by making a single turn around the object and bringing the end over the standing part and around the inside of the loop several times. — see illustration at KNOT

time 1 The running time or playing time of a contest.
2 a A time-out. **b** A signal used in calling for or signaling a time-out.
3 British term meaning the end of the playing time of a game. ⟨saved a . . . penalty kick nine minutes from *time* to atone for an earlier mistake — *London Times*⟩
— **against time** *of a race or time trial* With competitors individually timed over a course, each seeking to have the fastest time in contrast to competing directly against one another.

time advantage *wrestling* The amount of time a wrestler is in a position of advantage over his opponent. The time advantage for each wrestler is kept on separate clocks during the match and at the end if one wrestler has a margin of advantage of a full minute or more over his opponent, he is awarded one point. (also called *riding time*).

time cut see TIME THRUST

timed fire *shooting* Competition in which there is a time limit of 20 seconds for each 5 shots. — compare RAPID FIRE, SLOW FIRE

time hit *fencing* A hit made on a time thrust.

time-in The resumption of play at the end of a time-out.

timekeeper or **timer** An official in most team sports whose duty it is to keep track of the playing time elapsed and to control the game clock according to the rules or the instructions of the head official.

time line see DIVISION LINE

time on *Australian Rules football* Time added at the end of regulation playing time to compensate for a delay or interruption during the game.

time-out A brief suspension of play declared by an official in certain sports. In some sports (as basketball or football) a team is allowed a fixed number of time-outs (as 5 per game in basketball) which are usually taken to discuss strategy during the game. An official may declare a time-out at his own discretion (as in the case of injury or a rules dispute) or signal a time-out automatically (as after a foul or score), but official time-outs are not usually charged to either team. In football and volleyball either team may request a time-out anytime the ball is dead. In basketball only the team in possession of the ball may request a time-out.

timer 1 An official (as in track and field or auto racing) who times individual competitors.
2 see TIMEKEEPER

time thrust or **time cut** *fencing* A counterattack that is both a parry and a riposte and that is usually made against a compound attack so as to arrive ahead of the opponent's attack.

time trap see SPEED TRAP

time trial 1 A competitive event in which participants are individually timed over a set course or distance. The time trial may be a complete competition in itself, or it may be used to determine starting positions in a major race (as in auto racing).
2 A practice race (as in track and field or swimming) to determine ability and conditioning.

tin see TELLTALE (*squash racquets*)

tinsica *gymnastics* A stunt that resembles a cartwheel but that is made with a half twist so that the performer winds up facing in the same direction as when he started.

¹tip 1 To hit a ball or puck lightly or with a glancing blow.
2 To give someone advice or supposedly inside

tip

information for betting (as on a horse race). **3** British term meaning to pick or designate a particular competitor (as a racehorse) as a likely winner.

²tip 1 The higher or front part of something (as a ski).

2 Information reputed to be from a reliable source on the likely outcome of a contest (as a horse race).

3 Short for *foul tip, tip-off, tippet.*

tip-in A goal made by tipping or pushing a rebound into the basket or net.

tipoff 1 or **tapoff** *basketball* A jump ball that starts a period of play.

2 *speedball* An action identical to a basketball jump ball held when 2 opponents have simultaneous control of the ball.

tippet *fishing* A short section of fine line at the end of a tapered leader to which an artificial fly may be attached. The tippet is routinely replaced when it becomes worn or shortened after several flies have been tied on and subsequently cut off.

tipster A tout.

tip-top *fishing* The guide ring that is braced out from the tip of a fishing rod.

tip-up *fishing* Any of several devices used in ice fishing designed to hold a baited line and to signal when a fish bites. The signaling mechanisms of tip-ups can be separated into 2 main categories: a balanced piece of wood that tilts to vertical when the line is pulled or a flag mounted to a flexible metal strip that springs upward when triggered by the movement of the spool. (also called *tilt*)

title The distinction of being a champion in a sport, league, or division. ⟨won the *title*⟩ ⟨will defend his *title*⟩

titleholder or **titlist** Someone who holds a title; champion.

toad-in-the-hole see RUSSIAN POOL

toboggan 1 A relatively long flat-bottomed vehicle made of boards which are curved up at the front that is used for coasting down snow-covered hills.

2 see LUGE

tobogganing 1 The sport or pastime of coasting down a hill on a toboggan.

2 Luge competition.

toe 1 The outer end of the head or blade of a club or stick. — see illustration at CLUB

2 The corner of the butt of a gunstock that is lowermost when the gun is in firing position.

toeboard *track and field* A stopboard used in the shot put.

toehold *mountain climbing* A hold or place of support for the toes.

toe hold *wrestling* An illegal hold that involves any bending or twisting of the opponent's foot or toes.

toe loop jump or **tap loop jump** *skating* A jump from the backward outside edge of one skate assisted by a toe pick or toe point from the free skate with a full turn in the air and a return to the backward outside edge of the same foot. (also called *cherry flip*)

toe pick *skating* **1** or **toe rake** One of the sharp teeth at the front of a figure-skating blade that assists a skater in a jump or spin.

2 A touch of the toe picks to the ice to assist the takeoff and landing of a jump.

toe point *skating* **1** or **toe stop** A hard rubber pad mounted on the toe of a roller skate that assists the skater in the takeoff and landing of a jump.

2 A touch of the toe point on the floor to assist in the takeoff or landing of a jump.

toe raise An exercise (as in weight training) in which the performer stands flat on the floor or with the balls of his feet on a raised surface (as a book) and pushes himself up on tiptoe, often against the resistance of weights, to strengthen his calf muscles. (also called *heel raise*)

toe rake see TOE PICK

toe spin see SCRATCH SPIN

toe stand *gymnastics* A balance position in which the body is raised up on the toes with the arms held out to the side at shoulder level, the back arched, and the head back slightly.

toe stop see TOE POINT

toe Walley *skating* A Walley jump made with an assist on the takeoff with a toe pick or toe point from the free foot.

toe weight *harness racing* A small metal weight attached to the front toe of a harness horse to regulate the gait.

ton One hundred points or runs; century. ⟨their win . . . with Jeff Hopkins hitting a *ton* and former Glamorgan star Don Ward 65 in a total of 214–3 — *Cardiff (Wales) Western Mail*⟩

¹top 1 The first part. ⟨the score is tied in the *top* of the ninth inning⟩ ⟨the *top* of the batting order is due up⟩

2 The end of an English billiards table opposite the balk and toward which the players shoot in the beginning of a game. The top of an English billiards table is analogous to the foot of a pocket billiards table.

²top 1 To strike a ball just above the center and

touch football

send it rolling or bouncing along the ground.
2 To impart topspin to a ball.

topping lift *sailing* A line that runs up to the mast to support the main boom or the spinnaker pole.

topside On deck.

topsides The upper portion of the hull of a boat on each side above the waterline.

topspin A forward rotary motion around a horizontal axis imparted to a ball causing the ball to tend to move downward when traveling through the air, to pick up speed and take a low bounce after hitting a surface, or to continue rolling after striking another ball. (also called *overspin*)

top-spinner *cricket* **1** A bowled ball having topspin.
2 A bowler who employs topspin.

torero A matador or a member of his cuadrilla; bullfighter.

torpedo taper see FLY LINE

toss-up **1** *speedball* A method of starting play after a tie ball in which the ball is tossed high between 2 opponents who attempt to bat it to a teammate; tipoff.
2 see JUMP BALL

total bases *baseball* The total number of bases reached on base hits by a batter or team. A single is equivalent to one total base; a double, 2; a triple, 3; and a home run, 4.

totalizator or **totalizer** The machinery through which pari-mutuel betting is carried on and which dispenses tickets and automatically records wagers and calculates odds. As a wager is made, an operator pushes a button on the machine causing it to print a ticket with the competitor's program number, the number of the race, the track, the date, the amount of the wager, and a special code intended to frustrate would-be counterfeiters. There are usually several hundred individual machines at a track to handle wagers in various denominations. All machines are connected to a central computer which instantaneously records the wagers and computes the odds. The odds and usually also the total amount wagered on each competitor are shown on an electronic display board (*tote board*) in the track's infield where it can be seen by all bettors. At the instant a race begins, a switch is thrown which stops and locks all printing machines, even if one is in the midst of printing a ticket, so that no wagers can be made after the start of a race. — see also PARI-MUTUEL BETTING

total victory *sambo* A victory as a result of a

perfect throw of the opponent from a standing position or of the application of a painful submission hold during ground wrestling.

tote board *pari-mutuel betting* An electrically operated board located in the infield of a track on which the betting odds, race results, and times are displayed. (also called *odds board*)

¹touch *baseball* To get a hit or to score against a particular pitcher. ⟨*touched* him for a three-run homer⟩

²touch **1** *fencing* A hit.
2 *football* The end zone.
3 *rugby* The out-of-bounds area outside of and including the touchlines.
4 *soccer* The out-of-bounds area outside of but not including the touchlines.

touchback **1** *football* A situation in which a player downs the ball in his own end zone after it was propelled over the goal line by the opposing team (as on a punt, kickoff, or forward pass). The player's team then puts the ball in play at its own 20-yard line with a first down. A touchback is automatic if a kick continues out of the end zone over the end line. — compare SAFETY
2 *speedball* A situation in which the ball is driven over the end line by an offensive player without scoring. The ball is put in play by the defensive team with a pass or kick from the end line.

touchdown **1** *football* A score of 6 points made by carrying the ball across the opponent's goal line, by completing a forward pass to a teammate across the goal line, or by recovering a loose ball in the opponent's end zone.
2 *rugby* A situation in which a player downs the ball in his own in-goal. Play is restarted with the defending team putting the ball in play with a drop-out from within the 25-yard line. The rugby touchdown is analogous to the touchback in football.
3 *speedball* A score of 2 points made by completing a forward pass to a teammate beyond the opponent's goal line.

touch down *rugby* To touch the ball to the ground in the opponent's in-goal for a try or in one's own in-goal for a touchdown.

touché *fencing* A term used to acknowledge a hit.

toucher *lawn bowling* A bowl which touches the jack as a result of its delivery and not by being hit by another bowl or by the jack's being knocked against it.

touch football A variation of football played usually with 6 to 9 players to a side in which blocking is allowed but tackling is not and in which a defensive player must touch the ballcarrier between the shoulders and knees usually with both hands to stop play. Each team is given 4 downs in which to score or lose possession of the ball, and each member of a team is eligible to catch a forward pass.

touch-in-goal *rugby* The out-of-bounds area between a goal line and a dead-ball line.

touch-in-goal line *rugby* The extension of a touchline between the goal line and the dead-ball line.

touch judge *rugby* Either of 2 officials stationed on each side of the field who assist the referee in determining when and where the ball goes into touch and when a goal has been kicked.

touchline The sideline of a soccer or rugby field.

tour A series of professional tournaments (as of golf or tennis) held usually every week in a different city throughout the season and competed in by the same players.

Tour de France A bicycle race covering approximately 4000 kilometers (2500 miles) of France and Belgium and parts of Spain, Italy, Germany, and Switzerland that is held in 21 daily stages. The individual stages are timed, and the competitor with the lowest overall time is the winner. The Tour, which originated in 1903, is run over public roads, including both flat and mountainous areas, and is the most important cycling race in the world.

tourer Short for *ski tourer.*

touring Short for *ski touring.*

touring car A usually 4-, 5-, or 6-passenger sedan. — compare GRAND TOURING CAR, SPORTS CAR

touring ski A light narrow ski having a pronounced upturn at the front that is used in ski touring.

Tourist Trophy An annual motorcycle race held on the Isle of Man that consists of 6 laps over a 37-mile course. It was inaugurated in 1907 and is considered the most prestigious of all motorcycle races. The term has been taken over by other promoters for motorcycle races over a closed course from ½ to 2 miles long having left- and right-hand turns, a steep grade, and a jump.

tournament A series of games or contests that make up a single unit of competition of a professional tour or the championship play-offs of a league or conference. The most common tournament is the single elimination tournament in which competitors are paired off for individual rounds, with winners advancing to the next round and losers being eliminated until there is a single champion. Also popular is the round robin tournament in which each competitor competes against every other competitor one at a time; the competitor that finishes with the best won-loss record is the champion. On the professional golf tour, tournaments differ from those in other sports. A golf tournament normally consists of 4 rounds played on consecutive days with all players playing at the same time. Golfers are not competing directly against one another but are trying to play each round in the lowest possible score; the one with the lowest cumulative score at the end of the tournament is the winner. — see also DOUBLE ELIMINATION TOURNAMENT, ELIMINATION TOURNAMENT, LADDER TOURNAMENT, ROUND ROBIN

tournament casting Bait casting, fly casting, or skish competition.

tourney A championship tournament.

tour skiing see SKI TOURING

¹tout *horse racing* Someone who sells betting advice or tips.

²tout To sell a tip on a contest or solicit bets; to act as a tout.

tower **1** A diving platform and especially the 10-meter platform.

2 Short for *tuna tower.*

towing *soaring* The launching of a sailplane; the method by which a sailplane is launched. There are 3 principal methods of towing: having an airplane tow the sailplane up to a suitable height at which the tow line is released (*airplane tow*), having an automobile drive down a runway towing the sailplane until it is airborne (*auto tow*), and having an automobile tow the plane by means of a line that runs through a pulley to the sailplane (*auto-pulley tow*). The auto-pulley tow is useful where the runway ends at a cliff. The automobile can move away at right angles to the line of takeoff or even directly back toward the plane, and the pulley device can be located near the edge of the cliff. If the sailplane is being pulled behind an airplane, it has to ride below the altitude of the plane (*low tow*) or above it (*high tow*) to avoid the turbulence of the backwash from the propellers.

tow lift see SKI TOW

towline A line by which something is towed:
1 A line from a boat to a water skier.
2 A gangline.
3 A line connecting a sailplane with the towing airplane or vehicle.

toxophilite Someone who is interested in or expert in the use of a bow and arrow; an archer.

T position *skating* A position in which one skate is set perpendicular to the instep of the other.

trace 1 *dogsled racing* The line by which the dogs are harnessed to the sled.

2 *fishing* A leader.

3 *skating* The mark or figure made in the ice by a skate blade.

¹track 1 A usually oval course laid out for racing. In track and field, the standard outdoor track is ¼ mile long with 2 wide turns and often with one or 2 chutes to extend the straightaways. A track is usually of cinder or a rubberized composition material and composed of 6 to 8 running lanes. The length of an indoor track depends on the size of the facility, but a representative one

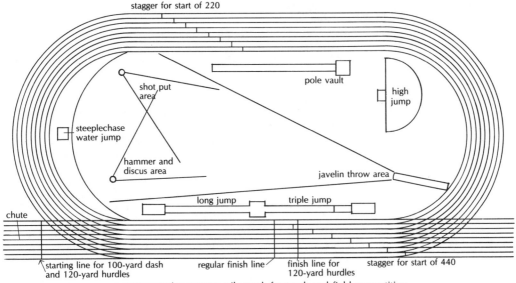

a representative quarter-mile track for track and field competition

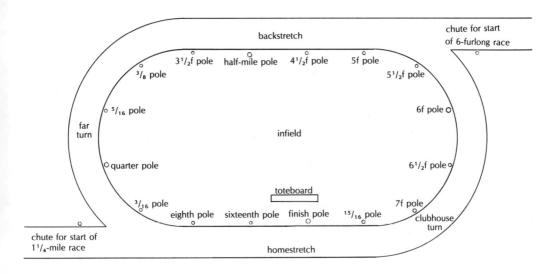

a representative one-mile track for horse racing

track

is about 1/10 mile. Indoor tracks are typically made of wood, dirt, cinder, or composition material. In horse racing the tracks vary from ½ to 1½ miles in length and usually have one or more chutes. A typical American track is oval with a 1-mile dirt track surrounding a turf course. Often inside the turf course is another turf course used for steeplechases and including a water jump. Auto racing tracks range from ¼ to 2½ miles long. Many smaller tracks are dirt, and most are made with a moderate banking on the turns. At some superspeedways, the banking may be extremely high. Cycling tracks are typically constructed of wood, are usually about 200 meters (220 yards) long, and have extremely high banking all the way around.
2 A cry of warning (as in skiing) to those ahead to move out of the way.
3 Track and field sports. ⟨lettered in football and *track*⟩; running events as distinguished from field events.
4 *bowling* A long section of an alley where the surface dressing has been worn off by continuous use.
²track *bowling* **1** *of a ball* To follow a particular line or track.
2 *of an alley* To become worn with a track.
track and field The sport consisting of athletic contests such as footraces, jumping events, and throwing events conducted on a running track and the enclosed field. The running events normally include dashes of 100, 200, and 400 meters (or corresponding U.S. distances of 100, 220, and 440 yards), runs of 800 meters (880 yards), 1500 meters (one mile), 5 kilometers (3 miles), and 10 kilometers (6 miles). There are walking races typically of 20 and 50 kilometers, hurdles races of 110 meters (120 yards) and 400 meters (440 yards), and a 3000-meter steeplechase. Teams normally compete in relay races of 400 and 1600 meters (400 yards and one mile) and occasionally medley relays in which each team member runs a different distance. In major competition, such as the Olympics, the marathon is run in conjunction with the track and field competition. The field events include the high jump, long jump, triple jump, and pole vault, throwing events (such as the shot put, hammer, discus, and javelin throws), and the decathlon (pentathlon for women).
trackman A track and field athlete.
track shoe see SHOE
trackside At or in the area immediately adjacent to a track.

track suit A sweatsuit.
traffic A concentration of participants or players and especially defensive players. ⟨to force difficult shots in *traffic*⟩
¹trail A path or route usually through woods and fields for use especially by hikers or ski tourers.
²trail **1** To be behind another competitor in a contest or in league standings.
2 To follow a teammate down the field, court, or ice especially on a fast break or a breakaway; to be a trailer.
trail bike A lightweight usually small motorcycle designed for off-the-road use on trails.
trailer An offensive player who follows the main action of a play to be in position to receive a pass from the ball or puck handler or to score on a rebound.
trailhead The point at which a trail begins.
trail leg or **trailing leg** *track and field* The leg that gives the impetus for the takeoff for a jump and that is usually trailing behind the rest of the body during the first part of a jump; takeoff leg.
trail official *basketball* The official who moves down the court behind the players and who stations himself in the backcourt. — compare LEAD OFFICIAL
¹train To prepare for a competition by undertaking a period of exercise designed to increase endurance and strength and to sharpen the specific skills needed for a sport. For athletes training may also involve regulation of the diet and restriction of social activities.
²train *surfing* A set of waves.
trainer **1** A member of the staff of a ball club who is responsible for administering first aid and treating the ailments and minor injuries of the team members.
2 *boxing* An individual responsible for the conditioning and development of a boxer and for strategy employed in a fight.
3 *horse racing* An individual who manages a racehorse for the owner and who is responsible for the training and health of horses under his care, for selecting the races for his horses, and often for claiming horses for the owner.
training camp A place often away from an individual's or team's home base where it trains for a contest or for a new season.
training table A dining table or an area in a school or college dining room set aside for athletes so that their diet can be controlled.
training track *horse racing* A special racetrack that is not used for racing but only for training or working out racehorses and that is usually

softer and deeper than a track for racing in order to develop a horse's stamina.

tramline British term for the alley on a badminton court.

trampoline

trampoline An apparatus that consists of a rectangular bed of canvas or webbing attached by springs to the inside of a 9-by-15-foot metal frame which stands about 3 feet high and that is used as both a springboard and a landing area for stunts in trampolining.

trampolining The sport of performing stunts on a trampoline. Trampolining forms a part of gymnastics and is a part of competition in some meets. A competitive performance normally consists of a routine of 11 different stunts involving both forward and backward flips and includes stunts begun from the feet as well as from lying or kneeling positions. (also called *rebound tumbling*)

transom The planking forming the stern of a square-ended boat.

¹**trap 1** *baseball* **a** The act or an instance of catching a ball immediately after the first bounce so that it is barely distinguishable from a catch made on the fly. **b** A piece of leather or leather webbing between the thumb and finger sections of a glove or mitt to form an extension of the pocket.

2 *basketball* A defensive maneuver in which 2 defenders converge quickly to double-team the ball handler in order to steal the ball or force a passing error.

3 or **trap block** or **trap play** *football* A play

in which a defensive lineman is allowed to penetrate the offensive line and then is blocked from behind or from the side while the ballcarrier runs through the spot vacated by the defensive player. (also called *mousetrap*)

4 The act or manner or an instance of gaining control of a moving ball in soccer or speedball by stopping, slowing, or deflecting the ball with some part of the body other than the hands. When the ball is stopped with the sole of the foot, the foot is merely placed on top of the ball to stop it and hold it in place. A trap made with the leg, waist, or chest normally involves allowing the body to give as the ball hits it to absorb the rebound force so that the ball will drop straight down where it can be immediately played with the feet. (also called *block*)

5 A mechanical device used for sailing clay pigeons in trapshooting and skeet shooting usually by means of a spring-loaded arm and often ranging in complexity from a hand-held instrument to an electric remote-controlled self-loading launcher.

6 The sport of trapshooting.

7 see STARTING BOX

8 Short for *sand trap, speed trap.*

player trapping the ball with his foot

²**trap 1** To stop a moving ball with the soles of the foot or by allowing it to bounce softly off a part of the body other than the hands or arms in soccer or speedball.

2 *baseball* To catch a ball immediately after the

first bounce in such a way that it is barely distinguishable from a catch made before the bounce.
3 *basketball* To double-team an opponent with the ball especially during a press.
4 *football* To block an opponent in a trap play.

trap block see TRAP (*football*)

trap blocker *football* The player who blocks the onrushing defender in a trap play.

trapeze *sailing* A wire running from the upper part of a mast that is attached to a wide belt or harness worn by a crew member so that he can stand out from the windward rail to exert more leverage when hiking out. — see illustration at CATAMARAN

trap gun A typically 12-gauge shotgun used in trapshooting. The trap gun usually has a long barrel and a tight choke because most targets are hit at a distance of 30 or more yards from the shooter. The gun used for rounds in which double targets are thrown must be capable of firing 2 shots.

trap house A shelter from which clay pigeons are launched. A single low trap house is located in front of the shooting stations in trapshooting; in skeet there is a trap house on each side of the shooting stations. — see also HIGH HOUSE, LOW HOUSE

trapped *golf* Bordered with sand traps. ⟨a heavily *trapped* green⟩

trap play see TRAP (*football*)

trap shoot A trapshooting match.

trapshooter Someone who engages in trapshooting.

trapshooting The sport of shooting at clay pigeons with a shotgun from 5 positions spaced 3 yards apart on an arc 16 yards behind a single, low trap house. The targets are thrown away from the shooting stations at angles unknown to the shooters but on a trajectory that gives them a height of between 8 and 12 feet when they are 10 yards from the trap. A round normally consists of 5 shooters at a time taking a number of

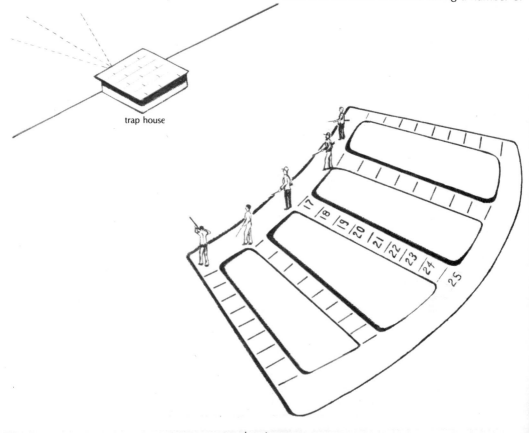

trap house

trapshooting range

shots from each of the 5 stations with one shooter stationed at each station. When each has had a turn (an *inning*), they move on to the next station and continue until all have shot from each station. The shooter is permitted to hold his gun at his shoulder in shooting position and call for the target to be released. In handicap matches, shooters with higher handicaps are positioned at greater distances from the trap. In rounds in which double targets are thrown, they are thrown in opposite directions at fixed angles. — compare OLYMPIC TRENCH, SKEET

trap shot 1 *golf* A shot made from a sand trap. **2** *handball* A half volley.

travel *basketball* To take more steps than permitted by the rules or to fail to keep the pivot foot on the floor while holding the ball; to commit a traveling violation. (also *walk*)

traveler *sailing* **1** A metal bar fixed traversely across the stern of a boat along which a ring attached to a block of the main sheet tackle moves when the sail is shifted from one side to the other. (also called *horse*)
2 A ring or clamp which is attached to the block of the main sheet tackle and which moves along the traveler bar.

traveling *basketball* A violation that occurs when a player moves his pivot foot or takes more steps than allowed while holding the ball and that results in loss of possession of the ball. A player with the ball who is standing is permitted to move one foot in any direction any number of times so long as the other foot (the *pivot foot*) remains in continuous contact with the floor. If a player catches a pass while running, he is allowed to take 2 steps if both feet were off the floor when he caught the ball, or one step if one foot was on the floor, without being called for traveling. If he is standing and holding the ball, the player is permitted to jump in the air providing he shoots or passes the ball before his feet again touch the floor. (also called *walking*) — see also PIVOT FOOT

travers *equitation* A dressage movement in which the horse is guided beside a wall with his head near the wall and facing in the direction of movement but with his body at an angle of about 30 degrees from the wall. — compare RENVERS

¹traverse 1 *mountain climbing* Sideways movement across a rock face or slope often to reach another route especially after the first route becomes too difficult to climb.
2 *skiing* **a** Movement diagonally across a slope rather than straight down the fall line. **b** The

position assumed in a traverse with the skis relatively parallel and edged into the hill and with the uphill ski slightly advanced.

²traverse To move in a traverse; to traverse across a slope or rock face.

traverse sidestep see SIDESTEP TRAVERSE

treble hook *fishing* A hook that has 3 bands, 3 points, and 3 barbs and that is usually formed by joining a single hook to a double hook. — see illustration at FISHHOOK

trenches see PIT (*football*)

tri Short for *trimaran*.

trial 1 *motorcycle racing* A competitive event in which individuals are judged on the skill with which they handle their motorcycle on a course with a series of obstacles or hazards such as water and mud, rocks, steep hills, and fallen trees. Each rider is observed at the hazards and is given penalty points for dismounting, touching the ground with one or both feet, and going out of bounds. Time is not a factor in a trial; the individual with the fewest penalty points is the winner.
2 *track and field* An attempt in a field event. In throwing events and in the long jump and triple jump, each competitor is given 3 preliminary trials, and those who have the best performances advance to the finals, which consist of 3 more trials. The result of any trial, whether preliminary or final, is credited to a performer for the meet. In the high jump and pole vault, competitors are not restricted to a set number of trials, but any competitor with 3 consecutive unsuccessful trials is eliminated.
3 Short for *field trial*.

trial heat *track and field* see HEAT

trial horse A competitor (as a yacht) against which another can compete in tuning up for a contest.

trialling British term for motorcycle trial competition.

triangle *billiards* see RACK

triangle pass or **triangular pass** A pass (as in soccer or field hockey) made to a teammate with the passer immediately cutting around the defender toward the goal for a return pass. — compare GIVE AND GO

triangular meet A meet (as in wrestling or track and field) in which 3 teams compete against each other simultaneously. The team with the greatest point total is credited with 2 victories, the second place team is credited with one win and one loss, and the team with the fewest points is charged with 2 losses.

triathlon 1 *track and field* A 3-event contest for women which consists of the 100-meter dash, the high jump, and the 4-kilogram (8 pounds 13 ounces) shotput.

2 A competition, popular in Britain, which consists of horseback riding, trapshooting, and fly casting.

tri-captain One of 3 captains of a team.

triceps extension *weight training* An exercise for the triceps muscle in which a barbell or dumbbell is held with bent elbows behind the head at shoulder level, raised straight overhead, and then lowered to the original position.

trick ski A short water ski without a fin and often having a rounded bottom for use in performing tricks while waterskiing.

trifecta *pari-mutuel betting* A variation of the perfecta in which a bettor must select the first 3 finishers of a race in the correct order of finish in order to win. (also called *triple*) — compare SUPERFECTA

trigger A small lever on a firearm that is squeezed with the finger to release the hammer or firing pin and fire the weapon.

¹trim 1 To adjust a sail to the desired angle to the wind.

2 To set a surfboard to plane on a wave at the desired angle by shifting the body weight.

²trim The position of a boat or surfboard in the water; the angle at which a sail is adjusted to the wind.

trimaran A sailboat that has 3 parallel hulls or planing surfaces. — compare CATAMARAN

trim tab 1 A small auxiliary airfoil attached usually to the trailing edge of a control surface (as an aileron or rudder) to permit minor adjustments for stability in flight.

2 **a** A small horizontal surface on the bottom of a boat to improve trim. **b** A small section on the trailing edge of a rudder on larger boats which can be adjusted at an angle to the rudder to help control lee or weather helm.

3 A small control surface behind a propeller on a motorboat to counteract the torque effect of the rotating propeller blades.

tri-oval *auto racing* A racetrack in the shape of a triangle with rounded corners — compare OVAL, ROAD COURSE

¹triple 1 Victories in 3 events or races on the same program by a single individual.

2 *baseball* A base hit on which the batter reaches third base safely.

3 *bowling* see TURKEY

4 *pari-mutuel betting* see TRIFECTA

5 Short for *triple jump.*

²triple *baseball* 1 To hit a triple. ⟨*tripled* in the ninth⟩

2 To cause a baserunner to score or a run to be scored by a triple. ⟨*tripled* home the tying run⟩

³triple 1 Involving 3 complete turns or rotations of the body. ⟨*triple* somersault⟩

2 *of a knot* Formed with 3 turns instead of one; formed with 2 additional loops. ⟨*triple* bowline⟩

triple bars *equitation* An obstacle for show jumping which consists of 3 parallel rails arranged one behind the other with each progressively higher.

triple bogey *golf* A score of 3 strokes over par for a hole.

Triple Crown 1 *baseball* The distinction of leading a league in batting average, home runs, and RBIs in a single season.

2 *horse racing* The distinction of winning the 3 most important races for 3-year-olds in a single year. In thoroughbred racing the races making up the Triple Crown are the Kentucky Derby, the Preakness Stakes, and the Belmont Stakes. Since thoroughbred fillies rarely compete against colts, there is a Triple Crown for fillies composed of the Acorn, the Mother Goose Stakes, and the Coaching Club American Oaks. In harness racing, the Triple Crown for trotters is composed of the Hambletonian, the Kentucky Futurity, and the Yonkers Trot; the pacing Triple Crown has the Little Brown Jug, the Cane Pace, and the Messenger Stakes. In Britain, the Triple Crown for thoroughbreds consists of the Derby, the Two Thousand Guineas, and the St. Leger.

triple-header A program consisting of 3 consecutive events.

triple-jump To attain a specified distance in the triple jump. ⟨he *triple-jumped* 53 feet⟩

triple jump *track and field* A field event in which each competitor jumps for distance from a running start employing 3 successive leaps and landing first on the takeoff foot (a hop), then on the other foot (a step), and finally on both feet (a jump). (also called *hop, step, and jump*)

triple option *football* An offensive play in which the quarterback has the option of either handing the ball off to the fullback up the middle, pitching out to a halfback running to the outside, or keeping the ball and running with it or passing it. The play is run on the same pattern on every down with the quarterback usually choosing his option according to the situation or the positions of the defenders.

L   hop   L   step   R   jump

triple jump

triple play *baseball* A play in which 3 players are put out.

triple-team To block or guard an opponent with 3 players at one time.

triple threat A football player who is particularly adept at running, kicking, and passing the ball.

tripping The act of tripping an opponent with any part of the body or with one's stick which is a foul in any sport.

troll *fishing* To trail a baited line or artificial lure behind a slow-moving boat.

trolling Fishing by trailing a lure or bait behind a slow-moving boat. Trolling is the usual method of fishing for freshwater game fish that live in deep water (as lake trout and salmon) and saltwater big game fish. The lures most often used are live or dead fish and spoons or other wobbling or spinning artificial lures.

trolling motor A small outboard motor designed to propel a small rowboat or canoe at a steady slow speed for trolling.

tromlet *gymnastics* A stunt performed on a pommel horse which consists of a movement from the middle to the end of the horse followed by a return movement back to the middle accomplished by double leg circles.

trompement *fencing* The avoiding of an opponent's parry especially by not allowing him to catch the sword blade and deflect it with his own blade.

¹trot **1** *equitation* A 2-beat gait in which the legs move in diagonal pairs. — compare PACE

2 A harness race in which the horses are driven at a trot.

3 Short for *trotline.*

²trot **1** To drive a horse at a trot.

2 *of a horse* To move at a trot.

trotline *fishing* A length of heavy line having a number of shorter baited lines attached at intervals that is fastened at both ends (as across a river) and left unattended. A trotline is illegal in some states.

trots Harness races.

trotter *harness racing* A standardbred whose natural or acquired gait is a trot.

trotting The sport of harness racing. In general usage, the term is used for racing of both trotters and pacers.

truck *sailing* The cap for the top of a mast.

trudgen stroke *swimming* A stroke executed in the prone position that combines the arm motion of the crawl and the scissors kick. The trudgen, named for the former British swimmer J. Arthur Trudgen who made it popular, is not as fast as the American crawl stroke, but it is less tiring and its use is generally limited to long-distance swimming.

true bearing see BEARING

true north North with respect to the north pole as distinguished from magnetic north.

true wind *sailing* The direction from which the wind is blowing as distinguished from apparent wind.

try *rugby* A score of 3 points under Rugby League rules or 4 points under Rugby Union rules made when the ball is grounded in the opponent's in-goal. A try, analogous to a touchdown in football, is followed by a placekick at the goal, which adds 2 points if successful.

try for point *football* An attempt to score an additional one or 2 points allowed to a team following a touchdown. The team scoring the touchdown is permitted one down from the 2-yard line in professional football or the 3-yard line in college football to placekick the ball through the uprights or to carry the ball or complete a pass into the end zone. A try for point by either means is worth only one point in professional football; in college football a successful kick is worth one point, while a successful run or forward pass will give the team 2 points.

TSD rally see RALLY

T stop *skating* A method of stopping in which the free foot is placed behind and perpendicular to the skating foot and the weight is transferred to the outside edge of the free foot so that the skate skids sideways on the surface to stop the skater.

tube see CURL (*surfing*)

tubing The sport or pastime of riding down a river or of sliding down a snow-covered slope on an inflated automobile inner tube.

¹tuck **1** A body position (as in diving or gymnastics) in which the knees are bent, the thighs drawn tightly to the chest, and the hands clasped around the shins. — see illustration at INWARD DIVE

2 *skiing* A position in which the skier squats forward and holds his ski poles under his arms and parallel to the ground that is usually used to minimize wind resistance in downhill racing.

²tuck *skating* To cross the rear foot behind the skating foot before the final thrust of a progressive.

tug-of-war A contest in which 2 teams pull against each other on opposite ends of a rope with the object to pull the middle of the rope over a mark on the ground to win. The rope is usually marked in the middle between the opposing teams, and the ground is usually marked with 2 lines 12 feet apart so that one team has to move the rope about 6 feet to win.

tumbler Someone who engages in tumbling.

tumbling A sport in which individuals perform acrobatic feats (as somersaults, handsprings, twists, and rolls) on a mat without the use of apparatus.

tunnel **1** *rugby* The area between opposing forwards in a scrum.

2 *surfing* see CURL

turbocharged *of a racing engine* Equipped with a turbocharger.

turbocharger *motor sports* A supercharger that consists of a turbine compressor driven by exhaust gases. The exhaust gases turn a turbine wheel which in turn drives the air compressor wheels that force air into the engine.

turbocharging *motor sports* The practice of equipping racing engines with turbochargers.

turf *horse racing* **1** A grass racetrack often located inside a larger dirt track.

2 The sport or business of horse racing.

turf accountant A bookmaker licensed to take wagers on horse racing in Great Britain.

turfman Someone who owns and races horses or who is an avid fan of horse racing.

turfski A short ski used in turfskiing.

turfskiing The sport of sliding down grass slopes on special skis with rollers on the bottom.

turkey *bowling* Three successive strikes in a single game.

turle knot A knot used to tie a fly to the end of a fishing leader that is formed by passing the end of the leader through the eye of the hook, tying a single or double slip knot and passing the loop over the fly, and then pulling the knot tight. — see illustration at KNOT

¹turn **1** An opportunity to participate or to make a play in a game or sport in which participants play in succession or in a scheduled order.

2 The point at which a course changes direction; the curved part of a running track or a racetrack.

3 a A circular movement of the body around the vertical axis. **b** *gymnastics* A movement around a bar that is less than a full circle.

4 a *skating* A quick reversal of direction while skating an edge that is made as a single uninterrupted movement. — see THREE TURN **b** *skiing* A change of direction either while moving or while standing still. — see CHRISTIE, KICK TURN, STEM TURN **c** *swimming* A reversal of direction at the end of the pool during which the swimmer must touch the wall with a hand or foot. — see FLIP TURN **d** The manner or technique of making a turn.

²turn **1** To make a turn (as in swimming, skating, or skiing).

2 To cover a distance by running or driving. ⟨*turned* a fast lap⟩

turnaround jump shot *or* **turnaround jumper** *basketball* A jump shot that is started with the back to the basket in which the shooter turns either at the start of the jump or in midair.

turn-in *football* A pass pattern in which the receiver runs a short way downfield and then cuts toward the middle of the field.

turn-out *football* A pass pattern in which the receiver runs a short way downfield and then cuts for the sideline.

turnover The act or instance of a team's losing possession of the ball (as in basketball or football) through error or a minor violation of the rules.

turn over To lose possession of the ball through a turnover.

turn the ball over *of a baseball pitcher* To throw a screwball.

turn the corner *of the ballcarrier in football* To cut upfield after running laterally (as to get outside the formation or around potential block-ers).

turn turtle *surfing* To grab the rails and wrap the legs around the surfboard and turn upside down in the water so that the board will be on top momentarily to offer some protection from a crashing wave.

turnverein An old name for an athletic club.

12-meter A racing sloop of the keelboat type that is constructed according to a formula which is based on the overall length, girth, sail area, and freeboard of the boat and expressed as 12 meters and that typically has a length of around 65 feet and a sail area of 1800 square feet plus a spinnaker. It is manned by a crew of 10.

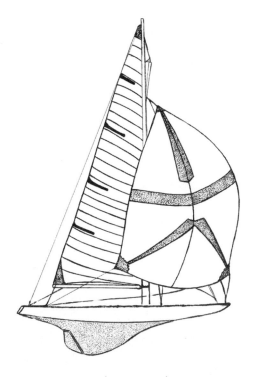

twelve-meter yacht

25-yard line 1 *field hockey* A line 25 yards from and parallel to the end line across each end of the field which serves as a restraining line during a penalty bully.

2 or **25-yards line** *rugby* A line 25 yards from and parallel to each goal line which serves as a restraining line during a drop-out.

24-second clock *basketball* A shooting clock used to indicate time remaining under the 24-second rule.

24-second rule *basketball* A rule in professional play that requires the offensive team to try for a goal within 24 seconds of inbounding or gaining possession of the ball (as after a basket or a turnover).

24-second violation *basketball* A violation of the 24-second rule.

21-yard line A line 21 yards from and parallel to the goal line at each end of a hurling or Gaelic football field which serves as a restraining line for opposing players during a kickout or puck-out.

20-point must system *boxing.* A scoring system in which the winner of a round is given 20 points and the loser any number less than 20. If the round is scored even, each boxer is given 20.

20-second rule *boxing* A rule that allows a boxer 20 seconds to climb back into the ring after being forced out. Failure to return within the 20-second limit results in a TKO.

twin bill A doubleheader.

twin double *pari-mutuel betting* A system of betting involving usually the last 4 races of a program in which the bettor must pick the winners of 2 successive races, exchange the ticket for the right to choose the winners of the next pair of races, and be correct in that choice in order to win. In effect, the pool is 2 daily doubles with the bettor having to pick the winners of 4 successive races.

twi-night doubleheader or **twi-nighter** *baseball* A doubleheader in which the first game is played in the late afternoon and the second in the evening.

twirl *baseball* To pitch in a game.

twirler A baseball pitcher.

twist 1 A rotation of the body (as in diving or gymnastics) about the vertical axis.
2 The spiral rifling of a gun barrel; the distance in which rifling makes one complete turn of a gun barrel. ⟨a 12-inch *twist*⟩
3 Spin given to a ball.
4 Short for *twist dive.*

twist dive or **twisting dive** *diving* Any of a group of competitive dives in which the diver performs a twist between the takeoff and the entry. — see also ARMSTAND DIVE, BACKWARD DIVE, FORWARD DIVE, INWARD DIVE, REVERSE DIVE

two-base hit or **two-bagger** A double in baseball.

200 or **200-meter dash** *track and field* A race run over a distance of 200 meters.

two mile

two mile or **two-mile run**   *track and field*   A race run over a distance of 2 miles.

two-minute drill   *football*   An offensive method of play often used by a team tied or trailing in a game in the closing minute or two of play in which several plays are called in one huddle in order to run off as many plays as possible. A short quick pass to the sideline is the most common play in a two-minute drill since it allows the receiver to get out of bounds and stop the clock.

two-minute warning   *football*   Notification made by the referee to each of the teams when only 2 minutes remain in a half. An official time-out is taken for the warning.

two old cat or **two o'cat**   A version of one old cat played with 2 batters in which a batter who is unable to safely return to home is permitted to occupy the base while the other player bats.

twosome   *golf*   A match between 2 players.

Two Thousand Guineas   A 1-mile stakes race for 3-year-old thoroughbred racehorses that has been held annually since 1809 at Newmarket, Cambridgeshire, England, and that is one of the English Classics and one of the races in the English Triple Crown.

two-time   *fencing*   A compound movement consisting of 2 simple actions.

220 or **220-yard dash**   *track and field*   A race run over a distance of 220 yards.

two-way   **1** Involving 2 participants. ⟨a *two-way* race for the pennant⟩
2 Exhibiting or using both good offensive and defensive play. ⟨a *two-way* player⟩

U

überstreichen *equitation* The act of giving rein to a horse for several strides to show that the horse is capable of maintaining a perfect canter independently.

Ultimate Frisbee A game played between 2 teams of 7 players using a Frisbee on a rectangular playing field 60 yards long and 40 yards wide with the object to pass the Frisbee across the goal line to a teammate for a score and to prevent the opposing team from scoring. The Frisbee is advanced only by passing it to a teammate. Players are permitted to attempt to prevent successful passes but may not physically impede opposing players. The play is not continuous; it stops whenever the Frisbee touches the ground or after a score. When the Frisbee is dropped or batted down by an opponent, the defensive team takes possession. The game is played in two 24-minute halves with unlimited substitutions allowed.

ultralight *fishing* Relating to or being tackle that is extremely light and delicate. An ultralight rod commonly weighs less than 3 ounces and uses line of less than 3 pounds tested strength.

ump Short for *umpire.*

¹umpire **1** An official who controls the game in lawn bowling and curling and who calls infractions, rules on the legality of equipment or a delivery, supervises measuring at each end, and rules on questions of interpretation of the rules. **2** An official in lacrosse or basketball who has equal responsibility with the referee for the conduct of the game and for conducting face-offs or center jumps, for calling infractions and fouls, and for administering penalties. Where there is a difference of opinion, the referee usually has the overall final authority. In many cases in both lacrosse and basketball, both officials will be called referees. In women's lacrosse, the game is conducted by a center umpire assisted by 2 goal umpires. **3** *Australian Rules football* see BOUNDARY UMPIRE, FIELD UMPIRE, GOAL UMPIRE **4** *badminton* An official who conducts the match and whose duties are like those of the umpire in tennis. **5** *baseball* An official responsible for the conduct of the game, determining the fitness of the playing conditions, indicating when time is out and when the ball is in play, calling balls and strikes, indicating foul balls, calling whether a runner is out or safe at a base, and deciding on interpretations of the rules. In major league professional play 4 umpires are usually used, one behind home plate, known as the umpire-in-chief, who calls balls and strikes and rules on plays at home plate, and one umpire at each of the other bases to call plays there. The umpire-in-chief has final authority for the conduct of the game. For the World Series, additional umpires are usually used in the outfield on each foul line to rule on foul balls. In amateur play, the use of only 2 umpires is common. One umpire is positioned behind home plate to call balls and strikes, foul balls, and plays at home plate and the other is in the infield to rule on plays at any of the bases. **6** *cricket* Either of 2 officials who have equal responsibility for control of the game and for ruling on illegal deliveries, for deciding when a batsman is out, and for awarding extras. Normally one umpire is stationed behind the nonstriker's wicket to watch the bowler's delivery and to be in position to judge whether a batsman is out leg before wicket, and the other umpire is positioned on the leg side approximately even with the striker's wicket. The umpires exchange positions when the direction of bowling is changed after each over. **7** *field hockey* Either of 2 officials who are positioned in each end of the field and who have equal responsibility for the conduct of the game, for calling infractions, and for awarding penalties. **8** *football* An official who takes a position in the defensive backfield on scrimmage plays and who is primarily responsible for checking players' equipment, watching for offensive or defensive holding, and watching for linemen illegally downfield on passing or kicking plays.

9 *polo* Either of 2 officials who are mounted and positioned in each end of the field and who have equal responsibility for the conduct of the game, for ruling on infractions, and for awarding penalties and goals.

10 *table tennis* An official whose duties are like those of the umpire in tennis.

11 *tennis* An official who is positioned at one end of the net usually high enough to observe all of the action on both sides of the net and who conducts the match, keeps and announces the score, and, with the assistance of the linesmen, indicates faults. The umpire is under the ultimate authority of the referee, who decides questions of interpretation of the rules and appeals.

12 *volleyball* An official who is positioned at the opposite end of the net from the referee to assist him by calling infractions such as players out of position, too many hits on a side, and whether the ball or a player touches the net.

²umpire To serve as umpire for a game or match.

umpire-in-chief see UMPIRE (*baseball*)

unanswered Not matched by corresponding scoring from an opponent. ⟨put in 10 *unanswered* points to give them a 17–8 lead⟩

unassisted **1** Made or performed without an assist. ⟨an *unassisted* double play⟩ ⟨an *unassisted* goal⟩

2 *of a tackle in football* Made with little or no help from teammates.

unattached *of an athlete* Not affiliated with a team or club (as in track and field).

unavoidable hinder A hinder (as in handball or paddleball) that cannot be avoided. — see HINDER

unbalanced line *football* An alignment of the offensive line typical of the single wing formation in which there are an unequal number of players on either side of the center. — see illustration at SINGLE WING

uncleat To release a mooring line from a cleat.

uncovered **1** *of an offensive player* Not guarded by a defensive player.

2 *of a line of attack in fencing* Not protected by the position of the sword.

under **1** *auto racing* Inside; on the lower part of a banked turn. ⟨went *under* Isaac on the first turn to move into second place — John S. Radosta, *New York Times*⟩

2 or **underneath** *football* To or on the scrimmage side of a defensive zone. ⟨the linebackers were dropping off 15 yards . . . so I threw

under them, to the backs — Johnny Unitas⟩

underarm sneak *wrestling* A move in which a wrestler lifts his opponent's arm, ducks his head under the arm, and lifts to force the opponent's shoulders forward and permit him to get behind the opponent. (also called *duckunder*)

underarm throw *lacrosse* A throw usually used as a shot that is made by swinging the stick down and underhand in a circle so that the ball travels forward close to the ground.

underbody The underwater part of a boat's hull.

undercard *boxing* The program accompanying a feature bout.

¹undercut *mountain climbing* A handhold which must be gripped from underneath.

²undercut To hit a ball with the racket or paddle face angled up so as to impart backspin.

underdistance *track and field* A training technique in which a runner practices at running distances less than that of his usual event in order to increase his speed. — compare OVERDISTANCE

underdog A competitor that is given little chance of winning a contest. — compare FAVORITE

underdraw *archery* To draw an arrow back just short of full draw which results in a loss of power on the shot and often results in the arrow's falling short of the target.

undergrip see GRIP (*gymnastics*)

underhand With the hand or arm moving forward in an arc below the level of the waist. ⟨pitched the ball *underhand*⟩ ⟨an *underhand* serve⟩

underhook *wrestling* A hold in which a wrestler hooks his arm under his opponent's arm or leg especially to counter a move by the opponent.

underhand

underlay *pari-mutuel betting* A situation in which the closing odds on a given competitor are lower than they were in the morning line.

underneath **1** *basketball* Under or near the basket. ⟨he started hitting from *underneath*⟩ **2** *football* see UNDER

underspin see BACKSPIN

¹understeer The tendency of an automobile to travel straight ahead on a turn or to turn less sharply than the driver intends.

²understeer *of an automobile* To tend to continue straight ahead on a turn or to turn less sharply than the driver intends.

understrung *of an archery bow* Having less than the recommended fistmele.

underswing *gymnastics* A swing on an apparatus with the body below the hands in a hang position.

undertow A seaward rush of water down a sloping beach after the water is thrown up on the beach by a breaking wave. The term is often confused with *rip current.*

underway *boating* Moving through the water under control; not at anchor or aground.

unearned run *baseball* A run scored as a result of a fielding or throwing error or as a result of catcher's interference or one that is scored after the defensive team has had an opportunity to make the third putout of the inning. — compare EARNED RUN

uneven parallel bars *gymnastics* **1** Two parallel wooden bars 2400 millimeters (7 feet 10½ inches) long that are supported at different heights above the floor on which swinging movements are performed in women's competition. The upper bar is 2300 millimeters (7 feet 6½ inches) high and the lower bar is 1500 millimeters (4 feet 11 inches) high. The distance between the bars is adjustable from 500 to 580 millimeters (19½ to 22½ inches). — see illustration at HIP CIRCLE **2** An event in competition in which the uneven parallel bars are used.

unhittable *of a pitched baseball* Thrown with enough speed or break to be very difficult to hit cleanly.

uniform The clothing or costume worn by participants in a game or sport. A uniform is normally required in team sports as a means of distinguishing the teams through the different colors or styles. A team normally has 2 sets of uniforms of different colors, one for home games and one for away games. A uniform usually consists of a shirt, pants, and often matching-color socks. In baseball, the cap is a part of the uniform and is to be worn at all times while a player is on the field. In sports in which helmets are worn, the helmet is normally a part of the uniform.

universal *mountain climbing* A light piton with a V-shaped blade — see illustration at PITON

unlap To put oneself back on the same lap as or one lap closer to a competitor by overtaking him during a race; to regain a lap lost to a competitor as a result of being lapped.

¹unlimited **1** *of a racing vehicle or craft* Not restricted as to the size or type of engine that may be used. **2** *of a racing class* For unlimited vehicles or craft.

²unlimited **1** A wrestling class which has no upper limit on weight; the class above the 191-pound limit. **2** An unlimited hydroplane.

unlimited hydroplane A hydroplane of the largest type that is driven by an underwater propeller (as opposed to a water jet) and that is powered by an inboard engine of unlimited displacement.

unload *of a football quarterback* To throw the ball ostensibly for a pass to get rid of it so as to avoid being tackled with it for a loss.

unmarked *of an offensive player* Not marked or guarded by an opposing player.

unnecessary roughness **1** The act or an instance of being excessively rough (as in checking) in ice hockey or box lacrosse which results in a minor penalty. In ice hockey it is also known as *roughing.* **2** *football* A general classification of illegal actions on the part of players including kicking, kneeing, tripping, or striking opponents, tackling a player who is obviously out of bounds, and throwing oneself against a player who is obviously out of the play either before or after the ball is dead, which is penalized by loss of 15 yards. For what the officials judge to be a flagrant foul, the offending player may be disqualified.

uno-goal polo A variation of water polo played in a pool at least 3 feet deep with a playing area of between 15 and 20 yards square. A team scores 2 points for putting the ball in its opponent's goal (an inflated inner tube), and fouls are penalized by a free throw worth one point.

unplayable **1** *of a playing surface* Temporarily unsuitable for play in the opinion of an official. **2** *of a ball or puck* Inaccessible.

unreturnable *of a shot in a wall or court game* Not able to be returned; out of reach of a player.

unsight To move to or be in a position to block

unsportsmanlike conduct

an official's or another player's and especially an opponent's view of the play.

unsportsmanlike conduct   Conduct that is not characteristic of good sportsmanship such as illegally hiding the ball or substituting something in place of the ball, giving unfair assistance to a player, unfairly distracting an opponent, fighting, using profanity or abusive language, and striking an official, for which the offender is penalized and often disqualified. Unsportsmanlike conduct is penalized in basketball by a technical foul; it is a personal foul in lacrosse. In football the team may be penalized 15 yards, and the player may be disqualified. In track and field, a player is disqualified for unsportsmanlike conduct.

unstring   *archery*   To remove the bowstring from the nock of a bow.

unweight   *skiing*   To reduce momentarily the force exerted by the skis on a slope prior to attempting a turn by shifting the weight or position of one's body. Two methods of unweighting are commonly employed. In the first, the skier quickly raises his body using a short jumping motion. At the peak of this movement the weight on the skis will be minimal although the skis do not actually leave the snow. This is known as *up-unweighting*. In the second, the skier quickly lowers his body from a relatively erect position. For an instant during this movement the weight is minimal and the skier is free to turn the skis. This is referred to as *down-unweighting*.

up   **1**   *baseball*   At bat.
2   *golf*   Ahead of an opponent in match play by one or more holes. ⟨a 2-*up* victory⟩
3   *horse racing*   Mounted on the horse or seated in the sulky.
4   *of a ball in court games*   Legally playable; not down.
5   *of a competitor*   Mentally prepared. ⟨to get *up* for a game⟩
6   *of a defender*   In a position close to the man being guarded. ⟨play *up* on a man⟩
7   Ahead; leading. ⟨*up* by 2 runs going into the ninth inning⟩

up and back   A strategy in doubles play (as in tennis) in which one partner plays at the net while the other plays in the backcourt as distinguished from both partners playing the same distance from the net.

up back   *football*   The running back nearest the quarterback in an I formation.

upcourt   *basketball*   In or into the part of a court in which a team's goal is located; toward the frontcourt.

upfield   **1**   In or into the part of the field toward which the offensive team is headed; downfield. ⟨the goalkeeper cleared the ball *upfield*⟩ ⟨the halfback took the handoff, turned the corner, and headed *upfield*⟩
2   In the part of the field from which a play starts. ⟨the quarterback hit his receiver with a 40-yard pass but a flag was thrown back *upfield*⟩

uphill   Upper; nearer the top of an incline. ⟨the *uphill* ski⟩

uphill christie   *skiing*   A parallel christie made by turning the skis uphill from a traverse and commonly employed for coming to a stop.

upland game   Birds (as pheasant, partridge, and quail) and small mammals (as rabbits, squirrels, and woodchucks) of upland areas as distinct from waterfowl and big game. Often the term *upland game bird* is used to distinguish the birds from the mammals.

upper arm hang   *gymnastics*   A position on the parallel bars in which the gymnast hangs between the bars supported by his upper arms while grasping the bars with his hands.

upper arm support   *gymnastics*   A position on the parallel bars in which the gymnast is supporting himself above the bars on his upper arms with his legs in the air.

uppercut   *boxing*   A relatively short punch to the head or body normally thrown from the waist level upward while keeping the arm bent.

upright   A vertical support for a crossbar.

uprights   A football goal.

upright spin   *skating*   A spin performed in the standing position.

uprise   *gymnastics*   A movement from a hang position on the rings or the horizontal bar or from an upper arm support position on the parallel bars to a straight arm support by swinging the body and at the peak of the swing pulling up with the arms. When the move up is at the end of a backward swing, it is a *back uprise;* if from a forward swing with the assist of a kip, it is a *front uprise.* (also called *stem*)

¹upset   To defeat the favorite in a contest.

²upset   A defeat of the favorite in a contest; a contest in which the favorite is defeated.

upwind   In the direction from which the wind is blowing; on the windward side of something (as game).

utility   *of a player in a team game*   Capable of serving as a substitute at any of several positions in the absence of regular players. ⟨a *utility* infielder⟩ ⟨a *utility* forward⟩

utilityman   A utility player.

V

Valdez *gymnastics* A movement from a sitting position up and back to a handstand position in a single smooth action. The performer sits with one hand on the floor behind him, one leg out straight on the floor in front of him, and the other leg bent so that the foot is near his body. With a push of the bent leg and a swing of the other leg and arm, the performer rises up and back, supported momentarily on the one hand on the floor, to finish in a 2-hand handstand.

Valdez

valet *horse racing* A jockey's attendant.

valve The device on a scuba diver's air tank which can be manually opened and closed in the manner of a water faucet to control the flow of air and to which the regulator is attached. The valve is opened fully when the regulator is attached; the regulator controls the flow of air. — see J VALVE, K VALVE

Van Alen Simplified Scoring System *tennis* Either of 2 scoring systems developed by James H. Van Alen to speed up play:

1 A system, often called the *no-ad game,* in which points are called 1, 2, 3, and 4 with the first side to win 4 points winning the game; there is no deuce and no advantage. A set is won by the side first winning 6 games. If the 2 sides are tied at 5 games apiece, a 9-point tiebreaker is played.

2 A system like that used for table tennis in which a set is won by the first side to score 31 points or, where time is a factor, 21 points. A side must win by at least 2 points. Service is changed after every 5 points and in doubles the service goes to the other side after the fifth, fifteenth, and twenty-fifth points. Serve also changes at the end of a set.

vane The fletching of an arrow.

vang Short for *boom vang.*

vantage see ADVANTAGE

Vardon grip or **Vardon overlapping grip** see GRIP *(golf)*

variation *see* DECLINATION

variometer An aeronautical instrument that uses a calibrated leak of air from a storage chamber to the outside air to measure the difference in the pressures and indicate rate of climb. The variometer is a necessary instrument in a sailplane to indicate to the pilot when he has encountered rising air. A common form of variometer uses a green and a red pellet in parallel tubes. When the craft is ascending, the green pellet rises in its tube; when descending the red pellet rises.

varmint Any animal or bird that preys on game or that is unprotected by game laws.

varsity The principal sports team or squad that represents a college, school, or club in competition with other colleges, schools, or clubs.

¹vault **1** *gymnastics* **a** A leap over an object (as a pommel horse or vaulting horse) made with a running start in which the hands are used to lift and support the body during the leap. **b** The manner or style of making a vault; the act or an instance of making a vault. **c** Vaulting competition.

2 An instance of making a pole vault.

²vault 1 To make a leap over an object (as a vaulting horse) by placing the hands on the horse for support and for a push off.

2 To attain a specific height in the pole vault. ⟨he *vaulted* 17 feet⟩

vaulter Someone who makes a vault in gymnastics or a pole vault in track and field.

vaulting The action or practice of making vaults over apparatus.

vaulting horse *gymnastics* An apparatus which consists of a padded leather-covered rectangular form 1600 to 1630 millimeters (about 5 feet 3 inches) long and 350 millimeters (13½ inches) wide that is used in vaulting competition. The horse used in men's vaulting is supported usually on 4 legs 1350 millimeters (4 feet 4½ inches) above the floor. It has 2 white lines marking off 3 sections on the top, a croup, saddle, and neck. The end sections (croup and neck) are each 400 millimeters (15½ inches) long. The horse is placed so that male gymnasts vault from end to end. Whether the hands are placed on the croup or the neck depends on the style of vault being attempted. The horse used in women's vaulting is 1100 millimeters (3 feet 7 inches) high and is placed so that the gymnasts vault over it from side to side. A pommel horse that has the pommels removed and that is adjusted to the proper height may be used as a vaulting horse. — see illustration at YAMASHITA

veer or **veer offense** *football* An offense that employs the triple option run from a pro-style T formation. — see T FORMATION; compare WISHBONE

velocity *baseball* Speed; the ability to throw the ball hard. ⟨the knuckleball pitcher . . . really has three strikes against him from the beginning. His high school coach looks for guys who can throw with *velocity*. — Wilbur Wood⟩

velocity stacks *auto racing* A set of short flared pipes mounted on the intake ports of each carburetor or the fuel injection system of a racing engine to provide each cylinder with an equal volume of air.

velodrome A track for cycle races.

venery 1 The act or practice of hunting.

2 Animals that are hunted; game.

vent valve *ballooning* A simple valve mounted on the top of a balloon that permits the balloonist to release gas or air from the balloon and thereby regulate lift.

verglas *mountain climbing* A thin sheet of ice covering a slope.

veronica *bullfighting* A pase in which the matador keeps his feet in place while he swings the cape slowly away from the charging bull and leads the bull by him on one side.

vet Short for *veteran*.

veteran An athlete who has extensive experience in a sport especially at the professional level. The term is commonly used of a skilled player with much experience as a starter in contrast with a journeyman, though at times the term may be used of any player with as little as 2 years experience in contrasting him with a rookie.

vice skip *curling* The player who plays third for his team and who is in charge of the head for his team when the skip is curling.

victory The winning of a contest; a contest that one or one's team wins.

victory lap An additional lap customarily taken after the end of a race by the winner in some sports (as auto racing, cycling, and track and field).

view halloo *fox hunting* A shout given by a hunter on seeing a fox break cover.

vigorish The percentage of the total amount of money bet that is kept as profit by a racetrack or a bookmaker. In wagering through a pari-mutuel system, the percentage, usually set by law (as at 15 percent), is automatically taken out before payoffs are calculated. The bookmaker's vigorish is determined by the odds he gives. If both sides of a wager put up 6 dollars to win 5, the bookmaker will earn one dollar on the wager regardless of which side wins.

violation 1 An infraction of the rules. In general use the term may be synonymous with *foul*.

2 A minor infraction of the rules which is less serious than a foul: **a** *basketball* An infraction of the rules other than a procedure infraction or personal contact such as walking with the ball, causing the ball to go out of bounds, making an improper dribble, or violating a time rule (as the 3-second or 10-second rules) that is penalized by loss of possession of the ball. **b** *lacrosse* An infraction of the rules such as delay of the game or causing the ball to go out of bounds that is penalized by loss of possession of the ball. **c** *soccer* An infraction such as improper substitution, unsportsmanlike play, offsides, interference, or improper charging which is penalized by an indirect free kick for the opposing team.

d *speedball* An infraction of the rules such as carrying the ball, touching a ground ball with the hands, making 2 successive overhead dribbles, or violating any of the kicking restrictions which is penalized normally by a free kick for the opposing team. If a violation is committed by a defensive player in his own end zone, it is penalized by a penalty kick.

visual exchange see EXCHANGE

vital point Any of several areas of the human body (as the temple, throat, heart, and liver) to which a blow is considered to have lethal potential in karate and jujitsu.

vitals *hunting* The organs (as the heart, liver, lungs, and brain) of an animal that are most necessary for life and that are key targets for the big-game hunter.

¹volley 1 A return of the ball or shuttlecock before it hits the playing surface. In tennis and paddle tennis a volley is not permitted on the serve but can be attempted at any other time during the exchange. In other court games (as handball, squash racquets, or paddleball) a volley can be attempted on any shot during the game including the serve. In volleyball and badminton a volley is the only legal return, as contact of the ball or shuttlecock with the court results in the loss of a point or the serve.

2 or **volley kick** *soccer* A kick of the ball before it hits the ground.

3 A rally (as in badminton).

²volley 1 To return a ball or shuttlecock before it hits the floor or ground; to make a volley.

2 To hit a ball or shuttlecock back and forth across a net (as for practice or to warm up). ⟨*volley* for serve⟩

volleyball A game played on a rectangular court between 2 teams of 6 players in which a large inflated ball is volleyed back and forth across a high net until the ball touches the floor or is hit out of bounds. The court measures 60 feet by 30 feet. Play is started by one team serving to the other team with each team thereafter allowed to hit the ball 3 times before it must cross the net. The first 2 preliminary hits are usually used to set up a teammate who attempts to spike the ball and drive it downward into the opponent's court. Points are scored only by the serving side; if the serving side fails to make a good return, the service passes to the other side. A single player serves during a team's turn; when the team regains service, all the players move to new positions so that a new player becomes the server. In this way, each player may have an opportunity to serve during the course of the game. A game is played until one team scores 15 points and has at least a 2-point advantage over the other.

volleyer Someone who volleys a ball and especially a tennis player noted for playing the volley.

volley kick see VOLLEY

volte *equitation* A school figure which consists of the horse's walking around a circle approximately 6 meters in diameter.

volume training see OVERDISTANCE

volunteer snooker An English version of snooker in which a player may elect (volunteer) to shoot at a ball other than the one he is on but at the risk of forfeiting penalty points if he fails to pocket the volunteered ball.

voodoo ball A baseball manufactured in the United States but stitched in Haiti.

vorlage *skiing* A position in which the skier leans forward from the ankles usually without lifting the heels from the skis.

V seat *gymnastics* A balance position in which the gymnast sits on the floor or on a balance beam and holds the legs and torso in the air in the form of a letter V.

wadcutter A target bullet having a flat top instead of a pointed or rounded nose that is designed to cut a clean hole in a target.

wader or **waders** *fishing* A waterproof garment consisting of trousers sometimes reaching to the armpits, with attached socks or waterproof boots or shoes that is worn over regular clothing while wading. Sometimes hip boots are referred to as waders.

¹waggle *golf* A preliminary movement of the clubhead back and forth over the ball before the backswing is begun that is often used as a method of releasing tension.

²waggle *golf* To move the clubhead back and forth over the ball when addressing the ball before a stroke.

wahine A female surfer.

waist line *mountain climbing* A line wrapped usually several turns around a climber's waist to which a climbing rope or descendeur may be secured.

waive To put a player on waivers.

waiver The act of a club's relinquishing claim to a player who is being dropped from the roster of another club in a professional sports league. Professional sports clubs have a system whereby the other clubs in a league have the right to claim a player before a club can drop or trade that player or sell his contract to a club in another league. The waiver is automatic unless a club makes a formal claim within a designated time limit. A club can pick up a player "on waivers" by buying his contract for the stipulated waiver price. When a club places a player on waivers it "asks waivers" on him, and it has the right to withdraw the player's name from the list a limited number of times if a claim is made. If a player is not claimed, he "clears waivers" and is then formally dropped from the club or can then be traded to a club in another league. Some leagues have an injured waivers system for players that are injured and that a club wishes to replace temporarily on the roster. A club may place a player on waivers simply to see if another club is interested in acquiring that player and then withdraw the player and try to work out a trade.

wake surfing Surfing in the wake of a boat instead of on an ocean wave.

¹walk 1 *equitation* A moderately slow 4-beat gait in which each foot strikes the ground separately and in which the horse is supported on 2 or 3 feet at any given time. The normal sequence of movements is one hind foot, the forefoot on the same side, the diagonally opposite hind foot, and the other forefoot.
2 *track and field* A race in which competitors are limited to using a fast walk in which the leg is kept straight when it is supporting the body and continuous contact with the ground is maintained by not raising one foot until the heel of the other foot is on the ground. (also called *racewalk*)
3 see BASE ON BALLS

²walk 1 *baseball* **a** *of a batter* To receive a base on balls. ⟨*walked* in the third inning⟩ **b** *of a pitcher* (1) To give up a base on balls to a batter. ⟨*walked* 4 and struck out 3⟩ ⟨*walked* the leadoff batter⟩ (2) To force in a run by giving a batter a base on balls with the bases loaded. ⟨*walked* in the winning run⟩
2 see TRAVEL

walker An athlete who competes in a walk.

Walker Cup A trophy presented to the winner of a golf competition between amateur men's teams from the United States and Great Britain that is held every 2 years. The competition is match play and consists of four 18-hole foursome matches and eight 18-hole singles matches. The trophy is named for George H. Walker, a former president of the United States Golf Association and organizer of the competition.

walking see TRAVELING

walking ring *horse racing* An oval area where horses are walked to warm up before a race. (also called *parade ring*)

walkover 1 *gymnastics* A stunt in which the

performer, from a standing position, leans forward (*front walkover*) or backward (*back walkover*), places his hands on the floor, brings one leg at a time overhead, pauses briefly in a handstand position, and continues through to bring the legs down one at a time to finish in a standing position.

2 *horse racing* **a** A race in which there is only one starter due to the scratching of the rest of the field and in which the horse need only walk the distance to win. **b** A race in which all of the starters belong to the same owner.

3 a A contest in which the winner is given the victory (as through disqualification of his opponent). **b** A one-sided contest.

wall 1 *equitation* A solid obstacle for show jumping typically constructed of light boxes painted to resemble a solid brick or stone wall. **2** *mountain climbing* A steep rock face pitched 60 to 90 degrees from horizontal. — compare GLACIS, OVERHANG, SLAB
3 *surfing* The steep face of a wave.

Walley *skating* A jump from the inner backward edge of one foot, with a full turn in the air, and a return to the outer backward edge of the same foot. On landing, the skater follows a curve in the opposite direction from the rotation of the turn.

wall game A game (as handball, squash racquets, or jai alai) that is played by hitting or hurling a ball against a wall of a court.

wall pass *soccer* A pass that is kicked back immediately to the passer so that its flight resembles that of a ball rebounding from a wall.

wall shot 1 see CAROM SHOT (*croquet*)
2 see ALLEY SHOT

wall-up *of a surfing wave* To build up to maximum height prior to breaking in a sudden crash.

waltz jump *skating* A jump in which the skater takes off from the outer forward edge of one skate, makes a half turn, and lands on the outer backward edge of the other skate. (also called *three jump*)

waltz position *skating* A position in dance skating in which the skaters face each other and the man holds the girl's right hand in his left hand and places his right hand at the back of her waist.

waltz three *skating* A three turn in which the free foot is placed on the surface just after the turn to continue the curve on that foot. (also called *dropped three*)

wand *archery* A long narrow target used in the wand shoot. A wand usually consists of a slat of soft wood 6 feet long and 2 inches wide but may

consist of a white strip painted vertically on the face of a board or circular target.

wand shoot or **wand shooting** *archery* Competition in which 36 arrows are shot at a wand from a distance of 60 yards for women and 100 yards for men.

warm-down A period of practice or a series of light exercises designed to allow a competitor to taper off from competition or hard exercise.

warm down To taper off an activity in a warm-down. ⟨I did four hard quarters and *warming down* my left knee started to hurt — Dave Wottle⟩

warm-up A period of practice or a series of exercises designed to loosen the muscles and increase the blood circulation of a competitor prior to hard exercise, a practice session, or competition.

warm up To engage in a warm-up prior to hard exercise or competition.

warm-up suit 1 A usually nylon 2-piece suit designed to keep a skier warm and dry.
2 see SWEATSUIT

warning line *fencing* A line parallel to and one meter from each end of the piste for foil fencing and 2 meters from each end in épée and saber fencing which serves to warn the fencer that he is nearing the end of the piste. — see illustration at FENCING

warning track or **warning path** *baseball* A usually dirt or cinder strip around the outside edge of the outfield to warn a fielder who is running to make a catch that he is approaching the fence.

wash *rowing* To move in front of another shell illegally so that the other crew is forced to row in one's wake.

washout 1 *bowling* A leave in which the 1, 2, and 10 pins, and sometimes the 4 pin, remain standing for a right-handed bowler or the 1, 3, and 7 pins, and sometimes the 6 pin, remain standing for a left-handed bowler. — see illustration of pin arrangement at BOWLING
2 see RAINOUT

wash-out 1 The disallowing by the referee of a goal in ice hockey or box lacrosse.
2 The signaling by a linesman that a delayed offside or a potential icing will not be called because the play by a defensive or attacking player changes the situation making the call unnecessary.

wash out see RAIN OUT

watch see CHECK (*Australian Rules football*)

water boy Someone who supplies players (as on a football team) with drinking water especially by bringing a water bucket to them on the field during a time-out.

water dog *hunting* Any dog trained to retrieve waterfowl.

waterfowl Swimming game birds (as ducks or geese) as distinguished from upland game birds.

waterfowler Someone who hunts waterfowl.

water hazard *golf* Any hazard, excluding casual water, in which water stands (as in a pond, lake, or sea) or runs either continuously of intermittently (as in a river or drainage ditch). When a player's ball lies in a water hazard, he must play it as it lies if he can. If he cannot play it from the water, the player may drop outside the hazard behind the hazard or not more than 2 club-lengths from the point at which the ball entered the hazard with a penalty of one stroke, or he may play another ball from the point of the last stroke, count both strokes, and take a one-stroke penalty. The player is not permitted to touch the club to the water before the stroke if he is attempting to play the ball from the water hazard.

water jump **1** *horse racing* A pool of water on a steeplechase course 12 feet across that is guarded at the approach side by a fence at least 2 feet high. The bottom of the pool slopes up from a depth of 2 feet behind the fence to ground level at the far side.

2 *show jumping* A pool of water 4 to 5 meters (approximately 13 to 16½ feet) across that is guarded on the approach side by a hedge or rail approximately 2 feet high. The bottom of the pool slopes up to ground level at the far side, and the far edge is marked by a white strip of soft wood or rubber about 2 inches wide.

3 *track and field* A pool of water 12 feet square on a steeplechase course guarded on the approach side by a 3-foot-high hurdle. The bottom of the pool slopes up from a depth of 2 feet 3¾ inches (2½ feet in college competition) just behind the hurdle to ground level at the far end.

water knot A knot often used for joining the ends of sling material that is formed by tying an overhand knot in one end and threading the other end through the knot in the opposite direction. — see illustration at KNOT

waterline The line on the hull of a boat where the surface of the water meets the hull when the boat is afloat.

water polo A game played in a rectangular pool or an enclosed rectangular area of water 75 to 100 feet long and 45 to 60 feet wide (20 to 30 meters long and 8 to 20 meters wide for international play) between 2 teams of 7 players each with the object to dribble and pass an inflated ball to a point near the opponent's goal and throw it past the opposing goalkeeper for a score and to prevent the opposing team from scoring. Unlimited substitution is permitted if it takes place while play is stopped. All movement in the water is by swimming, and players dribble the ball by keeping it in front of them while swimming a crawl stroke. The ball is passed and thrown at the goal only with one hand, and punching the ball is not permitted. Only the goalkeeper is permitted to touch the ball with 2 hands. Players may physically interfere with an opponent who is holding or moving the ball, but they are not permitted to hold, pull back, or dunk an opponent who is not actually holding the ball. Fouls consist of technical fouls (called *ordinary fouls* in international play), such as standing on the bottom or punching the ball, for which the opposing team is given a free throw, and personal fouls, such as holding or dunking an opponent who is not holding the ball or committing a technical foul to prevent a goal. A personal foul is charged against the guilty player in addition to giving the opposing team a free throw. As in basketball, a player is disqualified if he is charged with 5 personal fouls. In international play, a player is suspended from the game for a period of 30 seconds for each personal foul and his team plays shorthanded. Play is started at the beginning of each period with the referee throwing the ball into the middle of the pool and blowing his whistle to signal for players of both sides to sprint from their own goal lines to try to gain possession of the ball. In college play, the goalkeeper passes the ball out of the goal to a teammate to restart play after a goal has been scored. In the international game, play is restarted after a goal with a member of the team scored against passing the ball to a teammate from the middle of the playing area. The game consists of four 7-minute quarters (5-minute quarters in international play), and it is conducted by 2 referees (one referee in international play) assisted by 2 goal judges who are stationed at the sides of the pool.

water-ski To plane or glide over the water's surface on water skis while being towed by a motorboat.

water ski One of usually a pair of strips of wood or fiberglass having a slightly upturned front that typically measure 6 inches wide and 6 feet long and that are used in water-skiing. General-purpose water skis have a deep skeg or fin on the

wedge

lower edge at the rear for stability. Trick skis are usually shorter and wider than normal skis and usually have no fin so that they can be turned or pivoted while in motion.

water-skier Someone who water-skis.

waterskiing The sport of planing and jumping on water skis.

wave-kick *surfing* A stunt performed while riding on the nose of the surfboard in which the surfer either kicks or drags one foot in the wave.

¹wax A paraffin-base synthetic substance that is applied to the bottom of skis to alter the characteristics of the running surface. In downhill skiing, waxes of different densities are used to decrease the friction between the snow and the running surface, with a harder wax used in cold dry conditions and a softer wax in soft wet conditions. In ski touring, 2 and sometimes 3 layers of wax are employed. A tar-base wax is applied directly to the running surface to protect the ski from moisture and wear. A second optional layer, or *binder,* serves to help bind the base wax and running wax. The third layer, or *running wax,* serves to decrease friction when the skier is moving and to increase friction when the skier is standing or climbing according to the pattern of application to the running surface. — see also BASE, CLIMBING WAX, KLISTER

²wax **1** To apply wax to the running surface of skis. **2** To apply wax (as household paraffin) to the upper surface of a surfboard to increase traction for the feet.

waxing cork A section of cork used to work wax onto the surface of skis.

weak safety *football* The safety playing on the same side of the field as the weak side of the offensive line.

weak side **1** The side of a court or field away from the ball. **2** *box lacrosse* The side of an offensive pattern having the smaller number of players; the side opposite the point man. **3** *football* **a** The side of an unbalanced line having the smaller number of players. **b** The side of the line opposite the tight end.

weanling *horse racing* A recently weaned horse that is not old enough to be classified as a yearling. — compare YEARLING; see AGE

wear *sailing* To change from one tack to another when sailing close-hauled by turning the bow away from the wind; jibe. — often used in the phrase *wear ship*

weather Windward.

weather helm see HELM

¹weave A figure-eight movement by usually 3 or more attacking players in an arc in front of the goal (as in basketball or lacrosse) with constant passing of the ball at close range in order to make it difficult for defenders to keep up with their men and to make it possible for a player to get free for a shot. In the weave, the player with the ball usually cuts inside a teammate moving toward him in the opposite direction so that he will pass the ball to the outside to the teammate keeping himself between the defenders and the ball and momentarily shielding the teammate from the player trying to guard him.

²weave **1** To move in or execute a weave (as in basketball or lacrosse). **2** *of a boxer* To move from side to side to present a moving target to one's opponent.

webbing **1** *baseball* The lacing connecting the thumb and finger sections of a glove or mitt. **2** A network of straps inside a helmet to support the helmet off the head in order to cushion blows.

wedel To ski downhill by means of wedeln.

wedeln *skiing* A maneuver in which the skier swings the tails of his skis from side to side while skiing down the fall line.

wedge **1** *football* A wedge-shaped formation of blockers ahead of the ballcarrier on kickoff returns. Unlike the players in the old flying wedge, the players in the modern wedge are not linked together, and the formation is usually broken up quickly by members of the kicking team who delight in hurling themselves into a mass of onrushing opponents. **2** *golf* An iron club with an extreme loft for use in pitch and chip shots from close to the putting green. The normal pitching wedge has a loft of about 55 degrees from vertical and is used to pitch a ball up to the green from close range. A sand wedge used to make a shot in a sand trap, is essentially identical to a pitching wedge except the base is somewhat thicker to permit it to dig into the sand of the bunker. **3** *mountain climbing* A wedge-shaped block of wood, a nut, or an angle piton or bong which is wedged in a large crack to serve as an anchor or belay point. **4** *skiing* **a** A position used especially in stopping or slowing down in which the skis are pushed apart with the tips together and the inside edges in the snow. The wedge resembles a snowplow, but the skis are not so wide as in a snowplow. **b** A skiing technique in which students are instructed in the making of wedge stops and wedge turns from the beginning from which they progress to parallel turns.

5 *surfing* **a** A surfboard constructed with 2 diagonal stringers that meet at a point in the front. **b** The point where 2 waves meet at an angle.

wedge engine An internal-combustion engine having wedge-shaped combustion chambers.

wedge shot *golf* A shot made with a wedge.

weedless *of a fishhook or fishing lure* Designed with a lightweight wire guard that covers the point of the hook to prevent its catching in weeds and sticks but that is light enough to be pushed out of the way to expose the point when a fish takes the hook or lure in its mouth.

weigh To raise an anchor.

weigh-in **1** The official weighing of contestants (as in boxing, weight lifting, and amateur wrestling) before a competition usually to determine that the contestants' weights fall within the limits of their respective divisions or weight classes. The weighing in normally takes place on the day of the competition usually from one to 5 hours before the beginning of the competition, depending on the sport. When the competition lasts for several days, as at a national championship, competitors are weighed in every day. The weigh-in is a part of all divisions of professional boxing except the heavyweight division in which there is no weight limit. It has been retained for heavyweight fights, however, as part of the ceremony and prefight buildup.
2 *horse racing* The official weighing of the jockey and his saddle and equipment after a race.
3 *hunting* The official weighing of a kill in a competitive archery hunt.

weigh in **1** To take the weight of a particular competitor in a weigh-in.
2 *of a jockey* To be weighed with the saddle and equipment after a race. — compare WEIGH OUT

weigh-out The official weighing of a jockey, saddle, and any impost weights before a race.

weigh out *horse racing* To weigh a jockey before a race. — compare WEIGH IN

¹weight **1** *archery* The force required to pull a bow to full draw that is expressed in pounds.
2 *curling* The momentum required to send a stone to a particular spot on the ice.
3 *horse racing* A lead bar placed in a slot in saddle bags to bring the total weight carried by a horse to the required amount for a particular race.
4 *track and field* A shot, hammer, 35-pound weight, or 56-pound weight put or hurled for distance in a field event.
5 *weight lifting* **a** A disk having a specific weight that is placed on a barbell or dumbbell. **b** A barbell or dumbbell. ⟨he lifted the *weight* to his shoulders⟩

²weight *skiing* To shift the body weight to a specified ski in traversing or making a turn; to put force on a ski to make it follow a straight course and not slip sideways. — compare UNWEIGHT

weight belt *scuba diving* A belt that holds a number of lead weights that counteract the natural buoyancy of the body and allow a diver to maintain a chosen depth. — see illustration at SCUBA DIVER

weight class *wrestling* A classification into which competitors are grouped according to body weight. — compare DIVISION

WRESTLING WEIGHT CLASSES

(maximum weights)

high school	college	international
98 lbs	118 lbs	48 kgs (105.5 lbs)
105 lbs	126 lbs	52 kgs (114.5 lbs)
112 lbs	134 lbs	57 kgs (125.5 lbs)
119 lbs	142 lbs	62 kgs (136.5 lbs)
126 lbs	150 lbs	68 kgs (149.5 lbs)
132 lbs	158 lbs	74 kgs (163.1 lbs)
138 lbs	167 lbs	82 kgs (180.5 lbs)
145 lbs	177 lbs	90 kgs (198 lbs)
155 lbs	190 lbs	100 kgs (220 lbs)
167 lbs	unlimited	over 100 kgs
185 lbs		
unlimited*		

* (minimum 175 lbs)

---

weight-for-age race *horse racing* A race in which horses carry scale weights. — see SCALE OF WEIGHTS

weight forward line see FLY LINE

weight lifter Someone who competes in weight lifting; someone who trains or exercises by lifting weights.

weight lifting **1** A competitive sport in which individuals lift a barbell with the object to lift a greater weight than other competitors in a specific weight division. There are 2 forms of international weight lifting competition: Olympic lifting, in which only 2 lifts, the snatch and the clean and jerk, are employed, and powerlifting which involves the squat, deadlift, and bench press. In both types of competition, the competitors are permitted 3 attempts in each lift. Competition proceeds with the barbell loaded with successively higher weights with the increments in multiples of 2.5 kilograms (5.5 pounds). Each competitor selects the weight at which he will make his next attempt, and he is called in turn when that weight is on the bar. From the time he is called, the lifter must begin his lift within 3 minutes, or the attempt will be eliminated. The competition is conducted by 3 referees who rule on the validity of each lift. One referee serves as chief referee, who signals to the lifter when he may proceed with a step in a lift or may return the bar to the floor or a rack when the lift is over. The competitor with the highest single attempt in a lift will be designated the champion of that particular lift, but final placing is determined by the combined total of the best attempts in each lift. — see also DIVISION

2 Weight training.

weight man *track and field* An athlete who competes in a field event in which a weight is thrown or put.

weight program A program or plan followed in weight training.

weight throw see 56-POUND WEIGHT THROW, 35-POUND WEIGHT THROW

weight training A system of conditioning (as for track or football) in which an athlete lifts weights for strength and endurance usually concentrating on those muscles most used in his sport. The athlete normally follows a predetermined schedule of weight progression that permits him to increase stamina and strength in an orderly gradual manner.

welter Short for *welterweight.*

welterweight **1** A boxer who competes in the welterweight division. — see DIVISION

2 *horse racing* A weight of 28 pounds sometimes imposed in a steeplechase in addition to scale weight.

Western grip see GRIP (*tennis*)

Western roll *track and field* A method of high jumping in which the jumper leads with the leg farthest from the bar, brings his trailing leg up under the other leg, and crosses the bar on his side with both legs passing over the bar together. — compare FLOP, SCISSORS, STRADDLE

Western round *archery* A target round in women's competition in which each competitor shoots 48 arrows at a distance of 60 yards and 48 arrows at 50 yards.

wet fly *fishing* An artificial fly that is designed to be used below the surface of the water.

wet pitch A spitball in baseball.

wet suit A close-fitting usually rubber suit that is worn by a scuba diver and occasionally by a surfer or water-skier and that is designed to trap a thin layer of water between the suit and the skin where it is warmed by body heat to provide a layer of insulation from cold water. — see illustration at SCUBA DIVER

W formation *soccer* A formation of a 5-man forward line in which the outside forwards and the center forward play in a line close to the goal and the inside forwards play relatively far from the goal so as to present the appearance of the letter W. — compare M FORMATION

¹wheel **1** A sports league.

2 Leg. ⟨for a back with a bum *wheel,* [he] rolled spectacularly, leading all ballcarriers with 89 yards — Ron Reid, *Sports Illustrated*⟩ — often used in the plural ⟨believes he can play as long as his *wheels* hold out⟩

3 *judo* A throw in which the judoist grasps the opponent's lapels with both hands, upsets the opponent's balance with his foot, and turns the hands as he would in turning a steering wheel to bring the opponent to the mat.

4 *pari-mutuel betting* A system of betting on pools such as the daily double, quiniela, or perfecta in which a bettor matches a single competitor with all the other competitors in the same contest or in the next contest so that all possible combinations involving the first competitor are covered.

²wheel To bet a wheel in pari-mutuel betting; to pair a particular competitor with every other competitor.

Wheelchair Games An international program of sports competition similar to the Olympic Games

Western roll

wheel dogs

that is held for paralyzed individuals confined to wheelchairs. The events include archery, basketball, bowling, table tennis, swimming, and track and field events such as the discus throw and shot put. The games are intended not so much for individuals competing against each other as for individuals competing against their handicaps. (also called *Paralympics*)

wheel dogs *dogsled racing* The pair of dogs that are hitched closest to the sled and that are second in importance to the leader.

wheelie or **wheelstand** **1** The balancing of a drag-racing vehicle momentarily on its rear wheels as a result of applying power to the rear wheels suddenly. The lift results from a reaction to the great torque on the rear axle and is generally avoided since it wastes power which could be used otherwise to propel the vehicle forward. **2** *freestyle skiing* A stunt in which a skier jumps but keeps the tails of his skis in contact with the snow.

wheelie bar A device (as a bar or short frame with small wheels) projecting from the rear of a drag-racing vehicle that prevents the vehicle from tipping back too far during a wheelie.

wheelstand see WHEELIE

wheel sucker *cycling* A rider adept at utilizing the slipstream from another rider to conserve energy while keeping up with the front rider.

wherry *rowing* A narrow open racing or exercise boat rowed by one person with sculls.

¹whiff **1** To swing at a ball or puck and miss it. **2 a** *of a baseball batter* To strike out. **b** *of a baseball pitcher* To strike out a particular batter.

²whiff *baseball* A strikeout.

¹whip A flexible rod or lash with which an animal is driven. The whip used in harness racing and dogsled racing is relatively long while that used in horse racing is a fairly short flexible rod with a short loop of flexible leather at the end.

²whip **1** To drive an animal (as a racehorse) by hitting with a whip. **2** *archery* To put a serving on a bowstring. **3** To fish with an artificial lure.

whip in *fox hunting* To keep a pack of hounds from scattering by use of a whip.

whipper-in *fox hunting* A huntsman's assistant whose job it is to keep the hounds together in a pack.

whisker pole *sailing* A light pole extending from the mast to the clew of the jib to hold the jib out when sailing off the wind.

whistle *of an official* **1** To stop play (as because

of a violation or foul) by blowing a whistle. **2** To charge a player with an infraction or a foul. ⟨was *whistled* for charging⟩

whistle buoy see BUOY

white flag *motor racing* A solid white flag used to indicate that an official or emergency vehicle is on the course or, when shown at the start-finish line, to indicate that there is only one more lap in the race.

white hazard *billiards* A winning hazard in English billiards in which the white ball is pocketed and which counts 2 points.

white hope *boxing* A white contender for a title held by a black.

whiteout *mountain climbing* A condition in which a climber's sense of depth and orientation is lost because of the uniformly bright reflection of light from a snow cover and an overcast sky.

¹whitewash To hold an opponent scoreless; shut out.

²whitewash or **whitewashing** A shutout.

whitewater **1** The rapids of a river or waterway. **2** *surfing* The turbulent part of a breaking wave.

whitewater racing A usually slalom kayak or canoe race run over the whitewater of a river or specially prepared waterway. On a special waterway the course is usually a half mile long. On a river the course will normally be about 2 miles long.

whizzer *wrestling* An arm lock in which the wrestler, usually from a position beside and facing in the same direction as his opponent, encircles the opponent's near arm holding it under his own armpit and trapping it behind his own body.

whizzer

wick *of a delivery in curling* To carom off another stone.

wicket **1** *cricket* **a** A wooden frame at which

the ball is bowled that consists of 3 wooden stumps that stand 28 inches high topped by 2 short bails that fit into grooves in the top of the stumps. The stumps must be of equal diameter and of sufficient size that the ball cannot pass through; they are set up with a total width of 9 inches. There are 2 wickets on the field, one at each end of the pitch. The wicket is somewhat analogous to a base in baseball; a batsman is out if the wicket is knocked down by a bowled ball or if a fieldsman knocks down the wicket with the ball while the batsman is out of the crease. While the batsman is behind the popping crease, he is not subject to being run out. **b** The grassy strip 22 yards long and 10 feet wide between the 2 wickets on which the ball is bowled and on which the batsmen run between wickets; pitch. **c** A turn at bat for a batsman during an innings; a batsman who has had a turn at bat and has been put out during an innings. ⟨scored 215 runs for 5 *wickets*⟩

2 *croquet* Any of a number of stout wire arches placed in the ground around the court through which the balls must be hit. The wickets vary in size and height with the version of the game being played. For lawn croquet, the wickets are approximately 10 inches high and have an opening approximately 5 inches wide. For association croquet, they are 12 inches high and 3¾ inches wide. In regulation croquet and in roque, the wickets are 3⅜ inches wide and 9 inches tall in regulation croquet and 8 inches tall in roque.

cricket wicket and surrounding area

wicketkeeper *cricket* A player who is stationed behind the wicket which the bowler is attacking and who is analogous to the catcher in baseball. The wicketkeeper is traditionally the only player on the field to wear gloves for fielding. He wears a heavy glove on each hand and shin pads similar to those worn by the batsman.

¹wide **1** *of an arrow or bullet* Away from the center of the target.

2 *of a ball or shuttlecock* Hit beyond the side boundaries of a court.

3 *baseball* **a** *of a pitch* Out of the strike zone to the outside of home plate. **b** *of a throw* To either side of a base.

4 *of a delivery in curling* To one side of the line indicated by the skip.

5 *football* To or on the outside of an offensive line; toward the sideline.

6 *horse racing* To or toward the outside of a racetrack. ⟨tends to run *wide* in the turns⟩

7 *volleyball* Toward the sideline. ⟨a *wide* set⟩

²wide *cricket* A bowled ball that is delivered so high or wide of the wicket that in the judgment of the umpire it is out of reach of the batsman when he is in his normal batting position. A wide ball automatically counts as one run for the batting side unless the batsmen are able to score more by running. A wide does not count as one of the 6 deliveries that constitutes an over. It is possible for a batsman to be stumped on a wide or for either of the 2 batsmen to be run out. A batsman may also be called out for a hit wicket or for handling the ball or obstructing the field on a wide, but he may not be caught out if he hits the ball. Runs scored on a wide are counted as extras and are not credited to the batsman.

wide open **1** Characterized by a freewheeling offensive style of play in which a team risks losing the ball or puck or sacrifices defense in order to score.

2 *of a player* Not guarded by an opponent.

wide receiver *football* The split end or the flanker in an offensive formation.

Wightman Cup A trophy presented to the winner of an annual tennis competition between women's teams from the United States and England. The competition began in 1923 and is held alternately in England and the United States; it consists of 5 singles and 2 doubles matches. The trophy is named for its donor, Mrs. Hazel Hotchkiss Wightman, a former American singles champion.

wild **1** *of a baseball pitcher* Lacking control.

2 *of a throw* Far away from the intended target.

wild card A team in a conference that qualifies for the play-offs (as in football or basketball) by virtue of its having the best record of all of the conference teams that did not automatically qualify for the play-offs (as by being division champions).

wildcat **1** *of a cartridge* Having a bullet of standard caliber but using an expanded case or a case originally designed for a bullet of greater caliber.

2 *of a rifle* Using wildcat cartridges.

wildfowl A game bird and usually a waterfowl.

wildfowler Someone who hunts wildfowl.

wild-pitch *baseball* To deliver a wild pitch; to cause a run to score as a result of a wild pitch.

wild pitch *baseball* A pitch that is not hit by the batter and not stopped by the catcher, that in the opinion of the official scorer could not be controlled by the catcher with ordinary effort, and that enables a base runner to advance. — compare PASSED BALL

willow A cricket bat.

Wilson *skating* A jump in which the skater takes off from the outer backward edge of one skate, makes a full turn in the air, and lands on the outer backward edge of the other skate beginning a curve in the opposite direction.

Wimbledon The All England Lawn Tennis Championship played annually at the All England Tennis and Croquet Club, Wimbledon, London. The fixture, begun in 1877, became an open event in 1968.

¹win **1** A victory in a contest. Wins are recorded along with defeats in team sports to determine league standings. In baseball a win is also credited to the winning pitcher in order to record annual and career pitching statistics.

2 *pari-mutuel betting* First place at the finish. A bettor collects on a win bet only if the competitor wins the contest. — see also PARI-MUTUEL BETTING

²win **1** To gain the victory in a contest.

2 To gain a point in a contest (as tennis).

3 To finish first in competition involving betting. — compare PLACE, SHOW

¹wind **1** The ability to breathe properly especially during exertion. ⟨building up his *wind*⟩

2 *sailing* The direction from which the wind is blowing.

— **against the wind** or **close to the wind** or **into the wind** or **near to the wind** or **on the wind** In the direction from which the wind is blowing. — **before the wind** or **off the wind** or **with the wind** In the same direction as the main force of the wind. — **under the wind** **1** On the

windsurfing

side away from the direction from which the wind is blowing; to leeward. **2** In a place that is protected from the wind.

²wind To allow a horse to catch its breath.

windage An adjustment in the sight of a rifle or bow that moves it to one side or the other to correct for inaccuracy such as that caused by a crosswind.

wind-aided *track and field* Relating to a distance recorded in the long jump or triple jump or to a time recorded in any race run over a distance of 220 yards or less in which a wind of 4.47 mph or greater average velocity assisted the performer. Wind-aided times and distances do not qualify for official recognition as track-and-field records. ⟨ran a *wind-aided* 9 flat in the 100-yard dash⟩

winder A hard fast run and especially a warm-up run in which a sprinter gradually builds up to top speed.

windmill A supercharger.

wind shadow *sailing* The area of relatively dead air leeward of a boat.

Windsor round *archery* A target round in which each contestant shoots 36 arrows at a distance of 60 yards, 36 at 50 yards, and 36 at 40 yards.

wind sprint One of a series of short sprints in a training program designed to increase an athlete's wind and endurance.

windsurfer One who engages in windsurfing.

Windsurfer A trademark for a surfboard equipped for sailing with a mast and sail.

windsurfing The act or sport of handling a surfboard that is equipped with a collapsible mast and a triangular sail and that is ridden while standing up.

windup *baseball* A swing of the arms by a pitcher back and then up over the head or simply up over the head while facing home plate just before turning the body and throwing the ball. The windup, which is usually accompanied by a rocking of the body, sets a rhythm which the pitcher follows until the ball is released. The windup is normally eliminated in favor of a stretch when there are runners on base because the extra moment it takes to complete the windup would give the base runner too great an opportunity to steal. Once the pitcher starts the windup motion, he must continue through with it and throw the pitch to home plate or be charged with a balk. — compare STRETCH

windup

wind up

wind up *of a baseball pitcher* To go into a windup before delivering a pitch.

windward On the side facing the wind; facing the direction from which the wind is blowing. — compare LEEWARD

— **to windward** **1** To or on the windward side. **2** Into the wind; toward the direction from which the wind is blowing.

¹wing **1** An airfoil that resembles an airplane wing and that is mounted above the rear of a racing car to improve the car's traction.
2 Either of 2 forwards (as in hockey, soccer, or speedball) who play on the outsides of the forward line near the sides of the playing area.
3 An area on the side of the playing area normally occupied by a wing; the position played by a wing.
4 *basketball* Either of 2 players who normally play on each side of the free throw lane.
5 *football* A flanker.
6 *lacrosse* Either of 2 midfielders who play on either side of the center.
7 Short for *wing forward, winglock.*

²wing *wrestling* To get an opponent in a winglock and roll him over.

wing and wing Sailing on a run with the mainsail and jib fully extended on opposite sides of the boat.

wing area *lacrosse* Either of 2 rectangular areas along the sidelines that are bounded by the sidelines and parallel lines 20 yards from the center of the field within which the second attack and second defense must remain during a face-off.

wingback *football* **1 a** An offensive halfback in the single wing formation who lines up just outside the formation and serves as a pass receiver, blocker, or ballcarrier. **b** A flankerback.
2 The position played by a wingback.

winger A wing on a hockey, box lacrosse, or soccer team.

wing forward **1** *rugby* Either of 2 forwards who line up on the outside of the second or third rows during a scrum. (also called *flanker, flank forward*)
2 *soccer* An outside forward; wing.
3 The position played by a wing forward.

wing halfback *soccer* **1** Either of 2 halfbacks who play to the left and right of the center halfback and who normally guard the opposing inside forwards.
2 The position played by a wing halfback.

winglock *wrestling* A hold in which a wrestler, who is held by the opponent with an arm around his waist, grabs the opponent's arm pinning it to his own body and rolls to one side in an effort to force the opponent to the mat on his back.

wingman **1** A wing (as on a hockey or soccer team).
2 *Australian Rules football* Either of 2 center-line players who play to the left and right of the center.
3 *basketball* A guard or forward who plays the wing position.
4 *football* A flanker.
5 *lacrosse* A midfielder who normally plays near the side of the field and who lines up in the wing area during a face-off.

wingshooting The act or practice of shooting at game birds in flight.

wingshot **1** A shot at a flying game bird or target.
2 Someone who is skilled in wingshooting.

wing T *football* A variation of the standard T formation in which one of the halfbacks is used as a wingback. — see T FORMATION

wing threequarter *rugby* **1** Either of the 2 threequarter backs who play near the sides of the field.
2 The position played by a wing threequarter.

winner **1** A competitor who wins.
2 A shot in a court game that is not returned and that scores for the player making it.

winner's circle *horse racing* An enclosure near the finish line at a racetrack where the winning jockey and horse are brought for photographs and awards.

winning gallery *court tennis* Either of the galleries on each side of the court that are farthest from the net. A ball driven into the opponent's winning gallery immediately wins the point for the player making the stroke. (also called *last gallery*)

winning hazard see HAZARD

winning pitcher *baseball* The pitcher on the winning team who is given credit for the victory by virtue of the fact that he was pitching when his team gained the lead. A pitcher cannot be credited with the win if his team loses the lead and subsequently regains it after he has been removed from the game. For a starting pitcher to be the winning pitcher, he must have pitched at least 5 innings.

winter ball Organized baseball played during their off season by major league and minor league players who want to improve some aspect of their game or to work their way back into shape after an injury. Winter ball is played usually in an instructional league or in the organized league of a foreign country.

winter book *horse racing* A theoretical assignment of odds during the winter that reflects a handicapper's opinion of the chances of probable starters for a major race that is to be held the following season.

Winter Olympics or **Winter Games** A program of amateur competition in winter sports held in a different country every 4 years as an adjunct to the Olympic Games. The Winter Games originated in 1924, and they are usually held during the winter preceeding the Summer Games. Competition normally includes Alpine and Nordic skiing, figure skating, speed skating, biathlon, ice hockey, and bobsled and luge competition.

wipeout *surfing* A potentially serious fall from a surfboard caused by losing control, colliding with another surfer, or being knocked off by a wave. During a wipeout, the surfer is often in danger of being struck by the free surfboard or of being driven into the rough bottom by surf. The term is occasionally used to describe any fall (as in skiing, cycling, or motorcycle racing). (also called *gas-out*)

wipe out **1** *surfing* To experience a wipeout. **2** To defeat a particular opponent by a wide margin.

wire *horse racing* The starting line or the finish line of a racetrack.

wired *surfing* Thoroughly studied and understood. ⟨he has the local surf *wired*⟩

wire to wire From start to finish. The term originated in horse racing where the starting line and finish line were marked by overhead wires but is commonly used of any contest. ⟨took the victory by leading *wire to wire*⟩

wishbone or **wishbone T** *football* A variation of the T formation in which the halfbacks line up farther from the line of scrimmage than the fullback does so that the alignment of the 4 backs gives the appearance of a wishbone. The wish-

wishbone: C center; FB fullback; G guard; HB halfback; QB quarterback; SE split end; T tackle; TE tight end

bone is popular in college football, and the triple option is commonly run from it. — compare I FORMATION, T FORMATION

wobbler **1** *curling* A fast-moving stone that wobbles as it travels down the ice. **2** see SPOON

wolf vault *gymnastics* A vault over a long horse or pommel horse made by bringing one leg up in a squatting position and extending the other leg to the side.

wood **1** *golf* **a** A club having a long shaft and a large hardwood or metal head that is normally used in driving off the tee or from the fairway. The group of woods consists of 5 clubs numbered one (the *driver*) to 5 in order of increasing loft. The face of wooden clubs is usually reinforced and the head is sometimes weighted to increase driving power. — see also CLUB; compare IRON, PUTTER **b** A wood shot. **2** *bowling* **a** Pins. **b** Short for *dead wood.*

wood shot **1** A shot in a racket game in which the ball or shuttlecock is hit accidentally with any part of the frame of the racket. The shot is legal but usually quite ineffective. **2** *golf* A shot played with a wood; a drive.

Worcester *bowling* A leave in which all of the pins but the one and the 5 remain standing. — see illustration of pin arrangement at BOWLING

¹work *baseball* To pitch; to play as the pitcher. ⟨bring in a new pitcher to *work* to the next batter⟩

²work Playing time; playing experience.

working ball *bowling* A bowled ball that has sufficient speed and spin to make the pins scatter upon impact.

working sails *sailing* The general-purpose sails normally used on a boat as distinguished from special lightweight or heavyweight sails for unusually light or heavy wind conditions.

workout A period of practice or exercise to test or improve fitness.

work out To go through a workout.

works team see FACTORY TEAM

world-class Being of the highest caliber in the world. ⟨a *world-class* runner⟩ ⟨*world-class* soccer⟩

World Cup A world championship competition and the trophy symbolic of world championship in certain sports: **1** *golf* An annual event consisting of 4 days of stroke-play competition between 2-man teams representing more than 40 nations. The competition was originated in 1953 when it was known as the Canada Cup. Both team and individual

World Drivers Championship

scores are recorded, and a championship is awarded to the team and to the individual with the lowest scores.

2 *skiing* An annual series of international Alpine competitions for men and women. The winners of the cup are the skiers with the best overall scores in all events.

3 *soccer* The competition, held every 4 years, representing world supremacy in soccer and conducted in a final elimination competition made up of 16 teams who are winners from regional competitions. The competition is essentially open, but each nation is generally represented by its best professional players. The trophy itself is won permanently by any national team that is victorious 3 times.

World Drivers Championship An annual championship for international race car drivers based on their overall performance during a season of Grand Prix racing in formula one cars.

World Series A postseason play-off series between the pennant winner of the National League and the pennant winner of the American League for the championship of professional baseball in the United States. The World Series was begun in 1903 and since 1922 has been a best-of-seven (first team to win 4 games) series. Promoters in other sports have begun to use the term to apply to a variety of contests ranging from cycle races to golf matches, and it is also applied to an international softball competition.

worming Fishing with a worm as bait.

wraparound *gymnastics* A backward hip circle.

wraparound check *box lacrosse* A stick check in which the checker attempts to dislodge the ball from the opponent's stick by reaching around his opponent from behind and hitting his stick. A minor penalty can be called on the checker if he makes contact with his opponent with either his body or stick during a wraparound check.

wrench An auto racing mechanic. (also called *monkey*)

¹wrestle To engage in wrestling.

²wrestle A wrestling match; a period of wrestling.

wrestler Someone who engages in wrestling.

wrestler's bridge A bridge position assumed by a wrestler. — see BRIDGE

wrestling **1** A sport in which 2 unarmed individuals struggle hand to hand with each attempting to subdue his opponent. Wrestling is one of the world's oldest sports: some forms are known to have existed 5000 years ago. Modern wrestling has many traditional forms. On an international level, there are 2 principal forms of wrestling: freestyle and Greco-Roman. In freestyle the opponents attempt to throw each other to the mat and to secure holds which score points or which enable them to pin the opponent's back to the mat. In freestyle, a wrestler is permitted to apply holds on his opponent's legs and to use his legs to trip or throw his opponent and to apply holds. Greco-Roman wrestling is basically a development of the Greek style employed in the pentathlon in the original Olympic Games, and it is identical to freestyle wrestling except that holds on the body below the waist and the use of the legs to hold or trip an opponent are prohibited.

Wrestling is conducted in weight classes; a match in amateur wrestling consists of three 3-minute periods (in collegiate wrestling the first period is 2 minutes and the other 2 are 3 minutes each) with a 1-minute rest between. A wrestler wins the match by securing a fall (pinning the opponent's shoulders to the mat for a full second) or by accumulating the most points during the course of the match. In college wrestling, an individual is awarded 2 points for bringing his opponent to the mat under control (a *takedown*), one point for escaping from a hold applied by the opponent (*escape*), 2 points for a *reversal* in which he gets out of a hold and at the same time gains one over the opponent, 2 points for a *near fall* in which the opponent's shoulders are held close to the mat in a position that threatens a pin, and one point for having accumulated a full minute advantage in *riding time*. There are certain actions and holds which are illegal in both freestyle and Greco-Roman wrestling. These include choking, gouging, punching, elbowing, or kneeing an opponent, a headlock which covers the nose and mouth, a full nelson, a hammerlock in which the arm is bent at an angle greater than 90 degrees, and any hold used solely for punishment. In addition, there are a number of potentially dangerous holds which must be watched by the referee because they could result in severe injury if a limb is forced beyond the normal range of movement.

The match is conducted by a referee on the mat who signals for the wrestlers to start and stop, watches for illegal and improperly applied holds, signals when a wrestler has scored points, and indicates when one has secured a fall. Off the mat, a judge assists the referee by watching the holds and checking for scoring movements and falls. In college meets, wrestlers are awarded points according to their success in each match. For a victory by a fall or default, the wrestler scores 6 points; for a decision in which the margin of victory is 10 points or more, 4 points; for a decision with less than a 10-point advantage, 3 points; for a draw, each wrestler scores 2 points. In international wrestling, wrestlers are rated according to penalty points. If an individual wins a match by a fall, he has no penalty points. For a simple decision on points, he is charged with one penalty point. If the decision was with a margin of 8 or more points, he is charged with only half a penalty point, and if he wins by evident superiority (an advantage of 12 or more points) he is given no penalty points. Each wrestler is charged with 2 points for a draw. The loser of the match is given the difference between 4 and the number of points charged against the winner. For example a wrestler who loses by a fall is charged with 4 penalty points; one who loses a match by 8 points is charged with 3½ penalty points. — see also HOLD; compare INDIAN WRESTLING, JUDO, SAMBO, SUMO

2 An entertainment developed from wrestling that has some of the features of wrestling and that is staged in a boxing ring between professionals. The activity, usually called *professional wrestling* to distinguish it from the sport, relies principally on showmanship for its appeal. The participants frequently affect showy costumes and outlandish behavior, and a bout often pits a villain against a good guy in a confrontation of good and evil. Professional wrestling ostensibly has rules governing the number of participants permitted in the ring at one time and banning such actions as choking, kicking, gouging, punching, and biting adversaries, but they are usually purposefully ignored for the entertainment of spectators. An individual wins his match when he is able to pin his adversary for 3 seconds or when his adversary submits or is unable to continue the action. Promoters often stage tag team matches, matches between women wrestlers or with 2 against one, and even free-for-alls in which a number of participants start out in the ring with each seeking to be the only one left in the ring at the end. (also called *rassling*)

wristlock *wrestling* A hold secured on the opponent's wrist.

wrist pass see SNAP PASS

wrist shot *ice hockey* A quick shot made with the stick blade against the puck by snapping the wrist forward to move the stick instead of taking a backswing and sweeping the stick into the puck. — compare SLAP SHOT

wrist wrestler Someone who engages in wrist wrestling.

wrist wrestling A version of arm wrestling in which opponents interlock thumbs instead of gripping hands. As a competitive sport, wrist wrestling is conducted as an elimination event with all competitors paired within weight classes and with the winners of each round advancing to face other winners until there is one champion in each class. For the competition, which is conducted by a referee, the competitors interlock right thumbs placing right elbows on a high table or stand so as to form an arch. Under the arch, they hook the fingers of the other hands. An individual wins a match by forcing the opponent's arm to the table or by forcing the opponent to lift his other arm from the table or to release the grip with either hand.

wrong-field *of a hit in baseball* Made to the opposite field. ⟨a *wrong-field* double down the line — Peter Gammons, *Boston Globe*⟩

wrong-un A googly.

XYZ

X-ring *shooting* The innermost area of the innermost scoring ring on certain targets for smallbore competition that is used for breaking ties. When 2 or more shooters are tied, the victory is given to the one with the most holes in the X-ring.

yacht A sailboat or powerboat with a net weight of 5 or more tons that is privately owned and that is used exclusively for pleasure. The term is sometimes used of any sailboat, especially in connection with yacht racing.

yacht club An association of boat owners for promoting and regulating yacht racing especially among its members.

yacht racing The sport of racing sailboats. The term is usually used of all sailboat racing from large seagoing yachts to small dinghies.

yachtsman's anchor A traditional-style anchor commonly used on small sailboats. — see illustration at ANCHOR

Yamashita *gymnastics* A vault in which the gymnast performs a handspring in a piked position.

yank *of a manager or coach* To remove a player (as a pitcher or quarterback) from a game especially when that player is not very effective.

yard A spar attached to a mast for supporting a sail.

yardage *football* The total number of yards gained by a player or team.

yardage chain see CHAIN

yard line or **yard marker** *football* Any of a series of marked or imaginary lines one yard apart on the field that are parallel to the goal lines and that indicate the distance to the nearest goal line.

yardsman *Canadian football* Any of 3 assistants to the officials who are responsible for marking the progress of the ball and keeping track of the downs and whose duties are analogous to those of the chain crew in American football.

¹yaw Side to side movement (as of a plane or boat). — compare PITCH, ROLL

²yaw To undergo yaw.

yawl A 2-masted fore-and-aft-rigged sailboat that has the mizzenmast aft of the rudderpost. — compare KETCH; SCHOONER

yearling *horse racing* A racehorse during the period between January 1st of the year after the year in which it was foaled and the following January 1st that can range in actual age from

Yamashita

zone ride

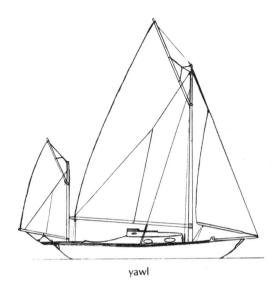

yawl

nearly newborn to nearly 2 years. — see also AGE; compare WEANLING

yellow card *soccer* A solid yellow card raised by a referee to indicate that a player has, in his judgment, committed a flagrant foul and is being cautioned.

yellow flag *motor racing* A solid yellow flag that calls for caution and no passing because of danger ahead. When waved the yellow flag indicates that there is great danger ahead and that the vehicles may have to stop.

yip *golf* To mishit the ball when making a putt with the result that the ball misses the hole.

yips *golf* Nervousness or excitement often from the pressure of competition that causes a golfer to choke and miss a relatively easy putt. ⟨I've still got 20–20 vision. . . . It's just the *yips* that makes me putt like I do — Sam Snead⟩

yoick see HOICK

Yonkers Trot A 1-mile stakes race for 3-year-old trotters that is held at Yonkers Raceway in New York and that is one of the races in the trotting

Triple Crown. — compare HAMBLETONIAN, KENTUCKY FUTURITY

yorked *of a cricket batsman* Bowled out with a yorker.

yorker *cricket* A bowled ball that lands at or near the batsman's feet where it is extremely difficult to hit.

York round *archery* A target round in men's competition in which each contestant shoots 72 arrows at a distance of 100 yards, 48 arrows at 80 yards, and 24 arrows at 60 yards.

young lion A competitor who is relatively new to major competition (as in auto racing) or to a tour (as in golf) but who performs unusually well and shows promise of greatness.

youngster see JUVENILE

Zamboni A trademark used for a 4-wheel ice resurfacing machine which scrapes the top of an ice surface (as on an ice hockey rink) and lays down a thin film of water to freeze.

¹zero *shooting* The adjustment required of a sight so that the bullet will hit the center of the bull's-eye for a given range.

²zero *shooting* To make a zero adjustment on a weapon; to adjust the sight on a weapon so that the bullet will hit the exact center of a target.

¹zone **1 a** An area of a field, court, or rink covered by a particular defender in a zone defense. **b** A zone defense.
2 Short for *attacking zone, defensive zone.*

²zone To employ a zone defense against an opponent.

zone blocking see AREA BLOCKING

zone defense A defense in a team sport characterized by having each player defend an assigned area of the playing surface and guard an opponent only when the opponent is in this area. — compare MAN-TO-MAN

zone press *basketball* see PRESS

zone ride *lacrosse* A ride in which some of the team members drop away from the opponents to cover a zone rather than an individual player. (also called *Maryland ride*)

APPENDIX

Abbreviations   492
Referee Signals   496
Scorekeeping   498

ABBREVIATIONS

Variation in the styling of abbreviations is frequent and widespread.
Most of the abbreviations in this list have been normalized to one form.

a alternate captain; assists; goals against

AAA Amateur Athletic Association

AAU Amateur Athletic Union

ab times at bat

ABA Amateur Boxing Association; American Badminton Association; American Basketball Association

ABC American Bowling Congress

ABL Amateur Bicycling League

ABLA Amateur Bicycle League of America

ac athletic club

ACA American Camping Association; American Canoe Association; American Casting Association

ACC Atlantic Coast Conference

ACCUS Automobile Competition Committee for the United States

ACU American Cycling Union; Association of Cricket Umpires

AFA Amateur Fencing Association; Amateur Football Alliance; Amateur Football Association

AFC American Football Conference; American Foxhound Club; Association Football Club

AFCA American Football Coaches Association

AFL American Football League

AFLA Amateur Fencers League of America

AGA Amateur Gymnastics Association

agp average goals against per period (ice hockey)

AHAUS Amateur Hockey Association of the United States

AHCA American Hockey Coaches Association

AHL American Hockey League

AHRA American Hot Rod Association

AIAW Association of Intercollegiate Athletics for Women

AIBA Association Internationale de Boxe Amateur (boxing)

AJBC American Junior Bowling Congress

AL American League (baseball)

ALBA American Lawn Bowling Association

alw allowance race

AMA American Motorcycle Association

APA American Paddleball Association

APBA American Power Boat Association

APTA American Platform Tennis Association

ARCA Automobile Racing Club of America

ARDC American Race Drivers Club

ARL American Roque League

ARRC American Road Race of Champions

ASA Amateur Softball Association

ASL American Shuffleboard League; American Soccer League

ASUUS Amateur Skating Union of the United States

ATA Amateur Trapshooting Association

ATP Association of Tennis Professionals

att attempts

avg average

AWSA American Water Ski Association

b back; backward edge (skating); bay; blinkers; bowled out; bowler; breezing (horse racing)

ba batting average

BAAB British Amateur Athletic Board

bb base on balls; bats both right-handed and left-handed

BCA Billiard Congress of America

BCF British Cycling Federation

bhp brake horsepower

bk balk

bl bats left-handed

blk black

bp batting practice; bonus points

br bats right-handed; brown

BRL Babe Ruth League

BSJA British Show Jumping Association

bt beat

bufly butterfly

c canoe; captain; catcher; caught out; center; colt

CASC Canadian Automobile Sports Club

cb center back; cornerback

cc cubic centimeters; cycling club

cf center field; center forward

CFL Canadian Football League

cg complete games (baseball)

ch center halfback; chestnut

chb center halfback

CHL Central Hockey League

chstnt chestnut

cid cubic inch displacement

clm claiming race

com completions

cp cover point

CSI Commission Sportive Internationale (auto racing)

ct court

d defeated; defense; disqualified (horse racing); draw; driving (horse racing)

DGWS Division for Girls and Womens Sports

dh dead heat; designated hitter

dis or **dist** distanced (horse racing)

dk b dark bay

dk br dark brown

dnf did not finish

dnp did not play

dp double plays

dq disqualified, fouled out

e easily (horse racing); end; entry (horse racing); errors; excellent skiing conditions; expert slope (skiing)

ECAC Eastern Collegiate Athletic Conference

EHL Eastern Hockey League

EL Eastern League

er earned runs

era earned run average

et elapsed time

f fair skiing conditions; mutuel field (horse racing); filly; flied out; goals for; forward

fa field goals attempted; fielding average; first attack

FA Football Association

fb fullback

fc fielder's choice

fd first defense; first down

ff foul fly

fg field goals

FEI Federation Equestrienne Internationale (Equitation)

FHAA Field Hockey Association of America

FIA Federation Internationale de l'Automobile (auto racing)

FIBA Federation Internationale de Basketball Amateur

FIBT Federation Internationale de Bobsleigh et de Tobogganing

FIE Federation Internationale d'Escrime (fencing)

FIFA Federation Internationale de Football Association (soccer)

FIG Federation Internationale de Gymnastique (gymnastics)

FIH Federation Internationale de Handball; Federation Internationale de Hockey

FIJ Federation Internationale de Judo

FIL Federation Internationale de Luge

FIM Federation Internationale Motorcycliste (motorcycle racing)

FINA Federation Internationale de Natation Amateur (swimming)

FIRA Federation Internationale de Rugby Amateur

1b first base

FIS Federation Internationale de Ski

FISA Federation Internationale des Societes de Aviron (rowing)

FITA Federation Internationale de Tir à l'Arc (archery)

FITT Federation Internationale de Tennis de Table

FIVB Federation Internationale de Volleyball

fl flanker

fm firm (horse racing)

fo force out

frgr frozen granular snow

fst or **ft** fast (horse racing)

ft free throws

g games; workout from starting gate (horse racing); gelding; goal-keeper; goals; good skiing conditions; guard

ga goals against

gb or **gbl** games behind leader

gd good (horse racing)

GLM graduated length method

GNAS Grand National Archery Society

gp games played

gr granular snow; gray

grd ground rule double

gs games started (baseball)

GT grand touring car

gwg game winning goals

h handily (horse racing); head (horse racing); hits; hooker; horse (horse racing)

hb halfback

hcp handicap race

hd hard (horse racing); head (horse racing)

hdle hurdles

hg workout handily from gate (horse racing)

hp hit by pitcher; horsepower

hr high run (billiards); home runs

hy heavy (horse racing)

i inside edge (skating); intermediate slope (skiing)

IAAF International Amateur Athletic Federation

IBA International Basketball Association

IBF International Badminton Federation

IBG International Boxing Guild

ICAAAA or **IC4A** Intercollegiate Association of Amateur Athletes of America

ICF International Canoe Federation; International Casting Federation

ICSPE International Council of Sport and Physical Education

IDRA International Desert Racing Association

if infielder

IFA Intercollegiate Fencing Association

IFWHA International Federation of Womens Hockey Associations

IGA International Golf Association

IGF International Gymnastic Federation

IGFA International Game Fish Association

ih inside home

IHF International Handball Federation; International Hockey Federation

IHL International Hockey League

IIHA Intercollegiate Ice Hockey Association

IIHF International Ice Hockey Federation

IKF International Kart Federation

il inside left forward

IL International League

ILTF International Lawn Tennis Federation

im individual medley

IMCA International Motor Contest Association

IMSA International Motor Sports Association

in or **inter** interceptions

inv invitational race (harness racing)

ip innings pitched

ir inside right forward

IRA Intercollegiate Rowing Association; International Racquetball Association; International Rodeo Association; International Rowing Association

ISA International Skeeter Association

ISC International Softball Congress

ISDRA International Sled Dog Racing Association

ISF International Softball Federation

ISIA Ice Skating Institute of America

ISRA International Ski Racers Association

ISU International Shooting Union; International Skating Union

ITA International Track Association

ITPA International Tennis Players Association

ITTF International Table Tennis Federation

IVA International Volleyball Association

IWFA Intercollegiate Women's Fencing Association

IYRU International Yacht Racing Union

JBBF Judo Black Belt Federation

jv junior varsity

k kayak; kicker; strikeout

l left; losses

lb left fullback; left on base; linebacker

lbw leg before wicket

ld left defense

l/d lift-drag ratio

le left end

Abbreviations

lf left field; left forward; left full-back; lock forward

lfb left fullback

lg left guard

lgw love games won

lh or **lhb** left halfback

LLB Little League Baseball

lob left on base

lp losing pitcher

LPGA Ladies Professional Golfers Association

ls left safety

lsgr loose granular snow

lt left tackle; light

LTA Lawn Tennis Association

ltb light bay

ltd limited skiing conditions

lw left wing

m maiden; mare; midfield; field goals missed

mat matinee race (harness racing)

mdn maiden race

med rel medley relay

mfh master of the foxhounds

mgr manager

min minutes played

ML Mexican League

mlb middle linebacker

MLPA Major League Players Association

MLUA Major League Umpires Association

mm machine made snow

mv muzzle velocity

mvp most valuable player

my muddy conditions (horse racing)

n novice slope (skiing)

NAA National Archery Association

NAAO National Association of Amateur Oarsmen

NAHL North American Hockey League

NAIA National Association of Intercollegiate Athletics

NASCAR National Association for Stock Car Auto Racing

NASL North American Soccer League

NASTAR National Standard Race

NAUI National Association of Underwater Instructors

NBA National Basketball Association; National Boxing Association

NBC National Basketball Committee

NBPRP National Board for the Promotion of Rifle Practice

NCAA National Collegiate Athletic Association

NCCS National Climbing Classification System

NCFA National Club Football Association

NCJA National Collegiate Judo Association

NFAA National Field Archery Association

NFC National Flying Club; National Football Conference

NFCAA National Fencing Coaches Association of America

NFL National Football League

NHC National Handball Club

NHL National Hockey League

NHPAA National Horseshoe Pitchers Association of America

NHRA National Hot Rod Association

NIFA National Intercollegiate Fencing Association

NIT National Invitational Tournament

NIWFA National Intercollegiate Womens Fencing Association

NJCAA National Junior College Athletic Association

nk neck (horse racing)

NL National League (baseball)

NLL National Lacrosse League

NMLRA National Muzzle Loading Rifle Association

no nose (horse racing); lifts not operating (skiing)

NORRA National Off Road Racing Association

NPA National Paddleball Association

NRA National Rifle Association

ns nose (horse racing)

NSA National Shuffleboard Association; National Ski Association

NSPS National Ski Patrol System

NSTA National Squash Tennis Association

NTGA National Tournament Golf Association

NWC National Wrestling Confederation

NWFL National Womens Football League

o outside edge (skating)

oe offensive end

of outfield

off offensive

og offensive guard

oh outside home

ol outside left forward

opn open race (horse racing)

opp opponent

opr lifts operating (skiing)

opt clm optional claiming race

or opponents' runs (baseball); outside right forward

os out stealing

ot offensive tackle; overtime

OTB Off-Track Betting

p pitcher; games or matches played; point; poor skiing conditions; punter

pat point after touchdown

pb passed ball

PBA Professional Bowlers Association

pc or **pct** percentage; winning percentage

PCHL Pacific Coast Hockey League

PCL Pacific Coast League

pdr powder snow (skiing)

pe physical education

per periods

pf personal fouls; prop forward

PGA Professional Golfers Association

ph pinch hit; pinch hitter

pim penalties in minutes

pkd pdr packed powder (skiing)

pm penalty minutes

po putouts

pos fielding position

pp post position; power play

ppg power play goals

pts points

PWBA Professional Women Bowlers Association

q or **qb** quarterback

r rebounds; right edge (skating); runs scored

rb right fullback; running back

rbi run batted in

RCA Rodeo Cowboys Association

rcb right cornerback

RCCC Royal Caledonia Curling Club; Royal Curling Club of Canada

rd right defense

re right end

reb rebounds

rf right field; right forward; right fullback

rfb right fullback

rg right guard

rh or **rhb** right halfback

rig ridgeling

ro roan

rp relief pitcher

rpg rebounds per game

rpm revolutions per minute

rs right safety

rt right tackle

Abbreviations

rw right wing
s spurs; stolen base
sa second attack; slugging average
sac sacrifice
sb stolen bases
sc spring conditions (skiing)
SCCA Sports Car Club of America
s'chase steeplechase
sd second defense
se split end
SEC Southeastern Conference
2b second base; doubles
sf soft (horse racing)
sh sacrifice hit
shg shorthanded goals
SHL Southern Hockey League
sho shutouts
SID Sports Information Director
sl slow (horse racing)
sly sloppy (horse racing)
so shutouts; strikeouts
ss shortstop; strong safety
SSAA Skate Sailing Association of America
st start; starting line
stk stakes race
str stretch
sv saves
SWC Southwest Conference
sy sloppy (horse racing)
t tackle; tie; time trial
tb times at bat; total bases; total bouts
tc total fielding chances; turf course (horse racing)
td touchdown
te tight end
tg tying goals
3b third base; triples
tko technical knockout
tl throws left-handed
TL Texas League
tp total points; touchdowns passing
tg three-quarter midget
tr throws right-handed; touchdowns running
TRA Thoroughbred Racing Association
TRPB Thoroughbred Racing Protective Bureau
TT Tourist Trophy (motorcycle racing)
u eased up (horse racing)
UEFA Union of European Football Associations
UFIB Union Federazioni Italiane Bocce (boccie)
UPGA United Professional Golf Association
USA United Soccer Association

USAAF United States Amateur Athletic Federation
USAC United States Auto Club
USAWF United States Amateur Wrestling Foundation
USBF United States Baseball Federation
USBGA United States Blind Golfers Association
USCSC United States Collegiate Sports Council
USET United States Equestrian Team
USFARS United States Federation of Amateur Roller Skaters
USFHA United States Field Hockey Association
USFSA United States Figure Skating Association
USGA United States Golf Association
USHA United States Handball Association
USHGA United States Hang Gliding Association
USHL United States Hockey League
USILA United States Intercollegiate Lacrosse Association
USISA United States International Sailing Association; United States International Skating Association
USJF United States Judo Federation
USKA United States Karate Association
USLTA United States Lawn Tennis Association
USMPBA United States Modern Pentathlon and Biathlon Association
USOA United States Olympic Association
USOC United States Olympic Committee
USPA United States Parachute Association; United States Polo Association
USPLTA United States Professional Lawn Tennis Association
USPSF United States Pigeon Shooting Federation
USPTA United States Paddle Tennis Association; United States Pony Trotting Association
USRPA United States Racing Pigeon Association
USRS United States Rowing Society
USSFA United States Soccer Football Association

USSGA United States Seniors Golf Association
USSRA United States Squash Racquets Association
USTA United States Trotting Association
USTFF United States Track and Field Federation
USTHF United States Team Handball Federation
USTTA United States Table Tennis Association
USVBA United States Volleyball Association
USWCA United States Womens Curling Association
USWF United States Wrestling Federation
USWFHA United States Womens Field Hockey Association
USWLA United States Womens Lacrosse Association
USWSRA United States Womens Squash Racquets Association
ut utility player
u/w underwater
VASSS Van Alen Simplified Scoring System
w wins; base on balls
WBA World Boxing Association
WBC World Boxing Council
WCT World Championship of Tennis
WFL World Football League
WHA World Hockey Association
WIBC Womens International Bowling Congress
WITF Womens International Tennis Federation
wp wild pitch; winning pitcher
WTT World Team Tennis
WUKO World Union of Karatedo Organization (karate)
x pt extra points
YBA Youth Bowling Association
yds yards
YRA Yacht Racing Association

495

Referee Signals

First Down

Time-Out

Time-In, Start the Clock

Personal Foul

Delay of Game

Grabbing Face Mask

Illegal Use of Hands

Intentional Grounding

Loss of Down

Offside

No Score, Incomplete Pass, or Penalty Declined

Crawling or Helping Runner

Roughing the Kicker

Clipping

Dead Ball

Pass Interference

Illegal Motion

Illegal Forward Pass

Illegal Procedure

Illegal Receiver Downfield

Unsportsmanlike Conduct

Touchdown, Field Goal, or Point After Touchdown

Safety

Referee Signals

Basketball

| Start the Clock | Time-Out | Jump Ball | Number of Points Scored | Number of Free Throws Permitted | No Score |

| Personal Foul | Holding | Charging or Pushing | Player Control Foul | Blocking | Illegal Use of Hands | Goal Counts |

| Technical Foul | Traveling | Illegal Dribble | 3-Second Violation | Bonus Situation (one and one) |

Ice Hockey

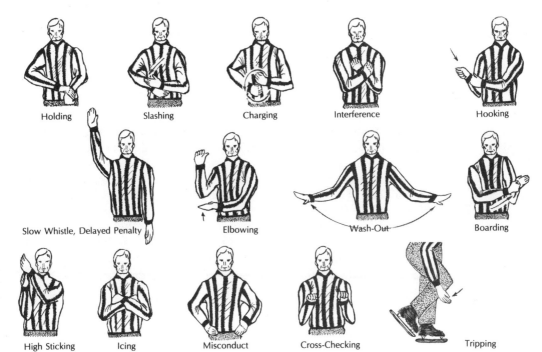

| Holding | Slashing | Charging | Interference | Hooking |

| Slow Whistle, Delayed Penalty | Elbowing | Wash-Out | Boarding |

| High Sticking | Icing | Misconduct | Cross-Checking | Tripping |

497

Scorekeeping

BASEBALL

The progress of a baseball game is normally recorded by means of a set of symbols which stand for various actions. The record is kept for the batting team to show what each player does as a batter and base runner, how he advances around the bases, and what action is taken by the fielding team. The score sheet typically consists of a line of boxes for each player in the lineup representing each player's turn at bat during an inning. The box itself represents the diamond with the lower left-hand corner representing home plate and the other corners, counterclockwise from home plate, representing the bases. When a player reaches first base, the fact is indicated in the lower right-hand corner of the box with the appropriate symbol to describe what happened, such as a base hit, an error, or a base on balls. On many score sheets, there is a diamond in the center of each box which is darkened when a player scores to help the scorer quickly spot the runs made by the team.

The following is a list of typical symbols used in keeping score:

—	single	W or BB	base on balls	SAC	sacrifice
=	double	F	fly ball caught	WP	wild pitch
≡	triple	FF	foul fly caught	PB	passed ball
≡ or HR	home run	HP	hit by pitched ball	BK	balk
K	strikeout (swinging)	E	error	S or SB	stolen base
Ϗ	strikeout (called)	FC	fielder's choice		

Each player position has a number which is used in showing defensive actions:

1 pitcher	4 second baseman	7 left fielder
2 catcher	5 third baseman	8 center fielder
3 first baseman	6 shortstop	9 right fielder

When a player is put out, the position number of the defensive player making the putout is given in the appropriate corner of the score box. On a forceout or a tag, the player throwing the ball as well as the player making the putout is listed. The notation 6–4 means that the shortstop played the ball and threw to the second baseman, who made the putout. This method helps the scorer keep track of assists. On a double play, the entire action is listed in one box (that of the second player put out on the play) and circled so that it will stand out. The first out of the double play is noted in the usual way. For an unassisted putout, the same number is repeated (as 3–3). Occasionally a number of different players will handle the ball on a putout, as when a player is caught in a rundown. In that case all numbers are given in order. For example, 5–2–5–1 indicates that the player was caught in a rundown between third base and home when the third baseman threw to the catcher, who threw the ball back to the third baseman (presumably while chasing the runner back to third), who threw it to the pitcher covering home for the tag.

Scorekeeping

Whenever a player is advanced because of the action of a batter behind him, that player's position in the batting order (not his playing position number) is placed in the appropriate corner of the box.

The following is a sample of how a score sheet might look for a team after six innings of a typical game. The players are listed on the score sheet according to the batting order. The player's uniform number is usually listed to one side of his name and his defensive position to the other side. The scorer uses a small circled number to indicate each out of the inning. On some score sheets, there may be provisions for keeping track of the ball and strike count on each batter. If the team were using a designated hitter (DH), he would be listed in the batting order but the pitcher would not be. If during an inning all members of a team get a chance to bat, an additional column would be used and designated as a continuation of that inning. If a game continues into extra innings, additional boxes are often provided; the boxes set aside for game totals for at bats, hits, runs, RBIs, and errors can be used if needed.

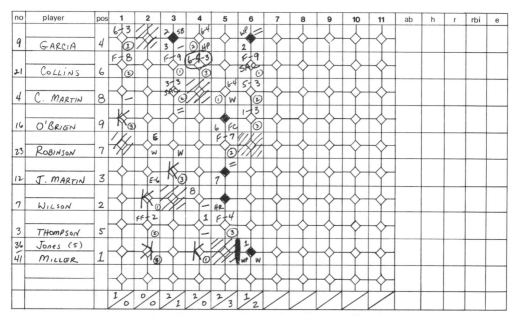

The following is an inning by inning summary of the sample game:

inning one   Garcia grounds to the shortstop, who throws him out at first base. Collins flies out to the center fielder. C. Martin gets a base hit (single), but O'Brien strikes out for the third out of the inning. The block beside Robinson's name is marked to remind the scorer that Robinson will be the first batter of the next inning.

inning two   Robinson gets a base on balls. J. Martin hits to the shortstop, who makes an error allowing Martin to get on base and Robinson to advance to second. Wilson strikes out, and

Scorekeeping

Thompson hits a pop foul that is caught by the catcher. Miller is called out on strikes for the third out, leaving two men on base.

inning three   Garcia leads off with a single. He steals second with Collins at bat. Collins flies out to the right fielder, and Garcia goes to third base on the play. Collins's position in the batting order (2) is placed in the upper left-hand corner of Garcia's box. C. Martin bunts to the first baseman, who fields the ball and tags Martin before he can reach first base. This sacrifice scores Garcia from third for the team's first run. O'Brien follows with a double and Robinson gets a base on balls, but J. Martin ends the inning with a strikeout.

inning four   Wilson and Thompson get back-to-back singles to begin the inning. Wilson is able to make it to third base on Thompson's hit. Miller again strikes out, this time swinging. Garcia is hit by a pitched ball and is awarded first base. Thompson moves to second, and the bases are now loaded. Collins grounds to the shortstop, who throws to the second baseman for the forceout on Garcia. The ball is then relayed to the first baseman to get Collins in the double play. Since the third out is a forceout, neither Wilson nor Thompson can score.

inning five   C. Martin walks and is put out at second base on O'Brien's grounder to the shortstop. O'Brien gets on base as a result of a fielder's choice (perhaps a missed double-play attempt). Robinson flies to the left fielder, who prevents O'Brien from advancing to second. O'Brien scores on J. Martin's double. Martin scores on Wilson's home run. Thompson pops up to the second baseman to end the inning.

inning six   Jones (a relief pitcher who replaced Miller in the fifth inning) gets a base on balls. A heavy solid line helps the scorer separate his at bats from those of Miller. Garcia doubles, driving Jones to third. On a wild pitch, Jones scores and Garcia reaches third base. Collins hits a sacrifice fly to right field, scoring Garcia. C. Martin grounds out to the third baseman, and O'Brien is thrown out at first after hitting the ball back to the pitcher.

By following the inning summary line at the bottom of the score sheet, one can see that through six innings the team has eight hits and six runs.

Scorekeeping

BOWLING

In tenpin bowling, each bowler is allowed two deliveries in each frame for an opportunity to knock down a maximum of ten pins. On the score sheet he is given credit for the number of pins knocked down with each ball.

For making a strike—knocking down all the pins with the first delivery—the bowler is given as a bonus the number of pins knocked down with his next two deliveries, and the bonus is added to the ten points he receives for that frame. For a spare—knocking down all pins with two deliveries—he is given as a bonus the number of pins knocked down with his next delivery. When a strike or spare is made, a mark (X for a strike and / for a spare) is placed in one of the small boxes at the top of the frame. (The X is usually placed in the left-hand box; the / goes in the right-hand box.) The score is not entered for that frame until the number of bonus pins has been determined.

If a player fouls on a delivery, an F is entered in the appropriate box (the left-hand small box if on the first ball or the right-hand small box if on the second ball), and he is not given credit for any pins that fall on that delivery. Often a G will be placed in the box if a gutter ball is rolled. When the bowler has a split remaining after the first delivery, that fact is indicated by a circle in the right-hand box. After the second delivery, that box will either show that the split was converted for a spare or have the actual number of pins knocked down, if all were not knocked down. If there is no split and all the pins are not knocked down with the second ball, an error is indicated by a short horizontal line in the second box.

The following is an example of how to score a typical game:

With his first delivery of the first frame, our bowler knocks down five pins. On his second delivery, he gets four more for a total of nine pins for the frame. A 5 is entered in the left-hand small box, and a 4 is put in the right-hand small box. In the larger area of the frame is the running total of the game after the first frame, 9.

NAME	1	2	3	4	5	6	7	8	9	10	TOTAL
	5 4										
	9										

In the second frame, the bowler gets six pins with his first delivery and three with his second, making a total of nine pins for the second frame and eighteen for the game thus far. In frame three, seven pins fall with the first ball; the second ball goes into the gutter so that the bowler gets no more pins. After three frames, his total stands at 25: 9 pins in the first frame, 9 in the second, and 7 in the third.

1	2	3
5 4	6 3	7 G
9	18	25

Scorekeeping

In the fourth frame, our bowler gets seven pins with his first ball and the remaining three pins with the second ball, giving him a spare. The spare is indicated by a mark in the right-hand box of the frame, but no cumulative score for that frame is given until the first ball of the next frame is rolled to determine the bonus.

2	3	4	
6 | 3	7 | G	7 | /	
18	25		

With the first ball of the fifth frame, the bowler knocks down six pins; with his second ball he gets the remaining four for another spare. Frame five is not yet complete, but frame four is. The six pins of the first delivery are added as a bonus to the ten made in frame four making the running total 41 pins. The six pins count both as a bonus in frame four and as part of the total pinfall in frame five.

3	4	5	
7 | G	7 | /	6 | /	
25	41		

In frame six, our bowler gets a strike (all ten pins with the first ball). This is indicated by an X in the small box of frame six. The total for frame six will be figured after the bowler has made two more deliveries. In the meantime, the ten pins of frame six are counted as the bonus for the spare in frame five giving the bowler 20 pins in frame five and a running total of 61.

4	5	6	
7 | /	6 | /	X	
41	61		

The bowler rolls another strike in frame seven. The X is placed in the box in frame seven, but neither frame six nor seven is complete yet. In frame eight, the bowler gets only eight pins with the first ball but leaves the 6 and 8 pins for a split. An 8 is entered in the left-hand box, and a circle is placed in the right-hand box to indicate the split. In reading over the player's score sheet later, anyone can see that if the player failed to make the spare in frame eight, it is because he had a more difficult situation than a simple leave. At this time frame six can be totaled since two additional deliveries have been made. In frame six the bowler got ten pins. On the next two deliveries he scored ten and eight pins respectively for a total of 28 for that frame and a running total of 89 pins.

5	6	7	8	
6 | /	X	X	8 | O	
61	89			

On the second delivery of the eighth frame, our bowler gets both remaining pins, converting the split to a spare. Frame seven is now complete with ten pins for the strike and ten pins for the bonus. This makes the player's total 109 through frame seven.

6	7	8
☒	☒	8 ∅
89	109	

With the first delivery of the ninth frame, the bowler knocks down seven pins; with his second ball he misses all the remaining pins for an error. The 7 is entered in the left-hand box, and in the right-hand box is placed a horizontal line. Both frames eight and nine are now complete. With seven pins on the first ball of the ninth frame as a bonus, the score for the eighth frame is 17, for a total of 126. The seven pins of the ninth frame makes the running total 133.

7	8	9	
☒	8 ∅	7 −	⌐
109	126	133	

In the final frame, the first delivery is a strike. This gives the bowler two more bonus balls in that frame. On the second delivery, he scores eight pins and on the final ball the remaining two pins. He now has a total of 20 pins for the final frame and a game total of 153. If the bowler had not gotten a strike or a spare in the tenth frame, he would have had only two deliveries for that frame just as for every other frame.

NAME	1	2	3	4	5	6	7	8	9	10	TOTAL
	5 4	6 3	7 6	7 /	6 /	☒	☒	8 ∅	7 −	☒ 8 2	
	9	18	25	41	61	89	109	126	133	153	153

Scoring for duckpins and candlepins is essentially the same. In both games, up to three balls are allowed in each frame, but a strike can still be scored only with the first ball and a spare only with the first two deliveries. Bonus pins are figured in the same way as for tenpins.